Civil Litigation

Civil Litigation

LUCILLA MACGREGOR,

CHARLOTTE PEACEY,

GEORGINA RIDSDALE

OXFORD

UNIVERSITY PRESS

OXFORD
UNIVERSITY PRESS

Great Clarendon Street, Oxford, OX2 6DP,
United Kingdom

Oxford University Press is a department of the University of Oxford.
It furthers the University's objective of excellence in research, scholarship,
and education by publishing worldwide. Oxford is a registered trade mark of
Oxford University Press in the UK and in certain other countries

© Oxford University Press, Susan Cunningham-Hill and Karen Elder 2020

The moral rights of the authors have been asserted

Ninth edition 2016
Tenth edition 2017
Eleventh edition 2018
Twelfth edition 2019
Thirteenth edition 2020

Impression: 2

Public sector information reproduced under Open Government Licence v3.0
(http://www.nationalarchives.gov.uk/doc/open-government-licence/open-government-licence.htm)

Published in the United States of America by Oxford University Press
198 Madison Avenue, New York, NY 10016, United States of America

British Library Cataloguing in Publication Data
Data available

ISBN 978–0–19–885844–7

Printed and bound in the UK by
TJ Books Limited

CONTENTS

ONLINE RESOURCES CONTENTS

○ **Case study documentation**

Documentation in support of the two fictional case studies in the manual

○ **Four additional chapters**

Enforcement of Judgments

Guide to Preparing Instructions to Counsel

Injunctions and Other Equitable Remedies

A Practical Guide to Court Hearings

○ **Annotated forms**

Key forms from the litigation process, with useful annotations to help you understand how they should be completed correctly

- N1 Claim Form
- N181 Directions Questionnaire
- Form N244 Application Notice

○ **Court forms**

Links to templates of the most commonly used court forms and which are referred to in this textbook.

○ **Litigation train**

An interactive timeline to help put the litigation process in context

○ **Online updates**

A summary of some key recent updates

○ **Podcasts**

Recorded by the original authors, these audio files will accompany and supplement your understanding of topics in Chapters 12, 15, and 19.

- Directions
- Part 36 offers
- Consent orders

○ **Answers to the self-test questions**

Answers to the self-test questions that appear at the end of a number of chapters in the manual

○ **Web links**

Direct links to some useful websites relating to civil litigation

○ **Test bank of questions**

A bank of customizable multiple-choice questions to help assess students' learning

○ **Case study materials**

Suggested answers to the questions in relation to the two fictional case studies in the manual

○ **Video clips**

Three video scenarios to accompany the two fictional case studies featured in the book and of general application

- Andrew James Pike—Mediation. Chapter 5
- Andrew James Pike—Interim Payment. Chapters 13 and 14
- Bollingtons Limited—Telephone application. Chapter 13
- Top Tips for success at interim applications

These video clips are accompanied by audio narrative which puts each clip into context. The audio narratives are also available as podcasts.

PREFACE

The aim when preparing this manual has been to provide a primarily practical but comprehensive text on the areas of civil litigation that any legal practitioner or student on the Legal Practice Course will encounter during his time in the dispute resolution department or in his studies for the civil litigation element of this core subject area. This text is designed for use by all practitioners in litigation, including students, paralegals, trainees, and newly qualified practitioners, and it will act as an up-to-date refresher for any practitioner re-entering the world of litigation in practice. This edition is current as at the time of writing. We also detail the SRA Standards and Regulations, which came into force in November 2019. These include the Codes of Conduct for solicitors and for firms (part of which—the Transparency Rules for firms—came into force on the 6 December 2018). We have also highlighted areas of practice or procedure where changes are expected (for example, the new disclosure pilot and the shorter and flexible trials scheme) so that practitioners can be alert to the changes and look out for them.

We believe that this manual provides a comprehensive and up-to-date guide for the study of civil litigation, enabling such a student to engage with the method of study required to prepare for practice, and advise his notional 'client'. It will also prepare and guide any legal practitioner about to undertake those early tentative steps advising 'real clients', ensuring that the professional obligations of legal practice (and contained in the SRA Standards and Regulations) are maintained, and furnish any new litigator with the skills to engage in the tasks that are likely to fall to him.

There are five important parts to the innovative approach of this manual. They are:

1. The 'litigation train'—a diagrammatic flow line that we illustrate at the beginning of relevant chapters in the manual that represents a stage of the litigation process. By the time a student of litigation in practice, including any student on a Legal Practice Course, has studied through to the end of the manual, the sections of this diagrammatic 'train journey' will together form a complete diagrammatic illustration of the path an action may take, from the first meeting with a legal representative, to trial.

2. This litigation train is also reproduced in the online resources, created for use with this manual, and is represented by three visual levels. Level 1 marks the main stages of litigation. By clicking on one of these stages, the student will be brought into Level 2. Level 2 of each stage is represented by six headings—'Client Issues and Funding', 'Professional Conduct', 'CPR and Practice', 'ADR', 'Costs—Proportionality and Reasonableness', and 'Time'. Clicking on each of these headings brings the student into Level 3, where details will be given of the main factors arising within the heading selected for the stage of the action selected.

   The diagrammatic litigation train will enable students, and practitioners, to see 'at a glance' how an action may progress and what might arise at that stage not only in terms of practice and procedure, but also the other considerations that a legal practitioner may need to engage with at that point in the action. These 'headings' at Level 3 comprise both the procedural matters to be undertaken and the ancillary matters that the practitioner will need to consider, including professional conduct, and the relationship with the client, other professionals, and other persons involved in the litigation at that stage. It will give the student a visual image and, in note form, a review of the action at that stage. It will also enable a student to see, and remind the practitioner, what might have taken place before that stage and what might be taking place later in the litigation. In this way a student will be able to focus his work and in so doing act in the best interests of his client at all times.

3. The wholly practical elements of the manual enable a student to understand and anticipate the activities and skills that he will need when undertaking the work of a legal representative. Notably these include the chapters 'A Practical Guide to Court Hearings' (included in the online resources), 'The First Client Meeting and Initial Considerations', 'Witness Statements and Documentary Evidence', and 'Trial, Settlement, and Appeals'. However, all the chapters provide practical guidance for the work to be undertaken for that part of the litigation process being dealt with in that chapter.

4. Included in the chapters are 'text boxes'—these are called: 'Practical Considerations', 'Costs', and 'ADR Considerations'. These highlight notable examples of how each of these elements might arise in practice at that part of the litigation.

5. The online resources—in addition to the litigation train noted in point 1, this resource includes:

   • video clips of parts of litigation 'in action', which include audio narrative putting each clip into context.

   • suggested solutions to the case study contained at the end of most chapters, which will also give additional exercises to aid learning or act as a review for young practitioners. These are available for lecturers to provide to their students;

   • some of the most common court forms, left blank;

   • some forms completed, and with notes to assist in the understanding of the detail and content of these forms as they are used in practice;

   • three audio podcasts to aid understanding and give an alternative medium to learn from in complex areas;

   • additional chapters on practical tips for court hearings, enforcement of judgments, the law, practice, and procedure of injunctions (to be read in conjunction with section 14.8 in the manual), and a guide to preparing instructions to counsel.

   • The authors take care to include the most up-to-date Civil Procedure Rules (CPR), forms, and procedures. Where significant changes occur during the year of an edition, these will be added to the online resources.

In this thirteenth edition we have updated the law and reference to the SRA Standards and Regulations whilst maintaining the overall structure of previous editions.

There have been two major events since the publication of the previous edition. The first is Brexit. The UK left the EU on 31 January 2020. We are now in a transition period until the end of 2020 by which time (it is currently expected) the UK and EU will have negotiated additional arrangements. Where some legislative changes have already been implemented as a result of Brexit, this is mentioned in context in specific parts of the text book.

The second major event has been the Coronavirus pandemic. As part of the nationwide lockdown, which commenced on 23 March 2020, the government enacted a large number of emergency Regulations. We have not included any reference to those Regulations as a vast majority are unrelated to the content of this book. Furthermore, it is anticipated that most, if not all, of these Regulations are temporary and will be revoked when the pandemic crisis is over. At the time of submitting to print, it is not known when this might be. As far as any changes to civil litigation is concerned, the most significant has been to the protocols as regards remote hearings. Other significant changes related to the requirements to include a declaration in a witness statement that it had been obtained remotely (see Chapter 17, paragraph 17.4.2.3) and an allowance by Medco to obtain a medical report following a remote video examination (previously prohibited). We welcome any constructive comments from lecturers, young practitioners, supervising partners, and students about how the text and the online resources can be improved.

The authors would like to acknowledge, and give thanks to, the original authors of this textbook, Susan Cunningham-Hill and Karen Elder.

The writing of this manual and the production of the video case studies and online resources, could not have been achieved without the cooperation and assistance of many friends and colleagues of the original authors.

In relation to the case study video clips: Ne'ema Bowen, and HH Judge John Rubery (retired).

We should like to thank the team at OUP for their patient help and guidance.

For any errors or omissions, we apologize and take full responsibility for them. The law is as stated on 6 April 2020.

Lucilla Macgregor
Charlotte Peacey
Georgina Ridsdale

ACKNOWLEDGEMENTS

Grateful acknowledgement and thanks are made to Practical Law Dispute Resolution, who have given us permission to reproduce extracts taken from Practical Law Dispute Resolution's *Practice note, Damages-based agreements in civil litigation (other than employment tribunal matters): overview* (up-to-date as at 4 May 2020). The choice of where the extracts have been placed in this text has been made by the authors, and not by Practical Law Dispute Resolution.

GUIDED TOUR OF THE BOOK

Civil Litigation manual is a pedagogically rich text which has been designed to facilitate your learning and understanding of civil litigation in practice. This 'guided tour of the book' will explain how to get the best from this book by illustrating each of the features used by the authors to explain the practical processes involved in civil litigation.

WITHIN EACH CHAPTER

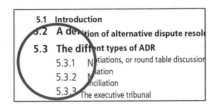

CHAPTER CONTENTS

A detailed contents list at the start of each chapter enables you to anticipate what will be covered and identify what the main topics of the chapter will be. Also use this feature to gain an understanding of how the topics fit together in the wider subject area.

LIST OF RELEVANT COURT FORMS

At the start of relevant chapters, a list of the commonly used forms for the topic examined in the chapter will be set out. These will help you know which forms should be used and when.

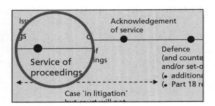

'LITIGATION TRAIN' DIAGRAMS

At the start of relevant chapters, these useful diagrams illustrate where you are in the overall litigation process and help you to see the 'bigger picture'. Use these diagrams to put your learning into context. By seeing these litigation trains as continuous you will see more clearly the progression of cases through the litigation process. You will be able to see, at a glance, where steps most commonly arise.

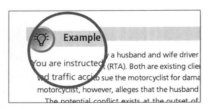

EXAMPLES

Look for the example icon to find relevant, practical examples of how the law has been or could be applied in common situations. These examples bring the subject to life and allow you to examine how principles, rules, and statutes work in practice.

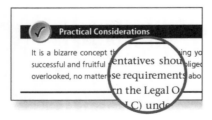

PRACTICAL CONSIDERATIONS BOXES

It can sometimes be difficult to see how the various rules and processes would work in practice. These boxes will help you gain an understanding of how things work in the day-to-day practical situations you are likely to come across as a trainee solicitor.

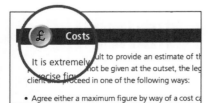

COSTS BOXES

In practice, it is vital to consider your client's costs and when any fees need to be paid. These boxes highlight any costs issues that apply at various times within the litigation process.

ONLINE RESOURCES ICON

Wherever this icon appears in the margin, more information is available in the online resources which accompany this text. This may be video footage, case study documentation, a series of self-test multiple-choice questions, or links to other useful websites or guidance. See the online resources contents at p. xvii for more information.

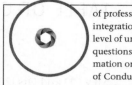

of professional conduct o
integration of all of thos
level of understanding, t
questions and general qu
mation on the Solicitors'
of Conduct, part of whic
and the remaining parts

END OF CHAPTER FEATURES

CASE STUDIES

Throughout the book, the authors refer to two fictional case studies, which provide a practical focus to the law and procedures described in the text. The documentation for these case studies appears in the online resources. See the online resources contents at p. xvii for more information.

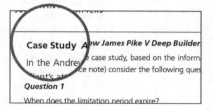

Case Study *A ew James Pike V Deep Builder*

In the Andre
nt's at te note) consider the following ques
Question 1

When does the limitation period expire?

KEY POINTS SUMMARY

The key points covered are summarized in a user-friendly list at the end of each chapter. Look to these summaries to help you consolidate your learning or to check your knowledge at revision time.

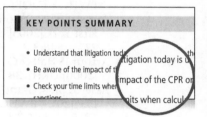

KEY POINTS SUMMARY

- Understand that litigation tod...
- Be aware of the impact of t
- Check your time limits whe
  ...ctions.

SELF-TEST QUESTIONS

These questions allow you to test yourself on particular areas of the law in preparation for your assessments or to assess your learning throughout the duration of the course. Use these questions to highlight areas where you might need to improve your understanding by re-reading the text or asking your lecturer. You will find suggested answers for each chapter provided as downloadable and printable documents in the online resources.

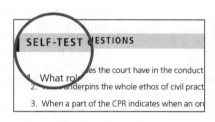

SELF-TEST QUESTIONS

1. What rol ...es the court have in the conduct
2. ...nderpins the whole ethos of civil pract
3. When a part of the CPR indicates when an or

FIGURES

Flowcharts, shaded boxes, or example forms provide a visual representation of what has been described within the chapter.

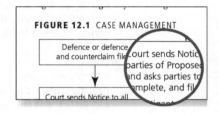

FIGURE 12.1 CASE MANAGEMENT

Defence or defence
and counterclaim file

ourt sends Notic
arties of Propose
nd asks parties to
mplete, and fil

Court sends Notice to all

TABLE OF CASES

TABLE OF CIVIL PROCEDURE RULES

TABLE OF STATUTES

TABLE OF STATUTORY INSTRUMENTS

TABLE OF INTERNATIONAL TREATIES

TABLE OF EUROPEAN LEGISLATION

1 INTRODUCTION

1.1 INTRODUCTION

This brief introductory chapter serves several purposes. Its aims are to:

- explain the philosophy of the manual and its pedagogical features;

- assist in broadening your research skills and knowledge;

- introduce you to the Civil Procedure Rules (CPR);

- highlight professional conduct considerations and how they are dealt with in this manual.

1.2 CIVIL LITIGATION—OUR APPROACH

1.2.1 WHAT IS OUR APPROACH?

It has been our intention, whilst writing this manual, to provide a practical yet informative approach to the study and practice of civil litigation for those studying civil litigation and those new to practice. As experienced tutors and litigators, we are aware of the need for a manual that gives students and practitioners an accessible and comprehensive explanation of the fundamental substantive and procedural issues whilst also providing a learning resource that illustrates, through practice-based case studies, diagrams, self-test questions, video clips, and podcasts, how civil litigation is conducted in practice.

Our experience of university student-centred learning has demonstrated that utilizing a wide range of interrelated learning resources is the most effective method of facilitating and reinforcing the understanding of key legal issues both progressively and holistically. This assists both students, in the preparation of their civil litigation assessments, and new practitioners, in their transition to becoming experienced litigators.

1.2.2 HOW IS THIS APPROACH ACHIEVED?

This innovative approach is reflected in our belief that students and practitioners should be aware that resolving disputes for clients encompasses not only a working knowledge of the

CPR, but also an awareness of the alternatives to litigation, coupled with an understanding of professional conduct obligations and legal skills. The overall picture is, therefore, one of integration of all of those. To enable those using this manual to gauge their progress and level of understanding, the online resources accompanying this manual contain case study questions and general questions. The online resources will also contain more detailed information on the Solicitors' Regulation Authority's (SRA) Standards and Regulations, Codes of Conduct and Transparency Rules which came into force in November 2019.

There are also text boxes dispersed through the chapters that highlight practical considerations, alternative dispute resolution (ADR) processes, professional conduct, and costs issues, all of which enhance the existing substantive text on these matters.

We have also selected relevant court forms that are used frequently in practice, along with other important relevant documents for you to consider. Some of the more common court forms have been annotated or completed to help you to understand how to deal with them. Some of these forms appear in the Appendices, whilst others can be found in the online resources.

The vocational approach is achieved in a number of ways. We seek to explain the law and procedure in an accessible and reader-friendly way. In general, we have not reproduced the actual CPR, although the manual aids the interpretation of the Rules. Any student or practitioner will need to examine the text of the CPR in dealing with any matter in litigation, but the manual will lead you to the relevant CPR. The CPR can be accessed at http://www.justice.gov.uk/courts/procedure-rules/civil.

The substantive parts of each chapter are supplemented by practical examples, charts, and templates, as well as a summary of key points, some general questions, and podcasts. We have also included two case studies that feature as stand-alone cases in the manual. These are an essential part of our practical approach because the case studies, which follow the paths of two actions through a likely litigation, can be used to check your understanding at the end of each chapter. These case studies are:

- the personal injury case study—*Andrew James Pike v Deep Builders Ltd*; and

- the debt/breach of contract case study—*Bollingtons Ltd v Mrs Elizabeth Lynch t/a The Honest Lawyer*.

The case study questions appear at the end of most chapters. The information and materials relevant to the case study questions, along with the suggested answers to these, appear in the online resources.

The case studies are designed to be studied progressively as you follow the reading of the chapters. Because these case studies are progressive, you will need to keep the 'path' of each action in your mind as you move on to the next set of questions between consecutive chapters. To get the most from the case study questions, in terms of the application of substantive knowledge and procedure, the key is to contextualize each case study in terms of what has gone before and what is likely to come next. This will help to develop your proactive skills as a practitioner and engender 'thinking outside the box'. Treat these fictional characters as your own clients!

To further assist in this contextualization, we have devised a teaching tool illustrated at the beginning of relevant chapters and in the online resources called the 'litigation train'. This depicts diagrammatically the fundamental steps to be taken in a case from start to finish, as well as highlighting important considerations at various stages of the action. As such, the 'train' is not associated in any way with the case studies, but rather offers a neutral 'checklist' of the likely procedural and practical steps that may be taken as a case proceeds to trial. The diagrammatic litigation train enables you to see 'at a glance' where the case sits in its path to trial and will, therefore, allow you to see the steps that may be taken at that stage.

As indicated, the litigation train features both at the beginning of chapters, commencing in Chapter 6, and in the online resources. The former illustrates a small section of the train relevant to the chapter, whilst the latter denotes three different levels of detail of the train, as follows, uncovered by the click of the mouse.

1. The first level displays the train in its entirety.
2. The second level sets out a variety of generic subheadings for each individual stage on the train.
3. The third level details the substantive information for each subheading.

The final part of the vocational approach—linked to both case studies—is the video clips that appear in the online resources. The clips should be viewed as learning aids in that they seek to illustrate, in a practical way, aspects of civil practice. The videos are not necessarily a depiction of how cases always proceed, and they should not be regarded as definitive examples of how advocacy should be conducted. Commentary is included on the clips, as well as 'top tips' from the advocate's and the court's perspectives. The participants relied on the documentation and information provided for the case studies as presented at the end of chapters and as featured in the online resources. The filming was based around a 'general framework for filming' document, but all participants devised the detail of their own script. It is important to remember that case law used to support legal submissions and the interpretation of the CPR in these clips may have changed since the filming of these videos. It is a timely reminder, therefore, that, when preparing for advocacy in practice, thorough research of the current law on both substantive and procedural matters is always required.

1.3 RESEARCH SOURCES

Legal research is an important part of your studies, but it is also a crucial skill that you will be required to exercise in practice. An accurate, relevant, and up-to-date research report to your supervising fee earner (covering both primary and secondary sources, primarily in electronic resources) will reflect well on you. The online resources provides invaluable links to related websites from which you can access further useful information. Here, we include a summary of useful practitioner resources which can be found both in text format and (in part) in electronic format.

1.3.1 PRACTITIONER WORKS

There is a proliferation of widely available resources for civil litigators which primarily focus on the CPR, Practice Directions, and Protocols, with useful commentaries on their application in practice. We seek to mention those works most commonly used by civil litigators in practice.

- *Blackstone's Civil Practice* (Oxford University Press)
- *The White Book* (Sweet and Maxwell)
- *The Green Book* (Butterworths)

1.3.2 JOURNALS AND NEWSLETTERS

Articles contained in journals and newsletters allow practitioners to keep up to date with current issues in all areas of the law. Many of these are now subscribed to electronically. There are general legal journals, such as the *Solicitor's Journal* and the *Law Society Gazette*, which contain legal news, letters, commentaries, and a legal update on a variety of topical legal matters. The journals and newsletters pertinent to civil litigation are *Litigation Funding* (Law Society Publishing) and *Civil Procedure News* (Sweet & Maxwell).

1.4 **A MATTER OF STYLE**

The use of the masculine he/his should be taken to include she/her. It is not intended to cause offence by adopting the masculine as the general descriptive phrase in this manual. Further, in using the masculine, we do not want to give the impression that all advocates and judges are male; far from it—the female stake in litigation practice on both sides of the bench is ever increasing!

1.5 **THE CIVIL PROCEDURE RULES (CPR)**

The CPR represents the cornerstone of the English and Welsh civil legal system. The CPR are also supported by Pre-Action Protocols, which provide guidance in relation to the pre-action behaviour of parties and High Court Guides (the supplemental information in respect of court practice in the High Court).

All of these aim to provide a comprehensive procedural code that will govern the conduct of all civil cases in all civil courts in this country, and will represent your primary source for the study and practice of civil litigation. The CPR has an explicit foundation in the concept of the 'overriding objective', which is looked at in some detail in Chapter 2, along with the whole philosophy of the civil courts system.

1.6 **PROFESSIONAL CONDUCT**

1.6.1 **INTRODUCTION**

A very important and pervasive area of practice is the professional conduct rules that govern the solicitors' profession and other legal practitioners alike. These were formerly contained within The SRA Handbook but have been recently replaced. The professional conduct rules are now contained in the SRA Standards and Regulations. This came into effect on 25 November 2019. All references to the Codes of Conduct applying to solicitors and firms will be those stated in the SRA Standards and Regulations.

1.6.2 **HOW WE DEAL WITH PROFESSIONAL CONDUCT IN THIS MANUAL**

The SRA Standards and Regulations apply to all individuals and firms regulated by the SRA. It is very important for all legal practitioners to understand the contents of the SRA Standards and Regulations, which set out:

- SRA Principles
- The Codes of Conduct for Solicitors
- The Codes of Conduct for Firms
- The Accounts Rules
- The Rules allowing solicitors to provide legal services to the public from businesses which are unregulated entities
- The Rules allowing individual self-employed solicitors (freelancers) to provide reserved legal services without being authorized as an entity
- The requirements for firms to have an authorized person who has practised for three years
- The changes to the assessment of character and suitability
- The Transparency Rules
- The transitional arrangements for the introduction of the Solicitors Qualifying Exam (not currently in force).

The SRA Standards and Regulations can be found at https://www.sra.org.uk/solicitors/standards-regulations/.

1.6.3 THE ELEMENTS OF THE NEW SRA STANDARDS AND REGULATIONS AND CODES OF CONDUCT

The SRA Handbook contained the previous Codes, the aim of which was setting and maintaining high professional standards—the standards the public expect. This purpose was set out in the SRA November 2015 Policy Statement: to protect consumers of legal services and to support the rule of law and the proper administration of justice.

The new SRA Standards and Regulations which came into force in November 2019, (which encompasses all those elements set out in paragraph 1.6.2 above) gives solicitors and firms more freedom and flexibility but at the same time radically shortens and simplifies the previous Handbook and Code.

The need to act with honesty and integrity, which are fundamental to acting as a solicitor, will be stand alone SRA Principles.

The new SRA Standards and Regulations are streamlined and simplified for the UK legal profession. It sets out the standards and requirements that the UK legal profession is expected to achieve and observe, for the benefit of both clients and in the public interest.

The changes are split across four areas:

- shorter, clearer principles (7);
- simplification of the rules, how the SRA approve firms and who can run them, and a revised enforcement approach;
- revised shorter and simpler accounts rules; and
- transparency, which includes better information, more choice, and ensuring that firms publish information on price, working on a digital badge, and publishing complaints data.

The SRA Standards and Regulations provides two separate codes, a Code for Solicitors and a Code for Firms. These replace detailed and prescriptive requirements with a framework for competent and ethical practice. The SRA Standards and Regulations enable a new opportunity for solicitors to freely deliver services outside of regulated firms. It simplifies the enforcement policies and provides greater clarity about what action the SRA will take when solicitors or firms fall short of the high standards required.

It also includes clear guidance for the public on what they can expect and what protections they have.

The SRA Standards and Regulations have two distinct strands with two separate Codes to underpin the new regulatory approach:

SRA Code for Solicitors, REL's (Registered European Lawyer), and RFL's (Registered Foreign Lawyer): All solicitors, no matter where they practise, will have to comply with this Code. It aims to clearly set out the professional standards and behaviours expected of solicitors.

SRA Code for Firms: This aims to provide more clarity to firms the SRA regulates about the business systems and controls they need to have in place, and what their responsibilities are as an SRA regulated business.

This approach requires firms and individuals to exercise their judgment in applying the SRA standards to their situation and in deciding the appropriate course of action. If the course of action a firm or individual decides upon is in question, this approach will require the SRA to assess the risk to the regulatory purpose (the need to provide appropriate protection to consumers, and to support the rule of law and administration of justice).

The SRA Standards and Regulations lay out a framework for an individual's ethical and competent practice. For firms, the SRA Standards and Regulations make it clear that managers are jointly and severally liable for any breaches by their firm and that employees can be personally liable for any breaches their activities cause.

This is underpinned by an enforcement strategy that ensures that action is taken in relation to serious breaches where these present a risk to the public interest.

The SRA Standards and Regulations have a revised set of Principles, as follows:

The Principles

The Principles, comprising *'the fundamental tenets of ethical behaviour'* which apply to all individuals and firms regulated by the SRA, have been reduced in number from ten to seven.

You act:

1. In a way that upholds the constitutional principle of the rule of law, and the proper administration of justice.

2. In a way that upholds public trust and confidence in the solicitors' profession and in legal services provided by authorised persons.

3. With independence.

4. With honesty.

5. With integrity.

6. In a way that encourages equality, diversity and inclusion.

7. In the best interests of each client.

In the event of any conflict between the Principles, then the Principle that best serves the public interest in the proper administration of justice will take precedence.

The SRA Standards and Regulations provide an approach to produce a Code that focuses on core professional standards and behaviours that will apply to all solicitors, wherever they work. The standards for firms are intended to be sufficiently broad to apply to all business models.

The SRA Standards and Regulations are drafted in an 'Outcomes' focused way and incorporates many of the Outcomes from the 2011 Code. These are set out as standards that solicitors, RELs, and RFLs need to meet. However, it no longer includes Indicative Behaviours. These were an integral part of the 2011 Code. Many individuals and firms found their status confusing, with many interpreting them as rigid requirements rather than indicators of ways in which they could achieve or evidence compliance with the Outcomes. However, in the 2019 SRA Standards and Regulations some of the Indicative Behaviours from the 2011 Code have become standards in their own right. Others have been moved to guidance, or, form the basis of case studies to encourage understanding, provide clarity, and support compliance. The SRA Standards and Regulations provide that the core provisions also apply to solicitors working in-house, with one section of the SRA Standards and Regulations containing provisions that are only relevant when providing services to the public rather than an employer. This puts solicitors working in-house on an equal footing with other solicitors, bound by the same core standards.

The SRA Standards and Regulations provide that the core standards (referred to by the SRA as *'the golden thread running through what it means to be a solicitor'*) are maintained, while allowing for flexibility of application. For example, each Code of Conduct has a section on conflict of interests, which succinctly sets out when a solicitor should not act, when he may act, and the conditions for acting in two substantive paragraphs. The equivalent section in the 2011 Code contains seven outcomes (with sub-paragraphs) and 14 Indicative Behaviours.

It remains to be seen whether this will leave more gaps for interpretation and understanding. Many solicitors may feel more comfortable with prescriptive rules.

Accounts Rules

The quite prescriptive Accounts Rules in the 2011 Code have been reduced. The key requirements remain (for example, rules in relation to holding and dealing with client money, operating a client account, and paying interest) but these have been significantly simplified. For example, there are two very brief paragraphs relating to the payment of interest, a subject which previously covered several pages of rules, and guidance notes. There is also a notable addition: the ability to use a third party managed account as an alternative to a client account. This is a significant move away from the traditional model of holding money in the client account apart from in very limited prescribed circumstances.

Authorisation/Assessment

The Authorisation Rules in the new SRA Standards and Regulations are divided into a set of rules for firms and amended regulations for individuals.

The Assessment of Character and Suitability Rules (previously referred to as the Suitability Test) make it clear that, when considering character and suitability, the overriding factors which the SRA will have in mind are the need to protect the public and the public interest and maintain public confidence in the profession.

The new rules reduce the categories of criminal conduct from three to two (criminal findings which are (1) *likely* to result in a refusal or (2) *may* result in a refusal).

Regulatory and Disciplinary Procedure Rules

The new Regulatory and Disciplinary Procedure Rules are less prescriptive in relation to the misconduct which may result in a disciplinary decision. The new rules simply refer to professional misconduct or serious breaches and provide that a financial penalty may be directed when this is appropriate to (1) remove any financial or other benefit from the conduct; (2) maintain professional standards; or (3) uphold public confidence in the profession. The focus has therefore shifted from describing the type of behaviour to describing the impact of the behaviour.

The SRA Standards and Regulations are not a radical departure from the previous Handbook in terms of the requirements placed on solicitors and law firms. If anything, it marks a liberalization of the current framework particularly around the ways in which solicitors can practise. It also seeks to enable a wider level of discretion or proportionality in the relationship between the regulator and the regulated.

It is important to acknowledge that professional conduct is a pervasive aspect of being a practitioner, and all practitioners should aim to achieve an integrated approach to this by assessing their professional conduct obligations at all times within all the work that they do.

2 A MODERN LITIGATION APPROACH

> Relevant parts of the CPR: 1

2.1 INTRODUCTION

The study and practice of what is commonly referred to as 'civil litigation' is probably somewhat misleading. A more accurate description would be 'dispute resolution', as there has been an emphatic move away from resolving disputes through the court system. Most firms describe their departments conducting litigation as the 'Dispute Resolution' department—encompassing all aspects of dispute resolution. Whilst students and practitioners are required to know how to conduct a case within the court framework, they are also expected to have an understanding of the philosophy and alternatives to litigation if they are to act in accordance with their professional obligations.

This chapter addresses the following:

- how we litigate in the 21st century;
- the concept of the overriding objective;
- the importance of time computation; and
- human rights and civil litigation.

2.2 CIVIL LITIGATION

2.2.1 WHAT IS THE PURPOSE OF CIVIL LITIGATION?

Civil litigation encompasses the 'machinery' and the 'mechanics' of how legal and equitable rights are asserted, determined, and enforced through the courts in the absence of agreement between the parties. The rules being upheld by the courts have their base in Christian and commercial ethics: what is good, but also what may have been agreed.

The courts therefore exist to do justice between persons who come to them. It has, however, been a long-term criticism of the courts that the very processes designed to ensure that justice may be achieved through the courts can also cause a delay and expense that may not be proportionate to the value or importance of the claim.

2.2.2 THE CPR AND REFORM

The Civil Procedure Rules (CPR) aim to promote the quest for justice in a timely, cost-efficient way, the manner in which we have conducted civil litigation has undergone some significant changes in the past 20 years starting with Lord Woolf's complete overhaul of civil procedure in 1998 and Lord Jackson's review for improvement in 2010. There are further reforms planned which have the aim of streamlining the court processes, enabling more work to be done online, increasing efficiency, accessibility, and saving administrative costs.

2.2.3 THE KEY FEATURES OF CIVIL PRACTICE IN THE COURTS

Civil litigation practice in the courts is conducted in accordance with the CPR. The ethos of this practice is set out below:

- The CPR have a fundamental objective—that is, a stated reason for their existence: the 'overriding objective': all cases must be conducted justly, fairly, expeditiously, and proportionately, and in compliance with court rules, practice directions, orders, and procedures. The whole culture, or ethos, of litigation has as its aim to be less adversarial and more inquisitorial. See paragraph 2.3 in this chapter.

- The ways in which litigation is funded by either claimants or defendants can play a major part in the way an action progresses. See Chapter 3. Financial considerations are, therefore, a key factor to take into account—the issue of 'proportionality' as regards costs is a keyword. See Chapter 4.

- There is a fundamental expectation that parties will attempt to resolve their dispute by making offers to settle or entering into an ADR process rather than proceeding to trial and to persist in their settlement attempts. See Chapters 5 and 15.

- Pre-Action Protocols indicate what steps (of 'best practice') should be taken before an action is commenced. See Chapter 8.

- The systems of judicial case and costs management once proceedings have been issued ensure that the courts govern the progress and ambit of an action. Cases are also 'tracked' by the court—to the small claims track, the fast track, or the multi-track. See Chapter 12.

- The disclosure of documents and both lay and witness evidence is controlled by the court, and the parties have an onerous duty to the court to comply with any requirements ordered. See Chapters 16, 17, and 18.

- Trials deal with relevant issues only, and the trial judge will usually expect the parties to provide chronologies, skeleton arguments, and reading plans to promote expediency at trial. See Chapter 19.

As the CPR are updated, all legal representatives need to keep a careful eye on these regular updates issued by the Ministry of Justice, available online at http://www.justice.gov.uk/courts/procedure-rules/civil/update, and they should also review recent cases emanating from such rule changes in the senior courts.

2.2.4 LITIGANTS IN PERSON (LIP)

Litigants in person are known as unrepresented parties, self-represented litigants, or self-represented parties. Today, LIPs must deal with a legal system that is designed primarily for legal representatives and as a result, the system is often complex and obscure for them. They may feel (and often are) at a disadvantage. Consequently they should be treated in a way that redresses that disadvantage and achieves fairness to ensure that cases are dealt with justly pursuant to the overriding objective (see paragraph 2.3) and that the right to a fair trial is maintained in accordance with Art. 6 European Convention on Human Rights (ECHR).

Legal representatives should, therefore, approach opposing LIPs with an understanding of these issues and of the courts' approach to LIPs. There are limits to what a LIP can and cannot do in litigation and that can depend on whether the LIP is an individual, a company, or a protected party such as a child. However, generally they can conduct their own litigation and represent themselves at trial (sometimes with lay assistance).

As you are now much more likely to come across a LIP as an opponent, you need to be aware of your duties, if any, to a LIP. A legal representative does not generally owe a duty of care to any opposing party to litigation, whether represented or not. Indeed, the legal representative's duty is to protect his own client's interests against the opposite party. That said, a legal representative's professional conduct duties do have some relevance to his dealings with an opposing LIP. All legal representatives must of course comply with their professional conduct obligations as discussed in Chapter 1 at paragraph 1.6.

Within the SRA Standards and Regulations (which sets out the Codes of conduct for solicitors and firms—see Chapter 1), all solicitors must act with integrity. The courts expect legal representatives to assist LIPs to some degree so that the complexities of litigation do not cause the LIP to be less fairly placed in the action. Acting for a client where the opponent is an LIP will have certain additional obligations on the legal practitioner to manage his duties to his client, the court, and the partial assistance expected to be given to the LIP.

The Principles must still be adhered to but the following should also be considered:

- Legal representatives must not take advantage of LIPs.

- Clients must receive the best possible information about how their matter will be priced as well as about the overall cost of their matter and any costs incurred. You should explain to the client at the outset the additional costs that can arise when proceedings become more protracted, and any other potential adverse costs implications as a result of having an LIP as the opposing party.

- Legal representatives must comply with court orders that place obligations on them. They must inform the client of circumstances in which the legal representative's duties to the court outweigh their obligations to the client.

The CPR apply equally to LIPs but in reaching a case management decision, the court may well take into account the fact that a party is a LIP. Clients should be made aware of this, so that they know what the matter is likely to involve in terms of time and cost.

In addition to our professional conduct rules and the CPR acknowledging the existence of LIPs and how best to help them, legal representatives can greatly assist the efficient progress of the litigation where one party is a LIP. Offering a LIP some practical assistance may in fact assist the client to progress the litigation. To this end guidelines have been prepared by the Bar Council, the Law Society, and CILEx to assist legal representatives when dealing with LIPs. Legal representatives can also help the court in directing attention to matters that need to be addressed at case management conferences and directions hearings where there is a LIP. Examples of assistance that could be considered (if in the interests of the client) include:

- providing a web link to a procedural rule, or a link to or copy of an authority (not just the citation);

- preparing all bundles and drawing orders where it would normally be for the opposing party to do, unless the LIP confirms he will do it;

- where a particular pre-action protocol applies, sending a copy of that protocol with the letter of claim;

- allowing the LIP sufficient time to get to grips with material, such as costs information for possible agreement, and providing skeleton arguments and other documents in good time before a hearing;

- providing details of sources of support for LIPs (such as the Citizens Advice Bureau and the Personal Support Unit. The judiciary has published a handbook to assist LIPs that covers the entire court process and gives advice on how best to approach each stage of litigation);

- defining the issues by filing and serving a list of issues as a matter of course;

- allocating responsibilities between the parties;

- explaining the steps to be taken and time limits. This can help to avoid future misunderstandings and delay;

- ensuring that the costs involved are fully explained; and

- ensuring adequate time estimates for hearings. This helps to avoid unnecessary adjournments where hearings take longer owing to the participation of a LIP who is unfamiliar with procedure.

It is the general experience of those in practice who run cases where a LIP is the opposing party that litigation can take longer to conclude either by way of settlement or trial and that costs can accrue somewhat unnecessarily. By acknowledging your opponent as a LIP, this will undoubtedly reduce those timeframes and legal costs.

2.3 THE OVERRIDING OBJECTIVE

This is the very first (and fundamental) Part of the CPR, entitled '*The Overriding Objective*':

1.1 (1) The Overriding Objective of these Rules is to enable the court to deal with cases justly and at proportionate cost.

(2) Dealing with a case justly and at a proportionate cost includes, so far as is practicable—

(a) ensuring that the parties are on an equal footing;

(b) saving expense;

(c) dealing with the case in ways which are proportionate—

(i) to the amount of money involved;

(ii) to the importance of the case;

(iii) to the complexity of the issues; and

(iv) to the financial position of each party;

(d) ensuring that it is dealt with expeditiously and fairly;

(e) allotting to it an appropriate share of the court's resources, while taking into account the need to allot resources to other cases; and

(f) enforcing compliance with rules, practice directions, and orders.

This 'overriding objective' is critical. It is the cornerstone of the CPR. The overriding objective is to be the starting point for all proceedings commenced and as the case proceeds. It is the rule to which all legal representatives will return whenever assistance is required in interpreting the CPR or in seeking to justify a step in the action.

2.3.1 WHAT IS THE EFFECT OF THE OVERRIDING OBJECTIVE?

The effect of the aims set out in the overriding objective means that interpretation of the rules must be purposive rather than a close analysis of individual words. The application of the rules and the use made of them by litigants must, 'in general', be justifiable in terms of the aims of the overriding objective. Words will, wherever possible, be given their natural meaning.

Words such as 'may' clearly imply a discretion, but words such as 'must' or 'should' do not. Care needs to be taken, however, even when seeing such words in a rule.

 Example

Whilst the word 'may' is included in a rule, implying a discretion, it may not be clear from the rule who has that discretion. In *McPhilemy v Times Newspapers Ltd (No 2)* [2000] 1 WLR 1732 the discretion in the word 'may' in CPR 32.5(5)—'any other party *may* put the witness statement in as evidence' (the rule relates to provisions applying when a party has served a witness statement, but later elects not to call that witness or use the statement at trial)—is with the court, not the 'other party', as mentioned in the rule. This is not obvious from the words of the CPR.

2.3.1.1 Dealing with a case justly, fairly, expeditiously, and proportionately, and in compliance with the court rules, practice directions, orders, and procedures

The court's primary concern must be to create justice, but this 'justice' must be further defined in terms of the need for a case to be: conducted without undue delay; fair to the parties; and proportionate to the value (or importance or complexity) of the action. Where the aims of the overriding objective seem, in certain circumstances, to contradict each other, the need to achieve 'justice' will override any apparent contradiction. So, for example, if a party requires an extension of time, this may contradict the aim to deal with cases expeditiously. In these circumstances, the aim to give 'justice' may override the need for expeditiousness if, on the particular facts, it is appropriate and 'just' to do so.

We can generally say that dealing with a case 'justly' involves an analysis of the remaining aims. Dealing with a case 'proportionately' will sometimes mean that what may be appropriate or 'just' in one case will not be appropriate or 'just' in another: for example, where the value or importance of one case is less than that of another. Proportionality is most often applied to the financial value of an action and the sum of costs that should (proportionately) be utilized to seek justice, but it can equally be applied to situations concerning the importance of the case or the availability of judicial time.

Where cases are to be dealt with 'expeditiously', this means not only 'efficiently' and within the rules, but also in a way that saves costs. 'Saving costs' also incorporates the concept of what is proportionate—that is, what is a suitable level of expenditure for that case.

We could add a further 'aim' to the CPR: that of requiring the parties and their legal representatives to cooperate wherever possible. This need to have a less adversarial, more cooperative litigation system is clearly anticipated in the greater importance given to other forms of dispute resolution by the CPR. It also implies a need for legal representatives to be less combative in their dealings with one another, and to cooperate with each other and the court in assisting a case to proceed efficiently.

2.3.1.2 What advice should be given to clients concerning the overriding objective?

It is important that clients should be advised at the outset of *their* retainer of their obligations and duties, and the expectations of the court in conducting actions within the aims of the overriding objectives. In advising clients about these aims, the client should also be advised of the possible consequences of a failure to abide by the overriding objective. These may include costs and/or interest sanctions, which may be applied as a penalty for the failure. Proportionality of costs is also something that will need to be highlighted to clients at the outset. This is discussed in more detail in Chapter 4, paragraph 4.3.

2.4 **THE COMPUTATION OF TIME**

Litigation is frequently about working within a framework of rules with associated time limits. As a legal representative, you will, therefore, need to know how to calculate a period of time for filing (lodging with the court) or serving (on a third party) that is either specified by the CPR and its Practice Direction (PD) or by a judgment or order of the court. However, CPR 3.9 permits the court to place emphasis on the efficient and proportionate conduct of litigation when considering whether a party who has exceeded a time limit set by the court should be able to avoid the penalty of missing a deadline. The manner in which the courts have applied CPR 3.9 has fluctuated over time, and initially, many parties were either struck out, had to pay additional costs, or were unable to rely on evidence. However, in more recent times, the court has moved away from such a robust application. A fuller discussion on relief from sanctions and CPR 3.9 can be found in Chapter 12 at paragraph 12.9, where the emergence of important case law on this point is examined. However, as a starting point, legal representatives must fully understand how time limits are calculated and whether such time limits can in fact be complied with.

We intend to deal with general time computation and not specific time limits imposed by the CPR, statute, or any service requirements. Those time limits are dealt with in the appropriate chapters later in the manual.

2.4.1 **PERIODS OF TIME EXPRESSED AS A NUMBER OF MONTHS**

If you must do something within 'four months', this implicitly means four calendar months (CPR 2.10).

For example, if you were to issue a claim form on 1 March, it would have to be served within four months after the date of issue—that is, on or before 1 July.

2.4.2 **PERIODS OF TIME EXPRESSED AS A NUMBER OF DAYS**

The key issues for you to be aware of here are the meaning of 'clear days' and the difference between 'more than five days' or 'less than five days'.

2.4.2.1 **'Clear days'**
Periods of time expressed in days, whether more or less than five days, implicitly mean 'clear days'. What this means is that in calculating the number of days in which you must do something, you must not include the day on which the period begins, and if the end of the period is defined by reference to an event such as a hearing, then you must not include the day of the event (CPR 2.8(2) and (3)).

For example, if your particulars of claim must be served within 14 days of service of the claim form and the claim form was served on 2 November, then the last day for service of the particulars of claim is 16 November.

2.4.2.2 **'More than five days'**
If a time period is stated to be more than five days, then bank holidays and Saturdays and Sundays are included.

For example, taking the case of the particulars of claim above, the weekends in November are included in the 14-day calculation.

2.4.2.3 **'Less than five days'**
Some periods of time are expressed to be five days or less, but bank holidays, Christmas Day, Good Friday, and weekends are excluded (CPR 2.8(4)).

For example, if you are to serve an application notice three days before a hearing and the hearing is on 20 February (a Monday), then the last day for service will be 14 February (a Tuesday).

Practical Considerations

Calculating time in these instances can be crucial, so ensure that you read the part of the CPR, judgment, or order carefully. There are occasions on which a step has to be taken within a period of days described as being 'beginning with' a certain day. If that is the case, then that start day is included in the computation of time.

2.4.2.4 An important exception

The main exception to the above points is where you are calculating the deemed date of service (see Chapter 9, paragraph 9.7.1).

2.4.2.5 Filing documents when the court office is closed

CPR 2.8(5) states that where the period of time for filing a document ends on a day on which the court office is closed, the document will be filed in time if it is done on the next day on which the court is open.

2.5 THE IMPACT OF HUMAN RIGHTS LEGISLATION ON CIVIL LITIGATION

2.5.1 HOW ARE THE CPR INTERPRETED?

When construing the rules, the courts primarily seek to give the words their natural meaning. Where the meaning is clear, the courts do not have the power to interpret a different meaning. However, if the application of the natural meaning of a rule applying traditional rules of construction means that a party's human rights would be infringed, the Human Rights Act 1998, s. 3(1), provides that 'so far as it is possible to do so, . . . [the words] must be read and be given effect in a way that is comparable with the Convention Rights'. The court therefore has the power to interpret the CPR in the light of human rights legislation. It is unclear—at least for now—how the impact of Human Rights on litigation practice will be affected by the UK leaving the European Union. See paragraph 2.5.2.4 below.

2.5.2 WHAT ARE THE MAIN PROVISIONS OF THE EUROPEAN CONVENTION ON HUMAN RIGHTS (ECHR) THAT HAVE A DIRECT IMPACT ON THE CPR AND THE LITIGATION PROCESS?

Articles 6, 8, and 10 of the ECHR are those that have the most direct impact on the CPR and that you, as a legal representative, will encounter most frequently in litigation practice.

2.5.2.1 Article 6—the right to a fair hearing

Article 6 makes it clear that any provision that restricts a person's right to submit his claim to a judge may breach the 'right to a fair hearing'. There are many situations in which a person's rights are restricted in this way: for example, where the dispute must be submitted to a tribunal (such as in employment disputes) or to an administrative process (that is, in setting the sum of maintenance that a parent must pay to the other parent with care of the child where the parents are divorced). When this occurs, three questions need to be considered to establish whether the restriction is one that contravenes the right to a fair hearing, as follows:

1. Does the case involve a determination of the person's civil rights and obligations?

2. Is the administrative determination of the person's rights subject to control by the courts?

3. Is the restriction of the person's right to access to the courts proportionate?

In nearly all of the situations in which we see the law apparently restricting a person's right to a fair hearing, we will see that they do not breach Art. 6 once the above three questions are considered.

2.5.2.2 Article 8—the right to respect for private and family life

Private and family life includes the relationship between spouses, parents and children, unmarried couples and their children, grandparents and grandchildren, and a person's sexual orientation, personal identity, and private space.

Article 8 may be invoked to protect personal and private information, correspondence, telephone conversations, and relationships between people. A balance sometimes has to be struck between the protection provided by Art. 8 and the right to a fair hearing under Art. 6. Where the confidentiality involves children (for example, in a family law hearing), it is generally thought that Art. 8 will take precedence, but where the confidentiality involves adults (for example, in the need for proper and fair disclosure in a civil action), Art. 6 will take precedence. In the latter situation, there are clear limits to any precedence of Art. 6. This has been clearly demonstrated in *Jones v University of Warwick* [2003] 1 WLR 954, in which video evidence of the claimant in personal injury actions has been held to be 'fair' where the video evidence is obtained secretly but in public places, but not fair if obtained secretly and of the claimant in his own home.

In *Long Beach Ltd and Denis Christel Sassou Nguesso v Global Witness Ltd* [2007] EWHC 1980 (QB), the court examined the balance to be achieved between the claimants' right to privacy under Art. 8 and the rights of the defendant to freedom of expression under Art. 10. The findings in this case were significantly influenced by the fact that the documents (over which the claimants sought the right to privacy) had already come into the 'public' domain as a result of the court proceedings and the public interest in publication.

2.5.2.3 Article 10—the right to freedom of expression

Article 10 provides a qualified right to freedom of expression. The right is qualified by the need to protect another individual's rights or reputation. This Article has altered the common law test applied in the grant of injunctions. A practical review of injunctions is contained in Chapter 14, paragraph 14.8, and there is an additional chapter 'Injunctions and other Equitable Remedies' available in the online resources.

Also, in defamation claims, there may be proceedings to restrain publication of information that would invade the privacy of another person. *Douglas v Hello! Ltd* [2001] QB 967, the case involving Michael Douglas and Catherine Zeta Jones, involved a breach of the couple's right to privacy of photographs taken of their wedding. In these cases, a balance has to be made between the potentially competing interests of protecting private and family life under Art. 8, and the right to freedom of expression and the protection of the rights and reputation of persons under Art. 10.

It is often a question of balancing the right of privacy with the right of freedom of expression. This balancing exercise was also considered in the case *HRH Prince of Wales v Associated Newspapers Ltd* [2006] EWCA Civ 1776, concluding that where it was obvious that the information was private (as it was here, being contained within a private diary), Art. 8 will prevail.

2.5.2.4 Brexit

At the time of writing there is a possibility that the Human Rights Act 1998 will be updated after Brexit but it is thought unlikely that any changes will take place in the near future.

2.5.3 RAISING HUMAN RIGHTS LEGISLATION IN CIVIL LITIGATION

2.5.3.1 Jurisdiction

Claims under the Human Rights Act 1998, s. 7(1)(a) in respect of a judicial act must be brought in the High Court. Other civil claims under the Human Rights Act 1998 can be brought in the County Court or the High Court.

Deputy district judges and masters (whether sitting in the High Court or in a County Court) cannot hear claims under the Human Rights Act 1998.

2.5.3.2 Statements of case

Form N1 (the claim form) and notices of appeal have boxes on the printed form in which the claimant must state whether a Human Rights Act 1998 point is being raised in the action or in the appeal. If it is, then full particulars of the point must be set out in the particulars of claim or appeal claim. See Appendix 3 for an example of a completed claim form used to commence a civil claim.

2.5.3.3 A declaration of incompatibility

The court may not make a declaration of incompatibility under the Human Rights Act 1998, s. 4, unless twenty-one days' notice has been given to the Crown (Human Rights Act 1998, s. 5, and CPR 19.4A(1)). Where this occurs, directions requiring notice will usually be made at the first opportunity and a Minister, or other person permitted by the Human Rights Act 1998, is entitled to be joined on application by the Minister or by direction of the court.

2.5.3.4 Claims for damages for a breach of a human right

Where a claim is made for damages for a breach of a human right, notice must be given to the Crown.

2.6 THE SINGLE COUNTY COURT

The Crime and Courts Act 2013 established the single County Court by making provision for the removal of geographical jurisdictional boundaries from the county courts. This single County Court will sit at various locations within England and Wales in a way similar to the High Court, and it has a single seal and a single identity to indicate its national jurisdiction. The courthouses in which it will convene will act as 'hearing centres' with court administrative offices attached to them.

KEY POINTS SUMMARY

- Understand that litigation today is underpinned by the overriding objective.
- Be aware of the impact of the CPR on how you conduct the resolution of a dispute for your clients.
- Check your time limits when calculating periods of time and beware that missing a deadline could result in severe sanctions.
- Take account of human rights issues when proceeding with a claim.

SELF-TEST QUESTIONS

1. What role does the court have in the conduct of litigation?
2. What underpins the whole ethos of civil practice in the courts?
3. When a part of the CPR indicates when an order should be complied with by reference to a number of days, is the date of the order and/or the date by which the order must be complied with included in calculating the number of days?

 Suggested answers to these self-test questions can be accessed in the Student Resources section of the online resources.

3 COSTS INFORMATION TO THE CLIENT AND FUNDING OPTIONS

3.1 INTRODUCTION

When a legal representative takes instructions from a client at the outset of a new matter, he is obliged to give to the client the best information possible about the likely costs of pursuing and ultimately resolving the dispute, as well as discussing with the client the best way of funding the action. This advice needs to be reviewed with the client throughout the duration of the matter.

This funding advice is inextricably linked to a legal representative's professional conduct duties generally and set out in the SRA Standards and Regulations (comprising the Codes of Conduct for solicitors and firms) with specific reference to funding advice. The Transparency Rules contained in the SRA Standards and Regulations deals with a firm's obligations regarding its charges. These Rules require regulated law firms to publish price and service information on their websites, including their complaints procedures.

This chapter will focus on the following:

- what information your client needs to know about costs generally and, in order to meet these professional obligations, the advice to be given; and

- the different types of funding options currently available that may or may not be offered to a client.

3.2 **PROFESSIONAL CONDUCT RULES**

The SRA Standards and Regulations contain the provisions that set out a solicitors and a firm's obligations regarding the information to be provided to clients about costs and funding.

3.2.1 **HOW DOES THE LEGAL REPRESENTATIVE COMPLY IN PRACTICE WITH PROFESSIONAL CONDUCT RULES?**

In order not to fall foul of your professional conduct obligations here, the SRA Standards and Regulations requirements must be dealt with at the outset of a new matter.

As the matter progresses, the legal representative has a continuous duty to update the client about costs and funding, as well as to ensure that he complies with the specific requirements under the Civil Procedure Rules (CPR) on costs.

 Practical Considerations

Case law has emphasized the need for legal representatives to comply with their professional conduct obligations and has highlighted the importance of keeping detailed attendance notes of any discussions about costs, as well as a written record of the costs information that has been provided to the client.

CPR, to a degree, overlap with the general provision of costs information to the client contained within the SRA Standards and Regulations, but they are more prescriptive and involve the cost information being provided to the court as indicated earlier, either in the form of costs estimates in fast-track cases or in the form of costs budgets in most multi-track claims. The courts have become increasingly robust in ensuring that costs incurred in an action are 'proportionate', 'justified', and 'fair'. Where costs incurred are considered not to be proportionate, justified, or fair, the likelihood is that they will not be recoverable or may not be allowed at all.

Additionally, clients involved in litigation need to be aware of the following issues. These will impact on the costs information that needs to be given to them.

- The loser generally pays the winner's costs—but this is not always the case because costs are ultimately at the discretion of the court.

- The court will look at the conduct of the parties when making a decision about who pays costs.

- Options other than litigation for resolving their dispute, such as mediation or another form of alternative dispute resolution (ADR) are considered.

- The fact that litigation is expensive is weighed.

- There should be a review of the cost–benefit analysis at key stages in the litigation, such as at disclosure, or when witness statements are exchanged. At these, and at other times, there should be an analysis of the case as it has progressed and this may include a review of the merits of the case (in relation to) the total costs of the action so far incurred, as well as the costs that are to be incurred from then on, together with a review of the client's resources or the terms of a funding or insurance agreement, the opponent's ability to pay any judgment against him, and the likelihood of enforcing a judgment against the opponent.

- Costs are quantified on two bases: standard and indemnity (defined in Chapter 4, paragraph 4.3.2).

- Costs are assessed pursuant to either a summary assessment or a detailed assessment. (These procedures are set out in Chapter 20 'Assessment of Costs Proceedings'.)

£ Costs

It is extremely difficult to provide an estimate of the overall likely cost of a matter to the client. If a precise figure cannot be given at the outset, the legal representative should explain the reason to the client and proceed in one of the following ways:

- Agree either a maximum figure by way of a cost cap to be reviewed.
- Identify a stage when a more meaningful costs estimate can be given.
- Consider whether it would be more appropriate to provide a fixed fee for a defined phase of the claim. For example, Phase I could include specific steps between first instructions and the commencement of the pre-action protocol phase. A carefully calculated fee is agreed with the client, and when the end of the first phase is completed, a Phase II fixed fee could be agreed up until a further stage in the action if appropriate, or alternatively, a costs estimate or cap could then be provided to the client. Fixed fees, costs estimates and caps can be used consecutively in any phase of an action, but if using a fixed fee or costs cap, these must be expressly agreed with the client in advance.

3.2.2 WHAT ARE THE CONSEQUENCES IF YOU BREACH PROFESSIONAL CONDUCT RULES?

The SRA Standards and Regulations include a regime of a defined enforcement strategy, as well as a disciplinary effect.

Essentially, this means that a breach of their requirements may render you liable to pay damages to the client and to a reduction of the bill, as well as conditions being placed on your practising certificate (if you are a solicitor), a fine, a suspension, or even being struck off the Roll. These sanctions are all separate from the client's right to pursue a negligence claim against you, if appropriate.

3.3 METHODS OF FUNDING A CLAIM AND IMPORTANT CHANGES

When you take initial instructions from your client, you will need to consider in some detail with him how he is going to fund his claim or his defence of a claim. There are a number of options that may or may not be available to your client, but it is best to sit down with your client and discuss each option with him and whether an option is available to him or not, with reasons, so as to find the most appropriate method of funding.

The most common methods of funding offered by legal practices are set out in the following paragraphs. Many of these methods stand alone or can be combined depending on your client's needs and the assessed risk in each case for both client and practice. Most legal practitioners will not offer any type of funding arrangement if the prospects of success are below 60 per cent. For a comparison of these different methods of funding see Table 3.1 at the end of this chapter.

3.3.1 'BEFORE THE EVENT' (BTE) INSURANCE

Many clients have existing insurance in respect of motor vehicles and property or even as a perk of a credit card facility. Under the terms of these policies, the client may have (sometimes unbeknown to him) legal expenses insurance that may cover payment of some or all of his own and his opponent's legal costs of a civil action, if necessary.

A legal representative should ask his client to check all existing insurance policies to ascertain whether such cover is provided, the extent of the cover, and whether it is appropriate. If your client is relying on such a policy to fund an action, it may be appropriate for the legal representative himself to look at the terms of the policy to identify the existence and ambit of those terms, as many BTE policies have intricate and sometimes difficult-to-understand policy exclusions or limits of indemnity which may not be sufficient to cover many multi-track cases. If your client has the benefit of BTE, then there is a presumption that he will use it rather than seek another method of funding.

3.3.2 PRIVATE FUNDS

Private funds are the traditional method of paying for litigation, and the client's ability to pay privately very much depends on his own resources available from capital and income. It is more usual for commercial clients to pay privately than individuals, although in either case it makes the provision of costs information to your privately paying client even more pertinent.

The client will pay the legal representative's costs of conducting the case at an agreed hourly rate, plus disbursements and VAT. (For a full discussion on how those costs are made up and assessed, see Chapter 4, paragraphs 4.3.2 and 4.4.) In accordance with the terms of the retainer set out in the client care letter, the client will usually be billed on an interim basis every month for work done.

The client should be informed at the outset of any claim that if he is successful, his costs are likely to be more than any amount of costs recoverable from his opponent. This is for several reasons:

- the opponent will always attempt to compromise your costs as a matter of principle;
- you will usually advise your client to accept, with your client's express authority, a lesser amount for your costs to avoid the further expense and time commitment of a detailed assessment of those costs; and
- in pursuing a claim on behalf of your client in accordance with your professional conduct obligations and doing the best for your client, you will almost certainly spend time on the case that will simply be irrecoverable if the matter proceeds to a detailed assessment: for example, attending on the client for an hour when your opponent may successfully argue that thirty minutes was reasonable, or spending six hours drafting and reviewing your client's witness statement when three-and-a-half hours may have been reasonable. Some aspects of your advice to your client in litigation are also rarely recoverable—for example, the time spent in advising him of the best method of funding available and your client care obligations to him in general.

In litigation, when a costs recovery order has been made in your client's favour, this will not generally cover the time spent on certain aspects of the case and thus, although it is work properly done on the file (for example, interviewing or taking a statement from a witness that you ultimately decide not to use) and is work for which your client should pay, it will not be part of the costs of the action.

In practice, there is an unwritten rule that there is usually to be expected, in most cases, a shortfall of at least 20–30 per cent in the recovery of costs.

3.3.3 UNION AND ASSOCIATION FUNDING

If your client is a member of a trade union or other association, he may have funding in place by virtue of his membership to cover his own legal fees, and possibly his opponent's legal fees if he loses. It is incumbent on the legal representative to ask the client at the first meeting whether he is a member of a union or association.

It may well be that further enquiries are needed to ascertain relevant cover, but care must be taken by the legal representative to ask the client in a clear and unambiguous manner about membership details. If it is the case that the client has union funding, it is very likely that the union will insist, in accordance with the terms of membership, that panel solicitors be appointed to represent the client. In this case, you must inform the client that if he is to take advantage of this, then he must terminate any retainer that he has with you, and you must forward to the client any relevant documentation. The benefit to the client of having union-backed funding is that the client does not have to concern himself with any part of his ultimate damages award being diverted to his legal representative, as is the position under CFA and DBA (see paragraphs 3.3.5 and 3.3.8).

3.3.4 **PUBLIC FUNDING (LEGAL AID)** – *Rare*

Public funding (now also more commonly known as Legal Aid) in civil matters is effected through the Legal Aid Agency (LAA).

The way in which Legal Aid works today is that it is only solicitors' practices that have a contract with the LAA that can undertake legally aided work.

In order to be eligible for Legal Aid, the client has to satisfy a financial eligibility test and a merits test before the level of service from the LAA is decided upon. Details of all of the materials governing public funding can be found in the Legal Aid Agency Manual at https://www.gov.uk/government/organisations/legal-aid-agency. If public funding is available, it can be offered, subject to the satisfaction of the means and merits test, on a partial contribution basis by the client out of his disposable capital or income paid to the LAA on a monthly basis, or the client can be wholly publicly funded with no contribution.

However, there are a number of excluded categories of work that cannot be funded by the LAA and these include (not exhaustively) all personal injury work (save for some instances of obstetric clinical negligence cases) and matters of a property, trust, probate, or commercial nature—that is, essentially, most areas of civil and commercial litigation. Because of these far-reaching exclusions, LAA funding is not looked at in any detail in this manual.

3.3.5 **CONDITIONAL FEE AGREEMENTS (CFA)**

3.3.5.1 What are CFA?

A CFA is essentially an agreement for litigation services under which the legal representative's fees and expenses, or any part of them, are payable only in particular circumstances, those circumstances being the success of a client's claim (Courts and Legal Services Act 1990, s. 58). CFA are available to claimants and defendants. They can stand alone or be used in conjunction with other forms of funding.

There are a number of different types of CFA, depending on the fee agreement between the client and the law firm. The most common types of CFA are those with a success fee and a discounted CFA with no success fee.

3.3.5.1.1 *CFA with a success fee*

A CFA agreement operates on the basis that the client and the law firm enter into a legally binding agreement where the client pays no legal costs to his legal representative throughout the duration of his case. If the client is successful, the legal representative is then entitled to charge an agreed percentage uplift to his base costs (these are the normal legal costs based on an hourly rate), known as an 'additional liability' or 'success fee'. Therefore, in the event of a 'win' for the client, the usual order for payment of the successful client's costs would be for the losing opponent (in personal injury litigation this is usually an insurance company) to pay most of those reasonable base costs and disbursements.

However, the client is not permitted to seek to recover any part of the success fee from the opponent. The client must bear this himself. In personal injury cases, the success fee (inclusive of VAT) can be set at a figure up to 100 per cent of the base costs, but the amount recoverable is limited to 25 per cent of the damages recovered by the client (excluding future pecuniary losses) and is net of any state benefits received by the client. In all other cases the success fee can be no greater than 100 per cent of the legal representative's fees.

[handwritten margin note: claimant must pay the success fee]

Example of the operation of a CFA with a success fee for a successful claimant

A claimant client and legal representative entered into a CFA with a success fee of 50 per cent representing the risk element alone (see paragraph 3.3.5.2.1 for an explanation of the calculation of the success fee) in respect of personal injuries sustained in a road traffic accident. The client agreed to pay all the disbursements himself. The client was successful and recovered damages of £30,000. The base costs incurred by his legal representative were £20,000 plus VAT. The opponent was ordered to pay the claimant's costs. Whilst the legal representative was permitted to agree a success fee of 50 per cent, he is limited to recovering no more than 25 per cent (of the relevant damages recovered at £30,000) inclusive of VAT from his client in the personal injury claim. Therefore, the claimant would secure payment from the opponent in respect of his disbursements. The claimant's legal representative would claim base costs of £20,000 plus VAT from the opponent and assess the success fee at £10,000 being 50 per cent of the base costs. However, that £10,000 represents more than 25 per cent of the damages recovered by the client and as such the legal representative will be limited to claiming a success fee of £7,500 inclusive of VAT from his client. Consequently, the client would only retain £22,500 of his damages payment.

Example of the operation of a CFA with a success fee for a losing claimant

Taking the facts of the previous example, if the client lost his action, he is again unlikely to secure an order for costs in his favour. Therefore, as he had lost, he would recover no damages and he would not secure the return of the disbursements paid personally. However, he would not be required to pay the £20,000 to his legal representative, nor would he be asked to pay the £7,500 success fee.

There are a number of exceptions to the new rule that the success fee can no longer be recovered from the opponent and these are as follows:

- in defamation, publication, and privacy cases—deferred for the foreseeable future; and

- in diffuse mesothelioma cases—under further review by the Lord Chancellor.

In these situations, if the client is successful, the success fee can be recovered from the opponent, but this will be subject to the usual arguments or scrutiny by the court on what that level of success fee should be.

3.3.5.1.2 *Discounted CFA*
Whilst discounted CFA more commonly feature in commercial cases, they are less common than CFA with success fees. They operate on the basis that an enhanced percentage on base costs is charged to the client as the litigation progresses and that the client pays as he goes along. If the client is successful, then there is no further enhancement, but if the client loses, then the legal costs are reduced, and a reimbursement may be made to the client.

With the demise of legal aid in civil litigation, part of the aim of the expansion of the use of CFA for funding purposes was to provide access to justice, and to encourage the risks of litigation to be shared between the client litigant and the person most able to assess the level of that risk—the legal representative. A legal representative is unlikely to take on an action if he stands too great a risk of not being paid if the action is lost.

3.3.5.2 The success fee
The success fee is the additional liability or enhancement to the legal representative's base costs. There are a number of categories of success fee:

3.3.5.2.1 *The discretionary success fee—how is it calculated?*
Primarily, there are two aspects to the calculation of the success fees. The success fee represents the risk factor to the legal representative of taking on the litigation and the fact

that the legal representative is, in effect, postponing being paid his legal costs until the resolution of the claim. Whatever percentage is attached to each of these elements, the global success fee, including risk and postponement, cannot be more than 100 per cent of the base costs.

How this global success fee is actually calculated depends on each case and firms have their own policy on this. Some firms undertake the risk assessment on a case-by-case basis, while others look at a cross-section of similar cases and consider the probability of success in that way. Generally, the success fee has to be reasonable. It is also possible, and indeed popular, to have staged success fees, starting low and increasing as the case progressed, or starting high and decreasing if admissions of liability were made.

However, as far as the success fee is concerned in **personal injury** matters, there is a cap on recovery of that success fee from the client as this cannot represent more than 25 per cent (inclusive of VAT) of the client's damages, excluding the future loss element, whether the matter settles before trial or goes to trial.

In the case of *Herbert v HH Law Ltd* [2019] EWCA Civ 527, the Court of Appeal ruled on two important issues in the context of an assessment of solicitor/client costs.

3.3.5.2.2 *Fixed success fees*

The low-value personal injury claims in road traffic accidents and low-value personal injury employers' and public liability claims do not have any fixed success fees but do have a sliding scale of fixed costs according to damages recovered once these cases have exited the low-value protocol process and entered the litigation forum. Whilst these cases remain within the online protocol system, there are, however, no fixed success fees.

3.3.5.3 The regulation of CFA

3.3.5.3.1 *What governs CFA?*

There are three sources of authority for the CFA regime:

- the Courts and Legal Services Act 1990, ss. 58 and 58A as amended by s. 44 Legal Aid, Sentencing and Punishment of Offenders Act 2012 (LASPO);
- the Conditional Fee Agreements Order 2013 ('the CFA Order') which revokes the Conditional Fee Agreements Order 2000; and
- the SRA Standards and Regulations, both the Code of Conduct for Solicitors and the Transparency Rules.

3.3.5.3.2 *What does the legal representative need to discuss when advising his client on entering into a CFA?*

There are a number of mandatory requirements that must be brought to the client's attention, and these are as follows:

- The CFA must be in writing.
- It must not relate to proceedings that cannot be the subject of an enforceable CFA (that is, criminal—excluding some environmental matters—and family proceedings).
- The success fee is not recoverable from the opponent under any circumstances.
- The maximum amount of the success fee must be expressly stated to the client, and must not exceed 100 per cent of the base costs for all claims with a cap on the amount of success fee recoverable for personal injury and clinical negligence cases of no more than 25 per cent of the damages awarded (excluding future losses) net of any sums recoverable by the Compensation Recovery Unit (see Chapter 7 at paragraph 7.6.3.1.1).
- You must explain to your client when he may be liable for his own and his opponent's costs.

- You must explain the client's entitlement to an assessment of costs when you intend to seek payment of costs from your client.
- You must disclose to your client whether you have any interest in any funding policy.

 Practical Considerations

Practically, it is advisable to consider matters from your client's perspective: a client receiving a model Law Society CFA with a success fee agreement is likely to be very much at a loss if he is expected to read and understand all of this material on his own. Additionally, he needs to know that this is still a legally binding contract, and that it represents the retainer between himself and the firm.

The requirements noted earlier make no mention of explaining to the client the detail of the success fee calculations. Essentially, you should explain the terms of the CFA with a success fee to your client in detail, probably at a meeting, and back up important aspects in writing. The aspects that you may wish to discuss are likely to include what happens on termination of the agreement, and why the success fee has been set at a certain level.

3.3.5.4 What happens if you fail to adhere to these requirements?

If you fail to adhere to the requirements set out previously, the result of which is to have an adverse effect on the client, or you fail to make appropriate enquiries of your client as to other existing methods of funding such as BTE before entering into a CFA, the CFA is very likely to be held unenforceable. What this means is that you may be deemed to have had an unenforceable contract with your client and, therefore, to have no legal basis upon which to charge for the work done. This would, effectively, prevent you from recovering your legal costs from either your client or his opponent.

If, however, you fail solely to comply with your professional conduct obligations, it is unlikely that this would make the CFA invalid. Any breach in this particular situation will not prevent you from recovering, if your client wins, any disbursements. It is only the legal costs and success fee that may remain irrecoverable.

3.3.6 'AFTER THE EVENT' (ATE) INSURANCE

3.3.6.1 What is ATE insurance?

ATE insurance has traditionally worked in one of two ways within the realms of litigation. Its most popular use has been to supplement a CFA either with a success fee or a discounted CFA. It is usually purchased to provide insurance to cover the case in which the client loses and is ordered to pay some or all of his opponent's legal costs and disbursements. It can also be purchased to cover payment of his own disbursements and can include cover for any shortfall of the costs recovery order against a losing opponent (the premiums for each level of cover can be significantly different). The second way in which it is used is as a stand-alone insurance policy without a CFA, whereby the client is seeking funding from a reputable insurer against his own and his opponent's legal costs and disbursements. This is very likely to continue to be the case.

In either of these scenarios, ATE insurance is only available after the dispute has arisen and should only be obtained if there is no other insurance or funding option available to the client. ATE insurance will, however, never cover the payment of a court order or judgment in respect of damages.

3.3.6.2 The premium

As with all insurance policies, the client is responsible for payment of the premium, and the level of the premium is usually based on the strength of the case and the level of cover required. In the ATE market for personal injury claims, the premium is not too onerous, usually totalling less than £500 for the basic cover in non-complex fast track cases. However, in commercial cases, it is not uncommon for premiums to be as much as 20–30 per cent of the amount of cover required. For example, if the client seeks cover in respect of an adverse costs order only, and his legal representative believes that the opponent's likely legal costs and disbursements are in the region of £20,000, then the premium will be approximately £4,000–£6,000. Insurance providers will generally fix the premium of ATE insurance in commercial matters on a case-by-case basis.

As you can see, premiums can be expensive, but some insurers will allow the staged payment of premiums. The usual stages that underwriters consider for triggering payment of these staged premiums are pre issue of proceedings, after completion of many of the standard directions during the litigation (see Chapter 12 on case management for details of these important steps in the action), pre trial, and post trial. With each stage comes a greater premium. Other insurers may agree that part or all of the overall premium be paid at the conclusion of proceedings. If the premium or any part thereof is payable by your client, you may need to consider with your client whether he should take out a loan to pay for the premium.

3.3.6.3 The recoverability of the premium
Section 46 of LASPO 2012 provides that the ATE premium is not recoverable from the opponent and must be borne by the client in the event of a win, save for in the following types of cases:

- defamation, publication, and privacy cases—deferred for the foreseeable future;
- mesothelioma cases—under review by the Lord's Chancellor's department; and
- clinical negligence cases where the value of the claim is in excess of £1,000 and the premium relates solely to the cost of medical experts' reports on liability and causation.

This leaves potential claimants and legal practitioners in a more disadvantageous position where CFA with success fees and ATE premiums are concerned: claimants are much more likely to have to look to their damages to pay the success fee if successful and legal representatives risk losing clients, if CFA with success fees are not offered, and if offered and the action won, they simply agree to forgo the success fee as a matter of discretion to retain the client, resulting in a much lower level of fee income.

However, claimants and their legal advisers are not left completely without access to justice and a 'fair deal'.

3.3.7 AN INCREASE IN DAMAGES AWARDED

To assist claimants meeting the additional costs and risks of litigation a 10 per cent increase in the award of general damages is permitted for all non-pecuniary loss claims, i.e. all personal injury cases where damages for pain and suffering or loss of amenity, physical inconvenience, discomfort, and mental distress are claimed. This increase in general damages is limited to these types of claims only.

3.3.8 DAMAGE BASED AGREEMENTS (DBA)

3.3.8.1 What are DBA?
A damages-based agreement (DBA) is a form of 'no win, no fee' arrangement between a legal representative and a client, which provides that the client will make a payment to the legal representative if the client obtains 'a specified financial benefit' (usually damages

paid by the losing side). The amount of the payment will be determined as a percentage of the compensation received by the client (s. 58AA, Courts and Legal Services Act 1990 (CLSA 1990)).

If the client is unsuccessful, the legal representative will not be paid for the work done under the DBA. The client will still be potentially liable for adverse costs, and these may be covered by after the event (ATE) insurance.

If the DBA does not comply with the relevant legislation and is, therefore, unenforceable, the client will not have to pay the legal representative anything under the DBA. In these circumstances, there would be no recoverable costs ordered from the losing side because of the application of the indemnity principle.

The Damages-based Agreements Regulations 2013 (SI 2013/609) (DBA Regulations 2013) describe a DBA as a private funding arrangement between a representative and a client, whereby the representative's agreed fee (the payment) is contingent on the success of the case and is determined as a percentage of the compensation received by the client (paragraph 2.1, DBA Regulations 2013: explanatory memorandum).

DBAs were introduced by section 45 of the Legal Aid, Sentencing and Punishment of Offenders Act 2012 (LASPO 2012), with effect from 1 April 2013. Section 45 amends section 58AA of the CLSA 1990 to allow DBAs in all civil litigation and not just in employment matters (as was previously the case).

The CLSA 1990, as amended by section 45 of LASPO 2012, also sets out a framework of requirements for DBAs, and makes provision for regulations and rules of court to provide further detail.

3.3.8.2 How do they operate?

The DBA Regulations 2013 cap is the percentage of the client's compensation that may be taken as a law firm's contingency fee or 'payment'. The cap is set at:

- 25% in personal injury claims;
- 35% in employment matters;
- 50% in all other matters.

The payment must include VAT. The firm will need to deduct from the payment any of its own fees that have been paid or are payable by another party and any counsel fee disbursements that it has incurred and that have been paid or are payable by another party. The caps apply only to proceedings at first instance.

Both CPR 44.18 and paragraph 7.11 of the explanatory memorandum to the DBA Regulations 2013 confirm that the indemnity principle applies to DBAs. As a result, if the claimant's solicitor is entitled to a contingency fee under the DBA that is less than the amount of recoverable costs, the recoverable costs from the losing defendant will be limited to the amount of the contingency fee.

3.3.8.3 The requirements of DBA

With the exception of DBAs in employment matters where the requirements are different, a DBA must:

- Be in writing (s. 58AA(4)(a), *CLSA 1990*).
- Specify the following (Regulation 3, DBA Regulations 2013):
  - the claim or proceedings, or parts of them, to which the DBA relates;
  - the circumstances in which the legal representative's payment, expenses, and costs, or part of them, are payable; and
  - the reason for setting the amount of the payment at the level agreed.

With the exception of DBAs in employment matters, a DBA must not require the client to pay anything other than (Regulation 4(1), DBA Regulations 2013:

- The contingency fee, referred to as 'the payment'.
- Any expenses incurred by the legal representative, net of any amount that has been paid or is payable by another party. The definition of 'expenses' in the DBA Regulations 2013 gives the expense of obtaining an expert's report as an example. The explanatory memorandum to the DBA Regulations 2013 refers to court fees as another example (paragraph 7.13, explanatory memorandum).

The payment must be net of the following:

- Costs (including fixed costs under CPR 45) that have been paid or are payable by another party to the proceedings by agreement or order (where costs are defined as the total of the legal representative's time reasonably spent multiplied by the legal representative's reasonable hourly rate).
- Counsel's fees that have been paid for as a disbursement by the legal representative, and that have been recovered or are recoverable from another party.

This means that any of the legal representative's fees that are recoverable from the other side and any counsel's fees incurred by the legal representative and payable by the other side must be set off against the contingency fee or payment. This will effectively reduce the amount that the client must pay to its legal representative out of the damages recovered (and the risk of non-payment by another party is the legal representative's, not the client's).

3.3.8.4 Uncertainties in the DBA Regulations

The DBA Regulations 2013 include relatively little detail. Despite this lack of detail, or possibly because of it, there are a number of issues and difficulties in understanding exactly how DBAs should work in practice, and it is understood that the take-up in use of DBAs outside the employment context has been relatively slow.

In 2019, the government said that it accepted that the DBA Regulations 2013 would benefit from additional clarity and certainty and that it would consider the way forward in light of the outcome of an independent review of the drafting of the Regulations, undertaken by Professor Rachael Mulheron and Nicholas Bacon QC. The latter published their proposals for reform in October 2019, including re-drafted regulations, an explanatory memorandum, and worked examples for commercial and personal injury claims. As at April 2020, the final outcome of that review is still awaited.

3.3.8.5 How does a DBA work in practice?

Remember that the payment is 25% or 50% of the monies actually received by the client from their opponent, not 25% or 50% of the monies the opponent has agreed, or been ordered, to pay. As a result, you should consider the potential need for enforcement and how enforcement proceedings would be funded when you first enter into a DBA.

In addition, since the contingency fee is calculated as a percentage of 'the sums ultimately recovered by the client', the amount payable to the law firm could be significantly reduced, or even eliminated altogether, in any of the following scenarios:

- The defendant was insolvent.
- Contributory negligence was a factor.
- A counterclaim reduced the sum recovered by the claimant.

The requirement for costs and counsel's fees, that have been paid or are payable, to be set off against the contingency fee appears to add another risk factor in relation to the amount that a law firm might end up with. The use of the word 'payable' suggests that if the losing defendant is ordered to pay costs and counsel's fees but fails to do so, the amount of costs and counsel's fees ordered will still have to be set off against the contingency fee that the law firm is entitled to receive (assuming that any damages are recovered in these circumstances). (The same appears to apply to expenses, given that the legal representative can only require the client to pay any expenses that it has incurred 'net of any amount which has been paid or is payable by another party ...'.)

If the legal representative and the client agree to enter into a DBA, they must decide at the outset who will meet the liability for adverse costs if the client is unsuccessful. If, as is often the case in Canada, the solicitors agree to bear any adverse costs order, then this additional risk can be reflected in the percentage recovery allowed in the event of success. Otherwise, if the client is unsuccessful, it will be potentially liable for adverse costs.

The client may choose to take out ATE insurance to cover these adverse costs. However, in the case of ATE insurance policies entered into from April 2013, it is no longer possible to recover the ATE insurance premium from the losing side and the client will have to pay for the premium (subject to a few exceptions where recoverability is still possible, including claims relating to insolvency where the policy was entered into before 6 April 2016, and publication and privacy proceedings).

It seems unlikely that the courts will make solicitors liable for the adverse costs where this has not been agreed between the solicitors and the client, although unfortunately the DBA Regulations 2013 do not address this issue expressly.

If the client loses the claim, the law firm will not receive any payment. However, the client will usually still be responsible for paying expenses (unless the firm has agreed otherwise).

In the light of the definitions of 'payment' and 'expenses' in the DBA Regulations 2013, it seems that in non-employment matters, the client will not be liable to pay counsel's fees if it loses. Therefore, counsel is likely to ask for an indemnity from the solicitors. As a result, solicitors should try to persuade counsel to enter into a DBA with the client whenever they are intending to do so themselves.

3.3.9 LITIGATION FUNDING

3.3.9.1 What is litigation funding?

Litigation funding, previously known as third-party funding, essentially involves the provision of funds by individuals or companies who have no other connection with the litigation (and who are not practising lawyers). This type of funding was originally labelled 'champertous', meaning that an independent body, which was financing an action on behalf of another, may be able to apply pressure in the litigation, ultimately distorting the concept of justice. This could be done by exerting influence over the decision to accept or reject offers or over general strategy.

However, with the demise of many forms of funding over the years, litigation funding is now a legal and viable form of funding in civil litigation matters. The litigation funder might fund some or all of the client's legal representative's fees, his disbursements and barrister's fees, and the cost of the ATE premium to cover the risk of having to pay the opponent's costs. It is not usually intended to cover the actual costs of the opponent, as ATE is designed for that purpose.

There is therefore an overlap with ATE here, as ATE can be purchased to cover some or all of the earlier stated costs. It may be cheaper for the client to fund some or all of these costs himself, knowing that he will get his money back from an ATE insurance policy if he loses. If litigation funding is employed, then the legal representative will need to ensure that his own retainer does not conflict with the litigation funder's agreement and that a confidentiality clause is in place.

3.3.9.2 How is litigation funding regulated?

Despite the fact that there is still no statutory regulation of these types of funding agreements, a voluntary code of conduct for litigation funders has been established and sets out the standards of practice and behaviour for funders. The code primarily addresses four main areas. The funder:

- must have adequate financial resources to cover his funding liability for 36 months;
- must have at least £2 million of capital and a mandatory annual audit;
- can only withdraw from a case in three specific circumstances; and
- is restricted from trying to control the litigation by the funding agreement.

A funder may provide the full legal costs of the proceedings, may partly fund the proceedings, or may fund only the disbursements. Protection from adverse costs orders is often, but not always, provided and, in some circumstances, the funder may provide no direct funding at all, but instead agree to cover a party's potential exposure to adverse costs. In return, the funder would expect to make a financial profit for its outlay. This profit is usually calculated at 15–45 per cent of the damages recovered.

The 'penalty' to the funder if the funded party loses is that he does not recoup his outlay and the court has a discretion to order that the funder—effectively, a non-party to the litigation—be ordered to pay the costs of the successful opponent, rather than the funded party. The court derives its authority from s. 51(1) and (3) of the Senior Courts Act 1981. The discretion is only exercised in exceptional circumstances.

 Practical Considerations

Because litigation funding is now a real alternative to CFA and probably DBA in the litigation market, when discussing funding options with your client, you will need to raise the possibility of this type of funding. A competent legal representative should also consider seeking costs against a non-party, especially in situations in which an unsuccessful opponent does not 'look good for the money'. Equally, a person considering supporting the litigation of another will require careful advice to avoid making himself a potential target for a costs application and to ensure he complies with the Code of Conduct for litigation funders.

3.3.9.3 Types of case suitable for litigation funding

Litigation funding is primarily used for commercial cases of large value. It is not generally thought appropriate for personal injury or non-monetary relief claims. As with DBA, litigation funders are unlikely to be interested in defendant claims unless there is a sizeable and realistic counterclaim having taken into account the likelihood of success of the claimant's claim.

If your client's claim is suitable, then the legal representative will need to investigate the prospects of the claim, and, if better than 60 per cent, approach either a broker or a funder directly on a confidential basis to ascertain a quote for the funding. The Association of Litigation Funders currently has eight funder members.

3.4 WHAT DO YOU TELL YOUR OPPONENT ABOUT FUNDING?

3.4.1 CFA AND ATE

If your client enters into any type of CFA either with or without a success fee not recoverable from the opponent, there is no CPR requirement to inform your opponent of either. This is because there is no additional costs burden to the opponent.

3.4.2 DBA AND LITIGATION FUNDING

DBA and litigation funding do not impose an additional burden on the opponent. Consequently, there is no statutory or CPR requirement to formally notify your opponent.

However, it is often tactically conducive to settlement and the smooth running of the case to let your opponent know by letter how your client's case is funded: if your opponent is informed that your client has funding either by way of a CFA, DBA, or a litigation funder, then this will alert them to the fact that the legal representative must genuinely believe the client's case has better than reasonable prospects of success.

3.4.3 BTE, UNION, ASSOCIATION, AND LEGAL AID

As regards BTE and union-backed cases, the funding pre-dated the dispute and does not, therefore, impose an additional liability to the opponent. However, it is best practice to inform your opponent of the funding arrangement.

In relation to legal aid, it is mandatory to inform the opponent that your client is legally aided. This is primarily because a legally aided opponent cannot be ordered to pay an opponent's costs. This is crucial for your client to know if they ever face this situation as an opponent to a legally aided case, as it will inevitably affect how the case is conducted on a proportionate, commercial, and financial basis.

3.5 MISCELLANEOUS POINTS

3.5.1 BARRISTERS AND CFA WITH SUCCESS FEES AND DBA

It is possible, though obviously less commonplace, to invite any barrister (known as counsel) instructed in an action in which the legal representative has a CFA with a success fee or a DBA with his client to enter into a similar CFA with a success fee or DBA with the legal representative.

It has to be appreciated, however, that the barrister is being asked to share the risk of the action in the same way as the client's legal representative, but that the barrister is probably taking on a greater risk, because it is the riskier cases that go all the way to trial. However, barristers who are asked to give early advice may be more likely to agree to a similar funding arrangement with the client.

It should also be noted here that there is no requirement for the disclosure of a CFA with a success fee or a DBA made between the legal representative and counsel.

3.5.2 COLLECTIVE CONDITIONAL FEE AGREEMENTS (CCFA) AND COLLECTIVE DBA

CCFA are based on exactly the same principle as CFA, both with and without success fees, and are used by legal representatives who act for clients who are routinely involved in litigation, such as trade unions and other associations or corporations. Instead of entering into a separate CFA with each new matter for the client, there will be one CCFA, which does not specify each individual matter, but instead provides for fees to be paid on a common basis in relation to a type of claim: for example, a tripping claim or a road traffic accident. Accompanying a CCFA with a success fee will be a risk assessment document in respect of each individual claim. These CCFA do not need to be formally notified to the opponent.

It is not thought that DBA are suitable for operation on a collective basis, and no mention has been made of this in the DBA Regulations.

KEY POINTS SUMMARY

- Before bringing a claim, consider ADR or, if available, whether the dispute might be resolved by a trade body or another means.

- If litigation is the only feasible option, undertake a risk assessment whether acting on behalf of the claimant or defendant. This risk assessment will include consideration of the likely costs recovered (by the firm or the client) and those unlikely to be recovered.

- On the basis of the value and risk assessment, consider what method of funding is suitable or available to your client, giving your client the advice they need to make a sound judgment of choice (where a choice is available).

- Discuss whether the client needs or wants insurance to bring or defend the claim and the timing of both.

- Consider whether insurance is available and, if so, at what cost.

- Review with the client what court fees or expert fees will be payable and when.

- Keep in mind your professional conduct obligations in relation to client care and information on costs.

- Maintain a detailed written account of the costs advice and information that you give to your client, and review it periodically.

SELF-TEST QUESTIONS

1. What is the difference between a CFA with a success fee and a DBA?

2. Why are DBA not suitable for many defendant claims?

3. What are the sanctions if you fail to provide costs information to your client in accordance with your professional conduct obligations?

 Suggested answers to these self-test questions can be accessed in the Student Resources section of the online resources.

TABLE 3.1 COMPARISON OF FUNDING OPTIONS

Funding option	Summary	Comparison
BTE	Legal expenses insurance is usually attached to home and motor insurance policies and can provide full or partial cover.	Sometimes the terms exclude certain types of civil claims and the cover is often restricted. Even if there is a limit on the cover it is usually beneficial to make use of the BTE and then move on to another form of funding such as a CFA, ATE, or private funds.
Private funds	Funds provided from client's own cash flow or capital.	Commercial clients are usually better placed to use this option. Many clients begin paying privately where there is no BTE or union funding in place and then move to one of the other options, such as CFA, ATE, or DBA if appropriate, or vice versa. This is probably the only funding option that does not require at least a 60% chance of winning as the client carries all the risk.
Union and Association Funding	Cover provided by virtue of the client's membership.	Once a claim has been accepted, cover is usually provided for the entirety of the claim, rendering it a very attractive funding option for the client. There is usually no need to look to any other type of funding to support the client in the litigation.

(contd.)

Funding option	Summary	Comparison
Conditional Fee Agreements	Client does not pay any legal costs until the point of winning, which is usually the recovery of damages at which point the legal representative's costs become payable. Costs orders against the opponent are usually secured in these circumstances in respect of the legal costs and disbursements but the client remains responsible for payment of the success fee.	CFA are not an overly attractive funding option for the client in lower value cases due to the non-recovery of the success fee. This method is used where the client has no other financial means of paying his legal costs. Generally the success fee is paid to the legal representative, to all intents and purposes, from the damages recovered, which can often significantly reduce the compensation to the client. Even if this is the only option open to the client, many clients will think hard as to whether the pursuance of the claim is financially viable. For this reason CFA are losing their appeal. They can be used alongside ATE and run consecutively with BTE and private funds.
ATE	Insurance that is purchased after the dispute has arisen to protect the client against an adverse costs order and/or to fund the litigation and disbursements. The premium is not recoverable from the opponent in the event that the client is successful in his claim.	A popular choice in some forms of litigation but not in others where the premium is high. In those cases the client will think hard about whether to purchase it due to the non-recoverability of the premium. ATE is often used alongside privately funded, CFA-, DBA-, and litigation-funded matters.
DBA	A contingent arrangement whereby the client does not pay for legal costs until the point of success. In the absence of a costs order in favour of the client, at that point the legal representative is contractually entitled to take payment of his fees (usually capped) from the actual damages recovered by the client.	These have had little presence in civil litigation, but it is thought that claims will need to be of a high value for a legal representative to offer this form of funding to a client. These can be used with ATE and run consecutively with privately paying matters or where BTE has expired. They are thought to be an alternative to CFA. Legal representatives are wary of the new DBA and they are rare in practice. Even if they become more popular they are thought to only be available to the high-value claimant market.
Litigation funding	The provision of funding by third parties who are not connected to the dispute.	This is realistically only intended for high-value commercial cases, which are a small percentage of claims. ATE can be used concurrently to support the client, with BTE and private funding being used consecutively.

4 THE NATURE, EXTENT, AND RECOVERY OF LEGAL COSTS

Relevant parts of the CPR and its PDs: 1, 3, 27, 35, 36, 44, 45, 46, and 48.

4.1 INTRODUCTION

The term 'legal costs', for the purposes of litigation, is intended to cover the amount of time that a legal representative spends on a matter. These are otherwise known as 'profit costs'. The term 'disbursements' covers counsel's fees, court fees, ATE premiums (although these have their own rules in relation to recoverability, as has been seen in Chapter 3 at paragraph 3.3.6), expenses, and payments to other third parties, such as experts, incurred from the outset of the retainer until it is terminated or concluded. For the sake of clarity, the term 'costs' is intended to cover both legal costs and disbursements.

The client has a contractual obligation to pay for all of his costs incurred in bringing or defending a claim subject to the type of funding arrangement into which he may have entered with his legal representative, as set out in Chapter 3, paragraph 3.3. These costs are known as 'solicitor and client costs' and are discussed in Chapter 6, paragraph 6.2.1. However, the client may be able to recover a proportion of those costs from his opponent either by agreement or by an order of the court. Once the client has established an entitlement to the recovery of his costs, the parties will endeavour to agree the amount. If they cannot agree, then the court will assess those costs. The procedures for assessing costs are not detailed in this chapter but are discussed in Chapter 20 on 'Assessment of Costs Proceedings'.

The way in which the court will deal with the recovery of costs is primarily based on the 'overriding objective' contained in CPR 1, the aim of which is to deal with cases justly. The overriding objective was discussed at some length in Chapter 2. However, three of the methods that the court is specifically encouraged to use to meet that objective have an obvious bearing on costs and are worth looking at again.

To deal with a case justly, the court must, so far as is practicable:

- ensure that the parties are on an equal footing;
- save expense; and
- dealing with the case in ways that are proportionate to the amount of money involved, complexity, and the parties' financial positions.

Therefore, as a starting point, it should be borne in mind that whoever pays the costs at the end of the day, those costs should be kept, overall, within sensible proportions, having regard to the case in question.

Against the background of the overriding objective, this chapter will focus on the control and recovery of costs including:

- the discretionary nature of costs awards;
- the general principle that the loser pays;
- how the court controls costs incurred;
- the basis upon which costs orders are made;
- the aspects of a legal representative's work that are recoverable and how they are formulated; and
- the different types of costs order.

4.2 THE GENERAL PRINCIPLES OF COSTS IN LITIGATION

There are three fundamental principles that underpin costs within the litigation framework. These are:

- the payment of costs by one party to another is at the discretion of the court;
- a general rule has emerged that the loser should pay the winner's costs; and
- Qualified One Way Costs Shifting (in personal injury cases only). This seeks to refine the above two general principles.

4.2.1 THE DISCRETIONARY NATURE OF COSTS

The court's discretion in the award of costs is founded on s. 51 of the Senior Courts Act 1981 and CPR 44.2, and is wide-reaching. The court is required to take into account all of the circumstances of the case, particularly regarding the following (CPR 44.2(4)):

- the conduct of all the parties;
- whether a party has succeeded on part of its case, even if that party has not been wholly successful; and

- any admissible offer to settle made by a party which is drawn to the court's attention and which is not an offer to which costs consequences under Part 36 apply.

CPR 44.2(5) further suggests that a party's conduct may include:

- conduct before, as well as during, the proceedings and in particular the extent to which the parties followed the Practice Direction on Pre-Action Conduct and Protocols or any relevant pre-action Protocol;

- whether it was reasonable for a party to raise, pursue, or contest a particular allegation or issue;

- the manner in which a party has pursued or defended its case or a particular allegation or issue; and

- whether a claimant who has succeeded in the claim in whole or in part exaggerated its claim.

As can be seen, it is the parties' conduct in virtually every aspect of litigation that is under scrutiny by the courts in the exercise of its discretion. This conduct issue should be highlighted to the client at the outset, and wherever it may need reiterating within a costs review during the action, in order that he understands how the recovery of his costs could be affected by his behaviour both before and during proceedings.

There is, however, one situation in which the court has no discretion in whether to make an award of costs between parties: that is, where a valid CPR 36 offer has been accepted (see Chapter 15, paragraphs 15.7.1 and 15.8.1).

4.2.2 THE LOSER PAYS THE WINNER'S COSTS

This second general principle is only a starting point and the courts frequently depart from it when considering costs at the end of a hearing, sometimes ordering only a partial costs recovery or no costs recovery at all. The main reason why the court may not order the loser to pay the winner's costs is, again, owing to the conduct of one or both parties. CPR 44.2 and 44.4 require the court to take into account the conduct of the parties to the litigation both pre and post issue.

There is a plethora of cases demonstrating how the court may exercise its discretion on costs and costs recovery, which you will find throughout this manual. Instances in which the court frequently departs from these general rules, as stated previously, and makes a different costs order, whether claimant or defendant could be any one of the following:

- failure to comply with a pre-action Protocol;

- failure to negotiate;

- refusal to enter into an ADR process, particularly mediation;

- rejection of a without prejudice or Part 36 Offer;

- exaggeration of a successful party's claim; and

- failure to succeed on the whole claim.

It is worth noting that these situations do not represent an exhaustive list of the occasions on which the court will exercise its discretion, but illustrate how wide the court's discretion can be.

4.2.3 QUALIFIED ONE WAY COSTS SHIFTING (QOCS)

In personal injury cases, including clinical negligence, a claimant will in general no longer have to pay the defendant's costs if the claim fails, but the defendant will continue to have to pay the claimant's costs if the claim succeeds. This can tentatively reduce the necessity for the claimant to purchase ATE (to protect against an adverse costs order) as this is effectively eliminated by these changes effected by Part 2 LASPO 2012 and CPR 44.13–44.17 and PD 44 Section II.

QOCS applies to all claimants in personal injury and clinical negligence actions no matter when the accident occurred (save for applications for pre-action disclosure made under s. 33 of the Senior Courts Act 1981 or s. 52 of the County Courts Act 1984), whatever their means, but there are exceptions to this new rule, as follows:

1. where the claim is found to be fundamentally dishonest (fraudulent);

2. where the claim is for the financial benefit of another (intended to catch property damage insurers or credit hire providers); and

3. where the claim has been struck out, where it discloses no reasonable cause of action, or where it is otherwise an abuse of the court's process.

In all these cases, it is very likely that the claimant will be required to pay the defendant's costs, either on the standard or the indemnity basis. However, as a proviso to this, it should be noted that CPR 44.14–44.16 permits orders for costs against the claimants in categories 1–3 to be enforced (either with or without the permission of the court), but only up to the level of the damages and interest recovered by that claimant. Therefore, if the claimant did not recover any damages, then that claimant will not be ordered to pay the defendant's costs under the QOCS rules.

However, the QOCS rules do not preclude a successful claimant being deprived of all or part of his costs or being ordered to pay all or some of the defendant's costs in other circumstances: a claimant can lose the QOCS protection where the defendant has made a successful Part 36 offer. (See Chapter 15 for full details of Part 36 offers.) What this means is that the claimant will be potentially back on risk for costs if he fails to beat the defendant's Part 36 offer at trial, but again only up to the amount of the claimant's damages and interest award. As seen in Chapter 3 at paragraph 3.3.6, if ATE is taken out in respect of this risk, then the claimant will be insured against payment of those costs, but he will have to meet the payment of the premium himself. This is, therefore, one of the reasons claimants still purchase ATE even in light of the QOCS rules.

 Practical Considerations

When advising a client on the recovery of costs in litigation, whether claiming or defending, it is best to reinforce with him that the primary obligation for payment of his own legal costs rests with him, but that the court has a discretion to order that some—but, most probably, not all—of those costs be paid for by his opponent in certain circumstances. It is better for the client to see the recovery of legal costs as a 'bonus' rather than 'the norm', because judges have such a wide discretion in the award of legal costs that it is becoming increasingly difficult to predict when and how much will be recovered. Clients should also be made aware that their conduct both before and during the litigation may also be called into question, and, if thought not to be in accordance with their duty to the court, then they may in fact be punished by costs orders against them or be at risk of falling into one of the excluded QOCS cases.

4.2.4 THE LEGALLY AIDED LITIGANT

Despite the fact that legal aid is restricted in civil matters, in cases in which it has been awarded and the legally aided litigant is unsuccessful in the litigation, what happens to the legal costs of the winning party?

The Civil Legal Aid (Costs) Regulations 2013 and LASPO 2012, s. 26, state that a legally aided litigant is generally protected against adverse costs orders. This is known as 'costs protection', but only extends to the ambit of the Legal Aid certificate and to the duration of the proceedings in which the litigant was legally aided. Therefore, if your client is successful against a legally aided opponent with full costs protection, he will rarely recover any of his legal costs.

A legally aided litigant can lose his costs protection in the following circumstances:

- when, on the report of his instructing solicitor informing the Legal Aid Agency (LAA) of a change in the merits of his case or his income, the certificate is withdrawn, leaving the remainder of the action without funding and consequently the litigant unprotected; or
- where the opponent of a legally aided litigant contacts the LAA, making representations about the conduct and/or merits of the legally aided party to the extent that the certificate is withdrawn or partially withdrawn.

 Practical Considerations

It is, therefore, very important that your client is made aware as soon as an opponent is in receipt of a Legal Aid certificate that he is very unlikely to secure any costs recovery in respect of that part of the proceedings in the event of a successful outcome to the dispute, whether at trial or otherwise. This may affect your client's decision to pursue the litigation or to accept (or reject) offers.

4.3 THE BASIS ON WHICH COSTS ARE AWARDED

In paragraph 4.2, we have looked at the basic principles and how the court decides who is to pay the costs of an action. Underlying those principles are two further considerations that the court and the parties have to bear in mind when deciding how much the winning party is entitled to recover.

4.3.1 THE INDEMNITY PRINCIPLE

The indemnity principle is a long-standing principle that the winning party cannot recover more from his opponent than he has paid to his legal representative in the course of the litigation. To this end, if a client care retainer letter is not sent to the client, it could be argued that, in the absence of a formal contract, the client has no liability to pay his legal representative's costs and therefore the losing party has no liability to pay the winning party's costs.

 Example

You act for a client in a privately funded personal injury matter and send a client care letter. You make a successful application to the court for an interim payment. The court also awards you your costs. When the court is assessing those costs at the end of the hearing, the amount that you are seeking to recover cannot exceed the amount of costs that you have incurred on behalf of your client in respect of the application. Consequently, if the total cost of making the application was £1500, you are limited to recovering that amount from your opponent.

There are, however, four notable exceptions to the indemnity principle, as follows:

- CFA have the potential to breach the indemnity principle on the basis that the purpose of the agreement was that the client paid the legal representative only nominal legal fees (see Chapter 3, paragraph 3.3.5, for more on the nominal amount that the client may have to pay if he loses) should he have lost the case. However, this potential trouble spot was catered for by s. 31 of the Access to Justice Act 1999, which permitted the winning CFA with success fee client to recover his base legal costs if the CFA was in the prescribed form.

- In-house legal representatives are presumed to cost the same as instructing an independent firm to act, although, in practice, this may not be the case. Nevertheless, the case of *Re Eastwood* [1975] 1 Ch 112 established this pragmatic approach and it has remained ever since.

- A legally aided party's legal representative is only entitled to prescribed rates, although he is entitled to a full recovery of costs from a losing opponent.

- Pro bono representation, whilst free of charge to the client, can, in certain circumstances, be paid for by the unsuccessful opponent in accordance with s. 194 of the Legal Services Act 2007.

Interestingly, the indemnity principle does apply to DBAs so that a party will not be able to recover, by way of costs, more than the total amount payable by that party under the DBA.

4.3.2 THE TWO BASES OF ASSESSMENT

The two bases of assessment are known as the 'standard basis' and the 'indemnity basis', and the court has the discretion to award costs using either one.

4.3.2.1 The standard basis

If the court awards costs to be assessed on the standard basis, CPR 44.3(2) states that only costs that are proportionate are to be allowed, but that if there is any doubt, then the doubt will be resolved in favour of the paying party. The key point here is that the costs must be reasonably incurred, reasonable in amount, and proportionate. (A discussion on proportionality merits its own stand-alone section and this is dealt with in paragraph 4.3.2.4.)

4.3.2.2 The indemnity basis

If the court awards costs on the indemnity basis, CPR 44.3(3) provides that if there is any doubt as to whether a cost has been incurred reasonably or is reasonable in amount, then the doubt is resolved in favour of the receiving party. The key point here is that proportionality is not taken into account under the strict interpretation of the CPR.

The word 'indemnity' is used here again, but it takes on a different meaning when used in assessing costs.

The 'indemnity principle' and 'indemnity costs' are two separate issues that those new to practice often find confusing: the former is the global background against which costs are assessed, as described previously; the latter is a formula that the court will use to calculate costs.

The same fundamental rule applies to costs assessed on the standard and indemnity bases: in each case, they must be reasonably incurred and reasonable in amount. Costs are usually awarded on the standard basis unless the court feels that there has been some culpable behaviour, in which case, indemnity costs may be awarded.

 Practical Considerations

Such instances of situations in which an indemnity costs order may be made include pursuing an unjustified claim, rejecting a CPR 36 offer (that is subsequently beaten), an abuse of court process, dishonesty, or repeated flouting of court orders. A party who is faced with an intransigent or obstructive opponent can increase his chances of securing a costs recovery order on the indemnity basis if, before proceeding with any application or step (that the party now has to take because of the opponent's intransigence or obstructive behaviour), a letter is written to that opponent, warning him that an application for costs on the indemnity basis will be sought.

In light of the comments on applications for costs on the indemnity basis, it is worthy of note that the case of *Hobson v West London Law Solicitors* [2013] EWHC 4425 QB commented that when the court is left to consider whether indemnity costs should be awarded, the parties must act in a proportionate manner in pursuing that application.

4.3.2.3 What does the court take into account when deciding the amount of costs on either basis?

In deciding what costs have been reasonably incurred, are reasonable in amount, and are proportionate for a standard basis assessment, and what costs have been unreasonably incurred or are unreasonable in amount for an indemnity basis assessment, the court, in accordance with CPR 44.4(3), will take into account the following (subject to the indemnity principle):

- the conduct of the parties at all times, including in particular (i) conduct before and during the proceedings and (ii) the efforts made, if any, before and during the proceedings in order to try to resolve the dispute;
- the amount or value of any money or property involved;
- the importance of the matter to the parties;
- the particular complexity of the matter, or the difficulty or novelty of the questions that it raised;
- the skill, effort, specialized knowledge, and responsibility involved;
- the time spent on the case;
- the place where and the circumstances in which the work or any part of it was done; and
- the receiving party's last approved or agreed budget.

4.3.2.4 Proportionality in relation to costs

As mentioned in paragraph 4.3.2.1, costs on the standard basis must be proportionate as well as reasonable.

The mere fact that costs may have been necessarily incurred does not make them proportionate. CPR 44.3 has also now been amended to include a definition of 'proportionate costs' as follows, and the costs incurred should bear a reasonable relationship to:

- the sums in issue in the proceedings;
- the value of any non-monetary relief in issues in the proceedings;
- the complexity of the litigation;
- any additional work generated by the conduct of the paying party; and
- any wider factors involved in the proceedings, such as reputation or public importance.

What this essentially means is that disproportionate costs will not now be allowed even if they were necessarily incurred.

It is, therefore, the authors' view that if a client wishes to pursue his case at a disproportionate cost, he can do so, but most probably this will be largely at his own expense. Wealthy litigants who, however, seek to put their opponent to excessive and disproportionate costs by tactical manoeuvres may face an indemnity costs order against them.

4.4 HOW LEGAL COSTS AND DISBURSEMENTS ARE FORMULATED

Now that we have looked at the fundamental costs provisions, we need to ascertain exactly what can be charged for and ultimately recovered from the opponent if a favourable costs order is made.

4.4.1 WHAT WORK CAN BE INCLUDED?

A legal representative's work is calculated and ultimately assessed by reference to time spent on a variety of tasks, including various attendances either by telephone or at face-to-face meetings with clients, opponents, counsel, experts, the court, and others. Time spent considering and preparing documentation, including statements of case, letters, reports, advices, schedules, and perusing original documentation, is also allowable. Much of a legal representative's work is taken up with these items of work in the run-up to an interim hearing or trial, and added to this will be time spent at the hearing. The total of all the work done on an hourly rate is known as the 'base costs' to which, if your client is funded by way of a CFA, will be added the success fee, as discussed is Chapter 3 at paragraph 3.3.5.

At paragraph 4.1, we discussed disbursements: these are to be added to the overall statement of costs or bill to be presented to the opponent at the conclusion of a successful action or application.

 Practical Considerations

It is crucially important to understand the importance of accurate time recording by legal practitioners in a dispute resolution department, both in respect of being able to bill a client on an interim basis, usually monthly, and in relation to being able to provide a costs estimate or costs budget to the court and to the client. Time recording is done electronically and allows a fee earner, at any time, to ascertain and control the level of costs being incurred. This will assist with the compliance of your professional conduct rules, particularly in relation to updating your client on the costs being incurred.

4.4.2 HOURLY RATES

Once you have identified what items of work have been done and what disbursements have been incurred, you will need to consider what hourly rate will be applied to the hours spent in undertaking those tasks. These are considered periodically by the Civil Justice Council Costs Committee (CJCCC), the 2010 Guideline Hourly Rates continue to apply (the Civil Procedure Rules Committee has cofirmed that a review and recommendation will take place this year). See Table 4.1 for the rates in force.

You can see that there are zonal rates in England and Wales that include groups of towns and cities: National 1 and National 2. These involve two bands covering the whole country, except London, with a further three bands for the City of London, Central London, and Outer London. The rates for London 3, Bands A and B, are presented as ranges following the format of *The Guide to the Summary Assessment of Costs*. These ranges go some way towards reflecting the wide range of work types transacted in these areas.

In addition, there are four levels of fee earner within these bands:

- Grade A—solicitors and Fellows of CILEx with over eight years' post-qualification experience (PQE), including at least eight years' litigation experience;
- Grade B—solicitors and legal executives with over four years' PQE, including at least four years' litigation experience, and suitably qualified and regulated costs lawyers;

TABLE 4.1 CURRENT GUIDELINE HOURLY RATES (£)

	Band A	Band B	Band C	Band D
London 1	409	296	226	138
London 2	317	242	196	126
London 3	229–267	172–229	165	121
National 1	217	192	161	118
National 2	201	177	146	111

- Grade C—other solicitors, legal executives, and fee earners of equivalent experience to include suitably qualified and regulated costs lawyers; and

- Grade D—trainee solicitors, paralegals, and fee earners of equivalent experience.

It is further recognized that, in certain complex, major litigation, the appropriate rate may exceed the guideline—sometimes by a significant margin. It is within the court's inherent discretion whether it is prepared to allow a greater hourly rate. This often arises when a party instructs a legal representative from outside his locality, in which case charging rates are much higher.

 Practical Considerations

The client needs to be aware that the figure to which he agrees in his retainer with his legal representative at the outset of the case (and any subsequent increase, decrease, or change in fee earner as the matter moves along) may be higher or lower than these guideline hourly rates. If it is the case that the client care letter denotes a higher hourly rate than the guideline figure, unless the court can be persuaded, it is likely that the Senior Courts Costs Office (SCCO) guideline figure will be adhered to. If the retainer letter figure is lower than the guideline figure, then, because of the indemnity principle, the client will be stuck with a costs recovery based on the lower figure in his client care letter.

4.4.3 WORK DONE BY COUNSEL

Work undertaken by counsel, including advocacy, drafting or amending documentation, and written, telephone, or conference advices, can be recovered against an opponent. However, it is essential that the legal representative negotiates counsel's fee (known as a 'fee note') with counsel's clerk in advance of incurring the fee—particularly if it will have to be justified in detailed assessment proceedings. Counsel also operates on an hourly rate basis, denoted by experience and seniority.

4.4.4 EXPERTS' FEES

It is important that the terms of engagement with the expert are agreed in writing before any work is undertaken. CPR 35.4(2) states that any party seeking permission to adduce expert evidence must provide a costs estimate of that evidence to the court.

4.5 THE DIFFERENT TYPES OF COSTS ORDER MADE BY THE COURT

As the litigation progresses, the court can make a variety of costs orders at interim hearings and at trial. At Table 4.2 at the end of this chapter, we list some frequently made costs orders that can be made both at interim hearings and at trial. At interim hearings (see Chapters 13–14), once the district judge or master has made his decision, he will then decide the costs order of the application or case management conference (but not the whole action). Most of the costs orders listed in Table 4.2 are also available to the trial judge after handing down his judgment at the final hearing.

4.6 THE COURT'S POWERS TO CONTROL COSTS RECOVERED BY ONE PARTY AGAINST ANOTHER

The courts are constantly looking at ways of reducing the cost of litigation and making it less unpredictable. In addition to the court's discretion in the award of costs, the court has developed a number of alternative costs orders and approaches that can be employed, usually in multi-track cases in which matters are particularly complicated.

CPR 44.2(6) permits the court to make the following orders of costs recovery:

(a) *a proportion of another party's costs;*

(b) *a stated amount in respect of another party's costs;*

(c) *costs from or until a certain date only;*

(d) *costs incurred before proceedings have begun;*

(e) *costs relating to particular steps taken in the proceedings;*

(f) *costs relating only to a distinct part of proceedings; and*

(g) *interest on costs from or until a certain date, including a date before judgment.*

In the next section we focus on two conventional approaches of cost capping and percentage-based or issues-based costs orders and the new costs management powers of the court.

4.6.1 COST CAPPING

'Cost capping' refers to the situation when the court places a limit on the amount that a party can recover from its opponent. It can do this prospectively or retrospectively, although the latter is rare. The court derives its general powers under s. 51 of the Senior Courts Act 1981 and CPR 3, 3.19–21 and also Section II at PD 3F.

The process of cost capping involves making an application to the court under CPR 23 (although oral applications can be made), usually at an early stage in multi-track actions, such as early directions or a subsequent early case management conference (CMC).

The evidence in support of the application usually takes the form of a witness statement detailing whether the costs capping order is in respect of the whole or part of the litigation and why the costs should be capped. It is usual to suggest here that, without cost capping, costs will be unreasonably or disproportionately incurred. A costs budget in the form of Precedent H is also usually required in relation to costs already incurred, as well as those to be incurred.

The court will exercise its inherent discretion as to whether to cap a party's cost in accordance with the overriding objective and CPR 3.19(5) and (6). There have been a number of cases where the court has refused to make a cost capping order even where there has been a real risk of disproportionality and has chosen instead to order costs management to deal with the potential issue of disproportionate costs.

If a costs cap is ordered, the court will have regard to CPR 3.19 and the circumstances to be taken into account, as well as to a party's right to continue his proceedings under Art. 6 of the European Convention on Human Rights. Once a cost capping order is made, as with any other type of costs order, the party is not limited to what he spends on litigation, but simply to what he can recover from the other party if he wins and obtains a costs order in his favour.

 Practical Considerations

At this stage, it is not entirely clear how costs management (see paragraph 4.6.3) and costs capping co-exist. There are separate court rules and no specific guidance on how they interact. It has been said that costs management is not costs capping, but it has also been said that the effect of costs management is to limit costs. It is worth noting that there is a difference in scope of the two rules at present. It is currently the case that costs management is not automatically imposed in all multi-track cases (although it is a requirement in most multi-track cases), and there is a discretion not to order it even where it applies. Whereas the power to costs cap extends to all multi-track cases, even complex and detailed commercial litigation. However, again, it is a matter of discretion and the guidance attached to the rules confines costs capping to 'exceptional cases' which, arguably, in an effective way severely limits the extent of costs capping. It remains to be seen if the rules and guidance are amended in the future.

4.6.2 PERCENTAGE-BASED AND ISSUES-BASED COSTS ORDERS

Percentage-based and issues-based orders are considered where there are a number of issues in the case upon which the judge at trial has to make a ruling. Often, there will be a clear and significant cost attached to either proving or disproving the issue. In the circumstances in which both parties are successful on some, but not all, of the issues, instead of awarding all of the costs of the action to the ultimately successful party, the court will award costs of proving the issues and disproving other issues to the respective parties. This is done by either making a party pay a percentage of its or its opponent's costs, or allowing costs incurred on the issues proved or disproved.

 Practical Considerations

In practice, the courts favour making percentage-based costs orders rather than issues-based costs orders because, once the trial judge has made the order (having had the advantage of hearing all of the issues in the case in detail), it is then for the costs judge to decipher the issues before deciding whether individual items are attributable to certain issues that have been allowed or disallowed. The courts are, however, less likely to make these types of costs orders in multi-track matters in light of the costs budget requirements.

4.6.3 COSTS BUDGETING

This is part of the court's costs management process.

4.6.3.1 Multi-track cases only

The position for all multi-track cases in the Queen's Bench or Chancery Division of the High Court and the County Court, excluding:

- the Admiralty and Commercial Courts;
- litigants in person; and
- any Part 7 claim valued at over £10 million, notwithstanding the fact that the court should retain a discretion to apply or not apply costs management both above and below the threshold.

is that both parties must file and exchange costs budgets either with the Directions Questionnaire if the claim is worth less than £50,000 or twenty-one days before the first case management conference (CMC) (CPR 3.13), unless the court orders otherwise. These are then considered by the court during the litigation. The aim is to give the court control over costs and to try and ensure that the parties are on an equal footing (see CPR 3.12–3.18 and PD 3E). This essentially means that all parties need to provide a detailed analysis of their likely costs in a prescribed costs form known as Precedent H for each phase of the proceedings. This form enables the parties to set out what they believe will be their costs for bringing or defending a claim to a conclusion up to and including trial. This includes the fees of the parties' legal representatives (including counsel), court fees, medical records fees, and experts' fees. This form can be found in the online resources, and it has its own prescribed statement of truth: 'This budget is a fair and accurate statement of incurred and estimated costs which it would be reasonable and proportionate for my client to incur in this litigation.'

The parties must also file and serve a Budget Discussion Report in Precedent R form no later than seven days before the CMC. This must include the figures which are agreed and not agreed, for each phase of the budget, as well as a brief summary of the grounds of dispute. This can be found in the online resources.

In practice the court now has cost management powers which it exercises throughout the litigation (rather than at the conclusion) either on paper, by telephone, or at costs management conferences which can be heard at the same time as CMCs. However in cases where costs budgets are mandatory, the court retains a discretion as to whether or not to require the parties to file them: the court can dispense with them or postpone them. However parties are advised to always be prepared to file and serve costs budgets rather than relying on the court discretion at a CMC.

At these conferences, if a party objects to another party's budget, the court can intervene and either approve the budget or order a revision by making a costs management order (CMO). If at any stage any party's budget exceeds the agreed or approved budget, the onus is on that party to notify the opponent and the court seeking further approval or a revised CMO. A failure to do so is likely to limit the recovery of costs to the agreed/approved budget unless there is good reason to depart from the approved budget. If there is not, there will be a loss to the party who exceeded the budget and failed to update their opponent and the court.

The High Court has imposed severe sanctions on a claimant who 'genuinely but mistakenly' thought it was acceptable to file a costs budget excluding the phases of trial preparation and trial, see *Page v RGC Restaurants Ltd* [2018] EWHC 2688 (QB).

The decision illustrates the risks of filing a 'materially incomplete' costs budget, even where a party considers it premature to budget for the later stages of the action. In these circumstances it seems the only safe course is to budget for the entire action, unless the court has made an order directing that budgets be limited to only part of the proceedings.

CPR 3.14 provides: 'Unless the court otherwise orders, any party which fails to file a budget despite being required to do so will be treated as having filed a budget comprising only the applicable court fees.'

Paragraph 6(a) of Practice Direction 3E provides that, unless the court otherwise orders, a budget must be in the form of Precedent H. It goes on to say that, in substantial cases, the court may direct that budgets be limited initially to part only of the proceedings and subsequently extended to cover the whole proceedings.

 Practical Considerations

What is often overlooked in practice is that once costs budgets have been filed, the making of a CMO, i.e. approving or not approving a party's budget, is discretionary (CPR 3.15). Therefore, it is not in every case that the filing of costs budgets will result in a budget being fixed by the court under a CMO, although the court is likely to pay close regard to the budgets provided when deciding what case management decisions are to be made. It is inevitable that case management and costs management are inextricably linked, and consequently, your reading of Chapter 12 on Case Management, will inform your understanding of the reasons costs budgeting is likely to form a core part of the strategy for tackling disproportionate costs and active case management.

It will, therefore, come as no surprise that there has been a plethora of case law on costs budgets, particularly in relation to the courts' approach to exceeded budgets, revising budgets and budgets that were not filed on time or at all. A recent decision in the case of *Seekings and another v Moores and others* [2019] EWHC 1476 where a defendant's application to revise it's costs budget upwards by a third was refused, highlights this. Such decisions are appearing on a monthly basis and serve as a warning to legal practitioners to note the CPR requirements on costs budgets and to take proactive steps and apply to the court in advance of a deadline or the upper limit of a budget to seek the court's approval for late service or a revised budget. Failure to do so will leave those defaulters in the hands of CPR 3.9 seeking relief from sanctions.

4.6.3.2 Effect on litigation practice and detailed assessment of costs

Chapter 20 deals with the assessment of costs after judgment, but it is worth noting here the implications of these costs budgets in relation to the detailed assessment of costs. Costs budgets now provide much less scope to challenge costs in detailed assessment proceedings if those costs fell within the agreed or approved budgets. CPR 3.18 states that where a CMO is made (but remember that CMOs are not always made), the court will have regard to the successful party's last approved or agreed budget and should not depart from that budget without good reason where costs are being assessed on the standard basis only. In *Harrison v University Hospitals Coventry and Warwickshire NHS Trust* [2017] EWCA Civ 792, the Court of Appeal confirmed that when a costs management order has been made, the future (estimated costs) element of the costs budget is binding on a subsequent detailed assessment. The figure for those costs should not be departed from (upwards or downwards) unless 'good reason' can be shown. This was the clear interpretation of CPR 3.18 and was in accordance with the purposes of costs management.

The reality is that during the course of proceedings, it will be open to the parties to consider, and where appropriate, challenge a Precedent R cost budget. If not challenged, they may not be capable of challenge at detailed assessment.

By the same token, a close account will need to be made of a client's case so as to avoid unrecoverable costs. It is to the advantage of the parties and indeed clients, that a better understanding and accurate picture of costs is grasped earlier and during litigation. It is also helpful to have a clearer understanding of work undertaken by opponents by viewing their Precendent H. It can be indicative of the approach taken.

4.7 FIXED COSTS

Not all costs will be assessed by the court; in some circumstances costs are 'fixed'. The CPR deal with many kinds of fixed costs in CPR 45. In this section, we explain four of the most common types of fixed costs.

4.7.1 FIXED RECOVERABLE COSTS IN ROAD TRAFFIC ACCIDENT (RTA) CLAIMS

CPR 45.9–45.15 and PD Section II set out the fixed recoverable costs regime for road traffic claims that settle in a total sum of up to £10,000 before the issue of proceedings. These fixed costs do not apply to cases where the new Low Value RTA Pre-Action Protocol applies, and consequently, there will be few cases in which these will arise.

The costs that are recoverable are limited to:

- fixed costs relating to the agreed damages—that is, £800 plus 20 per cent of the damages up to £5,000, plus 15 per cent of the damages between £5,000 and £10,000, and a 12.5 per cent London weighting;

- VAT; and

- disbursements from a specified list in CPR 45.12.

 Example

You practise in Exeter and have negotiated a settlement during the Personal Injury (PI) Protocol phase of your client's PI claim arising out of a road traffic accident earlier in the year. During your handling of the claim, you obtained your client's doctor (GP) and hospital notes, and instructed a consultant orthopaedic surgeon to prepare a report, which was disclosed to the defendant. You also obtained a copy of the police accident report book, on receipt of which you instructed an enquiry agent to locate witnesses, but none were found.

Damages have been agreed at £8,000 pre issue.

Your fixed costs are as follows:

- £800; plus
- £1,000 (being 20 per cent of £5,000); plus
- £450 (being 15 per cent of £3,000); plus
- VAT on £2,250; plus
- recovery of the GP and hospital note fee, the fee for the medical report, and that for the police accident report book.

Unfortunately, you are unlikely to recover the enquiry agent's fee because it does not fall within any of the disbursements in CPR 45.12.

4.7.1.1 Fixed recoverable costs—the future

Jackson LJ has set out the next stage in costs management in his 'Review of Civil Litigation Costs: Supplemental Report fixed Recoverable Costs' dated July 2017.

In the Supplemental Report, Jackson LJ makes two key proposals:

1. extending the fixed recoverable costs regime (FRC) to cover all types of cases in the fast track— including holiday sickness and noise induced hearing loss claims, and non-personal injury claims such as defended debt cases, tracked possession claims, housing disrepair and other money claims;

2. imposing a fixed recoverable costs regime on cases with values in excess of £25,000.

Jackson LJ recommends the introduction of a new 'intermediate track' which will encompass claims between £25,000 and £100,000. The proposed procedure for these cases will include a trial of no more than three days, with no more than two expert witnesses giving oral evidence on each side.

Within the 'intermediate track', Jackson LJ proposes a streamlined procedure and a grid system of FRC which includes four 'complexity bands' to reflect the amount of work. The costs recoverable will naturally be scaled accordingly.

Unsurprisingly, mesothelioma and other asbestos-related lung disease claims are to be excluded from the intermediate track, as are clinical negligence claims, multi-party cases, actions against the police, child sex abuse claims, and intellectual property cases. Furthermore, a case allocated to the intermediate track initially can potentially be taken out of it if the nature of the case changes fundamentally.

Jackson LJ has also made it clear that any reforms that he proposes must fit with other civil justice initiatives, including the whiplash reforms and the increase in small claims personal injuries limit.

Consultation on the reforms commenced in March 2019 and closed in June 2019. No implementation has taken place, and some time has passed since it was first expected. Information from the Ministry of Justice states that the feedback is being analysed.

If Jackson LJ's most recent proposals are accepted, he recommends a review after four years, at which point consideration should be given to extending the intermediate track to include monetary claims above £100,000 and claims for non-monetary relief. Jackson LJ retired in March 2018. It remains to be seen what will come of his proposals and whether his civil cost reforms will be driven forward with the same zest and ambition witnessed under Jackson LJ's tenure.

4.7.1.1.1 *The introduction of a fixed costs pilot study*

A pilot scheme introducing voluntary capped costs of £80,000 for High Court (in certain Business and Property Courts) for cases worth up to £250,000—as recommended by Sir Rupert Jackson has been introduced to run from 14 January 2019 for a period of two years.

The voluntary capped costs pilot started in January 2019 and runs for two years in certain Business and Property Courts for cases valued upto £250,000.

The aim of the scheme will be to see whether there is a demand and to see whether it would lower the costs of litigation and speed up the resolution of claims, increasing certainty of costs exposure and streamlining the proceedures in the pilot courts.

This is in effect a pilot only for cases with a value of £100,000 to £250,000 because it runs in the High Court, and cases with a value of £250,000 will be exempt. Other cases exempt are those that require more than a two day trial, involve allegatons of fraud, require extensive disclosure, witnesses or expert evidence or involve many issues and multiple parties.

Statements of case will be limited in length and witness statements, if ordered, will also be limited in length. There will be no costs management, automatic disclosure or expert evidence. The court will at a Case Management Conference (CMC) decide whether to make any orders necessary in relation to disclosure and evidence in order to resolve the matter.

The trial is expected to take place not more than eight months after the CMC which should not exceeed two days.

Not more than twenty-one days after the conclusion of the trial, the parties will produce a schedule of costs by reference to various stages of the litigation, which will be assessed summarily by the court.

A cap applies to each stage, together with an overall cap £80,000 (exclusive of VAT, court fees, wasted costs, and costs of enforcement).

Where a Part 36 offer is made by the claimant but not accepted, costs will not be set at large; instead, the stage caps will increase by 25 per cent, and the overall cap will increase to £100,000.

Sir Rupert wrote:

'If the pilot is a success, I recommend that the capped costs regime used during the capped costs pilot (with any modifications found necessary) should become available for any suitable case in the Business and Property Courts or the business and property lists of the county court up to a value of £250,000. This could be done by creating a "capped costs list" in those courts.

'It may well become appropriate to extend the regime to cases up to £500,000, but that must be for future consideration.'

4.7.2 LOW-VALUE PERSONAL INJURY CLAIMS IN RTA AND LOW-VALUE PERSONAL INJURY, EMPLOYERS', AND PUBLIC LIABILITY CLAIMS

These Low-Value Pre-Action Protocols stipulate the requirements for the low-value claims of up to £25,000 that can be dealt with. The whole process is undertaken online and is described as proceeding through three stages or until settlement is no longer possible, and then it reverts to the court system. There are Protocols for each of these types of case. (See Chapter 8 on Protocols and Chapter 9, paragraph 9.2.8 for further detail.)

The fixed costs for each of these three protocol claims are set out in CPR 45 Section III, where at CPR 45.18 fixed costs throughout each of the three stages are set out in Table 6 in relation to RTA protocol claims which settle within the protocol itself. Similarly, for employers' liability (EL) and public liability (PL) protocol cases, the fixed costs are set out in Table 6A. There are also stipulations regarding the costs of disbursements and provision for the cost of additional advice on the value of a claim.

If any of these protocol claims are incapable of settlement, then, as previously stated, the parties are at liberty to step out of the Protocol and issue proceedings through the courts in the normal way. However, there are fixed costs entitlements (except where it is a EL/PL disease case) in respect of these litigation costs, described as 'fixed recoverable costs'. These are not to be confused with those costs at CPR 45.9–15 in Section II also described as 'fixed recoverable costs' set out in paragraph 4.7.1.

CPR 45 Section IIIA deals with these fixed recoverable costs. Similarly, they are subdivided at CPR 45.29A–L into Table 6B for RTA claims, Table 6C for EL claims, and Table 6D for PL claims. Provision is also helpfully made in respect of defendants' costs in those cases where the fixed costs regime would otherwise apply (including those cases where a defendant successfully counterclaims—see Chapters 10 and 11 for further details of counterclaims) and the costs recoverable by both parties in related interim applications (see Chapters 13 and 14 for further details on interim applications).

We should also highlight here that these protocol fixed costs cases do not escape the operation of CPR 36 offers to settle with corresponding costs penalties. Chapter 15 details the complex requirements of Part 36 offers, but with the complete overhaul of Part 36 in April 2015, there are now specific provisions for the costs consequences of Section IIIA low-value RTA, public liability (PL), and employers' liability (EL) claims that have stepped out of the Protocol. There is also a new Section II within Part 36 that deals solely with RTA, EL, and PL Protocol offers to settle.

4.7.3 FAST-TRACK FIXED COSTS

CPR 45.37–45.40 and PD 45 Section VI deal with fast-track trial costs.

It is only the costs of the fast-track trial that are fixed; the costs of the rest of the matter from date of instruction are not, unless your client's claim falls within those fixed costs in paragraphs 4.7.1 or 4.7.2.

These trial costs that the court may award are based on the value of the claim, although the court does have the power to award more or less than the fixed amounts. A common example of this is where your client asks you to attend the trial with him, in addition to your trial advocate. This is often for comfort or a 'belt and braces' approach. CPR 45.39 indicates that the additional fee of £345 will only be recoverable by your client if it was 'necessary' for you to attend to assist your trial advocate.

4.7.4 FIXED COSTS ON A SPECIFIED DESIGNATED MONEY CLAIM

Fixed costs can be recovered in an action in which a defendant to a claim for a specified sum of money admits the whole sum claimed, and it pays it on receipt of the claim form and particulars of claim. Details of the fixed costs allowed can be found in CPR 45.1, and a further discussion on this is in Chapter 10, paragraph 10.5.1.

4.8 WASTED COSTS ORDERS

Wasted costs orders are governed by s. 51(6) of the Senior Courts Act 1981, as substituted by s. 4 of the Courts and Legal Services Act 1990 and CPR 46.8 and PD 46.8.

These are costs orders whereby the court has held that the conduct of a legal representative has been shown to have been improper, unreasonable, or negligent. The result of this is that the legal representative is ordered to pay either his own client's costs by way of an indemnity, where those costs have been disallowed as against the other party, or to pay the costs of his opponent.

PD 46.5.1 sets out the three factors to be considered by the court in hearing such an application as follows:

1. The legal representative must have acted improperly, unreasonably, or negligently.

2. His conduct must have caused a party to incur unnecessary costs.

3. It must be just, in all of the circumstances, to make the order.

The court's discretion to make a wasted costs order follows a two-stage formula:

- whether, on the evidence of the applicant alone, a wasted costs order is likely; and

- whether such a costs order is justified, notwithstanding the cost involved.

The respondent adviser to the application is given the opportunity to object to the application, but the burden rests with the applicant, although there is no burden on the respondent to excuse himself.

As for the timing of the application, wasted costs orders are usually dealt with at the end of the trial when the judge is hearing cost applications. The reason for this is that the conduct can be scrutinized in the context of the whole proceedings and the issue of proportionality can also be considered.

Wasted costs orders are only designed to apply to a small number of cases, which according to case law defines improper, unreasonable, and negligent conduct as being a breach of professional duty, vexatious, and incompetent, respectively.

In so far as the test for 'unnecessary' is concerned, the way in which the court will deal with this is by looking to the 'but for' test—that is, 'but for' the conduct of the legal representative, would the costs, on a balance of probability, have been incurred?

 Practical Considerations

It is not always clear when to proceed with a wasted costs order. Conduct that might be considered appropriate for wasted costs orders probably includes failing to attend a court appointment, breaching court orders, negligently misstating a case, continuing with an action after it has become hopeless, and where a real loss has been suffered as a result of the legal representative's conduct. This is not a complete list of the occasions on which the court might consider a wasted costs order.

However, where a wasted costs order is made and the client is not present in court to hear the order, the party's legal representative must notify the client in writing of the costs order no later than seven days after the legal representative receives notice of the order (CPR 44.8).

KEY POINTS SUMMARY

- Bear in mind the overriding objective, reasonableness, and proportionality.

- Costs orders are discretionary, but the principle 'the winner is awarded his costs against the loser' is the starting point against which the discretion can be exercised. This has further been amended in personal injury cases with qualified one way costs shifting.

- Remember the wide variety of costs orders that can be made, both at an interim stage and the final stage of an action and advise your client accordingly.

- Understand the difference between 'standard' and 'indemnity' costs.

SELF-TEST QUESTIONS

1. What basis of costs is the usual basis upon which costs are awarded?

2. Is proportionality taken into account when assessing costs on the indemnity basis?

3. What are the general principles in costs in litigation and how have these been amended?

4. What is the likely consequence if a party exceeds his agreed or approved costs budget?

 Suggested answers to these self-test questions can be accessed in the Student Resources section of the online resources.

TABLE 4.2 THE DIFFERENT TYPES OF COSTS ORDER MADE BY THE COURT

Costs in any event	These can be made at trial (and are often known as costs of proceedings) or at interim hearings. It means that whatever other costs orders are made at trial or other interim hearings, a party in receipt of this costs order has an absolute entitlement to the costs of that particular application or hearing.
Costs in the case/application	These are usually made at interim hearings, particularly CMCs and pre-trial reviews.
	A party in receipt of this costs order will only get his costs of the application or hearing if he gets a cost order in his favour at trial.
Costs reserved	Here the court postpones making a decision on costs, usually until trial or another substantive hearing. If it does not make a later costs order regarding the reserved costs then the costs will be costs in the case.
Claimant's/defendant's costs in the case/application	This is often used where one party has been successful at an interim hearing but the court is not minded to give that party a costs in any event order but neither is it minded to make a costs in the case order. When the court makes such an order it has the effect of allowing the party who was successful on application a costs in any event order only if he secures a costs of proceedings order at trial. If he does not obtain a costs of proceedings order at trial then each party bears their own costs of the application to which this order relates.
Costs thrown away	Where a judgment or order is set aside, or the whole or part of any proceedings are adjourned, the party in whose favour the costs order is made is entitled to costs he has incurred as a consequence.
Costs of and caused by (an amendment)	This is the usual order the court makes in respect of an application to amend a statement of case. The order requires the party making the amendment to pay the other party's costs of preparing for and attending the hearing and any consequential amendments to his own statement of case.
Costs here and below	This order is often made on appeal and allows the party who is successful on the appeal to recover his costs of the appeal and the lower court.
No order as to costs/each party to bear their own costs	Each party is to bear its own costs of the part of the proceedings to which the order relates, whatever costs order the court makes at trial.

5 ALTERNATIVE DISPUTE RESOLUTION

Relevant parts of the CPR and its PDs: 1, 3, 24, 26, and 44.

5.1 INTRODUCTION

Alternative dispute resolution has been available in this country for many years and has now become an important and necessary consideration as an alternative to litigation. The court now has a duty, as part of its active management of cases, to further the overriding objective, which includes, under CPR 1.4(2)(e), encouraging ADR as a method of dispute resolution.

This chapter will deal with the methods by which the Civil Procedure Rules (CPR) encourage parties to settle their disputes at an early stage and, ultimately, without proceeding to trial. It will also look at the methods of dispute resolution that may be available, including a more detailed look at the most common of them. This chapter covers:

- the different types of ADR;
- the integration of ADR into the CPR;
- the Civil Justice Council's ADR working group report;
- the philosophy of ADR; and
- a detailed look at mediation.

5.2 A DEFINITION OF ALTERNATIVE DISPUTE RESOLUTION (ADR)

There is no single overarching definition of ADR, but it has been said that a starting premise must be that it is a voluntary process and must, therefore, be consented to by the parties to a dispute. However, the Glossary to the CPR defines ADR simply as a 'collective description of methods of resolving disputes otherwise than through the normal trial process'. These descriptions are of limited help, because it appears that they exclude negotiations and any type of process which is not voluntary.

For the purposes of this manual, we seek to include the most prevalent ADR processes. All of these are looked at in this chapter.

5.3 THE DIFFERENT TYPES OF ADR

5.3.1 NEGOTIATIONS, OR ROUND TABLE DISCUSSIONS

Whether you negotiate over the telephone or arrange a meeting to sit around a table to try to resolve a dispute, this can be done at any time, but should always be conducted on a 'without prejudice' basis. The legal representative for each party usually carries out telephone negotiations. 'Round table' meetings more commonly involve each party attending with his legal representative and, possibly, counsel. Breaks can be taken during the negotiation to give each party the opportunity to have confidential discussions with its legal team.

This forum gives the client the opportunity to have his case aired and to appreciate the strengths and weakness of his opponent's case. It is usually—but not always—the first step taken in trying to resolve a dispute before proceeding with one of the other alternatives listed here.

This is a non-adjudicative form of dispute resolution.

5.3.2 MEDIATION

The process of mediation is confidential and conducted without prejudice to impending or continuing litigation between parties. It may take place at any time before or during litigation and can normally be set up at very short notice, although, like other forms of negotiation, the timing may be critical. The process is also non-binding until a final written agreement has been signed by the parties. The parties can walk away from it at any time before a settlement is concluded, although the court may, to a degree, investigate their behaviour during any mediation, as well as their attitude towards it.

The parties appoint a neutral intermediary who endeavours to facilitate a settlement. The mediator does not act as judge or arbitrator, nor does he rule on the merits and neither will he suggest or impose the settlement terms. Rather, by shuttling between the parties, exploring their positions, and bringing them together as and when appropriate, the mediator helps the parties to find common ground. As the settlement emerges from consensus, one of the key advantages is that the parties then 'own' the settlement and do not see it as having been forced upon them by a court or third party.

It is often capable of achieving commercially sensible solutions, which can leave both parties satisfied—not something that a court decision following great expenditure and a 'gloves off' approach can often achieve. The solution may also be in the form of relief that the court itself had no power to order. If successful, it will probably be a great deal cheaper than a trial. Even if unsuccessful, both parties are likely to benefit by knowing more about the strengths and weaknesses of each other's position, and this may promote settlement at a later date.

There is no formal regulation of mediation as yet in this country, but the Civil Mediation Council exists to drive mediation forward in the UK in terms of accreditation of mediators. The EU Mediation Directive has, however, defined five key provisions relating to mediation in cross-border disputes for civil and commercial matters. Whilst it is a generally accepted view that mediation in the UK complies with the Directive, the UK Government effectively revoked the implementation of the Directive on the Brexit exit day (31 January 2020).

This is a non-adjudicative form of dispute resolution.

5.3.3 CONCILIATION

As with mediation, conciliation is based on a neutral intermediary liaising with the parties, but usually the conciliator will be more proactive and may suggest his own solutions. This method of dispute resolution is common in employment disputes, often through the Advisory, Conciliation and Arbitration Service (ACAS).

This is a non-adjudicative form of dispute resolution.

5.3.4 THE EXECUTIVE TRIBUNAL

The 'executive table' is usually used to resolve commercial disputes. A panel is formed from senior representatives of the parties who have not themselves been involved in the dispute. The representatives sit together with a neutral adviser. The process is similar to a mini-trial, although, in reality, it is not a trial at all. The parties present their cases to the executives, who then have an opportunity to evaluate the respective claims. Rather than making a determination, however, the panel members then retire and endeavour to negotiate a settlement on a commercial basis. If the executives struggle to come to an agreement, the independent adviser issues a non-binding advisory opinion.

This is a non-adjudicative form of dispute resolution.

5.3.5 EARLY NEUTRAL EVALUATION (ENE)

Under early neutral evaluation (ENE), a third party—usually an independent legal representative or a judge as permitted by CPR 3.1—considers the issues and advises on the likely outcome. If a judge is chosen to provide the evaluation, he will not determine the action if it goes ahead. Having the view of an independent arbiter, respected by both parties, may then act as a spur to settlement—or at least enable the parties to re-evaluate their cases or appreciate the critical issues and the likely outcome if they do not settle.

This is a non-adjudicative form of dispute resolution.

5.3.6 JUDICIAL OR EXPERT DETERMINATION

If pursuing judicial or expert determination, the parties jointly instruct and make written submissions to a senior judge (often one who has retired) or Queen's Counsel (QC), who then makes a written appraisal. The parties are required to agree the form and extent of the instruction in advance, and whether the appraisal is to be binding or not. It is extremely important that the client understands the nature and extent of the instruction, especially if it is to be binding, because this will ultimately determine the case. These decisions cannot generally be appealed, but can be challenged on limited grounds—usually where the expert has materially departed from his instructions. Legal representatives must, therefore, exercise great care when drafting the instructions or 'mandate' to the expert determiner.

In practice, expert determination can be on a preliminary issue, such as liability, leaving the parties to negotiate or mediate the quantum part of the claim.

This is a form of adjudicative dispute resolution.

5.3.7 ARBITRATION

Arbitration features heavily in many industries, including the construction and football arenas, and appears commonly as the dispute resolution clause in many national and international commercial agreements. The 1996 Arbitration Act governs current arbitration practice in this country, it introduces mandatory and non-mandatory provisions.

The arbitrator is usually a solicitor, barrister, architect, or quantity surveyor, who conducts the arbitration on a private basis according to a timetable set by him in discussion with the parties, with a view to coming to a final and binding decision known as a 'final award'. The process involves meetings between the arbitrator and the parties, as well as the presentation of statements of case, written submissions, and documentary evidence.

Once the award has been made, the arbitrator does not release it until he has been paid by the parties. The award can be enforced in the High Court if not paid, or, set aside by a High Court judge on the application of the disgruntled party to a specialist division of the High Court.

The main features of arbitration are that it is expensive, as is litigation, because you must use an expert arbitrator, and it can be fairly long-running as a dispute resolution process. However, your client may have no option but to arbitrate if there is a valid arbitration clause in the contract and, if this is the case, litigation cannot be considered (unless both parties agree). The common practical effect of this is that if a party attempts to litigate a matter where there is a valid contractual arbitration clause, then the opponent can usually apply to the High Court under s. 9 of the Arbitration Act 1996 to stay proceedings whilst the arbitration continues.

This is a form of adjudicative dispute resolution.

5.3.8 ADJUDICATION

If adjudication is pursued, either by virtue of a contractual term, agreement between parties, or pursuant to the Housing Grants, Construction and Regeneration Act 1996, as amended by the Local Democracy, Economic Development and Construction Act 2009, a party serves on his opponent a 'notice of intention to proceed to adjudication' and nominates an adjudicator (usually a surveyor, architect, engineer, solicitor, or barrister). The adjudicator will issue directions on paper as to when full written submissions are to be made to him. These submissions are known as the 'referral notice' on the part of the party who commences and the 'response to referral' on the part of the defending party. The adjudicator may require a site inspection or a directions hearing. There are strict time limits imposed under the 1996 Act (as amended), which regulates the principles of adjudication.

The most important features of adjudication are that:

- the contract must be a 'construction' contract;
- there must be a dispute to refer, not only a difference—that is, a dispute can arise only once the subject matter of a claim, issue, or other matter has been brought to the attention of the opposing party, and that party has had an opportunity to consider, admit, modify, or reject it;
- the adjudicator must come to his written decision within twenty-eight days of the service of the referral notice (subject to a short extension if agreed);

- the adjudicator has limited jurisdiction on costs, dependent on whether the parties have agreed to confer jurisdiction on the adjudicator to award costs, therefore each party must bear its own costs, no matter who is successful; and

- the adjudicator's decision is binding unless and until it is appealed to the High Court. As such, the losing party must comply with the decision until such time as it may be appealed. If he does not, then an application for a CPR 24 summary judgment can be made.

This process is frequently used in construction and engineering disputes, both between contracting parties and professional advisers, such as architects and engineers. There are exclusions as to the type of contract to which this process can apply—notably, domestic building matters and food processing plants, to name but a few.

This is a form of adjudicative dispute resolution.

Table 5.1 at the end of this chapter offers a summary of some of the advantages and disadvantages of the different types of ADR process to help you to identify which method is most appropriate for your client. The summary is not, however, exhaustive.

The most commonly used process as an alternative to litigation in England and Wales for general civil disputes is *mediation*, and, for this reason, much of this chapter will focus on mediation as a form of dispute resolution.

5.4 **THE BENEFITS OF ADR**

Litigation conducted in an adversarial and combative manner can prove time-consuming and expensive. The process can last many months, or even years, and because the parties are vying to 'win', litigation can end up driving them further apart. The parties become focused on seizing the tactical initiative and undermining each other's case in whatever way they can. In this way, the parties can sometimes forget, if they were in a commercial relationship, why they were in business together in the first place.

Whilst the media hype concerning ADR can sometimes give the mistaken impression that ADR is a panacea, it is true that ADR does have a number of major attractions.

- ADR (save for arbitration)—and mediation in particular—is relatively inexpensive by comparison with litigation.

- Most forms of ADR, in terms of the final meeting or hearing, rarely take more than a day or two, although complex arbitrations can be lengthy.

- Because non-adjudicative ADR is not based on 'winners' and 'losers', it tends to encourage the parties to talk more freely. The intention is to provide the parties with a neutral, non-threatening, and totally confidential environment in which they can explore their respective cases, as well as their business relationship.

- ADR, save for arbitration and adjudication, is more flexible than litigation. The basis of any settlement arrived at is not limited by the legal remedies available from the courts; rather, settlements can be used to regulate the parties' relationship in the future. For example, a party who has suffered loss arising from a breach of contract may be prepared to forgo the normal legal remedy of damages in return for more preferential trading terms going forward. This may be particularly important if the defendant does not actually have the means in the immediate future to meet an expensive damages claim, in which case a victory at trial is likely to be a pyrrhic one.

- Many forms of ADR (again save for arbitration and adjudication)—notably mediations—are conducted in total confidence and on a 'without prejudice' basis. Therefore, the content of the settlement discussions cannot (although there are exceptions) be disclosed to a court or to other third parties. This contrasts with the open arena in which litigation is conducted and the media publicity that is often attendant.

- Many forms of ADR (save for arbitration and adjudication) are only possible if both parties agree, and, unless the parties choose otherwise, settlements cannot be imposed on them. Only once a settlement is reached does it become binding. Before that time, the parties can withdraw or revert to litigation. In litigation, the parties are bound by the rulings of the court, however unfair they consider them to be.

- The whole purpose of ADR is to promote early settlement. Even if it does not achieve this aim, it will often provide the parties with a better understanding of the psychology of their opponent and the issues that they see as important. This knowledge may prove useful in any subsequent settlement negotiations.

The key words are, therefore, speed, flexibility, cost, consensus, confidentiality, and settlement.

5.5 THE ENCOURAGEMENT OF ADR

Whilst it is expressly recognized in the Pre-Action Protocols that no party can or should be forced to mediate or enter into any form of ADR, it is strongly encouraged, with various provisions in the CPR and possible cost consequences for failing to engage in the process. As judicial decisions continue to be given over parties' engagement with ADR, the debate also continues as to whether ADR should be made compulsory (see 5.5.2.3 below).

There is provision and scope for ADR during the Pre-Action Protocol period, and the CPR also give guidance and direction on the use of ADR within proceedings. HM Courts and Tribunals Service has also made strides to help mediation as a form of ADR become more accessible to parties. Commercially ADR is becoming more intrinsic in 'business to consumer' disputes both within the UK and the EU.

5.5.1 ADR AND THE PROTOCOLS

A standardized approach has been undertaken for all Pre-Action Protocols, including the Practice Direction on Pre-Action Conduct and Protocols. They all embody similar paragraphs requiring the parties to consider whether ADR is appropriate and, if so, in what form, warning that the court may, at a subsequent hearing, require evidence that ADR was considered pre-issue. Each Protocol and the Practice Direction on Pre-Action Conduct and Protocols summarizes the appropriate ADR methods, which are commonly discussion and negotiation, and mediation.

The Protocols state that if proceedings are issued, the parties may be required by the court to provide evidence that ADR has been considered. There could be cost sanctions for unreasonable refusal to participate in ADR.

 Practical Considerations

Best practice suggests that a degree of discussion with your opponent should be attempted in advance of any type of ADR. This could take the form of a 'without prejudice' chat or negotiations with your opponent's legal representative over the telephone, or a face-to-face discussion and a Part 36 offer.

5.5.2 ADR AND THE CPR

Judicial encouragement of ADR is now prevalent in the CPR. Proceedings can be stayed if the parties wish to attempt ADR and/or the court considers ADR to be appropriate. The CPR encourage the use of ADR in the following ways and at the following prescribed stages of litigation—but remember that the Court Guides for High Court matters also deal with the divisional courts' requirements for ADR.

In *Lomax v Lomax* [2019] EWCA Civ 1467 it was held that the court had the power pursuant to CPR 3.1(2)(m) to order early neutral evaluation (ENE) even though one party had not consented to it.

5.5.2.1 Staying proceedings for ADR after filing Directions Questionnaires

In all Part 7 claims (for a definition of a Part 7 claim see Chapter 9, paragraph 9.3), after the defendant has served its defence, a court officer will provisionally track the claim and then serve a Notice of Proposed Allocation. This Notice, amongst other things, requires the parties to complete a Directions Questionnaire (DQ) in either form N180, for cases in the small claims track, or form N181 for cases in the fast track and multi-track (for the detailed rules, see CPR 26.3 and Chapter 12). The DQ requires legal representatives to confirm that they have explained to their client the need to try to settle, the options available and the possibility of cost sanctions if they refuse to try to settle. The DQ also asks the parties specifically about settlement and whether they would like a one-month stay (or such a period as the court deems appropriate) in which to attempt to settle the case by ADR or other means (CPR 26.4(1)).

If all of the parties request a stay, or the court, of its own initiative, considers that such a stay would be appropriate, the court will direct that the proceedings be stayed for at least a month (CPR 26.4(2)). Judicial comments published to date indicate that if one of the parties requests a stay in order to attempt ADR and the party opposing a stay cannot show good reasons why ADR is unlikely to work, the court is likely to order a stay.

Where a stay is ordered, the onus is then on the claimant to notify the court if a settlement is reached. If no notification is given by the end of the period of the stay, the court will go on to make such directions as to the management of the case as it considers appropriate.

5.5.2.2 Case management conferences (CMCs) and pre-trial requirements

Even if ADR is not attempted at the DQ stage of the proceedings, the door remains open to a reference to ADR, and possibly a stay of the litigation for that purpose, throughout the litigation process.

Intrinsic to current-day litigation is the concept of 'case management'. It, therefore, seems likely that the courts will ask parties attending CMCs whether they have attempted ADR and to justify their position if not.

The point of raising ADR on all of those occasions is to ensure that alternatives to litigation receive proper consideration. It will no longer be sufficient to tick the box in the DQ, indicating that ADR has been considered or rejected as unsuitable. On occasions such as the first CMC and the pre-trial hearing, you should be prepared to explain, in some detail, why your client does not consider ADR to be appropriate or, possibly, why it was tried and failed (without exceeding the realms of confidentiality).

Practical Considerations

Best practice would suggest that in cases involving many parties, in which the availability of individuals attending an ADR process final meeting or hearing is difficult to coordinate, the court is generally agreeable to granting stays for ADR for periods of three to six months.

Practical Considerations

ADR in practice is more overarching than the Protocols and CPR actually suggest, because ADR can effectively take place at any time. It is not limited to the Protocol phase, or to points in an action dictated by CMCs or pre-trial matters. Mediation, for example, can take place during lengthy trials.

The key point here is that, as a legal representative, you should be constantly considering when and how and what form of ADR can be used to avoid trial and/or judgment.

5.5.2.3 ADR and its future relationship with the CPR

In October 2017, the Civil Justice Council ADR Working Group concluded that ADR has not yet become a sufficiently integral part of the civil justice system in England and Wales.

It stated that currently, the court rules and pre-action protocols contain a number of prompts and signposts, encouraging parties to make use of ADR to avoid court proceedings as listed above in paragraph 5.5.2. However, any sanctions, other than a stay which is not really a 'sanction' only really take effect at the end of the case, when costs liability is decided and costs are assessed. The courts have held that there can be cost consequences for a party who unreasonably refuses an offer to mediate a dispute or even fails to respond to an offer of mediation. This can mean not recovering all of the costs, despite being successful.

The report notes that although these attempts are 'well crafted and well thought out', they are not working sufficiently well. So, further thought was given whether ADR should be made compulsory. The majority view is that compulsion may be too heavy-handed. But it is noteworthy that a minority of the working group consider that the current requirements should go further. They would like to see the introduction of ADR as a condition of access to the court in the first place, or at the very least as a condition to progress beyond its interim stages. The report suggests that the courts should promote the use of ADR more actively at and around the allocation and directions stage. This is often the first time a judge considers the dispute and makes case management directions about the future conduct of the case. The working group suggests that the court should be more interventionist and judges should be able to mark disapproval at a much earlier stage of the case with costs sanctions.

The working group's final report was published in 2018. Its conclusions are set out below in paragraph 5.5.7.

5.5.3 ADR AND HM COURTS AND TRIBUNALS SERVICE

A number of County Court hearing centres in England and Wales have piloted and set up voluntary mediation schemes for fast, and multi-track cases, but not all hearing centres offer these schemes.

The way in which these schemes operate in fast and multi-track cases is that, on the filing of a defence to a two-party action, the court writes to the parties asking if they will agree to submit to a fixed three- or four-hour mediation for a fast- or multi-track case at court, usually to take place outside court hours and therefore between 4 p.m. and 8 p.m. for a fixed fee per party.

If both parties agree, the court allows the mediation to take place in the court building, with both parties attending, along with an accredited mediator. The process is wholly independent from the court and, if settlement is reached, a consent order is drawn up there and then, and placed with the court file to be sealed, and the action comes to an end. If settlement is not reached, the court file is returned to the court for consideration by the district judge.

However, in all small claims, on the filing of the DQ (here in form N180) where the parties have both indicated a desire to attempt mediation in claims of less than £10,000, the court will ask the parties if they are willing to participate in a telephone mediation for up to one hour at a time to suit the parties and the appointed mediator. Should settlement ensue, a consent order is drawn up the following day, signed by the parties, and submitted to the court to bring the action to an end. Should settlement not occur, then the mediator will inform the court and the matter will be listed for a final hearing to be adjudged either orally or on paper. See Chapter 9, paragraph 9.2.1.2 for further details.

5.5.4 ADR AND COST CONSEQUENCES

A party who refuses to enter into an ADR process may well be penalized in costs if the matter proceeds to trial and they are successful. They may not secure a costs order in their favour. In deciding the level of costs to award at trial, the court must have regard to 'the efforts made, if any, before and during the proceedings in order to try and resolve the dispute' (CPR 44.4(3)(a)(ii)).

There have been many costs awards made based on a party's refusal to mediate and what is to be taken into account by the court. The most prominent of these was *Dunnett v Railtrack* [2002] 2 All ER 850, which was the first case in the courts to seriously penalize a successful party for refusing to mediate appropriately, and *Halsey v Milton Keynes NHS Trust* [2004] EWCA Civ 576, which still provides the most comprehensive guidelines on what the court will take into account when assessing whether a party was justified in refusing to mediate.

The court will consider in such circumstances:

- the nature of the dispute;
- the merits of the case;
- the extent to which other settlement methods were attempted;
- whether the cost of ADR would be disproportionately high;
- whether any delay in setting up the ADR would have been prejudicial; and
- whether ADR had reasonable prospects of success.

Over the years since *Halsey*, the courts have made some important extensions as follows:

- The Court of Appeal extended the *Halsey* principle to cover a failure to engage with mediation at all. It held in *PGF II v OMFS Company 1 Ltd* [2013] EWCA Civ 1288 that, as a general rule, a failure to respond at all to an invitation to participate in ADR is in itself unreasonable, regardless of whether there was a good reason for refusing ADR. This case, therefore, sends a clear message: reject mediation if inappropriate, but engage with the idea. Simply not responding to an invitation to mediate, as in this case, puts the successful 'refusing' party at risk of not recovering a proportion of his costs.

- The High Court in *Reid v Buckinghamshire Healthcare NHS Trust* [2015] EWHC B21 (Costs) (28 October 2015) held that the costs sanctions which may follow when a party unreasonably refuses to mediate can apply equally where the party refusing to mediate is the losing party. In this case the losing party was ordered to pay the winning party's costs on the indemnity basis as the penalty.

- In *Thakkar v Patel* [2017] EWCA Civ 117 the Court of Appeal held that a judge had been entitled to make a costs order against the defendants reflecting that it had been reasonable for the claimants to refuse an offer to settle at an early stage in the proceedings and the fact that the failure to mediate was mainly the fault of the defendants.

 Practical Considerations

Best practice would suggest that it is a question of knowing the strengths and weaknesses of your client's case, and balancing those with proportionality in terms of time and costs. It is not simply a matter of railroading your client's case to trial if it is strong, but nor is it necessary to agree to an ADR process where it is clearly inappropriate. Examples of the former would be if, rather than risk trial, you were to consider an application for summary judgment or a strike-out at an early stage (where your opponent's case is weak or misconceived); an example of the latter would be if you were to evaluate your client's conduct against the *Halsey* guidelines: perhaps where mediation is sought within weeks of the trial date, or negotiations had been suggested and refused, or the client feels it has a particularly strong case. In these instances, cases decided prior to 2014 had suggested that a refusal to mediate could be reasonable. But the situations where this is likely to be the case are ever decreasing. In any event, it is apparent that, as a matter of course, all members of the legal profession should now routinely consider with their clients whether their disputes are suitable for ADR and ensure their clients understand what the court may consider as a reasonable or unreasonable refusal to mediate. These considerations should be made at regular intervals during the whole dispute. In view of the extent of the cost consequences, it is advisable that this is evidenced in writing.

 Costs

There should be clear documentary evidence (attendance note or letter) on your file of the occasions on which you considered ADR with your client and your opponent. The suggestion of ADR can be a very useful and valuable weapon to use to attempt to defeat an application for costs, even if that party has lost the litigation.

5.5.5 THE MEDIATION HANDBOOK

In the quest to continue educating legal representatives and clients alike on the benefits of ADR, The Mediation Handbook has been described as a 'neutral, authoritative manual', which aims to provide a practical guide to using mediation for both legal representatives and clients, as well as guidance for identifying cases that may be suitable for mediation. It includes:

- an insight into the role of the mediator;
- sample mediation documents; and
- a list of Civil Mediation Council (CMC) accredited mediation providers.

The Mediation Handbook is frequently referred to in judgments by the courts when they consider contentions that a party has unreasonably refused to mediate. It is therefore suggested that legal practitioners should familiarize themselves with its contents.

5.5.6 LEGISLATION AND ADR

The ADR Directive requires British businesses to ensure that ADR is available for any contractual dispute between a consumer and a business. In addition, the ODR Regulation provides for the establishment of an online dispute resolution (ODR) platform to assist consumers in resolving disputes with retailers in relation to contracts for the sale of goods and services within the EU.

5.5.7 ADR AND THE FUTURE

The Civil Justice Council ADR Working Group published its final report in November 2018. The report made 24 recommendations including the setting up of a Judicial-ADR Liaison Committee, increasing public awareness of ADR, ensuring ADR is widely available through proper resourcing and continued court and government encouragement of ADR.

The report stated that it did not support a compulsory requirement to engage with ADR as a precondition to taking a particular step. It also did not support the introduction of Mediation Information and Advice Meetings (MIAMs), as used in family proceedings, for civil proceedings.

It therefore remains the case that, whilst ADR is firmly encouraged by the courts with costs sanctions for unreasonably refusing to engage with the process, it is not compulsory.

5.6 **IS ADR ALWAYS SUITABLE IN DISPUTE RESOLUTION?**

ADR may not be appropriate to resolve every dispute. Consider the following:

- A client's commercial objectives may be best achieved by embarking on litigation. The commencement of proceedings may exert more pressure, at least initially, than a suggestion that the parties attempt ADR.

- The litigation may be necessary because the prime remedy needed is an emergency injunction, which can only be obtained from the courts, or because the parties are looking for a definitive court ruling on a particular issue in order to establish a binding precedent (public interest).

- There may be little point in delaying litigation if the opposing side is not yet ready to talk settlement in realistic terms, for example, where there is no final prognosis available in a personal injury case.

- Your client's case may be strong enough to justify an application for summary judgment. In those circumstances, pursuing the litigation by way of an interim application route may well result in a quicker conclusion or settlement than a reference to ADR.

Even if ADR is considered appropriate, there may be a particular type of ADR that is best suited to a client's case or in which the client may achieve a tactical advantage. Likewise, the timing of a reference to ADR may itself be a delicate matter. Whilst there is now a duty imposed on all parties to a dispute to consider ADR pre-issue, sometimes, ADR will be most effective after litigation has progressed to a point at which the issues have been crystallized in the statements of case. These can be difficult decisions that need to be taken on a case-by-case basis. All legal representatives need to be trained to assist clients in making the right decision in line with their personal and commercial objectives.

5.7 **PREPARATION FOR ADR GENERALLY**

As is apparent from this chapter, from the outset of any dispute, the parties should now actively consider whether ADR is likely to be of benefit and, if so, how the process is to be handled. This is an exercise that is likely to involve the client and legal representative collaborating closely, since the issues are likely to be commercial, or personal, as well as legal. Even if a client is intractably opposed to ADR, it can no longer bury its head in the sand and ignore it: if it cannot justify its opposition, it may well find itself penalized in costs, as suggested earlier.

So what issues need to be considered at the outset?

1. A realistic appraisal of the case is essential, because ADR is likely to be ineffective if the key issues have not been identified and evaluated. As part of this process, the legal representative and client need to consider any commercial and/or personal objectives and whether they might be better achieved by ADR or litigation. The likely costs, timescale, and pressure points may all have a bearing here.

2. Careful consideration needs to be given to any settlement discussions to date, the likely readiness of the opposing side to negotiate realistically, and the timing of any attempt at ADR. Reconsider the points made in paragraph 5.6: if ADR is a possibility, the merits of the different types of ADR should be considered. (Table 5.1 at the end of this chapter may assist.)

3. If some form of intermediary, mediator, expert, or judge is needed, the identity of that person should be discussed. Does the intermediary require expert knowledge of a particular field to grasp the issues, or would a generalist be better suited? Does the legal

representative already know a suitably qualified individual, or would it be better to approach one of the leading ADR bodies or courts? Can agreement be reached with the opposition regarding the appointment of the intermediary?

4. The selection of the ADR team to represent a client and/or prepare submissions for the client also requires careful planning. Usually, it will be the client and the legal representative in attendance, but consideration should be given to whether an expert, counsel, or witnesses may be required. (These would only ever be necessary to clarify issues.)

5. Finally, the negotiation strategy needs to be thought through in advance and parties who have not experienced ADR before should be informed about the process, so that they are not caught unawares. Clearly, your strategy and tactics may vary once the process gets underway and depending on how it develops, so it is important to remain flexible and open minded.

5.8 MEDIATION AS A FORM OF ALTERNATIVE DISPUTE RESOLUTION

Mediation is becoming more predominant in dispute resolution both within our own jurisdiction and in Europe. The Mediation Directive, in this regard, applies to European cross-border disputes (rather than disputes arising within any one member state such as the UK) and was implemented by May 2011. Many of its regulations are similar in essence to mediation practice in this country. However, following Brexit on 31 January 2020, the UK government has effectively revoked the implementation of the EU Mediation Directive Cross Border Mediation (EU Directive) (EU Exit) Regulations 2019.

The remainder of this chapter will concentrate on aspects of mediation in practice within the UK that are important to bear in mind when conducting a piece of litigation and when advising a client.

5.8.1 THE INTERPLAY OF MEDIATION AND LITIGATION

Mediation is a flexible process and can, therefore, be used at any time: before proceedings are issued, during proceedings, even during a lengthy trial. However, whilst the ethos of the CPR was to encourage the use of ADR and mediation in particular, some thought is required as to the exact timing of the mediation.

It may be the case that there are glaring evidential gaps in relation to liability, causation, and quantum, such as experts' reports to help to assess responsibility and value. Without such a report, it would be pointless to try to compromise any of those issues, because agreement could only ever be 'subject to' its findings. The main focus of mediation is to resolve disputes more quickly and cheaply than litigation. This may not be the case if mediation is entered into too early.

5.8.2 THE COST OF MEDIATION

One of the advantages of mediation is that there will be cost savings if resolution is reached. There will also be time savings to the client, whether it is a personal or commercial matter. The cost and time savings will be greater the sooner mediation is entered into (subject to it being an appropriate time to mediate), compared to proceeding through to trial.

However, there is still a cost implication to the client in entering into mediation, and, depending on the value of the claim, it could even be seen as disproportionate to mediate. Nevertheless, even if this is the case, it will be wholly disproportionate to litigate. The client must, therefore, not be misled on the benefits of mediation and, whilst it is considerably cheaper and quicker than litigation, the costs of the mediator are borne jointly and severally between the parties. A party's legal representative's time, the preparation, and any expenses must be met by that party (subject to any agreement reached during the mediation itself).

Mediators are usually either solicitors or barristers, or other professionals, such as architects, surveyors, and engineers, who have been specially trained by accredited bodies such as the Centre for Dispute Resolution (CEDR)—http://www.cedr.com—and the ADR Group (ADRg)—http://www.adrgroup.co.uk. These accredited bodies can be contacted to find a suitable mediator or, alternatively, individuals can be approached directly. The Civil Mediation Council has set up an online Mediation Directory, which allows users to search for civil mediator providers by county at http://www.civilmediation.justice.gov.uk/.

The mediator's fees are usually based on a fixed fee for a day or half a day and are dependent on experience. The piloted schemes mentioned in paragraph 5.5.3 are subject to a nominal fixed fee payable by the parties to the court, although each party is still bound by its retainer with its own legal representative in respect of the preparation for, and attendance at, the mediation.

5.8.3 HOW DO YOU 'SELL' MEDIATION TO YOUR CLIENT?

The following are some of the major selling points of mediation of which the client should perhaps be made aware at a meeting when the ADR options are being discussed.

- It has been said that mediation leads to a sudden outbreak of common sense, because the aim of mediation is to solve problems, not to find fault—that is, what the client actually wants and can live with, as opposed to what the issues are in the case.

- Mediation provides the forum to 'get things off your chest'. Sitting down face to face with the opponent and telling them what has happened, and the effect that the wrongdoing or breach has had goes a long way to diffusing the situation and sets the stage for the real work of reaching a settlement.

- Mediation also provides the equivalent for the client of a day in court. Whilst it is an informal and private process with an impartial third party present, the client feels that, within the four walls, he is telling the world that he has been wronged. The presence of the mediator seems to fulfil the client's emotional need in this regard.

- It gives the client the chance to see his case unfold before the mediator and his opponent, and to acknowledge the strengths and weaknesses of both parties' cases. It also gives the client an opportunity to see his legal representative in action, because it is usually the legal representative who conducts the opening statement on behalf of the client. The client has a chance to see his case being presented and feels as though something is finally happening.

- Mediation gives each party an opportunity to hear its opponent's case, facts, and issues. The key point here is that all of the parties hear the same information even if they perceive it differently. It is then the mediator's job to define and clarify certain facts and issues.

- Mediation has a way of unearthing the real issues in a case. Sometimes, this requires some digging around by the mediator to get to the root of the problem, because it has been masked by ancillary ones.

5.8.4 WHAT DOES THE CLIENT NEED TO KNOW ABOUT MEDIATION?

The client needs to know full details of the mediation process, including preparation and procedure, how long is required, and what it can achieve in terms of time and cost savings. The length of the mediation will determine the cost, and, therefore, thought should be given to whether a full day is, in fact, necessary, or whether a shorter period—for example, five hours—would suffice. However long the mediation day is anticipated to last, it is always worthwhile blocking out time in your own and your client's diaries in case it should overrun. It would undermine the process if progress were to be made towards settlement during the mediation day, but the parties have to leave for other commitments.

It is often appropriate, when discussing mediation with the client, to provide details of the costs incurred to the date of the prospective mediation and an estimate of costs to trial. The client may already have had this costs information if the claim is a multi-track case, as it is likely that a costs budget has been or will need to be prepared in any event, as examined in Chapter 4 at paragraph 4.6.3. It would also be advisable to undertake a risk analysis on the prospects of success and proportionality.

It should also be made clear to the client that what is discussed in mediation is confidential and on a 'without prejudice' basis.

It is, however, very important—especially for those who are new to the mediation process—that the client understands what he will achieve. The client should not be led to have enhanced expectations about a 'victory' at the hands of his opponent. Mediation is not about 'point scoring'; rather, it is about getting on with life and business, and laying the dispute to rest.

As such, it is the legal representative's job to manage those expectations. Mediation is about compromise, and it is very unlikely that as matters settle at mediation, either party will be elated with the outcome. It is, however, still a preferable process than proceeding to trial, at which a third party, the judge, decides the case for the parties, and at which there is always a 'winner' and 'loser' on the issues in the case.

5.8.5 PREPARATION FOR THE MEDIATION DAY

5.8.5.1 The appointment of the mediator

The parties may be able to agree on a known individual to act as mediator. Alternatively, they may approach one of the recognized mediation bodies to obtain a list of possible candidates to act as mediator, as set out in paragraph 5.8.2. Consideration should be given to whether the mediator needs specialist skills and whether a legal or other professional is required. Sometimes, the appointment of joint mediators may be appropriate. The urgency of the mediation may, of course, determine which mediators are available. Curricula vitae (CVs) are usually requested, along with dates of availability.

Once the parties have agreed on the identity of the mediator, he is informed and contacts both parties simultaneously to confirm his appointment. Most mediators or mediation bodies will require the parties to enter into a mediation agreement. Each party enters into the agreement with the mediator in advance of the mediation day, although it is common that these are left for signing on the morning of the mediation. The agreement will usually cover some basic ground rules, which predominantly include confidentiality and fees. A sample mediation agreement can be seen in the online resources.

5.8.5.2 Procedural steps

5.8.5.2.1 *The mediator's requirements*

On the agreed appointment of the mediator, the mediator will write to the parties simultaneously, confirming his understanding as to who they and their legal representatives are, when and where the mediation is to take place, the anticipated duration of the process, and his specific requirements as to documentation. It is very important that a person with authority to settle from each party is present at the mediation. It is frustrating if that person has only a limited authority, although having a client representative at the end of the telephone is a better alternative.

5.8.5.2.2 *The position statement*

The mediator will usually require a position statement as part of the specific documentation from each party. These will be copied to the opposite party and the mediator seven days before the mediation (although this time limit varies in practice). The parties need to consider who will be responsible for the preparation of these submissions, and, frequently, this is a role assigned to the legal representative. Generally, mediators will want submissions kept fairly short, giving only a summary of the case and each party's stance in relation to the issues.

Practical Considerations

The parties should try to agree a core bundle of documents to send to the mediator along with the position statements, because this limits the amount of reading time. The preparation of the core bundle will usually fall to the party who would be the claimant in any litigation.

5.8.5.2.3 *Preliminary discussions with the mediator*

Before the day of the mediation, the mediator may wish to discuss with the parties or their lawyers any difficulties that he has with his understanding of the case, the manner in which the initial presentation of their cases is to be made, and possibly details of any previous failed settlement attempts. These discussions are confidential to each party.

It also gives the mediator a chance to get to know the legal representatives or client ahead of the day, and this will ultimately save time and money. These discussions are usually done over the telephone, but are not always necessary.

5.8.6 THE MEDIATION DAY(S)

The following describes the likely procedure during a mediation day. However, it is important to remember that each mediation day is different and that the discretion lies with the mediator as to how it is conducted. For example, if the relationship between the parties was particularly acrimonious, the mediator may decide to dispense with the opening joint session or to curtail it significantly.

5.8.6.1 The initial joint meeting

The mediation may take place at a neutral venue or at one of the party's legal representative's offices. Once the mediator is ready, the parties will be called into a room, where the mediator will outline the mediation process and establish the ground rules. It is at this stage that the parties or their legal representatives will normally be asked to make short opening statements of their cases. In essence, this will amount to a short summary of the written submissions, again with a view to clarifying the issues in the case. An opening joint session can be seen in the online resources video clips.

5.8.6.1.1 *Private 'caucuses' or 'sessions'*

Once the submissions are complete, the mediator may choose to keep the parties together or invite them into separate rooms, where they can speak privately. These private meetings are called 'caucuses', and nothing said in caucus can be revealed to the other side without the permission of the party in caucus. The caucuses are useful means of exploring the business relationship between the parties, of finding out where they are coming from, flushing out the issues that each side sees as key, and perhaps looking at why previous settlements have failed.

The mediator may well engage in 'shuttle diplomacy', moving between rooms in a series of private sessions, looking for common ground or areas in which the parties feel able to make movement.

5.8.6.1.2 *Joint meetings*

The mediator will not simply wish to act as messenger for the parties. At times during the process, the parties may be brought together for joint meetings so that they can negotiate directly or tackle issues that are proving to be a stumbling block. Likewise, the mediator may wish to meet with the legal representative or the experts separately, or to meet with the parties in the absence of their lawyers. The process is voluntary, however, and the mediator cannot compel a party to do anything with which he does not feel comfortable.

5.8.6.1.3 *The settlement*

If the mediation results in a settlement, the mediator will normally be keen to have the terms written up into a formal agreement there and then. This may be a task delegated to the parties' legal representatives or it may be something that the mediator takes on. It is normally desirable to record the agreement in writing as soon as terms are agreed and whilst there is still an impetus to settle. Once the settlement has been written up and the parties have signed up to it, it becomes binding and can be enforced in the usual way through the courts as examined in the Online Chapter 'Enforcement of Judgments'. A closing settlement meeting can be seen in the online resources video clips.

KEY POINTS SUMMARY

- ADR must be considered, and considered seriously—if it is not to be tried, have a good reason why not and, even if it gets rejected early on, do not be afraid to reconsider later.

- Change your mindset—aim for resolution, not a judicial determination.

- Understand the different types of ADR and which one may be best suited to the client's case.

- The CPR expect parties to engage with ADR and there can be cost penalties for an unreasonable refusal to consider ADR.

- Consider when is best to mediate. It will be different in every case.

- Make sure that your client understands what he can expect from mediation and curtail those enhanced expectations.

- Be prepared for mediation in terms of written submissions and documents. Whilst mediation is a flexible process, there is no excuse for sloppy or inaccurate presentation.

- If settlement is achieved, ensure that the agreement or order drafted is legally binding and enforceable.

SELF-TEST QUESTIONS

1. What type of ADR process is voluntary but imposes a decision on the parties?

2. How can mediation in low-value cases be used effectively and proportionately?

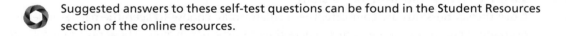 Suggested answers to these self-test questions can be found in the Student Resources section of the online resources.

TABLE 5.1 A COMPARISON OF ADR PROCESSES

Type of ADR process	Positive features	Negative features	Common use in
Negotiation/round table discussions	Voluntary, without prejudice, flexible, legal representation not essential, arranged at short notice, and inexpensive.	Inequality of parties, and parties often become entrenched in their own positions.	All types of disputes at any stage.

Type of ADR process	Positive features	Negative features	Common use in
Mediation	Voluntary, confidential, non-binding, proactive intervention of neutral third party, ascertains what your opponent really wants, free to leave at any time, can be arranged quickly, and cheaper than proceeding to trial.	Both parties must be willing to make it work, and there is still a cost implication to the parties.	All types of disputes (save for test cases) at any stage even during trial. Can also be used either consecutively or concurrently with adjudication if appropriate.
Conciliation	Voluntary, without prejudice, proactive intervention of independent third party, gain a better understanding of opponent's dispute.	Usually no formal written submissions required, and this can sometimes hamper the process by clouding issues.	Usually a precondition in many contracts to arbitration or litigation and is common in employment matters.
Executive Tribunal	Voluntary and can be quick and effective. Very low cost implication.	The opinion does not have to be followed, and the executives can remain entrenched in their respective positions.	Commercial matters with reasonably sized commercial entities.
Early Neutral Evaluation	Voluntary and non-binding, usually occurs early on in a dispute, focuses on central issues and relevant law only.	If a judge is wanted it may take time to arrange. Still, a cost implication as submissions and documentation needs to be prepared.	Larger technical building and engineering or commercial cases.
Expert Determination	Binding but voluntary process. Decision can be obtained quickly and written submissions are not onerous.	Decision cannot be enforced as a court judgment. A fresh action in contract would have to be raised. Selection of agreed expert and the limits of his instruction can be problematic.	In ongoing contract where there is an ongoing business relationship to preserve, mostly used in cases with technical issues.
Arbitration	Specialist arbiter to hear the case, private, can prohibit litigation, finality of award provides commercial certainty.	Expensive and time-consuming (similar to litigation), but award if unpaid can be easily enforced through the courts.	Construction and engineering claims.
Adjudication	Quick, choice of specialist adjudicator, adjudicator has no jurisdiction to award costs (less risk in a difficult case), retains a business relationship or ongoing contract thereby reducing disruption, private.	Adjudicator has no jurisdiction to award costs (limits recovery), no automatic right to interest, only binding until appealed; to enforce the decision you must issue fresh proceedings and apply for P24 Summary Judgment, costs implication on enforcement.	Construction and engineering claims, and some professional negligence claims. Can also be used either consecutively or concurrently with litigation if appropriate.

6 THE FIRST CLIENT MEETING AND INITIAL CONSIDERATIONS

> Relevant parts of the CPR and its PDs: 7, 19, and 21.

6.1 INTRODUCTION

As a legal representative new to practice, you will be expected initially to assist in clients' cases and ultimately to handle your own files. New cases for existing and new clients are usually fielded through an existing fee earner in the practice or through the firm's receptionist to the litigation (otherwise known as 'dispute resolution') department, where cases are allocated to the various fee earners. In smaller firms, this may mean only one or two fee earners.

In every new matter for every client, your professional conduct duties, particularly client care issues, should be at the forefront of your mind as a legal representative before you proceed to undertake any work for the client. These can be addressed to some degree in advance of the first attendance on the client.

The first meeting that you have with a new client is likely to take some time and there will usually be a number of action points that arise as a result of the meeting.

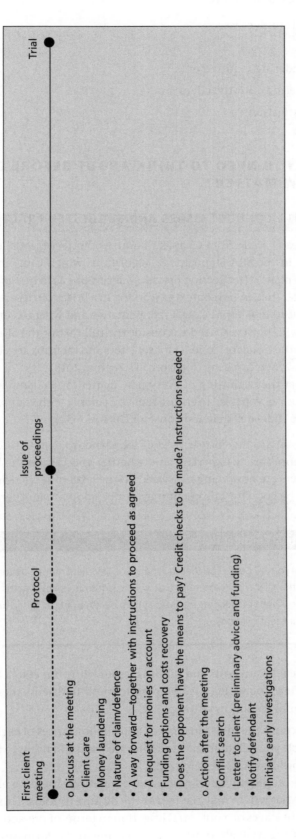

LITIGATION TRAIN: THE FIRST CLIENT INTERVIEW AND INITIAL CONSIDERATIONS

First client meeting

Protocol

Issue of proceedings

Trial

o Discuss at the meeting
• Client care
• Money laundering
• Nature of claim/defence
• A way forward—together with instructions to proceed as agreed
• A request for monies on account
• Funding options and costs recovery
• Does the opponent have the means to pay? Credit checks to be made? Instructions needed

o Action after the meeting
• Conflict search
• Letter to client (preliminary advice and funding)
• Notify defendant
• Initiate early investigations

All of these aspects require you, as the legal representative, to spend time with, and incur a cost to, the client.

This chapter will focus on:

- professional conduct issues;

- client care;

- money laundering requirements;

- the first meeting with the client; and

- initial investigations.

6.2 WHAT DO YOU NEED TO THINK ABOUT BEFORE DEALING WITH EVERY NEW MATTER?

6.2.1 PROFESSIONAL CONDUCT ISSUES AND SUGGESTED PRACTICE

As you are already aware from Chapters 1 and 3, your professional conduct duties, as a whole, are contained in the SRA Standards & Regulations which came into force on 25 November 2019—see Chapter 1). This section provides suggestions as to best practice when a new client is engaged in order that, in the context of working in a litigation department, you have a complete picture of what to look for as a legal representative and what to consider when acting in new matters. You will, however, need to consult the full text of the SRA Standards & Regulations which include the Codes of Conduct for solicitors and for firms, together with the Transparency Rules for firms which came into force on 6 December 2018.

Remember, at the beginning of every new matter for a client, and throughout the matter until its conclusion, you need to ensure that you comply with your professional conduct duties.

Best practice indicates that you consider the following:

(a) Whether you are the correct level of fee earner to deal with each matter, whether you have the appropriate expertise, and whether you can do the best for your client. Legal practitioners are now being measured on the level of service provided to each client and what may be good for one client may not be good for another.

 Practical Considerations

If you feel that you are out of your depth in handling any client matter, discuss this with your supervising partner and the client. It is essential that your client knows your status and experience as a legal representative when you become involved in his case. (We discuss this in more detail in paragraph 6.3 as part of your client relations.)

(b) Discuss the relevant costs and funding issues with your client, both right at the start and as the matter progresses. It is best practice both to discuss these with your client and to give this information in writing.

Taking into account the individual needs and circumstances of each client, all relevant information to enable your client to make an informed decision needs to be provided, and an explanation as to how these will be delivered.

An example of 'providing all relevant information' could be ensuring that you explain procedurally what will or may happen as the dispute unfolds. This could include highlighting the different stages of a potential litigation in terms of pre-action protocol right through to trial, discussing ADR alternatives, and placing any information given in the context of costs and time frame. The client can then decide, armed with this information, the nature and extent of the services he requires from your practice.

Practical Considerations

When explaining general client care obligations to your client, you should stress that the relationship between the client and yourself as a legal practitioner is a two-way process. You should, therefore, highlight to your client that he has to make a time commitment to his own case. It is important to control his expectations early on and to ensure that he appreciates that, with his cooperation, you will endeavour to do your best for him.

(c) It is best practice to explain to your client the distinction between 'solicitor and client costs'—that is, the sum that the client must pay to his own legal representative—and 'costs between the parties' (otherwise known as '*inter partes* costs')—that is, costs that may be awarded, at the discretion of the court, between the parties once litigation has commenced. This distinction is important, because, as can be seen from Chapter 4, paragraph 4.3, the amount that a client is able to recover from his opponent, should he receive a favourable costs order, is very likely to be less than the client is liable to pay his own legal representative—subject of course to the type of funding arrangements the client has. The client will, therefore, usually be left with 'irrecoverable costs' from litigation. The client must fully understand his liability for those.

(d) Discuss your firm's complaints-handling procedure, to ensure your client is aware of the procedure and knows how to make a complaint if they are unhappy with the service they receive. You also need to ensure that all complaints are dealt with promptly and fairly.

 Practical Considerations

It is a bizarre concept that, when establishing your client retainer and setting out the terms for a successful and fruitful relationship, you are obliged to raise the issue of complaints. This must not be overlooked, no matter how awkward you feel about discussing this aspect.

Legal representatives should also be aware of the Provision of Services Regulations 2009 (as amended by the Provision of Services Regulations (Amendments etc) (EU Exit) Regulations 2018), which impose requirements to give information to your client on additional client care issues over and above the SRA requirements. These concern the Legal Ombudsman (LEO). The LEO was established by the Office for Legal Complaints (OLC) under the Legal Services Act 2007, and it provides a free complaints resolution service to clients and can deal with complaints about many categories of lawyers, including barristers and solicitors.

The 2018 Regulations were introduced to address deficiencies arising as a result of the UK's exit from the EU. However, the 2009 Regulations (as amended by the 2018 Regulations) still provide protection for UK businesses and consumer rights.

(e) You are prohibited from acting where a conflict of interest arises between you and your current clients and/or two or more current clients.

You can, therefore, never act where there is a conflict, or a significant risk of conflict, between yourself and your client.

 Example

You are instructed by a husband and wife driver and passenger, respectively, of a vehicle involved in a road traffic accident (RTA). Both are existing clients, as your private client department dealt with their wills. They want to sue the motorcyclist for damages for the personal injuries they each sustained. The motorcyclist, however, alleges that the husband was either wholly or partly to blame for the collision.

> The potential conflict exists at the outset of the retainer, even before the allegation against the driver has been made, because there is clearly a risk that the innocent passenger may have a claim in negligence against the husband driver.

(f) You must maintain the confidentiality of your client's affairs at all times unless your client (or former client) agrees to the disclosure of confidential information or it is permitted by law. Further, you are also under a duty to make your client aware of material information within your knowledge. However, your duty goes further than this, because you are not permitted to act if, by acting, you are putting confidentiality at risk at some point in the future. Perhaps the key point to make here is that the duty of confidentiality will always override the duty of disclosure.

6.2.2 MONEY LAUNDERING REGULATIONS

We thought it appropriate to discuss briefly here how you deal practically with your obligations under the Money Laundering Regulations 2007 (and subsequently updated by further Regulations in 2017 and 2019) as a legal representative in a litigation department. We do not intend to set out your money laundering obligations in detail. A link to further advice from the Law Society can be found in the online resources.

When you enter practice, your firm will be required to provide staff with appropriate training on their legal obligations, and information on how to recognize and deal with money laundering and terrorist financing risks (reg. 21).

Money laundering within the litigation and dispute resolution framework is not as prevalent as in other areas of practice, because litigation can probably be classed as fairly low risk. However, you are still required to identify your client's name and address, usually by a passport or driver's licence and a utility bill for an individual. For a company, you will need to consider the appropriate individual identification requirements for the company directors and, where the company is limited, undertake a company search and personal identification documents for the relevant directors and shareholders. You are required to report any reasonable suspicions to your money laundering reporting officer.

The Money Laundering Regulations 2007 brought additional burdens to legal representatives in the identification of beneficial owners of client trusts, companies, and partnerships (reg. 5), the customer due diligence measures (reg. 7) to be applied to high-risk (reg. 14) and low-risk (reg. 13) situations and revised administrative and training requirements.

6.3 WHAT DO YOU NEED TO DO BEFORE COMMENCING A NEW MATTER?

Based in part on the theoretical considerations in paragraph 6.2, there are some essential tasks that you must undertake before you take substantive instructions from your client, whether a new or an existing client. These items will be mirrored in each new matter that arises, but as you undertake repeat work for an existing client, you will get to know your client and some of these items will become easier to deal with.

6.3.1 SEND A CLIENT CARE LETTER

This is otherwise known as a 'retainer letter' or Terms of Engagement. Attached to this letter are the firm's standard terms and conditions of acting, such as when bills will be rendered, interest provisions for late payments, VAT, storage of client files and documents, dispute resolution and jurisdiction clauses, etc.

The client care letter, along with the standard terms and conditions, must be sent out to the client before he has his first meeting with you, and before you commence work on his behalf.

Usually the legal representative will speak with the client over the telephone to ascertain the general background to the dispute and either offer a free, time-limited meeting or a fixed-fee meeting. As the client care letter and standard terms and conditions are sent out in advance of the first meeting, you will not be able to set out—other than to highlight in a general way—the client's objectives for that particular matter, what the main issues are, the options available, or what steps should be taken, nor be able to give an estimate or fixed-fee indication of the costs of the matter. These will have to be set out in a subsequent letter after the first interview.

Client care obligations became more onerous with the implementation of the Consumer Contracts Regulations 2013 ('the Regulations'). The Regulations give any individual or individuals, who are clients, the right to cancel the contract (being the client care letter and standard terms and conditions) without giving any reason in situations where the legal representative contracts with the individual client away from the office. The Notice to Cancel is usually referred to in the client care letter and set out in full in the standard terms and conditions.

The consequences of not complying with these Regulations are very serious; it is a criminal offence to do work for an individual if the necessary notices and procedures have not been given or followed. Further, the contract is treated as unenforceable. This effectively means that the legal representative cannot be paid.

The Law Society has published a Practice Note to provide an explanation of how the Regulations apply to solicitors and their clients which provides helpful guidance for practitioners.

The burden of proof is on the legal representative to establish compliance. A number of examples are set out below:

 Example 1

- The legal representative sees an individual in the office. He hands out the client care letter and the standard terms and conditions of the firm.
- The individual reads and signs them in the office.
- No cancellation period applies and work can be commenced immediately.

 Example 2a

- The legal representative sees an individual in the office who takes the client care letter and the standard terms and conditions of the firm away with him to consider.
- The individual then signs and returns them to the firm.
- Cancellation period applies and work cannot be commenced until the expiry of the fourteen-day cancellation period.

 Example 2b

- The legal representative sees an individual in the office who takes the client care letter and the standard terms and conditions of the firm away with him to consider.
- The individual then brings them back to the office and signs them there (and does not just hand them in signed).
- No cancellation period applies and work can be commenced immediately.

Example 3a

- The legal representative attends the individual's home/hospital/other location away from the office, where he gives the individual the client care letter and the standard terms and conditions of the firm.
- The individual reads, signs, and returns them to the legal representative away from the office or returns them by post or email.
- Cancellation period applies and work cannot be commenced until the expiry of the fourteen-day cancellation period.

Example 3b

- The legal representative attends the individual's home/hospital/other location away from the office where he gives the individual the client care letter and the standard terms and conditions of the firm.
- The individual then brings them to the office and signs them (and does not just hand them in signed).
- No cancellation period applies and work can be commenced immediately.

Example 4a

- The legal representative talks to the individual initially on the telephone and then sends out the client care letter and the standard terms and conditions of the firm by email or post.
- The individual signs and returns them by email or post.
- Cancellation period applies and work cannot be commenced until the expiry of the fourteen-day cancellation period.

Example 4b

- The legal representative talks to the individual initially on the telephone and then sends out the client care letter and the standard terms and conditions of the firm by email or post.
- The individual then brings them to the office and signs them (and does not just hand them in signed).
- No cancellation period applies and work can be commenced immediately.

It is hugely important to remember that if the legal representative does not give notice and follow these procedures, then no work can be undertaken during the fourteen-day cancellation period. If work is undertaken during that period, it is a criminal offence, and the firm does not get paid.

The Regulations only apply to clients who are individuals. If a firm acts for a corporate or business entity such as a limited company/LLP/PLC/partnership/sole trader in their business capacity, they fall outside the Regulations. No cancellation rights or periods apply, and, consequently, there are no cancellation notices required.

It is also worth noting that emailing the client care letter with the standard terms and conditions to the individual is only permitted if the individual expressly agrees to receive them by email.

Practical Considerations

In practice legal representatives can bypass the burden of the Regulations as follows: they notify the individual that because they have cancellation rights, unless he agrees, the legal representative cannot start work. The individual is invited to indicate in writing that he expressly agrees that the legal representative can begin work. If the individual does agree, then the legal representative must inform the individual that if he does in fact proceed to give notice to cancel within fourteen days, the firm is at liberty to charge for the work done to the date of cancellation. The legal representative then hands/sends to the individual the client care letter and standard terms and conditions of the firm, which include a written provision that, if he signs, he agrees for work to be commenced straight away.

6.3.2 REQUEST MONIES ON ACCOUNT

As can be seen from Chapter 3, paragraphs 3.2 and 3.3, the question of how a client is to proceed with or defend a claim needs to be identified right at the beginning of the retainer. However, you are not usually able to help your client to decide how he is able to fund matters until you have attended on him and taken detailed instructions at a first meeting. This first meeting needs to be paid for by the client, unless your firm offers free first interviews or is under a general retainer with a trade union, insurance company, or other association.

It is, therefore, good practice to explain why and how a first meeting, the time needed to review any documentation, and any early work to be undertaken need to be paid for and to ask your client to provide monies on account to cover these. The amount will depend on the type of matter and your hourly rate.

It is good practice to ask for the monies in the form of a cheque, banker's draft, or an account transfer to the client account for money laundering reasons. For every new matter that you have for a client, your accounts department, on your instruction, will need to open an account for the client and matter. The account will have a client account and an office account.

The monies on account are client monies. Once you receive the monies, you should ask your accounts department to place it in the client account. The monies stay there until you render a bill to your client. The monies will then be transferred across to the solicitor's account for that matter, and any balance due can be requested from the client. If there is a surplus in the client account, that can remain there until the next bill is rendered.

Refer to the SRA Standards & Regulations Accounts Rules for guidance on handling client money and client accounts.

6.3.3 COMPLY WITH MONEY LAUNDERING REQUIREMENTS

The identification documents for an individual highlighted in paragraph 6.2.2 are usually dealt with by your firm's receptionist, who will copy them when the client attends the office. Sometimes, the client will bring them with him to your first meeting. If your client is a limited company, then a company search can be done online with Companies House for a nominal fee. In either case, you will need to examine the identification documents to ascertain whether you are satisfied that your money laundering obligations have been complied with. Consequently, it is not enough merely to undertake a company search against your limited company client. Once the identity of the directors has been ascertained, passports and utility bills are required for those directors. If another company holds shares in your client company or the shareholders differ from the directors, then if their shareholding exceeds 25 per cent, further investigations are necessary of those shareholders before you can conclude your money laundering obligations.

 Practical Considerations

A common problem arises when you have made a request for the identification documents and they are not forthcoming. The work that your client has instructed you to do may be urgent, such as making an application to set aside default judgment, or going on record as acting and attending a hearing on his behalf. Best practice and compliance with the Money Laundering Regulations 2007 suggest that you are not permitted to act further until you have received such documentation. You may feel that this puts you in difficulties with your professional conduct duties of acting in your client's best interest. However, this frequently occurs in practice, and a nominal amount of work can be done whilst the documentation is awaited—but, at some early point, you will need to inform your client that you will be unable to do any further work until the documentation is received.

It is, therefore, essential that the question of identification is dealt with when you first speak to your client over the telephone.

6.3.4 UNDERTAKE A CONFLICT SEARCH

Your secretary or accounts department will usually undertake a conflict search. Alternatively, larger firms' case management systems have a conflict check provision. Most firms have detailed file opening forms to be completed by the fee earner. On this form, you will need to state the identity of your client's opponent. A check will be carried out to see if anyone in the firm:

- is acting, or has acted, for that opponent, or
- whether another member of the litigation department is acting against the same opponent.

You may need to discuss this with the fee earner who is acting or has acted for the opponent or the other competing client, as well as with your supervising fee earner and the firm's compliance officer, in accordance with the firm's conflict policy.

6.3.5 ASK FOR ANY RELEVANT DOCUMENTATION

In order to enable you to be of more assistance to your client at the first substantive meeting (and ultimately to save time and cost to your client), it is sensible, when arranging the first meeting, to ask for any paperwork that he has in relation to the case itself and in relation to the potential funding of the case, such as insurance policies (see Chapter 3, paragraph 3.3).

For example, if your client has a breach of contract action, contractual documentation should be provided in advance of the first meeting or telephone call to allow you to consider what the relevant terms of the contract are, such as provisions for interest, exclusions, and dispute resolution and jurisdiction clauses. If your client has been injured, any existing insurance policies should be supplied to ascertain whether he has any legal expenses cover for any part of his claim, as identified in Chapter 3 at paragraph 3.3.1.

With such documentation available to you before you take substantive instructions, you have the opportunity to form preliminary views, devise a list of questions, and consider funding options.

6.3.6 PRE-INTERVIEW QUESTIONNAIRES

Some firms—particularly smaller firms or firms that undertake a lot of personal injury work—send out client questionnaires before the first meeting with the client. These are pro forma questionnaires and are designed to act as an aide-memoire and checklist, particularly for professional conduct, client care, and money laundering requirements.

There are advantages and disadvantages to using these questionnaires. As a legal representative, you will need to recognize your firm's policy on this.

6.4 THE FIRST CLIENT MEETING

Preparation is the key to a good client meeting, and we would suggest that you allocate enough time to prepare fully before attending your client. This will include a review of all of the information that you have received and a double check on your professional conduct (especially costs), client care, and money laundering duties. It may also be helpful to prepare your own agenda to form the basic structure for the meeting.

In practice, meetings can be challenging for the legal representative who is new to practice—especially if you are to conduct the meeting on your own. In the early part of your legal career, it is more likely that you will sit in on meetings with other, more experienced, fee earners.

Often, in repeat business with existing commercial clients, there will be no face-to-face meeting, but only an email or telephone call to provide new instructions. However you receive those first substantive instructions, you must still have regard for paragraphs 6.2 and 6.3.

The following sets out some suggestions as to what should and may happen at a first meeting with your client.

6.4.1 CLIENT ETIQUETTE AND PRELIMINARY MATTERS

Client interviewing is a skill that you will develop as you become more confident and experienced in your legal career. If you are having a face-to-face meeting with your client, ensure that you know the date, time, and place of the meeting, because these can take place in the office or at another venue. Wherever the location, of course, you must always be on time.

There are the usual pleasantries in the first few minutes of a client meeting, such as enquiring as to the client's well-being and journey (if he has travelled), offering refreshments, and generally making the client feel at ease. If the meeting is to take place at your offices, either book a conference room or, if the meeting is in your room, make an attempt to tidy and remove from sight any confidential information, and do notify your secretary that you do not want any interruptions.

You may need to deal with any outstanding professional conduct and client care issues, but these can be done either at the outset or the conclusion of the meeting.

6.4.2 THE FORMAT OF THE MEETING

Whether the meeting is undertaken by telephone or in person, there are six main tasks for you to perform during the attendance.

6.4.2.1 Identify what your client wants you to do for him

You need to identify what your client's objectives are, but, at the same time, ensure that your client does not have any enhanced expectations. Your client needs to know the implications of embarking on steps that could involve him in litigation or another form of dispute resolution and all of the financial risks that go with that, but he must be realistic as to the likely cost and the prospects of success.

Your client's goal may be straightforward: for example, in a breach of contract case, this may simply be recovery of losses, or in a personal injury matter, it may be compensation. Your client may, in fact, want something different: for example, in a breach of contract case, it may be rectification of reputation damaged by the breach, or in a personal injury matter, it may be an apology and assurance that the defective piece of equipment has been repaired so as to avoid damage to others.

6.4.2.2 Take full details of your client's version of events

Without wishing to oversimplify any case, there will nearly always be two differing accounts of how the accident happened, how the contract was breached, or why someone was negligent. Your client will need to recount to you his version of events in his own words and it is important that you allow him to do this. Please see the Andrew Pike case study in the online resources for an example of an initial attendance note.

Practical Considerations

You will spend some time writing this down as your client speaks and, therefore, do not be afraid to ask your client to clarify anything for you. As your client recounts the facts, you may wish to ask questions—but remember that clients are not always clear on what is relevant to their case, so do not be too keen to interrupt, because they are unlikely to be satisfied that what they have to say on a particular point is not important until they have been given the opportunity to tell you. There is a balance to be struck, because some clients will talk continuously if you allow them to.

This attendance note will, in effect, form your client's proof of evidence and later be used to prepare the particulars of claim (or defence) if proceedings are issued. Examples of these documents can be seen in Chapter 11 and in the Appendices at the end of the manual. It may also be useful at this point to ask for any additional documentation in relation to your client's case. For example, if your client has been injured in an RTA, it may be helpful if he draws a sketch plan of the site of the accident, and the direction and position of the vehicles.

6.4.2.3 Explain some basic legal principles

The key to helping your client to resolve his dispute is to identify from the outset the relevant legal issues. Most cases are based on actions in contract and/or tort. Every case is made up of legal components, and your client will need to have a basic understanding of these components and how they fit into pursuing or defending his claim.

Any legal action must have a cause of action and can, theoretically, be divided up into three legal parts, known as 'liability', 'causation', and 'quantum'. Some, or all, of these may be in dispute in a case. For example, if your client were to have a contractual dispute, he would need to prove that there was a contract (cause of action) that the opponent had breached (liability), that the breach caused the losses (causation), and the nature and extent of those losses (quantum). These legal components are discussed in more detail in Chapter 7, paragraph 7.5.

These three legal components are looked at in light of the underlying principle that the claimant has to prove his case against the defendant on a balance of probabilities by way of either original and/or documentary evidence, and lay witness or expert evidence. (See Chapter 17, paragraph 17.2, for a fuller discussion on burdens of proof and evidence.) Most disputes will include the preparation and service of at least one type of evidence on your opponent for use at trial.

In essence, you will need to explain to your client in basic terms, avoiding too much technical legal language, that he may have three hurdles to overcome if he is to be successful in his case—namely, who was responsible, who caused the losses, and what those losses were—and that he will have to prove his case on the basis of what was more likely than not to have occurred. It will also be usual for you to undertake some kind of risk assessment when discussing these fundamentals of his case. (See paragraph 6.4.3.6 for an outline of how you should approach a risk assessment.)

6.4.2.4 Discuss how his dispute can be resolved

Remember that your client may never have been involved in any type of dispute and its resolution before. If he has, then some of the following suggestions may already be familiar to him.

You will need to explain to him briefly and in simple terms the ethos of dispute resolution, as highlighted in Chapter 2—particularly in relation to the overriding objective, and the principles of proportionality and reasonableness in terms of costs.

He needs to be clear that litigation is a last resort and that his problem may be better resolved by one of the alternatives to litigation. Alternative dispute resolution (ADR) is discussed in detail in Chapter 5, and most commonly includes negotiation and mediation. You should, however, point out to him what he can expect from litigation, if that is the way that his matter is to ultimately proceed, and discuss the necessity and purpose of the Protocol phase (see Chapter 8, paragraph 8.3), as well as outline how a case gets to trial.

> **ADR considerations**
>
> When discussing the possible ADR options, it is important to highlight to your client not only the benefits of ADR, but also the potential costs consequences of failing to consider ADR—most notably, costs sanctions if he should win.

Tied in with this, as with paragraph 6.4.2.3, is your risk assessment, and this is discussed in paragraph 6.4.3.6.

6.4.2.5 Answer difficult questions

First and foremost, if you are unsure of the correct answer to a client's question, then always inform your client that you will need to check the position—perhaps by undertaking some research or by speaking to a more experienced fee earner—and that you will then get back to him, either in writing or by telephone.

During a first meeting with a client, there will always be a number of questions that he will ask. Most of them can be easily dealt with: for example, 'What can I recover?' However, there are questions that clients usually always ask and which are very difficult to answer with any degree of certainty at this early stage. These include:

- **'Have I got a good case?'** The best that you can do is answer the question based on the information that you have at that particular time, and consider making the advice provisional on further investigations and, therefore, preliminary.

- **'How much will I get?'** You are unlikely to be able to put a precise figure on this, although at a later stage, after further investigations and the collating and exchange of evidence, you will be able to give a bracketed figure.

- **'How long will it take?'** Again, the answer to this question will very much depend on the conduct of the opponent and to which method of dispute resolution your client agrees. A bracketed time period can probably be identified.

- **'How much will it cost?'** The costs question is the only question here that must be addressed with some degree of accuracy, as discussed in paragraph 6.2.1 (see also Chapter 3, paragraph 3.2).

6.4.2.6 Summarize and explain what happens next

Towards the end of the meeting, once both you and your client have discussed the case as described previously, it is good practice to summarize your client's case, the options available to him, and how you can help him. This will enable you to ensure that you have all of the correct material facts and to reassure your client that you fully understand the main issues.

In order for your client to feel that his meeting has been worthwhile, you will need to set out what you will both do following the meeting. All of this should, of course, be followed up by a letter, but it is important that your client feels satisfied that something is being done when he leaves. The problem or dispute still belongs to the client, but a client can feel that he is sharing the burden by feeling satisfied with your understanding and your suggestions as to a way forward. At the end of each meeting with the client, or in a letter following the meeting, the client should be told when he will hear from you again. Good file management practices dictate that you diarize your file to the date upon which you intend to contact the client further. In the interests of good client relations, you must then do so, because he will be expecting to hear from you. Even if there is nothing to report, contact should be made and an explanation for any delay that has occurred provided.

6.4.3 SPECIFIC CONSIDERATIONS ON FIRST TAKING INSTRUCTIONS

Each case that you take on, or in which you assist, will differ to some degree from the last. However, there are certain aspects that can fundamentally shape a case that should also be considered at the first meeting in addition to the six tasks set out previously. In many cases, these will not feature heavily, but in others, they may require some detailed consideration, research, or even counsel's advice.

As you start your legal career, it may be helpful to prepare a checklist of these points to which you can refer mentally during the meeting. This may remind you to consider and act upon them, or to consider and dismiss them.

6.4.3.1 Limitation and jurisdiction

Both limitation and jurisdiction are dealt with in some detail in Chapter 7, paragraphs 7.4 and 7.2. It is essential, however, in every case and for whichever party you act, that you consider whether there is a limitation issue looming and, if so, what can be done about it to protect your client's interests.

Similarly, if an accident happened abroad, or a contractual dispute involves foreign parties and issues, you will need to turn your mind to any jurisdictional issues.

6.4.3.2 Funding

Unless you are acting frequently for an existing client, you will need to discuss the variety of funding options at the first meeting (see Chapter 3). Remember to make a detailed note of what was discussed and how this is to be followed up.

6.4.3.3 Who is your client?

A legal representative is entitled to act for any person able to instruct him to bring or defend proceedings. There are a variety of different litigants and you will need to ensure, whether you act for the claimant or the defendant, that you know whether your client is one of the following:

- an individual over the age of 18;
- a child or a protected party (CPR 21.1);
- a limited and public limited company, including a limited liability partnership;
- a partnership or sole trader (CPR 7.2A and PD 7.5A–5C);
- the estate of a deceased person (CPR 19.8);
- another incorporated or unincorporated association, including a trade union, a building society, a charity, a local government body, or a club; or
- a trust or trustee (CPR 19.7A).

There are a number of reasons why you need to know who your client is at this early stage, as follows:

- You will need to consider whether the person from whom you are taking instructions has the authority and capacity to give those instructions. There is a detailed discussion on capacity for children and protected parties in Chapter 7, paragraph 7.3.2, and in Chapter 9, paragraph 9.5.
- The identity of your client is necessary to enable you to identify your client properly for the purposes of money laundering compliance.
- If proceedings do eventually ensue, you will need to know how to describe the parties on the claim form (see Chapter 9, paragraph 9.6 and Table 9.2).
- You will need to serve those proceedings and there are different rules for service on all of the different types of legal entity listed here. (This is dealt with in Chapter 9, paragraph 9.7 and Table 9.3.)

For a fuller discussion on legal entities, see Chapter 7, paragraph 7.3.

6.4.3.4 Who do you sue?

In most cases, this will be fairly straightforward. However, in some instances, this may require a little more thought, as follows:

- **Retailer or manufacturer?** For example, if your client purchased a defective portable gas stove, there may be three causes of action to consider: a claim in negligence against any person who puts defective goods in circulation; a consumer claim under the Consumer Protection Act 1987 (as amended by the Consumer Rights Act 2015) against a producer of defective goods; or a claim in contract against the seller by the buyer. Under the last two options, there are some strict limitations, so it is as well to know which is your best cause of action and against which defendant; although, wherever possible, proceedings may be taken against both. Clear client instructions will help you to decide which is the most appropriate course of action.

- **Employer and employee?** Where your client was injured by the negligent act of an employee, then the employer will be vicariously liable for the acts of that employee—but only if the employee was acting in the course of his employment. What is deemed to be 'in the course of employment' has, over the years, been extended to include employees not following instructions and even deliberate acts of negligence, but each case will have to be looked at individually (see Chapter 7, paragraph 7.5.1.2).

- **Agent or principal?** This dilemma will feature in commercial cases usually involving contracts. It is best illustrated by way of an example.

 Example

A carpet cleaning company (the principal) appoints a sole trader (the agent) to secure carpet-cleaning contracts for commercial premises. The business relationship is formalized by an agency agreement. The carpet-cleaning services are performed, but damage several carpets at your client's office. The correct opponent in this case would be the carpet company, by virtue of the agency agreement, because the agent concluded the contract on behalf of the principal and not himself. It is essential that the agent acted within his actual or ostensible authority. If he did not, then unless the principal ratified the actions of the agent, the action will lie against the agent if it was clear to the contracting party that the agent was acting for himself.

- **Motorist and insurer?** If your client was injured in a road traffic accident (RTA) by the negligent driver of an insured vehicle, whilst your client has no common law right to sue the insurer, the insurer has a right to conduct the claim on behalf of the defendant driver. This is usually by way of an express term contained in the contract of insurance entitling the insurer to 'step into the shoes' of the person that it is insuring and to bring or defend an action in the name of the insured—a principle that is known as 'subrogation'. In certain circumstances, it is also possible for a claimant to sue the insurer under the provisions of the European Communities (Rights against Insurers) Regulations 2002, SI 2002/3061 (see Chapter 9, paragraph 9.6.5.1).

 Example

Roger Smith was driving his BMW 3 series and was stationary at a set of traffic lights. A Mondeo, being driven by Peter Anderson, collided with the rear of Roger Smith's car. The car was not owned by Peter, but by his father Simon Anderson, who was fully comprehensively insured with Peter as a named driver with Albatross Insurance Company. Albatross Insurance is entitled to conduct the defence of the claim on behalf of Simon Anderson, but if proceedings are issued, then Roger will need to issue them against Peter Anderson, because he was the negligent driver.

6.4.3.5 Is the opponent worth suing?

At this first client meeting, it is essential that you discuss with your client, once you have identified who the opponent is, whether that opponent is financially capable of satisfying any judgment or order (including costs) made in your favour.

In commercial cases, there are certain limited methods of trying to ascertain the solvency of your client's opponent, which include a bankruptcy search at the Insolvency Register or winding-up search at the Royal Courts of Justice, a company search, a credit search, a Land Registry search, a search of the Register of Judgments, Orders and Fines, or instructing a private investigator to gain a picture of the opponent's ability to pay. Often, your client will have some general information on his opponent from industry rumour. It is important that the question of whether the defendant has the money to satisfy a judgment is kept under review throughout the action.

In personal injury cases, most opponents are insured, and so the concern over the opponent's ability to pay is not so troublesome—but see paragraph 6.4.3.7 for the uninsured position in road traffic cases.

6.4.3.6 Risk assessment

A risk assessment needs to be undertaken periodically throughout a client's case, and the first one will be done either at the first meeting or in the follow-up letter of advice. In order to undertake a thorough risk assessment, you will need to consider and weigh up:

- the substantive legal argument;
- the strength of the three component parts of liability, causation, and quantum, and how you will prove or defend each part evidentially;
- the prospects of success;
- the prospect of losing;
- the cost of proceeding; and
- the likelihood of costs recovery.

Conducting a risk assessment will usually entail a full file review.

Let us consider an example of an RTA in which your client was injured. Acting for the claimant, you will need to include the following in your risk assessment:

1. The cause of the action and who is the opponent—that is, you must acknowledge that this is a negligence action against another road user.

2. What, as a matter of law, your client must establish—that is, that there was a duty of care owed to him, that this was breached by the other driver's negligent driving, that the negligent driving caused the losses, and that the losses were of a specific nature and amount.

3. What facts your client will have to establish—that is, that your client was another road user, details of the other driver's negligent driving, that, by colliding with the claimant, he suffered losses, and the details of those losses.

4. What evidence your client will need to establish these material facts—that is, your client's own evidence in a witness statement (and perhaps other independent witnesses) attesting to his presence on the road, the other driver's negligent driving, the fact of the collision, and the fact that he suffered losses. The losses will need to be proven by documentary and expert evidence.

5. What the strengths and weaknesses of your client's case are—which will depend on any additional information or facts, and these are different in every case. For example, in relation to the liability argument, who was responsible for the accident? If the other driver received a conviction as a result of his driving in relation to the accident and that conviction is relevant to the issues (of liability and quantum) in the case, then this conviction may be used to support your client's case (s. 11 of the Civil Evidence Act 1972

permits you to make use of the conviction by stating it in your particulars of claim). However, in the absence of a relevant conviction, if the opponent had independent witness evidence to support his case, then this would be potentially damaging to your client's case.

6. What the likely value of this case is and the cost of pursuing it—as a legal representative new to legal practice, you will need assistance in both these. Ascertaining these figures requires litigation experience. In respect of the value of the case, you will need to consult practitioner texts such as *Kemp and Kemp on Damages*, *Current Law*, and the *Judicial College Guidelines*, or you may even seek counsel's advice. A more senior fee earner will help you to consider the total costing of the matter.

 Practical Considerations

The value of your client's case and its likely costs are difficult figures to assess, but doing so will get easier with experience. If you do find yourself at a meeting with a client on your own at the outset of your legal practice, always inform your client that your views are subject to review by a more senior fee earner and are, as such, preliminary. It may well be the case that, owing to the lack of information and evidence, your views would be preliminary in any event at that stage. Do not forget that, in the more complex cases, it may be prudent to seek counsel's advice on any aspect of the substantive case. The dangers of giving robust advice on the merits of a claim without conducting a thorough investigation can be seen from the case of *Levicom International Holdings BV v Linklaters (a firm)* [2010] EWCA Civ 494, where the Court of Appeal held that Linklaters had been negligent when they initially advised the claimant (without all the requisite information available to them) that their chances of success 'were not less than 70 per cent'. Based on that advice, the claimant rejected the defendant's offer and commenced arbitration proceedings. Later, counsel's advice on behalf of the claimant was much less positive, and a less valuable settlement was concluded.

In commercial cases, in addition to the risk assessment, you should also consider the commerciality of pursuing the claim or defence on behalf of your client. Commercial clients often settle cases purely for commercial reasons (cash flow or preservation of a business relationship), but there are also those commercial clients who choose to pursue matters on a point of principle (such as business reputation, industry hierarchy, or just plain stubbornness).

6.4.3.7 The Motor Insurers' Bureau (MIB)

This section is particular to RTAs in which your client has been injured in a collision with either an uninsured or untraced driver. The MIB is an independent body voluntarily set up and financed by motor insurance companies to deal with claims in which injuries were caused by drivers who have no, or no relevant, insurance or in hit-and-run cases.

The MIB has made two main agreements with the government, which can be viewed online at http://www.mib.org.uk. If you are ever consulted by a client in one of these two situations, then it is advisable that you read the agreements in full, because they both contain quite a list of formalities with which you must comply.

The claim will otherwise proceed in line with any other RTA personal injury matters with the usual conduct and procedural requirements.

6.4.3.8 The Criminal Injuries Compensation Authority (CICA)

The CICA is a statutory body that administers the Criminal Injuries Compensation Scheme (CICS). The Scheme provides compensation payments to victims of violence, such as assault or rape, and covers both physical and psychological injuries valued at a minimum of £1,000. This process is most commonly used where the offender is penniless or not known, and is, therefore, an alternative to litigation.

Unlike the CPR, the CICS covers injuries sustained in Scotland, but the limitation period for all injuries wherever they were sustained is two years from the date of the incident. The process is by way of an application form to the CICA.

The Scheme will assess the injuries in a similar manner to that used by the courts when assessing damages for personal injuries, but there are some important differences.

If you are ever consulted by a client injured as a result of a criminal offence, you should obtain full details of the Scheme, including the application form and various guides, from http://www.cica.gov.uk. The CICA will obtain medical records and request that the applicant be medically examined.

6.5 ACTION BY YOU AFTER THE FIRST INTERVIEW

There will usually be a number of action points for you to follow up after the first meeting if the case is to be taken forward. Legal representatives should be proactive in their approach to litigation, although what exactly will need to be done will very much depend on the type of case. The following are some basic suggestions of what you might need to do, but remember—whatever the action or steps in a case that you take on behalf of your client, you must have his express instructions to do so.

6.5.1 WRITE TO THE CLIENT

A legal representative should always confirm in writing to his client what was discussed at the meeting. This will usually span the following:

- **The funding arrangements.** If a CFA, after the event (ATE) insurance, or a DBA is to be entered into, the copies of the agreement and/or broker forms (to secure a quote for the insurance) should be included and explained in the letter. A further meeting may be necessary to go through these documents with your client before signing him up, in order to comply with best practice and your professional conduct duties and obligations. If the client is to pay privately and/or is only funding disbursements, then you will require further monies on account to cover the work that you are about to do.

- **The return of the signed client care letter (if the client is a corporate entity) and any outstanding money laundering identification documents.**

- **The nature of the client's problem, the advice given (including any risk assessment), and the client's instructions.** Often, at first meetings, clients do not usually give initial instructions on the advice given at the meeting, because they need time to think about it. If this is the case, then the letter will be requesting instructions, usually regarding investigations and moving the claim forward.

- **Costs information.** In most standard client care letters there is a section for detailed calculations for costs estimates for both litigation and ADR options. This must be completed at the time the client care letter is sent. If it is not appropriate to complete this detailed estimate, owing to lack of information or the fact that the client has instructed you to undertake a very limited amount of work, then it may be appropriate to place a cap on legal costs and disbursements to be incurred. This can be reviewed when the cap has been met and a full costs estimate or a further costs cap given at that later stage. Alternatively, as mentioned in Chapter 3 at paragraph 3.2.1, a fixed fee for a defined phase of the claim can also be given. In any event, costs information needs to be addressed with the client in this letter to the client.

- **A request for documentation from your client, such as original documents and photographs.** It is also advisable to remind your client to preserve any relevant documentation as evidence to prove part of his claim: for example, return taxi fares to hospital for out-patient appointments in a personal injury claim, or photographs of renovations in a building dispute. Additionally, your client will need to appreciate the nature of the exchange of information and documentation in the Protocol phase and in litigation itself, and that even documents that harm his case may need to be disclosed. This may have been touched on at the first meeting, but it is more likely to be dealt with at subsequent early meetings and correspondence in the run-up to, and the duration of, the Protocol. (For details of your client's disclosure duty, see Chapter 8, paragraphs 8.4 and 8.8, and Chapter 16, paragraph 16.4.)

- **Details of when you will next contact your client and what you are doing until you next do so.**

 Practical Considerations

Your client will believe that he is singularly the most important client that you have and, to maintain good client relations, you should provide your client with a time frame within which you will work and report back to him. Even if there is nothing with which to update your client, you should tell him just that. Your client wants to know what you are doing and, if paying privately, how you are spending his money.

6.5.2 DRAFT YOUR CLIENT'S STATEMENT OR PROOF OF EVIDENCE

After you have seen your client, the notes of what your client said in the interview can be formulated into the basis of a statement. This should be done as early as possible, especially in personal injury cases. It is even common practice to send the first draft with the letter of advice (see paragraph 6.5.1), and to ask for it to be signed and returned. In commercial cases, this is not usually done at this early stage, although a detailed proof of evidence is prepared from which a statement can be formulated later.

6.5.3 NOTIFY YOUR OPPONENT

In most cases, it will be sensible either to call or to write to your opponent or their legal representative (if they have appointed one) to inform them that you have been instructed by your client and that all further correspondence should be directed to you.

This contact also gives you the opportunity to inform your opponent that you intend to comply with Protocol and provides the forum to discuss how you are to proceed in this regard. (See Chapter 8, paragraph 8.2, for a full review of Protocols.)

In some cases, it is appropriate to ask your opponent whether they intend to dispute your client's claim, because this may save a great deal of time and money in the furtherance of the claim by undertaking the investigations detailed in the next section.

6.5.4 INITIATE EARLY INVESTIGATIONS

At this early stage, but subject to funding arrangements being in place, there will usually be a variety of investigations that can be carried out to enable you to give firmer views on how successful you think your client will be. Some of the information necessary for you to give a firmer view on success will come from your client—particularly in commercial cases, in which the client will be in possession of contractual documentation. If not, then your opponent will be, and the securing of such documentation is usually completed through the 'full and frank' exchange of documentation in the Protocol phase (see Chapter 8, paragraph 8.4).

These early investigations can serve a dual purpose, because they can also provide the type of evidence that your client will need to prove his claim at trial. Remember (see paragraph 6.4.2.3): your client's claim has three legal components—that is, liability, causation, and quantum—all of which must be proved if your client is the claimant, or disproved if your client is the defendant (unless, of course, your opponent has admitted them).

Before undertaking any investigations, you will need to outline to your client the nature of the investigation and the approximate cost, and receive his express instructions to proceed.

Practical Considerations

You will need to discuss with your client which investigations are appropriate for his case. If he has a case that is difficult on liability, then it may be more proportionate and reasonable for you to advise that only the liability investigations be done, and the results considered and assessed by you, before proceeding with the causation and quantum investigations. Some investigations, however, provide evidence for more than one of the component parts: for example, a medical report can provide evidence that the type of injury sustained was caused by the negligent act, as well as document the nature and extent of that injury to enable you to assess its value later.

6.5.4.1 Liability investigations

Liability investigations will differ slightly, depending on the type of case that you are preparing.

6.5.4.1.1 *A personal injury matter*

These early investigations are likely to include:

- interviewing witnesses to the accident and preparing draft witness statements (see Chapter 17, paragraph 17.4);

- obtaining a copy of the police accident report book (or an extract if there is a pending prosecution), which should contain any statement taken from the parties, measurements, a sketch plan, and photographs of the site of the road accident;

- attending any proceedings relating to any prosecution;

- obtaining a certificate of conviction if the other driver was convicted as a result of the collision and the conviction is relevant to the issues of the case;

- attending any inquest in a fatal accident case should someone involved have been killed, at which the coroner will try to decide—based on post-mortem evidence, and that of witnesses and police officers (which evidence may be useful for any civil case)—whether the death was accidental or whether there are grounds for a criminal prosecution;

- requesting a copy of the accident report book from your client's employer and a copy of the report of the Health and Safety Executive (HSE) on the incident, as well as the employer's general Health and Safety guidance and information;

- attending the scene of the accident yourself to inspect the area and take photographs; and

- considering steps that may be needed to preserve evidence.

6.5.4.1.2 *Commercial cases*

These early investigations are likely to include:

- identifying potential parties and causes of action—remembering that commercial cases often have a number of likely parties and/or causes of action, depending on the nature of the dispute (for example, in a building case, if your client instructed an architect and a structural engineer to design and build a commercial warehouse that turned out to be structurally dangerous and, therefore, unfit for purpose, the cause of action may lie against one or both of the professional parties);

- obtaining copies of all of the relevant contracts and any revisions to those contracts;

- verifying the insurance position of the potential opponents;

- seeking to preserve for inspection any original evidence, such as a defective machine or piece of equipment (for example, a faulty alarm box, which led to the failure of a sensor, which, in turn, led to water-damaged stock);

- seeking to identify and preserve the relevant electronic documents and ascertain where they are stored;

- requisitioning reports or letters written by third parties (for example, an open letter written by the manufacturer of an inadequate part of a gearbox that was supplied through a chain of contracts to your client, stating that the part manufactured has limitations of use); and

- considering the type of expert that you need and finding one (for example, if your client purchased an unsatisfactory precision piece of engineering for steel cutting, you would need to locate the appropriate type of engineer to prepare a report).

6.5.4.2 Quantum investigations

Again, the nature of quantum investigations will vary.

6.5.4.2.1 *A personal injury matter*

In a personal injury matter, you will need to:

- obtain your client's hospital, GP, and X-ray notes;

- obtain curricula vitae (CVs) from appropriate experts; and

- write to your client's employer for information on loss of earnings and employment details.

6.5.4.2.2 *A commercial matter*

In a commercial matter, you will need to:

- obtain letters or quotations for the replacement cost of goods damaged;

- write to third parties for information (for example, if your client is pursuing a claim alleging that an ex-employee poached customers in breach of a confidentiality and restrictive covenant clause in the contract of employment, enquiries could be made with those customers regarding the liability issue of poaching and how much business was lost); and

- consider instructing an accountant or another appropriate expert to quantify your client's business losses.

Once in possession of all relevant information, you will then be able to discuss with your client the implications of the information that you have secured, with a view to moving into the Protocol phase.

KEY POINTS SUMMARY

- Not just with every new client, but with every new matter, you will need to go through your professional conduct obligations, including client care and money laundering, as well as undertaking a conflict search and considering how your client is going to fund the claim.

- Conflicts can arise as litigation progresses, so be alert to the possibility.

- The impressions gained by a client at a first meeting are very important. The key words are: professionalism, competency, empathy, confidence, honesty, and reliability.

- Follow up preliminary views at a first meeting with your further views after you have received further information or undertaken research.

- Keep your client updated with what you are doing.

- Never act without instructions.

Case Study *Andrew James Pike v Deep Builders Ltd*

Consider the materials available in the online resources in relation to this chapter and answer the following questions.

Question 1

Read the attendance note on Andrew Pike. Consider the viability of Andrew Pike's claim at this stage, based on the information contained in the attendance note.

Question 2

Using the partially completed letter in the online resources, complete the letter of advice to your client in light of the issues raised in the attendance note.

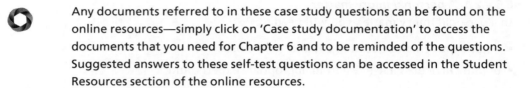

Any documents referred to in these case study questions can be found on the online resources—simply click on 'Case study documentation' to access the documents that you need for Chapter 6 and to be reminded of the questions. Suggested answers to these self-test questions can be accessed in the Student Resources section of the online resources.

7 PRE-ACTION SUBSTANTIVE MATTERS

Relevant parts of the CPR and its PDs: 2, 3, 7, 17, 19, 21, 25, 29, and 40.

LITIGATION TRAIN: PRE-ACTION SUBSTANTIVE MATTERS

First client meeting
Pre-Action or Protocol phase
Issue of proceedings
Trial

o Discuss at the meeting
• Client care
• Money laundering
• Nature of claim/defence
• A way forward—together with instructions to proceed as agreed
• Request monies on account
• Funding options and costs recovery
• Does the opponent have the means to pay credit checks? Instructions needed

o Action after the meeting
• Conflict search
• Letter to client (preliminary advice and funding)
• Notify defendant
• Initiate early investigations

o Consider the following matters
• Jurisdiction
• In which court should the potential action proceed?
• Does my client/opponent have legal capacity?
• Limitation
• Issues on liability, causation, and quantum
• What is my client seeking to recover?

7.1 INTRODUCTION

A student's or a practitioner's role in the dispute resolution (or litigation) department is to assist in the procedural and theoretical aspects of a client's case. These latter aspects can include consideration of matters that can determine where an action proceeds and whether it is capable of proceeding.

The contents of this chapter are purposely substantive in nature and may be considered by you, to varying degrees, either before you see your client on a new matter, at the first meeting, or, more commonly, after you have received detailed instructions and are able to reflect on the overall issues in the case.

In practice, it is crucial that you allow them to become part of your 'checklist' of items that may or may not feature in your client's case. It is also self-evident that the decision 'where to claim' should also consider the costs of the claim in a particular jurisdiction, the conduct of the claim in a jurisdiction, and the outcome and enforcement of a claim in a jurisdiction.

The following matters may be considered:

- the location of witnesses;
- the location of documents and other evidence. Consider the provisions for enforcing production of documents in the intended jurisdiction;
- whether an injunction or other pre-emptive remedy should be sought in the action;
- the length of time a claim may take to proceed in the intended jurisdiction and the consequences of any delay for your client;
- whether the availability or non-availability of public funding in the intended jurisdiction is an issue;
- the cost provisions in the intended jurisdiction and how they are applied;
- the enforcement provisions of judgments in the intended jurisdiction and how effective they are and whether a foreign judgment would be readily enforceable in that jurisdiction; and
- the remedies available in the intended jurisdiction.

    This chapter will consider:

- jurisdiction and governing law;
- the capacity to sue or be sued;
- limitation;
- the legal components of an action; and
- remedies.

7.2 JURISDICTION AND GOVERNING LAW

7.2.1 IN WHICH COUNTRY SHOULD PROCEEDINGS BE COMMENCED?

7.2.1.1 Jurisdiction

It is important to be sure, firstly, that the courts in England and Wales have jurisdiction to hear a potential action, and secondly, that the courts in England and Wales are the appropriate place in which to hear the dispute. In any action in which the client or opponent is based abroad, or in which the cause of action arose outside of that jurisdiction, questions of jurisdiction must be considered.

EU Regulation 1215/2012 came into force on 10 January 2015 and in effect, recast the Brussels Regulation. The Brussels Regulation 44/2001 continues to apply to cases commenced before 10 January 2015. This chapter concentrates on pre-action substantive matters for new cases and thus will apply only the new rules. Any practitioner with a case that may have issues of jurisdiction will need to study the regulations in detail to ensure the correct rules are identified. Essentially under the new rules Art. 25 gives jurisdiction to the courts of the member state chosen by the parties. There is no requirement that either party is domiciled within the EU for Art. 25 to apply—so even where the parties are not EU members, any clause that states that they have chosen the jurisdiction of the courts of a member state will be effective. However, the detail of these rules needs to be studied as there are exceptions—certain land disputes, for example—and there are special rules relating to employment, consumer contracts, and insurance. Art. 29 may deprive a court of jurisdiction where there are parallel proceedings. Pursuant to Art. 29, the court 'first seised' (i.e. where proceedings are first commenced) has priority. Where the two sets of proceedings involve the same cause of action and are between the same parties, any other member state court must stay its proceedings until the jurisdiction of the first court is established and, at that point, must decline jurisdiction. Under Art. 4 the basic rule is that the defendant must be sued in his local court which in the case of an individual is where he is domiciled and in the case of a company, where it has its seat. There are however alternatives to the basic rule under Art. 4 allowing a defendant who is domiciled in a member state to be sued in another member state. In contract matters, Art. 7(1) provides that a person domiciled in a member state may be sued in the courts of the state for the place of performance of the obligation in question. In cases relating to tort, Art. 7(2) provides that a person domiciled in a member state may be sued in the courts of the state where the harmful event occured. It is important to remember that Art 7(1) and Art 7(2) are alternatives to the basic rule under Art. 4 and a claimant may still choose to follow Art. 4. These rules may be subject to change as part of the UK's exit from the EU.

7.2.1.2 Contractual disputes

In addition to the considerations in paragraph 7.2.1.1, in breach of contract actions, it will be important to ensure that there are no provisions in the agreement that provide that the parties must arbitrate rather than litigate. Where this is the case, the parties will not be permitted to litigate unless by mutual consent. Parties will be bound by a valid arbitration clause in their agreement. The agreement will usually cover both the 'seat' for the arbitration (that is, where it should take place) and the governing law. These could be either national (that is, specifying that the arbitration should take place in England and Wales, and be subject to the laws of England and Wales) or international clauses.

Often, in commercial agreements, there will be staged alternative dispute resolution (ADR) clauses under which the parties have agreed to try a form (or forms) of ADR, usually culminating in arbitration. These clauses are enforceable, subject to the usual arguments of incorporation and reasonableness, and often include (depending on the nature of the agreement) suggested ADR methods, such as conciliation, followed by mediation, then adjudication, and, finally, arbitration. (See Chapter 5, paragraph 5.3, for a brief discussion on the variety of ADR processes.)

 Practical Considerations

Although a detailed study of the statutes and regulations concerning proceedings outside the jurisdiction of the court is beyond the scope of this manual, there are some basic guiding principles that can be used to alert the new legal representative to the need to consider 'jurisdiction' in more detail and to ask the assistance of a supervising partner, as follows:

- Is there a binding agreement that contains a jurisdiction clause to be applied?

- Is there a 'governing law' clause in the agreement?

- Does a party reside or have its business outside the jurisdiction?

- Was the agreement concluded outside the jurisdiction?

- Determine the costs of both your enquiries and the costs of service outside the jurisdiction, and obtain your client's instructions to incur those costs.

- Have you advised your client of the additional time that it may take to issue or serve outside the jurisdiction of England and Wales?

- If your opponent is a limited company registered abroad, does it have a UK division registered in the UK or a UK trading site?

- Might determination of the action outside the jurisdiction be preferable in terms of convenience, cost, or justice?

- Have you checked the provision for the enforcement of any judgment that may be obtained in the proceedings?

7.2.2 IN WHICH COURT SHOULD PROCEEDINGS BE COMMENCED?

The High Court and the County Court have concurrent jurisdiction over most claims. Where there is concurrent jurisdiction between the High Court and the County Court, a claimant generally has freedom to choose in which court to issue his proceedings. However, this general freedom must also take account of those parts of the Civil Procedure Rules (CPR) that exercise restrictions on parties.

In some circumstances, including the following, it can be seen that the complete 'freedom' (of which court to choose) provided by statute is restricted in practice by the CPR.

- CPR Practice Direction (PD) 7A.2.1 (amended) states that all claims for money may only be issued in the High Court where the sum claimed exceeds £100,000 (except in a personal injury case, £50,000).

- PD 7A.2.2 states that a claim for personal injuries may not be issued in the High Court unless the value of the claim is £50,000 or more. In determining the value of the claim, interest, costs, a reduction for contributory negligence against the claimant, the value of any counterclaim or set-off, and the recoupment of benefits under the Social Security (Recovery of Benefits) Act 1997 are all to be disregarded in accordance with Art. 9 of the High Court and County Courts Jurisdiction Order 1991, SI 1991/724 (which cross-references CPR 16.3(6)).

- PD 7A.2.3 states that a claim must be issued in the High Court or in the County Court where a statute requires it.

- Although PD 7A.2.1 permits a specified sum claim with a value exceeding £100,000 to be issued in the High Court, PD 29.2.2 restricts a claimant's right to *continue* proceedings issued in the High Court if the claim has a value of £100,000 or less. Unless one of the exceptions set out in that paragraph applies, the claim will usually be transferred to the County Court. These exceptions include that:

- the claim is one that, by statute, should be heard in the High Court;

- the claim falls within a specialist list, as defined by CPR 2.3(2)—these include claims that would be heard in the Commercial Court, the Mercantile Courts, the Patents Courts, or the Technology and Construction Court (TCC);

- the claim is one relating to professional negligence, fraud or undue influence, defamation, malicious prosecution or false imprisonment, claims against the police, claims under the Fatal Accidents Act 1976, or contentious probate claims; and

- there is an anomaly in the value of claims that may be brought in the High Court. Clinical negligence claims may only be brought in the High Court if their value is over £100,000 (whereas for personal injury claims—which exclude clinical negligence claims—the limit is £50,000) (Art. 2 High Courts and County Courts (Jurisdiction) (Amendment) Order 2009 and Order 2014 at Art. 2(7).

It is clear that any practitioner wishing to issue a claim in the High Court will need to justify doing so using one or more of the above provisions.

 Practical Considerations

Deciding in which court to issue proceedings should always be taken with care and consideration because the penalties for issuing in the wrong court can be severe. In the worst-case scenario, the wrong decision could result in an action for professional negligence. In most situations, when a genuine mistake has been made and a claim has been commenced in the wrong court, the court will either take the initiative to transfer the action or will do so upon the application of a party. The court will usually effect the transfer, but may impose cost penalties on the claimant representing the costs of the transfer. These penalties can include a continuing penalty as to costs; although the court has the power to reduce the whole costs of the claim by up to 25 per cent (Senior Courts Act 1981, s. 51(8) and (9)). Equally, in cases in which the claimant knew, or ought to have known, that the claim was being commenced in the wrong court, the court has the power to strike out the claim (County Courts Act 1984, ss. 40(1)(b) and 42(1)(b); CPR 3.4).

7.2.2.1 Rome II

EC Regulation 864/2007 contains the law relating to non-contractual obligations (known as 'Rome II'). This contains provisions that apply to tortious claims in EU member states. Its application will have most impact in general litigation, in personal injury claims in which a party has been injured abroad, and in product liability cases. Its provisions will affect questions of liability (and grounds for exemption from liability), and the existence, nature, and assessment of damages in such cases.

The practical significance of the provisions is that a court will now have to hear evidence and consider how damages are assessed in the jurisdiction in which the accident or the harmful physical impact occurred.

The full scope of Rome II is outside the remit of this book, but it is noted for completeness and so that practitioners can be aware that further knowledge should be sought in such cases. The progress of the negotiations for the UK's exit from the EU need to be kept under review as they will, in due course, impact on these rules.

7.2.3 THE POSITION AFTER THE UK LEAVES THE EU

One of the core values of the EU is that there should be commonality between the legal systems of all of the members of the EU. This is dealt with through a series of conventions and other treaties (see paragraph 7.2.2 above).

What happens if there is an agreement?

At the time of writing, there is no concluded deal as to what will happen after the UK leaves the EU. Under the draft withdrawal agreement of 14 November, the EU and the UK have agreed that the provisions referred to above—covering jurisdiction, judgments, proper law, lawyers, insolvency, etc.—will all remain the same as they were when the UK was part of the EU. Accordingly, if there is such an agreement, things will likely continue as before.

What may happen after Brexit if there is no agreement?

The government has set out its intentions in a paper, the draft political declaration, but these are only intentions. The government accepts that in the event there is no deal, there will be no agreed EU framework for ongoing civil judicial cooperation between the UK and EU countries. The UK would become a third-party country, and this would mean that EU countries would not consider the UK to be covered by EU rules.

It is perhaps worth saying that there are also issues as to what will happen when the UK formally leaves the EU, presumably in 2021. Without an agreement, it is likely that the existing regime will no longer apply to cases pending before the courts after the UK has left the EU, as EU rules on the recognition and enforcement of judgments will cease to exist in the UK, and will no longer apply between the UK and EU. Furthermore, it is not clear whether a case decided in the UK on or before the UK has left the EU under the current system would be recognized and enforced in another EU country after the UK has left the EU. This is just to make life even more complicated.

The concern is that if companies are no longer able to enforce UK judgments in the EU, even more may take steps to change their jurisdiction clauses in their contracts from the UK to France or Germany.

This will not only have an impact on the volume of litigation in England and Scotland, but will also mean less transactional work, as there will be fewer contracts drafted under English law.

7.3 **LEGAL CAPACITIES**

7.3.1 **INDIVIDUALS OVER THE AGE OF EIGHTEEN AND MENTAL CAPACITY**

A person who is over the age of eighteen or who is not a patient under the Mental Health Act 1983, and has capacity under the Mental Capacity Act 2005, has the capacity to sue and be sued in his own name. If a person is not over eighteen or does not have the requisite mental capacity defined under the Mental Capacity Act 2005, then they are a 'protected party' and they cannot litigate in their own name (subject to CPR 21.2(3)). Issuing a claim by a person who, in fact, does not have the mental capacity to give proper instruction to understand and to conduct litigation can have serious consequences. This was very clearly illustrated in the case *Joanne Dunhill (by her litigation friend Paul Tasker) v Shaun Bergin* [2012] EWCA Civ 397, where the court was considering, on appeal, whether to set aside a settlement on the grounds that the claimant did not have the requisite mental capacity. The Court of Appeal concluded that the correct question was not whether the claimant had proper capacity to approve the settlement agreement, but whether she had the mental capacity to litigate at all.

7.3.2 **CHILDREN AND PROTECTED PARTIES (CPR 21)**

CPR 21 governs the provisions that apply when acting for or against a child or a protected party. CPR 21.1(2) defines a 'child' as 'a person under 18' and a 'protected party' as 'a party, or an intended party, who lacks capacity to conduct the proceedings'—that is, a person who, by reason of mental disorder within the meaning of the Mental Health Act 1983, is incapable of managing and administering his property and affairs. CPR 21.2.1 provides that a protected party must have a litigation friend to conduct proceedings. A child will usually also conduct litigation through a litigation friend, though in respect of children the court does have the power to permit the child to conduct the litigation—CPR 2.2(3).

The court will not generally exercise this power—one of the key reasons for this being that a child does not have contractual capacity (for example, to pay his legal representative's fees!).

7.3.3 COMPANIES

Companies are legal 'persons' and, therefore, can sue or be sued in their own name. A company is one registered under the Companies Acts. When suing or being sued, it must do so in the full, registered, company name. If the company is in liquidation, then that fact must be added to the name—that is, '(in liquidation)'. A company that is not required to use 'limited' or 'plc' (or the Welsh equivalents) in its name should be referred to by its name, followed by an appropriate description.

7.3.4 LIMITED LIABILITY PARTNERSHIPS (LLPs)

Limited liability partnerships (LLPs) were created by the Limited Liability Partnerships Act 2000 (LLPA). Like a company, an LLP is a legal person separate from its members and, like a company, it must sue or be sued in its own name, which must be the registered name. Many legal practices now operate as LLPs, so are now incorporated rather than partnerships. Litigators need to take care when issuing proceedings against such bodies and ensure that any proceedings are issued correctly. The case of *Insight Group v Kingston Smith* [2012] EWHC 3644 (QB) gives some guidance on the issues arising.

7.3.5 PARTNERSHIPS

Partnerships are not legal entities, and the liability of partners is generally joint and several (Partnership Act 1890, ss. 9 and 12). Partners may sue or be sued in their individual names. Alternatively, partners carrying on business within the jurisdiction may sue or be sued in the name of the firm and the words '(a firm)' added to the case title. A party suing or being sued by partners in the name of the firm may serve notice on the firm, requiring all of the partners who were partners at the time that the cause of action arose to disclose their names and addresses. Failure to disclose is likely to result in an order for disclosure, with an order that the action be stayed (or the firm be debarred from defending) if disclosure is not made.

7.3.6 SOLE TRADERS

A sole trader may be sued, but may not sue in his trading name. A claimant sole trader should sue in his own name, adding the words 'trading as' (or 't/a') and the trading name. A defendant sole trader whose real name is not known may be sued in the business name, followed by the words '(a trading name)'.

7.3.7 ASSOCIATIONS

These may include trade unions and employers' associations, building societies, charities, local and central government bodies or departments, and other public bodies. All of these may be sued or sue in their name. Clubs, however, may not; these may sue or be sued in the names of the members of the club, or representative proceedings may be brought. An incorporated club may sue or be sued in its own name.

7.3.8 TRUSTS AND TRUSTEES

A claim by or against a trust is brought by or against all of its trustees. The beneficiaries of the trust need not be parties to the action (CPR 19.7A), but any judgment or order made in the action will bind the beneficiaries unless the court orders otherwise.

7.3.9 ESTATES OF DECEASED PERSONS (CPR 19.8)

Under the Law Reform (Miscellaneous Provisions) Act 1934, s. 1(1), most causes of action subsisting against or vested in an individual survive his or her death. If a party to a claim dies (or is adjudged bankrupt), the court has the power, under CPR 19.5(3), to add or substitute as a party in the action the person to whom the interest or liability of the deceased or bankrupt party has passed.

7.3.9.1 Where the death of the party is before the claim is issued

The claim must be brought or defended by the personal representatives of the deceased person. If the claim is made against a deceased defendant before there has been a grant of probate or letters of administration, the claim form cannot be served until the court (usually upon the application of the claimant before the expiry of the time limit for service of the claim form) has appointed a person to represent the deceased defendant.

7.3.9.2 Where the death of the party is after the claim has been commenced

The surviving party in the action needs to make an application to the court either to substitute the deceased party for the personal representatives of the estate of the deceased party, or, if no personal representatives have been appointed, to direct a person to represent the estate of the deceased party or to order the action to proceed without the deceased party being represented.

Where an action is continued by or against a deceased person, the court has power to order that any interested parties should be served with notice of the action (CPR 19.8A), and, in so doing, that person will be bound by any judgment or order made in the action. If the person so served files an acknowledgement of service, they will become a party to the claim.

These provisions must be distinguished from the restricted circumstances in which a party may voluntarily assign its interest (or liability) in the action to another. Such assignments are, however, outside the scope of this book.

7.4 LIMITATION

7.4.1 THE PURPOSE OF LIMITATION PERIODS

The primary purpose of limitation is to protect a defendant from the potential injustice of having to face a claim that has gone stale and for which reliable, or any, evidence may be difficult to obtain. It also provides an end to the time during which a person has an 'expectation' or concern that an action may be brought against him.

7.4.2 HOW IS 'LIMITATION' APPLIED TO ACTIONS?

7.4.2.1 From the claimant's perspective

Satellite litigation may come up on issues arising to clarify whether a limitation period has expired or not, or from applications in which the claimant seeks to proceed with the action and seeks the court's discretion to permit the action to continue.

Periods of limitation may vary in different jurisdictions; the periods of limitation within the jurisdiction may also vary, depending on the type of claim. The issue of the claim form stops the 'limitation clock' ticking and where the limitation period is nearing its end for the action, there will be a need to issue as a matter of urgency to avoid the claim becoming statute-barred.

 Practical Considerations

Where protective proceedings have to be issued to avoid an action becoming statute-barred, it must be remembered that further investigation can take place before service of the claim form—but care must be taken to serve within the lifespan of the claim form issued. Any application to extend the life of the claim form must be made 'within the period specified by CPR Rule 7.5'—that is, before the expiry of the time for service. Only in exceptional cases can the life of the claim form be extended after the end of the period specified by CPR 7.5 (CPR 7.6(3)—see Chapter 9, paragraph 9.7.1.5).

7.4.2.2 From the defendant's perspective

Limitation is a procedural defence, but it must be specifically stated in the defence itself. It will not arise and apply to the claimant's action automatically. The consequence, therefore, of the expiry of the limitation period for an action is that the defendant, in most cases, acquires an unassailable defence provided he has pleaded it in his defence.

7.4.3 LIMITATION PERIODS

Most limitation periods are laid down in the Limitation Act 1980 (LA 1980), as amended. Some procedural rules impose time limits that act rather like limitation periods.

A claim that is outside the provisions of the LA 1980 is not subject to a strict period of limitation. It may, however, be subject to a time limit by analogy to the Act, or it may be subject to the defences of laches and acquiescence.

The main limitation periods are as outlined in Table 7.1.

TABLE 7.1 LIMITATION PERIODS

Class of claim	Limitation period
Fraudulent breach of trust	None (LA 1980, s. 21(1))
Recovery of land	12 years (LA 1980, s. 15(1))
Recovery of money secured by mortgage	12 years (LA 1980, s. 20(1))
Speciality	12 years (LA 1980, s. 8(1))
Recovery of money due under statute	6 years (LA 1980, s. 9(1))
Enforcement of a judgment	6 years (LA 1980, s. 24(1))
Contract	6 years (LA 1980, s. 5)
Recovery of trust property and breach of trust	6 years (LA 1980, s. 21(3))
Recovery of arrears of rent	6 years (LA 1980, s. 19)
Tort (except those listed below)	6 years (LA 1980, s. 2)
Note: This includes claims under s. 2(1) of the Misrepresentation Act 1967	
Defective Premises Act 1972 (DPA 1972) claims	6 years (DPA 1972, s. 1(5))
Personal injury claims	3 years (LA 1980, s. 11(4))
Fatal Accident Act 1976 claims	3 years (LA 1980, s. 12(2))
Claims under the Consumer Protection Act 1987	3 years (LA 1980, s. 11A)
Carriage by Air Act 1961 (CAA 1961) claims	2 years (CAA 1961, Sched. 1)
Claims for personal injury or damage to vessel, cargo, or property at sea	2 years (Merchant Shipping Act 1995, s. 190(3) and Sched. 6)
Disqualification of company directors	3 years (Company Directors Disqualification Act 1986, s. 7(2))
Contribution under the Civil Liability (Contribution) Act 1978	2 years (LA 1980, s. 10(1))
Contributions under the Maritime Conventions Act 1911	1 year (Merchant Shipping Act 1995, s. 190(4))
Carriage of Goods by Road Act 1965 (CGRA 1965) claims	1 year (CGRA 1965 , Art. 32(1))
Defamation and malicious falsehood	1 year (LA 1980, s. 4A)
Applications for judicial review	3 months (CPR 54.5)
Unfair dismissal under the Employment Rights Act 1996 (ERA 1996)	3 months (ERA 1996, s. 111(2))
Applications for new business tenancies under the Landlord and Tenant Act 1954 (LTA 1954)	Not less than 2 months nor more than 4 months (LTA 1954, s. 29(A)(3))
Actions for an account	Period applicable to claim on which account is based (LA 1980, s. 23)

7.4.4 WHICH LIMITATION PERIOD APPLIES TO AN ACTION?

It is sometimes difficult to determine into which category a particular case may fall. It is possible that the nature of the claim itself may affect the application of a limitation period. If the action arises from fraudulent behaviour, the court will consider whether it was the fraudulent behaviour of a party or of another. Where the fraud is that of a person who is not a party, then the defendant will normally be able to rely on a limitation period applying. But if the fraudulent behaviour is that of a party, then it is more likely that the court will determine that no limitation period applies. Claims that are a mixture of tort and contract can also cause difficulties.

A full examination of the more complex issues arising from limitation is outside the scope of this manual, but any legal representative acting in an action in which 'limitation' is raised will need to examine the law applying in detail (see *Blackstone's Civil Practice* in this regard).

The court has a discretion to dis-apply the limitation period in personal injury actions under s. 33 of the LA 1980. In these circumstances, the court will decide whether it would be equitable and whether it would be prejudicial to the defendant, taking into account all of the circumstances of the case. There may be good reasons not to rely on what appears to be a limitation defence, where a fair trial can still take place despite the delay. Two recent cases have considered the application of s. 33 LA—in *Kara Rayner v Wolferstans (A firm), Medway NHS Foundation Trust* [2015] EWHC 2957 (QB), the judge allowed the claimant to proceed with her personal injury claim seven years after the statutory period of limitation had expired, where the judge found that the claimant had been prejudiced by delays not of her making. This case is a clear example of the court assisting a 'deserving' claimant. In *Collins v Secretary of State for Business Innovation & Skills* [2013] the court would not exercise its discretion, as it decided that the evidence was sketchy and unreliable, and there would be real prejudice to the defendant if the limitation period was dis-applied. Limitation is far from straightforward and it is difficult to predict if and how the court will exercise its discretion, often being influenced by the cogency of the evidence and prejudice to the parties.

7.4.5 FOREIGN LIMITATION PERIODS

Where the rules of private international law provide that the law of any other country is to be taken into account in any claim in England or Wales, the law of that other country relating to limitation must be applied under the Foreign Limitation Periods Act 1984.

7.4.6 WHEN DOES THE 'CLOCK' BEGIN TO RUN ON LIMITATION PERIODS?

There are a number of important features that you will need to consider when dealing with a case with an actual or potential limitation problem. These are addressed in this section and will be followed by a summary of the practicalities of dealing with cases that are near to the expiry of their limitation period.

7.4.6.1 The time runs from the accrual of the cause of action

Time begins to run from the earliest time at which an action may be brought—that is, time runs from the point at which facts exist establishing all of the essential elements of the cause of action.

A distinction is drawn between mere procedural requirements and substantive elements. This can sometimes be a difficult distinction to draw. The difference between the accrual of a cause of action in contract and tort can be problematic, because for contract, there is no need for damages to have been caused before a claimant is able to sue in contract—the cause of action accrues on the date of the breach and the six-year limitation period runs from this date. For an action brought in tort—for example, in negligence—the limitation period runs from the date on which the damage is suffered (because the 'loss' is an essential component of the tort of negligence). For such actions, therefore, the cause of action accrues when the alleged act of negligence causes loss. Damage may be caused much later than the date of the breach.

In *Haward v Fawcett* [2006] UKHL 9, the House of Lords considered the three-year limitation period prescribed by LA 1980, s. 14A, and the extent of knowledge required by the claimant to start the period running. LA 1980, s. 11(4)(b) deals with the date at which the claimant is deemed to have knowledge of a loss. The case *Hoey v Sir Robert Lloyd & Co Ltd & Others* (2011) EWCA Civ 1060 considered the principles that should be applied to consider when the claimant 'had knowledge'—he would need to have knowledge of his injury, but also that it was linked to the negligent acts of the defendant.

It concluded that, for time to start to run, the claimant must have knowledge of the 'factual essence of the act or omission' that caused the loss. It was not necessary for the claimant to know the precise details of the alleged negligence, or for him to identify conclusively that the defendant's acts or omissions were the cause of his loss. It was sufficient that the claimant had enough information to make it reasonable for him to commence investigations into the potential claim against the defendant, and s. 14A gives the claimant three years in which to complete those investigations. This section of the LA was strictly applied in the case *Boycott v Perrins Guy Williams* [2011] All ER (D) 113 (Oct).

A more recent case was *Munroe K Ltd v Bank of Scotland* [2018] EWHC 3583 (Comm). The case is a timely reminder showing that s. 14A does not extend the limitation period until each and every breach is identified and a claimant cannot postpone the date of 'knowledge' under s. 14A of the Limitation Act by choosing which breach of duty it relies on.

 Practical Considerations

In order to avoid claims being time-barred, limitation should be considered from the outset and continually reassessed to ensure that a claim is made at the right time. Where a limitation period is approaching expiry, practitioners should consider stopping the clock by entering into a standstill agreement with the potential defendant.

7.4.6.2 Potential parties to an action must exist

There must be a party capable of suing and a party capable of being sued. For example, a company may have been removed from the Register of Companies in the intervening period between the accrual of the cause of action and the issue of proceedings. However, in these circumstances, a company may be restored to the Register for the purposes of making or defending a claim, but the limitation period will run from the date of breach (or whatever the cause of action) and not the date of registration.

7.4.6.3 Persons under disabilities

Where the claimant is a person under a disability, being either a child or a protected party (see paragraphs 7.3.1 and 7.3.2), the limitation period does not start to run until:

- if a child, from the date of the child's eighteenth birthday; or

- if a protected party, if they were of unsound mind at the time of the cause of action (or the unsound mind was caused by the cause of action), from the date on which they are no longer of unsound mind (whenever that may be medically certified). If the person was of sound mind at the time of the cause of action, the limitation period will continue to run.

7.4.6.4 Fraud, concealment, and mistake

In claims based on fraud, the limitation period does not begin to run until the claimant discovers (or could, with reasonable diligence, have discovered) the fraud. The limitation period will also not run whilst the defendant deliberately conceals a relevant fact. Where the claim is for relief from the consequences of a mistake, time does not run until the mistake is discovered, or could have been discovered with reasonable diligence.

7.4.6.5 Latent damage

The Latent Damage Act 1986 created greater fairness in situations in which the limitation period may expire before a party is even aware that a claim exists. In claims in tort (other than for personal injuries), the Latent Damage Act 1986 provides new sections (inserted into the LA 1980, ss. 14A and 14B). The provisions added to the LA 1980 by the 1986 Act provide two periods of limitation: one that is six years from accrual (the usual period for claims in tort), and another that is three years from the 'starting date'—that is, the earliest date at which the claimant knew that the relevant damage was sufficiently serious to justify proceedings, enabling a claim to subsist, and when it could be attributed to the act of negligence and the identity of the defendant.

To prevent defendants being potentially 'at risk' of a claim indefinitely, s. 14B of the LA 1980 provides a long-stop period for bringing proceedings of fifteen years from the act or omission alleged to constitute the negligence causing the claimant's damage.

7.4.6.6 The discretionary extension of limitation periods

Discretionary provisions to extend the statutory limitation period apply in:

- judicial review proceedings (the three-month time limit can be extended if good reasons are shown);

- defamation claims (the one-year limitation period can be extended if it can be shown, on a balance of prejudice between the claimant and the defendant, to be equitable to allow the limitation period to be extended); and

- personal injury claims, in which a wide discretion is provided in s. 33 of the LA 1980 to extend the limitation period. See also paragraph 7.4.4.

7.4.6.7 Practical pointers when calculating the limitation period

As stated, time 'runs' from the day following the day of accrual of the action. Parts of a day are ignored. Time 'ends' when the claimant delivers his request for the issue of a claim form, accompanied by the claim form and fee, to the court office. The court will not issue a case until all of the necessary documents for issue, and the appropriate fee, have been lodged at court. If the court office is closed on the final day of the limitation period, the action will still be 'in time' if all of the documents and the fee are lodged on the next court business day. If documents and the fee are sent to the court by post, receipt of the documents and fee will be date stamped on receipt and the action will still be 'in time' even if the court does not issue on the day on which it receives the documents. Clearly, in any case in which the limitation period is about to end, it is crucial for the practitioner to ensure that the court receives the documents and fee on time. This is a situation in which the practitioner would make a personal attendance at court to issue the proceedings.

7.4.7 HOW DO THE PROVISIONS OF AMENDMENT AND SUBSTITUTION AFFECT THE LIMITATION RULES?

Amendment and substitution are governed by CPR 17.4 and 19.5. These provisions of the CPR are, to a degree, overlapping, in that they both deal with amendments to a statement of case after the expiry of the relevant limitation period. CPR 17.4 deals with applications to allow an amendment to include a new cause of action, or to allow an amendment of the name of a party where there has been a mistake in the name given to a party. CPR 19.5 deals with the provisions applying to add or substitute parties after the expiry of the limitation period.

There is a clear overlap in the provisions, and both need to be examined where a new party is to be added after the expiry of the limitation period. Confusion has arisen whether the mistake in naming the wrong party is one concerning the actual identity of the party, rather than a mistake in the name given to the party. In general, the cases seeking to clarify this have upheld the view that a mistake as to name is within the provisions, but not a mistake as to the identity of a party.

7.4.8 LIMITATION PERIODS APPLYING WHERE THE CLAIM SEEKS A CONTRIBUTION FROM AN ADDITIONAL PARTY

A claim for a contribution under the Civil Liability (Contribution) Act 1978 must be brought within two years from the date on which the person seeking a contribution is 'held liable … by a judgment' (LA 1980, s. 10).

The provision was not clear whether the time ran from the date of judgment or the date on which damages are assessed, and these may often be at different times. In *Aer Lingus v Gildacroft Ltd & Sentinel Lifts Ltd* [2006] EWCA Civ 4, the Court of Appeal clarified that the time runs from the date of assessment of the damages.

 Practical Considerations

Limitation is one of a series of 'key dates' that should be logged with any new instructions. On receiving any new instructions, the expiry of the relevant limitation period should always be checked and noted. Equally, in new instructions from a defendant to proceedings, the relevant limitation period should always be checked and noted, because a defendant who takes a step in the action beyond filing his acknowledgement of service and raising limitation in his defence will be unable to raise the issue later in the action.

7.5 THE LEGAL COMPONENTS OF AN ACTION

In Chapter 6, we looked at the concept of an action having three legal components: liability, causation, and quantum. Here, we aim to focus on these in more detail.

 Practical Considerations

Whilst we have divided the legal components into three parts, not every claim will have an issue on all three parts. Part of your role as a legal representative is to ensure that your client understands, in very basic terms, why he has a good, or not so good, case. This will inevitably require an explanation from you on the prospects of success in relation to the claim. To help you to provide this advice, we consider that breaking the case down into legal components will allow you to see the case as a whole and advise the client accordingly.

7.5.1 LIABILITY

Liability is the first hurdle that your client will have to get over—unless, of course, the opponent has admitted liability. You will first have to ask yourself, and your client, who was responsible for the breach of contract or accident. In most cases, this will be fairly self-evident. In those cases in which it is not, the most common liability issues that you will come across as a legal representative are as follows.

7.5.1.1 Joint and several liability

Where two or more persons are liable to another, they may be either jointly liable, severally liable, or jointly *and* severally liable. A contract that provides that more than one person will be liable will usually set out the parties' liability. If the contract fails to state the nature of the parties' liability, then determining that liability will be a matter of construction.

7.5.1.1.1 *Joint liability*

Where parties are jointly liable, then either is liable up to the full amount.

7.5.1.1.2 *Several liability*

Where liability is several, then the parties are liable only for their respective shares.

7.5.1.1.3 *Joint and several liability*

Joint and several liability is a mixture of both of these. The person to whom the parties owe the joint and several liability may elect to pursue the whole claim against either one of those liable (as in joint liability), but as between those liable, the liability is several and thus any party pursued by the recipient of the liability may seek a contribution from his co-obligors in the share of each of their liability (several liability).

7.5.1.1.4 *Who should the claimant sue?*

For joint debts, the general rule is that all of the joint debtors should be made parties to the action. Where the claimant fails to do this, the defendant may make an application for his joint debtor to be added to the action as an additional party. The claimant then has the option of joining in that additional party as a defendant to his action.

For joint and several liability debts, the claimant can choose whether to sue one or more of those who are jointly and severally liable.

7.5.1.2 Vicarious liability

'Vicarious liability' is an employer's liability for the acts of its employees. In common law, an employer is vicariously liable for the tortious acts of its employees if they are carried out 'in the course of employment'. This has, in recent times, had a wide definition, but will not extend to employees acting 'on a frolic of their own'. The court will look at, amongst other factors, the relationship between the employer and the third party, and whether the act of the employee was in sufficiently close connection to his employment. The connection between the tortious person's actions and 'course of employment' has been subject to recent review by the courts (*Catholic Child Welfare Society v Various Claimants (1) and the Institute of Christian Brothers (2)* [2012] UKSC 56), and the concept of vicarious liability has widened and can, on the facts of a case, include actions that may not be considered to be 'in the course of employment' and to other persons akin to an employee though not an employee. A detailed look at these points is outside the scope of this manual, but practitioners should be aware of this and, when an issue arises in practice, be prepared to undertake research to check the position and advise accordingly.

 Practical Considerations

When considering who is responsible for the wrong done to your client, you will need to turn your mind to whether the person who carried out the breach is the person with legal liability or, indeed, whether there is an additional person or entity that may also be to blame. Be aware that you may need to make some enquiries before you secure a definitive answer.

7.5.2 CAUSATION

Causation is very often either overlooked or simply assumed to be unproblematic in the success of a case. This is a misconception, because causational factors can condemn a case to complete or partial failure.

We have found it helpful to divide causation into two categories: liability causation and quantum causation.

By 'liability causation', we mean whether the negligent acts caused the accident or breach. In many cases, this will be uncomplicated, but you should ask yourself the question in any event.

 Example

Did the negligent driving of the opponent (such as driving through a red light or driving too fast) cause the collision in which your client was injured, or was it the opponent's defective vehicle that caused the accident (the fact that the brake pads were worn and the tread was bare on the front two tyres), or both? It is important that you consider this, because it will affect what you say to your opponent, and how you state your client's claim in the letter of claim and in any proceedings that may result. Remember that only facts in issue can be dealt with at trial.

By 'quantum causation', we mean whether the breach caused the loss. At first glance, this may seem unlikely to feature in many cases, but consider the following example.

 Example

Did your client's former solicitor's failure to issue proceedings for breach of contract within the limitation period cause the loss that your client is seeking (by depriving him of the opportunity to pursue a claim through the courts), or was his case so poor on liability (your client failed to perform his part of the contract) that it would have failed in any event?

7.5.3 QUANTUM

In paragraph 7.6.3, we look at the different types of damages that your client can recover in a civil claim. Here, we will seek to remind you of the theoretical basics that you would have come across in your academic studies in contract and tort.

The general principles that we would like to remind you of are as follows.

- In contract cases, the damages must not be too remote from the breach. What this means is that the losses must have flowed naturally from the breach or have been in the reasonable contemplation of the parties at the time that the contract was made as being the probable result of the breach.

 Practical Considerations

In practice, you are likely to come across this in commercial contract cases, in which you will need to consider whether the losses were consequential losses. Many contracts have incorporated into them purported valid exclusion clauses in this regard, excluding any consequential losses. In these cases, you will need to examine the clause carefully (considering whether the clause is, in fact, incorporated into the contract and reasonable) and discuss with your client the circumstances surrounding the making of the contract, as well as the true nature of the losses that occurred and whether they would really fall into the category of consequential losses.

- In cases in tort, the damages must also not be too remote, and this is, in part, based on the damages being a reasonably foreseeable consequence of the tort.
- In both contract and tort cases, the claimant has a duty to mitigate his loss. If he fails to do so, then his damages claim may be reduced. The duty only arises at the time of the breach of contract or commission of the tort.

Example

In a personal injury case, the claimant may fail to attend physiotherapy sessions, consequently prolonging his rehabilitation period. In a breach of contract case, the claimant may fail to secure a replacement machine (for the defective machine supplied by the defendant) and so allow a significant loss of production claim to accrue.

 Practical Considerations

If the defendant wishes to make an allegation that the claimant has failed to take all reasonable steps to mitigate his loss, then he should raise this initially in his response to the letter of claim, then state it in his defence. The burden of proof in this circumstance will lie with the defendant.

7.6 REMEDIES

7.6.1 THE PURPOSE OF A REMEDY

There are several remedies that may be sought in a civil action. The aim of any action will be to:

- establish, or seek to change, a legal status;
- determine legal rights and duties;
- rectify an infringement or denial of legal rights; and
- seek a declaration of the state between the parties with no further remedy.

In all of these cases, the courts seek to create justice between the parties. The decision, or order, of the court will be based on the law, the evidence, the cogency of the evidence, and the rules of the court.

The remedy that the court decides is called a 'judgment', or an 'order'. In Chapter 9 it will be seen that, in the drafting of a claim form, the remedy that the claimant seeks must be set out. This does not, however, restrict the court in the making of a remedy that it sees to be just and appropriate; although remedies can only be granted in accordance with principles of law. The court does not have an inherent jurisdiction to make any order that appears to be just (but compare this with the outcomes available in ADR when the parties may agree terms that may be far more flexible, pragmatic, or commercial).

Any action commenced in the courts must have a viable cause of action to succeed. The basic outline of the cause of action will be set out in the particulars of claim (the claim will be expanded upon in the witness statements), and to succeed, it must include all of the elements that the action needs. For example, for negligence, there must be a duty of care, a breach of that duty, and, for this part of the allegation, the claimant will need to list all of the aspects of the defendant's conduct that the claimant says fell below the appropriate standard of care. There must be consequential loss or damage, and the claimant must provide details as to how the defendant's conduct caused, or materially contributed towards, his injury (causation) and provide details of the loss or injury (loss).

7.6.2 WHAT REMEDIES ARE AVAILABLE?

The principal remedies available in civil proceedings are:

- legal remedies—usually damages, these are legal rights to which the person seeking them is entitled as of right on sufficient proof of the infringement; and

- equitable remedies—usually injunctions or specific performance, the court may award these at its discretion when a legal remedy would be inadequate or is unavailable. Such discretion to award an equitable remedy is exercised by the court in accordance with established principles.

7.6.3 DAMAGES (INCLUDING THE CRU)

Damages are a monetary payment for an infringement of a legal right. The amount to be paid reflects the sum required to compensate for the loss caused by the defendant's breach or wrongdoing (compensatory damages).

Where the damages arise from a breach of contract, the contract may provide how the damages are to be calculated. Where the infringement of a legal right has caused no loss, the damages may be only nominal.

Damages are categorized in a number of ways: tort and contract; specified and unspecified sums. The most common judgment given is for a sum of money; the money due will either be a debt or damages. Interest may be awarded on a money judgment, but this relief is ancillary to the principal remedy, rather than an independent remedy. Damages in contract aim to put the claimant in the position in which he would have been had the contract been performed satisfactorily. Damages in tort aim to put the claimant in the position in which he would have been but for the commission of the tort. Contributory negligence (that is, when the claimant has contributed to the harm caused to him) will reduce the damages awarded by an appropriate percentage of up to 100 per cent (under the Law Reform (Contributory Negligence) Act 1945).

7.6.3.1 Personal injury damages

Although personal injury damages are tortious cases, the basis for assessment of damages for personal injury cases is a specific field of 'damage assessment'.

Personal injury damages are divided into two categories:

- special damages—all of which are past quantifiable damages that arose from the commission of the tort up to the date of trial; and

- general damages—that is, all other damages, the sum of which is assessed by the court based on the evidence adduced.

The 15th edition of the Judicial College Guidelines contains details for the assessment of damages. This is updated every two years. As a result this percentage uplift should be applied when considering the value of a client's potential claim by reference to case law. The publication also gives further guidance on minor injuries, chronic pain, death, repetitive strain injury cases, and sexual abuse cases. It is a very useful guide for all legal practitioners undertaking personal injury work.

7.6.3.1.1 *Personal injury damages—the Compensation Recovery Unit (CRU)*

The CRU is a department of the Department for Work and Pensions (DWP). It seeks to recover state benefits that a claimant has received as a result of their injury or disease where the claimant is receiving damages for loss from a defendant or insurer. The aim of the scheme is to ensure that a claimant is not, in effect, compensated twice.

The elements of the scheme are contained in the Social Security (Recovery of Benefits) Act 1997, the Social Security Act 1998, and the Social Security (Recovery of Benefits) Regulations 1997 (SI 1997/2205).

The aims are as follows:

- to ensure that a person does not receive compensation in respect of the same injury or disease twice;

- to ensure that a defendant (or compensator) cannot make a compensation payment (unless it is an 'exempt' payment) to a claimant without first applying to the CRU for a

Certificate, and, when making any payment to the claimant, must pay to the DWP an amount equal to the total amount of the recoverable benefits on the Certificate;

- in some circumstances the defendant (or compensator) may deduct some, or all, of the amount he pays to the DWP from the compensation award to the claimant (this is known as 'off-setting');

- the defendant (or compensator) is responsible for payment of all relevant benefits paid to the claimant;

- the period in respect of which listed benefits can be recovered starts on the day following an accident or injury (or when benefits are first claimed as a consequence of the accident or injury) and ends on: (i) the day on which a compensation payment is made in final discharge of the claim, (ii) the date on which an agreement is made between the compensator and the claimant under which an earlier compensation payment is treated as having been made in final discharge of any claim, or (iii) the date five years after the relevant period begins—which ever comes first (the 'relevant period').

A useful summary of the scheme appears on the DWP's website at www.dwp.gov.uk/cru.

Most social security benefits are paid for three main reasons and cover:

1. loss of earnings if a person is rendered incapable of work;
2. the cost of care arising from a condition; and
3. loss of mobility arising from a condition.

Benefits falling within each category can be deducted from specific heads of damage in the claimant's action against the defendant. Thus, there are certain benefits that can be deducted from damages paid to a claimant by the defendant in respect of loss of earnings (during the relevant period). Loss of earnings does not include compensation awards in respect of future loss of earnings or a 'Smith and Manchester' (handicap on the open labour market) award, loss of congenial employment, or loss of pension rights. Claims in respect of the cost of care will not include damages paid for the cost of future care of the claimant, the loss of ability to undertake DIY tasks, loss of housekeeping capacity, for special diets, or for aids or equipment. Claims in respect of loss of mobility will similarly not apply to the element of damages that deals with the claimant's future costs.

No benefits can be deducted from general damages. Benefits can only be offset against special damages and only like for like. A full list of the benefits that fall within the remit of the CRU rules for loss of earnings, the cost of care, or loss of mobility can be found on the DWP website.

The claimant or defendant may, at anytime, ask for a Certificate of Deduction of Benefits to be reviewed. The decision of any review can also be appealed by either party. Details of how to do this, timeframes, and the review and appeal process can be found on the DWP website

7.6.3.1.2 *Personal injury damages—the recovery of NHS charges*
The CRU is also responsible for collecting from a defendant or insurer the cost of any NHS treatment that a claimant has received following an accident. The sums that may be recovered are set by the government (DWP department) and are revised from time to time by way of an annual amendment to the Personal Injuries (NHS Charges) (Amounts) Amendment Regulations.

7.6.3.2 Contract damages
The aim of damages in contract is to put the claimant in the position in which he would have been but for the breach. The assessment of this principle is made on two different bases:

- to restore the claimant to the position in which he would have been had the contract been properly performed (loss of bargain); or

- to compensate the claimant for expenditure rendered futile by the breach.

When the sum due is known (for example, for the supply of goods that have not been paid for), this would be a 'specified' claim. In contract, however, there may be other losses that are unspecified, which, on the basis of evidence before it, are assessed by the court. These may include damages for loss of profit, distress, or inconvenience. These may relate to 'expectation' loss, 'reliance' loss, or 'restitution'. Where a claim constitutes a claim for a specified sum and unspecified sums, it is called an 'unspecified sum claim'.

7.6.3.3 Nominal damages

Nominal damages may be awarded where there has been an infringement of a legal right, but where there have been no losses arising from the infringement. If actual damage to the claimant is an essential element of a cause of action (for example, for actions in negligence), then a failure to prove any damage will result in the action being dismissed.

7.6.3.4 Aggravated damages

Aggravated damages are defined in the CPR Glossary as 'additional damages', which the court may award as compensation for the defendant's objectionable behaviour. They are intended to compensate for 'injured feelings' (meaning that a company, which has no feelings, may not be awarded aggravated damages). An award is most often made when the defendant's behaviour was designed to injure the claimant's pride or dignity.

The court may increase the sum because of the way in which the defendant may have behaved and because of the additional hurt caused by the objectionable way in which the defendant caused the loss (aggravated damages).

Any claim for aggravated damages must be specifically stated.

7.6.3.5 Exemplary damages

In exceptional circumstances, the court may award enhanced damages as a penalty. These damages are distinct from aggravated damages, but they may be awarded alongside aggravated damages. These damages are defined in the CPR Glossary as 'Damages which go beyond compensating for actual loss and are awarded to show the court's disapproval of the defendant's behaviour'.

Again, as with a claim for aggravated damages, any claim for exemplary damages must be specifically sought in the claim. They will only be made in exceptional circumstances, which include:

- oppressive, arbitrary, or unconstitutional behaviour by government servants;
- where the conduct of the defendant, as well as being objectionable, was designed to make a profit in excess of the compensatory damages that are payable; and
- where exemplary damages are expressly provided by statute.

7.6.3.6 Provisional damages

Provisional damages may be awarded in cases where the claimant *may suffer* a change in his condition, that change being a risk that the injuries he suffered may change in the way identified. For example, the injury may cause an early onset of arthritis, arthritis not yet being a part of the claimant's injury. Section 32A of the Senior Courts Act 1981 provides that an award for provisional damages may be made when conditions are satisfied—the claimant has suffered injury—and there is a chance or risk of developing a serious disease or deterioration in his condition—the court will exercise its discretion when and if to make such an award. The requirements for an award of provisional damages in a personal injury claim were considered and restated (the case did not change the application of s. 32A) in *Chewings v Williams & Abertawe Bro Morgannwyg University NHS Trust* [2009] EWHC 2490 (QB). The 'risk' (of change or deterioration) must be measurable, not merely fanciful.

7.6.4 THE DELIVERY UP OF GOODS

A final judgment ordering the delivery up of goods may take one of three forms permitted by the Torts (Interference with Goods) Act 1977, s. 33(2):

- an order for the delivery of the goods and payment of any consequential damages—a discretionary remedy that will generally often only be made when the goods in question are unique or exceptional;

- an order for the delivery up of the goods, but giving the defendant the option of paying a set value for the goods, together with any assessed consequential damages, if any (but any payment of the set value by the defendant extinguishes the claimant's title to the goods); and

- a judgment for damages and not for the return of the goods (but, again, any payment of the set value by the defendant extinguishes the claimant's title to the goods).

7.6.5 INJUNCTIONS

An injunction may be either mandatory (that is, requiring some act to be done) or prohibitory (that is, requiring some conduct to stop or prohibiting threatened conduct). Any injunction is an equitable and, therefore, discretionary remedy and cannot be obtained 'as of right'. The court may award damages in place of an injunction, and will always do so if damages are a suitable and adequate remedy. See also the Additional Chapter 'Injunctions and other Equitable Remedies' in the online resources, and Chapter 14, paragraph 14.8.

7.6.6 SPECIFIC PERFORMANCE

An order for specific performance is an equitable remedy and requires the performance of the obligations of a party. Again, it will be awarded if damages would not be an adequate remedy and the principles of equity are met. Specific performance is sought most often in claims related to land, but it can also be ordered in relation to goods that are rare or unique. Specific performance and damages may be awarded.

7.6.7 RECTIFICATION

Rectification to reflect the parties' true position is also a discretionary remedy. It is not the bargain that is rectified, but the written record of the bargain. An order for rectification is retrospective, and the agreement is seen to be in the form rectified from the date on which it was originally made.

7.6.8 ACCOUNTS

A party alleging that an account is inaccurate must give notice of the objections of the account in his claim. The objections must give full particulars and specify the ground on which it is alleged that the account is inaccurate. Accounts are a common remedy between principal and agent, between partners, and in claims involving jointly owned property.

7.6.9 DECLARATIONS

The power to make a final binding declaration is contained in CPR 40.20, and the power to make interim declarations in CPR 25.1(b). The court will consider the justice to both parties in making a declaration and whether the declaration will serve a useful purpose. A declaration may make findings of fact, as well as of legal rights.

7.6.10 **RESTITUTION**

Claims for restitution can be made in law and in equity, and are based on the principles of unjust enrichment. Restitution deals with the principle of unjust enrichment at another's expense (in contrast to contract, in which the underlying principle is agreement and compensation is for breach of the agreement).

Restitution is used to restore the claimant to his previous position by making good the loss that he has suffered. The claim is for repayment of benefit received by the defendant, not for loss suffered by the claimant. Such a claim can arise when the damages are less than the benefit received by the defendant. The most common claims in restitution are for payment of money had and received, which covers both money paid under a mistake and money paid where there has been a total failure of consideration.

Restitution is viewed as separate and distinct from the laws of contract and tort, although it is, to a large extent, based on remedies and obligations found in contract and tort. The law of restitution does not depend on the existence of a breach of contract, but it may be an alternative action. Enrichment may be either positive (that is, the receipt of money or goods) or negative (that is, the saving of a necessary expenditure).

The remedy to which the claimant is entitled under the law of restitution is generally a personal remedy, which requires the defendant to pay to the claimant the value of the enrichment that the defendant has obtained at the claimant's expense. Alternatively, a claimant may be able to:

- seek a proprietary remedy, such as a declaration that the defendant holds an identifiable asset on trust for the claimant;

- assert a lien over an asset; or

- assert that he should be subrogated to the rights of a third party over the property of the defendant.

The courts have recognized a number of circumstances in which the law of restitution may be utilized—for example, an action for money had and received, or an action for money paid, services rendered, rescission, an account of profits, subrogation, and tracing.

A defendant may seek to defend a claim for restitution where he can show that the benefit was received by him as a valid gift, or as part of a valid agreement, or an equitable or statutory obligation owed by the claimant to the defendant. He may also seek to defend such a claim against him if he can show 'a change of position' as a result of the benefit alleged: for example, if he has donated the money to charity and he is neither a wrongdoer, nor has he acted in bad faith. There are other defences, and a practitioner acting for a client making or defending an action in restitution will need to study this area of law in detail.

7.7 **YOUR CLIENT'S DISCLOSURE OBLIGATIONS**

Full particulars of the disclosure obligations of a party to litigation are contained in Chapter 16. These obligations are onerous, and a client should be made aware of the need to preserve documentary (or real or electronic) evidence as these documents (or things) might assist in any future action or may assist his opponent. For this reason, 'disclosure' and the client's obligations in this respect can be considered to be a pre-action substantive matter.

KEY POINTS SUMMARY

- Identify the type of action that you have and consider jurisdictional and limitation issues at the outset.

- If acting for a child, diarize any imminent 18th birthday to enable you to deal with the consequential procedural matters.

- Break your case down into the three legal components to help you in risk assessment and evidential issues.

Case Study *Andrew James Pike v Deep Builders Ltd*

In the Andrew Pike case study, based on the information contained in the online resources (the client's attendance note) consider the following questions.

Question 1

When does the limitation period expire?

Question 2

In which court and area should you issue proceedings, and why?

Question 3

What remedy is Mr Pike seeking? Provide details for your answer.

Suggested answers to these case study questions can be accessed in the Student Resources section of the online resources.

8 PRE-ACTION PROTOCOLS

> Relevant parts of the CPR and its PDs: 3, 25, 31, 35, 36, and 44.

8.1 INTRODUCTION

In this chapter, we will look at Protocol practice in general, the aims of Protocol, the content of two Protocols (the Personal Injury Protocol and the Construction and Engineering Protocol), and the Practice Direction on Pre-Action Conduct and Protocols (PDPACP). Clearly, for any action covered by a Protocol, it would be essential to look at that Protocol in detail. The aim in looking at two Protocols is to give a flavour of Protocols in practice. Because Protocols are all in a similar (but not the same) format, a closer look at two diverse ones will help the understanding of others. We will also consider the consequences of non-compliance with Protocol or the PDPACP, and the occasions on which it may be appropriate to issue proceedings without complying with Protocol practice. We also look at some pre-action applications that may be made under the CPR.

LITIGATION TRAIN: PRE-ACTION PROTOCOL AND PROTOCOL PRACTICE

First client meeting

Pre-action or Protocol phase

Issue of proceedings

Trial

General steps to note

- Letter of Claim or Letter before Claim
- Copy documents to accompany
- Acknowledgement from defendant
- Response from defendant
- Exchange of information and documentation
- Consideration of expert evidence
- Potential meeting of parties
- Negotiations—including P36 offers
- ADR process

Note: In the context of this chapter, all references to the 'claimant' or the 'defendant' mean 'potential claimant' or 'potential defendant', because proceedings have not yet been started.

8.2 WHAT ARE 'PRE-ACTION PROTOCOLS'?

The word 'protocol' or 'Protocol' in terms of litigation is both legal jargon and a document containing specific guidance for the conduct of pre-action work for cases falling within the ambit of the specific Protocol. Legal professionals will refer to the term 'protocol' to mean work undertaken before any proceedings have been commenced, but also to mean *a* 'Protocol'—comprising specific guidance on pre-action work to be undertaken.

All the Pre-Action Protocols and the PDPACP seek to encourage a pattern of behaviour between litigants before proceedings are commenced. In many cases where this work is undertaken a settlement may be achieved and litigation is not commenced at all—'seeking settlement' (where it can be achieved with appropriate pre-action work) is a key aim of Protocol practice. Work conducted in this pre-action stage under the guidance of the Protocols and the PDPACP also encourages and enables parties to enter into a form of alternative dispute resolution (ADR) to seek a settlement. In cases where settlement is not achieved at this stage and proceedings are, by then, ultimately issued, the Protocols in place and the PDPACP aim to ensure that cases are well prepared for management by the court in litigation. It should be noted that there is an emphasis that all pre-action work (seeking to further the aims of Protocol) should also be proportionate.

8.2.1 THE CASE-SPECIFIC PROTOCOLS

It is important to remember that the Protocols do not have the same status as the Civil Procedure Rules (CPR). The Protocols have been designed to give guidance for steps to be taken before litigation in specific types of cases. There is not a specific Protocol for every type of case: so far, they have been promulgated for:

- resolution of travel package claims;
- clinical disputes;
- personal injury claims;
- defamation;
- construction and engineering disputes;
- professional negligence (see the note below at the end of this paragraph);
- judicial review;
- housing disrepair;
- possession claims based on rent arrears;
- disease and illness (this protocol is currently subject to review);
- possession claims based on mortgage or home purchase plan arrears in respect of residential property;
- the Practice Direction on Pre-Action Conduct and Protocols (PDPACP);
- dilapidations;
- low-value personal injury claims in road traffic accidents and employers' liability and public liability claims. (**Note:** these procedures provide a claims procedure for cases that fall within the claims process. Such claims are handled by the Claims Portal.) (For further detail on this procedure see Chapter 9, paragraph 9.2.8.); and
- the Pre-Action Protocol for Debt Claims.

The more general guidance contained in the PDPACP probably indicates that there will be fewer case-specific Protocols in the future. However, the Protocol for Debt Claims came into force on the 1 October 2017. Further detail of this Protocol is contained in paragraph 8.2.4. The Civil Justice Council (CJC) has set up a working party to consider a proposed new pre-action protocol for boundary disputes.

Note: On 1 May 2018, the Civil Procedure Rule Committee published an amendment (http://email.practicallaw.com/c/13OUKoUCMlSWMy4EeeQr9GAo9) to the Professional Negligence Protocol, stating that a letter of claim should, in addition to including the information set out in paragraph 6.2 http://email.practicallaw.com/c/13OUKt06l7M83qmPHj15tTSX5 of the Protocol, indicate whether the claimant wishes to refer the dispute to adjudication. If they do, they should propose three adjudicators or seek a nomination from the nominating body. If they do not wish to refer the dispute to adjudication, they should give reasons.

8.2.2 THE PDPACP

A party, which includes additional parties to an action arising under CPR 20 (and the parties' legal representatives), needs to consider the impact of the Practice Direction on Pre-Action Conduct and Protocols (the PDPACP) which applies to all cases where there is no case specific protocol.

The PDPACP (and all the case specific Protocols) expect parties to exchange information and make appropriate (and proportionate) attempts to resolve the dispute without issuing proceedings. In complying with objectives of the PDPACP (and other Protocols) in seeking to identify the issues, narrow the issues, and seek to resolve legal, factual, or expert issues, the parties are expected to take such steps as are proportionate (to the dispute). Protocol practice must not be used to obtain an unfair advantage over another party.

Such steps to achieve these objectives (PDPACP paragraph 3) may include:

- Seeking to understand the position of the parties.
- Making decisions how to proceed.
- Attempting to identify and settle the issues without issuing proceedings.
- Considering ADR (to assist with settlement or the identifying or narrowing of issues).
- Taking steps that support the efficient management of subsequent proceedings if litigation is commenced.
- Taking steps to reduce costs.

Supporting these objectives may include taking the following steps in the pre-action phase of a dispute:

- By the parties setting down, in writing, the concise details of their claim. These exchanges will be carried out in an order and timescale that the PDPACP suggests (though there is nothing to stop the parties agreeing other sensible, efficient, proportionate timescales for this exchange of information). These steps will include the Letter of Claim and the Letter of Response.
- Disclosing key documents relevant to the issues in dispute.
- Taking steps to obtain relevant and necessary expert evidence.
- Seeking to agree a form of ADR process and embarking on the process.

8.2.3 RECOVERING PRE-ACTION COSTS INCURRED

When the parties have complied with the aims and objectives of Protocol practice but a claim has been subsequently issued the parties may recover costs reasonably incurred in complying with the relevant Protocol, but only to the extent that such costs are proportionate

(PDPACP paragraph 5). The extent of recovery of those costs will be discretionary and in accordance with costs recovery principles (see Chapter 4).

If a case settles as a result of protocol (and proceedings have not therefore been issued), the court will not have jurisdiction over costs and the parties should seek to deal with costs in any settlement agreement. If the parties have agreed who is to be liable for costs but have not agreed the sum of those costs they may commence 'costs only' proceedings under CPR Part 8.

If a prospective claimant decides not to pursue their claim as a result of the steps taken in complying with protocol, then the costs incurred by the prospective defendant in responding and itself complying with protocol will not, generally, be recoverable. However, if a claim has been issued, but then stayed to enable the parties to engage in protocol procedures (for example, when an action has been issued for protective reasons, for example the period of limitation for the claim was near its end), the defendant may be entitled to recover its costs if the claimant subsequently discontinues the claim.

8.2.4 THE PRE-ACTION PROTOCOL FOR DEBT CLAIMS

The Pre-Action Protocol for Debt Claims came into force on 1 October 2017.

It applies to any business (including sole traders and public bodies) claiming payment of a debt from an individual (including a sole trader). It does not apply to business-to-business debts unless the debtor is a sole trader.

It includes a template Information Sheet and Reply Form to be provided to debtors in all cases.

The Protocol does not apply:

(a) where the debt is covered by another Pre-Action Protocol such as Construction and Engineering or Mortgage Arrears; or

(b) to claims issued by Her Majesty's Revenue and Customs that are governed by Practice Direction 7D (Claims For The Recovery Of Taxes And Duties).

This Protocol's aims are very similar to the aims of all other Protocols (see paragraph 8.3 below) to:

(a) encourage early engagement and communication between the parties, including early exchange of sufficient information about the matter to help clarify whether there are any issues in dispute;

(b) enable the parties to resolve the matter without the need to start court proceedings, including agreeing a reasonable repayment plan or considering using an ADR procedure;

(c) encourage the parties to act in a reasonable and proportionate manner in all dealings with one another (for example, avoiding running up costs which do not bear a reasonable relationship to the sums in issue);

(d) support the efficient management of proceedings that cannot be avoided.

8.2.4.1 Initial information to be provided by the creditor

The creditor should send a letter of claim to the debtor before proceedings are started. The letter of claim should, as the protocol states:

(a) contain the following information—

    (i) the amount of the debt;

    (ii) whether interest or other charges are continuing;

    (iii) where the debt arises from an oral agreement, who made the agreement, what was agreed (including, as far as possible, what words were used) and when and where it was agreed;

(iv) where the debt arises from a written agreement, the date of the agreement, the parties to it and the fact that a copy of the written agreement can be requested from the creditor;

(v) where the debt has been assigned, the details of the original debt and creditor, when it was assigned and to whom;

(vi) if regular instalments are currently being offered by or on behalf of the debtor, or are being paid, an explanation of why the offer is not acceptable and why a court claim is still being considered;

(vii) details of how the debt can be paid (for example, the method of and address for payment) and details of how to proceed if the debtor wishes to discuss payment options;

(viii) the address to which the completed Reply Form should be sent;

(b) do one of the following—

(i) enclose an up-to-date statement of account for the debt, which should include details of any interest and administrative or other charges added;

(ii) enclose the most recent statement of account for the debt and state in the letter of claim the amount of interest incurred and any administrative or other charges imposed since that statement of account was issued, sufficient to bring it up to date; or

(iii) where no statements have been provided for the debt, state in the letter of claim the amount of interest incurred and any administrative or other charges imposed since the debt was incurred;

(c) enclose a copy of the Information Sheet and the Reply Form attached to the Protocol as Annex 1; and

(d) enclose a Financial Statement form (an example Financial Statement is attached to the Protocol as Annex 2).

The letter of claim should be clearly dated towards the top of the first page. It should be posted either on the day it is dated or, if that is not reasonably possible, the following day.

The letter of claim should be sent by post. If the creditor has additional contact details for the debtor, such as an email address, the creditor may also send the letter of claim using those details. If the debtor has made an explicit request that correspondence should not be sent by post, and has provided alternative contact details, the creditor should use those details when sending the letter of claim. (Note that a condition in a creditor's standard terms does not constitute an explicit request.)

If the debtor does not reply to the letter of claim within thirty days of the date of the letter, the creditor may start court proceedings, subject to any remaining obligations the creditor may have to the debtor (for example, under the Financial Conduct Authority's Handbook). Account should be taken of the possibility that a reply was posted towards the end of the thirty-day period.

8.2.4.2 Response by the debtor

The debtor should use the Reply Form attached to the Protocol in Annex 1 for their response. As the protocol states, the debtor should request copies of any documents they wish to see and enclose copies of any documents they consider relevant, such as details of payments made but not taken into account in the creditor's letter of claim.

If the debtor indicates that they are seeking debt advice, the creditor must allow the debtor a reasonable period for the advice to be obtained. In any event, the creditor should not start court proceedings less than thirty days from receipt of the completed Reply Form or thirty days from the creditor providing any documents requested by the debtor, whichever is the later.

If the debtor indicates in the Reply Form that they are seeking debt advice that cannot be obtained within thirty days of their reply, the debtor must provide details to the creditor as specified in the Reply Form. The creditor should allow reasonable extra time for the debtor to obtain that advice where it would be reasonable to do so in the circumstances.

Where a debtor indicates in the Reply Form that they require time to pay, the creditor and debtor should try to reach agreement for the debt to be paid by instalments, based on the debtor's income and expenditure. In trying to agree affordable sums for repayment, the creditor should have regard where appropriate to the provisions of the Standard Financial Statement or equivalent guidance. If the creditor does not agree to a debtor's proposal for repayment of the debt, they should give the debtor reasons in writing.

A partially completed Reply Form should be taken by the creditor as an attempt by the debtor to engage with the matter. The creditor should attempt to contact the debtor to discuss the Reply Form and obtain any further information needed to understand the debtor's position.

8.2.4.3 Disclosure of documents

The Protocol makes clear that 'early disclosure of documents and relevant information can help to clarify or resolve any issues in dispute. Where any aspect of the debt is disputed (including the amount, interest, charges, time for payment, or the creditor's compliance with relevant statutes and regulations), the parties should exchange information and disclose documents sufficient to enable them to understand each other's position.

If the debtor requests a document or information, the creditor must:

(a) provide the document or information or

(b) explain why the document or information is unavailable, within thirty days of receipt of the request.'

8.2.4.4 Taking steps to settle the matter and alternative dispute resolution

'If the parties still cannot agree about the existence, enforceability, amount or any other aspect of the debt, they should both take appropriate steps to resolve the dispute without starting court proceedings and, in particular, should consider the use of an appropriate form of ADR.'

'Where the parties reach agreement concerning the repayment of the debt, the creditor should not start court proceedings while the debtor complies with the agreement.' On 1 May 2018, the Civil Procedure Rule committee made a minor amendment to this Protocol, directing parties to the Money Advice Service website, where copies of the most up to date versions of the Standard Financial Statement can be obtained.

8.2.4.5 COMPLIANCE WITH THE PROTOCOL

The Protocol asserts that 'if a matter proceeds to litigation, the court will expect the parties to have complied with the Protocol. The court will take into account non-compliance when giving directions for the management of proceedings. The court will consider whether all parties have complied in substance with the terms of the Protocol and is not likely to be concerned with minor or technical infringements, especially when the matter is urgent.'

8.2.4.6 Taking stock

Where the procedure set out in the Protocol has not resolved the matter, the parties should undertake a review of their respective positions to see if proceedings can be avoided and, at the least, to narrow the issues between them.

The creditor should give the debtor at least fourteen days' notice of their intention to start court proceedings, unless there are exceptional circumstances in which urgent action is required (for example, because the limitation period is about to expire).

Debt collection is one area of litigation where there is often justification for less pre-action investigative work and for the prospective claimant to be able to seek debt recovery quickly. In these circumstances it may be more appropriate to give the prospective defendant less time to respond to the letter of claim but you will have to be prepared to justify to the court why shorter time periods were reasonable.

Some clients in commercial work, particularly debt collection work—may want to take immediate action and issue proceedings without compliance with the Protocol for Debt Actions. This is usually because of their wish to safeguard, as far as they can, their cash flow position and often because they may have been seeking to recover the debt themselves for some time before consulting a legal practitioner and, therefore, feel that the debtor has 'had enough time'. It is to be noted that the new Protocol 'expects' parties to have complied with it. However the Protocol does not apply to all debt matters. It applies to any business (including sole traders and public bodies) claiming payment of a debt from an individual (including a sole trader). It does not apply to business-to-business debts unless the debtor is a sole trader.

As stated at the beginning of this section, the 'Protocol does not apply where the debt is covered by another Pre-Action Protocol such as Construction and Engineering or Mortgage Arrears; or to claims issued by Her Majesty's Revenue and Customs that are governed by Practice Direction 7D (Claims For The Recovery Of Taxes And Duties).'

'The Protocol is also intended to complement any regulatory regime to which the creditor is subject. To the extent that compliance with this Protocol is inconsistent with a specific regulatory obligation (such as a principle, rule or guidance contained in the Financial Conduct Authority's Handbook) that regulatory obligation will take precedence. The Protocol should also be read in conjunction with industry and government guidance relating to good practice in the recovery of debt.'

Where the Protocol does apply, parties are expected to have complied with it and a failure is likely to be met with sanctions or penalties being imposed by the court. However, compliance is not compulsory, and where a client insists on the issue of proceedings without reference to the Protocol, the legal practitioner will need to explain to his client the potential consequences of failing to comply (as detailed in paragraph 8.6). If the client continues to choose not to comply, then you must ensure that you have a detailed note on your file and a letter to your client pointing out those consequences of non-compliance. You are entitled to continue to act, however, as compliance with Protocol is not compulsory.

The litigation train in this chapter sets out a flowchart of matters to consider and the path to follow in the pre-action stage of an action.

8.3 THE AIM OF THE PROTOCOLS OR PROTOCOL PRACTICE

The broad objectives of the Protocols are:

- To encourage the exchange of early and full information about a prospective claim in order that the parties may understand the position or claim of their opponent.
- To enable parties to avoid litigation by agreeing a settlement of a claim before the commencement of proceedings.
- To support the efficient management of proceedings where litigation cannot be avoided.

In the same way that costs penalties may follow for a litigant who unreasonably refuses to participate in a form of ADR or who refuses a reasonable pre-action offer, costs penalties may also follow for litigants who unreasonably do not comply with Protocol (see Chapter 4, paragraph 4.2.2, for further examples).

The concept of Protocol practice is relevant to a range of initiatives for good litigation and pre-litigation practice—especially:

- the predictability of the time needed for steps that should reasonably be taken pre-proceedings, and
- a standardization of relevant information, including documents to be disclosed.

8.4 WHAT ARE THE COMMON FEATURES OF THE PROTOCOL PHASE?

There is a pattern to all of the Protocols in place. Each contains:

- a template for the recommended contents of a letter of claim, so that appropriate enquiries can be commenced upon receipt;
- guidelines for the contents of a letter of response. See Chapter 10, paragraph 10.3.2, for guidance on the content of a letter of response;
- guidelines for parties to provide pre-action information to each other, using standard forms and questionnaires;
- guidelines for parties to give pre-action disclosure;
- guidelines to encourage parties to instruct a single, agreed, expert—instead of each party having its own expert witness;
- guidelines to encourage the parties to try to settle their dispute without resorting to litigation—for example, by mediation, or another form of ADR; and
- a suggested bar on starting proceedings until a certain period has elapsed from the sending of the initial letter of claim.

8.5 HOW DOES THE COURT ENCOURAGE COMPLIANCE WITH PROTOCOL PRACTICE?

The need to undertake pre-action work within the spirit of the Protocols cannot be over-emphasized.

A party who unreasonably fails to comply with the aims of Protocol practice is likely to face penalties and or sanctions by the court in any subsequent litigation. The court will consider imposing such sanctions or penalties when:

- It makes the case management directions order (see Chapter 12).
- It makes decisions on costs or interest on sums due.

In deciding the amount of costs, pre-action conduct is one of the factors that the court will consider (CPR 44.4(3)(a)(i)).

The sanctions or penalties the court may impose (PDPACP paragraph 15) include:

- Making an order that the parties are relieved of the obligation to comply, or further comply, with Protocol.
- Staying the action while particular steps are undertaken.
- Applying sanctions.

The sanctions that may be imposed for non-compliance with Protocol (PDPACP paragraph 16) include:

- Making an order that the party at fault pays part, or all, of the costs of the other party or parties.
- Making an order that the party at fault pays those costs on an indemnity basis (CPR 44.3(3), and see Chapter 4).
- If the party at fault is the claimant who has been awarded a sum of money, depriving the claimant of interest on that sum for a specified period or reducing the rate of interest on that sum that would otherwise have been awarded.
- If the party at fault is the defendant, and the claimant has been awarded a sum of money, awarding interest on that sum for a specified period at a higher rate (up to 10 per cent above base rate) than would otherwise have been awarded.

The courts will be robust in seeking an explanation of a party's pre-action conduct if it has failed to meet the aims and objectives of protocol. The case of *Webb Resolutions Ltd v Waller Needham & Green (a firm)* [2012] EWHC 3529 (Ch) is a reminder that the court will be robust in seeking to impose a sanction where it believes that a party has not complied with the letter or spirit of protocol unless there was good reason not to do so. However, the court has also made it clear that compliance with protocol should be 'proportionate' and 'appropriate'. The court will take a pragmatic view when considering an action by a litigant asking the court to impose sanctions or penalties for an opponent's non-compliance. In *Higginson Securities (Developments) Ltd & Another v Hodson* [2012] EWHC 1052, the court held that a failure to comply with an advised step in the pre-action phase was 'justified', and imposed no penalty for the failure. This case also highlighted the need for parties to incur costs in the pre-action stage 'proportionately' (to the complexities of the case and the amount of money that is at stake). See *Sainsbury's Supermarkets Ltd v Condek Holdings Ltd and Others* [2014] EWHC 2016 (TCC). In this case the claimant took no steps to comply with protocol. After the claims were struck out, the court ordered the claimant to pay part of the defendant's costs in the indemnity basis. Again, look at the case of *CIP v Galliford Try* (unreported, 3 June 2014) (TCC), in which the claimant was awarded its pre-action costs in relation to a defence pleaded by the defendant but abandoned shortly before the hearing. However, the court refused to award these costs on the indemnity basis as there had been some compliance with protocol by the defendant.

 Practical Considerations

The following are useful guidelines to ensure that Protocol practice is followed.

- Always engage with the opposing party at the earliest opportunity.

- Always write a full letter of claim and give a reasonable time in which the potential defendant can respond (other than debt collection work where the 'short form' letter before claim should be used).

- If proceedings have to be issued before Protocol steps (for example, because of the limitation period), always give a clear indication of the reasons for issuing at this stage and suggest that directions are sought to provide a stay for Protocol practice to run its course, or give full reasons why the Protocol cannot be followed.

- Protocols are not inflexible, and where it is not possible to adhere to the 'letter' of a Protocol, it should be possible nonetheless to adhere to its 'spirit'. For example, where time limits can justifiably and reasonably be varied, they should be varied to take account of the particular characteristics of the dispute.

- Reasonable early exchange of documents is essential, as is the move towards attempting to use agreed experts. Consider exchanging experts' reports early or seeking to engage an agreed expert.

- Take care not to overstate the case or to fail to mention issues that were known at the time but which 'tactically' have not been mentioned at an early stage.

- If an opponent is failing to engage with Protocol, make this clear as soon as possible, in open correspondence. Where necessary (or at every occasion on which there has been non-compliance), state that a claim for costs or indemnity costs will be sought in any subsequent action for the non-compliance (see Chapter 4, paragraph 4.3, for a definition of indemnity costs).

- Do not reject the opponent's proposals without giving your considered (and reasonable) reasons.

- Remember that Protocol does *not* mean that you have to bend and concur with every request made. Protocol is essentially an exchange of letters, detail of the claim, and a settlement meeting. Once those obligations are concluded, you are at liberty to refuse to continue corresponding with the opponent until proceedings have been issued.

- Undertake a full 'stocktake' when Protocol has been exhausted and before issuing proceedings.

8.6 WHEN WOULD IT BE APPROPRIATE TO ISSUE PROCEEDINGS WITHOUT REFERENCE TO PROTOCOL PRACTICE?

There are essentially three situations in which it may be appropriate to take steps in the action without the cooperative communication with the opponent anticipated in any Protocol practice or when proceedings should be issued without reference to Protocol, as follows.

8.6.1 WHEN THE END OF THE LIMITATION PERIOD FOR THE ACTION IS CLOSE

When the end of the limitation period for the action is close, the claimant should issue 'protective' proceedings to avoid the action becoming statute-barred. To comply with Protocol practice and the overriding objective, the claimant should inform the defendant of the reason for his early issue. The claimant then needs either to:

- serve the proceedings and suggest to the opponent that the court be asked to grant a stay of the action for Protocol practice to be observed; or
- diarize the time by which the claim form must be served (within four months after issue—or six months after issue if the defendant resides outside the jurisdiction of the court) and suggest that the parties continue to conduct their exchanges in accordance with Protocol practice in the intervening time and before serving the claim form. (See also Chapter 7, paragraph 7.4.)

8.6.2 WHEN AN INTERIM REMEDY IS REQUIRED TO PROTECT OR PRESERVE EVIDENCE OR THE ASSETS OF THE PROPOSED DEFENDANT

When an interim remedy is required for the protection or preservation of evidence, or of the assets of the proposed defendant, once the interim application has been heard, the claimant should consider seeking directions to enable Protocol practice to be engaged with and conducted. An interim application that could be required before engaging in Protocol might be that for a search order or freezing injunction. (See also Chapter 14, paragraph 14.7.)

8.6.3 WHEN THE PROPOSED DEFENDANT MAY ATTEMPT TO ISSUE PROCEEDINGS OUTSIDE THE JURISDICTION OF THE COURT TO AVOID THE COURTS OF ENGLAND AND WALES ASSUMING JURISDICTION OF THE ACTION

Some actions may have a choice of jurisdiction, and if it is felt that a party may issue proceedings to avoid the jurisdiction of the courts of England and Wales, it may be reasonable and justifiable to issue proceedings quickly. Again, once the proceedings have been issued, the claimant should seek directions of the court to consider how best to incorporate Protocol practice.

8.7 PRE-ACTION DISCLOSURE APPLICATIONS

An application for pre-action disclosure is a step that can be taken pre-action—in the Protocol phase of an action—but making such an application is not part of Protocol. Where the circumstances for seeking pre-action disclosure are met under the provisions of CPR 31.16, such an application is one made under the CPR, not Protocol, even though the intended purpose of the application may be to seek pre-action disclosure of documents that Protocol suggests should be exchanged. It is one of the instances in which a party can seek an order of the court for compliance with a pre-action step.

An application for pre-action disclosure is sometimes necessary to investigate a potential claim fully, and if the documents needed are not forthcoming from the opponent, an application for pre-action disclosure may be required.

A court order (for pre-action disclosure) can only be made in limited circumstances—usually where:

- the respondent is likely to be a party to the proceedings;
- the applicant is likely to be a party to the proceedings;
- the documents, or classes of document, requested would be disclosed under standard disclosure rules; and
- disclosure now would fairly assist in disposing of the claim without the need to issue proceedings and save costs.

(For more details on applications for pre-action disclosure, see Chapter 14, paragraph 14.6)

An order made will specify the documents, or classes of document, which must be disclosed. The respondent must specify any documents that he no longer has or which he claims the right or duty to withhold from inspection.

Orders can be made against a person who is a non-party, but only where the document sought will support the applicant's case (or adversely affect the other party's case) and disclosure is necessary to dispose of the claim fairly or save costs. (For further details, see Chapter 14, paragraph 14.6.)

Both potential parties to a claim should fully identify if there are any other potential parties, and their names, addresses, and details of insurers (if known). A delay in notifying such information could lead to a delay in progress, and such delay could be construed as a failure to abide by the Protocol practice.

8.8 PRE-ACTION APPLICATIONS TO INSPECT PROPERTY

These applications are also contained within the CPR, not the Protocols, although the application is made in the Protocol phase. Again, the intended purpose of the application may be to seek a party's compliance with something that clearly falls within the aims of Protocol—but, as with applications for pre-action disclosure, when the application can meet the criteria set out in the CPR for the application it will be an application under the CPR, not Protocol. In these situations the court will also have the power to enforce compliance.

CPR 25.5 deals with the ability to inspect property before the commencement of proceedings against a potential party to the action or against a non-party. This may be required when dealing with an accident at work claim. If the injury was caused by machinery, it may be prudent to inspect this machine before it is altered, adjusted, repaired, or removed. To obtain such an order, it must be shown that the property:

- is, or may become, the subject matter of the proceedings or
- is relevant to the issues that will arise in relation to those proceedings.

 Practical Considerations

The template letter of claim supplied in the Protocol does not include a request that evidence should be preserved intact. This may be due to CPR 25.5, but it may be worth considering including this request in either the letter of claim or in the first letter to the proposed defendant.

8.9 PART 36 OFFERS TO SETTLE

An offer can be made before proceedings are commenced, and, provided that it is not withdrawn, it will have the same impact and cost consequences as a Part 36 offer made after the issue of proceedings if rejected. (For further detail on offers to settle, see Chapter 15.)

8.10 THE PERSONAL INJURY (PI) PROTOCOL

In this section, we will take a closer look at the Protocol that is in place for PI cases. The aim, as with all Protocols, is to encourage better and more standardized pre-action work.

8.10.1 FOR WHICH CASES IS THE PI PROTOCOL DESIGNED?

The PI Protocol is primarily designed for personal injury claims which are likely to be allocated to the fast track (at the moment PI cases with a value between £1,000 and £25,000). The government is committed to increasing the small claims limit for PI claims to £5,000, thereby reducing the number of lower value PI claims being allocated to the fast track. This proposed change has been running alongside reports of the government's plan to ban the right to claim for whiplash injuries or at least to cap the amount recoverable. This latter aim has been implemented with the the Civil Liability Act 2018 (CLA 2018) enacted in December 2018. It brings significant reforms to the personal injury market. The CLA sets out to change the small claims track limit for personal injury claims. The new limit will increase from £1,000 to £5,000 for road traffic accident claims and to £2,000 for all other injury claims.

For whiplash claims, the CLA 2018 will introduce a set tariff of damages for low-value whiplash injuries to the neck, back, and shoulder of up to two years. The tariff amounts will be set by regulations, but are expected to be significantly lower than the current level of common law damages.

The changes under the CLA 2018 due in April 2020 have now been further delayed until August 2021 due to COVID 19.

The PI Protocol is not intended to apply to claims which proceed under:

- The Pre-Action Protocol for Low Value Personal Injury Claims in road traffic accidents (claims which exit this procedure prior to Stage 2 will proceed under this Protocol in accordance with paragraph 1.3). (For further detail of this claims procedure, see Chapter 9, paragraph 9.2.8).

- The Pre-Action Protocol for Low Value Personal Injury (Employer's Liability and Public Liability) Claims (claims which exit this procedure prior to Stage 2 will proceed under this Protocol in accordance with paragraph 1.3);

- The Pre-Action Protocol for the Resolution of Clinical Disputes; and,

- The Pre-Action Protocol for Disease and Illness Claims.

Although the PI Protocol is designed for fast-track cases, paragraph 1.1.2 states that if at any stage the claimant values the claim at more than the upper limit of the fast track, the claimant should notify the defendant as soon as possible. However, the 'cards on the table' approach advocated by this Protocol is equally appropriate to higher value claims. The spirit, if not the letter of the Protocol, should still be followed for claims which could potentially be allocated to the multi-track.

Annex A of the protocol includes an illustrative flowchart of the likely progression of a claim under this Protocol.

Practical Considerations

It is essential to come to a conclusion as soon as possible about to which track a potential case would be likely to be allocated. The court makes a final determination of which 'track' a case will be allocated to, but legal representatives should undertake all of the relevant Protocol steps before such an allocation is made. It is therefore important to know where the case may fall, because a failure to abide by the Protocol in a case in the fast track may have significant cost consequences for you or your client. Even for a case falling within the multi-track, you will have to justify any steps taken that diverge from Protocol.

8.10.2 WHAT PRE-ACTION STEPS ARE RECOMMENDED BY THE PI PROTOCOL?

8.10.2.1 Early contact

The claimant is encouraged to contact the prospective defendant as soon as practicable to advise that investigations are underway, giving as much detail as possible at that stage. It may be some weeks before the claimant is in a position to prepare a full letter of claim (see paragraph 8.10.2.2), but any early contact apart from putting the prospective defendant on notice may enable useful questions to be asked about the selection of experts, the availability of documents, or the intention to abide by the Protocol. Such a letter could also usefully make enquiries about the prospective defendant's views on seeking to mediate or resolve the potential dispute by way of another form of ADR. The letter should say how long it is likely to be before a formal letter of claim might be sent.

An early letter of this kind will not start the timetable of time limits proposed in the Protocol.

8.10.2.2 The letter of claim

The time limits of Protocol-compliant steps are started once the formal letter of claim is sent to the proposed defendant.

The letter should contain the information described on the template at Annex B1:

- a clear summary of the facts on which the claim is based;
- an indication of the nature of all injuries that have been sustained;
- an indication of the way the injuries sustained impact on the claimant's day-to-day life;
- an indication of other financial losses, with an indication of the heads of damage unless this is impracticable;
- a request to identify the name of the proposed defendant's insurers;
- the documents that the prospective claimant proposes to disclose (if any) and seeks from the prospective defendant; and
- the date on which the letter must be acknowledged (under the Protocol, this is within twenty-one days).

The letter needs to be phrased in such a way that the defendant (possibly an individual) can easily understand it. It also needs to stress the requirement that this should be passed to the defendant's insurer (if there is one) immediately. If the details of the insurer are known, then a copy should be sent to the insurer at the same time. The letter should also state when a reply is expected—usually within twenty-one days. It should state clearly on the letter that it is the letter of claim for the proposed action.

The PI Protocol has a template letter of claim annexed to it as Appendix B1.

Practical Considerations

Although the PI Protocol has a template letter of claim, it should not be thought that the letter of claim should contain only those matters set out in the template. Each particular case will be different, and there will be other matters that can usefully, and effectively, be raised and added to the template letter. It is, therefore, useful to see the template letter as a template for the bare minimum that the letter should contain. For example, where no earlier attempt has been made to agree a medical expert, the letter of claim could include proposals to set in motion the process for agreeing a medical expert. The letter of claim could also set out any proposed alterations to the Protocol timetable, as well as the reasons for the suggested alterations. Similarly, if earlier correspondence had not made any reference to the claimant's willingness to embark on a form of ADR, this could be a useful time to do this and, at the same time, to set out the suggested ADR timescale.

8.10.2.3 Details of any Conditional Fee Agreement (CFA), After the Event Insurance (ATE), or Damages Based Agreement (DBA)

If the claimant has a CFA, or ATE insurance, or a DBA, there is no impact on the defendant, as the success fee and ATE premium are not recoverable from the opponent. There is, therefore, no CPR requirement to inform your opponent of these funding arrangements. However, it may be tactically conducive to settlement and the smooth running of the case to let your opponent know how your client's case is funded: if your opponent is informed that your client has funding either by way of a CFA, DBA, or a litigation funder, then this will alert them to the fact that the legal representative must genuinely believe the client's case has better than reasonable prospects of success.

8.10.2.4 Sufficient detail of the value of the claim

The priority at the letter of claim stage is for the claimant to provide sufficient information for the defendant to assess liability *and* sufficient information for the defendant to assess the likely value of the claim.

8.10.2.5 Rehabilitation

There is a duty on both the claimant and defendant to consider, at a very early stage, any reasonable needs on behalf of the claimant for rehabilitation and/or medical treatment.

The Protocol reads:

> The claimant or the defendant or both shall consider as early as possible whether the claimant has reasonable needs that could be met by early rehabilitation treatment or other measures.

The parties should, therefore, consider at an early stage (even before liability is resolved) how those needs might be met. The provision of any report obtained for the purposes of assessment of provision of a party's rehabilitation needs shall not be used in any litigation arising out of the accident, the subject of the claim, save by consent.

The Rehabilitation Code 2015 applies regardless of the severity of the claimant's injury (although the Code recognizes the differences in practice in the handling of a low-value claim and a claim of more serious or catastrophic injuries. For the latter reference should be made to the Serious Injury Guide which came into effect on 12 October 2015). Both parties and the insurer have duties to consider rehabilitation (and the insurer will pay the costs of any rehabilitation report). (For further detail of the Code, see Chapter 18, paragraph 18.8.3.) Consideration of rehabilitation options should be an ongoing process throughout Protocol.

8.10.2.6 The defendant's response

Note: There is further detail of the defendant's pre-action responses in Chapter 10, paragraph 10.3.

The defendant (or his insurer) needs to reply by acknowledging the letter within the time limit (for example, twenty-one days). If there is no response within the twenty-one days, then proceedings can be started. It can be sensible to try to make direct contact with the defendant (or his insurer) to find out the reason for any delay. This may not be caused by the defendant (or his insurer) trying to avoid the issue; it is more likely to be the tardy process of the letter of claim being passed from the defendant to his broker, then to the insurer, and ultimately being allocated to a case handler, which can often take more than twenty-one days.

Once a response has been made, the defendant (or his insurer) has three months in which to investigate the claim. The reply must deal with liability, either admitting or denying it. If the defendant denies the claim, then his reasons for denial must be given.

8.10.2.7 The early disclosure of documents

Disclosure of the defendant's documents can clarify the issues that are in dispute. The claimant can send a list requesting documents that are considered relevant, and which are believed to be in the defendant's possession and should be disclosed. Where there is a denial of liability, the reply should include a list of all documents material to the issues and likely to be ordered to be disclosed by the court.

If the defendant admits liability, but alleges contributory negligence, the defendant should disclose the documents that are relevant to his allegations.

Annex C of the PI Protocol sets out tables of the expected documents for disclosure in different PI actions.

8.10.2.8 The selection of experts

Whilst the use of experts in the Protocol phase is not governed by the CPR (Part 35, in particular), it is still intended that an agreed expert is used by the parties either pre or post the issue of proceedings. (For further details on joint experts, see Chapter 18, paragraph 18.8.)

However, the treatment of joint experts during the Protocol stage is fundamentally different from the treatment of experts during the course of litigation. This is because the PI Protocol suggests that the expert is jointly selected by the agreement of both parties, although there is nothing stopping the parties from agreeing to the joint instruction of a medical expert pursuant to CPR 35.

Joint selection under the Protocol, however, is effected by the claimant or defendant (usually the claimant) putting forward a list of suggested joint experts. If, within fourteen days, no objections are raised by the opponent, then one of the mutually acceptable experts can be approached to examine the claimant medically, and he will be an 'agreed' expert. The claimant will pay the fee in its entirety.

Once a jointly selected report has been prepared, it is only sent to the claimant. If the claimant decides to rely on the report, then he must disclose it to the defendant. Both parties can ask the expert written questions on relevant issues, such questions usually being copied to the opponent. Answers to the questions will be sent to both parties.

If a defendant has agreed to the joint expert, but then wishes to instruct his own expert witness in any subsequent proceedings, he is not entitled to rely on such a report unless:

- the claimant agrees that he may do so or
- the court so directs or
- the claimant's expert's report has been amended and the claimant is not prepared to disclose the original report.

Under the Protocol, however, if the parties cannot agree on the identity of a jointly selected expert, then the parties may instruct experts of their own choice. If proceedings are subsequently issued, the court will decide whether either party has acted unreasonably and, if so, the court will consider whether any expert evidence is required (and, if so, in what fields and how many), and will consider whether costs penalties should be imposed.

The key features, therefore, of joint selection are that there is likely to be a letter agreed by the parties instructing the medical expert to prepare a report, but that the report belongs to the claimant and is paid for by the claimant. It is, therefore, the claimant's decision whether he wishes to rely on it and subsequently to disclose it to the defendant. The agreement by the defendant to agree a particular medical expert gives him no entitlement to see the report unless the claimant discloses it. Any report prepared by a joint expert selected in the Protocol phase is, therefore, not a joint report for the purposes of CPR 35.

Annex D of the PI Protocol contains a template letter of instruction to a medical expert.

8.10.2.9 ADR

There are no rules regarding which methods of ADR to adopt. Discussion and negotiation are usually considered first, then perhaps early neutral evaluation (ENE) and mediation. However, with any of these options, it will not be easy to proceed fully before receiving expert evidence—especially the medical report—because full awareness of the injuries is needed to assist in quantifying the claim (see further Chapter 5, paragraphs 5.6 and 5.7).

8.10.2.10 If settlement fails, what next?

If the PI Protocol fails to secure settlement, then the claimant can proceed to issue his claim, although, in practice, the parties usually reflect on what has been achieved during the Protocol phase rather than rush to issue. This may involve seeking counsel's opinion.

8.10.2.11 If an admission is made

If protocol procedures secure an admission of liability from the prospective defendant the prospective claimant should send the prospective defendant:

- any medical reports obtained in the Protocol stage on which the prospective claimant wishes to rely;

- a schedule of any past and future expenses and losses which are claimed (even if the schedule is provisional). The schedule should contain as much detail as reasonably practicable and should identify these losses that are ongoing. If the schedule is likely to be updated before the settlement is concluded it should say so.

The prospective claimant should delay issuing proceedings for twenty-one days from disclosure of the above information (unless to do so would make the claim statute barred) to enable the parties to consider whether the claim is capable of settlement (Paragraph 8).

8.10.2.12 Stocktake

Where the protocol procedures have not resolved the dispute between the parties, each party should undertake a review of its positions and the strengths and weaknesses of its case. The parties should then consider together the evidence and the arguments in order to see whether litigation can be avoided, or, if that is not possible, for the issues to be narrowed before proceedings are issued. Where the prospective defendant is insured and the pre-action steps have been taken by the insurer, the insurer would normally be expected to nominate solicitors to act in the proceedings and to accept service of the claim form and other documents (this is not mandatory; Paragraph 11.1).

8.11 THE CONSTRUCTION AND ENGINEERING PROTOCOL

8.11.1 GENERAL OBSERVATIONS

The Construction and Engineering Protocol is one of the shorter Protocols and with the November 2016 revisions (which was updated again in February 2017), this has become even shorter in many ways. As a legal representative, you should be aware that this Protocol applies to all construction and engineering disputes, including professional negligence claims against architects, engineers, and quantity surveyors. The Professional Negligence Protocol would, therefore, be inappropriate to use in such negligence cases for these professions.

This is the only Protocol that suggests parties may wish to meet before any proceedings are issued. There is no longer an obligation here to meet however. This Protocol also includes a provision that the Protocol can be dis-applied by agreement between the parties. Further, the changes include provisions that costs consequences will only be imposed under this Protocol for 'flagrant/very significant' disregard of the Protocol.

8.11.2 THE LETTER OF CLAIM

Like the majority of the Protocols, the commencement of the Protocol is signified by a letter of claim containing enough basic information to enable the defendant to investigate the claim further. The Protocol suggests that only an outline or summary of the claim is necessary. The following information should be included:

- the parties' full names and addresses;
- a list of principal contractual or statutory provisions relied on;
- a summary of the claim and relief claimed, including the value of the claim with a proportionate level of breakdown;
- the name of any expert instructed by the claimant and the issues to which that evidence will be directed; and
- confirmation as to whether the claimant wishes the Protocol referee procedure to apply.

8.11.3 THE DEFENDANT'S RESPONSE

The defendant has fourteen days in which to acknowledge the letter of claim and has a total of twenty-eight days from the date on which he received the letter of claim in which to send a response to the claimant.

The response will indicate the following:

- a brief and proportionate summary of the Defendant's response to the claim/s made;
- a brief summary of any proposed counterclaim;
- the name of any expert instructed by the defendant and the issues to which that evidence will be directed; and
- the names of any third parties the Defendant intends to or is considering to submit to the Pre-Action protocol process.

If the defendant either fails to acknowledge within the fourteen days or to provide a full response within the twenty-eight-day period, then the claimant is able to commence proceedings without fear of sanctions. Clearly, if a counterclaim has been raised, then the claimant will be required to respond to that within the same time limit as the defendant's response.

8.11.4 THE PRE-ACTION MEETING

If the parties agree to the pre-action meeting, this can often incur the greatest expense. This should take place within a time period of a further twenty-one days after receipt of the defendant's response (or after the claimant's response to a counterclaim).

There is no prescribed format or purpose for the meeting, which could even take the form of a mediation. However, generally, it is envisaged that the purpose of the meeting is to narrow issues and identify how the issues can best be resolved. Obviously, ADR is strongly suggested in the Protocol, but it is acknowledged that if the parties see litigation as the only way forward, then the Protocol contains provisions for the parties to agree:

- whether expert evidence is required, on what issues, and whether this should be joint;
- the extent of disclosure; and
- the conduct of any potential litigation, having regard to minimizing delay and cost.

It is also worth noting that the Protocol permits any party who attended the pre-action meeting to disclose the following facts to the court if proceedings ultimately ensue:

- where and when the meeting took place;

- who attended, who did not and why, and any agreement reached; and

- whether ADR was discussed.

This is notwithstanding the fact that the court recognizes that these pre-action meetings are without prejudice.

 Practical Considerations

As a legal representative, you will need to be careful in disclosing the facts of the meeting to the court. Legal representatives may be expected to supply information to the court that meets these requirements whilst at the same time protecting the 'without prejudice' status of the meeting.

The Protocol will be concluded at the completion of the pre-action meeting or if no meeting takes place, fourteen days after the expiry of the period in which the meeting should have taken place.

8.11.5 THE PROTOCOL REFEREE PROCEDURE

The Protocol referee can only be appointed by agreement between the parties who feel they need guidance on complying with the Protocol. If the Parties confirm agreement (in their respective letters of claim and response), then the Technology and Construction Solicitors Association (TeCSA) will administer it. The application fee, however, is substantial.

The referees are not judges but usually senior solicitors or barristers. The procedure provides for the applicant to give (with its application) brief details of the directions it seeks on no more than four sides of A4 paper. If the nominated referee accepts the appointment, there is provision for the respondent's reply within five working days of the notice of appointment (also on no more than four sides of A4 paper) and a reply within two working days thereafter (this time, on no more than two sides of A4 paper).

The referee is to reach a written decision no later than ten working days after receipt of the notice of appointment, although the parties (but not the referee) can agree to extend this. The referee can give directions for future conduct of the Protocol process, find whether there has been non-compliance with the Protocol and, if so, whether that non-compliance demonstrates a flagrant or significant disregard for the terms of the Protocol.

The referee's decision is binding on the parties and must be complied with until the dispute is determined by legal proceedings or agreement between the parties.

As this part of the Protocol has only recently been implemented, it is not yet clear what the take up will be for the optional referee procedure. It is clearly only intended for higher value more complex claims in light of the fee involved.

8.12 THE LOW-VALUE RTA, EMPLOYERS' LIABILITY, AND PUBLIC LIABILITY CLAIMS PROCEDURE

This claims procedure is designed to be outside the court processes and may apply to low-value personal injury claims in road traffic accidents and employers' liability, and public liability claims with a value up to £25,000. For details of this procedure, see Chapter 9, paragraph 9.2.8.

KEY POINTS SUMMARY

- Be familiar with which Protocols apply to which types of case, and understand how to comply reasonably and proportionately with the guidance for best practice in the pre-action work for that type of case.

- Be familiar with the guidance laid down in the Practice Direction on Pre-Action Conduct (PDPACP), because this guidance applies both to cases that have a specific Protocol and those that do not.

- Do not be afraid to request amendments to any of the Protocols to suit your case. As long as you act reasonably and within the spirit of the Protocol generally, you cannot be criticized.

- Ensure that your client understands what the Protocol phase is all about and that he understands the possible consequences of failing to abide by Protocol or within the spirit of Protocol.

- Understand the interplay of the CPR in some pre-action applications that can be made in the Protocol (pre-action) phase.

Case Study *Bollingtons Ltd v Mrs Elizabeth Lynch t/a The Honest Lawyer*

Bollingtons Limited is an existing client of the firm. Mr Green of Bollingtons has been in to see you. View a copy of your file note and the invoice for the supply of beer in the online resources.

Question 1

What information would go in your letter before claim to Mrs Lynch?

Question 2

What points would you cover in your first letter to your new client Bollingtons Ltd? Consider which matters it would be advisable to reiterate, advise on, request from, or send to the client. Please ensure that you are certain who the client is. Consider whether you should justify and explain the steps that you have taken, and what professional conduct points could arise at this stage in this case study.

Case Study *Andrew James Pike v Deep Builders Ltd*

Consider the following questions.

Question 1

Does the PI Protocol apply in this case? If it does, explain why. If it does not, also explain why and suggest which other protocol that might apply.

Question 2

Consider the Template Letter of Claim in Annex B1 of the PI Protocol and the provisions of paragraph 5. What amendments, either by way of additions or deletions, would you make to this letter to ensure it was a PI Protocol compliant letter in Andrew Pike's claim?

Question 3

If, by way of example only, Andrew Pike's claim was valued at less than £25,000, and there had been an admission of negligence but no agreement as to quantum, which Protocol or other claims procedure may apply? Please give your reasons.

 Any documents referred to in these case study questions can be found in the online resources—simply click on 'Case study documentation' to access the documents that you need for Chapter 8 and to be reminded of the questions. Suggested answers to these self-test questions can be accessed in the Student Resources section of the online resources.

9 STARTING YOUR COURT ACTION AND SERVING IT ON THE DEFENDANT

LITIGATION TRAIN: STARTING YOUR CLAIM AND SERVING IT ON THE DEFENDANT

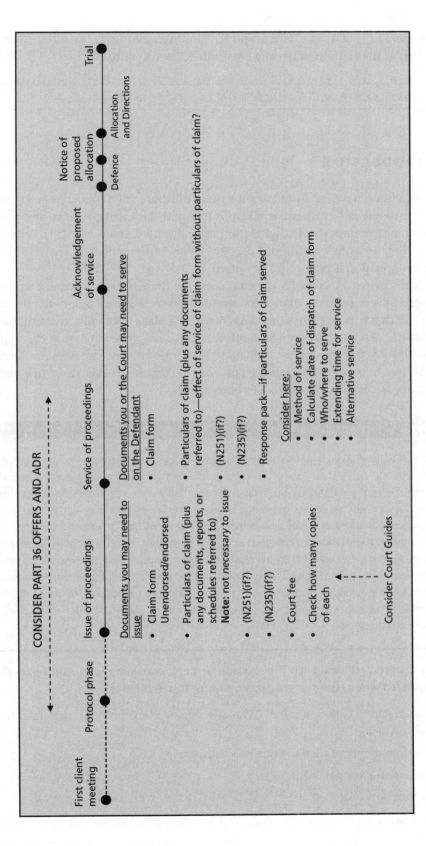

Relevant court forms relating to this chapter:

- N1 Claim Form;
- N208 Part 8 Claim Form; and
- Forms EL1, ELD1, PL1, RTA1, and RTA3 all referred to as the CNF (Claim Notification Form) if the claim is under the low-value RTA procedure.

Relevant parts of the CPR and its PDs: 1, 6, 7, 27, 28, and 29.

9.1 INTRODUCTION

No resolution has been found to your client's dispute. If Protocol has been undertaken, this will be despite all of the steps taken in line with Protocol guidance and perhaps an early (but failed) attempt to settle with alternative dispute resolution (ADR). Perhaps it is because your client is faced with an intransigent opponent. If your client wishes to proceed to seek justice, litigation is now your last option.

Clearly, when we consider the emphasis that there is for pre-action preparation of a case to create every possible chance for a resolution to be found before issuing a claim, it will be clear that it is only those more difficult, less black-and-white cases that *will* proceed to litigation. Obviously, there will be those cases that proceed because the opponent has no intention of cooperating in finding a settlement or because he does not have the funds to settle. But, in general, the cases that proceed to litigation will be those in which both parties feel they have a good case—to win or to defend.

 Practical Considerations

This very generalized overview of the nature of the cases that do proceed to litigation is worth bearing in mind. It is rare that a party will want to proceed to litigation and face the heavy burden and uncertainty of it without feeling, in his own mind, that he has a good case. As the legal representative for such a client, you need to manage his expectations very carefully. A client may have a very firm conviction that he has a good case or that he has the moral high ground, but this does not necessarily mean that there is a good case in law. It is these 'certain' clients who nonetheless have a difficult case to prove who are perhaps the most difficult to manage. It is also these clients who will look to complain if things do not go as they expected, so all advice and risk assessment analysis needs to be carefully explained, and supported with a file note and correspondence. There is a balance to be struck between positive support and risk assessment: you may be doubtful, but do not overlook the fact that your client may win.

This chapter will deal with the procedural steps, considerations, and issues that need to be considered when commencing proceedings. It will include:

- the 'tracks' created by the CPR—the 'small claims track', the 'fast track', and the 'multi-track';
- the documents needed to issue proceedings;
- parties and joinder; and
- service provisions.

The initial stages of an action (issue, service of the claim form, and service of the particulars of claim) are largely within the control of the claimant—the claimant will decide, within the time limits he has, when to serve and will choose a method of service available to him.

However, once a defence has been filed, the court's proactive case management processes will begin. In effect the court will 'take over' the management of the case. But that is the continuing story (see Chapter 12); for now, we are assuming that the decision to commence proceedings has been taken by your client *and* that you have your client's instructions to proceed. This chapter will tell you how you will take the necessary steps towards the process of litigation.

9.2 THE TRACKS

The CPR have divided litigation into three different 'tracks'. The aim of these divisions is to ensure that the overriding objective of litigation is maintained—that is, to ensure that litigation is conducted justly (which includes at a proportionate cost), fairly, efficiently, proportionately, and in compliance with the rules. The court will allocate a case to a track but legal representatives are able to determine which track a client's case is likely to be allocated to, as the division between the tracks is largely according to value. The legal representative may also seek to influence, by representations made to the opponent and to the court (usually when completing the Directions Questionnaire (DQ) for the case), to which track the case is allocated (see Chapter 12, paragraph 12.6.3). Cases will be *tried* by the courts also according to value and complexity. In this way, court resources will be allocated to those cases that, in terms of value or importance, justify the time employed on them and also in a way that ensures that judges hear cases that they have the experience to hear or that justify his time (bearing in mind his experience and seniority) in hearing them.

An awareness of the likely track allocation is important because it will bring with it an appreciation of the likely management decisions the court will make for the case. For example, for a case likely to be allocated to the small claims track, the legal representative will be aware that only very limited costs for legal representation are recoverable. He will clearly need to take this into account when advising his client so that the client is also aware of this. Equally, if the claim is likely to be allocated to the fast track, the client needs to be made aware of the likely timescale of such an action and of the tight control that the judge will exercise to manage the case, to ensure that it can be concluded within 30 weeks of allocation to the fast track and a one-day trial time. To ensure this, the time and resources that the court will allocate to a fast-track case may appear, to the client, to be very restricting. The client needs to understand the reasons.

Multi-track cases encompass, by value, a huge range of cases (of a value of £25,000 upwards) and although a case may be allocated to the multi-track, if it is at the lower end of the spectrum by value, it may be necessary to discuss with clients the likelihood or merits of attempting to agree a fast-track regime for the case. It may also be necessary to advise the client that such a case (at the lower end of the spectrum in terms of value in this track), although allocated to the multi-track, is likely to be tried by a circuit judge or district judge, and will be restricted in terms of the resources and time that the court will allocate to it, so that the time spent on the case is proportionate to the value claimed.

The following represents a brief overview of the tracks. Further details of the court's case management powers that start when the case is allocated to track can be found in Chapter 12.

9.2.1 THE SMALL CLAIMS TRACK

CPR 27 governs the procedure of cases in the small claims track. The notes that follow are an overview of the main characteristics of cases in this track. A legal representative involved in a small claims track case will need to study the provisions in CPR 27.

9.2.1.1 What cases are likely to be allocated to the small claims track?

Cases that have an upper limit value of £10,000 will be those allocated to the small claims track, except in the following cases:

- personal injury cases, in which the upper financial limit in this track is £1,000 in value of damages for pain, suffering, and loss of amenity; (this limit is expected to rise—see Chapter 8, paragraph 8.10.1);

- claims by a residential tenant against his landlord for repairs or other work to the premises, with an upper limit of £1,000 in value of those repairs and an upper limit of damages;

- cases involving claims against landlords for harassment or unlawful eviction; and

- disputes involving an allegation of dishonesty that is disputed will not usually be suitable for the small claims track.

Once the court office has determined that a case is suitable for the small claims track, it will send Form N149A to the parties, who will then be required to complete the DQ Form N180. (Form N181 will be used for cases allocated to the other tracks.)

 Practical Considerations

In cases that fall below the financial limits of the small claims track by an admission of part of the claim by the defendant, the claimant should consider making an application for judgment on the admission under CPR 14.1(4) in order to recover costs, because these may amount to more than will be permitted in the small claims track. CPR 46.11 states that a case that has been in another track before transfer to the small claims track will have those costs provisions applying in its previous track. This provision will not apply, however, in the circumstances of a part admission, because the case will not have been 'previously allocated'.

9.2.1.2 What are the main features of cases in the small claims track?

The main characteristics of small claims track cases are as follows:

- Hearings will be less formal. The court has the power (under CPR 27.8) to conduct the hearing in a way that it considers is fair. Evidence will often not be taken on oath, and the court may limit cross-examination. The judge may act as 'advocate' and may ask questions of witnesses, and he may limit or exclude cross-examination. The hearing will be tape-recorded, and a party may obtain a transcript upon payment of the fee. CPR 27.10 permits the court, at the request of the parties, to hear the case without the parties being present—that is, as a 'paper' hearing.

- Lay representation is permitted, and it is common for parties to represent themselves. Lay representatives or lawyers may represent companies.

- Costs are restricted and, in general, will be fixed costs, any court fees paid, and the reasonable expenses of the successful party in attending the hearing, including a sum, not exceeding £95, for lost earnings or loss of leave. The total fees of any experts permitted will be restricted to £750 (PD 27.7.3). The court may also award such other costs as it thinks reasonable if it thinks that a party has behaved unreasonably.

 Costs

Although the court has a wide discretion to award costs in the small claims track, it will rarely do so outside the fixed costs listed. The power to award additional costs in the face of 'unreasonable behaviour' could include making a wholly false claim, paying the whole sum just before the hearing, or deliberate delay. Where the party seeking these discretionary costs is legally represented and the party against whom these costs are sought is not, the court will look very carefully before making any additional discretionary order for costs. Clients instructing a lawyer to represent them in cases in this track need to be aware of this, even in the face of what appears to be 'unreasonable behaviour'.

- Some procedural rules do not apply—these include CPR 25 (except those parts relating to interim injunctions) and CPR 31 (disclosure and inspection in this track is governed more informally). Appendix A of Practice Direction (PD) 27 sets out the documents that will normally be required. CPR 32, 33, 35, 36, 39, and 18 also do not apply to this track. These, in general, deal with evidence, offers to settle, and requests for further information.

- The path a small claims track case will take from issue of the case to its final hearing is short-circuited, and the district judge may well set a final hearing date when the case is allocated to this track and a directions order for the case is made. The hearing itself will usually be before a district judge or deputy district judge. All small claims will automatically be referred to mediation where both parties have consented to mediation on their DQs. The action will be automatically stayed if the parties have been referred to mediation with permission to apply for the purposes of carrying into effect the settlement agreement, if one is achieved at the mediation, unless the parties have agreed that the claim is to be dismissed or discontinued. For small claims where the parties have not consented to enter mediation or the mediation has failed, the court will decide whether the claim will be determined at a hearing or as a paper hearing. A paper hearing will save the time and cost of a hearing. Judges have the power to order a hearing where they think it appropriate to hold a hearing, but paper hearings are likely to be granted in the vast majority of cases in this track.

9.2.1.3 Can small claims track judgments be set aside or appealed?

9.2.1.3.1 *Setting aside*

A party in a small claims track case who was neither present nor represented at the hearing, and who had not given notice to the court and the other party that he would not be attending under the provisions of CPR 27.9(1), may apply to have any decision made at the hearing set aside and the claim reheard. To do this, the party will need to make his application to set aside not more than fourteen days after the order has been served on him (CPR 27.11(2)), and he will need to establish that:

- he had a good reason for not attending or not being represented, or that he had not given notice to the court to proceed in his absence, and

- he has a reasonable prospect of success.

Therefore, a party, no matter how good his case, will have no right to have the order set aside if he was deliberately absent from the hearing. If the court does make an order to set aside, it may continue to rehear the case immediately after its decision on the application to set aside or it may list an alternative date and give such further directions as it sees fit.

Any other party who is 'unhappy' with the judgment of a small claims track hearing will need to consider whether he has grounds to appeal.

9.2.1.3.2 *Appealing*

The provisions for appeal in the small claims track are similar to those in the fast track and multi-track, but simplified. Any appeal can only be with the permission of the court that decided the case or the appellate court.

9.2.2 **A 'EUROPE-WIDE' SMALL CLAIMS PROCEDURE**

This procedure enables a simplified procedure for cross-border civil and commercial debt collection and small claims procedures. These are known as the European Order for Payment (EOP) and the European Small Claims Procedure (ESCP). They are both paper-based processes, using the standard forms and procedures set out in CPR 78. With the UK's intended exit from the EU, it is not known what cross-border cooperation there will be in these matters after the UK has left the EU or after any negotiated 'transition' period that is determined for the UK's exit from the EU.

9.2.2.1 The European payment order procedure (EPOP)

The EPOP was adopted under EC Regulation 1896/2006. The purpose of the EPOP is to speed up and reduce the cost of debt collection in cross-border uncontested money claims. This is achieved essentially by creating a payment procedure between member states that obviates the requirement for prior recognition of the resultant payment order by member states before enforcement.

The procedure serves as an option to claimants. In the UK, should a claimant not wish to proceed with EPOP, he is free to proceed with his own debt collection under the CPR.

9.2.2.2 The European Small Claims Procedure (ESCP)

The ESCP was adopted under EC Regulation 861/2007. The purpose of the ESCP is to simplify and speed up small claims litigation in cross-border cases, with the ultimate aim of reducing costs. As with the EOP, this is achieved by means of a procedure that eliminates the need for the issue of further proceedings to recognize and enforce the eventual judgment.

Again, as with the EOP, it is an optional process for claimants to take. It can, however, only be used where the value of the claim does not exceed €5,000.

9.2.3 THE FAST TRACK

CPR 28 governs the procedure of cases in the fast track. The notes that follow are an overview of the main characteristics of cases in this track. A practitioner involved in a fast-track case will need to study the provisions in CPR 28. The stages of a fast-track action will also be considered in greater detail later in the manual.

9.2.3.1 What cases are likely to be in the fast track?

Cases in this track will be those cases that:

- have a monetary value of between £10,000 (£1,000 in the personal injury, landlord and tenant, and other claims detailed in paragraph 9.2.1.1) and £25,000;

- have no monetary value (these could include a claim for an injunction, specific performance, or a declaration), which the court considers suitable for this track (and which do not require the more complex treatment that may be given in the multi-track);

- any other case, irrespective of its monetary value, which the court considers is suited to this track; and

- cases that the parties elect to be in this track (and where the court agrees that it is appropriate to manage the case in this track).

9.2.3.2 What are the main features of cases in the fast track?

The main characteristics of fast-track cases are as follows:

- There will be tight court control with strict time limits. When a case is allocated to the fast track, the court will set a programme for the case that enables the trial to take place within thirty weeks of allocation. The trial 'window' (a period of time—usually three weeks—within which the trial date will ultimately be set) will be set at allocation.

- Costs will be strongly linked to 'proportionality'. Increasingly, the CPR are looking to impose (and increase the scope of) fixed costs in this track. The fast track provides a 'no frills' procedure for medium-sized cases that do not justify detailed or extensive preparation. In effect, there will be no more than seven months available in which to make the case ready for trial.

Once a case is issued and the court office indicates that it is likely to be allocated to the fast track, it will issue a notice of intended allocation in Form N149B(FT). On receipt of this, the parties will need to consider the following procedure and standard directions:

- Accept allocation to this track and download and complete the DQ. In the fast track, the DQ will be in form N181. Parties must send a copy of the completed form to the court and all parties. Parties are under an obligation to consult with each other when completing their DQ. In considering and completing the DQ, parties may have regard to the standard directions set out in CPR 28. Parties are encouraged to agree directions, and where these agreed directions enable the case to proceed within fast-track principles, the court is likely to make the directions orders requested.

- The court will restrict expert evidence, and if expert evidence is permitted, the emphasis will be on joint experts and written, but not oral, evidence from the expert(s) at the trial. Any party seeking expert evidence will need to provide justification for it and provide an estimate of the likely cost. Cost capping is likely to be applied to any expert evidence in this track.

- Evidence of fact will also be restricted so as to enable the case to be heard within the short trial time of one day for cases in this track. A witness's statement will invariably be ordered to stand as his evidence-in-chief.

- Requests for further information (usually to clarify another party's case) will be controlled and time limits imposed to respond will be tight—usually within fourteen days of the order.

- The filing of pre-trial checklists will be standard. As a further incentive to settle, the hearing fee paid on the filing of pre-trial checklists will be refunded if a settlement is reached at least fourteen days before the trial date.

- Trial timetables will often be set. Simple trial timetables will set a limit for the time that each party will have in which to submit its evidence and give its closing submissions. More complex trial timetables will set the time allowed and the order of each stage of the trial—the whole providing for a five-hour trial period, to include judgment and summary assessment of costs.

- Trial bundles will be standard and a direction may be made for a case summary to be lodged.

- The parties will submit costs schedules before the trial and the judge will be expected to deal with costs at the end of the trial by way of summary assessment. The court's power to award costs in fast-track trials is limited by CPR 28.2(5), which sets fixed amounts for the costs of the trial depending on the amount recovered.

- Trials will be heard by circuit judges or district judges.

 Costs

The emphasis for fast-track trials is to provide an efficient, speedy resolution to disputes that have not been settled by other means. Costs are restricted and clients need to be kept fully informed of the amount of time that their legal representative can justifiably spend on the case. Where a client has not been kept fully informed of this and a high legal bill is incurred, even where the client may have won the action, the courts are unlikely either to impose a full costs recovery order against the losing party, and in circumstances in which the legal representative cannot show that the client has been kept fully informed of what is a 'reasonable level of time spent', the courts are unlikely to allow those costs to be recovered from the client either.

9.2.3.3 Can fast-track judgments be set aside or appealed?

The provisions for setting aside default judgments in the fast track are those set out in CPR 12 and 13, and these are dealt with in Chapter 14, paragraph 14.2. Appeals procedure against judgments is contained within CPR 52 and is dealt with in Chapter 19, paragraph 19.7.4.

9.2.4 THE MULTI-TRACK

CPR 29 governs the procedure of cases in this track. The notes that follow are an overview of the main characteristics of cases in this track. A legal representative involved in a multi-track case will need to study the provisions in CPR 29. The stages of a multi-track action will also be considered in greater detail in the relevant sections of this manual.

9.2.4.1 What cases are likely to be in the multi-track?

Cases in the multi-track will be those cases that:

- have a value over £25,000;

- have a value of less than £25,000, but in which the trial will last for more than one day; and

- are complex or important cases of any, or no value, where it is appropriate for them to be dealt with in this track.

Cases in the multi-track may be issued in the County Court or the High Court (or District Registry of the High Court), but note CPR 7A 2.1 and 2.2 (see paragraph 9.3.3).

The financial value of cases in the multi-track will not be the only criterion to be applied when considering its suitability for this track, and CPR 26.8 sets out additional criteria that will be applied to the allocation of cases to this track. These include:

- the nature of the remedy sought;

- the likely complexity of the facts, law, or evidence;

- the number of parties or likely parties;

- the value of any counterclaim or other CPR Part 20 claim (additional claim) and the complexity of any matters relating to it;

- the amount of oral evidence that may be required;

- the importance of the claim to persons who may not be parties to the proceedings; and

- the views expressed by the parties (although the court is not bound by these views).

The court has the power to take any other factors into account when considering whether to allocate a case to this track. Cases within the financial criteria of the track may still find that they are transferred for trial to the equivalent of a fast-track judge, because the case does not require the experience of judges hearing the multi-track trials. In general, cases with a value of £100,000 or less will be transferred to the County Court hearing centre for trial.

Cases that are likely to stay and be *tried* in the High Court or a district registry in this track will be:

- cases of a high financial value (exceeding £100,000);

- cases involving issues of public importance;

- test cases;

- clinical negligence cases; and

- cases in which there is a right to trial by jury, including deceit cases.

9.2.4.2 What are the main features of cases in the multi-track?

The main features of cases in the multi-track include the following:

- Once a case has been identified by the court office as one suitable for the multi-track, it will issue a notice of intended allocation to the parties in form N149C (MT). As with the fast-track cases, the parties will be expected to download and complete the DQ in form N181. Again, parties should consult with one another as to the directions they seek, using a menu approach to the directions they seek and by reference to the standard and model directions suitable for cases in the multi-track directions that are available online. Cases in this track at the lower end of the spectrum in terms of value are likely to have directions orders that are similar to those in the fast track. As with all the tracks, judicial case management is tight, but in this track, the courts will employ a greater range of management decisions, because the value of cases in this track is so broad. The case management decisions in this track will be designed to reflect this range. The more complex cases may have several CMCs and a pre-trial hearing. The lower-value, simpler cases will have directions applied to them that are the same as, or not very dissimilar to, fast-track directions.

Directions that are tailored to the requirements of each case are more likely to be made in this track if it is proportionate to do so.

- Statements of case are still intended not to be technical. Simplicity and clear English is the key with all documents drafted for trials under the CPR, and the multi-track is not excluded from these aims.

- There will be a focus on precise issues. As with all tracks, the courts will expect parties to narrow the issues in dispute.

- Stays for the purpose of ADR will be encouraged. In this track, the procedural judge, who will have experience of these cases, may use CMCs as mediation-style hearings to promote settlement, and will attempt to restrict and identify the issues to be tried.

- If a multi-track case is being dealt with in the Commercial Court or the Technology and Construction Court, a judge will be assigned to that case, and he will handle all CMCs and pre-trial reviews. The High Court also encourages this, and judges can reserve future CMCs or pre-trial reviews, or hearings, for a case to themselves. As with any CMC in this track or the fast track, it should be a legal representative (or counsel) who has knowledge of the case who attends, and, when attending, he should ensure, as far as possible, that he has authority to act on the matters likely to arise at the CMC. Where the person attending does not have this knowledge and authority, and this causes an adjournment of the hearing, the courts will be more ready to impose a wasted costs order in this track.

- The court will exercise greater flexibility with expert evidence in this track and will more commonly allow parties to have their own experts or experts in more than one field. However, the principles of the overriding objective will still apply—notably, that of proportionality.

- Costs budgets must be filed by the parties in accordance with CPR 3.13.

- Case summaries and skeleton arguments are commonly ordered in the directions in this track for CMCs, and interim and final hearings.

9.2.4.3 Can multi-track judgments be set aside or appealed?

The provisions for setting aside judgments in the multi-track are those set out in CPR 12 and 13, and these are dealt with in Chapter 14, paragraph 14.2, for default judgments. Appeals against judgments procedure is contained within CPR 52 and is dealt with in Chapter 19, paragraph 19.7.4.

9.2.5 ISSUING A CLAIM IN THE COUNTY COURT

There is a single County Court. Cases in the County Court will be issued either in:

1. The County Court Money Claims Centre (CCMCC), unless special procedures are provided in the Rules or PDs (see PD 2C and PD 7A.4A.l). All County Court money claims under CPR 7 should be issued in the CCMCC.

   Once claims have been issued, they are likely to be managed in the CCMCC until a hearing is required. Proceedings will then be sent to an appropriate County Court hearing centre. There is a discretion for a court officer to send the case to a preferred hearing centre, the defendant's home court, or such other court as may be appropriate at any time if he considers the claim should be referred to a judge for directions (CPR 26.2A).

   Or

2. A County Court hearing centre unless any rule, PD, or amendment provides otherwise (PD 2C.2). These include:

   (a) Probate claims.

   (b) Technology and Construction Court claims.

(c) Intellectual property claims.

(d) Proceedings under Parts 1 to 11 of the Insolvency Act 1986.

(e) Proceedings under s. 67(1) and (2) of the Race Relations Act 1976.

(f) Proceedings under the Companies Acts or the Limited Liability Partnerships Act 2000 in respect of which the County Court has jurisdiction.

(PD 2C.3.1(3) and 3.3)

Also, claims of a debtor or hirer for an order under s. 129 of the Consumer Credit Act 2006 (known as a 'time order') must be made at the County Court hearing centre where the claimant debtor or hirer resides or carries on business (PD 7B.4.3).

A full list of all of the County Court hearing centres in England and Wales can be found on the HM Courts and Tribunals Service website under 'Court Finder'.

Or

3. Certain claims may be started at any County Court hearing centre. These include:

- Certain Consumer Credit Act 2006 claims.

- Possession claims.

- Accelerated possession claims.

- Landlord and tenant claims.

- Applications for certain types of injunctions.

(PD 2C.4)

Or

4. Part 8 claims which may be started at any County Court hearing centre unless a rule, practice direction or enactment provides otherwise. However, when a claim is given a hearing date, the court may direct that the claim be transferred to another County Court hearing centre, if appropriate (PD 2C.6).

9.2.6 ISSUING A CLAIM IN THE HIGH COURT

The High Court has three divisions:

- Chancery Division.
- Queen's Bench Division.
- Family Division.

And within the Chancery Division and the Queen's Bench Division there are 'specialist courts'. Cases in the Family Division are not within the scope of this manual.

The Chancery Division typically deals with claims involving:

- Equity.
- Trusts.
- Commercial fraud.
- Tax.
- Intellectual property.
- Land.
- Business disputes.
- Contentious probate.
- Regulatory work.
- Bankruptcy.
- Professional negligence.

Some claims must be brought in the Chancery Division and these are listed in the Chancery Guide at paragraph 18.1. There are some County Court hearing centres that can handle Chancery Division matters and some claims in Chancery may be issued in the County Court in those hearing centres (PD 7 A.2.5).

The Queen's Bench Division typically deals with claims for:

- Defamation.
- Breach of contract.
- Negligence.
- Personal injury.
- Land possession claims.
- Non-payment of debts.

Some claims must be brought in the Queen's Bench Division, and these are listed in the Queen's Bench Guide at paragraph 1.5.5. Certain cases may also be brought in one of the specialist courts of the Chancery Division or the Queen's Bench Division, but these are also outside the scope of this manual.

Cases brought within the High Court may be brought in the High Court in London or one of the District Registries (see Chapter 7 paragraph 7.2).

9.2.7 LORD JUSTICE BRIGGS INTERIM REPORT 2017

The courts are committed to continuing the introduction of many of the reforms suggested in LJ Briggs report (published on 12 January 2017). These include further modernization reforms, for example introducing a single integrated IT system to allow electronic case management and an online self-service system for all court users to complete court and tribunal forms and pay fees digitally, or to start claims for debt repayment, personal injury, or housing disputes. Legal representatives should be alert to the announcement of possible changes and also check whether electronic filing of claims is required as it is compulsory for users in certain courts and optional in others.

9.2.8 THE CLAIMS PROCESS FOR LOW-VALUE ROAD TRAFFIC CLAIMS, EMPLOYERS' LIABILITY CLAIMS, PUBLIC LIABILITY CLAIMS, AND DISEASE AND EMPLOYERS' LIABILITY CLAIMS

This claims process is contained within the Pre-Action Protocol for low-value personal injury (employer's liability and public liability) and includes claims for personal injury in:

- road traffic accident claims (injury arising out of the use of a vehicle);
- employers' liability (EL) claims; and
- public liability (PL) claims.

with a value up to £25,000. Cases in this portal are handled by Claims Portal Limited. The claims process for cases in this portal is intended to speed up matters where liability (but not quantum) is admitted and that are relatively straightforward up to this value. 'Straightforward' in this context would not include, for example, claims in which contributory negligence is alleged or those in which issues of causation are raised. It is thought that many of the higher-value claims within the bracket up to £25,000 will exit this procedure into litigation on grounds of complexity.

9.2.8.1 Low-value RTA claims procedure

A brief resume of this procedure is detailed here:

- This procedure came into force on 30 April 2010 and was extended to also include EL and Pl claims in July 2013.
- It applies in those cases with a value of damages between £1,000 and 25,000 (in RTA actions with the claim for personal injuries of at least £1,000, excluding vehicle damage). The

following claims are excluded from the procedure: Motor Insurers' Bureau claims, deceased party (claimant or defendant) claims, claims where the claimant is bankrupt, claims where the defendant is insolvent and there is no identifiable insurer, or claims where the claimant or the defendant is a protected party or a vulnerable adult. In respect of disease or personal injury claims, claims where there is more than one defendant are also excluded, as are claims where the accident or alleged breach of duty occurred outside England and Wales, and claims involving clinical negligence and any mesothelioma claim.

9.2.8.1.1 *The most relevant sections from the Protocol*
These are:

1.1 'Admission of liability' means that the defendant admits that:

- (a) the breach of duty has occurred;
- (b) the defendant thereby caused some loss to the claimant, the nature and extent of which is not admitted; and
- (c) the defendant has no accrued defence to the claim under the Limitation Act 1980.

If causation is an issue, the claim should exit the Portal:

(1) 'Employer liability claim' means a claim by an employee against their employer for damages arising from:

- (a) a bodily injury sustained by the employee in the course of employment or
- (b) a disease that the claimant is alleged to have contracted as a consequence of the employer's breach of statutory or common law duties of care in the course of the employee's employment, other than a physical or psychological injury caused by an accident or other single event.

Disease claims (within the value) are, therefore, likely to start in the Portal, but most will probably exit if causation is not admitted.

Most EL claims are likely to exit the Portal for a number of reasons:

- (a) lack of information to investigate;
- (b) time taken to investigate—there is often more complexity for EL claims; and
- (c) the difficulty of obtaining a report from the policyholder and documents within the Portal time periods.

PL claim means a claim for damages for personal injury arising out of a negligent breach of a statutory or common law duty of care made against:

- (a) a person other than the claimant's employer or
- (b) the claimant's employer in respect of matters arising other than in the course of the claimant's employment, but
- (c) it does not include a claim for damages arising from a disease that the claimant is alleged to have contracted as a consequence of breach of statutory or common law duties of care, other than a physical or psychological injury caused by an accident or other single event.

Again, most PL claims are likely to exit the Portal for a number of reasons:

- (a) the lack of time to investigate for the defendant and obtain an accident report. The insurer also needs time to obtain the records from the policyholder;
- (b) the complexity of the claim—often more information is required from the claimant before an admission can be made; and
- (c) most insurers will not admit causation readily and without seeing the GP/hospital records.

9.2.8.1.2 *Commencement procedure—Stage 1*
The standard forms used in the process set out by this Protocol are available from Her Majesty's Courts and Tribunal Service (HMCTS) website at www.justice.gov.uk/forms/hmcts.

- Depending on the claim being made (whether an RTA, PL, or EL claim), Forms RTA1, EL1, ELD1, or PL1 will be used; these are called a Claims Notification Form (CNF) (see Appendix 11). Before commencing a claim in the Portal, legal representatives are required to undertake 'previous claims' checks on potential claimants and to confirm to the defendant that this has been done.

- The procedure is dealt with online and the CNF form is completed and submitted online.

- The CNF is also submitted electronically to the insurer and by first-class post to the defendant. The insurer must acknowledge receipt of the CNF the next day, but has fifteen days to respond in full.

- If the claim is admitted, costs of £200 are payable for Stage 1 of an RTA claim (£300 for an EL or PL claim) within ten days.

9.2.8.1.3 *The procedure in cases where the CNF procedure does not settle the action*
The case re-enters pre-action Protocol if:

- the insurer had failed to respond to the CNF;
- liability has been admitted but subject to an allegation of contributory negligence (in an RTA claim, other than on the issue of the wearing—or not—of a seat belt);
- liability is denied;
- it is alleged that the CNF is incomplete;
- it is alleged that the claim is overvalued; or
- if the fixed costs on an admission have not been paid within ten days.

9.2.8.1.4 *CNF procedure—Stage 2*
This will occur when liability has been admitted on the CNF and fixed costs paid. In this situation:

- The claimant completes the Medical Report Form EPL3 and sends it to an appropriate expert who completes the form, dealing with injury (diagnosis), opinion, and prognosis. The expert also deals with any seat belt issues if raised.

- A medical report in soft-tissue injury claims brought under the RTA Pre-Action Protocol may be sought from a not for profit company, MedCo Registration Solutions (MedCo). Medico-legal experts and medical reporting organizations (MROs) will need to be registered with MedCo in order to provide medico-legal reports for RTA soft-tissue injury claims. Users will be able to use the MedCo Portal to search for individual experts or MROs and they will receive a number of randomly generated results from which to choose, to prevent the potential for conflicts of interest between those commissioning and those providing medico-legal reports. There is an accreditation requirement for medico-legal experts and MROs (this is intended to improve the quality of medical evidence and reports). The claimant confirms the content of the Medical Report Form.

- The claimant's legal representative completes the Settlement Pack Form (EPL4)—this will include the agreed Medical Report Form and sets out calculations and a settlement figure the claimant feels is justified.

- The insurer has fifteen days in which to accept or make a counter-offer. If a counter-offer is made, the claimant has twenty days within which to consider it.

- If the action is concluded, the agreed sum is paid plus an additional sum of £300 (for an RTA claim), and £600 (for EL or PL claims) costs for this stage. (Note: the relevant Stage 1 fixed costs will already have been paid for Stage 1.)

9.2.8.1.5 *CNF procedure—Stage 3*

This stage will be implemented where there has been a settlement on liability but not on quantum. In this situation:

- The claimant's legal representative sends the insurer a Court Proceedings Pack (Form EPL6).

- Proceedings are commenced by a modified Part 8 procedure.

- The final assessment hearing can be a paper or oral hearing.

- The fixed costs for this stage are £250 (if a 'paper' hearing) plus an additional £250 advocate's fee (if the matter is listed for a hearing) (this fixed cost is the same for all claims in the Protocol). Please see the online resources for examples of sample documents and correspondence of a claim in the Portal. These documents provide an example of a completed CNF (PL1) and the accompanying correspondence. Note that in this example the defendant is acting in person and failed to respond to the claim within the time limits. As a consequence of this, the matter reverted to the Personal Injury Protocol and may ultimately result in litigation. You will see in the letters the degree of explanation given in the correspondence to a defendant acting in person.

9.3 THE DOCUMENTS NEEDED TO COMMENCE AN ACTION

The most common way in which to start civil proceedings is by issuing a claim form (Form N1), although there are still several different ways in which an action may be commenced depending on the type of action, as follows:

1. A claim form under CPR Part 7—Form N1—is the standard (and by far the most common) method under the CPR. There are specialist versions of Form N1 for use in Admiralty claims and in the Commercial Court in the Queen's Bench Division of the High Court.

2. A claim form under CPR Part 8—Form N208—can be used in proceedings in which there are no substantial factual disputes (for example, in a claim by or against a child or patient that has been settled before the commencement of proceedings and the sole purpose of which is to seek approval of the court to the settlement), or where a Practice Direction directs the use of a Part 8 claim form (for example, in actions seeking a company director's disqualification). (See paragraph 9.3.6 for further discussion on the Part 8 procedure.)

3. A CPR Part 20 claim form—Form N211—can be used for additional claims and other subsidiary claims.

4. An arbitration claim form—Form N8—is available for use in applications under the Arbitration Act 1996.

5. Special claim forms—Forms N5, N5A, and N5B—are available for starting a claim in possession cases and for actions seeking relief from forfeiture.

6. A specialist claim form—Form N2—is available for use in probate proceedings.

7. A 'petition', rather than a claim form, is used in family proceedings, the winding up of a company, or administration proceedings and bankruptcy actions.

8. An originating application form can be used in actions under the Insolvency Act 1986.

9. An interpleader notice is to be used in some County Court interpleader proceedings.

10. 'Informal' applications may be available under a specific statutory authority (for example, an application under the Deeds of Arrangements Act 1914, s. 7).

Although each of these forms of initiating proceedings is quite common, a legal representative new in the litigation department is unlikely to have much experience of many different methods of initiating proceedings outside the use of Form N1 procedure. However, one of the other proceedings that may more commonly be used is the Part 8 proceeding. We will, therefore, look at the Form N1 procedure in some detail for Part 7 claims, and highlight the main features of Form N208 for a Part 8 procedure.

9.3.1 THE CLAIM FORM N1 FOR PART 7 PROCEDURE

Unless, under the CPR, another method of commencing proceedings is required or permitted, an action will be commenced using the claim form in Form N1. The definition of 'starting proceedings' is when the court issues, at the request of the claimant, a claim form prepared by, or on behalf of, the claimant. Issuing a claim involves the court sealing the claim form with its official seal. This is important because it:

- *stops* time running for limitation purposes (it is 'issue', not service, that is the relevant date for limitation purposes) and
- *starts* time running for service.

CPR 7 and 16.2 govern the claim form requirements. The front page of the claim form is essentially an administrative document. It assists the court office to see 'at a glance' for which court the claim is intended, the names of the parties, the nature of the action (for example, contract or tort), the value of the action (which will determine the court fees that will be payable to issue the claim), the addresses of all of the parties to be served, and the fee paid. The fees payable can be found in form EX50 – Civil and Family Court Fees available on www.gov.uk. See paragraph 9.2.5 in respect of designated money claims which will all be issued out of the CCMCC.

See the online resources for a completed and annotated Form N1.

> ### ✓ Practical Considerations
>
> It is always worth remembering these basic facts about the front page of the claim form. Those new to litigation commonly and consistently tend to put far too much detail on the front page of the claim form—especially at the section headed 'Brief details of claim'. The judges who will be managing the case and hearing the trial of the action will rarely, if ever, read the front page of the claim form. The detail of the claim should be reserved for the particulars of claim.

9.3.2 WHAT INFORMATION SHOULD BE INCLUDED ON FORM N1?

CPR 16.2 states that the claim form must include all of the following.

1. It must set out the names and addresses of the respective parties, including the parties' titles and postcodes. (The postcode can be obtained from Royal Mail, online at http://www.royalmail.com.)
2. It must contain a concise statement of the nature of the claim.
3. Where possible, it must state the value of the claim (CPR 16.3) by stating that the claimant expects to recover:
   - not more than £10,000 (but note the exceptions to this—in a claim for personal injuries or in a claim by a tenant against his landlord for repairs where the figure is stated as 'not more than £1,000'—see paragraph 9.2.1), which will indicate a case that is likely to be allocated to the small claims track; or
   - more than £10,000 (or £1,000), but not more than £25,000, which will indicate a case that is likely to be allocated to the fast track; or

- more than £25,000, which will indicate a case that is likely to be allocated to the multi-track; or

- the claimant cannot say how much is likely to be recovered.

If the claim is to be issued in the High Court, it must include one of the following statements:

- the claimant expects to recover more than £100,000 or

- some other enactment (giving details) provides that the claim may be commenced in the High Court.

If the claim is for personal injuries, that the claimant expects to recover £50,000 or more.

The statement of value on the claim form does not limit the court to award a judgment in that sum. The statement of value determines the court fee that will be payable on the issue of the claim form (Form EX50 – Civil and Family Court Fees available on www.gov.uk).

In computing the value to place on the claim form, the following are disregarded:

- interest (for unspecified sum claims);

- costs;

- any potential finding of contributory negligence (unless admitted);

- any potential counterclaim or set-off (unless admitted); and

- any amounts to be recovered from state benefits under the Compensation Recovery Rules contained under the Social Security (Recovery of Benefits) Act 1997, s. 6.

If the claim is for a sum set out in a foreign currency, then the claim form must specify the sterling equivalent and the source of the conversion rate used.

4. On the back page of the claim form, the claimant has the option of stating his case in full in accordance with the drafting requirements for the particulars of claim (see Chapter 11, paragraph 11.4) if there is room to do so. Where the particulars of claim are included in this section, the claim form is called an 'indorsed' claim form. In these circumstances, the statement of truth must also be completed. If, as is often the case, there is insufficient room to set out the claimant's case fully, the claim form will merely indicate whether the particulars of claim are 'attached' or 'to follow'. The options available for the claimant are:

- to serve the indorsed claim form, together with the documents detailed in paragraph 9.3.5;

- to serve the 'unindorsed' claim form—in which case, the particulars of claim must be served within fourteen days of service of the claim form (see paragraph 9.3.5); or

- to serve the unindorsed claim form with the accompanying particulars of claim, together with the other documents set out in paragraph 9.3.5.

The claimant will also need to indicate whether a Human Rights Act 1998 issue is being raised in the claim on this reverse side of the claim form (and, if so, the human rights issue being raised must be specifically stated in the particulars of claim).

9.3.3 IN WHICH COURT SHOULD THE CLAIMANT CHOOSE TO ISSUE?

There is an apparent 'conflict' between the law and the CPR in the choice of court. The provisions relating to jurisdiction need to be considered when completing the claim form.

As stated in Chapter 7, the High Court and County Court have, in general, jurisdiction for all cases, whatever the value in contract and tort. Under the law, therefore, a party may issue his claim in the High Court or the County Court. However, the CPR provide that a case should not be issued out of the High Court unless the value exceeds £100,000 (PD 7A.2.1), and if the claim is for personal injuries, should not issue out of the High Court unless the value of the damages claimed exceeds £50,000 (PD 7A.2.2). (See also Chapter 7, paragraph 7.2.2.)

 Practical Considerations

As long as you can justify your decision (in terms of the overriding objective) to issue in the chosen court, the court will not penalize you. The prime point to note is to act reasonably.

9.3.3.1 Summary

For the practitioner undertaking less specialist litigation, the important rules can be summarized as in Table 9.1.

 Practical Considerations

If a claim is issued in the High Court when it should have been issued in the County Court, the court will often exercise its powers of management contained in CPR Part 3 and, specifically, the powers for transfer contained within CPR Part 30. The powers under these provisions include a power to rectify such an error (and order a transfer), as well as a power to strike out. A practitioner cannot be certain which of these powers the court will decide to exercise. The court will consider whether the error was deliberate or a bona fide mistake. It is important that the court is informed if an error is noted as soon as practicable. Care must always be exercised when deciding in which court to issue, because the consequences could be significant. If a mistake is made very close to the end of the limitation period, an order to strike out the claim issued in error could be a grave mistake. Even if the order to strike out were well within the limitation period, the issue fees would have to be paid again. If an order to transfer is made that rectifies the error, then the party at fault will usually be ordered to pay the costs involved in the transfer.

It should be noted that the court officials who deal with issue will generally accept the papers for issue even if they believe that the case has been issued in the wrong court, because these court officials have no power to make judicial decisions.

9.3.4 DOES INTEREST NEED TO BE SPECIFIED ON THE CLAIM FORM?

In specified sum claims, only the sum of interest accrued needs to be stated on the claim form, but the sum of interest will not be part of the 'value' of the case for tracking purposes.

TABLE 9.1 TYPES OF CLAIM

Type of claim	Jurisdiction
A money claim	May be commenced in the High Court only if the claimant expects to recover more than £100,000 (PD 7A.2.1).
A money claim issued in the High Court (Royal Courts of Justice)	May be commenced in the High Court, but the claim will usually be transferred to the County Court if the claim is worth less than £100,000, unless one of the exceptions stated in PD 29.2.2 applies.
A claim for personal injuries	May be commenced in the High Court only if the value of the claim is £50,000 or more (PD 7A.2.2).

9.3.5 WHAT OTHER DOCUMENTS ARE NEEDED TO START THE ACTION?

Although the claim can be issued by sending (or taking) to the court the completed Form N1, the court will not issue the claim until the following steps are taken and the further documents are lodged:

- the court fee—the fee to be paid will vary according to the sum claimed. The level of fees to be paid can be found in the Civil Proceedings and Family Proceedings Fees (Amendment) Order 2016. The fee to issue proceedings for the recovery of money is approximately 5 per cent of the value of the claim for all claims over £10,000. The fees payable for claims with a value of less than £10,000 are set out in the Civil Proceedings, Family Proceedings and Upper Tribunal Fees (Amendment) Order 2016—court fees valid from 21 March 2016. There is a discount of 10 per cent being applied to these fees where the claim is initiated electronically using the Secure Data Transfer facility or Money Claims Online;

- sufficient copies of the claim form for service on each of the defendants, together with a copy for the court file. Where there is more than one defendant, each copy of the claim form will have the relevant address of the defendant (including his postcode) on the front of the form in the bottom left-hand box. The address needs to be an appropriate address for service on that defendant (see the service provisions in paragraph 9.7); and

- where there is a party acting through a litigation friend, the litigation friend's certificate of suitability (Form N235).

Once the relevant documents have been received, the court issues the claim by sealing the claim form and enters details of the claim in the court 'issue book'. It enters a claim number against these details in the issue book and stamps the number on each claim form. The court will then send a notice of issue to the claimant. Form N205A will be used for a specified sum claim, Form N205B will be used for a non-specified sum claim, and Form N205C will be used in a non-monetary claim.

The court may then effect service of the claim form on the defendant(s) or return the documents to the claimant for service (see paragraph 9.7.2).

The claimant has the option of filing with these documents the particulars of claim, in which case, the response pack (Form N9) will be included in the documents served on the defendant. The court will supply Form N9 for this purpose. If the claim form is served on the defendant(s) without the particulars of claim, the defendant need take no action in response and the response pack (Form N9) is not served until the particulars of claim are served.

The claimant must serve the particulars of claim within fourteen days of service of the claim form. Service of the particulars of claim must be accompanied by the response pack (and if it is not, there has not been effective service).

Once he has been served with the particulars of claim and response pack, the defendant must now take steps to respond to the action (see Chapters 10 and 11 for detail of the particulars of claim and see the court forms available in the online resources).

9.3.6 THE FORM N208 PART 8 PROCEDURE

Part 8 procedure is intended for cases in which the nature of the relief or remedy sought, or the lack of factual dispute, makes using standard Part 7 Form N1 procedure unnecessarily cumbersome: for example, Part 8 will be used if a case concerning a child litigant is 'settled' in the Protocol phase of the action. Such a settlement will not give a sufficient discharge to the paying party unless the court has approved the settlement. To do this, an application will be made in Part 8 proceedings using Form N208. Similarly, a CPR 8 application may commonly be made when your client is seeking a declaration, for example, that a contractual term is incorporated into an agreement. Part 8 proceedings are also used in 'costs only' applications and in the new low-value personal injury cases arising out of road traffic accidents (see paragraph 9.2.8).

Part 8 procedure differs from Part 7 in that the witness evidence upon which the claimant wishes to rely must be served with the claim form and 'particulars' (which may be a summary of the witness statement). This procedure does not require the formal particulars of claim. The defendant does not need to file a formal defence, but the defendant will need to file their witness evidence with their acknowledgment of service. A failure to file witness evidence will mean that the non-serving party will be unable to make representations at any hearing unless the court grants permission to do so. DQs are not required (because all Part 8 claims are 'treated' as allocated to the multi-track). Costs budgets are only likely to be required if the case would otherwise be a Part 7 multi-track case or if the court requests costs budgets. Judgment in default is not available.

Though seemingly much simplified, Part 8 procedure cannot be used as a means of avoiding Part 7 Form N1 procedure and can be used only when:

- the claimant seeks the court's decision on a question that is unlikely to involve a substantial dispute of fact; or
- when a Practice Direction, or rule, requires that Part 8 procedure be used and the ruling or Practice Direction has modified or disapplied parts of the procedure for the action to enable this procedure to be used. Sections A, B, and C of the CPR PD 8 set out general provisions about claims and applications to which Part 8 applies.

9.3.6.1 What forms are needed for a Part 8 application?

Form N208 must be used for Part 8 claims and applications. Form N208 must state on it:

- that Part 8 applies;
- the question that the claimant wants the court to decide, or the remedy sought and the legal basis for the claim to that remedy;
- details of the claim if being made under an enactment; and
- the capacity of the representative if the claim is being made in a representative capacity.

Any evidence supporting the claim must be served with Form N208, and this must contain a statement of truth. Additionally, the service requirements are the same as those set out for Part 7 claims—except in the situations in which a defendant is not being named in the Part 8 claim and permission has been granted to issue without naming a defendant.

9.3.6.2 Responding in Part 8 claims

CPR 8.3 sets out the procedure for responding to a Part 8 claim. The defendant must acknowledge service in Form N210. If he objects to the use of the Part 8 procedure, he needs to set down his reasons. If a defendant wishes to rely on written evidence, he must file this with his Form N210. If the defendant fails to return Form N210, he may attend the hearing of the claim, but may not take part in it unless the court gives permission.

9.3.6.3 The hearing of Part 8 claims

Any evidence at the hearing is usually written evidence that has been served as set out in paragraphs 9.3.6.1 and 9.3.6.2. The court has power to permit oral evidence, but it will be rare that this will be required (because when it is, the Part 8 procedure is probably not appropriate for the claim).

9.4 CAN MORE THAN ONE CLAIM, OR MORE THAN ONE PARTY, BE INCLUDED IN ONE CLAIM?

9.4.1 JOINDER

CPR 7.3 reflects the statutory requirement of s. 49(2) of the Senior Courts Act 1981 that 'as far as possible, all matters in dispute between the parties are completely and finally determined, and all multiplicity of legal proceedings with respect to any of those matters is avoided'.

Generally, it is for the claimant to decide which causes of action he wishes to pursue against which parties. Where he has more than one claim against the same party, he has the right to issue separate claims for each (and to pay separate fees in respect of the issue of each). However, CPR 7.3 permits more than one cause of action to be claimed on one claim form and, therefore, in terms of economy and the provisions of s. 49(2) of the Senior Courts Act 1981, he would be best advised to issue all claims that he has against the defendant in the one action unless it would be inconvenient to do so.

Where there is more than one defendant, the claimant will usually issue against all defendants that he alleges are liable to him in the claim in the one action. His decision to do this will depend on a number of factors, including the nature of the liability of the defendants (whether they are jointly liable, or severally liable, or jointly and severally liable—see Chapter 7, paragraph 7.5.1), and whether all of his potential defendants are worth suing and his claim can be more easily satisfied against one. CPR 19.1 provides that 'any number of claimants or defendants may be joined as parties to a claim'. No guidance is given about which claims it might be considered convenient to dispose of in the same action. The court will take into account the overriding objective—in particular, the objectives of saving expense, and ensuring that cases are dealt with justly, expeditiously, and fairly. Thus, in general, claims involving common questions of law or fact between different parties, or different causes of action involving the same parties should be dealt with in the same proceedings.

Where there are joint claimants, they must have the same legal representative (and have no conflicting interests between them). Co-defendants may choose whom they wish to represent them.

Even though a party may issue a multiple of claims in the one action, and/or multiple parties may be joined in the action, the court has a discretionary power in CPR 3.1(2)(e) to order separate trials, and it will do so if, in separating the claims or the parties, the cases will proceed more efficiently.

Further, parts of CPR 19 need to be considered if it seems convenient to allow 'representative' actions. These provisions allow a single action to proceed that would bind all parties into an identified group. CPR 19.7 also deals with situations in which the persons that may be the subject of the action are unascertained or as yet unknown—this may apply in actions in an estate of a deceased person and persons unknown or not yet born, who may have an interest in the estate.

CPR 19.4 also contains the rules that relate to a person who wishes to intervene in an action and be added as a party. This may arise when the party who wishes to 'intervene' would be affected by any judgment that may be made in the action.

9.5 PROCEEDINGS BY AND AGAINST CHILDREN OR PROTECTED PARTIES

9.5.1 HOW DOES A CHILD OR PROTECTED PARTY EITHER MAKE OR DEFEND A CLAIM AGAINST HIM?

With the exception set out in CPR 21.2(3), a child or a protected party must sue and be sued by a litigation friend. Under the provisions of CPR 21.2(3), the court may grant permission for a child to conduct proceedings without a litigation friend. In practice, this is only likely to arise if the child is very close to becoming of age, and can show that he has the skill, knowledge, and understanding to conduct those proceedings. Any defendant faced with an application by a child to conduct proceedings himself will wish to be assured that any costs payable are secured in some way.

9.5.2 WHO MAY BE A LITIGATION FRIEND?

A child's litigation friend is normally a relative with no interest in the litigation adverse to that of the child. A protected party's litigation friend is usually a deputy appointed by the Court of Protection.

Unless the court appoints a litigation friend, the person who is to act as the litigation friend must follow the procedure set out in CPR 21.5. These provisions include:

- filing an official copy of his authority to act if his authority to act has been given under Part VII of the Mental Health Act 1983 or

- filing a certificate of suitability, which certifies that the person seeking to be the litigation friend satisfies the conditions set out in CPR 21.4(3) and

- serving the certificate of suitability on each party and filing a certificate of service when the certificate of suitability has been served.

The court may appoint the litigation friend upon the application of the person wishing to be the litigation friend or upon the application of a party. The claimant will need to make the application if the defendant in his action requires a litigation friend and no appointment has been made.

9.5.3 WHEN DOES THE APPOINTMENT OF A LITIGATION FRIEND TERMINATE?

When a child (who is not otherwise a protected party) attains the age of eighteen, the litigation friend's appointment will cease automatically and the litigation friend has no further authority. When a protected party ceases to be such, the appointment of his litigation friend continues until it is ended by a court order—the application to do this may be made by the former protected party, the litigation friend, or a party.

Once the appointment of the litigation friend has terminated, the new party (being the former child who is now of age or a former protected party) must:

- serve notice on the other parties, stating that the appointment of his litigation friend has ceased;

- state his address for service; and

- state whether he intends to carry on the proceedings.

He must do so within twenty-eight days of the date on which the appointment of his litigation friend ceased. If he fails to do this, then the court, or another party, may seek to strike out his claim or defence.

On his appointment as litigation friend, the litigation friend undertakes to pay any costs that the child or protected party may be ordered to pay in relation to the proceedings (subject to any right that he may have to be repaid from the assets of the child or protected party) (CPR 21.4(3)(c)). The liability for the costs continues until either the former child or protected party has served his notice, or when the litigation friend serves notice that his appointment has ceased. Where a person takes on the role of a litigation friend for a child party without any court order being made (CPR 21.4(3)) and has not provided an undertaking to pay any costs order which the child party may be ordered to pay, that litigation friend will be expected to be liable for such costs as the relevant party, if they had been an adult, would normally be required to pay—see *Barker v Confiànce Ltd and others* [2019] EWHC 1401 (Ch).

 Practical Considerations

Once a child attains the age of eighteen or a former protected party is no longer a protected party, then he becomes a new client for the purposes of client care and any CFA entered into with the litigation friend. The new client must then receive the standard retainer and client care correspondence that all new clients receive. If a funding arrangement is to be entered into with the new client, then notice of this must be given to the court and the other parties to the action in the normal way.

9.5.4 WHAT IS THE POSITION WITH REGARD TO EXPENSES INCURRED BY THE LITIGATION FRIEND IN CONDUCTING THE ACTION?

A litigation friend is entitled to recover money paid and expenses incurred from any monies secured by the action provided that they have been reasonably incurred and are reasonable in amount (CPR 21.12(1)). The criteria that the court will use to determine the reasonableness of their expenses are those set out in CPR 44.4. The litigation friend may not receive more than 25 per cent (of the sum awarded) if the claim is concluded by settlement or judgment in a sum not exceeding £5,000, unless the court directs otherwise.

9.5.5 SERVICE WHERE A PARTY IS A CHILD

Service of proceedings where that party is a child must be in accordance with CPR 6.13 (for service of the claim form) and CPR 6.25 (for service of an application for an order appointing a litigation friend and service of documents other than the claim form).

9.6 HOW ARE THE PARTIES IN AN ACTION DESCRIBED?

9.6.1 THEIR TITLES

The words that should be used to describe the parties in an action are set out in CPR PD 16.2.6.

- Under the CPR, the party who makes a claim is known as 'the Claimant'.
- The party against whom proceedings are brought is 'the Defendant' (CPR 2.3(1)).
- Parties to applications are referred to as 'Applicant' and 'Respondent' (CPR 23.1).
- Parties to petitions are referred to as 'Petitioner' and 'Respondent'.

TABLE 9.2 PARTIES AND THEIR DESCRIPTIONS IN STATEMENTS OF CASE

Class of party	Form of description
An individual	The full name if known and the title by which he or she is known
A child, or a protected party within the Mental Health Act 1983	The child's (or protected party's) full name followed by the full name of the litigation friend, that is, Jane Bloggs (a child by Joe Bloggs her litigation friend or if a protected party: by Joe Bloggs her litigation friend)
A child conducting the proceedings himself (where the court has permitted this under CPR 21.2(3))	Master Thomas Green
A child once he has adopted the proceedings on attaining 18 years of age	Miss Hilary Green (formerly a child but now of full age)
An individual who is trading under another name	Joe Bloggs t/a Blogg's Store
An individual who is suing or being sued in a representative capacity	Joe Bloggs as the representative of Jane Bloggs (deceased)
An individual who is being sued in the name of a club or other unincorporated organization	Joe Bloggs, suing/being sued on behalf of the Brown-town Tennis Club
A firm (other than an LLP)	Bloggs and Co (a firm) or the full name of each partner
A corporation (other than a company)	The full name of the corporation
A company	The full name of the company with an indication of its legal form (that is, Ltd, LLP, plc) and if registered outside the jurisdiction, the place of registration

Parties to Part 20 counterclaims and other additional claims are known by their names in the main statement of case (if they were a party), but if they have been brought in under CPR 20, they are known as 'third party' or 'fourth party', etc.

Table 9.2 details the description to be given to parties in an action depending on their form of 'identity'.

For further clarification of the identity of a party, see Chapter 7, paragraph 7.3.

9.6.2 WHAT HAPPENS IF A MISTAKE IS MADE IN THE NAME GIVEN TO A PARTY?

The court may substitute a new party for an existing party. Remedying the name of a party may even occur after the limitation period has expired, but this is limited to situations in which the mistake is in the name, not the identity of the party (CPR 19.5, and see Chapter 7, paragraph 7.3). The provisions for substitution of a party to rectify such a mistake apply when the mistake was genuine. In situations in which there has been a mistake as to the identity of the person, the proper course of action will be to reissue proceedings.

9.6.3 WHAT HAPPENS IF A PARTY DIES?

Under the Law Reform (Miscellaneous Provisions) Act 1934, s. 1(1), most causes of action subsisting against or vested in an individual survive his or her death. If a party to a claim dies (or is adjudged bankrupt), the court has the power under CPR 19.5(3) to add or substitute as a party in the action the person to whom the deceased (or bankrupt party's) interest or liability has passed.

Further details of the effect that the death of a party may have either before proceedings are commenced or during proceedings are set out in Chapter 7, paragraph 7.3.9.

9.6.4 CAN A CLAIM BE MADE AGAINST A PERSON WHO IS NOT KNOWN?

There are limited circumstances in which a claimant can avoid the requirements set out in PD 7A.4.1, which provides that the claim form should include the full name of each party. When a claimant does not know the identity of the defendant, but can identify him by a description that is sufficiently clear to determine who would be within that description, then he may seek permission to commence the claim by the description of the defendant (as yet unknown). This is useful in some intellectual property claims and is outside the scope of this book.

9.6.5 PARTIES IN CLAIMS FOR LOSS AND DAMAGE ARISING FROM A ROAD TRAFFIC ACCIDENT (RTA)

In an RTA claim, the usual procedure will be for the claimant to issue proceedings against the person(s) whom he alleges owed the claimant a duty of care and who has breached that duty of care, as a result of which breach the claimant has suffered loss. These are the normal provisions for a claim in tort. However, there are further provisions that may need to be considered concerning a claim arising from an RTA, as follows.

9.6.5.1 A claim against the insurer of a vehicle

Under the European Communities (Rights against Insurers) Regulations 2002, SI 2002/3061, a claimant who is resident in the European Economic Area (EEA)—that is, any member state of the EU, but also Iceland, Liechtenstein, Norway, and Switzerland—bringing proceedings in tort arising out of an RTA may issue proceedings against the insurer of the vehicle alleged to be responsible for the accident. This right is in addition to the right to issue proceedings against the driver of the vehicle. In most circumstances, the claim will be made against the driver, not the insurer, but it will be the insurer who will meet any judgment in the claim. The judgment may be enforced directly against the insurer, provided that notice has been given to the insurer either before or within seven days of proceedings being commenced (Road Traffic Act 1988, s. 152).

Practical Considerations

The notice under s. 152 of the Road Traffic Act 1988 is a vital part of any claims arising from an RTA and should form part of the aide-memoire or list of 'key dates' that will be created for any new claim of this nature. The letter of claim written in the Protocol phase of such an action is not sufficient notice by itself unless the notice specifies that it is 'notice under the provisions of s. 152 of the Road Traffic Act', and the letter of claim is written directly to the insurers and not simply 'handed to the insurers' by the insured. If notice has not been given and the insurer takes the point—that it has not been served—the claimant is left with no alternative but to discontinue the defective claim and issue fresh proceedings, giving proper notice under s. 152.

9.7 SERVICE OF THE PROCEEDINGS

9.7.1 WHAT (AND WHEN) IS 'SERVICE'?

9.7.1.1 What is 'service' of the claim form?

'Service' involves formally notifying the defendant(s) of the action against them. It is worth noting here, to avoid confusion, that CPR Part 6 distinguishes the requirements for service of the claim form from 'other documents'. Section II of Part 6 sets out the rules for service of the claim form and Section III sets out the detail for service of 'other documents'. 'Other documents' are defined as all those documents that require service that are *not* the claim form. In this regard, Section II of Part 6 (which sets out the rules for service of the claim form) states that the 'claim form' includes other documents that can be used to commence an action, for example, petitions.

Having a valid service of the claim form, in the manner specified by the court rules (and as it has been interpreted by case law), is a precondition to the exercise of the court's jurisdiction. In certain circumstances, the need to 'serve' the claim form may be dispensed with. It is also worth noting that what is sometimes described as the fiction of service is preserved—that is, the fact that a person has (or has not) *received* a document does not necessarily mean that the person has (or has not) been *served* with the document. The rules provide for a 'deemed service' rule. The 'deemed' date of service will be on the second business day after completion of the 'relevant step' required to effect service by the chosen method (CPR 6.14). The 'relevant step' for effective service for each method is set out in CPR 7.5. For limitation purposes the 'deemed' date of service of the claim form is less important than the date of 'dispatch' (which will be the 'relevant step' required for that method of service), as it is 'dispatch' that must be completed 'on time' (that is, within the limitation period). The deemed date of service is needed for the defendant to determine when the acknowledgement of service and/or defence is due. The interplay between CPR 7.5 and CPR 6.14 has been considered in a number of cases concerning valid service of a claim form, most recently in *Jones v Chichester Harbour Conservancy and others* [2017] EWHC 2270 (QB). In this case Master McCloud held that a claim form had been validly served where it was posted within the period of its validity under CPR 7.5, as extended by a court order, despite the date of deemed service under CPR 6.14 falling outside that period. The master's decision in *Jones* provides welcome clarification to the 'tension' between CPR 7.5 and CPR 6.14 and gives effect to a sensible reading of those rules. However, further clarification may be required before the position is absolutely clear and practitioners can rely fully on *Jones*. This does, unfortunately, mean that the safest option is to ensure the date of deemed service falls within the four-month period.

Parties in an action must give an address for service when responding to a claim (CPR 6.23).

9.7.1.2 When does service take place?

9.7.1.2.1 *Time periods for serving the claim form*

The rules relating to the service of a claim form (which must be an original sealed claim form, not a photocopy of a sealed claim form—see *Hills Contractors & Construction Ltd v*

Struth [2013] EWHC 1693 (QB)); the only exception to this requirement is where the claim form is served by fax or email in accordance with PD 6A) are as follows:

- A claim form issued for service within the jurisdiction must be served within four months after the date of issue (CPR 7.5(1)).
- A claim form issued for service outside the jurisdiction must be served within six months after the date of issue (CPR 7.5(2)).

9.7.1.3 Can the parties extend the period of service of the claim form?

The parties can agree between themselves to extend the time for service of the claim form (CPR 2.11). This was extensively considered in *Thomas v Home Office* [2006] All ER (D) 243 (Oct).

In order to extend the time for service, the parties may:

- agree to the extension in writing (CPR 2.11)—and this must be more than an oral agreement to extend the time recorded by a written note on each legal representative's file. A specific exchange of letters is recommended, which includes a precise deadline; or
- create a single document—that is, an agreement, signed by both parties, which sets out the determination to extend to a precise deadline.

When such an extension is agreed, it will be the claimant who will bear the risk of the court subsequently concluding that the agreement to extend was not valid.

9.7.1.4 Extending the time of validity for service of the claim form and/or seeking an order for alternative service

The courts have traditionally not shown much sympathy for a claimant or legal representative who has issued his claim form and then waited until the end of the period of validity of that claim form to serve it, but then encountered difficulties. It is, therefore, vital to understand the rules of service and to adhere to them strictly, so that good service is achieved—especially when service has been left late and is very near to, or at, the end of the period of validity of the claim form. The defendant can be pro-active if the claimant is slow to serve. Under CPR 7.7 a defendant can serve a notice on a claimant when a claim has been issued but not yet served. The notice requires a claimant to either serve the claim form or discontinue the case. If the notice is not complied with a court may dismiss the claim or make any order it sees fit. (See *Brightside Group Ltd v RSM UK Audit LLP* [2017] EWHC 6 (Comm)) for a recent decision considering CPR 7.7). CPR 7.7 enables a defendant to 'flush out' at an early stage whether a claim that has been issued against it is going to be pursued and to ensure early sight of it.

9.7.1.5 Extending the period of validity of the claim form

CPR 7.6 states that an application to extend the period of validity of the claim form must be made 'within the period specified by rule 7.5' (that is, within the period of validity of the claim form). Only in exceptional cases can the life of the claim form be extended after the end of the period specified by CPR 7.5 (see CPR 7.6(3)). The case of *Cecil & Others v Bayat* [2011] EWCA Civ 135 is a recent case that emphasizes the fact that applications to extend the life of the claim form should not be used where the reasons for non-service are practical, and where an application is being made it should be made before the time of validity has expired.

9.7.1.6 Is it sensible to wait to serve a claim form?

Once the claim form has been issued, whether pre-emptively to avoid an issue arising from expiry of the limitation period or on occasions on which it has been issued, but the particulars of claim are not yet drafted, it is still usually better to serve promptly. The claim form could be served with an explanation, and where the parties can agree an extension of time for the claimant to serve his particulars of claim, this may be achieved, by consent, under CPR 2.11 (see paragraph 9.7.1.3). Clearly it would be safer to obtain this consent to extension of time for service of the Particulars of Claim *before* service of the claim form.

In *Viner v Volkswagen Group Limited* [2018] EWHC 2006 (QB), Senior Master Fontaine refused the claimants' application to extend time to serve a claim form that had been filed but not served. This case highlights to claimants and litigation practitioners the need to be cognizant of the period of time in which a claim form must be served after filing.

9.7.1.7 Seeking an order for 'alternative service'

In certain circumstances in which service may not have been effectively achieved within the period of validity of the claim form, it may be possible (including retrospectively) to seek an order that service has, in fact, been successfully effected by 'an alternative method'. CPR 6.15 enables the court, for good reason, to make an order permitting service by an alternative method or at an alternative place. The court has the power to order this *retrospectively*. By CPR 6.15(2), the court may order that steps *already* taken to bring the claim to the attention of the defendant by an alternative method or at an alternative place have the effect of being 'good service'. There is every reason to believe that the courts will entertain such applications sympathetically when it is quite clear that the defendant has had notice of the proceedings and that the failure of good service may have been by some *understandable or reasonable* misunderstanding. It is doubtful, however, that the courts will agree to rectify a position in which the claimant (or his legal representative) has failed to serve properly by a basic misunderstanding of the CPR.

 Example

In a personal injury claim in which the claimant's legal representative has been corresponding with the defendant's insurer, it may be that the legal representative has had many cases with this particular insurer and that, in previous cases, this insurer has nominated its in-house lawyer to accept service. However, in this particular instance, the insurer has not expressly done this; although the claimant had sent the documents to the in-house lawyer in the 'normal' way, and the insurer had taken no issue on the point and continued to correspond on the claim with the claimant's legal representative. However, after the four-month period of validity has expired, the insurer takes the point, and declares that purported service is bad and that service has not been effected. It is thought that, in these circumstances, the courts *may* grant an order under CPR 6.15(2), allowing the 'service' on the insurers' in-house lawyer to be declared 'good [alternative] service'.

If and when the court makes an order under CPR 6.15(2) that service has been effected (by an alternative method), it must specify the date on which the claim form is deemed to have been served (by the 'alternative method'). This is contained in CPR 6.15(4)(b).

9.7.2 THE METHODS OF SERVICE

The methods of service that may be used are set out in CPR 6.3. Where the claim form is served within the jurisdiction, the claimant must complete the step required by Table 9.3 in relation to the particular method of service chosen, before midnight on the calendar day, four months after the date of issue of the claim form.

It is clear that it is the taking of the 'step required' that is the relevant time in which to determine whether service has been effected in time (that is, within the period of validity of the claim form), not the date on which the document is deemed served by the method

TABLE 9.3 THE METHODS OF SERVICE

Method of service	Step required
First-class post, document exchange, or other service that provides for delivery on the next business day	Posting, leaving with, delivering to, or collection by the relevant service provider
Delivery of the document to, or leaving it at, the relevant place	Delivering to, or leaving the document at, the relevant place
Personal service under CPR 6.5	Completing the relevant step required by CPR 6.5(3)
Fax	Completing the transmission of the fax
Other electronic method	Sending the email or other electronic transmission

chosen. If the claim form is posted or dispatched by midnight on any day within its validity period (four months within the jurisdiction), then it will be deemed served on the second business day after the 'step required', and it will not matter that the deemed date of service is outside the four-month validity period of the claim form. The relevant step required for different methods of service is shown in Table 9.3.

9.7.2.1 The 'default' position of service—by the court

In the High Court (but not the specialist divisions) and the County Court, the court will serve the claim form and accompanying documents unless the party lodging the document *expressly* indicates that it wishes to effect service. When a party is legally represented, his legal representative will usually arrange service. If the court is to serve, it will decide the method of service and this will usually be by first-class post. After service, the court will issue to the claimant (or his legal representatives) a certificate of service, and if the documents are returned by post, notice will be given to the claimant (or his legal representatives). In the County Court Business Centre, for all money claims, if the claimant wishes to effect service himself, the court copy of the claim form must have the words 'SOLICITOR SERVICE' boldly printed on the front page.

 Practical Considerations

Before issuing proceedings, it will be necessary to obtain specific instructions from the client regarding the method of service that he wishes to employ, so that monies on account for service can be obtained—for example, for the costs of engaging a process server—and so that the express request can be made to the court for 'documents to be returned (to the legal representatives acting) for service'.

Where the claimant elects to serve the documents, he must file at court a certificate of service in Form N215 within twenty-one days of service.

9.7.2.2 A clarification of 'personal service' under CPR 6

CPR 6.5 clarifies 'personal service' under CPR 6.5(3). The claim form must be served personally if a court order, a Practice Direction, or another enactment provides that it must be personally served. In all other cases, a claim form may be served personally unless service is to be effected on a party's legal representative or upon the Crown.

Under CPR 6.5(3), personal service is effected on:

(a) *an individual by leaving it with that individual;*

(b) *a company or other corporation* [which will include an LLP] *by leaving it with a person holding a senior position* [defined in PD 6A.6.2] *within the company or corporation* [for example, a person in a 'senior position' of an incorporated company is defined as a treasurer, the secretary of the company (or corporation), the chief executive, a manager, or other officer—and the definition of a person in 'a senior position' of an unincorporated association is also defined in PD 6A.6.2]; *or*

(c) *a partnership (where partners are being sued in the name of their firm) by leaving it with—*

(i) *a partner; or*

   a person who, at the time of service, has the control or management of the partnership business at its principal place of business.

 Practical Considerations

Personal service will often be completed by a process server. The person serving the document(s) should hand the document(s) to the individual and inform the individual of the contents of the document(s) in general, not specific, terms. When instructing a process server or agent to effect service for the first time, ensure that he has the experience and knowledge to effect service according to the rules.

9.7.2.3 What happens if the document(s) being served are handed back to the process server by the person who is to be served?

This happens quite commonly in practice: quite often, the person against whom proceedings have been brought is not entirely happy about the event, and he may simply, once he is told the general nature of the documents being served on him, hand them back (or throw them on the ground). There is no post-CPR authority on the point, but in *Nottingham Building Society v Peter Bennett and Co* (1977) The Times, 26 February, the Court of Appeal held that once the document was handed over and the person had been told of the general nature of the document, it had been duly served. There is no reason to suppose that the courts would make any different finding on the point under the provisions of the CPR.

9.7.2.4 Service by or on partnerships

Where the claim is by or against two or more persons who were partners and who had carried on business within the jurisdiction (at the time that the cause of action accrued), under the provisions of PD 7A.5A.2, the term 'partners' includes both those claiming to be entitled as partners and those alleged to be partners.

Further, under the provisions of PD 7A.5A.3, where a claim is commenced by a partnership, it should be in the name of the partnership that was in existence when the cause of action accrued.

When acting in a claim against a partnership, it may be necessary to obtain details of the names and last known addresses of each of the partners at the time that the cause of action arose. This is known as a 'partnership membership statement', and the partnership has fourteen days in which to provide such a statement when requested to do so (PD 7A.5B). PD 7A.5A.3 provides that 'where the partnership has a name, unless it is inappropriate to do so, claims must be brought in or against the name of the partnership'. This is a rule of convenience; that is, the use of the name of the firm name is merely shorthand for listing the partners individually. It may be inappropriate to start proceedings using the partnership name where, for example, there have been multiple changes of the name of the partnership or multiple mergers so that it would be clearer to identify the partners by their individual names. Similarly, if it seems likely that your client may have to seek enforcement of any judgment debt against the personal assets of one or more partners it is safer to issue against the partners by name of the partners. A compromise solution to what may be a cumbersome claim form would be to sue in the firm name but to set out the individual names of the partners in an attached schedule (making reference to the schedule in the claim form).

This is required because CPR 6.9 provides that where partners are sued in the name of a partnership, service should be at the principal or last known place of business of the partnership or at the partners' 'last known residence'.

However, where service is being made on an individual as a partner of the firm being sued, a notice must also be given specifying whether the person being served, is being served as:

- a partner;
- a person with control or management of the partnership business; or
- both of the above.

This information is contained in Form N218. It is advisable to include this notice with the document(s) being served.

 Practical Considerations

Where service is being effected on a person who may not be a partner, but who is stated to have 'control or management', it would be prudent to include Form N218 with the documents for service on every occasion and also whenever a partner is being served at his home or 'last known residence'.

9.7.2.5 Companies and limited liability partnerships (LLPs)

Service on a company may be by any method permitted under CPR 6—(CPR 6.3(2) (claim form) and 6.20(2) (other documents)). Additionally, section 1139(1) of the Companies Act 2006 (Commencement No. 8, Transitional Provisions and Savings) Order 2008, SI 2008/2860 provides that 'a document may be served on a company registered under the act by leaving it at, or sending it by post to, the company's registered office'.

Service on a limited liability partnership (LLP) may be served by any method permitted under CPR 6 (CPR 6.3(2) (claim form) and 6.20(2) (other documents)) and, additionally, by any of the methods of service permitted under the Companies Act 2006 as applied by the Limited Liability Partnerships Act 2000.

Where service is to be to an overseas branch of a company registered in England and Wales or on an overseas registered company, s. 1139(2) will continue to permit a document to be served at the UK branch on a person who is authorized to accept service or at any place of business in England and Wales. In the recent case *SSL International plc v TTK LIG Ltd* [2011] EWCA Civ 1170, the court rejected an attempt by the claimant to rely on CPR 6.5(3)(b) to serve a claim form on an Indian company that did not carry on business within the jurisdiction and concluded that personal service on one of the directors who was present within the jurisdiction was not effective service on the company. It is a reminder that the rules of service will be strictly applied.

Section 1139 of the Companies Act 2006 also applies to a limited liability partnership (LLP). Therefore, an LLP can be served at its registered office. Service under the provisions of s. 1139 is an additional place of service on a company or LLP and is effective even if the company or LLP has legal representatives acting, who have signified that they have instructions to accept service of proceedings.

 Practical Considerations

Where service is to be effected under s. 1139 rather than the CPR, note that the 'deemed date of service' (see paragraph 9.7.6) does not apply. The wording in the statute is 'in the ordinary course of post' and service is assumed to have occurred 'unless the contrary is proved'. Because this is a rebuttable presumption, it is again different from the 'deemed date of service' rule in the CPR. Also, under the Companies Act 2006, service by second-class post is permitted, whereas it is not under the CPR.

CPR 6.5(3) provides that a document is served personally on a company or other corporation by leaving it with a 'person who holds a senior position'. A list of who is such a person is set out in PD 6A.6.2 (with regard to a registered company), and appears in paragraph 9.7.2.2.

For an unregistered company or corporation, such a person might include:

- the mayor;
- the chairman;
- the president;
- the town clerk; or
- a similar officer.

 Practical Considerations

When instructing a process server to effect service on such a body, it would be prudent to provide the process server with a list of the people who are eligible to accept service.

9.7.2.6 Service on the Crown

Personal service cannot be made on the Crown.

9.7.2.7 What steps must be taken to ensure that the address for service is the correct one?

Where a claimant has reason to believe that the address of the defendant—whether he is being served as an individual, or as a partner in an (unincorporated) partnership or in the name of a business—is an address at which the defendant no longer resides or carries on business, the claimant must take 'reasonable steps' (and make 'reasonable enquiries') to ascertain the defendant's current address (CPR 6.9(3)).

In *Smith v Hughes*, sub nom *Cranfield v Bridgegrove Ltd* [2003] EWCA Civ 656, [2003] 3 All ER 129, the Court of Appeal held that the words 'last known address' were plain and un-qualified. It did not matter that the defendant was no longer there.

Since that case, however, it must be borne in mind that CPR 6.9 now states that where the claimant has reason to believe that the address is an address at which the defendant no longer resides, he must now make 'reasonable steps to ascertain the defendant's cur-rent address'. In *Davies (R on the application of) v Kingston Upon Thames County Court* [2014] EWHC 4589, the court determined that 'reasonable steps' would include knowing that the defendant was no longer at the address for service but had a 'postal re-direction' service in place.

 Practical Considerations

The practical effect of this is that, where the claimant does have reason to believe that the defendant no longer resides at the address that he has, it appears that it would be safer to make an application for an order for 'alternative service' under CPR 6.15 than to rely on the court's interpretation of the 'reasonable steps' that have been made under CPR 6.9(3). An application under CPR 6.15 could seek, for example, an order for service at an alternative place (such as place of work) or by an alternative method (for example, care of a relative).

9.7.2.8 Service by first-class post (or an alternative service that provides for delivery on the next working day)

By this provision, a courier service or any 'next day delivery service' can be used. But it would be prudent to obtain a 'proof of posting' receipt in order to establish the fact of deemed service by the method.

9.7.2.9 Leaving the document at a specified place

The provisions for this must be distinguished from personal service: personal service requires the document(s) to be handed to an individual, while leaving document(s) at a specified place requires that it be placed through the letterbox or left at reception. Confus-ing the two can result in ineffective service, as in *Cherney v Deripaska* [2007] EWHC 965 (Comm). In this case, the claim form was 'served' on a security guard at an address that was not 'the last known residence' of the defendant, nor was the security guard an agent for the defendant for personal service to be effective, nor was it effective service by being left at a specified place.

9.7.2.10 Service through the document exchange (DX) system

Service through the document exchange (DX) system may only take place when:

- the party's address for service includes a DX number;
- the DX number is on the party's writing paper; and
- neither party nor his representative has indicated that he will *not* accept service by this method.

9.7.2.11 Service by fax or other electronic means of communication

Under the provisions of PD 6A.4, service by fax or other electronic means may only take place when:

- a party or his legal representative has expressly (in writing) indicated that he is willing to accept service by this means and

- a party has given the fax number or email address to which documents should be transmitted;

- a fax number on the legal representative's writing paper or on a statement of case is 'express notice', unless a contrary intention is given and

- service on the party 'express notice' is satisfied by express prior written consent or by the number appearing on a statement of case or in a response to a claim that has been filed at court.

Thorne v Lass Salt Garvin [2009] EWHC 10 (QB) considered the requirement to obtain a party's express consent to serve by fax. The court held that service was invalid because the claimant had not first obtained the defendant's agreement, in writing, to accept service by fax. Although the defendant was a firm of solicitors, at the time of alleged service, it was not acting as its own legal representative; therefore, the existence of the firm's fax number on the notepaper did not (in these circumstances) indicate its agreement to accept service by fax. The judgment emphasizes the importance of strict compliance with the provisions relating to service.

There is no requirement to send a hard copy of a document served by fax, but if a hard copy does follow, it would be prudent to confirm which method of service is being employed, so that there can be no confusion as to the date of dispatch of the claim form for limitation purposes, or the 'deemed date of service' from which the defendant can calculate when his defence is due.

It is also worth remembering, in preparing to serve document(s) by fax or other electronic means of communication, that the fax number must be 'in the jurisdiction'.

 Practical Considerations

Previous correspondence by fax or email in a claim will not constitute 'express consent' (see *Kuenyehia v International Hospitals Group Ltd* [2006] EWCA Civ 21 and *Hart Investments Limited v Fidler* [2006] EWHC 2857, (TCC)). In the former case, the Court of Appeal confirmed that a failure to obtain express written consent could not 'happen' in this way, and in the latter case, service by fax on the second defendant's liquidator was held to be equally ineffective through lack of express consent. The detail of these cases goes to show quite how easily a mistake can be made, through a failure to abide by the strict letter of the procedural rules for service requirements.

9.7.2.12 Service by email

The appearance of an email address on notepaper is not deemed to be 'express consent', as it can be in some circumstances for service by fax. For this to be implied, the email address will need to appear on a statement of case filed at court.

For any situation in which service is proposed to be effected by email, it is good practice to check whether there are any limitations of format or size of document to be sent. It is also good practice to confirm whether incoming emails are checked on a daily basis and who checks them—it could be that the email does not reach its intended recipient as quickly as other methods of service.

Considering the potential for error in email transmission and the fact that the deemed time for service is the same day if a business day and sent before 4.30 p.m. or the next business day, many firms will not accept service by email. Despite the fact that express notice is strictly required where email addresses appear on a firm's notepaper, it will often be accompanied by a notice 'not to be used for service'.

As with faxes, there is no requirement to send a hard copy of a document served by email, but if a hard copy does follow, it would be prudent to confirm which method of service is being employed, so that there can be no confusion of the 'deemed date of service'.

The Supreme Court has recently considered a claimant's attempts to serve by email in *Barton v Wright Hassall LLP* [2018] UKSC 12, a case concerning an unsuccessful attempt to serve proceedings by email. By a majority, the Supreme Court decided not to retrospectively validate Mr Barton's—who was a LIP—attempt at service. Mr Barton was not treated more favourably because he was a litigant in person and the Court did not accept the rules about electronic service were obscure. The Court emphasized the danger of leaving service to the last minute.

9.7.2.13 Contractually agreed methods of service

CPR 6.11 provides that a claim form may be served by a contractually agreed method where:

- the contract provides that if a claim form is issued in relation to the contract, it may be served by a method specified in the contract, and

- the claim form contains only a claim in respect of the contract.

Practical Considerations

A contractual method of service is commonly used in contracts in which the transaction is based outside the jurisdiction, and in which it would save time and expense to serve in the agreed way (for example, on a nominated firm of solicitors). In using a contractually agreed method, it is prudent to check and take care that the claim arises out of the contract.

9.7.3 EXAMPLES OF THE EFFECT OF THESE SERVICE RULES

To help you understand these examples, remember that the date of dispatch is the key date for limitation, and the deemed date of service is the key date from which the defendant calculates when his defence is due.

Example 1

A claim form expires on Friday 31 October. On that day, it is placed in a postbox at 11.30 p.m., addressed to the defendant at his usual address. The defendant is deemed served on Tuesday 4 November (the second business day after completion of the relevant step—see CPR 6.14 and 7.5). The claim form has been served 'in time'—that is, within its validity period—because the 'step required' was undertaken before the end of the period of validity of the claim form.

Example 2

A claim form expires on Saturday 1 November and is handed to the defendant personally on that day. The defendant is deemed served on Tuesday 4 November (see CPR 6.14 and 7.5). Again, the claim form has been served 'in time'—that is, within its validity period.

Example 3

A claim form expires on Friday 31 October. It is transmitted by fax that afternoon at 4.15 p.m. Provided that the transmission of the fax is completed, the claim form has been served 'in time'—that is, within its validity period—because the time given in which to complete the transmission of the fax is until midnight on Friday 31 October. The deemed date of service will be on the second business day after dispatch—that is, Tuesday 4 November.

Note: Under PD 6A.10, it is quite clear that the deemed date of service of 'other documents' by fax, email, and personal service must be completed before 4.30 p.m. This is not noted in any part of the CPR or the Practice Direction in relation to service of the claim form. The authors are, therefore, interpreting the rules in relation to the dispatch of a claim form to cover any method of service set out in Table 9.3 and that the step to effect service by the method chosen should be before midnight. There are no provisions in the new rules that indicate that the date when the 'step required' is made can ever count as the first business day, even when that step is effected before 4.30 p.m.

 Example 4

A claim form expires on Friday 31 October. At 3.00 p.m. that afternoon, the claim form is given to the accounts clerk at the defendant company's registered office in purported performance of effecting personal service. Here, there has not been valid service of the claim form, because the method chosen has not been done correctly—the accounts clerk not being within the definition of 'a senior person'.

Note: In this situation, CPR 6.15(2) may act to 'save' the situation.

 Example 5

In an action, the defendant has indicated that service may be on his nominated solicitor, but there has been no confirmation of this by the legal representatives. Service is duly effected on the firm within the time of validity of the claim form. Here, again, valid service has been effected, because for service on nominated solicitors where the nomination has been given by the defendant, there is no need to obtain the express consent of the legal representative for service on it to be good service (CPR 6.7). There has to be express consent for service on nominated solicitors, but that consent may be given by the defendant or the legal representatives.

 Example 6

Service has been effected personally on the defendant within the time of validity of the claim form, but, in this case, the legal representatives of the defendant had indicated that they have authority to accept service on their client's behalf. In this situation, there has not been good service, as consent to service on nominated legal representatives now excludes personal service on the defendant, and service must be effected on the nominated solicitors (CPR 6.7).

9.7.4 **WHEN MAY A PARTY SERVE DOCUMENTS ON A PARTY'S LEGAL REPRESENTATIVE?**

It is important to know when service is required on a party or whether it may be effected on its legal representative. It is often more convenient to serve on an opponent's legal representative, because it will be with that representative that you will probably have had all of your correspondence. Usually, when service can be effected on the legal representative, no other form of service will be valid.

Where the legal representative works from within the EEA, service must still take place on the legal representative where service on the legal representative has been notified to the serving party as the means of service on their client.

9.7.4.1 Are there any occasions on which service cannot be effected on the legal representative of a party?

The general rule is that any document may be served personally (CPR 6.5(2)). However, when a solicitor has been properly authorized to accept service, this will override the general rule, and service *must* be made on the firm of solicitors authorized to act unless:

- the document is one that must be served personally—this is when a court order requires it, or when the document or order contains a penal notice. In these situations, service on the person to be served is the only effective method of service; or
- the contractual provision relating to the action provides for a method of service that excludes service on solicitors authorized to act.

9.7.4.2 When does a legal representative have 'authority' to accept service?

CPR 6.7 operates to prevent any other method of service being effective where the legal representative, who is acting, is authorized to accept service except in the circumstances noted in CPR 6.5(1). The important point to note is that the legal representative must have the necessary express authority. Notice of this authority can be given:

- by the legal representative;
- by the party; or
- by the party's insurer when the action is subrogated to the insurer.

 Practical Considerations

Where notice has been given by the party to be served or his insurer, it is usual to seek confirmation from the legal representative in writing that he has that authority and will accept service, despite the implication from the CPR that notice may be given by the person to be served or his insurer.

An 'assumption' should never be made that a legal firm has the authority and instructions from its client to accept service on its client's behalf. Instructions authorizing a legal representative to accept service on his client's behalf must always be expressly given by the client (preferably in writing) and be expressly confirmed to the opponent wishing to serve documents. When a legal representative is acting in such a matter, and has been so acting during the course of all pre-action work and negotiations, it could be easy for an 'assumption' to be made that they will accept service on their client's behalf. But despite the fact that all correspondence on the matter has been directed to the legal representative, this does *not* mean that they have authority to, or will, accept service of proceedings—specific confirmation is required. It may be significant in the case of *Integral Petroleum Electrical Industries Ltd v Alstom UK* [2014] EWHC 430 (Comm) that the Commercial Court treated service of particulars of claim on the defendant's legal representatives by email as valid service, despite the fact that the legal representatives had not agreed to accept service by email and that the purported service was five days late. The court held that the case fell within CPR 3.10, which provides that an error of procedure does not invalidate any step in the proceedings unless the court so orders.

9.7.5 WHEN SERVICE ON A PARTY'S LEGAL REPRESENTATIVE IS NOT AVAILABLE, WHO MUST BE SERVED AND WHERE CAN THEY BE SERVED?

Save where service is to be on a person's (or firm's) legal representative who has been authorized to accept service on their behalf, service will be on the party, as set out in Table 9.3.

9.7.5.1 What steps must a party take to ensure that the address that they will use is a suitable place at which to serve?

The claimant must make 'reasonable enquiries' to ascertain the defendant's current address. 'Reasonable enquiries' is not specifically defined and will be given its natural meaning. The consequences of getting methods of service muddled or not taking enough care with ensuring proper service can be severe. In *Cherney v Deripaska* [2007] EWHC 965 (Comm), some problems arising with service were highlighted. In this case, among other things discussed, a defendant's 'occasional' residence did not fall within the definition 'usual or last known residence'. In *Cranfield v Bridgegrove Ltd* [2003] EWCA Civ 656, the Court of Appeal held that where the party had not provided an address for service, the meaning of 'last known address' could include a place at which the defendant used to live, even though it was known that he had left there (provided that 'reasonable enquiries' had been made to discover his current whereabouts).

In the case of *Relfo Ltd (in liquidation) v Varsani* [2009] EWHC 2297 (Ch), the court noted that it was possible for an individual to have more than one residence and that a party wishing to serve should look at the 'quality' of usage of the property, not simply how much time the defendant spent there.

If the defendant is in prison, he should be served in prison, not at his 'last known address'.

In effect, whenever the defendant's whereabouts is known and service on him could, therefore, be effected, it must be.

 Practical Considerations

If the defendant is thought not to be at his 'last known address', it may be more prudent to apply under CPR 6.15(2) for alternative service than to risk a conclusion that service has not been effective because the 'reasonable enquiries' were not sufficient. See examples in paragraph 9.7.3.

9.7.5.2 What happens if the documents are returned before the claimant has entered judgment?

If the document(s) served are returned undelivered before the claimant has obtained judgment, service will not be effective. In that situation, the claimant will have actual knowledge that the defendant has not received the document(s), and a valid certificate of service could not be completed.

Where this happens, the claimant will either have to try another method of service or apply to the court under the provisions of CPR 6.15 for an order for service by an alternative method.

However, if the document(s) are not returned before judgment is entered, service will be deemed to have taken place (provided that the provision as to 'reasonable enquiries' is met) even if, in fact, the defendant had never received them.

9.7.6 THE IMPORTANCE OF EFFECTIVE SERVICE

Provided that the 'step required' to effect service by the correct chosen method is achieved before the expiry of the period of validity of the claim form, it does not matter that the deemed date of service may be outside this period of validity. It is necessary to calculate the deemed date of service of the method chosen, because that is the date from which a party can calculate the appropriate period for taking a step in the action—for example, to seek a default judgment should the defendant fail to respond.

Remember, where service is by a method outside the CPR, the date of service may not have the benefit of the 'deemed service' rule.

The key to service is:

- do it on time and
- do it properly.

9.7.7 CONTESTING EFFECTIVE SERVICE

Defendants need to be able to determine whether service upon them is valid service and if not, whether it is worth contesting jurisdiction on the ground that service is invalid. If the claimant has left it until near the end of the limitation period to issue, taking a point on invalid service could dispose of the claim for good. The decision has to be made quickly, and if arguing jurisdiction on this ground, the defendant must:

- acknowledge service on Form N9 with box 3 ticked ('I intend to contest jurisdiction') within fourteen days. If the defendant files the acknowledgement of service without box 3 ticked, any defects of service are waived; and

- file an application within a further fourteen days under CPR 11(4).

The following are examples where it may be possible to dispute jurisdiction on the grounds of ineffective service:

- where only a photocopy of the claim form has been served;

- where service has been by an inappropriate method (for example, service by fax or email without express permission or by the deeming provisions in PD 6A.4.1(2));

- where service has been out of time (that is, more than four months after issue for service within the jurisdiction or six months after issue for service outside the jurisdiction);

- where service has been out of time but the claimant has obtained an extension of time from the court under CPR 7.6(2), but where the defendant feels that there appears to be good reason for the failure to serve within the appropriate four- or six-month period;

- where service has been on the wrong person (for example, on the defendant, but the defendant's solicitors had indicated that service should be effected on them—CPR 6.7); or

- where service has been at the wrong address and the claimant has made insufficient enquiry.

9.7.8 SERVICE OF DOCUMENTS OTHER THAN THE CLAIM FORM

CPR 6.20–6.29 provide separate rules for service of 'other' documents. These rules cover service of all other documents created in the action that require service *other than* documents used to initiate the proceedings (this, therefore, includes not only claim forms, but also petitions) other than the claim form. Essentially, many of the provisions for service of 'other' documents are repeated in these sections of CPR 6.

KEY POINTS SUMMARY

- Understand the criteria that will be applied to cases to place them into one of the three tracks.

- Look out for Europe-wide procedures and Money Claim Online procedures.

- Make sure that all documents required to start an action are in place and correctly completed. Decide who the parties are and describe them correctly.

- Understand and apply the rules for joining parties or causes of action together in the one claim.

- In relation to service—decide on the appropriate method of service, and ensure it is carried out properly and on time.

Case Study *Bollingtons Ltd v Mrs Elizabeth Lynch t/a The Honest Lawyer*

Question

Assume that it is now 7 October 20??. There has been no response to the letter before claim. Locate a blank claim form and complete it. A debt action such as this is relatively straightforward and this is the kind of case in which it would be appropriate to include the particulars of claim on the reverse side of the claim form itself—that is, an indorsed claim form. You will need to consider, and deal with, the claim for interest. You do not need to complete any calculations for interest, but make any provision in your draft for what you would have done. You will need to consult Chapter 11 to inform your drafting.

Case Study *Andrew James Pike v Deep Builders Ltd*

The insurers of Deep Builders Ltd have indicated that they accept that Mr Deep was acting in the course of his employment at the time of the accident but deny any negligence, alleging that Andrew Pike was responsible for the accident. You have obtained a medical report from Mr Edgar Higgins. Please read this in the online resources.

Question

Look at the draft particulars of claim available in the online resources. Consider this partially completed document and complete the remaining sections so that it meets the requirements of the CPR. You will need to consult Chapter 11 to inform your drafting.

Any documents referred to in these case study questions can be found in the online resources—simply click on 'Case study documentation' to access the documents that you need for Chapter 9 and to be reminded of the questions. Suggested answers to these case study questions can be accessed in the Student Resources section of the online resources.

Relevant court forms relating to this chapter:

- N9 Response Pack
- N211 Part 20 Claim Form

Relevant parts of the CPR and its PDs: 3, 9, 10, 11, 12, 14, 15, 18, 20, 24, 25, and 43x.

10.1 INTRODUCTION

It would be wrong to believe that the defendant will take a reactive role in the action, seeking only to fend off the claimant's case, sitting back and waiting to see if the claimant can establish his case. In modern litigation, the defendant will take a more proactive role. Additionally, the expectation that the parties will have engaged in Protocol should ensure that only the cases where both parties believe that they have a reasonable 'claim' or 'defence' or 'defence and counterclaim' commence litigation, and, thus, the defendant is very likely to have substantive responses to make to the claimant's claim. The Civil Procedure Rules (CPR) deny the defendant the right, in his defence, simply to deny the allegations against him.

LITIGATION TRAIN: ACTING FOR A DEFENDANT, RESPONDING TO THE CLAIM, THE CONSEQUENCES OF FAILING TO RESPOND

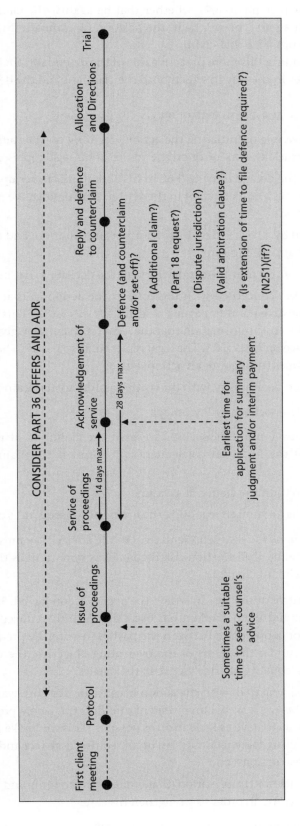

A defendant is charged with the duties of explaining any defence that he files and setting down why he submits that the claimant's allegations are false or cannot be substantiated.

Where the defendant makes an additional claim (which may be a counterclaim) in his defence (see paragraph 10.6.2), whether that be against the claimant or against another person not yet a party, he will be in the position of 'claimant' in that action, so will have the burden of proof for that claim.

Notwithstanding this more proactive role of the defendant, there are distinct differences and similarities in the way in which both the claimant and the defendant are 'involved' in the action.

The claimant, as a client, will, or may:

- take an active role in initiating the action, deciding on the cause(s) of action that he intends to pursue either alone or on the advice of his legal representative;

- decide who the defendant(s) will be in his action. It is never up to the defendant to join another party as a co-defendant in the action. That prerogative is the claimant's and only the claimant's;

- be motivated by a desire to seek justice and compensation, and to 'right a wrong' that he alleges has happened to him;

- exert some control over the action through the decisions that he takes;

- perhaps be less concerned with the costs of the action in that he hopes that the court will order the defendant to pay his costs if he is successful. This view may manifest itself despite all the costs information that the legal representative gives to his claimant clients and the advice on costs risks. The legal representative needs to be aware of managing this view at all times throughout an action; and

- potentially be 'economical with the truth' in order to maintain the strengths of his case.

The defendant, as a client, will, or may:

- have a defensive mindset, seeking to resist the claim, or, at the very least, to reduce significantly the financial consequences for him if the claimant should succeed in his claim;

- be seeking to limit the claimant's claim;

- have concerns for himself regarding the financial consequences of the action against him.

Note: The burdens for legal representatives in the advice they must give to their defendant clients on costs and the litigation risk is equally as important as the burden upon them to advise their claimant clients.

- have less control of the way in which the action is conducted. This 'difference' between the claimant and the defendant has been significantly reduced by the CPR and the requirement for cooperation between the parties in both the pre-action and the litigation stages. Also, under the terms of the overriding objective, the court will be looking to maintain an 'equality of arms' between the parties;

- simply be less 'engaged' with the action because he does not want to be involved in it at all. He may be angry at his involvement and find the whole procedure something with which he wants to have as little to do as possible. This can make the legal representative's job harder. Acting for defendants can often require more tact and perseverance in obtaining timely instructions; and

- potentially withhold information (that is damaging to him), and he may also be 'economical with the truth' in order to strengthen his case.

Whilst the procedural rules embodied in the CPR apply equally to claimants and defendants, it would be wrong to say that acting as legal representative for either is the same. In practice, legal representatives have had a tendency to specialize in 'claimant work' or 'defendant work', but this division is by no means universal. Firms that regularly handle both claimant and defendant work need to engage with the differing skills that apply to acting for one party and with the other.

It is unlikely in modern litigation that the service of a claim form upon the defendant will be the first that he knows of the claim being made against him. It is probable that he will have received earlier correspondence from the claimant and, if Protocol has been fully followed by the claimant and the defendant, the essence of each party's case will have been set out by each of them before proceedings have been started. This information will be formally contained in the letter of claim and in the response to the letter of claim, but also possibly in other pre-action correspondence. The parties may have engaged in some disclosure of evidence, had meetings, disclosed or exchanged experts' findings, and participated in some form of alternative dispute resolution (ADR) in the pre-action stage.

This chapter, in considering the options open to a defendant faced with a claim against him, will cover:

- the emotional responses of the defendant;
- the defendant's pre-action position;
- the way in which a defendant may fund the litigation;
- the essential steps needed to respond to a claim;
- the substantive responses to the action; and
- tactical responses to the claim.

10.2 THE DEFENDANT'S RESPONSE

There is a wide spectrum of responses that the defendant, as your client, may take to the action issued against him.

- He may **deny liability**—that is, he may entirely refute the liability allegations made against him. In order to do this, he will need to be able to proffer an alternate version of the story that the claimant has put forward. He will need to be able to give a version that satisfies the court that the claimant's case is not made. He may seek to achieve this by challenging the evidence of the claimant or by adducing evidence of his own that supports his version of how the 'event' (the allegations of the claimant) happened.

- He may **deny causation**—that is, he may accept some involvement in the events set out by the claimant, but deny that his actions either caused the breach or accident, or that the breach or event caused the damages and losses that the claimant alleges. To do this, he will need either to refute and challenge the claimant's case on causation, or to adduce evidence of his own that substantiates his denial.

- He may **deny quantum**, either by:
  - stating that he denies the nature and extent of the injuries or damage, and seek to suggest that the claimant contributed to his injuries; or
  - both admitting and denying—that is, by admitting parts of the claimant's case, but denying other parts of it.

- He may **seek a settlement**—in which case, he will be motivated to bring the action to an end as quickly as possible.

Clearly, in acting for a defendant, 'what' the defendant seeks to do will affect 'how' he will achieve it. A defendant can alter or affect the way in which the claim continues by the way in which he responds to it, and, thus, it is extremely important that the legal representative has clear instructions from the defendant and that the defendant fully understands the steps that will be taken on his behalf by the legal representative.

10.3 **THE DEFENDANT'S PRE-ACTION BEHAVIOUR**

10.3.1 **WHAT IS A DEFENDANT'S LEVEL OF ENGAGEMENT IN PROTOCOL?**

Chapter 8 deals with much of the pre-action work to be undertaken by the parties if they abide by Protocol. This section concentrates on, and will act as a reminder of, Protocol practice—but from the defendant's perspective.

Within Protocol, the defendant will need to ensure that he acknowledges the claimant's letter of claim (or letter before claim) within the time the letter has stipulated, because, under most Protocol practice, a failure to acknowledge the letter of claim will enable the claimant to proceed to issue proceedings. In those circumstances, it is highly likely that the defendant's failure to abide by Protocol practice will come back to haunt him in an unfavourable costs order within the litigation, especially if the court regards the failure to have significantly increased the costs or been the main reason why the action was started, when, had he cooperated, there may not have been a need for the action to have been started at all.

Having acknowledged the claimant's letter of claim, the defendant will then have a period of time in which to investigate the claimant's claim so that he can respond to the allegations. The period of time that the defendant should have to undertake these investigations will vary, but will be suggested in a Protocol applying to the action, or in the Practice Direction on Pre-Action Conduct and Protocols (PDPACP). The courts will expect the parties to act 'reasonably' and in accordance with the spirit of Protocol practice, and in accordance with the aims of the overriding objective. The parties may agree between themselves a reasonable time for the defendant to 'investigate' and be in a position at the end of that period to send a formal letter of response, or they may use the time suggested by the Protocol applying to the case. The steps taken by both parties in the pre-action stage should be 'reasonable' and 'proportionate'.

Once the defendant has investigated the claimant's allegation, he should reply fully to the letter of claim with a formal letter of response.

10.3.2 **THE CONTENTS OF A LETTER OF RESPONSE**

The letter of response should:

- say whether the claim is accepted in whole or in part, and make proposals for settlement; or
- state that the claim is not accepted, with detailed reasons.

In either of these two situations, the defendant needs to define which parts he accepts (if any) and which he refutes. Where he refutes the allegations, he needs to give detailed reasons for his conclusions.

- Where the claimant's allegations are being refuted, in addition to giving detailed reasons, the defendant should enclose documents for which the claimant has asked. If any documents requested by the claimant are not being sent, the defendant will need to give his reasons why they are not being supplied.
- The defendant may also request documents from the claimant (and the claimant should respond to this request within a reasonable time, and if the documents requested are not being sent, give reasons why not).
- The defendant should also state whether he is prepared to enter into a form of ADR, which might include:
  - discussion and negotiation;
  - early neutral evaluation (ENE) by an agreed third party; or
  - mediation.
- Although a party cannot be compelled to enter into a form of ADR, we have seen in Chapter 5 that the courts will take account of a party's response to the possibility of

settling the dispute by a form of ADR when considering the appropriate costs order that may be made in the action (see also Chapter 15, which contains details of the powerful use that a defendant may make of CPR Part 36 offers to settle).

- The parties should also take steps to consider any expert evidence that may be required and seek to agree on the use of an independent expert. Any steps that the parties make towards agreeing the use of experts does not, however, preclude the court from making any order as to expert evidence that it feels is appropriate. Both claimants and defendants in litigation should be advised by their legal representatives that any expert engaged in Protocol may not be permitted in the litigation, and that the costs of engaging that expert may not be recoverable.

- The defendant may, if he wishes to do so, notify the claimant if he has entered into a relevant funding arrangement that falls within the meaning of the pre-2013 CPR 43.2(1)(k) (which remains in force for pre-commencement funding arrangements pursuant to CPR 48.1).

10.3.3 IS THE DEFENDANT BOUND BY THE MATTERS THAT HE RAISES IN HIS LETTER OF RESPONSE IN ANY SUBSEQUENT LITIGATION?

In the Protocol phase, neither party is restricted to the matters and allegations that they raised in their letter of claim or letter of response. However, if the changes or additions to a party's case arise from an intent to mislead the other party during the Protocol phase, the court is likely to impose costs sanctions against the misleading party.

 Practical Considerations

Notwithstanding the professional conduct implications of inconsistencies between the defendant's letter of response and his subsequent defence, a significant departure from the defendant's original position contained in the letter of response can reduce his credibility. This may also encourage a claimant's application for summary judgment or strike-out (see Chapter 14, paragraph 14.3, and see paragraphs 10.7.1 and 10.7.2).

10.3.4 WHAT IS THE POSITION IF THE DEFENDANT MAKES AN ADMISSION DURING PROTOCOL?

The CPR encourage admissions, because they narrow the issues between the parties, usually save costs, and they will perhaps aid settlement being achieved. However, legal representatives should be aware of the importance of admissions and the consequences of them. In *Mack v Clarke* [2017] EWHC 113 (QB), the court considered the issues surrounding admissions confirming that CPR 14.1(5) was intended to reduce costs and delay and narrow the issues through unequivocal and clear concessions of claims or parts of claims.

10.3.4.1 What constitutes an admission?

An admission may be made of the truth of an allegation or of the facts stated, and it may be express or implied. It may be found in correspondence, or in oral discussions between the parties and their legal representatives, or between a party and a third party. An admission can also be inferred by conduct.

10.3.4.2 What are the consequences of a pre-action admission?

The consequence of a formal admission (for example, made in response to a notice to admit, in writing in open correspondence) will be that neither party will need to adduce evidence at trial of the issue or fact admitted. Informal admissions, such as an implicit acknowledgement of a state of affairs, are treated as pieces of evidence and further evidence may be adduced to disprove the informal admission or to explain away its apparent result. Equally, an admission made without knowledge of a material fact will have little evidential value.

10.3.4.3 Is a potential party always bound by a pre-action admission?

A party will not be bound by a previously made admission in the following circumstances:

- an admission made in previous proceedings that have not been placed before the current court as adopted and true;

- an informal admission that is not proved;

- an admission made by a person not authorized to make it unless there existed ostensible or apparent authority (of the agent), in which case the admission may bind (the principal), but he may have a right to claim an indemnity from the person who made the unauthorized admission; and

- an admission that is not clear and unambiguous.

10.3.4.4 Can admissions be withdrawn?

A formal admission may be withdrawn in certain circumstances, as follows:

- It may be withdrawn with the permission of the court (CPR 14.1(5)). The court will consider the overriding objective when considering such an application and will consider such issues as prejudice to a party, the reasons why the admission was made, the stress that a party was under when the admission was made, the interests of the public in permitting the withdrawal of the formal admission, and the time at which the application to withdraw from the admission is made.

- A pre-action admission can be withdrawn at any time without requiring the permission of the court, unless it is a personal injury, clinical negligence, or disease and injury claim (see the commentary in the White Book at paragraph 14.1.8 and the Pre-Action Protocol for Personal Injury Claims C2A-004).

- In exercising its discretion as to whether to allow an admission to be withdrawn the court will have regard to the guidance set out in the case of *Braybrook v Basildon & Thurrock Univeristy NHS Trust,* October 7, 2004 (Lawtel). That guidance is now codified in the Practice Direction to Part 14 at paragraph 7.2.

- Three important cases have considered the effect of formal admissions: *Sowerby v Charlton* [2005] EWCA Civ 1610; *The Governing Body of Charterhouse School v Hannaford Upright* [2007] EWHC 2718; and *Stoke on Trent City Council v John Walley* [2006] EWCA Civ 1137. These cases have held that:

  – permission may not be granted if it is made late (and close to the trial);

  – permission may be granted when the admission was made by mistake; and

  – permission will depend upon whether the admission was made pre-action or not.

- Following the outcome of these cases and further consultation, CPR 14.1A states that a person may withdraw a pre-action admission:

  – with the consent of the person to whom the admission was made; and

  – after commencement of proceedings with the permission of the court.

- These conditions apply when:

  – the admission was made in proceedings listed under the rule—that is, personal injury, clinical disputes, and disease and illness claims; and

  – the admission was made after a letter of claim has been sent, or if before, the admission states that it has been made under the provisions of CPR 14.

- The rule also makes provision for these pre-action admissions to be dealt with in subsequent litigation as follows:

  – that any party may apply for judgment on a pre-action admission that is covered under the rule; and

  – the party who made the admission can apply to the court to withdraw it (and the court will apply the criteria noted here when considering the application).

The case of *Moore v Worcestershire NHS Trust* [2015] EWHC 1209 (Q3) is a recent reminder of this important concept. However, in this case the defendant was allowed to withdraw an admission because it 'arose by mistake'.

10.3.5 WHAT IS THE POSITION OF AN EXPERT ENGAGED BY A PARTY IN PROTOCOL?

It will be for the claimant to decide whether any expert report that he has obtained in Protocol will be disclosed to the defendant (see also Chapter 8, paragraph 8.10.2.8, and Chapter 18, paragraph 18.12.1). A favourable report may increase the chances of achieving a settlement, but it will also give the defendant plenty of time to 'pick holes' in the claimant's expert report. Although there is encouragement in Protocol to seek to agree the use of a jointly selected expert, this does not mean that the claimant is forced to do so and, in any event, he may have engaged an 'advisory expert' (see Chapter 18, paragraph 18.8.1) to help him to formulate his case. The defendant also may wish to engage the assistance of his own expert. In personal injury claims, the claimant should not unreasonably refuse to be examined by the defendant's nominated expert.

Where the claimant has proffered the names of experts in Protocol, and where the defendant has not rejected an expert from that list and the claimant so instructs that expert, the defendant will not be permitted to engage his own expert within proceedings unless the court permits.

10.4 HOW MAY A DEFENDANT FUND THE COSTS INCURRED IN DEFENDING THE CASE AGAINST HIM?

A defendant has the same methods of funding his action available to him as those that are available to the claimant and he may agree or negotiate any of these with his legal representative. Essentially, these include:

- a private retainer with his legal representative; or
- a conditional fee agreement (CFA)—the definition of what would be deemed a 'success' in such an arrangement (where a success fee is included in the agreement) will be specifically set down in the CFA contract with his legal representative. It may vary from succeeding in resisting the claim to attaining a reduction in the sum of the claim. Notice of such a funding arrangement may be given to the claimant. (The 'success' fee element of a CFA entered into after 1 April 2013 is not recoverable from the claimant, and, in such circumstances, there is no requirement to give notice of the funding arrangement to the opponent.); or
- a damage-based agreement—probably only an option for a defendant as a method of funding for any substantial counterclaim he is pursuing.

Further details of these funding arrangements are outlined in Chapter 3, paragraph 3.3.

Defendants are under the same obligations to abide by the principles of the overriding objective to ensure that the litigation is conducted with 'a view to controlling expenses' and in conducting the action 'proportionately'.

A defendant who is engaged in litigation, but feels that the claimant may be unable to satisfy any costs order made against him, may, in certain circumstances, apply to the court for an order for security for costs within the provisions of CPR 25.12 (see paragraph 10.7.3 and Chapter 14, paragraph 14.7).

10.5 THE STEPS AND TIME LIMITS FOR RESPONDING TO A CLAIM

The defendant need not take any action in response to the claim issued against him until the particulars of claim have been served on him. Remember that the claimant is not obliged to serve the particulars of claim at the same time as the claim form, but if he does serve the claim form without the particulars of claim, he must serve the particulars of claim within fourteen days of serving the claim form (see Chapter 9, paragraph 9.3.5). When the claimant serves the particulars of claim, it will be accompanied with the response pack in Form N9A or Form N9C, which are supplied by the court. Form N9A will be used when the claimant's action is for a specified sum; Form N9C will be used when the claim is for an unspecified sum.

Time begins to run from the deemed date of service (see Chapter 9, paragraph 9.7.1.1) of the particulars of claim on the defendant (CPR 9.2). The defendant has fourteen days from that date in which to:

- file or serve an admission or
- file a defence (which may be combined with a counterclaim) (this may use Form N11 or be drafted separately) or
- file an acknowledgement of service.

Each of these options is now considered.

10.5.1 ADMITTING THE CLAIM AND REQUESTING TIME TO PAY

Forms N9A and N9C make provision for admissions to be made. Admissions may be made of the whole claim or a part of it. Where only part is being admitted, the defendant will need to file a defence to that part of the claim that is not admitted, otherwise the claimant will be able to apply for judgment in default of that part. In either case, the forms also make provision for the defendant to make provision to pay the sum admitted or to ask for time to pay.

Where the defendant seeks time to pay the sum admitted, he must also complete those parts of the form that require details of his assets, income, and outgoings. The completed form will be sent to the claimant, who may raise objections to the defendant's instalment payment offer that he will include in the form. Where the claimant raises objections to the offer, the court will either set the level of instalments or set the matter down for a disposal hearing. The specific detail and order of instalment offers and terms are set down in CPR 14.

Where the defendant admits the whole claim within fourteen days of service of the particulars of claim, he will be liable for the fixed costs of the action. Details of the sum of these fixed costs will be contained in the bottom right-hand box on the front page of the Form N1 claim form. Where the defendant admits the whole claim, the admission in one of the Forms N9 will be sent directly to the claimant rather than filed at court and the claimant will be able to obtain judgment on the claim by filing a request for judgment in either Form N225 or Form N227.

Where the defendant has requested time to pay, the claimant will have to respond to the offer and either accept it or raise objections. If the admission is of the whole claim, or the claimant accepts the instalment offer, the court will proceed to issue the judgment order in Form N30. The judgment will include accrued interest and the fixed costs. The judgment is also registered in the Register of Judgments. Because registration of a judgment debt may affect a defendant's creditworthiness, it is worth noting that a defendant may avoid registration of the debt if he has admitted the whole claim and paid the sum due and fixed costs within fourteen days of service of the particulars of claim.

If the defendant's admission is for part of the claim, but has an offer to satisfy the whole claim, the claimant has the option of accepting the sum offered. If he does accept the sum offered, the matter will proceed as stated and the court will proceed to make the judgment order. If the offer is rejected, the case will proceed as a disputed claim.

In unspecified sum claims in which the defendant has filed an admission of the claim, the matter will be stayed and set down for a disposal hearing for the court to determine the sum of the claim. Directions will be given as to the evidence to be filed and exchanged in advance of the disposal hearing.

Where the defendant is a child or protected party, the court must approve any admission, or part-admission, or offer to pay by an instalment option. (For further details of child or protected party applications, see Chapter 9, paragraph 9.5.)

10.5.2 FILING A DEFENCE

If the defendant intends to defend the action against him, he will need to file and serve his defence. The defence may be drafted on Form N11 or be a separately drafted document (see Chapter 11, paragraph 11.5). CPR 15 contains the rules for the filing of the defence and service upon every other party in the action. These rules include provisions that:

- a defendant who wishes to file a defence should do so within fourteen days after service upon him of the particulars of claim;
- a defendant who files an acknowledgement of service within fourteen days (after service upon him of the particulars of claim) must serve his defence within twenty-eight days after service upon him of the particulars of claim; and
- the time limits of fourteen days and twenty-eight days do not apply when the defendant resides outside the jurisdiction (the alternative time limits are set down in CPR 6.33), or when the defendant is disputing jurisdiction, he need not file a defence (CPR 11), or when the claimant makes an application for summary judgment, the defendant need not file a defence before the hearing of the claimant's application (CPR 24.4).

Forms N9A, N9C, and N9D provide space for a defence to the claim to be made. Where a party is legally represented, the defence will usually be separately drafted in the form and structure detailed in Chapter 11, paragraph 11.5.

 Practical Considerations

Acting for a defendant will require as many, if not more, matters to be discussed with the client than may be discussed with a claimant to establish whether he has a claim. Although the claimant will have formulated the substance of the claim, a defendant has a variety of options that may be available to him to respond and defend the claim (see further paragraph 10.6). A defendant should admit what should be admitted. Costs penalties and professional conduct Principles will apply if there has been any deliberate, or careless, intention to mislead the court or if a defendant is reluctant to admit those parts of the claim that clearly should be admitted. Ambiguous claims can be amended or put right, and it is important that you, as the legal representative, seek to balance the interests of the overriding objective and the need to be 'cooperative' in litigation with what may be in the 'best interests' of the client. Where a claim is being 'denied', the legal representative should consider whether there is evidence that is credible and admissible to support the defence. It is not simply a case of waiting to see if the claimant can establish his case.

Further, clients may not always understand the intricacies of their actions—for example, in claims for misrepresentation. Misrepresentation arises where something is said with the *intention* of inducing a contract and *does* induce a contract. Clients will not always understand the difference between pre-contractual enquiry and true misrepresentation. These misunderstandings have to be managed by the legal representative. These and many other matters may arise in acting for a defendant in even the simplest of actions.

10.5.2.1 Extending the time for service of the defence

The time limits for filing a defence may be extended by agreement between the parties. The parties can agree an extension up to a maximum of a further twenty-eight days. When such an agreement is made, the defendant must inform the court of the period of the extension (CPR 15.5). If any greater extension of time is required, whether the claimant consents or not, an application must be made to the court. The application must be justified in terms of the overriding objective.

 Practical Considerations

In any dispute resolution department, any legal representative has to be more than simply able to undertake the procedural requirements of litigation—he must also be commercially aware. In commercial matters, one or both sides to the claim may be in business and an awareness of the implications of this are important if the legal representative is to 'serve' his client's best interests. The action may have a significant cash flow impact on the business; the parties to the action may need to, or wish to, continue their business relationship. These, and other, business-related issues need to be understood and 'managed' within the action.

Once the defence is filed, the court's case management role is started with the notification of intended allocation and direction of the issuing of the DQ (directions questionnaire) to all parties. Chapter 12 sets out the detail and consequences for the parties of this step.

10.5.2.2 If no defence is filed and served

If the defendant fails to file a defence within the period specified, in most actions, the claimant will be able to obtain default judgment (CPR 12.3). This precludes the defendant from defending the claim further (see Chapter 14, paragraph 14.2, for details of how the claimant can secure default judgment and what the defendant can do to have it set aside). Default judgment is not permitted if the claim is for delivery of goods that are subject to an agreement regulated by the Consumer Credit Act 1974, or in CPR Part 8 proceedings, or in any other case in which a Practice Direction provides (CPR 12.2).

If a defence is not filed and the claimant fails to seek default judgment, six months after the date on which the defence should have been filed, the claim will be stayed (CPR 15.11).

10.5.3 FILING AN ACKNOWLEDGEMENT OF SERVICE

The form of acknowledgement of service is used by a defendant for three reasons. The defendant will file and serve the acknowledgement of service when he is unable to file his defence within fourteen days of the service upon him of the particulars of claim, but intends to defend some or all of the claim, or he may file it when he admits some or all of the claim, but wishes to have time to pay, or he may file it when he intends to signify (and take no other step in the action) that he disputes the jurisdiction of the court to hear the action.

The acknowledgement of service form is included with Form N9 (A, B, C, or D) and must be filed at the court out of which the claim is issued. It will ask for the following information:

- the defendant's full name—if the defendant's name has been incorrectly stated in the claim, the defendant will set out his correct name in the acknowledgement of service; and

- the defendant's full address for service, including postcode—this may be a personal or a business address, and if the defendant is legally represented, his legal representative will state the firm's address for service. Service of the claim on a partnership may be acknowledged by any of the partners served or someone authorized to acknowledge on behalf of the partnership, and if served on a company, the form of acknowledgement may be signed by a director or a person holding a senior position in the company (the person signing also indicating his position in the company).

See the online resources for a copy of the acknowledgement of service.

10.5.3.1 Disputing all or part of the claim

The defendant must tick one of two boxes on the form confirming whether he intends to defend all or part of the claim. He must then file his defence within the time limit now available to him by having filed the acknowledgement of service (see paragraph 10.5.2). The filing of the acknowledgement of service is also the trigger point for some interim applications—for example, either party may make an application for summary judgment, or the claimant may make an application for an interim payment. If the defendant admits the claim but wishes to have time to pay or pay by instalments he will complete a means form with the form of acknowledgement.

10.5.3.2 Contesting jurisdiction

If the defendant intends to contest the jurisdiction of the claim against him, he must tick the box confirming this. If a defendant intends to do this, he must take care not to take steps in the action beyond acknowledging service of the claim form (CPR 11). He must then, within fourteen days, make an application, supported with written evidence, disputing the jurisdiction of the court (CPR 11(4)). The defendant need not—in fact, should not—file his defence until after the court has heard his application. A defence will be required from him if his application disputing jurisdiction has failed, usually within fourteen days of the court's decision declaring that the action is correctly being dealt with within the jurisdiction. Sometimes, the application is clear: for example, there may be a valid agreement for the matter to be submitted to arbitration. Sometimes, the application disputing the jurisdiction of the court may be made because there is a choice, in which case, the court will exercise its discretion in accordance with the principles of the overriding objective.

If the defendant does not make an application to the court under the provisions of CPR 11(4), he will be treated as if he has accepted that the court does have jurisdiction to hear the claim.

See also Chapter 9, paragraph 9.7.7, for examples where the defendant may seek to challenge jurisdiction on the grounds of ineffective or invalid service of the claim form.

10.6 THE DEFENCE OF A CLAIM

10.6.1 COMMON DEFENCES

A defence is required when a defendant wishes to defend all or part of a claim. Once filed, a copy of the defence must be served on every other party. The time limits for the filing of a defence are set out at CPR 15.4 and in paragraph 10.5.

'Defences' can be broadly subdivided into the following categories, which can be used exclusively or concurrently if appropriate:

- **Procedural defences.** These could include, for example:
  - a submission that the court does not have jurisdiction or
  - a submission that the claim is outside the limitation period.
- **Defences to the cause of action.** These could include submissions that state:
  - that the claim does not disclose a cause of action or
  - that, on the evidence, the cause of action is not established on the balance of probabilities or
  - that, on the grounds of the defence, the defendant is absolved from liability.
- **Defences to the claim for damages.** These could include submissions that:
  - the claim does not set out all of the required elements for a claim for damages; or
  - on the evidence, the elements of the remedy sought are not, on the balance of probabilities, substantiated; or
  - on the facts, the loss was not caused by the breach (causation); or
  - on the facts, the loss was not foreseeable; or
  - on the facts, the claimant has failed to mitigate his loss; or further
  - in a negligence or breach of contract action, the claimant was also negligent or in breach, and contributed to his loss and damage.

It can be seen that some of these defences will act as defences to the claim itself, while others will seek to reduce (or eliminate) the liability that the claimant alleges has arisen, but 'liability' itself is accepted. We refer to the latter case as an admission of 'primary liability' coupled with an allegation of contributory negligence against the claimant. (See Chapter 11, paragraph 11.5, for details on how to draft some of these defences.)

One of the options that may be part of the defendant's case may be to seek to pass the blame or liability of the claimant's action to another. This is dealt with next.

10.6.2 **PART 20 CLAIMS**

A defendant faced with an action against him may have:

- no issue with the fact that the claimant has suffered a loss, but he may feel that responsibility for some or all of those losses does not lie with him, but with somebody else;
- a claim of his own that he would like to bring that arises out of the same set of circumstances.

In these circumstances, a defendant can use the provisions set out in CPR 20. CPR 20 essentially enables the defendant to make four types of additional claim, the nature of each of which is examined here. The correct terminology for this type of claim is an 'additional claim', but you will often see it referred to as a 'Part 20 claim'.

By way of definition, an 'additional claim' is any claim other than that initiated by the claimant against the defendant. This could also be called the 'main action'. Although CPR Part 20 claims are procedurally connected with the main action, they can be entirely separate claims. A settlement or action terminating the main action will not usually terminate an additional claim unless it is included in the agreement or order terminating the main action. It will depend on the nature of the additional claim and whether it is worth pursuing it after the settlement or termination of the main action. For example, if the defendant has sought a contribution or indemnity, the dismissal or striking out of the main action will render it pointless continuing with the claim for a contribution or indemnity, because there will be no sum to which to contribute or to indemnify.

10.6.2.1 A counterclaim brought by the defendant against the claimant (CPR 20.4)

A counterclaim is a claim in its own right that lies against the claimant in the action. It could form the basis of a separate claim by the defendant against the claimant in separate proceedings, but in these circumstances the defendant does not have the choice of issuing his own proceedings against the claimant, because when there is already litigation existing between the parties (because of the main action started by the claimant), the defendant must—apart from for reasons of convenience, efficiency, and cost-effectiveness—bring his counterclaim in the same set of proceedings where the counterclaim arises from the same, or substantially the same, set of facts as the claimant's claim.

The subject matter of the counterclaim need not be precisely the same as the proceedings started by the claimant against the defendant, but the claimant and the defendant must sue and be sued in the same capacity.

Determining whether the defence has a true counterclaim requires careful legal and factual analysis, as follows:

- A defendant's case that amounts to a simple dispute of the facts set down by the claimant in the action is not a counterclaim. An example of this could be where the defendant disputes the terms of the contract that form the basis of the claimant's case.
- If the defendant's case against the claimant amounts to a simple defence to the allegations against him, these are matters that would be raised in the defence, not in any counterclaim. An example of this situation would be where the defendant alleges contributory negligence on the part of the claimant. This also is not an 'additional claim' under CPR Part 20. In this situation, the defendant should set out his allegations in the defence, stating what duty or act the claimant failed to discharge or undertake that contributed to the losses that he sustained.
- Any situation in which the defendant has a separate claim that has all of the requirements of a true action against the claimant (where related to the facts of the main action), would be a counterclaim within the provisions of CPR Part 20.
- Where the defendant blames someone else and claims to have no personal responsibility for the claimant's loss or damage, such a claim would be included in the defendant's defence and would not be a counterclaim. An example of such a situation would be if, in

a road traffic accident (RTA), the defendant were to claim that the RTA was wholly caused by the claimant or someone else, or in a breach of contract action, if the defendant were to claim that he acted as agent rather than principal, or where the defendant claims to be absolved from the claim by an exclusion clause. These are defences, not counterclaims.

 Example

A claimant issues proceedings against a defendant for non-payment on an information technology (IT) service and maintenance contract. The defendant denies the allegations, stating that the IT works had not been effected correctly and that, as a result, his company has suffered loss of production.

The defence here is the allegation that the claimant had not performed his part of the contract properly, and the counterclaim is the monetary losses to the defendant, which he incurred as a result of those breaches by the claimant. The flowchart in Figure 10.1 at the end of this chapter illustrates this.

Therefore, the key features of a counterclaim are as follows:

- It is brought by an existing defendant in an action against the claimant.
- It arises out of the same, or substantially the same, facts as the claimant's claim against the defendant.
- It is a monetary claim in its own right.
- It is not a defence.
- The court heading identifying the parties will not change. It will be identical to the court heading on the particulars of claim.

A 'simple' counterclaim by the defendant against the claimant (such as that described in the previous example) is a situation in which it can be seen quite clearly that the party's claims against each other should be heard in the same action, avoiding the potential situation of two courts reaching different conclusions based on the same facts. However, if the claims are so different from one another that there is no overlap of evidence or facts, and the combining of the actions is unlikely to result in a saving of costs or time, it may indicate that the claims should be independently processed.

See Chapter 11, paragraph 11.6.1, for an example of a drafted counterclaim.

10.6.2.2 A counterclaim brought by the defendant against a person other than the claimant (CPR 20.5)

This type of additional claim is against a person who is not already a party to the action, but against whom the defendant has a monetary claim that arises out of the same set of facts. Therefore, much of paragraph 10.6.2.1 will apply in terms of identifying a true counterclaim as opposed to a defence, but, of course, the additional party will not be the claimant, because it must be a person who is not already involved in the proceedings.

The easiest way to explain this is by way of an example.

 Example

The claimant, Pearl Fisher, is injured in an RTA whilst driving in the course of her employment with Purcell Logistics Ltd and issues proceedings against the defendant, Scott Butler. The defendant denies negligence and alleges contributory negligence against the claimant. The defendant wants to make a counterclaim, because his truck was badly damaged, as were the materials in the truck. The counterclaim technically lies against the claimant's employer, owing to the principle of vicarious liability, but the employer is not a party to the action. If the defendant wants to pursue a counterclaim formally, then he will need to issue a Part 20 claim against the claimant's employer under CPR 20.5. The flowchart in Figure 10.2 at the end of this chapter illustrates this.

Practical Considerations

In practice, as would have been identified during Protocol correspondence between the claimant and defendant, what, in fact, would happen in this example is that the claimant's legal representative would have passed details of the counterclaim on to her employer's insurer, which would subrogate the counterclaim. It would confirm that the claimant was driving in the course of her employment and, in order to deal with the defence of the counterclaim proportionately and reasonably in this case, it would agree with the claimant's and defendant's legal representatives that it would allow the claimant's legal representative to conduct the defence to the counterclaim, indemnify them in respect of any costs, and abide by any judgment and costs orders made in respect of the counterclaim.

In such actions, the title of the action will change. The heading of a claim with a CPR Part 20 claim could look like that detailed here. (Note that the defendant refers to the Part 20 defendant as a 'third party'.)

MRS PEARL FISHER   Claimant

and

MR SCOTT BUTLER   Defendant

and

PURCELL LOGISTICS LTD   Third Party

These additional claims do not operate as a defence to the action either.

10.6.2.3 An additional claim brought by the defendant seeking a contribution or an indemnity (CPR 20.6)

A defendant may make such a claim for a contribution, or an indemnity or other remedy, from an existing party, usually another defendant, in which case the claim will be called a 'Contribution Notice'. Such a claim may arise between joint tortfeasors, joint contractors, joint sureties, joint debtors, or joint trustees. The sum of the 'contribution' will be based either on the facts of the joint responsibility, or on the basis of the degree of blame for the claimant's loss and damage. A claim for a contribution will usually seek to share the liability. A claim for an indemnity, however, seeks to pass on the entire liability to the indemnifier; an indemnity may arise under a contract, under statute, or by virtue of the relationship between the defendant and additional party. A party can also seek to claim both a contribution and an indemnity from its co-defendant.

Example

Claims for contribution are frequently found in road traffic actions, as follows:

The claimant had emerged from a set of traffic lights at a crossroads and was waiting to turn right in the junction. He was stationary. Two vehicles travelling in the opposite direction collided with him. The claimant issued proceedings against both defendants. The first defendant served a contribution notice, requesting that the second defendant agree to a 60:40 liability split in favour of the first defendant, in accordance with CPR 20.6.

Claims for indemnity are frequently found in commercial claims, as follows:

The claimant contracted with an architect to design a home for him. He also engaged a building company to construct the property. The property was defective, and the claimant issued proceedings against both the architect and the building company. In the architect's defence, he denied the claimant's claim and blamed his co-defendant for all of the claimant's losses. The architect in this situation served an additional claim for an indemnity against the building company. The flowchart in Figure 10.3 at the end of this chapter illustrates this.

In such actions, the court headings identifying the parties will not change. These additional claims do, however, operate as a type of defence to the claimant's claim.

10.6.2.4 An additional claim brought against other persons (CPR 20.7)

Such a claim is made in the first instance by a defendant to the action who wishes to blame someone other than the claimant for the claimant's losses. The new additional party will be called a 'third party'. If that third party then wishes to blame someone else, whether that 'someone else' is a party to the action or not, then that 'someone else' is called a 'fourth party'—and so on. These allegations and counter-allegations can become complex in, for example, large building and construction contracts—although the number of additional parties continues with the allegations and counter-allegations, it remains 'convenient' to hear all of the claims together (or as managed by the court), because all relate to the same facts (that is, the subject of the construction contract).

 Example

A garden centre contracted with a greenhouse supplier to supply and install two large warehouse greenhouses for indoor plants. The heating system did not work, to the extent that it overheated and killed the plants. The garden centre issued proceedings against the greenhouse supplier for loss of revenue. The greenhouse supplier defended the claim, blaming the electrical contractor that it had engaged to install the heating system. The electrical contractor denied liability and blamed its subcontractor—an individual who had actually undertaken the works. The flowchart in Figure 10.4 at the end of this chapter illustrates this.

When this occurs, the heading of the action will continue to 'evolve' as new parties are added and additional claims are made, and it might look like this:

DALE GARDEN CENTRE LTD	Claimant
and	
WIRRAL GREENHOUSES LTD	Defendant
and	
S & S ELECTRICAL SOLUTIONS (A FIRM)	Third Party
and	
MR BERNARD TALBOT T/A TALBOT ELECTRICIANS	Fourth Party

See Chapter 11, paragraph 11.6.2.1, for a drafted third-party claim.

These additional claims do operate as a defence to the claimant's claim.

10.6.2.5 How to issue an additional claim

10.6.2.5.1 *A counterclaim against the claimant*

Where the counterclaim is a 'simple' one, being a counterclaim made by the defendant in the main action against the claimant, the defendant may raise the counterclaim:

- without the permission of the court, provided that he files it with, or at the same time as, his defence (CPR 20.4.(2)(a)). Practically, the counterclaim is drafted so that it follows directly on from the defence. This can sometimes be confusing for those new to practice, as the counterclaim has the appearance of being part of the defence. It is, however, a separate legal document with its own cause of action and loss claimed. Again, see paragraph 11.6.1.1 in Chapter 11 for a draft counterclaim attached to a defence; or

- at any other time with the court's permission (CPR 20.4.(2)(b)). Here the counterclaim will more obviously stand alone as a separate legal statement of case. The only difference to the example given in paragraph 11.6.1.1 is that the full title of the action and the heading will need to be inserted at the top of the document.

In either of these cases a fee is payable for the counterclaim that is equivalent to the fee for issuing a fresh claim, although there is no claim form to complete.

10.6.2.5.2 *A counterclaim against a person other than the claimant*

Where the defendant wishes to seek an additional claim by way of a counterclaim against a person who is not a party to the proceedings, he must apply to the court for permission to do so (CPR 20.5). When he makes an application, it must be accompanied by a statement of case (of the additional claim), and will set out details of the stage that the main proceedings have reached, the nature of that claim, and details of the nature of the claim against the new party. The statement of case will be headed 'Defendant's Counterclaim against a Third Party'.

If the court makes an order permitting the addition of the new party, it will also give directions for managing the case. These directions are likely to include provision for service of all statements of case on the new party, together with a response pack and an order stating the time allowed for responding to the additional claim, together with directions of the role that the new party will take in the action (if any). Further case management directions will also be given for disclosure, exchange of witness statements, etc.

A fee is also payable here and, again, there is no claim form.

10.6.2.5.3 *An additional claim for a contribution or indemnity*

Where the defendant seeks a contribution or indemnity from someone who is already a party to the action, he may file a Contribution Notice setting out the grounds of the additional claim, and serve that on the claimant and the additional party without the permission of the court, provided that he files the notice and claim at the same time as filing his defence (CPR 20.6). He may also serve notice of an additional claim for a contribution or an indemnity against a person who later becomes a party to the proceedings, provided that he serves the notice within twenty-eight days of the new party being added to the claim. In any other circumstances, the defendant must seek the court's permission, by way of an application, to seek a contribution or indemnity.

No fee is payable and no claim form is issued.

10.6.2.5.4 *An additional claim against persons not party to the proceedings*

Where an additional claim is made against someone who is not yet a party to proceedings, the defendant can make this additional claim without the court's permission if the additional claim is issued before or at the same time as he files his defence, or at any other time with the court's permission on a without-notice application (CPR 20.7). The statement of case could be headed 'Defendant's Additional Claim against a Third Party'. Again an example of how to draft this document can be found at paragraph 11.6.2.1 in Chapter 11.

A fixed fee is payable, though the sum differs in the High Court and the County Court. There is also an additional (Part 20) claim form to complete (N211).

Please see the online resources for a copy of a Part 20 claim form.

10.6.2.6 The service of additional claims

When permission of the court is not required, a counterclaim made in these situations in which the permission of the court is not required must be filed at court with the defence and served on each party. Any additional claim issued by the court at a later date must be served on the person against whom it is made within fourteen days of issue by the court.

When permission of the court is required, the court will make directions for the service of the additional claim when it gives permission for the additional claim to be made within the main action.

In either case, service of the additional claim will be accompanied by:

- a form for defending the claim;
- a form for admitting the claim;
- a form for acknowledging service; and
- a copy of every statement of case already served in the main action and any other documents that the court has directed should also be served (CPR 20.12).

10.6.2.7 What response does a claimant or other person give to the counterclaim (CPR 20.4 and 20.5)?

Save where CPR Part 20 states to the contrary, the provisions of the CPR apply to counterclaims as if they were claims. In this way, a 'defence to the counterclaim' must be served within fourteen days of the date of service of the counterclaim. Failure to do this will enable the defendant to seek judgment in default on the counterclaim.

Whilst defending the counterclaim, a reply to the defendant's defence can be raised. The statement of case is known as a 'reply and defence to counterclaim' and forms one document. The reply is optional and is only usually prepared where something has been raised in the defence (and counterclaim) that requires a response, so that the issues between the parties are defined. PD 15 at paragraph 3.2A, however, states that the deadline for filing a defence to counterclaim (where a reply is also to be filed) may be extended by the court to correspond with the date for filing the DQ where that date is more than fourteen days after the notice of proposed allocation is deemed served for small claim track cases, and twenty-eight days for fast-track and multi-track cases, in accordance with CPR 26.3(6)(b). When there is no counterclaim, the usual time for service of the reply is on the filing of the DQ with the court. Once a reply and defence to counterclaim has been served, the court is very likely to case manage the claim and the counterclaim together.

See Chapter 11, paragraph 11.7, for a drafted reply.

10.6.2.8 What action must an additional party take in an additional claim (CPR 20.6 and 20.7)?

For additional claims brought by the defendant, the additional party must serve a defence (if already a party to the action), or an acknowledgement and defence if not already a party to the action.

If the additional party fails to acknowledge or defend the additional claim, he will be deemed to admit the main action and be bound by the outcome of it so far as it relates to him by the additional claim made against him by the defendant.

See Chapter 11, paragraph 11.6.2, for a drafted additional claim.

10.6.2.9 CPR Part 20 claims and costs

The general rule is that the loser should pay the winner's costs. As we have seen in Chapter 4, there are many factors that influence the order for costs that the court will make. Where an action has included additional claims, then the issue of costs demands special attention. In some situations, with additional claims, the defendant may be in the unenviable position of incurring costs in defending the main action, but also incurring costs in pursuing his additional claim. The issue of who has 'won' an action in which there are multiple claims may make it difficult to deal with the issue of costs orders between the parties, as well as the sum of those costs orders. These types of costs order are outside the scope of this book, but are 'flagged up' here as an area in which careful study and attention must be paid in any dealings with an action that includes an additional claim.

10.6.3 THE DEFENCE OF 'SET-OFF'

The law relating to set-off is complex, because it is based on legal doctrines (legal set-off and equitable set-off) and case law. Here, we set out only the basic principles in relation to the simplest and most common type of set-off: the legal set-off.

A legal 'set-off' is a money claim that a defendant has against the claimant. It is for an ascertainable amount and is usually used as a defence with a view to reducing significantly, or even extinguishing, the claimant's claim against the defendant. A defence of set-off is permitted under CPR 16.6. Another feature of a set-off is that it is 'separate' to the cause of action that the claimant has brought against the defendant in his particulars of claim.

Example

Sole Trader A supplies goods totalling £20,000 to Limited Company B in July. In August, Limited Company B supplies goods to the value of £30,000 to Sole Trader A. Neither company pays for the goods. Both transactions had a separate written contract. If A were to sue B, it is likely that B would raise a defence of set-off that, in this case, would completely extinguish A's claim if successful. B would then counterclaim, seeking the remaining £10,000. Therefore, in this example, B has both a defence of set-off and a counterclaim.

Here, the court could award the claimant judgment on his claim, but order a stay of execution pending the determination of the counterclaim.

Practical Considerations

In practice, you may come across contracts that stipulate that the debtor has no right of set-off against the creditor. You will need to consider the clause carefully, taking into account whether it may be held to be unreasonable and rendered ineffective under the Unfair Contract Terms Act 1977. The purpose of these clauses is to cover the situations in which contracting parties undertake reciprocal business.

A defendant who has an unquantified set-off against the claimant that is not connected with the claimant's claim is not usually entitled to a set-off, although the doctrine of equitable set-off would need to be examined. This is outside the scope of this manual.

Legal set-offs are therefore most successfully used by defendants in mutual debt-type claims as in the previous example—but compare the following example.

Example

A building contractor undertakes building works for a homeowner. The homeowner alleges that the works are of unsatisfactory quality and refuses to pay. The contractor issues proceedings for the amount owed, and the homeowner defends on the basis of poor workmanship and seeks to set-off, by way of a counterclaim, the value of the remedial works to rectify the job against what he owes the contractor.

This second example can be distinguished for two reasons: firstly, the second example concerns a set-off for an unquantified amount, because the value of the remedial works would need to be ascertained; and secondly, the counterclaim operates as a set-off within the claimant's action. Although the situation of the homeowner in this second example is not strictly a set-off, these types of scenario can also be treated as set-offs in practice.

10.7 COMMON TACTICS AVAILABLE IN DEFENDING A CLAIM

In addition to defending a claim, a defendant has a selection of tactics to employ where appropriate and proportionate to do so. The tactics listed here are not exhaustive, however, and all are also available to a claimant, save for the security for costs application (unless the claimant is defending a counterclaim), which rests exclusively with the defendant.

10.7.1 MAKING AN APPLICATION FOR SUMMARY JUDGMENT

An application for summary judgment may be made by the defendant under the provisions of CPR 24 when he believes that he can show that the claimant's case is so weak on the facts that it has no real prospect of succeeding. (See Chapter 14, paragraph 14.3, which deals with applications for summary judgment.)

An application for summary judgment can also be made for part of a claim, and in this way, the issues between the parties can be narrowed and be used by a defendant who wishes to restrict the claim being made against him. The requirements for summary judgment for part of a claim are the same as an application for summary judgment on the whole.

A defendant's application for summary judgment can be made at any time after he has filed his acknowledgement of service indicating an intention to defend the action (in whole or in part).

10.7.2 MAKING AN APPLICATION TO DISMISS THE CLAIM

A defendant may make an application to dismiss the claim under the provisions of CPR 3 (to strike out the claim or to dismiss the claim as a sanction). This could arise if the claim raises no proper cause of action, or is an abuse of process, or on the basis that there has been a failure to abide by an order of the court.

Examples of each of these could include:

- that the claim sets out no known 'cause of action' in law;
- that withdrawing, in bad faith, an admission previously made could be construed as an 'abuse of process';
- that attempting to relitigate a cause of action previously tried could also be an example of an 'abuse of process'; and
- a failure to abide by a court order or inordinate delay on the part of a party.

The court has the power to make orders under the provisions of CPR 3 on its own initiative, but the provisions can be used upon the application of a party. On occasion, an application under CPR 3 will be made in conjunction with an application for summary judgment under CPR 24—but note the distinction between the two applications set out in Chapter 14, paragraph 14.3.2.

 Practical Considerations

The provisions in CPR 3 will be exercised sparingly. In situations in which CPR 3 may apply, the court may determine that it would be more 'just' or appropriate to use the provisions of CPR 18 (see paragraph 10.7.4) to clarify the inadequate case. Alternatively, in the interests of 'justice', a court may also allow a party to amend its case rather than impose an order to strike out the claim.

10.7.3 MAKING AN APPLICATION FOR SECURITY FOR COSTS

A defendant has often not chosen to be embroiled in the litigation (although his behaviour may have been deliberately such that the claimant had no other option but to commence proceedings). Defending his position against the claim will cost him money. These costs can be considerable. Equally, a defendant will be at risk of an order for damages being made against him.

A defendant's armoury to protect against a judgment for damages against him will be in the steps that he can take to:

- prove his version of the 'story' that gives rise to the claim and absolve himself from any liability;
- show that a head of damage or a part of the loss is not recoverable so as to limit the claim against him; and
- show that the sum claimed should be as low as possible—that is, by showing a failure to mitigate by the claimant.

A defendant's armoury to protect him from the legal costs that he may incur in defending his claim includes:

- making a carefully pitched CPR Part 36 offer to transfer some of the risks of the costs of the action to the claimant (offers to settle and the consequences of such offers are detailed in Chapter 16);
- making an application for security for costs under the provisions of CPR 25.12. An application for security for costs is an interim application that a defendant (who may include

the claimant in an action if the defendant has lodged a counterclaim against him) can make in the circumstances set down in CPR 25.12. Such an application must be supported by written evidence (CPR 25.12(2)). The court may make such an order if the conditions set out in CPR 25.13(2) are met. In addition, the court must be satisfied that it is just to do so (CPR 25.13(1)(a)). It may be unjust to make an order when to do so would stifle the claimant's claim: for example, by restricting his financial viability or flexibility such that he is no longer able to fund and pursue his claim.

• A successful application for security for costs will result in the claimant (or sometimes a third party) being ordered to pay a sum of money into court, or other form of security by a bond or guarantee. The sum so held by the court office can then be used to meet all or some of any costs order that the claimant is ordered to pay to the defendant in the conclusion of the action.

10.7.4 MAKING A PART 18 REQUEST FOR FURTHER INFORMATION

CPR Part 18 covers a situation in which a party's case may not have been made clear or explained in sufficient detail in his statement of case. One way in which to remedy this is to make a request for further information. The rule, subject to any rule of law or procedure to the contrary, enables a party to make a request of another party for:

• clarification of any matter that is in dispute in the proceedings and/or

• additional information in relation to any such matter.

A defendant who wishes to make an application for further information is not thereby given additional time to file his defence unless the opponent agrees or an application is successfully made for additional time. Where a claimant's case is so badly drafted as to make filing a defence to it difficult, the defendant may often be better advised to make an application to strike out the case or to seek summary judgment than to use the provisions under CPR Part 18.

10.7.4.1 Procedure

Before making an application to the court for an order under Part 18, the party seeking clarification should first make a written request for the clarification that it seeks. It is generally good practice to create this request in formal form, so that it can be used as the application to the court if there is no, or a negative, response to the written request. The written request should allow the other party a reasonable time in which to respond (PD 18.1). The Practice Direction also gives guidance on the content of the formal request (PD 18.1.2–18.1.7).

Any response to the request should be in writing and should respond only to the matters raised in the request. In this way, the request and the response will clearly set out the issues arising from the Part 18 procedure. The response should contain a statement of truth.

If the respondent to the request objects to complying with the request, he should respond and say so with his reasons (PD 18.4).

If the respondent does not comply with the written request, and the party raising the request is not satisfied with the reasons and decides to proceed, he should file the application at court, and consider whether and what evidence should be filed. He must serve the other party with the application unless that party has made no response to the written request, in which case, the court can hear the application without a hearing. If the other party has responded to the request, but has objected to answering, the court will list the matter for a hearing.

The criteria that the court will apply in considering the matter will be whether the requests are reasonably necessary and proportionate to enable the requesting party to prepare his case or to understand the other party's case.

Details of the drafting of a request for further information are found in Chapter 11, paragraph 11.8.

KEY POINTS SUMMARY

- There are a variety of 'tactics' available to a defendant that may have the outcome of dismissing the claim (summary judgment) or securing him against the risks of the costs of defending the action (security for costs).

- A defendant need not take any action in response to the claim until he has been served with the particulars of claim.

- A defendant must take some step in response to the particulars of claim within fourteen days— either by filing his defence or returning the form of acknowledgement of service.

- If a defendant intends to dispute the jurisdiction of the court, he must file the acknowledgement of service indicating that intention, but he must not take any other step in the proceedings.

- Be aware of the different types of additional claim and the defence of set-off.

- There are occasions on which more than one step may be taken and care needs to be taken to determine which is the most appropriate.

- Understand the position of admissions made by a party.

- Note the position when a case may be transferred to another district registry of the High Court or County Court hearing centre and when it will be automatically transferred.

SELF-TEST QUESTIONS

1. What are the elements of an action and in what way might a defendant seek to respond to them?

2. If a defendant makes a pre-action admission, how will the admission be treated in any subsequent litigation?

3. Which applications may be made by a defendant who believes that the claimant's case is very weak or does not (as it has been set down) reveal any substantive cause of action?

4. When will an application for security for costs *not* be successful?

5. When *must* a defendant respond to a claim made against him? What are the steps that he can take and when must he take those steps?

 Suggested answers to these self-test questions can be found in the Student Resources section of the online resources.

Case Study *Bollingtons Ltd v Mrs Elizabeth Lynch t/a The Honest Lawyer*

The claim form endorsed with the particulars of claim has been correctly served in accordance with the CPR. The date upon which the defendant should have filed her acknowledgement of service and defence has passed. Default judgment has now been entered by the claimant's solicitors, although your client does not know that this has happened.

Acting for the defendant, you have today been telephoned by Mrs Lynch, a new client to the practice. You made a detailed note of your conversation, which appears as the attendance contained in the online resources.

Question 1

What are the initial steps that you would take regarding the claim form and particulars of claim?

Question 2

What issues will you need to cover in your first letter to your client?

 Any documents referred to in these case study questions can be found in the online resources—simply click on 'Case study documentation' to access the documents that you need for Chapter 10 and to be reminded of the questions. Suggested answers to these self-test questions can be accessed in the Student Resources section of the online resources.

FIGURE 10.1 COUNTERCLAIM BY DEFENDANT AGAINST CLAIMANT IN BREACH OF CONTRACT ACTION. SEE EXAMPLE IN 10.6.2.1

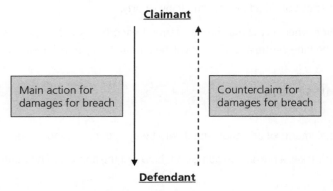

Note here that the title of the action remains the same.

FIGURE 10.2 COUNTERCLAIM BY DEFENDANT AGAINST SOMEONE OTHER THAN THE CLAIMANT IN PERSONAL INJURY CLAIM WHEN CLAIMANT DRIVING IN THE COURSE OF HIS EMPLOYMENT. SEE EXAMPLE IN 10.6.2.2

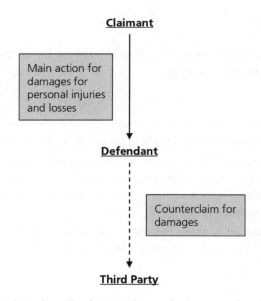

Note here that title of action changes but no court fees for additional claim, that is, the counterclaim.

FIGURE 10.3 ADDITIONAL CLAIM BY DEFENDANT SEEKING A CONTRIBUTION OR INDEMNITY IN BUILDING DISPUTE. SEE EXAMPLE IN 10.6.2.3

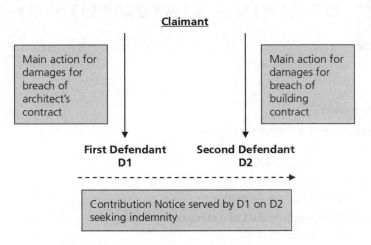

Note here that the title of the action remains the same.

FIGURE 10.4 ADDITIONAL CLAIM BY DEFENDANT AGAINST SOMEONE NOT YET A PARTY TO THE PROCEEDINGS IN BREACH OF CONTRACT ACTION. SEE EXAMPLE IN 10.6.2.4

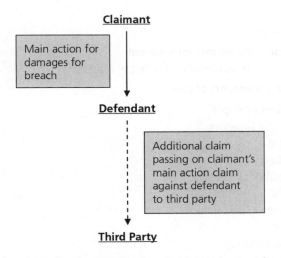

Note here that the title of action changes and a court fee is required to issue a Third Party claim, that is, the additional claim.

11 DRAFTING STATEMENTS OF CASE

Relevant parts of the CPR and its PDs: 1, 14–20, 22, and 32.

11.1 INTRODUCTION

Drafting statements of case requires a logical and clear mind. Legal representatives will draft many statements of case, with the aim of producing accurate, relevant, and compelling formal court documents. This chapter provides key formulae to help those new to practice produce competent statements of case.

Whilst a claim form is a statement of case, how to complete this standard form has been dealt with in Chapter 9, paragraph 9.3.2. The online resources feature the claim form N1, accompanied by drafting tips on the form itself. There is also an example claim form in Appendix 3.

Here, we examine some statements of case. This list is not exhaustive, but represents those statements of case that you will come across most frequently in practice:

- particulars of claim;
- defences;
- additional claims;
- replies; and
- Part 18 requests.

11.2 THE PURPOSE OF A STATEMENT OF CASE

Whenever preparing a statement of case, there are a number of cardinal rules to remember in relation to the purpose of the statement of case, as follows.

11.2.1 PROVIDE AN OUTLINE

The court requires only an outline of a party's case on liability, causation, and quantum. In essence, this means the statement of case needs to set out the cause of action, the exact nature of the allegation(s) being made, and the financial consequences. The temptation is to provide each and every detail that you have in relation to each of these points, but these are to be left to form the basis of the main witness statements in the action.

11.2.2 PROVIDE CLARIFICATION

The purpose of the statement of case is to clarify matters in dispute so that the issues can be clearly identified by the court and the parties to the action.

11.2.3 SET OUT FACTUAL DETAILS

All matters being alleged are stated so that all parties in an action know in advance what is being alleged by each party against them. Generally, it is only the facts of a case that are 'stated'—that is, facts relating to the nature or background to a case, the issues, the allegations, and losses.

However, because the CPR encourage considerable pre-action work being undertaken, the parties will normally be in a position to refer to some evidence in the statement of case and, on occasions, to exhibit it. There are some CPR requirements, for example PD 16.7.3(1), which stipulate that a written contract should be attached to the particulars of claim. This makes the art of drafting considerably simpler. It will also have the benefit of adding weight to a case for the party who can refer to or exhibit strong evidence in favour of his case. It may, however, be a question of reasonableness, judgment, or a mandatory requirement as to the relevancy or the inclusion of the evidence to be included or annexed.

11.2.4 IDENTIFY LEGAL REQUIREMENTS

Every piece of litigation must have a legal basis upon which a claim can be founded: for example, a claim in tort must be considered to exist before a negligence claim can proceed. However, generally, the law is not to be stated in the statement of case, because the judge is presumed to know it. Nevertheless, there is no prohibition against doing so and the law, in terms of a statute or regulation, may be stated where it is thought necessary. For example, if there is a particularly unusual point of law to be taken, or a little-known piece of legislation or a statutory defence, then the relevant law can be stated. This is particularly prevalent in accident at work claims (see the example in paragraph 11.4.1.3).

11.3 THE STANDARD REQUIREMENTS OF A STATEMENT OF CASE

In paragraph 11.4, we have set out a series of 'formulae for drafting' specific to different types of civil action. Here, it is the intention to highlight some general practical, but important, drafting hints that are particular to all statements of case, as follows:

- The statement of case should import the court heading of the action and state what type of statement of case it is directly below the court heading.
- The statement of case should always be in the third person: 'the claimant', 'the defendant', etc.
- Numbered paragraphs should always be used, frequently with subparagraphs or even subheadings if a paragraph is long. The judge, opposing lawyers, and any expert witnesses in the case do not want to lose the 'thread' and have to reread the statement of case. This may only irritate those who read it. Paragraph numbers also make reference to specific parts of a statement of case much simpler.
- The statement of case is the draftsman's opportunity to be articulate and clear on paper. When reading older statements of case, take care not to pick up on and replicate antiquated language such as 'hereinbefore' and 'bequeath'.
- There is a requirement to include a statement of truth on every statement of case. The statement of truth is said to add weight to a statement of case and should act to restrict the action to legitimate issues rather than statements of 'hopeful' allegations, which may have little chance of succeeding at trial. Increasingly, the judges are making costs orders (CPR Part 44) that reflect the numbers of issues with which a party may have proceeded to trial, and considering whether this was a sensible, proportionate, fair, and just thing to do (CPR Part 1).

11.3.1 THE STATEMENT OF TRUTH

All statements of case must contain a statement of truth in accordance with CPR 22, which also provides additional occasions when a statement of truth must be provided in other documents.

A failure to provide a statement of truth on a document where one is required will mean that although the document will remain effective unless it is subsequently struck out, the party may not rely on the statement as evidence of any matter set out in it (CPR 22.2).

The form of the statement of truth for a statement of case is set out in Practice Direction (PD) 22.2.1 and 22.2.2 as follows:

> [I believe] [the (claimant or as may be) believes] that the facts stated in this [name the document being verified] are true. I understand that proceedings for contempt of court may be brought against anyone who makes, or causes to be made, a false statement in a document verified by a statement of truth without an honest belief in its truth.

11.3.2 WHO SHOULD SIGN THE STATEMENT OF TRUTH?

Practice Direction 22.3 sets out who should sign the statement of truth. In general, it should be the party or his legal representative, but best practice indicates that, for all statements of case, the party itself should sign the statement of truth. PD 22.3 will need to be looked at where the party is a company, a partnership, or an insurer.

11.3.3 WHAT ARE THE CONSEQUENCES OF MAKING A STATEMENT OF TRUTH WHEN THE CONTENTS OF THE DOCUMENT, OR ANY PART OF IT, ARE KNOWN TO BE FALSE?

Proceedings for contempt may be brought against a person if he makes, or causes to be made, a false statement of truth. Proceedings for contempt may only be brought by the Attorney General or with the permission of the court (CPR 32.14 and PD 32.28).

11.4 THE PARTICULARS OF CLAIM

The principal rules surrounding the drafting of a particulars of claim can be found in CPR 16 and its Practice Direction. On the reverse side of Form N1 can be found a space in which to draft the particulars. It is not mandatory and usually not sensible or appropriate to draft the particulars of claim in that section of the claim form in every case; rather, it will be a question of common sense in terms of how much you have to say and whether there is enough room to set out your case clearly. It will usually only be a fairly straightforward claim, such as a debt claim, that can be fitted on the reverse side of the claim form.

Drafting can get quite technical, but it is important to remember a guiding principle— that is, 'tell the story'. The story is told to the defendant from the claimant's point of view, and is essentially very simple, as follows:

1. 'This is who we are ...'
2. 'This is who you are ...'
3. 'This is what happened ...'
4. 'It is your fault/breach ...'
5. 'This was the result of what happened ...'
6. 'And so this is what I want from you ...'

Remember, the claim must set out those facts and allegations that, if proved, would give the claimant the right to the remedy sought as a matter of law.

Against this simplistic theory of drafting a particulars of claim, the drafting formulae can now be brought into play. These will assist in the drafting of each of the most common statements of case and, if followed, can provide a good basic structure for even the most complex of cases, whether of high or low value.

11.4.1 THE FORMULAE

11.4.1.1 A claim for a breach of contract

A claim for a breach of contract should deal with the following matters in the following order:

1. The parties (and, if appropriate, the name of the parties' representatives) to, and the date (if written) or approximate date (if oral) of, the agreement.
2. The nature and purpose of the agreement and the consideration.
3. Any relevant express or implied terms of the contract that the claimant alleges have been breached by the defendant, generally stating any express terms first and then any implied terms.

4. The facts concerning each breach alleged (with sufficient details to identify what is the alleged breach).

5. Losses that flow from the alleged breach (with particulars of the losses).

6. Interest (see the worked example in paragraph 11.10 for a fuller consideration).

7. The 'prayer'—that is, a brief summary of what is being claimed. It does not add anything new to the document. For example:

AND THE CLAIMANT CLAIMS—

1. The sum of £ ...;

2. Interest.

8. A statement of truth and relevant authorization paragraph, if appropriate.

9. The date of the document and the 'author' (which may be the firm acting).

A detailed discussion of a worked example of a breach of contract claim is examined in paragraph 11.10. An example of a particulars of claim in a breach of contract claim is also included in Appendix 4.

11.4.1.1.1 *Example of breach of contract claim*

IN THE COUNTY COURT MONEY CLAIMS CENTRE   Claim No. CM67Y34566

BETWEEN

DALE AND CO LTD   **Claimant**

AND

MPR LTD   **Defendant**

<u>PARTICULARS OF CLAIM</u>

1. The Claimant is a private limited company carrying on business as a manufacturer of wood products.

2. The Defendant is a private limited company supplying woodworking machinery.

3. By a written Purchase Order dated 10 . . . . , the Defendant agreed to supply and the Claimant agreed to purchase an MPR X20 woodcutting machine ('the X20') for the total cash price of £45,000 plus VAT payable by an initial deposit of 20% on the placement of the order and the balance due on delivery of the X20. The Claimant made the deposit payment on 25th . . . . in the sum of £9,000 plus VAT and paid the balance plus VAT on 1st . . . . Payment was therefore made in full by the Claimant. A copy of the Purchase Order is attached to this Particulars of Claim.

4. There were implied terms of the agreement that the X20 would be of satisfactory quality and fit for the purpose for which it was provided—namely, as a specialist woodcutting machine capable of achieving a high degree of accuracy and speed.

5. The X20 was delivered on the due date, and installation and commissioning of the X20 was completed on or about 17. . . .

6. In breach of the implied terms, the X20 was neither of satisfactory quality nor fit for the purpose for which it was supplied.

PARTICULARS OF BREACH

6.1. The X20 seized up within five hours of installation.

6.2. The speed of the X20 was much slower than the more inferior model (the X18) in the range.

6.3. The operating cycle had been jarring, which caused the head synchronization and changing process to become significantly slower than the X18.

6.4. The X20 was supplied as a precision piece of machinery with four adjustable heads, but two of those adjustable heads regularly fell out of alignment by 0.3mm during the production process, with the result that the X20 was rendered unsuitable for the production of products that required precision woodcutting.

The Claimant will seek to rely on the engineer's service reports for the period January . . . . , October . . . . , and the evidence of a jointly instructed expert at the trial of the matter.

7. By reason of the breach of the implied terms, the Claimant has suffered loss and damage.

PARTICULARS OF LOSS AND DAMAGE

The purchase price plus VAT	£52,875
Loss of production costs resulting from 125 hours of down time due to the failure of the X20	£10,000
Loss of business and goodwill	To be quantified

8. Further, the Claimant claims interest pursuant to s. 69 of the County Courts Act 1984 on the amount to be found due to the Claimant at such a rate and for such a period as the court thinks fit.

AND THE CLAIMANT CLAIMS—

(1) Damages pursuant to paragraph 7 above;

(2) Interest pursuant to s. 69 of the County Courts Act 1984.

STATEMENT OF TRUTH

I believe the facts stated in these Particulars of Claim are true. I am duly authorized by the Claimant to sign this statement on its behalf. I understand that proceedings for contempt of court may be brought against anyone who makes, or causes to be made, a false statement in a document verified by a statement of truth without an honest belief in its truth.

Signed . . . .

Managing Director

Dated this . . . .

11.4.1.2 An action in negligence—a road traffic accident (RTA)

An action in negligence relating to a road traffic accident (RTA) should deal with the following and usually in this order:

1. Sufficient details to identify the incident should be set out, including a simple description that a collision occurred, on a particular date, at a particular time and place, and between the parties. Where an existing duty of care applies by implication, there is no

need to state this: for example, where the RTA occurred on the public highway, then there arises a clear duty of care by all road users to other road users and pedestrians. Where the existence of the duty of care is less obvious, it may be necessary to state it in the document;

2. A statement, with details of the negligence of the defendant, including specific examples of his negligence;

3. Any relevant previous convictions. When a conviction of an offence is relevant to the issues of the case, it may be pleaded. When this occurs, details of the conviction, its date, the court in which it was made, and the relevance to the cause of action in which that conviction is stated should be stated;

4. The fact that the claimant suffered injury as a result of the negligence, along with brief details of those injuries, referring to the appended medical report(s);

5. That losses have been sustained as referred to in a schedule of losses containing full details of those losses;

6. Interest pursuant to the relevant statute;

7. The 'prayer' for the relief sought, as earlier: damages and interest;

8. A statement of truth and authorization (if appropriate), as earlier; and

9. The date of the document and the 'author' (which may be the firm acting).

11.4.1.2.1 *Example of a negligence—RTA particulars of claim*

IN THE COUNTY COURT MONEY CLAIMS CENTRE   Claim No. CR345267

BETWEEN

MISS CHLOE WHITFIELD   Claimant

and

MR STEPHEN BROAD   Defendant

PARTICULARS OF CLAIM

1 The Claimant was the driver of an Audi A4 motor car, registration number GH51 OLM. The Defendant was the owner and driver of a Ford Focus, registration number VG52 BLU.

2. On 16 July 20??, in the vicinity of the Cloversmead Shopping Centre, the Claimant was driving down Hayhurst Avenue and turned left into Warrington Way, when a collision occurred with the Defendant's car.

3. The collision was caused by the negligence of the Defendant.

PARTICULARS OF NEGLIGENCE

The Defendant was negligent in that he:

(i) failed to keep any or any proper lookout.

(ii) failed to stop, or slow down, or swerve, or in any other way to control his motor car so as to avoid the accident.

(iii) was driving at a speed that was excessive in the circumstances.

(iv) drove through a red light on Warrington Way.

(v) was speaking on his mobile phone.

4. As a result, the Claimant has sustained injuries and suffered loss and damage.

PARTICULARS OF INJURY

The Claimant's date of birth is 20 November 1984. The Claimant suffered a whiplash injury and fractured her sternum. She suffers from headaches, pain in the neck and chest, and numbness in the outer upper arms. The Claimant held twice-weekly yoga classes at the local community centre, but has been unable to resume these classes since the accident. The injuries and symptoms are fully described in the attached medical report, prepared by Mr Christopher Kartby, consultant orthopaedic surgeon, dated . . . . . .

PARTICULARS OF LOSS AND DAMAGE

The Claimant refers to the attached Schedule of Losses for details of her special damages.

5. The Claimant claims interest pursuant to s. 69 of the County Courts Act 1984 at such a rate and for such a period as the court thinks fit.

AND THE CLAIMANT CLAIMS—

(1) Damages;

(2) Interest pursuant to s. 69 of the County Courts Act 1984.

STATEMENT OF TRUTH

I believe that the facts stated in these Particulars of Claim are true. I understand that proceedings for contempt of court may be brought against anyone who makes, or causes to be made, a false statement in a document verified by a statement of truth without an honest belief in its truth.

Dated this . . . .

Note: For a personal injury claim it is a CPR requirement to (a) plead the claimant's date of birth (PD 16.4.1(1)), (b) attach the medical expert's report (PD 16.4.3), and (c) attach a schedule of past and future losses and expenses (PD 16.4.2).

11.4.1.3 An action in negligence—a factory accident

An action in negligence relating to a factory accident should deal with the following matters, and usually in this order:

1. The relationship of the employer and employee should be established (or that of the factory owner and the visitor), and the application of any relevant statutory provisions (for example, the Factories Act 1961, but only if the breach amounts to an act of negligence) should be set out;

2. Details of the accident at the premises, with brief particulars as to how it happened;

3. An allegation that the accident was caused by the negligence (or breach of statutory duty of the owner, or employer, or employee, with particulars and any specific statutory provisions);

4. That, as a result of the alleged negligence (breach of statutory duty) the claimant suffered injury and loss, with particulars of both and annexed medical report(s) and schedule of losses;

5. Interest;

6. The 'prayer' for relief—damages and interest (as earlier);

7. A statement of truth and authority (if appropriate); and

8. The date of the document and the 'author' (which may be the firm acting).

Practical Considerations

Often, accidents at work are caused by the incompetence of a fellow employee. Consider the situation in which, acting for a claimant employee, you enter into Protocol with a potential employer defendant claiming damages for personal injuries. The employer fails to confirm that the fellow employee was acting in the course of his employment. If it is necessary for you to commence proceedings, you will need to issue against both the fellow employee and the employer until such time as the employer confirms vicarious liability either in correspondence or on the filing of his defence, at which point you can amend your particulars of claim to remove the fellow employee. This course of action is necessary to ensure that you have a cause of action against an appropriate party.

11.4.1.3.1 *Example of a negligence—factory accident particulars of claim*

IN THE HIGH COURT OF JUSTICE   Claim No. 202X-D-8976

QUEEN'S BENCH DIVISION

STOKE ON TRENT DISTRICT REGISTRY

BETWEEN

MR SIMON HERBERT   Claimant

and

ARISTA LOGISTICS LIMITED   Defendant

PARTICULARS OF CLAIM

1. The Claimant was employed by the Defendant as a forklift truck driver at Gladstone Lock warehouse, Regent Road, Stoke on Trent. The nature of the Claimant's work is regulated by the Provision and Use of Work Equipment Regulations 1992, SI 1992/2932, and the Manual Handling Operations Regulations 1992, SI 1992/2793.

2. On 29 September 2014, in the course of his employment, the Claimant was loading a steel rod of approximately 3.5 metres in length and weighing just over 100 kilos onto his forklift truck. By reason of the weight of the rod, it had to be loaded mechanically, and by reason of its length, it had to be placed on the forklift truck lengthways. Accordingly, it could not be placed across the forklift truck, but had to be positioned on the forks pointing away from the mast of the forklift. By reason of its length and despite using long forks, it would not stay on the forks unless strapped on. The Claimant and his colleague were attempting to strap the steel rod onto the forks of the forklift truck in order to secure it for transportation to the back of a lorry when it rolled off the forks and dropped directly onto the arch of the Claimant's left foot.

3. The accident was caused by the negligence and/or breach of statutory duty of the Defendant or its employees.

PARTICULARS OF NEGLIGENCE/BREACH OF STATUTORY DUTY

The Defendant was negligent in that it—

(i) Failed to devise and implement for the Claimant a safe system of work;

(ii) Failed to ensure that the Claimant had received adequate training and/or health and safety information, negligently and/or in breach of its statutory duty under regs 8 and/or 9 of the Provision and Use of Work Equipment Regulations 1998;

(iii) Failed to provide competent staff (the Claimant's case is that an overhead crane ought to have been used in order to load the metal rods onto the lorry);

(iv) Failed to exercise any or any adequate care for the safety of the Claimant;

(v) Failed, so far as was reasonably practicable, to avoid the need for the Claimant to undertake the said manual loading operation, in particular by not providing any, or any suitable, mechanical lifting equipment, negligently and/or in breach of its statutory duty under reg. 4(1)(a) of the Manual Handling Operations Regulations 1992;

(vi) Failed, so far as was reasonably practicable, to make a suitable and sufficient assessment of such manual handling operation, negligently and/or in breach of its statutory duty under reg. 4(1)(b) of the Manual Handling Operations Regulations 1992;

(vii) Failed to ensure that lifting equipment—namely, the forklift truck—was suitable for the purpose for which it was used, negligently and/or in breach of its statutory duty under reg. 5 of the Provision and Use of Work Equipment Regulations 1992;

(viii) Failed to ensure that the said forklift truck was used only for operations, and under conditions, for which it was suitable, negligently and/or in breach of its statutory duty under reg. 5 of the Provision and Use of Work Equipment Regulations 1992.

4. By reason of the above, the Claimant has suffered personal injury, loss, and damage.

PARTICULARS INJURY

The Claimant, who was born on 26 January 1990, sustained two broken bones in his left foot. Full details of the Claimant's orthopaedic injuries are contained in the medical report of Mr Mark O'Brien, dated 15 September 20??, annexed. The Claimant also now suffers from post-traumatic stress disorder as a result of the crush injury to his left foot. A psychiatric report of Dr Nichola Davies, dated 29 October 20??, is also attached.

PARTICULARS OF LOSS AND DAMAGE

The Claimant sustained a variety of financial losses and these are detailed in the attached Schedule of Losses.

AND THE CLAIMANT CLAIMS—

(1) Damages;

(2) Interest at such rates and for such periods as the court deems fit.

Dated this . . . .

STATEMENT OF TRUTH

I believe that the facts in these Particulars of Claim are true. I understand that proceedings for contempt of court may be brought against anyone who makes, or causes to be made, a false statement in a document verified by a statement of truth without an honest belief in its truth.

Note: These particulars of claim include a claim for breach of statutory duty because the breach amounted to a negligent act. See paragraph 11.4.1.3.

11.4.1.4 A debt action for goods sold and delivered, but not paid for

A claim for goods sold and delivered, but not paid for, should deal with the following matters and usually in this order:

1. The nature of the goods sold and delivered, the date of the delivery, any invoice details (with attached copy), and the price;

2. The fact that the goods have not been paid for, and that payment is still due and owing;

3. Interest pursuant to statute or under the terms of the contract;

4. The 'prayer' for relief—the price of the goods and interest;

5. A statement of truth with relevant authorization (if appropriate); and

6. The date of the document and the 'author' (which may be the firm acting).

The particulars for debt claims are usually very short and appear on the reverse of the claim form.

The following example shows the particulars as seen on the reverse of a claim form in a straightforward debt action. A claim form that contains the particulars of claim in this way is known as an 'indorsed claim form'.

11.4.1.4.1 *Example of an indorsed claim form*

---

1. The Claimant claims the sum of £15,000 plus VAT in respect of electrical components supplied and delivered to the Defendant in accordance with the terms of a written contract made between the parties dated 25 April 20??, a copy of which is attached to these particulars of claim.

2. The Claimant delivered the goods on the agreed delivery date of 1 February, but the Defendant has failed to pay the invoice, a copy of which is attached.

3. The total sum of £15,000 plus VAT of £3,000 remains due and owing.

4. The Claimant claims interest at the contractual rate of 8% per annum from the due date of payment to judgment or sooner payment in the sum of £xxx and continuing at a daily rate of £x.

AND THE CLAIMANT CLAIMS—

(1) The sum of £18,000;

(2) Interest in the sum of £xxx and continuing at a daily rate of £x, pursuant to the contractual interest rate.

I believe the facts stated in these Particulars of Claim are true. I understand that proceedings for contempt of court may be brought against anyone who makes, or causes to be made, a false statement in a document verified by a statement of truth without an honest belief in its truth. I am duly authorized by the Claimant to sign this statement on its behalf.

. . . .

Dated . . . .

Note: A debt claim such as this is for a specified sum. It is a CPR requirement that, for specified sums, the Particulars of Claim must include a detailed break down of the interest claimed at a daily rate (CPR 16.4(2)(b)).

11.5 THE DEFENCE

The principal rules concerning the drafting of the defence can be found in CPR Parts 15 and 16, and their associated Practice Directions. As mentioned in Chapter 10 (paragraph 10.5.2), the use of Forms N9B (a claim for a specified sum, N9D (a claim for an unspecified claim or a non-money claim), or N11 (a general defence), included in the response pack and served with the particulars of claim, may be used to file a defence. These forms can be found in the online resources.

The use of these forms is not mandatory and often there is insufficient space in any but the simplest claim to prepare a fully pleaded defence on the forms. These forms are usually only ever completed by litigants in person—that is, those without legal representation. In practice, the defence will be prepared as a separate document.

A defence is required when a defendant wishes to defend all or part of a claim. Once filed, a copy of the defence must be served on every other party. The time limits for the filing of a defence are set out at CPR 15.4 (see also Chapter 10, paragraph 10.5).

Under CPR 15.5, the defendant and the claimant may agree that the time for filing a defence be extended for a period up to a maximum of an extra twenty-eight days. Where the claimant consents to the requested extension, the defendant must notify the court in writing of the agreement to extend time. Any need for further time must be made by application to the court under CPR 3.1, because the CPR do not afford any authority to the claimant to agree to any further extensions of time (see also Chapter 10, paragraph 10.5.2.1).

11.5.1 THE FORMULA

The defence should deal with every material allegation contained in the particulars of claim. This is because a defendant who fails to address an allegation at all will be deemed to admit it (CPR 16.5(5)). The simplest way in which to do this is to respond to each paragraph of the statement of case in the order in which it appears, and to deal with each allegation in each paragraph.

For each response, the defendant has four options (CPR 16.5):

- he may **admit** the allegation;
- he may **deny** the allegation with reasons;
- he may **refuse to admit or make no admissions** to the allegation and request the claimant to prove such allegations or facts; or
- he may seek to **shift the blame to another party or third party**.

11.5.1.1 Admissions

Allegations that can be admitted *should* be admitted: for example, if there was a collision or a contract, in accordance with your client's instructions, you should be able to admit that fact. However, care should be taken not to admit that which should not be admitted (see the 'Professional Conduct' box). Conversely, a failure to admit statements that should have been admitted may have costs consequences for the defendant (see Chapter 10, paragraph 10.3.4.2).

11.5.1.1.1 *Example of an admission in an RTA claim*

'Paragraph 1 of the Particulars of Claim is admitted.'

11.5.1.2 Denials

Where an allegation is denied, in accordance with your client's instructions, the defendant needs to put his side of the story forward. A bare denial is not acceptable under the CPR. It is therefore important to remember, when drafting the defendant's version of events, that he needs to give an explanation of *how* and, in some cases, *why* the event happened, not simply to justify his own position. This will often involve allegations that the accident or breach and the resultant losses were caused by the negligence or breach of either the claimant or somebody else.

For example, in an action for damages arising from an RTA, it is likely that the *fact* of the collision can be admitted. The defendant, in his defence, may be saying that the collision was not his fault (that is, he may be denying the allegation), but if he has admitted that a collision occurred, his defence needs to explain how the accident happened. Simply denying the allegations of the claimant does not do this; rather, the defendant needs to explain by blaming someone else or by some other event *how* the accident did happen. This explanation in this example will need to set out clearly allegations of contributory negligence.

 Practical Considerations

This is an aspect of drafting that those new to practice find difficult, because there is a tendency to try to justify why the defendant was not doing what the claimant is alleging he did in its particulars of negligence, or breach of contract, or statutory duty. When planning out what you are going to say, do not attempt to justify his position by saying 'it was not the defendant who was driving negligently because he did not drive too fast, he did keep a proper lookout, etc… ', but instead put the ball back into the claimant's court by saying 'it was not the defendant who was driving negligently, it was the claimant, and this is what the claimant did to show that he drove negligently: he drove too fast; he did not keep a proper lookout, etc. …'

The theoretical reason why we do not recite why the defendant personally did not drive negligently relates to burdens of proof, which is discussed in Chapter 17, paragraph 17.2.1.

A defendant can also deny a claim if the limitation period for the action has expired: for example, in a breach of contract action, proceedings must be issued within six years of the date of the breach. For the defendant to take advantage of this defence, he must state limitation as an issue in the defence. If he fails to do so, then he will not be able to rely on it unless he seeks to amend his defence.

For further discussion on limitation periods generally, see Chapter 7, paragraph 7.4.

11.5.1.2.1 *Example of a personal injury RTA claim (as in paragraph 11.4.1.2)*

'3. It is denied that the Defendant drove negligently as stated in paragraph X. The collision was caused or contributed to by the Claimant.'

11.5.1.2.2 *Example of a breach of contract claim (as in paragraph 11.4.1.1)*

'4. Paragraph 5 of the Particulars of Claim is admitted, save for the fact that it is denied that the X20 was delivered on time, and that the installation and commissioning processes were completed satisfactorily, or at all.'

11.5.1.3 Refusing to admit, or making no admissions and requiring the claimant to prove an allegation or fact

The defendant may refuse to admit allegations that he can neither deny nor admit usually because he has no knowledge of those elements. For example, in a claimant's claim for personal injuries, this will include both general and special damages, and the defendant will have to consider what he has to say in relation to the cause, and the nature and extent, of the losses.

In relation to the claim for general damages, at this early stage of the litigation, the defendant is usually unlikely to be in a position to deny that the claimant has been injured. Remember that the purpose of the defence is to deny liability for them. By the time of the preparation of the defence, the defendant will have seen the claimant's evidence of his general damages—namely, the medical report. If the defendant has not either agreed the claimant's medical report or obtained his own medical report, or a joint report, then he is not in a position either to admit or deny either the causation, or the nature and extent, of those injuries until such time as he has his own evidence or has agreed that of the opponent.

In these circumstances, it is usual for the defendant to make no admissions as to the cause, or nature or extent, of the injuries, because he simply has no knowledge of these, but to ask the claimant to prove the cause, nature, and extent of those injuries. By making no admissions and stating that the claimant must prove the allegation or fact, the defendant is effectively refusing to admit a statement by the claimant, the effect of which is to leave the claimant with the burden of proving his allegation or fact. Thus the claimant will have the burden of providing evidence for his losses.

In relation to the special damages claim, in straightforward cases, the defendant will probably try to agree only the amount with the claimant (either part of or all the claim for special damages) at some stage in the action before trial because the evidence has been seen and is usually not wholly contentious. The defendant's assertion that he is not liable for them remains and therefore he is said 'to admit special damages subject to liability'.

In theory, therefore, it would be perfectly acceptable to admit the claimant's financial losses if, for example, the pre-action work had enabled the defendant to see evidence of the claimant's claim for special damages. The defence will make it quite clear that the defendant denies being the cause of those losses.

11.5.1.3.1 *Example of 'no admission' in the RTA personal injury claim (as in paragraph 11.4.1.2)*

'4. No admissions are made as to any of the Claimant's injuries as set out in paragraph 4 of the Particulars of Claim and in the medical report of Mr Kartby, dated … The Claimant is put to strict proof of the nature and extent of those injuries.'

The Court of Appeal has provided recent guidance in *SPI North Ltd v Swiss Post International (UK) Ltd & Anor* [2019] EWCA Civ 7 on the extent of a defendant's duty to make enquiries of third parties before that defendant may 'not admit' an allegation.

11.5.1.4 Shifting the blame

The 'option' for the defendant in drafting his defence of 'shifting the blame' is a hybrid and is usually linked to the option to deny outlined in paragraph 11.5.1.2. The defendant, in giving his explanation as to 'how' the events described by the claimant happened, may seek to attack the claimant's statement of case by alleging, in his own version of events, that the blame lay elsewhere. If this is to be done, then, again, the defendant's version of events needs to be set out.

For example, in an RTA claim, the defendant may seek to assert in his defence that the collision did not occur through the defendant's negligence, but rather as a result of the claimant's own negligence. The statement of case would then need to particularize the allegations of negligence of the claimant.

When someone other than a party in the proceedings is alleged to have been negligent, then that third party will have to be made aware of the allegations being made against them, as set out in CPR Part 20, and separate proceedings will need to be concurrently issued. This is known as an 'additional claim' and is discussed in Chapter 10, paragraph 10.6.2.

11.5.1.4.1 *Example of an RTA personal injury claim (as in paragraph 11.4.1.2)*

PARTICULARS OF NEGLIGENCE

The Claimant was negligent in that she:

(a) failed to keep any or any proper lookout;

(b) drove too fast in the circumstances;

(c) drove into a collision with the Defendant's vehicle; and

(d) failed by means of the brakes, steering, gears, or otherwise to manage and control her car so as to avoid the collision.

11.5.1.4.2 *Example of a breach of contract claim (as in paragraph 11.4.1.1)*

'5. It is denied that the X20 was neither of satisfactory quality nor fit for purpose, as alleged in paragraph 6 of the Particulars of Claim. The Defendant states as follows:

    (i) in relation to 6.1 of the Particulars of Claim, the Defendant contends that the Claimant's operative, Timothy Grave, failed to follow the operator's manual steps 1–3, causing the X20 to seize;

    (ii) … … … …

 Practical Considerations

To provide a 'safety blanket' when drafting a defence to ensure that all that is to be denied has in fact been denied, legal practitioners and counsel employ a useful phrase usually at the beginning of the defence as follows: 'Save to the extent set out below, the defendant joins issue with the claimant's particulars of claim.'

For an example of a defence, please see Appendix 5.

11.5.2 WHAT IF THE PARTICULARS OF CLAIM HAVE BEEN POORLY DRAFTED?

The structure illustrated in paragraph 11.5.1 has set a framework for drafting a defence to a well-articulated particulars of claim. In practice, many are not so well set out—especially those that are drafted by litigants in person. Rather than trying to respond to each and every paragraph, no matter how long or confusing the particulars of claim may be (which will only create an unintelligible defence), a more effective way to deal with the inadequate statement of case would be to draft the defence as if it were a particulars of claim, with an introductory paragraph informing the court and your opponent what you are doing. To give you the added protection of not failing to respond to any allegation, make use of the traverse clause and use it as your comfort zone. (Here, you would not be using it to cover up poor drafting.)

11.5.2.1 Example of an extract of a poorly drafted particulars of claim

1. I bought a Ford KA from Andersons in July for £3,750. When I took it back I told Mr Sharpe that it vibrated. He said it was nothing to worry about so I went home. Three weeks later the car broke down on the motorway. The RAC man said the cambelt had gone. I asked Mr Sharpe for my money back but he refused.

2. I felt that I have been duped and that I should be entitled to my money back, as I only had the car for 4 months.

I believe that the facts stated in the Particulars of Claim are true. I understand that proceedings for contempt of court may be brought against anyone who makes, or causes to be made, a false statement in a document verified by a statement of truth without an honest belief in its truth.

11.5.2.2 Example of an extract of a properly drafted defence

The Defendant responds to the entirety of the Particulars of Claim as follows:

1. The Defendant is a sole trader carrying on business as a retailer of new and used cars.

2. By a written agreement dated . . . , the Defendant sold the Claimant a used Ford KA for £3,750. At the time of the sale the Claimant was aware that the sale price had been reduced to reflect the fact that the car had not had its 30,000-mile service.

3. There were the following relevant terms of the agreement:

   (i) that in consideration of the Defendant having reduced the purchase price to £3,750, the Claimant would have the car serviced by a third party;

   (ii) that the Defendant gave the Claimant a 3-month warranty in respect of faults developing in the Ford KA.

4. In or about July 20??, after expiry of the warranty period, the Claimant returned the Ford KA and complained that it was vibrating. The Defendant inspected the car and identified that the wheels needed tracking. This was done without charge to the Claimant.

5. At the end of November 20??, the Claimant complained that the cambelt had broken and demanded a refund of the purchase price. Her request was refused for the reasons stated above.

6. No admissions are made to any of the breakdown allegations or the causes of those breakdown allegations. If, which is not admitted, the cambelt did break, it did so after the expiry of the 3-month warranty.

7. It is therefore denied that the Claimant is entitled to a refund of the purchase price or to any losses for the reasons set out in this Defence.

I believe that the facts stated in this Defence are true. I understand that proceedings for contempt of court may be brought against anyone who makes, or causes to be made, a false statement in a document verified by a statement of truth without an honest belief in its truth.

11.6 ADDITIONAL CLAIMS

Here, we are going to look at two of the four possible additional claims identified in Chapter 10: the counterclaim against the claimant (CPR 20.4), and the additional claim against another person (CPR 20.7).

11.6.1 A COUNTERCLAIM AGAINST THE CLAIMANT

The nature of this counterclaim is covered in Chapter 10, paragraph 10.6.2.1. This is the situation in which the defendant alleges that he has (usually) a monetary claim against the claimant that may arise from the same set of facts as appear in the particulars of claim and defence, or it may be an entirely separate matter. A counterclaim is capable of standing alone as an action in its own right, but it is raised as a counterclaim for convenience, and to save time and money. The rules, therefore, for drafting a counterclaim are the same as those for drafting an initial statement of case—that is, the particulars of claim.

11.6.1.1 Example of a counterclaim in an RTA personal injury claim (as in paragraph 11.4.1.2)

COUNTERCLAIM

1. The Defendant repeats paragraphs . . . to . . . of its defence.

2. By reason of the matters raised in the defence, the Defendant has suffered the following loss and damage:

PARTICULARS OF SPECIAL DAMAGE

Repair costs to car   £2,000

3. The Defendant further claims interest at such a rate and for such a period as the court deems fit.

AND THE DEFENDANT COUNTERCLAIMS—

(1)   Damages in the sum of £2,000;

(2)   Interest as above.

I believe the facts stated in this counterclaim are true. I understand that proceedings for contempt of court may be brought against anyone who makes, or causes to be made, a false statement in a document verified by a statement of truth without an honest belief in its truth.

. . . .

Dated . . . .

11.6.2 AN ADDITIONAL CLAIM AGAINST ANOTHER PERSON

The nature of this type of additional claim is covered in Chapter 10, paragraph 10.6.2.4. Here, there are two sets of documents that you will need to prepare: the 'Part 20 claim form', and the 'defendant's additional claim against the third party'.

The drafting of the Part 20 claim form follows the same principles as those set out in Chapter 9, paragraph 9.3.2, for the main action claim form. In this chapter, we will therefore focus on the defendant's additional claim against the third party. This statement of case can be adapted for further derivatives of additional claims under CPR 20.7: for example, a third party's claim against a fourth party, and so on.

The key to drafting these additional claims is set out as follows:

1. The opening paragraph of this statement of case should summarize the original and existing statements of case already served—that is, the particulars of claim against the defendant and the defence (and counterclaim).

2. The additional claim should also state and annex to it copies of all of these statements of case.

3. The additional claim should expressly deny the claim being made against the defendant.

4. The additional claim should then go on to make allegations against the third party and explain why the defendant is blaming him.

5. The additional claim should state the losses the defendant is seeking. These cannot be particularized at the time of drafting the additional claim. As such, all the defendant can do is to state that he seeks to recover the amount which the claimant may recover against him in the main action. This is done by way of an indemnity or contribution in the prayer, or by a request for damages generally.

11.6.2.1 Example of a defendant's additional claim against a third party

---

IN THE HIGH COURT OF JUSTICE   Claim No. 202X-R-2456

QUEEN'S BENCH DIVISION

MANCHESTER DISTRICT REGISTRY

BETWEEN

MILLARD AND CO LTD   **Claimant**

AND

SMT LTD   **Defendant**

AND

COLVILLE CONTRACTORS (A FIRM)   **Third Party**

DEFENDANT'S ADDITIONAL CLAIM AGAINST THIRD PARTY

1. This action has been brought by the Claimant against the Defendant. The Claimant claims from the Defendant damages and interest for an alleged breach of contract for the manufacture and supply of stainless steel cladding ('the Cladding'), as appears from the Particulars of Claim, a copy of which is served with this Additional Claim, along with the written contract, dated 17 September 20??.

2. The Defendant denies that it is liable to the Claimant on the grounds set out in its Defence, a copy of which is also served with this Additional Claim. These Particulars of Additional Claim set out the Defendant's Additional Claim against the Third Party on which the Defendant will rely if it is found liable to the Claimant.

3. By a written purchase order no. 55648 dated 1 October 20??, a copy of which is annexed to this Additional Claim made between the Defendant and the Third Party, the Third Party agreed to manufacture and deliver the Cladding for a price agreed at £132,500.

4. It was an implied term of the agreement that the Cladding would be of satisfactory quality and fit for its purpose.

5. On 5 January 20??, the Third Party, pursuant to the purchase order, manufactured and delivered the Cladding to the premises of the Claimant at Runcorn Works.

6. In breach of the above implied term, the Cladding was neither of satisfactory quality nor fit for purpose.

PARTICULARS OF BREACH

  6.1. The Cladding buckled when fixed to the rear elevation of the Claimant's commercial unit at Runcorn Works.

  6.2. The Cladding rusted and detached from the entrance area to the said commercial unit.

  6.3. Over the entire unit, the Cladding has discoloured and deteriorated to the extent that water ingress has occurred.

---

7. As a result of the matters set out above, the Defendant has suffered loss and damage to the extent of its liability (if any) to the Claimant, any costs that it may be ordered to pay to the Claimant, and its costs incurred in defending the Claimant's claim.

AND THE DEFENDANT ADDITIONALLY CLAIMS—

(i) An indemnity or contribution in respect of the Claimant's claim;

(ii) Alternatively, damages.

STATEMENT OF TRUTH

I believe that the facts stated in these Particulars are true. I am duly authorized by the Defendant to sign this statement. I understand that proceedings for contempt of court may be brought against anyone who makes, or causes to be made, a false statement in a document verified by a statement of truth without an honest belief in its truth.

Signed . . . .

Dated. . . . .

11.7 **THE REPLY**

11.7.1 **WHAT IS A REPLY?**

A 'reply' is a statement of case that responds to a defence, as discussed in CPR 15.8 and 16.7 and in Chapter 10, paragraph 10.6.2.7. It deals in essence with any matters raised in the defence to which the claimant feels that he should respond and which were not covered in the particulars of claim. There is no obligation on the claimant to serve a reply and, as such, no admissions are to be implied from the absence of one.

As with the drafting of a defence, the reply can respond to each, but not necessarily all, of the paragraphs of the defence in a structured and clear manner, explaining and clarifying (both by way of additional factual information) and taking issue with its contents.

 Example

In a simple debt action for the supply of flour to a commercial bakery, in which the formula described in paragraph 11.4.1.4 has been followed correctly, no details of any contract terms other than type of goods, delivery date, and price are relevant to the pleaded claim at this stage. The defendant defends the claim and refuses to pay the amount due, on the basis that the flour supplied and delivered was not of satisfactory quality, and he particularizes the problems—in this case, mite infestation.

Whilst there is no counterclaim raised in this scenario, the claimant may wish to respond by way of a reply and set out any relevant facts that could be brought to the attention of the court that might have a bearing on the success of his action, such as a contract term that the quality of the flour be maintained by storage in airtight containers and, in his reply, asserting the fact that the defendant kept the flour in open sacks.

A reply is not, however, an opportunity for the claimant to rectify any mistakes made in the particulars of claim; that is something that is left to the formal process of amendment (see paragraph 11.9).

11.7.1.1 Example of a reply based on the 'Example' box

> 1. Save as is expressly admitted or not admitted below, the Claimant joins issue with the Defendant on its Defence.
>
> 2. As to paragraph . . . of the Defence, the Claimant avers that a term of the said agreement, at clause . . . , between the parties was that the quality of the flour was to be maintained by storage in airtight containers.
>
> 3. As to paragraph . . . of the Defence, the Defendant refers to a report from a Mr . . . , an independent quality assurance inspector, who examined the flour for contamination. At paragraph 7 of the report dated . . ., Mr . . . states that 'the flour was contained in open sacks. . . .'
>
> I believe that the facts stated in this Reply are true. I am duly authorized to make this statement on behalf of the Claimant. I understand that proceedings for contempt of court may be brought against anyone who makes, or causes to be made, a false statement in a document verified by a statement of truth without an honest belief in its truth.
>
> . . . .
>
> Dated . . . .

11.8 THE PART 18 REQUEST FOR FURTHER INFORMATION

For a reminder of what a Part 18 request is, see Chapter 10, paragraph 10.7.4.

The doctrine of proportionality and the greater burden under the CPR for parties to state their cases in detail should mean that requests for further information are needed less frequently. They should be used with some caution.

 Example

A particulars of claim alleges that an agreement was made whereby the defendant agreed to supply the claimant with a quantity of mixed Mediterranean vegetables at a price of £10 per box and that, despite numerous requests by the claimant, the defendant has refused to supply any of the vegetables. The claimant, therefore, had to buy them elsewhere at a greater cost. The particulars are vague and incomplete in relation to the date of the agreement, whether it was written or oral, who made it, the amount of the order in terms of number of boxes and overall price, and the delivery date.

11.8.1 WHAT IS THE FORM AND CONTENT OF THE PART 18 REQUEST?

There is no requirement that the Part 18 request should be in a particular form, although guidance is given in PD 18.1.2–18.1.7. It should be expressed to be a request under the provisions of CPR 18.

It may be in a letter form, as suggested previously, or drafted as a stand-alone formal document with the court heading. It is often thought helpful to make the request in formal form, so that if there is no response to the request, it can form the basis of the application to the court for an order for the information sought.

In formal form, the document can also allow space for the recipient's reply (this is a different document from the reply discussed in paragraph 11.7) and, therefore, be prepared in tabular form. The reply to a CPR 18 request must contain a statement of truth, because it is a statement of case in its own right.

Whether made by letter or in formal form, the request must:

(a) be headed with the action title and number;

(b) state that it is a request made under CPR Part 18;

(c) identify the party making the request and the party to whom the request is made;

(d) set out, in numbered paragraphs, each request and identify which part (by repeating the words) of the other party's statement of case is either unclear or upon which clarification is sought; and

(e) state the date by which a response is expected and state that an application will be made to court if there is a failure to respond.

11.8.1.1 Example of a Part 18 request in respect of the 'Example' box

---

IN THE COUNTY COURT AT CARDIFF   Claim No. 1NT 443576

BETWEEN

MR CAMERON STUART   Claimant

AND

MR WILLIAM STODDARD   Defendant

DEFENDANT'S PART 18 REQUEST FOR FURTHER INFORMATION OF THE PARTICULARS OF CLAIM

This is a request made on 1st October 20?? by the Defendant of the Claimants for further information and clarification of their Particulars of Claim. The Defendants expect a response by 25th October 20??

<u>Under paragraph 1</u>—'By an agreement made in or about March 20??, the Defendant agreed to supply the Claimant with a quantity of mixed Mediterranean vegetables at a price of £10 per box.'

Please state:

1. The alleged date of the agreement;

2. Whether it is alleged that the agreement was oral or written;

3.   (a) If the agreement was oral, who made the agreement and what was said;

     (b) If the agreement was written, the terms of the agreement, along with a copy of the contract or documentation relied on in support thereof;

4. The date on which it is alleged that the Defendant agreed to supply the boxes of mixed Mediterranean vegetables;

5. The quantity of the said vegetables to be supplied.

<u>Under paragraph 3</u>—'notwithstanding several requests to do so. . . . '

Please give full particulars of:

6. The date/s of every such request;

7. Whether such requests were made orally or in writing;

8. (a) If orally, by and to whom the requests were made, the content of the request/s and the answer/s;

8. (b) If in writing, the details of the request/s and any documentation in support thereof.

<u>Under paragraph 6</u>—'. . . the Claimant had to purchase the same elsewhere at a greater cost.'

> Please state:
>
> 9. From where is it alleged that the Claimant purchased the mixed Mediterranean vegetables;
>
> 10. The quantity and price of the mixed Mediterranean vegetables.
>
> Dated . . . .

11.9 AMENDMENTS TO STATEMENTS OF CASE

CPR 17 generally sets out the position on amendments to statements of case. A party may amend a statement of case at any time before it has been served on any other party. Once served, a statement of case may only be amended with the consent of all parties or the permission of the court, unless the amendment relates to the removal, addition, or substitution of a party, in which case, the procedure set out in CPR 19.4 must be followed.

An amended statement of case must be marked as amended and set out as under PD 17.2.1. The original text need only be shown if the court considers it appropriate and desirable. If the substance of the statement of case is changed by the amendment, it should be reverified by a statement of truth.

The judge is not permitted to give judgment on the basis of a claim not set out in the statement of case. If this is done, a retrial will be ordered.

For the purposes of the Limitation Act 1980, an amendment to add or substitute a new party or to add a new cause of action is deemed to be a separate claim and to have been commenced on the same date as the original claim.

 Costs

The party applying to amend its statement of case will usually be responsible for its own costs, as well as any costs of the opponent, especially if the opponent then needs to amend his statement of case as a result of the amendment. Again, it is good practice to ask your opponent to agree to the proposed amendment before making an application to the court for permission. If your opponent unreasonably refuses, then it will be incumbent on you to raise this at the hearing on the question of costs, because the time and cost incurred by you and your client may have been unnecessarily incurred.

11.10 A DETAILED WORKED EXAMPLE

To demonstrate the thought processes behind drafting a statement of case, a detailed worked example of what should be considered when drafting an effective breach of contract claim is set out here. There are nine important stages.

11.10.1 THE ESSENTIAL INGREDIENTS

The essential ingredients of a successful claim for damages for breach of contract, leading to full recovery, are as follows:

1. That there was a contract, which involved:
   - an agreement;
   - between C and D;

- a promise;
- consideration; and
- an intention (to create legal relations);

2. that there was, in the contract, a material term—that is, one that D is alleged to have breached, or one that entitles C to the relief sought;

3. that C has performed any obligation that was a precondition to the performance of D's obligation, or to his entitlement to relief;

4. that D was in breach of his obligation;

5. that C has suffered loss and damage;

6. that such loss and damage was caused by D's breach;

7. that the loss is not too remote—that is, that it was reasonably within the contemplation of the parties at the time that they entered into the contract as a likely consequence of the breach, in the light of their knowledge at that time; and

8. that the claim is not statute-barred.

11.10.2 THE PARTIES

This stage is partly a matter of setting out essential ingredients to do with the parties and partly a matter of story-telling. If either party has a business or is a company, then you will almost always state what that party's business is. This may be an essential ingredient if you have to establish any of the following—for example:

- that a party entered into the contract in the course of his business;
- that a party was dealing as a consumer;
- that a term should be implied into the contract; or
- that a party held himself out as having a particular skill or expertise.

If the terms of a contract are to be inferred from the previous course of dealing between the parties, then this will need to be established. If there have been significant pre-contract negotiations, then these will have to be set out. If the claimant is making a claim for the loss of or damage to his property, then he needs to state his ownership of the property.

11.10.3 THE CONTRACT

To set out the contract properly, you must:

- state that there was a contract (or agreement);
- state the date (or the approximate date) of the contract;
- identify the parties to the contract;
- state whether either party acted through employees and, if so, identify them;
- confirm the form of the contract, whether written or oral, or partly both, or implied from a number of circumstances;
- attach any documents evidencing the contract;
- if the contract is oral, state how it was made (for example, by phone), between whom, and when and where;
- confirm the subject matter of the contract—that is, what it sought to do or what was promised; and
- identify the consideration.

11.10.4 THE DEFENDANT'S KNOWLEDGE

Where you are relying on the defendant's knowledge of certain facts to show that the loss and damage that you seek was within the contemplation of the defendant and so is not too remote, you need to state those facts and allege that he had that knowledge. The material time is the time at which the contract was made, so it is usual to confirm the date of the contract.

11.10.5 THE TERMS

At this stage, you should set out any material terms that have not already been covered when setting out the contract (see paragraph 11.10.3). It is a matter of judgment whether a term is really part of the basic subject matter of the contract (in which case, it belongs in the setting out of the contract) or whether it is a separate term. You should state whether the term is an express or implied term, and then set out its effect. The best practice is to paraphrase concisely, rather than to copy out the exact words of the term—but this is pointless if it will not make the term any more clear or concise. Do not set out terms that are not relevant.

If relying on an implied term, you should state the basis on which it is implied, unless it is obvious, or is implied by statute.

Where relying on express terms and implied terms, it is usual to set out the express terms first.

11.10.6 PERFORMANCE OF THE CONTRACT

It may be that the defendant was only obliged to carry out his obligations under the contract if the claimant had first performed his part of the bargain. If this is the case, then these obligations need to be set out.

11.10.7 THE BREACH

Breach of contract must be expressly alleged and particularized. You should start by alleging that the defendant was in breach of contract and then set out in full what it is that constitutes the breach. It may be an act or an omission, or a state of affairs, or the fact that some representation was untrue. If the defendant's breach brought the contract to an end, then this must be expressly stated by using the word 'repudiated'. If the defendant has repudiated the contract, thereby giving the claimant the right to treat the contract as at an end and the claimant has done so, it will be necessary to state that the claimant accepted the repudiation.

Where the breach consists of an act, omission, or event, you should state the date on which it occurred.

It may also, at this stage, be necessary to state any additional facts that entitle the claimant to the relief sought.

11.10.8 THE LOSS AND DAMAGE

It is essential to allege causation, as well as damage. This may take a considerable amount of explanation. It is sometimes not obvious why the breach alleged should have led to the loss claimed.

Particulars of the loss and damage must be given. You should state the nature of the loss and the basis on which the claimant wants damages to be assessed, set out the financial losses in an itemized schedule (if there are many), and quantify each item as far as possible.

11.10.9 INTEREST

Interest must always be stated in the particulars of claim. If it is not, the court is unlikely to award interest.

The sum of interest accrued in a specified sum claim only must be stated on Form N1, as well as in the particulars of claim.

Interest may be pleaded as follows:

- under the terms of the contract, if there was a contractual provision;

- under s. 35A of the Senior Courts Act 1981 (if the action is a High Court action)—that is, at 8 per cent (note this is expected to change and be much reduced—you should look out for the announcement of a change to the rate of interest during the course of this year);

- under s. 69 of the County Courts Act 1984 (if the action is in the County Court)—that is, at 8 per cent (note this too is expected to change and be much reduced—you should look out for the announcement of a change to the rate of interest during the course of this year); or

- under the Late Payment of Commercial Debts (Interest) Act 1998 (as amended by the Late Payment Directive 2011/7/EU)—that is, at 8 per cent above base rate. Compensation can also be claimed under the provision of this statute in addition to interest depending on the value of the claim.

If there is a contractual provision for interest, then there is a choice as to whether interest is stated under the contract or the Court Acts. It is not, however, permitted to state the Late Payment of Commercial Debts (Interest) Act 1998 (as amended) as an alternative to a contractual term for interest. If there is no contractual provision, then any one of the applicable statutes mentioned here can be applied.

If interest is stated on the terms of a contract, then express reference to the term in the contract needs to be made. Also, the rates of interest set out in the contract must be stated and the calculations given (both the total interest that has arisen and the continuing daily rate).

If interest is claimed under one of these statutes, then the claim must be for a specified sum. The statement for interest must state the authority (the relevant statute) and must also calculate the amount of interest that has accrued since the accrual of the cause of action (that is, the date of the breach) to the date on which the proceedings are issued, and thereafter a daily rate is calculated so that the court can readily calculate the sum due when judgment is given (if that is the outcome).

If the claim is for an unspecified sum (for the court to award), then interest is simply pleaded generally, requesting the court to award an appropriate amount.

KEY POINTS SUMMARY

- Remember that all statements of case are designed to provide an outline. Do not be tempted to include all of the details of your case.

- Even in the more complex cases, if you stick to the 'formulae', they will serve as a good basic structure for your case.

- Be ready to acknowledge that some drafting may be very complicated and best left to counsel. This is not 'passing the buck', but rather acting in your client's best interests by avoiding unnecessary amendments and adverse costs orders.

- Well-drafted statements of case will reflect well on you in the eyes of the judge if the matter ever gets to trial and should help to clarify the main issues in the case.

- In practice, it is common for practitioners to rely on precedent statements of case. Be aware of antiquated language and ensure that every paragraph used has a purpose for your own statement of case—such reliance must be undertaken intelligently.

- Do not forget the strategic use of a Part 18 request when acting for either the claimant or the defendant on service of their particulars of claim or defence. (See the online resources.)

Case Study *Andrew James Pike v Deep Builders Ltd*

Question

The insurer of Deep Builders Ltd has indicated that it accepts that Mr Deep was acting in the course of his employment, but denies negligence, alleging that Andrew Pike was responsible for the accident. Andrew Pike's solicitors have obtained a medical report prepared by a consultant orthopaedic surgeon. You undertake research and the information provided by the client leads you to believe that total damages on a full liability basis would be in the region of £45,000–60,000. Settlement was not achieved in the Protocol.

The claim form has already been drafted. You will also have drafted the particulars of claim (see the Andrew Pike case study question in Chapter 9).

Now, acting for the defendant, read the attendance note and consider the points that you believe the defendant needs to raise to defend this case and how it can deal with its own losses. Then draft the defence and any other statement of case that you feel is appropriate.

 Any documents referred to in these case study questions can be found in the online resources—simply click on 'Case study documentation' to access the documents that you need for Chapters 9 and 11 and to be reminded of the questions. Suggested answers to these self-test questions can be accessed in the Student Recources section of the online resources.

Relevant court forms relating to this chapter:

- Forms N180 and N181 Directions Questionnaire

- Form N263 and N264 Directions Report and the Electronic Disclosure Questionnaire

- Form N170 Pre-Trial Checklist

- Precedent H (costs budget form) and Precedent R (budget discussion report).

- Forms N149A, N149B, and N149C Notice of Allocation forms for each track

> Relevant parts of the CPR and its PDs: 3, 26, 27, 28, 29, and 44.

12.1   INTRODUCTION

This chapter considers the way in which the court 'actively manages' cases. All disputed cases will be subject to a level of court management and enforcement of its directions orders.

The chapter aims to give you an understanding of the time at which active case management commonly occurs and will address:

- the ethos of case management;

- allocation (to track);

LITIGATION TRAIN: CASE MANAGEMENT OVERVIEW

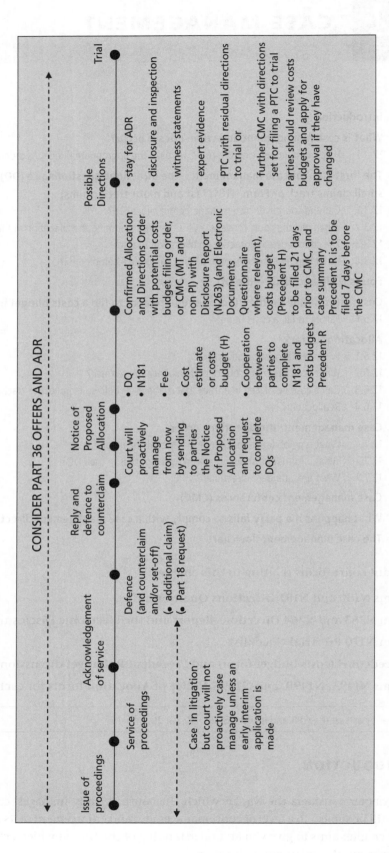

- case management directions through the tracks; and
- the ways in which the court will seek to ensure that its orders for the management of a case are complied with.

12.2 WHAT IS CASE MANAGEMENT AND WHEN DOES IT OCCUR?

'Case management' includes all of the ways in which the court will control the progress and disposal of actions. The bulk of the rules relating to these processes are contained in Civil Procedure Rules (CPR) Parts 3 and 26–29, and the Practice Directions that accompany them. Case management can be exercised at any time in an action's process through to trial, but there are times in the litigation process when it most commonly occurs:

- at allocation (when the court will confirm or allocate the case to a track and when the court will commonly make a directions order);
- at further case management conferences (CMC);
- whenever a party makes an interim application and the court makes further or amended directions at the conclusion of the interim application hearing; or
- on, the few, occasions when the court will impose orders or sanctions of its own volition.

Once a case is issued, the court will 'manage' (in other words 'control') the action throughout, from beginning to its end—this may include management decisions made after trial where continued directions are needed to resolve remaining issues concerning costs or enforcement. It is important to understand that case management is management by the court. This management will be exercised by the district judges, masters, and circuit judges and in some cases, by case officers. Any orders made in this way will read 'Before legal advisor –*surname of case advisor– sitting at – named County County* on the .... Day of .... 20?? it is hereby ordered....' PD 2E formalizes the matters that may be exercised by a legal adviser. The powers enable legal advisers in the County Court Business Centre and the County Court Money Claims Centre to deal with some matters that previously had to be dealt with by District Judges. These include such tasks as correcting procedural errors under CPR 3.10 where a claim has been served by the court contrary to the claimant's instructions, on applications to extend time for service of the claim form under CPR 7.6 (again subject to some exceptions), on applications for an order permitting service at an alternative place under CPR 6.15(2). This is not a full list of tasks that a court legal advisor can undertake.

The case advisors will be supervised by the judge. The type of orders that case advisors can make generally include consent orders or other such orders that are unlikely to be appealed.

12.2.1 HELPING, OR INFLUENCING THE COURT, TO MAKE THE APPROPRIATE DIRECTIONS ORDER FOR A CASE

Parties (and their legal representatives) usually have a voice in the case management decisions and the directions order on that is made for a case. The parties will usually seek to influence the court's decision in the information (or requests) they include in their completed DQ. It is ultimately the court that will control how a case will progress. But the court will have regard for, and consider, all justified requests by a party. Any request for a specific order or particular timescale for a case should be fully justified according to the principles of the overriding objective (CPR 1.3). In order to assist the court to make the right directions order for a case, legal representatives should have or include (probably in their DQ):

- a good understanding of the issues in the dispute;
- provide relevant information to the court promptly when such information is required;
- respond promptly to any contact from the court to monitor compliance with directions;
- ensure that any necessary applications are made promptly;
- keep the court informed of any significant delays in the implementation of any directions orders made; and
- continue to try to resolve the dispute.

The range of ways in which the courts will monitor and control cases can include:

- identifying disputed issues at an early stage, and how those issues are to be presented and proved;
- giving directions to ensure that the progress of the case is efficient;
- fixing dates and a timescale for each step to be undertaken to make the case ready for trial (essentially these comprise the directions order that sets out the steps that each party must take as the case progresses to trial);
- combining several aspects of management in one stage;
- controlling costs (which may include the filing of costs budgets in the form of Precedent H);
- disposing of cases summarily where they disclose no case or defence;
- expecting the parties to cooperate with each other on a number of fronts (see Chapters 3–6 and 16);
- dealing with matters without the parties having to attend court; and
- ordering a stay to encourage the parties to settle.

The aim of 'case management' is included within the ethos and the aims of the overriding objective—(CPR 1.1)—that is, ensuring that cases are dealt with justly (which includes 'enforcing compliance with rules, practice directions, and orders'), fairly, expeditiously, and proportionately (to the value and as to costs). To accommodate these objectives, in multi-track non-PI cases a menu approach will be taken to the directions orders a case may need, and for cases in the fast track and PI multi-track, fixed or standardized management directions and timetables are used as much as possible. In both the fast track and the multi-track, it will be for the parties to seek directions and management decisions that better suit their cases if these can be justified (within the provisions of the overriding objectives). Requests for 'tailor-made' directions will usually be set out in, or accompany, the directions questionnaire, Forms N180 or N181 (see paragraph 12.3). The courts can entertain requests for specific directions at any time, but if an application is made late, the justification for it will have to be strong and very persuasive.

The court has power to encourage and to compel parties to comply with court decisions. A failure to meet the directions and orders set can result in a variety of costs penalties. These may include an order to pay the other party's costs of a hearing or application of a 'wasted costs' order against the legal representatives (see Chapter 4, paragraph 4.8), an 'unless' order (in which the penalty for failing to comply is set down in the order), or an order to strike out that party's case or defence. CPR 3.9 requires the court to consider 'all the circumstances' of the case, so as to enable it to deal justly with any application for relief from a sanction the court has imposed on a party, including the need (a) for the litigation to be conducted efficiently and at a proportionate cost and (b) to enforce compliance with rules, practice directions, and orders. (See also paragraph 12.9.)

12.3 THE 'FIRST STEP' OF CASE MANAGEMENT—THE DIRECTIONS QUESTIONNAIRE (DQ)—(FORM N180: SMALL CLAIMS TRACK OR FORM N181: FAST AND MULTI-TRACK CLAIMS)

The first step in case management by the court will usually be taken once a defence is filed. Refer to the 'litigation train' at the beginning of this chapter. On the filing of the defence, the court will send a Notice of Proposed Allocation to all parties indicating the track to which the case is likely to be allocated (CPR 26.3). This will be accompanied with a Notice to download and complete the appropriate DQ (N180 for the small claims track and N181 for fast-track and multi-track cases). These must be completed and filed at the court and on each party within twenty-eight days of the deemed date of service of the Notice. Litigants in person will receive a paper copy of the DQ from the court rather than a notice.

12.3.1 CAN THE COURT EVER CASE MANAGE BEFORE ALLOCATION?

In some circumstances, steps will be taken on a case *before* the Notice of Proposed Allocation and the notice to file DQ are sent out to the parties. These provisions are listed in CPR 26 and predominantly include the occasions on which a case may be *automatically* transferred to the defendant's 'home court' (CPR 26.2).

CPR 26.2 (for cases in the High Court) and CPR 26.2A (for cases in the County Court) deal with the provisions for the automatic transfer of a case to the defendant's home court once a defence is filed:

- those that are defended;
- those that are for a specified sum; and
- those that are against individuals.

If there is more than one defendant, then the transfer will be to the home court of whichever of the defendants is an individual, or if there is more than one defendant who is an individual, the transfer will be to the home court of the first defendant to file his defence.

The definition of the defendant's 'home court' includes:

- for the High Court, the district registry for the district in which the defendant resides or carries on business, or where there is no such district registry, the Royal Courts of Justice; and
- for the County Court, the County Court in the jurisdiction in which the defendant resides or carries on business.

Other than the provisions mentioned that deal with an automatic transfer to another court, the procedure for and transfer between courts of other claims is dealt with in CPR 30.

Where the court orders a transfer, the court from which the claim is to be transferred must give notice of the transfer to all parties (CPR 30.4(1)).

12.3.2 WHEN WILL THE COURT CONVENE A CMC BEFORE CONFIRMING THE ALLOCATION OF THE CASE TO A TRACK?

→ *Case Management conference*

In most fast-track cases, there will be no need for a CMC. The case will be confirmed to the fast track and the directions order made after the filing of completed DQ by the parties (this will be within twenty-eight days of the deemed date of service of the Notice of Proposed Allocation). Equally in many (less complex) multi-track PI cases there may be no requirement for a CMC to be listed. However, for more complex high-value PI cases and for most non-PI multi-track cases the courts will list the case for a CMC after the Disclosure Report (and potentially the Electronic Disclosure Questionnaire) (see Chapter 16, paragraph 16.6) and costs budget have been filed. Where a CMC has been listed, the Disclosure Report must be filed at least fourteen days before the CMC and the costs budget at least seven days before the CMC. When a CMC has been listed, the court will then deal with case management and make the directions orders. The court may also treat any hearing that has occurred *before* it has received completed DQ as a CMC, and thus may dispense with the filing of completed DQ. In this way, the court will use some of the time of the hearing that is being heard to allocate the case to a track and make a directions order. This might happen if, for example, a party has made an application to the court for an interim injunction or for summary judgment (see Chapter 14): such applications can be made before a defence has been filed and so could be heard before the Notice of Proposed Allocation and the completed DQ have been sent.

A CMC may also be ordered in a case if the requests by the parties in their DQ (or by one party) for specific, tailor-made directions are either not agreed, or the request does not seem sufficiently justified.

12.3.3 THE COURT'S GENERAL PRACTICE ON ALLOCATION TO TRACK

After a defence is filed (or in a case in which there are multiple defendants, when the time limit for the filing of defences by all defendants has expired—CPR 26.3(2)), the court will send each of the parties a Notice of Proposed Allocation to track and request that they download, complete, and file a DQ in Form N180 (for cases in the small claims track) or in Form N181 (for all fast-track and multi-track cases). (As already stated, litigants in person will receive a paper copy of the DQ from the court rather than a notice to download the form and complete it.)

Fees are not required on the filing of DQ. (They are included in the issue fee.) Details of fees to be paid in litigation are contained in the Civil Proceedings and Family Proceedings Fees (Amendment) Order 2015, which sets out details of the fees payable in both the High Court and the County Court.

The notice to download, complete, and file a DQ will usually give the parties twenty-eight days in which to complete and return the DQ (fourteen days in the small claims track—CPR 26.3(6)). Parties may not, of their own accord or by agreement between themselves, vary the time permitted for the completion and filing of the form. Parties are expected to complete DQs, because the information sought from the parties on this form will enable and assist the court to make the best use of the available resources, including the amount of 'judicial time' that should be spent on the case, and order the appropriate directions for the case. In this way, the procedural judges will be able to make decisions and directions for the future conduct of the case that are 'proportionate (to the value of the claim and to the costs of pursuing it)', 'fair', and 'expeditious'. Normally, if the parties have completed the sections in the DQ properly and fully, it will provide the court with additional information about the progress (if any) that the parties have made towards resolving the dispute through alternative methods, and the progress that has been made in preparing evidence and settling the identity of any expert that may be needed and details of the appropriate directions order that the parties themselves feel are appropriate for the case.

12.3.4 WHAT HAPPENS IF ONE OR BOTH PARTIES FAIL TO FILE A COMPLETED DQ?

In practical terms, it is unlikely that the claimant will fail to complete his DQ. There are many rules and safeguards within the CPR that are intended to prevent parties from filing cases in court as 'threats' to their opponent, but with which they have, in reality, no real intention of proceeding. These include the need to sign statements of truth, and the costs penalties of unreasonably starting a case or raising issues that are not, or should not, be proceeded with. These sanctions and safeguards should mean that the number of cases in which the claimant intentionally fails to complete and file the DQ is few. It could happen that the claimant has simply failed to diarize the date on which the completed DQ should be filed at court, but even in these circumstances, the provisions requiring parties to consult with one another and to cooperate in completing their DQ (PD 26.2.3) should mean that where one party may have forgotten the deadline date, they are likely to be reminded of the need to complete and file it by the other party. It is important to note that even though the CPR seek to ensure that the parties consult and cooperate in the filing of the DQ, this consultation process cannot be used to delay the filing of the completed forms. In genuine cases in which there is a good reason for the delay in completing and filing the forms, and more time is needed (and can be fully justified), then the party (or parties) may apply to the court for further time. With the court's increased emphasis on compliance with court rules, legal representatives should never consider that extra time will be readily granted.

12.3.4.1 If completed DQ are not returned by any of the parties

If completed DQ are not returned by any of the parties, the court will order that unless a DQ is filed by a certain date (usually within seven days from the date of service of the order), the claim, defence, and any counterclaim will be struck out (CPR 26.3(7A), 26.3(8), and PD 26.2.5).

12.3.4.2 If completed DQ are filed by one (or some) of the parties, but not the other(s)

If the completed DQ are filed by only one (or some) of the parties, but not all involved, the case will be referred to the procedural judge and he may:

- confirm the proposed allocation to track should he feel that there is enough information supplied within any DQ that have been returned; or

- order that the parties attend a CMC. These are now automatically conducted by telephone (PD 23A.6(2))—see paragraph 12.6). The court may also order that the costs of the parties attending be paid by the party that failed to file its DQ.

In reality, if it is the claimant who has failed to file his DQ, the more likely order will be along the lines of that in paragraph 12.3.4.1, because the court is unlikely to see any benefit in progressing a case which the claimant does not seem to wish to pursue. Where the defendant has included a counterclaim in his defence and he has filed his completed DQ, then the court may, if it is appropriate to do so, either order an allocation hearing that all parties must attend, or make an order that will enable the defendant's counterclaim to proceed.

12.4 FORMS N180 AND N181—THE DQ

Form N180 is used in all cases in the small claims track, and Form N181 for all cases in the fast track and multi-track. DQ are not required in the specialist courts—claims in the Commercial Court, Technology and Construction Court, and Mercantile Courts use different forms and procedures. Legal representatives in any claim issued in the specialist courts should consult the specialist court guides for details of the procedure in these courts. Please see the blank DQ in Form N181 in the online resources. See also the 'Case study documentation' section of the online resources and the 'Annotated forms' section, in which there are some practical notes to aid completion of the form.

12.5 COSTS INFORMATION ON THE DQ OR THE REQUIREMENT TO FILE A COSTS BUDGET IN PRECEDENT H

Chapter 20 on 'Assessment of Costs Proceedings', at paragraph 20.3.5.8, notes that a legal representative's costs estimate made in the DQ may be binding in fast-track and multi-track cases where there has been no Costs Management Order (CMO). (This is where the court has formally recorded the extent to which the costs budgets are agreed or approved by the court.) CPR PD 44.3.2 states that if there is a difference of 20 per cent or more between the estimate given and the final costs being claimed, that party may be asked to provide a statement of the reasons for the difference. It will also be very pertinent to any costs recovery that the client had been made aware of the difference and had authorized it. CPR PD 44.3.4 also provides that the court 'may' take the estimate into account.

In cases where there are no CMOs, a costs estimate made in the DQ should be as accurate as possible and must be served on the client. If steps are taken on the case that would increase this estimate, a full file note should be made, the client informed, and his instructions to incur the additional costs obtained.

As suggested previously, for all **multi-track cases** the parties will have been ordered to file a cost budget in Precedent H, but there may not always be a residual CMO. Where there is a CMO the costs budget must be filed at least twenty-one days before the first CMC (CPR 3.13). The deadline for filing a cost budget had previously been seven days before the first CMC. The extended time frame is intended to encourage parties to agree cost budgets. (See Chapter 4, paragraph 4.6.3.)

12.5.1 FAILURE TO FILE A COSTS BUDGET

CPR 3.14 provides: 'Unless the court otherwise orders, any party which fails to file a budget despite being required to do so will be treated as having filed a budget comprising only the applicable court fees.'

Paragraph 6(a) of Practice Direction (PD) 3E provides that, unless the court otherwise orders, a budget must be in the form of Precedent H annexed to the PD. It goes on to say that, in substantial cases, the court may direct that budgets be limited initially to part only of the proceedings and subsequently extended to cover the whole proceedings.

The High Court has imposed severe sanctions on a claimant who 'genuinely but mistakenly' thought it was acceptable to file a costs budget excluding the phases of trial preparation and trial, see *Page v RGC Restaurants Ltd* [2018] EWHC 2688 (QB).

The decision illustrates the risks of filing a 'materially incomplete' costs budget, even where a party considers it premature to budget for the later stages of the action. In these circumstances it seems the only safe course is to budget for the entire action, unless the court has made an order directing that budgets be limited to only part of the proceedings.

12.6 ALLOCATION TO TRACK

Once a defence has been filed, the court will give Notice of the Proposed Allocation to track (see Chapter 9, paragraph 9.2, and paragraph 12.6.2, in this chapter) and direct that the parties download and complete the appropriate DQ. The court may dispense with the need for DQ to be completed; this may happen when another application (for example, an application for summary judgment or for strike-out) has been treated as an allocation hearing (see paragraph 12.3.2). Pursuant to CPR 26.3(6), the specified date for filing any documents required by the Notice of Proposed Allocation (and this will usually be a requirement to complete and file the DQ) will be at least:

- fourteen days after the Notice of Proposed Allocation is deemed served (for small claims track cases); or

- twenty-eight days after the Notice of Proposed Allocation is deemed served (for fast-track and multi-track cases).

On receipt of the completed DQ, the procedural judge will either confirm the track and make a directions order or will order a CMC to be listed. Where a CMC is listed, the parties will also be ordered to file a Disclosure Report (and possibly an Electronic Disclosure Questionnaire) and costs budget (see paragraph 12.3.2). A case can be 'down-tracked' in a case where both parties and the court agree that this is appropriate (see paragraph 12.6.3). A 'procedural judge' may include a master (for cases proceeding in the Royal Courts of Justice), or a district judge and circuit judge in the district registries and county courts. The parties have the opportunity in their replies to the questions in the DQ to influence the directions order that the judge will make to manage the case. Any request for a tailor-made directions order for the particular case will need to be justified by the party requesting it. The ultimate power to make case management decisions rests with the procedural judge.

The court will now automatically hear CMC over the phone wherever possible. (See the Additional Chapter 'A Practical Guide to Court Hearings' in the online resources.)

On occasions, the hearing of another application could be *treated* as the first CMC, where the court will confirm allocation to track and make the directions order. Legal representatives should always attend any such hearings fully prepared to discuss with the judge issues of allocation and the appropriate directions order to be made for the future management of the case. Where such a first CMC is listed or a hearing has been heard before the court has formally confirmed the allocation to a track, a legal representative who attends the hearing should, wherever possible, be the person who is responsible for the case (or at least part of the legal team responsible for the case). In any event, he must be familiar with the case, and have sufficient authority to deal with issues that may arise so as to be able to provide the court with any information that it might seek in order to make its decision on matters of allocation to track and the directions order appropriate for the case. See PD 26.6.5.

The majority of cases proceed between the filing of the defence and trial with a directions order that is more or less in standard form, but, when necessary, tailored to the needs of the particular case.

12.6.1 WHEN WILL ALLOCATION TAKE PLACE?

Generally, confirmation of the allocation to track—which includes both the allocation to track and any directions—will be made once the procedural judge has considered the DQ returned or, in cases where a first CMC has been listed at this hearing after the Disclosure Report, Electronic Disclosure Questionnaire, and costs budget have been filed, or possibly when the time limit for the filing of DQ has expired (see paragraphs 12.3.4.1 and 12.3.4.2).

If one or more of the parties have requested it, or if the court decides that it is appropriate to do so, the action can be 'stayed' for a period of time (in the fast track often for a period of one month) to enable ADR to be tried. In these circumstances, confirmation of allocation will not be made until after the period of stay ordered.

In cases in which the case is to be transferred to another court or hearing centre or to a specialist court, allocation decisions will be taken after the transfer by the procedural judge in the court or hearing centre to which the case is transferred—although note CPR 26.3(3), under which the court in which the claim was started will issue the Notice of Proposed Allocation request to the parties to file DQ before transferring the case. Unless the transfer is to one of the specialist courts, the notice will instruct that the completed DQ be returned to the court or hearing centre to which the case is transferred. A case transferred to a specialist court will be processed in accordance with the rules and procedures of the specialist court to which the case has been transferred.

12.6.2 WHAT DOES THE COURT CONSIDER WHEN ALLOCATING TO TRACK?

There are nine basic principles that the court will consider when allocating a case to the appropriate track. These are set out in CPR 26.8(1) and PD 26.7 and include:

- the financial value of the claim—that is, the sum that represents the 'financial value' of the case for tracking purposes, disregarding any amount not in dispute, any claim for interest or costs, and any claim of contributory negligence (CPR 26.8(2)). This principle is important to bear in mind in practice at all times. Both the Protocol phase of litigation, the rules of litigation and drafting statements of case, are designed to encourage parties to narrow the issues between them and, in doing so, the value of the claim may well be reduced. Narrowing the issues, admitting or agreeing what can be agreed, or being realistic in terms of the sum claimed in the Protocol phase can have significant impact on the 'value' of the claim for tracking purposes. Where the court believes that the amount being claimed by the claimant (or the defendant in any counterclaim) exceeds what that party may reasonably be expected to recover, it can make an order directing that the party justify the amount being claimed (CPR 26.5(3));

- the remedy sought;
- the complexity of the claim—which may include complexities of law, fact, and/or evidence; and
- where there is no financial value, the court will allocate the case to the most appropriate track, having regard to matters such as complexity, numbers of witnesses, the importance of the claim to persons who are not parties (in effect, those matters listed in CPR 26.8(1)).

12.6.3 CAN A CASE BE PLACED IN A TRACK THAT IS ABOVE, OR BELOW, ITS INDICATIVE TRACK?

A case can be placed in a different track. The criteria for cases to be heard in the small claims track should not be seen only as a question of value, although 'value' is the guiding principle that sets a case in that track. The small claims track is intended to provide a proportionate procedure for the most straightforward claims. Although a claim may exceed the small claims track financial limit, parties should consider whether it would, in fact, be more proportionate, more just, and more efficient for the case to be heard in the small claims track rather than the track that its value would indicate.

The court may also place a case in a track higher than its financial value would indicate if it is appropriate to do so (having regard to the matters listed in CPR 26.8(1)).

In practice, there may be cogent reasons why a party may wish to have his claim allocated to the 'highest' track, because it may mean that:

- the matter will be determined by a more senior judge;
- there may be more flexibility to recover more costs; and
- there may be more flexibility in the directions orders that can be made, and more flexibility in the amount of oral evidence to be given and the amount of expert evidence that may be permitted.

12.6.4 REALLOCATION

The court has discretion to reallocate a claim to a different track (CPR 26.10). This may happen if there has been a change in the circumstances, or nature, or value of the claim.

If a party is unhappy with the allocation order that has been made, he may appeal the order if he (or his legal representative) had been present at a CMC hearing (if such took place), or apply to the court to reallocate. In either case, the party should have clear reasons for asking the court to reallocate. An appeal would be with permission to a circuit judge, or, if by application, either by letter or Form N244, usually to the district judge who made the original order.

If a reallocation order is made, it is also likely to result in a change of the directions order made for the future management of the case. Any appeal or application by a party for reallocation should therefore also take account of, and suggest where appropriate, the changes that may be needed in the case management directions.

12.7 CASE MANAGEMENT: THE DIRECTIONS ORDER

Once the judge has confirmed or allocated a case to track he will then also make the case management directions order. This will set down all of the steps which the parties need to comply with, and when they must comply, in order to make the case ready for hearing. The directions order may indicate the steps which the parties need to comply with all the way to trial, or (more commonly) will set directions orders up to the point of the issuing of pre-trial checklists (Form N170—see paragraph 12.7.3.3), at which time the court will undertake a similar review of the action and set a further directions order of the steps that are required to manage the case on to trial.

12.7.1 WHAT TYPE OF DIRECTIONS ORDER WILL GENERALLY BE MADE?

Details of the most likely directions that may be made in an action will be contained in the CPR applicable to the track in which the case is placed (CPR Parts 27–29).

When making directions, the court will be seeking to apply the principles of the overriding objective. The aim of the directions made will be to ensure that the case proceeds on its path to trial properly, efficiently, and proportionately. Accordingly, every attempt will be made to clarify the issues in dispute (and encouragement is evident for the parties to seek to narrow the issues in dispute) and to control the evidence.

In the DQ, parties must either set out agreed directions or proposed directions. Parties can have reference to the 'standard directions' (contained in PD 28, and see paragraph 12.7.3) or in the schedule of typical directions orders contained in the menu options found in the CPR for multi-track non-PI cases (PD 29). Where inadequate information has been given in the DQ, the court is likely to set down standard directions and timescales.

12.7.2 WHAT INFORMATION SHOULD BE GIVEN BY THE PARTIES IN THEIR DQ?

If the parties have cooperated with each other, as they are required to do, in the preparation of their DQ, and, further, they have agreed the directions that they feel are needed for the management of the case either to trial or to the next CMC (which will probably be a pre-trial review), the procedural judge may simply endorse their proposals and make the directions order proposed.

In order to obtain the court's approval in this way, any proposals should:

- if appropriate, deal with the filing of a reply to a defence;
- if appropriate, deal with any amendments to a statement of case;
- make provisions for disclosure and inspection—its extent, as well as the time allowed;
- propose directions concerning the exchange of evidence of fact and expert evidence (if any). If there is expert evidence, the proposals should include a direction concerning the type of expert permitted, the timing of exchange of reports (if more than one), questions to the expert, and any meeting between experts (again if more than one expert has been permitted). In the fast track, the normal order for any expert evidence will be for a single joint expert;
- include dates on which any requests for further information may be made and complied with;
- state when the trial period should be set and the date for the sending out of pre-trial checklists (PTCs, Form N170) and the pre-trial review or hearing;
- if appropriate, set a date for a further CMC; and
- consider a stay for ADR.

The court may accept or reject the proposals, but, in making its directions order, will have regard to the proposals put forward by the parties. The ultimate responsibility for case management directions remains with the court.

In the fast track and PI cases in the multi-track, the order will normally be for 'standard directions'.

12.7.3 WHAT ARE 'STANDARD DIRECTIONS'?

'Standard directions' are established under the CPR. They represent the case management directions that apply generally to the average, relatively un-complex, claim. These can be found in the PD for each track. They seek to ensure that the claim will progress efficiently, proportionately (as to the value and costs), and justly.

12.7.3.1 In the small claims track

Standard directions in the small claims track are set out in CPR 27.4(3) and PD 27, Appendix B. These include:

- the requirement to exchange copies of all documents on which a party will rely usually at least fourteen days before the hearing;

- a requirement that the parties should file at court (for cases which will be determined as 'paper' hearings without the parties attending) or to bring originals of the documents to a hearing (where the court has determined that a hearing be listed);

- if appropriate a notice of the date and time of, and time allowed for, any final hearing;

- a note encouraging parties to communicate with each other, with a view to settling the dispute, coupled with a requirement that they should notify the court in writing if they do settle; and

- a note that no expert report will be permitted unless express permission has been granted.

PD 27, Appendix C, sets out the special directions that may be made or requested in this track. The purpose of special directions is to enable the case management of these low-value claims to be more effective, just, and proportionate (to their value and to the amount of costs being incurred). They may include directions regarding the issues on which the court requires evidence, the nature of the evidence required, and the way in which the evidence will be presented. (This is not a definitive list of special directions that could be made, but it gives useful guidance to any practitioner who is assisting a party who is conducting or defending a claim in this track, or a party who is acting in person.)

Because some of the CPR on matters relating to expert evidence, witnesses of fact, disclosure, and inspection do not apply to the small claims track (CPR 27.2), it may be necessary for the court to specify, or for the parties to seek, special directions because of the particular needs of the case, although it must be borne in mind that the overriding objective applies to the small claims track and that any request for special directions must meet with this objective. If the number of special directions needed, or some other reason, means that it is appropriate to do so, the court may, of its own initiative or upon the application of a party, reallocate a case from the small claims track to the fast track. It may also add, vary, or revoke any special directions made.

One of the most common special directions that may be sought may be a special direction that the parties exchange witness statements before the final hearing (this being a standard direction in both the fast track and the multi-track). Before making any such order, the court will have regard to the matters set out in the PD 27.2.5. These considerations include:

- whether there is to be a hearing and whether either or both parties are represented;

- the amount in dispute;

- the nature of the matters in dispute;

- whether it would be better for a party to be asked to clarify his case better before the hearing; and

- the need to provide for 'justice' without undue formality, cost, or delay.

12.7.3.2 In the fast track

The case management directions order in cases allocated to the fast track will generally (but not always) be given in two stages:

(a) when allocation to track has been confirmed and the first directions order is made and

(b) on the filing of pre-trial checklists (PTCs) in Form N170—(see paragraph 12.7.3.3).

On both occasions, the court will expect a degree of cooperation between the parties and will make the directions order wherever possible without a CMC. Where a CMC does have to take place, this will be by telephone (PD 23A.6.2). The court will also readily impose costs sanctions if the requirement for a CMC has been necessitated by either a lack of cooperation of a party or the default of a party in the completion of the DQ. Also, if a CMC has to take place, the parties have a duty to attend that hearing, having considered what directions order they wish the court to make.

The court will take account of the steps that the parties have already taken in the Protocol period to make the case ready for trial.

The Appendix in PD 28 contains the form of fast-track standard directions and, wherever possible, the court will base its directions order on those set out in the Appendix.

One of the principles that guide the decisions that the court will make for a fast-track case directions order will be the court's duty under CPR 28.2(2) to set a case management timetable and to fix a trial date (or trial period). This trial date or trial period shall not be longer than thirty weeks from the date of the directions order. Where parties recommend an agreed directions order to the court, they must equally ensure that the agreed directions order provides specific dates for steps to be completed, include a trial period (that must not be longer than thirty weeks from the date of the directions order), and include provisions about disclosure of documents and the management of both fact and expert evidence.

A typical timetable for the preparation of a fast-track case to trial would be a directions order that provided for:

- disclosure within four weeks (from the date of the directions order);
- an exchange of witness statements within ten weeks (from the date of the directions order);
- an exchange of expert reports within fourteen weeks (from the date of the directions order), together with any additional directions that may be needed—for example, concerning questions to the expert, or who is to pay the expert's fees;
- the date on which PTCs will be sent out by the court—typically, twenty weeks (from the date of the directions order);
- the date on which the PTCs must be returned—typically, twenty-two weeks (from the date of the directions order); and
- the date of the trial or trial period—typically, thirty weeks (from the date of the directions order).

If a party is dissatisfied with the directions order, or the parties have agreed that there should be changes made to the order, or if, for other reasons, changes are appropriate, an application for the change should be made at the earliest opportunity. This would be by notice of application to the court on Form N244, with reasons. Such an application will usually be heard by the master or district judge who made the original order. If an application is made later than fourteen days from the date of the order, the court will assume that the directions order made was appropriate at the time and therefore any changes will need to be justified. If the original directions order was made at a CMC at which the party was present or represented (or at which the party had had due notice of the hearing), he must appeal the order if he seeks changes. In any other circumstance, the party may apply to the court to reconsider the directions order made. In these circumstances, the application will usually be heard by the judge (or at least a judge of the same level) who made the original directions order.

Not satisfied with Directions order ?

 Practical Considerations

If a case requires special directions, it will be essential in practice to be prepared to state, and justify (within the provisions of the overriding objective), what special directions you think your case needs and make a request to the court for the special directions at the earliest opportunity. This will probably be in or accompanying the DQ.

12.7.3.3 The pre-trial checklists (PTCs) Form N170

Where the case management directions order for a case allocated to the fast track has been given in two stages, the initial directions order will usually give directions up to the point at which the court sends out PTCs to the parties. This form has a similar function to the DQ—that is, it seeks information from the parties that enables the court to determine the appropriate directions order that should be made guiding the case from that stage and on to trial. It also enables the parties to seek specific tailor-made directions if justified. Again, the parties should cooperate with one another in the completion of the PTC.

There is a fee for the filing of the PTC, this is the first part of the trial fee, (the second part is payable prior to trial as directed by the court). If the case settles or is discontinued a part (or in some situations, the whole) of the fee can be reclaimed. This is set out in paragraph 2.1 of the Civil Proceedings and Family Proceedings Fees (Amendment) Order 2015. Even when the court has not made a two-stage directions order to trial, both the pre-trial fees will be payable by the claimant within fourteen days of the specified dates. If the case is proceeding on a defendant's counterclaim alone, he will need to pay this hearing fee. If the hearing fee is not paid, the court will issue a reminder to the party, but CPR 3.7 and 3.7A enables the court to strike out the claim for non-payment after the reminder.

The purpose of the PTC is to:

- check the directions order to date has been complied with; and

- provide more detailed information about the trial requirements so that it can make a directions order dealing with the steps necessary to make the case ready for the trial and to include any directions for the trial itself.

The completed PTCs will be placed before the procedural judge, who will decide whether to make a trial directions order from the completed lists or to call a pre-trial review (or pre-trial directions) hearing or CMC. The court will also again consider whether there should be a stay for any further attempt at settlement by a method of ADR.

A typical directions order that may be made on receipt of the completed PTCs includes:

- confirming or fixing the trial date;

- directions concerning evidence, the number of witnesses, expert evidence (if permission has been granted at allocation directions or subsequently), or for expert evidence to be adduced;

- indicating whether a trial timetable and trial estimate are required;

- provisions concerning the preparation of the trial bundle; and

- any other relevant directions (for example, the provision of an interpreter, specific IT facility, etc.).

The trial judge can be pragmatic in his requirements for individual trials and such 'hands-on' directions were given in the case of *Multiplex Construction (UK) Ltd v (1) Cleveland Bridge UK Ltd (2) Cleveland Bridge Dorman Long Ltd* [2008] EWHC 231 (TCC), in which the TCC trial judge ordered that each party were to share the time allocated for the trial equally, that parts of the evidence were to be left to the trial judge's private reading, and that post-trial hearings were to take place to provide the parties with parts of his judgment and to discuss issues in the case. This style of case management is becoming more prevalent in the specialist courts.

12.7.3.4 In the multi-track

A multi-track directions order is, in practice, appropriate for cases in this track:

- that are worth more than £25,000;

- in which the trial is estimated to last for more than a day; and

- in which each party will need to adduce expert oral evidence either in more than one field of expertise, or from more than one expert in a particular field.

Multi-track claims can be heard in either one of the County Court hearing centres or the High Court, or one of its district registries, but unless there are particular factors of the case (complexity, legal principle), any case that is worth less than £100,000 will invariably be listed *for trial* in a County Court hearing centre. Cases on the multi-track will generally be dealt with either in the Royal Courts of Justice or other trial centres in the district registries.

12.7.3.4.1 *Case management directions in the multi-track*

Cases on this track are typically more complex and are of higher value than the cases in the small claims track or the fast track; accordingly, the case management directions order for these cases is likely to be more flexible and more likely to be tailored to meet the specific requirements of the case. The degree of flexibility available for actions within this track will reflect the wide variety of actions—from complex but quite low-value claims to claims involving great sums of money, or claims that raise matters of public importance. The emphasis is again on 'efficiency', 'fairness', and 'proportionality (to the value and to costs incurred)', and in claims that are less complex, the court will seek to make standard directions without the need for a CMC. Such claims will be given a directions order with tight timetables that are similar to the standard directions in the fast track. As in the fast track, parties are under a duty to be well prepared for hearings and to give consideration to the directions orders that they may require. Again, parties are expected to cooperate with one another in agreeing the directions that they seek.

At the time that the DQ (in Form N181) is filed for cases in this track, the procedural judge will decide whether to make the directions order or to fix a CMC and direct that the parties file a Disclosure Report, Electronic Disclosure Questionnaire, and costs budget before that CMC (see paragraph 12.3.2). The procedural judge will also consider whether to order a stay (whether sought by one or more parties in the action or not) while ADR procedures are attempted to settle the case or to narrow the issues.

If a party feels that the directions order is wrong or wishes to seek amendment to it, the rule that applies in the fast track concerning the directions order (that the court will assume that the directions order was correct for the circumstances of the case when made) applies equally in the multi-track and unless a prompt application to vary is made (within fourteen days, under PD 29.6.2(2)), and is fully justified, changes are unlikely to be made.

12.7.3.4.2 *What is a 'usual directions order' in a multi-track case?*

The directions order in cases allocated to the multi-track will generally (but not always) be given in two stages:

(a) when the court has confirmed the allocation and makes its first directions order with all the steps the parties must comply with up until the date of filing of the PTC; and

(b) on the filing of PTCs (Form N170—see paragraph 12.7.3.3) where the court will then make the directions order with the steps the parties must comply with from then on to make the case ready for trial (including orders for the trial itself).

As in the small claims track and the fast track, the court aims to set an efficient and proportionate and fair path for the action to trial. The court will usually consider:

- whether there is a need for an order to clarify the points in issue. This may be undertaken either by making orders for further information to be filed (CPR 18), or for amended statements of case to be prepared and filed and served;

- whether there should be an order for a stay to enable the parties to engage in a form of ADR;

- whether a Costs Management Order (CMO) should be made;

- what should be the scope of any disclosure and inspection;

- the number of witnesses of fact that are required and provision for the exchange of witness statements. Orders can be made to restrict the issues on which evidence will be given;

- whether there is a requirement for expert evidence. The court will further consider whether this should be by single joint experts or by each party having their own expert, and consider in which fields of expertise expert evidence is required. The court will consider what provisions need be made concerning expert evidence (for example, 'questions to an expert' or 'meetings between experts') and whether there needs to be a provision for oral evidence by the expert(s) at trial. As with witnesses of fact, orders can be made to restrict the issues on which expert evidence will be given;

- whether it is appropriate, on grounds of costs, efficiency, fairness, or proportionality, for there to be an order for a 'split trial' (between matters of liability and quantum), or whether there should be a trial of one or more preliminary issues (see Chapter 16, paragraph 16.2.2);

- whether there should be another CMC or pre-trial review hearing and when;

- whether it is possible to fix a trial period; and

- at which court, or before which calibre of judge, the matter should be listed for trial.

Parties will refer to the suggested draft directions contained at http://www.justice.gov.uk/courts/procedure-rules/civil/standard.directions when drafting their proposed directions order submitted with their completed DQ.

For an example of a Directions Order please see Appendix 6.

12.8 CASE MANAGEMENT CONFERENCES (CMC)

A first CMC may be held after the filing of DQ, the disclosure report, and the costs budget where the court will confirm allocation to a track and consider a directions order (usually in two stages; see paragraph 12.7.3.4.2). It may also have arisen immediately after the hearing of an early interim application (see paragraph 12.3.2). Often, the parties will also be prompted to try (or to try again) some form of ADR procedure to settle the case. In any event, the procedural judge will seek to use the hearing to progress matters efficiently, justly, and proportionately, and not only to make a directions order but also, for example, by encouraging parties to narrow the issues in dispute, or to order that certain issues shall not be proceeded with. CPR 32.2(3) gives the court power to limit evidence and the issues that the case proceeds with.

 Practical Considerations

It is important to remember that no mention must be made by the parties at the CMC of any CPR Part 36 offers that have been made in the action, or the details of any attempts at ADR.

Attendance at CMC should be by a legal representative who is familiar with the issues of the case and who has the appropriate authority to deal with matters arising at it (CPR 29.3(2) and PD 29.5.2).

 Practical Considerations

If the person attending the CMC does not have sufficient knowledge, or experience, or authority to deal with matters arising at the hearing, and the hearing has to be adjourned because of that lack of knowledge or authority, then a wasted costs order will usually be made.

If parties have been ordered to attend and the party is a company, it should be someone from the company who has knowledge of the history of the case.

At the CMC, the court will:

- make a review of the steps taken by the parties to progress the action;

- review how far the parties have complied with any previous directions or orders;

- decide on further directions or orders (that are within the spirit of the overriding objective);

- seek to encourage consensus, wherever possible, on issues, directions, orders, or future conduct; and

- record any agreements.

If the court feels that it will assist the efficiency of the CMC or the progress of the action, an order may be made in advance of the CMC, or before the hearing of any next CMC, for a case summary to be prepared by the parties and lodged at court. The court may equally order that certain documents (in a 'case management bundle') be prepared and lodged for the hearing. The Court Guides for High Court matters may also specify certain requirements for CMC.

12.9 WHAT HAPPENS IF A PARTY FAILS TO COMPLY WITH A CASE MANAGEMENT DIRECTION?

The court retains control of actions, and has powers of coercion and sanctions to ensure that, so far as possible, parties comply with the orders made. These include the following provisions and powers to:

- strike out a party's case—that is, the most draconian measure that is used in only the most serious cases of default or breach;

- make an 'unless order'—that is, the court will make an order against the defaulting party to compel compliance, but if they fail to do so, the 'unless' provision will apply. This 'unless' provision could be an order to strike out all or part of that party's case. In either track, where the directions order for trial has been set and the times allowed are 'tight', the court will be prepared to impose an 'unless' order on a party even after only one breach (see Chapter 13, paragraph 13.10);

- make adverse costs orders—the court may also provide that those costs orders be payable immediately;

- make an order for indemnity costs or increased interest on damages or costs;

- make an order that a defaulting party pay money into court;

- debar a party from proceeding with an issue, or from amending its statement of case, or from filing additional evidence;

- restrict the numbers of witnesses that may be called (including an expert witness); and

- refuse to grant any application for further time.

In respect of any of these orders and sanctions, the court will consider wasted costs orders against the legal representative if the reason for the party's default rests with the legal representative.

If both parties, or more than one party, in an action are in default, the court will consider a sanction order against either or both parties in default.

If a party defaults, it can apply to the court for relief from sanctions (CPR 3.9). This rule is intended to ensure that the parties focus on compliance with rules and court orders ('compliance' is part of CPR 3.9). The case of *Mitchell v News Group Newspapers Ltd* [2013] EWHC 2355 (QB) gave the following guidance on the approach the courts should follow where a party applies for relief from a sanction imposed following a breach of a court rule or an order:

- Where non-compliance is trivial and an application for relief from sanctions is made promptly, the court will often grant relief.

- The defaulting party must persuade the court that there was good reason for the default.

- If the party believes that the order was wrong when made, then the appropriate application is an appeal or an application to revoke or vary the order.

Generally any application for 'relief from sanctions' should only be made where there has been 'a material change of circumstance'. The more recent case *Thevarajah v Riordan* [2015] EWCA Civ 14 has added detail to this general overview of the courts' approach to an application for 'relief from sanctions'—and stated that a party who has finally complied with an order cannot use this as a reason for being relieved of sanctions the court had imposed on it for failing to abide by an order on time or as directed.

CPR 3.8 should be noted and does provide some leeway as it enables parties to agree extensions of time (to comply with an order), in writing, for up to twenty-eight days, without court approval, *provided* such extensions do not put a hearing at risk.

'Relief from sanctions' under CPR 3.9 was also considered in the case *Page v RGC Restaurants Ltd* [2018] EWHC 2688 (QB) referred to in paragraph 12.5.1 above. (See also Chapter 13, paragraph 13.11.) This case discussed the vital difference between disapplying the sanction under CPR 3.14 itself, where the court 'otherwise orders', and seeking relief from sanctions under CPR 3.9. On an application under CPR 3.9, the court's starting point is that the sanction has been properly imposed and complies with the overriding objective. That is a significant fetter on the court's ability to grant relief. That fetter does not apply where the court considers whether to dis-apply the sanction under CPR 3.14.

In this case, the judge considered whether to make an order dis-applying the sanction under CPR 3.14 in whole or in part. Both sides agreed that for this purpose the court must adopt the structured approach set out in *Denton v TH White Ltd* [2014] EWCA Civ 906 i.e.: (1) to identify the seriousness and significance of the breach; (2) to consider why the breach occurred; and (3) to evaluate all the circumstances so as to deal justly with the matter, taking in account the need for litigation to be conducted efficiently and at proportionate cost and to enforce compliance with rules, practice directions, and orders.

Applying this test, the judge concluded that:

1. The breach was moderately serious and moderately significant.

2. The claimant's advisors genuinely but mistakenly thought it was acceptable to file a budget which left over the trial preparation and trial phases to be considered later. That amounted to 'negligence', but not 'gross negligence'.

3. There was a clear distinction between what happened in relation to the phases of trial preparation and trial and what happened in relation to the earlier phases. It would be unjust to apply the CPR 3.14 sanction to the earlier phases. Applying the sanction to the trial preparation and trial phases would have severe consequences for the claimant and would fully serve the important considerations of encouraging efficiency, proportionality, and compliance.

The judge considered but rejected the claimant's application for relief from sanctions in respect of this more limited sanction.

 Practical Considerations

Legal representatives have a duty to help to further the overriding objective (CPR 1.3). It is, therefore, inappropriate to 'sit back' and let an action stagnate: delay by one party does not justify any delay by any other party.

12.10 **THE CASE MANAGEMENT FLOWCHART**

Figure 12.1 will guide you through the most significant aspects of case management.

FIGURE 12.1 CASE MANAGEMENT

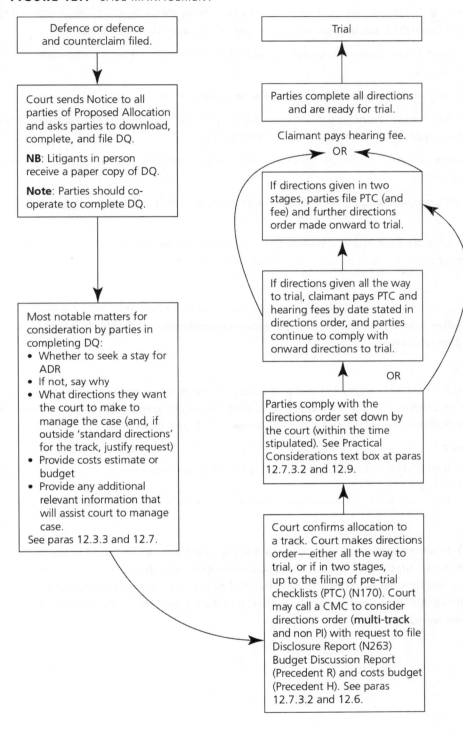

KEY POINTS SUMMARY

- Often the court's first step in 'active case management' will occur when a case is allocated to track and the court makes the first directions order to provide a timetable of the steps the parties must comply with, either in one stage (to trial) or in two stages: firstly, those steps to be undertaken up to the filing of form N170, and then secondly, from then on, to (and including) the trial.

- Parties are expected to cooperate in completing their DQ and to assist the court in the preparation of the directions order.

- The court will look to impose 'standard directions' wherever possible.

- Details of the standard directions applicable to each track can be found in the CPR and accompanying Practice Directions pertaining to the track (CPR 27–29).

- Any directions outside standard directions will need to be justified within the provisions of the overriding objective.

- Parties must be prompt in applying to the court for tailored directions orders and fully justify their request.

- The court will impose sanctions if a party fails to comply with the directions order set down unless extensions of time have been agreed in accordance with CPR 3.8(4).

Case Studies *Andrew James Pike v Deep Builders Ltd/Bollingtons Ltd v Mrs Elizabeth Lynch t/a The Honest Lawyer*

Question 1

Complete the DQ for the claimant in each of the two case studies. When completing the form consider whether the defendant (in each of the case studies) would be likely to agree the order sought or may seek to ask for a different order. (You do not need to complete the DQ for the defendant.)

Question 2

Prepare a suitable directions order that you feel the claimant could seek from the court for each of the two case studies.

 Any documents referred to in these case study questions can be found in the online resources—simply click on 'Case study documentation' to access the documents that you need for Chapter 12 and to be reminded of the questions. Suggested answers to these self-test questions can be accessed in the Student Resources section of the online resources.

13 INTERIM APPLICATIONS—GENERAL CONSIDERATIONS

It may also be appropriate to access and read the additional chapter 'Injunctions and other Equitable Remedies' contained in the online resources when reading parts of this chapter.

Relevant court forms relating to this chapter:

- N244 Notice of Interim Application

- N260 Statement of Costs

> Relevant parts of the CPR and its PDs: 1, 3, 23, 25, and 24.

13.1 INTRODUCTION

This chapter will consider the following:

- the nature of interim applications;

- interim applications made with and without notice, and those made with and without a hearing;

- common procedure; and

- time estimates.

It would be useful to read the Additional Chapter 'A Practical Guide to Court Hearings' in the online resources alongside this chapter and to refresh your memory by reviewing Chapter 4 for details of the likely costs orders that may be made in an interim application.

An interim application is any application made to the court that requires a judicial decision. This is usually in the time between a case being issued and the final trial or determination of the action. Because it is the courts that will manage or control the path that an action takes to trial (see Chapter 12), many steps that a party may wish to take will require a 'judicial decision' before those steps can happen; that is, the court will have to consider whether it will permit, or order, the step that the party is requesting. These requests are known as 'interim applications'. Some interim applications are very significant to a case (for example, an application for summary judgment) and some interim applications are less significant to the case (for example, an application for more time to do something).

13.2 WHY DOES A PARTY MAKE AN INTERIM APPLICATION?

Interim applications are often made in the following circumstances:

- applications of a minor procedural nature—for example, for more time in which to do something;
- applications for more significant case management decisions—for example, applications relating to disclosure, exchange of evidence, or directions; or
- applications for specific remedies—for example, for specific disclosure, interim injunctions, and interim payments.

Interim applications can be used for a variety of purposes:

- they may enable an action to progress to trial more quickly;
- they may preserve evidence; or
- they may be used to exert pressure on an opponent.

The more significant interim applications may, by their very nature, have a direct impact on the outcome of the action and may, in themselves, result in a determination of the action or a settlement being reached. Apart from the numerous encouragements and incentives contained in the Protocols and in the CPR for litigants to resolve their disputes without recourse to the courts, many of the more significant interim applications can be seen as part of the armoury with which a party—often the stronger party—can force its opponent to the negotiating table and to settle on terms that are favourable to that stronger party. In this way, interim applications can be used tactically to gain the upper hand. The court will always consider the aims of the overriding objective, so it is also important for any party making an interim application to be prepared to give his reasons and justify the application to the court within the terms of the overriding objective—that is, that making the application is 'just', 'fair', 'proportionate' (as to cost and value), efficient, and in compliance with court rules, procedures, and practice directions. An application that is made by a party that cannot be justified in this way will run the risk of an adverse costs order as well as a failure to secure the order requested.

Because of the significance of the outcome of some interim applications, the process of making them and the evidence supplied to support them needs to be considered every bit as carefully as the trial itself.

13.3 THE NATURE AND PURPOSE OF SUPPORTING EVIDENCE IN INTERIM APPLICATIONS

Interim applications can be included in the generic definition that we have given them— that is, 'any application that requires a judicial decision in the time between commencement and trial'—but there are many different kinds of application that can be made. The procedure for each interim application is not generic, and although there are common traits, it is very important for any legal representative making or responding to an interim application to have sought out and considered the CPR that applies, so as to be sure of the procedure and requirements for that particular interim application.

Another very important matter to understand in relation to interim applications is that although the evidence or arguments that need to be made to support or oppose the application will always have to be carefully thought out and be properly prepared, the quality of the evidence, in terms of the 'weight' attached to it, can often be quite 'light', as the evidence is being presented in writing and not orally and will not be subject to cross-examination (see Chapter 17, paragraphs 17.4.3 and 17.5).

Legal representatives commonly put forward many persuasive arguments in support of their client's interim application or to oppose the other party's application, but it is very important to remember that these arguments are often little more than assertions (however powerfully or persuasively made), as they do not comprise 'evidence' with as much credible 'weight' attached to it.

Oral evidence by witnesses is rarely permitted in interim applications. Care must always be taken, therefore, that in the making of interim applications the party making the application (or the party seeking to challenge the application) is aware of, and able to determine, what evidence is merely an 'assertion' and what evidence is supported by fact. Any party who seeks to oppose an interim application can often make very good use of the distinction in trying to persuade the master or district judge that the application should not be granted when it is based merely on an 'assertion', rather than evidence supported by fact, or is able to argue that the evidence supporting the application should be more carefully tested at trial by cross-examination and not at an interim application hearing.

It is very important, therefore, to consider the inclusion of material evidence in an interim application so as to add 'weight' to the persuasive assertions that the legal representative may make at the hearing of the application. An assertion that is supported by contemporaneous material evidence can be, and often is, sufficiently persuasive to meet the criteria of the interim application, and be sufficient to address the master's or district judge's discretion and persuade him to make the order or not make it.

Apart from appreciating the need to be persuasive in seeking or opposing any interim application, it also has to be remembered that all interim applications are 'procedural' in nature. An interim application can only be made if it is provided for in the CPR. Therefore, for any interim application to succeed, the rule providing for it must be complied with in full.

Making or responding to interim applications is where the practitioner can reveal his real understanding both of the issues affecting his client's case and his powers of persuasiveness. Preparing the written evidence for the application is the practitioner's chance to demonstrate his skills of 'advocacy on paper'. Similarly, making or responding to the application at the hearing is the practitioner's chance to practise skills of advocacy in a 'real' environment (albeit usually by a telephone conference hearing). (See the Additional Chapter 'A Practical Guide to Court Hearings' in the online resources.)

13.4 THE NATURE OF INTERIM APPLICATIONS

There is no single CPR that applies to all interim applications.

The court's general power to make interim orders is contained in CPR 3.1(2). The court's power to grant interim remedies is contained in CPR 25.1. However, the power to make orders is not restricted to these sections and other parts of the CPR will apply. It will often be necessary to consider the Court Guides (if you are dealing with a High Court matter) applying to the court in which the action lies for further specific procedural guidance for the application that is to be made.

CPR 23 and the accompanying Practice Direction (PD) provides general rules for interim applications.

Practical Considerations

The fact that there is no all-encompassing part of the CPR that covers the procedure for all interim applications may create some difficulties for a practitioner who is new, or inexperienced, in litigation. For some applications, whilst the procedure for making the application is neatly contained in a section of the CPR designed specifically for the application, others will be contained within the 'ethos' of the overriding objective, and they may also be a part of a particular CPR. Ensuring, therefore, that the application being made has covered all the procedural requirements for it to succeed is not always easy to ascertain. Often, both identifying a possible application that can be made, and knowing what procedure and weight of evidence is required to make it successfully, will be a question of experience.

It is important to remember that before any interim application is sought, the client's 'informed' instructions must be obtained. Thus the client will need to be advised of the consequences of any step taken or responded to, as well as the cost of making the application and the likelihood of recovery of those costs. With that guidance, the client must then give specific instructions to take the step that has been identified as necessary or important to make and in the client's best interests. If a costs budget has been filed, it may be necessary to also seek approval to amend the costs budget to include the additional costs involved in making, or opposing, an un-budgeted-for interim application.

13.5 COMMON PROCEDURE

The specific CPR that contains the power or the procedure to follow in some interim applications will take precedence over any general rule. The generic rules of procedure that will apply where there are no specific rules for the application being made are contained in CPR 23 and are as follows:

- Any interim application should be made as soon as it is apparent that it is necessary or desirable to make it (PD 23A.2.7).

- Wherever possible, an interim application should be made and heard at any hearing that has already been listed (PD 23A.2.8). Most commonly, this will be at a case management conference (CMC—see Chapter 12).

- The interim application should generally be made to the court in which the action is proceeding (CPR 23.2). If a trial has been fixed, the interim application should be made to the trial court. If the application relates to enforcement, it should be made to the court dealing with enforcement. If the application is being made pre-action, it should be made to the court in which the action is likely to be commenced.

- The application notice states the intention of the party applying. This notice should always be prepared (CPR 23.2) and, save in very exceptional circumstances, this notice should be filed at court even if the application is being made without notice (CPR 23.3). The formal requirements for application notices are set out in PD 23A.2.1—this refers to Form N244, which may be used to make the application. (See the online resources for a description of Form N244 and annotated notes for its completion.)

- Generally, an interim application should be an 'on notice' application unless there is good reason for it to be 'without notice' (CPR 23.4(2)).

- If there is a time limit for making an interim application, the application is treated as being made on the day on which the application notice and fee are received by the court (CPR 23.5).

- All of the evidence being relied on for the interim application should be filed at court, ideally at the same time as filing the application notice (PD 23A.9.3). If the evidence is already with the court, then further copies need not be filed.

- The application notice, evidence, and order should be served at least three clear days before the hearing (CPR 23.7(1)(b)). If the matter is to be heard by way of a telephone conference hearing, then these documents should be served within five days of the hearing date.

- A draft order (of the application sought) should be filed at court, and if it is long or complex, it should also be supplied on disk (PD 23A.12.1). If the matter is a multi-track case, then a case summary must also be served. Both the draft order and a case summary must be filed and served no later than 4 p.m. at least two clear days before the hearing.

- Supporting evidence is not always required when it is a case management directions order that is being sought, although reasons and costings should normally be given that seek to justify the application.

- The court may allow urgent applications to be dealt with on short notice (PD 23A.3 and 23A.4).

- Most interim applications are dealt with by the master or district judges, although some applications may be referred to a judge for hearing (CPR 23.1). If a particular master, or district judge, or judge has heard an earlier interim application, the matter can be referred to that master, district judge, or judge if it would be helpful to do so. The master or district judge may also refer the matter to a judge (PD 2 and PD 23A.1).

- A fee is payable unless the applicant can obtain exemption on the ground of financial hardship.

- If the court is to serve the respondent, the applicant must file sufficient copies of the application notice, supporting evidence, and draft order for it to do so. The court will then serve these documents, together with notice of the hearing date and time.

- If the respondent wishes to rely on evidence to respond to the interim application, such evidence should be filed at court at least two days before the hearing. This would include a case summary if the case is a multi-track case, as stated earlier.

- If an application for costs is being made in the application, the party's cost schedule (Form N260) must be lodged at court and served on the other party at least twenty-four hours before the hearing.

Note: Reference should be made to Chapter 4 for detail of the most common costs orders and cost procedure in interim applications.

13.6 TIME ESTIMATES

The court will expect the applicant to give an assessment of the likely time that the hearing of the interim application will take. Where the application is to be on notice, the court also expects the parties, wherever possible, to cooperate in agreeing a time estimate for the hearing. The estimated time is included in the application notice (Form N244).

 Practical Considerations

The time estimate should not only include the time for both parties to make their representations, but should also include time for the judge to make a decision and time for any applications for costs to be considered. In more complex matters, the estimate should also include time for the judge to read the papers.

13.7 COSTS AND INTERIM APPLICATIONS

It is important to provide accurate costs estimates for any interim application no later than 24 hours before the hearing usually in Form N260. Where an interim application is envisaged at the costs budgeting phase of case management, the costs of it should be included in the contingency section of the Precedent H. This will therefore form the basis of the costs estimate contained in the N260. From a practical point of view, the importance of budgeting accurately and making timely revisions cannot be overestimated. See *Cleveland Bridge v Sarens (UK) Ltd* [2018] 2 Costs LR 333.

On 25 February 2019, the Civil Procedure Rule Committee (CPRC) announced the commencement of a two-year *voluntary* pilot scheme under PD 51X for a new statement of costs for summary assessment, together with the introduction of two new forms N260A and N260B for use in the pilot scheme. The pilot runs from the 1 April 2019.

13.8 NOTICE AND HEARING PROVISIONS FOR INTERIM APPLICATIONS

13.8.1 APPLICATIONS WITH NOTICE

Applications on notice may occur with a hearing. They may also occur without a hearing when, for example, the parties have agreed that the order sought should be made or the court considers that a hearing is not appropriate (CPR 23.8). Most of the applications for which a hearing is listed will be heard by telephone, or by video conferencing (see the Additional Chapter 'A Practical Guide to Court Hearings' in the online resources).

These general rules apply, but remember that the procedure set out in a CPR specific to the interim application being made will take precedence over the general rules in CPR 23.

> ### ✓ Practical Considerations
>
> The CPR state that the notice of the interim application, the supporting evidence, notice of the hearing date, and the draft order should be served on the respondent 'at least three days before the hearing' (note: five days if the matter is being heard by way of a telephone conference hearing). However, it is important also to note the words 'as soon as practicable' that are contained in PD 23A.4.1. If, as the legal representative for the applicant in an interim application, you have filed your application at court in good time, and have received back from the court the date and time of the hearing that is some time ahead (for example, more than five days), you could be severely criticized by the court for holding back serving the application and notice of hearing on your opponent until much nearer the time of the hearing or telephone appointment (the aim being to gain the tactical advantage of time and giving the respondent limited time in which to respond). It would be wrong to choose to comply with that part of the rule for service that requires service 'at least three clear days before the hearing' and not that part which expects service 'as soon as practicable' in order to gain a perceived advantage of surprise. The criticism by the court could mean that the application is dismissed or adjourned, or, if the master or district judge does hear the application in these circumstances, he may make adverse costs orders against the applicant for the failure to serve 'as soon as practicable'.

13.8.2 APPLICATIONS WITHOUT NOTICE

Applications without notice can be made. These may be with or without a hearing.

The basic principle of litigation is that an order should not be made against a party without him having an opportunity to be heard. However, there will be occasions on which it is necessary to do so, such as:

- when giving notice may defeat the purpose of the application, or could create an injustice through delay or action that the respondent may take to defeat the application—examples include search orders and freezing injunctions (for further details of these, and other, injunctions, see the Additional Chapter 'Injunctions and Other Equitable Remedies' in the online resources. See also Chapter 14, paragraph 14.8);

- when the opponent is not yet on the court record—examples of this could be when the claimant seeks more time in which to serve the claim form, or when a defendant seeks permission of the court to issue an additional claim (CPR 20) (on the occasions on which permission is needed); or
- when the defendant can only be identified by description and not by name—an example may occur in intellectual property claims.

PD 23A.3 sets out a list of occasions on which an interim application may be made without notice. These include when:

- there is exceptional urgency;
- the overriding objective is best furthered by the application being made without notice;
- the parties consent;
- the court grants permission;
- a date for a hearing has been fixed and a party wishes to make an application at that hearing, but does not have sufficient time to serve an application notice; and
- where a rule, PD, or court order permits.

The evidence in support of an application without notice must include the reasons why notice was not given. For further detail of without notice applications, see Chapter 14, paragraph 14.8. Please also refer to the Additional Chapter 'Injunctions and Other Equitable Remedies' in the online resources.

13.8.2.1 What may happen if an application is made without notice when it is not appropriate to do so?

If an application is made without notice in circumstances when the court concludes that it was not appropriate to have done so, the application will probably be dismissed or adjourned until proper notice is given. A wasted costs order is likely to be imposed if the legal representative is at fault.

13.8.2.2 When does the respondent hear of the order made?

CPR 23.9 states that when an order has been made on a without notice application, unless the court orders otherwise, it must be served on the respondent. This service will include the application notice, the evidence that supported the application, and the order that has been made. Usually, the court will effect service—but see CPR 6.3 and 40.4 for details of these service provisions, and the option that the applicant has of effecting service himself.

The notice to the respondent will include a statement setting out the respondent's right to make an application to set aside or vary the order that has been made (CPR 23.10), but such application by the respondent must be made within seven days after the date of service.

13.8.3 APPLICATIONS WITHOUT A HEARING

Applications without a hearing are otherwise known as 'paper applications' and are discussed in some detail in the Additional Chapter 'A Practical Guide to Court Hearings' in the online resources.

13.9 'CARELESS' NEGOTIATIONS—THE STATUS OF THINGS SAID IN THE PRE-HEARING DISCUSSIONS

It is important to make a careful file note of any discussions between the legal representatives that take place either on the telephone before the hearing, or, if an attendance at court is required, whilst waiting. It is important to note that no form of privilege will cover the pre-hearing discussions unless they are stated to be 'without prejudice'. Care needs to be taken, in any pre-hearing discussions, not to make careless concessions or unsubstantiated assertions of fact, because these could come back to haunt you as informal admissions and may bind the client, or be used to challenge your client's or another witness's testimony at the trial. Please see the Bollington Beer case study in the online resources, as this demonstrates how pre-hearing discussions can be misconstrued.

Practical Considerations

It is important to remember that the 'without prejudice' rule only covers discussions that take place 'with a view to settlement' and that this will not, therefore, cover general case management discussions. This is important to remember so as to avoid making an 'informal admission', or an acknowledgement of a state of affairs in an 'open', not 'without prejudice', forum—a reminder that was reinforced in *Stax Claimants v Bank of Nova Scotia Channel Islands Ltd* [2007] EWHC 1153.

13.10 AN UNLESS ORDER

13.10.1 WHAT IS AN 'UNLESS ORDER'?

If the court concludes that the opponent in an interim application has failed adequately to comply with the obligations of a previous order or within the general ethos of litigation practice (he may have failed to respond to an early request to comply), or if the court doubts the bona fides of the opponent, it will often make an order and, at the same time, specify a sanction to be imposed if the order is not complied with—this is an 'unless' order. An order that imposes a sanction for non-compliance will specify the date and time by which the steps of the order must be complied with (CPR 2.9). The sanction part of the order may take the form of an 'unless' provision. PD 40B.8.2 lays down formulae for drafting unless orders. Compliance with the time limits set in court orders is regarded as fundamental to litigation practice under the CPR, and the courts will not shirk from making unless orders within the terms of a first order so as to ensure that the strict timetable for the action can be met.

Example

Your opponent has failed to serve his list of documents in accordance with the direction of the court for standard disclosure made at a recent CMC. You have requested the list and warned that an application will be made to the court if it is not forthcoming. The list still does not materialize and you are forced to apply to the court, requesting an order that your opponent be compelled to serve his list of documents within fourteen days, failing which he should be deprived of the opportunity to defend the action.

If your application is successful, the order might be drafted as follows:

- 'The defendant is to serve its list of documents by 4 p.m. on 25 May 20??, failing which he shall be debarred from defending the claim further ...'; or

- 'Unless the defendant serves its list of documents by 4 p.m. on 25 May 20??, its defence will be struck out ...'.

Costs

If, in your warning letter, you had also said that if you had to make an application to the court for an order compelling your opponent to comply you would seek an order for costs on the 'indemnity' basis, the court may also consider making a costs recovery order on the application on this enhanced basis.

13.10.2 RELIEF AFTER A FAILURE TO COMPLY WITH AN UNLESS ORDER

If an unless order is made against a party and the order is not complied with, the sanction will automatically be imposed, even if, at a later date, the party complies with the order. Consider the previous example: if the defendant did not serve his list by 25 May, but served it on 29 May, his defence would still be struck out by virtue of the breach of the 'unless' order. In *Christie v Magnet Ltd* [2016] EWCA Civ 906, Lord Justice Gross stated that an '. . . unless order means what it says. If a party does not comply with it, the sanctions automatically follow. Even if the consequences in the individual litigation are not immense, the consequences for the system are.'

It can be seen that an unless order is made as a last resort normally due to one or both of the parties failing to comply with a previous order, rule or practice direction. Also, unless orders are frequently made in cases where one of the parties makes an application to the court for their opponent to comply with a previous court order or direction.

An urgent application should be made for relief from sanctions if there is a breach of an unless order but there is a real risk that the court will reject the application unless there is a particularly good reason for it, such as if the circumstances were outside the party's control. See also paragraph 13.11 below.

13.11 RELIEF FROM SANCTIONS—CPR 3.9 AND CPR 3.8

CPR 3.9 provides a means whereby a party can apply for 'relief from a sanction' imposed by the court—that is, ask the court to consider CPR 3.9(1) and not to strike out the case, or to make the adverse costs order or impose whatever sanction has been imposed. The application must be made as soon as practicable and be supported by evidence. The court is very likely to take a robust and 'minimal tolerance' approach to any failure to comply with a court order. See Chapter 12, paragraph 12.9, for further details of the application of CPR 3.9.

In *Denton v TH White Limited, Decadent Vapours Limited v Bevan, Utilise TDS Limited v Davies* [2014] EWCA Civ 906 (*Denton*) the Court of Appeal has set out guidance on how the courts will consider applications for relief from sanctions under CPR 3.8.

This guidance states that in considering applications under CPR 3.8, the courts must:

- Identify and assess the seriousness and significance of the breach—if the breach is not serious or significant the court is likely to grant relief (from sanctions) and not consider any further guidelines.

- Consider why the breach occurred. The likelihood is that where reasons were cogent (for example serious illness or an accident) the court may consider relief.

- Evaluate all the circumstances of the case to enable the court to deal justly with the application, including the two factors set out in CPR 3.9: the need for litigation to be conducted efficiently and at proportionate cost, and the need to enforce compliance with rules, practice directions, and orders. The relevant factors will be case specific and 'promptness' (of the application for relief) may be a relevant consideration.

Essentially the courts will be seeking to ensure that a party does not try to take advantage of their opponent's mistakes (or misfortune) by unreasonably refusing to agree extensions of time or opposing applications for relief from sanction. But a party who does not obey the courts' orders and time limits without very good reason will not find the courts sympathetic. The more recent case *Thevarajah v Riordan* [2015] EWCA Civ 14 has added detail to this general overview of the courts' approach to an application for 'relief from sanctions'—and stated that a party who has finally complied with an order cannot use this as a reason for being relieved of sanctions the court had imposed on it for failing to abide by an order on time or as directed.

In *Motley & Others v Shadwell Park Ltd* (2017) CA (Civ Div), the Court of Appeal held that the judge had correctly considered the three stage test in *Denton*. Further in *(1) Chelsea Bridge Apartments Ltd and (2) Alan Ward v (1) Old Street Homes Ltd and (2) Anthony Donnellan* (2017) Ch D (Deputy Master Cousins) 04/09/2017, the court highlights the importance of complying with court orders, rules, and practice directions as a failure to do so carries with it the real risk of strike out. However, in the case of *Khandanpour v Chambers* [2019] EWCA Civ 570, the Court of Appeal allowed an appeal from an order refusing relief from sanctions regarding late payment of a sum ordered as a condition of setting aside a default costs certificate saying that 'a sense of perspective' was necessary and consideration of past conduct in relief applications. It can be seen that the court has the power under CPR, r. 3.4 to strike out a case in the event of non-compliance even in cases where there is no provision for strike out in the specific rule, practice direction or court order.

CPR 3.8 allows parties some greater flexibility and enables them to agree extensions of time to comply with directions orders when appropriate, when to do so will not put a hearing (date) at risk or affect the efficient, proportionate, and fair progress of the action.

See also Chapter 12, paragraph 12.9.

KEY POINTS SUMMARY

- An interim application is a step in the action between issue and trial that requires a judicial decision.
- There are some interim applications that can be made pre action.
- Interim applications require strict adherence to the requirements set down in the CPR.
- The key rules are CPR 1, 3, 23, and 25 or a CPR that deals specifically with a type of interim application.
- Applications are usually made in Form N244.
- Applications may be applications with notice, applications without notice, with a hearing, or without a hearing.

SELF-TEST QUESTIONS

1. What is the general purpose of interim applications?
2. The evidence submitted in support of an interim application is usually written evidence. What is the effect of this?
3. In terms of any interim application, what two most important matters must the person applying ensure that he can do or has done?
4. When would an interim application be made without notice?
5. What is the purpose of an 'unless order' and when might one be made in connection with interim applications?

 Suggested answers to these self-test questions can be accessed in the Student Resources section of the online resources.

14 INTERIM APPLICATIONS—COMMON TYPES

Relevant court forms relating to this chapter:

- **N244 Notice of Interim Application**

- **N260 Statement of Costs**

Relevant parts of the CPR and its PDs: 12, 13, 23, 24, 25, and 31.

14.1 INTRODUCTION

This chapter will consider the interim applications that a legal representative may most commonly come across in practice. This chapter should be read in conjunction with Chapter 13. We will consider both the procedure for these specific interim applications, as well as the form of the evidence needed to make or oppose them.

The interim applications that will be considered in this detail will be:

- an application to set aside default judgment;

- summary judgment;

- interim payment;

- an application for specific disclosure;

- an application for security for costs; and

- an application for an injunction.

It should be noted that the number of interim applications that can be made is far greater than those listed (see Chapter 13, paragraph 13.2). Some will follow the generic procedure detailed in Chapter 13; others may have a specific CPR covering the procedure and criteria for the application. It is important to remember that in nearly all interim applications (except, for example, those that require secrecy), a legal representative will be expected to ask his opponent to concede voluntarily to the relief or order being sought before proceeding with an application to the court. A failure to do this will usually result in an adverse costs order being made.

14.2 SETTING ASIDE A DEFAULT JUDGMENT

Before considering this interim application, you need to know when default judgment can be obtained by the claimant.

14.2.1 WHAT IS A 'DEFAULT JUDGMENT' AND HOW IS IT OBTAINED?

Default judgment enables the claimant to obtain an early determination of his action, without a trial and where a defendant fails to file an acknowledgement of service or a defence within the time limits prescribed by the court rules. Where the application is being sought under CPR 13.2 (considered in paragraph 14.3 below) it is judgment by an administrative, rather than a judicial, act, so the request for default judgment by the claimant is not itself an 'interim application' though it may appear to look like one. An application for default judgment under CPR 13.3 (see paragraph 14.2.3) does require 'a judicial decision' so is a true interim application. This application must not be confused with an application for summary judgment (considered at paragraph 14.3 below).

Any application or request for default judgment will need to have careful regard for the relevant time limits within which the defendant should have either lodged his acknowledgement of service or filed his defence. The following should also be noted and CPR Part 12 considered in detail in relation to the following circumstances:

- The claimant may obtain judgment in default of an acknowledgment of service only if at the date that judgment is entered, the defendant has not filed an acknowledgmemnt of service or a defence and where an acknowledgment of service has been filed but at the date on which judgment is entered a defence has not been filed. Note that the key date is the date of entry of judgment, not the date judgment is applied for (CPR 12.3(1) and CPR 12.3(2)).

- Default judgment does not apply, for example, when there is an application pending to strike out the claim, or when an application for summary judgment is pending (CPR 12.3), or when the situations set down in CPR 12.2 arise.

- The procedure is modified for certain claims—for example, where the claim includes a claim for 'any other remedy'.

- A defendant cannot obtain a default judgment on a counterclaim against a claimant on the basis of failure to acknowledge service, because CPR 10 does not apply to counterclaims, but it is important to know that default judgment may be obtained on a counterclaim once the time for filing the defence to the counterclaim has expired (CPR 12.3.2(b)).

- Special rules apply if a defendant is a child, patient, or state. In these situations, an application for default judgment must be supported by evidence (CPR 12.11.3).

- If a claimant, rather than the court, had served the claim form, default judgment cannot be entered until a certificate of service is filed.

- There is also special provision in the rules for obtaining default judgment against defendants sued in the alternative and those sued jointly, or jointly and severally. These provisions will either deal with the disposal of the whole claim, or enable default judgment to be obtained against one defendant and the action to proceed against the remaining defendants (CPR 12.8).

14.2.1.1 The procedure for securing a default judgment
Depending on the type of claim, default judgment is sought either by:

- filing a request (CPR 12.4 (1) or (3)) or
- an application to the court (CPR 12.4(2), 12.9, *and* 12.10).

14.2.1.1.1 *By request*
If default judgment is sought by filing a request:

- Form N225 will be filed if the claim is for a specific amount of money or for delivery up, in which case the defendant is given the alternative of paying a specific amount;
- Form N227 will be filed if the claim is for a sum of money to be determined by the court;
- the relevant completed form will be lodged at the court and no fee will be required;
- the request will be dealt with by the court administratively (rather than judicially); and
- if the requirements are made out, judgment will be entered.

14.2.1.1.2 *By application*
If default judgment is sought by application to the court:

- Form N244 will be completed, with supporting evidence;
- a fee will be payable;
- notice of the application must be given to the defendant (as soon as practicable after it is filed, or at least three clear days before the hearing) unless the defendant has failed to lodge an acknowledgement of service or an exception under CPR 12.11(4) applies; and
- at the court hearing, if the requirements are made out, judgment will be entered.

14.2.2 WHEN MAY AN APPLICATION BE MADE TO SET ASIDE A DEFAULT JUDGMENT?

Whilst the request for default judgment may not be an 'interim application', an application by the defendant to set aside the default judgment obtained *is* an interim application and requires a 'judicial decision' before it can be granted. CPR 13 sets out the rules and procedure for applications to set aside a default judgment. It makes a distinction between the two sorts of default judgment that may be sought under CPR 12—that is, those that the court *must* set aside (CPR 13.2) and those that the court *may* set aside (CPR 13.3).

The court *must* set aside a default judgment when a ground listed in CPR 13.2 has been established—that is, when the defendant can show that the default judgment was wrongly entered by the claimant in that:

- it may have been entered too early;
- it was made after the defendant had made an application to strike out the claim or had applied to dismiss the claim summarily, but where the application by the defendant has not yet been concluded;
- it may have been entered even though the whole claim (including interest and costs) had already been paid or settled; or
- it was entered after the defendant had filed an admission, but had made a request for time to pay, and that request has not yet been dealt with.

In each of these situations, the defendant's request to set aside the default judgment need only establish one of the grounds listed and the default judgment will be set aside.

The court *may* set aside a default judgment that has been entered by the claimant in all other situations. CPR 13.3 provides that the court has discretion to set aside the default judgment entered. A defendant who wishes to seek an order to set aside a default judgment will need to act promptly and satisfy the two grounds set out in CPR 13.3.1—that is, in addition to 'acting promptly', he must:

- show that he has a real prospect of successfully defending the claim or
- establish some other good reason why the judgment should be set aside and the defendant be permitted to defend the claim.

Additionally, under CPR 13.3.2:

- in considering whether to set aside or vary a judgment entered under CPR 12, the matters to which the court *must* have regard include whether the person seeking to set aside the judgment made an application to do so promptly. (Emphasis added)

The case of *Standard Bank plc v Agrinvest International Inc*, 14 January 2011, CA, is a case which clearly demonstrates that 'acting promptly' is every bit as important as the other criteria set down in CPR 13.3. In this case Lord Justice Moore-Bick set out some important observations on the necessity of timeliness in making applications to set aside default judgment. He confirmed that where there had been a lack of timeliness, even when a potentially successful defence had been put forward, the application may still be rejected.

14.2.3 WHAT EVIDENCE IS REQUIRED TO SET ASIDE A DEFAULT JUDGMENT?

14.2.3.1 Where the court must set aside the default judgment

An application need only submit the chronology or the facts that bring the application under the provisions of CPR 13.2. These facts may include copies of supporting evidence and, usually, there is sufficient space within Part C of the application notice (Form N244) in which to set out this detail. The court may be prepared to consider the application as a 'paper hearing' without notice (see the Additional Chapter 'A Practical Guide to Court Hearings' in the online resources). In any application to set aside default judgment under the provisions of CPR 13.2, the consent of the other party should be sought, and if it is obtained, the application can be submitted as an agreed application. The court will then almost certainly consider the application as a paper application, and no hearing will be listed. In all cases in which it is clear that the defendant can establish a ground under CPR 13.2, the claimant would be well advised to consent to the application, because he may otherwise incur penalty costs for his failure to cooperate in such an application.

14.2.3.2 Where the court has discretion to set aside a default judgment

For applications to set aside under CPR 13.3, evidence must be submitted. The evidence that the defendant needs to produce to succeed in the application will need to address the court's discretion, which will be used to consider whether to make the order. The supporting evidence will, therefore, need to address the following:

- The prospects of success of the defence—this could be achieved by presenting a witness statement that sets out the basis of the intended defence. One of the most persuasive ways of doing this would be to exhibit a draft of the intended defence to the witness statement (provided that the legal representative has the client's approval to incur the additional costs of drafting the defence).

- If the ground set out in CPR 13.3.1(b) is being relied on, the witness statement needs to address the 'other good reasons' why the defendant should be permitted to proceed and defend.

- The defendant will also need to set out in what way he has acted 'promptly' in making the application, or provide any valid and excusable reasons that he may have for any delay.

In the case *Hockley v North Lincolnshire & Goole NHS Trust* (unreported, 19 September 2014) the defendant had failed to file an acknowledgement of service within the fourteen days permitted by CPR 10.3(1). The claimant made a request, and obtained, default judgment on his claim. The defendant made a successful application to set aside the default judgment under CPR 13.3(1). The claimant appealed, seeking to restore the default judgment. In considering this appeal the court considered CPR 3.9 (see Chapter 13, paragraph 13.11, on relief from sanctions) and held that the defendant's breach (failure to adhere to the time limits of CPR 10.3(1) and file his acknowledgment of service on time) was 'serious'. The judge also noted that in making the application to set aside the default judgment the defendant had not filed a draft defence (or other document) with the application so as to allow the court to conclude that there was 'a real prospect' of defending the claim. It was held that the three-stage 'test' in *Denton* (see Chapter 13, paragraph 13.11) had considerable relevance. The case serves as a reminder that evidence in support of an application to set aside under this ground is crucial.

14.2.4 THE PROCEDURE FOR MAKING AN APPLICATION TO SET ASIDE A DEFAULT JUDGMENT

The claimant may still be invited to consent to the application before it is made. An application to set aside a judgment in default is made in the normal way in Form N244. Under CPR 13.4, the application will be transferred automatically to the defendant's home court if not already issued from that court when:

- the claim is for a specified sum; and

- the defendant is an individual.

If the defendant does not fall within the criteria of CPR 13.4, he could apply for a transfer to his home court as part of his application to set aside, but the application will be heard in the court in which the claim was issued; if the defendant makes this application, it will be transferred to the preferred hearing centre for the hearing of the defendant's application.

Supporting evidence may be contained in Part C of Form N244 or in a separate witness statement. It is unlikely that the evidence will be contained in a statement of case available in the case, because at this stage, the only statement of case is likely to be the claimant's particulars of claim. The application must be submitted promptly and will, in nearly every case, be 'on notice' with the requisite current fee. Please see the witness statement in the Bollington Beer case study in the online resources.

14.2.5 ORDERS THAT MAY BE MADE IN AN APPLICATION TO SET ASIDE A DEFAULT JUDGMENT

Where the application is made in a case in which the court must set aside, any order made for payment to the claimant will also be set aside.

In applications in which the court has a discretion to set aside, the court will consider the evidence supporting the application, and may make such orders and directions as it thinks are appropriate. This can include dismissing the application or granting the application, either conditionally or unconditionally. If the application is granted, the action will proceed as directed.

14.3 SUMMARY JUDGMENT

14.3.1 SUMMARY JUDGMENT AND THE EUROPEAN CONVENTION ON HUMAN RIGHTS (ECHR)

Summary judgment is available both to claimants and to defendants. It seeks to avoid the occasions on which an opponent's case shows no reasonable prospects of success. It provides a quick and efficient solution to the case. It is, therefore, clearly distinguished from a default judgment, which relies on a 'default' on the part of the defendant.

An order for summary judgment will prevent the opponent from having 'his day in court' and would, therefore, potentially be a breach of Art. 6 of the ECHR; the court's powers are, therefore, strictly controlled, and it will only make the order when the criteria for it are precisely met. Unless the strict criteria have been met, the court *cannot* make an order for summary judgment. In these situations, the court does, however, have the power to make lesser orders (see paragraph 14.3.5.2).

Any judgment or order made that denies a party a trial of the issues contravenes the basic core principle of domestic law and human rights. But this right is not an absolute one: the courts will frequently require the party who wishes to avoid an order for summary judgment against them to show that they have a claim or a defence with 'real prospects'—and that there is 'no other compelling reason' why the matter should be heard at a trial. Article 6 of the ECHR does not say that every piece of evidence must be tested at trial. The fact remains, however, that in any situation in which an injustice may occur, the court must be careful to ensure that due regard is given to these points before refusing a party a right to a 'fair hearing'. The CPR seek to embrace these issues. But the courts have limited scope to make an order that could breach the human right to a fair trial. This arises most clearly in applications for summary judgment. There will be occasions in applications for summary judgment on which the court can only make an order that is, in reality, a compromise—a balancing act, ensuring that cases are dealt with efficiently, but also fairly.

There is an advantage in a successful application for summary judgment in that it secures a quick determination of the action. But the disadvantages of a failed application must also be borne in mind. An application for summary judgment that has failed may, in addition to the likelihood of bearing an adverse costs order (these can be substantial and will be payable promptly), also result in delays, because until the application has been heard, further progress of the action is suspended.

14.3.2 WHEN IS SUMMARY JUDGMENT USED?

CPR 24 sets out the procedure when the court may make a decision on a claim or a particular issue without the delay and expense of trial. This has the benefit of precluding a claim that has no real merit proceeding to trial. It may apply at the same time as an application to strike out under CPR 3.4. Sometimes a combined application can be made under both CPR 3.4 and CPR 24. It is worth making a note of the differences between CPR 3.4 (applications to strike out a claim) and CPR 24.2 (applications for summary judgment).

CPR 3.4 provides that a claim, or part of a claim, may be struck out when:

- the statement of case discloses no reasonable grounds for bringing or defending the claim; or
- the statement of case is an abuse of the court's processes; or
- where there has been a failure to comply with a rule, Practice Direction (PD), or order.

CPR 24.2 provides that the court may grant summary judgment against a claimant or a defendant (for all or part of a claim) when:

- the claimant has no real prospect of succeeding on the claim or issue; or
- the defendant has no real prospect of successfully defending the claim or issue; and
- in respect of either of the grounds above, there is no other compelling reason why the case should be disposed of at trial.

In an application for summary judgment, the court may strike out the claim or defence if it is so weak on the facts that it will not succeed.

There is clearly an overlap between the two provisions, but the substance for each is not identical. Although there will be situations in which a combined application can be made, this will not always be the case and the practitioner must not assume that an application for summary judgment should always be conjoined with an application to strike out, or vice versa.

 Practical Considerations

If a combined application is being made, then the general requirements for any interim application set out in Chapter 13, paragraph 13.4, will apply, and the exact wording of each provision will have to be stated and the evidence submitted to establish both applications. The witness statement supporting a combined application will need to show, for example, both that a statement of case discloses no reasonable grounds for bringing or defending the claim (CPR 3), and that there is no real prospect of successfully defending the claim or issue and that there is no other compelling reason why the case should be disposed of at trial (CPR 24). A failure to address the exact requirements of both CPR 3 and 24 will result in a failure of that part of the application not complied with.

14.3.3 THE PROCEDURE FOR SUMMARY JUDGMENT

An application for summary judgment is one of the interim applications the procedure of which is neatly contained in a part of the CPR designed specifically for that interim application. In this case, procedure is set out in CPR 24.4, which includes provisions that:

- either party can make the application, although it may not be made by the defendant until the claimant has served his particulars of claim, and the defendant has served either his acknowledgement of service or his defence;
- if the claimant has failed to comply with any Pre-Action Protocol, an application for summary judgment by the claimant will not usually be entertained by the court until after the defence has been filed or the time for doing so has expired (in the latter situation, the application will often be an application for default judgment rather than summary judgment);
- if the application is made by the claimant on the defendant lodging his acknowledgement of service and before the defence is filed, then the defendant need not file his defence until after the hearing of the summary judgment application;

 Practical Considerations

Although the defendant need not file his defence before a claimant's application for summary judgment is heard, any defendant who intends to oppose the claimant's application for summary judgment would often be well advised to give specific details of the nature of the defence that they intend to raise, or indeed to attach a draft of their intended defence to the evidence that they lodge to oppose the application, because this will give the court the clearest possible opportunity of seeing the defence that is intended and showing that the claimant has not met the criteria required to be successful in the application.

- a defendant may make an application for summary judgment against the claimant's claim at any time after issue;

 Practical Considerations

The ideal time for a defendant to make an application for summary judgment against the claimant's claim would be at, or immediately before, allocation. This would delay allocation until after the application has been heard. In practice, however, the court will often move on to matters of allocation at the summary judgment hearing, if the application for summary judgment has failed. The application for summary judgment will be heard first. This power is provided for within the court's general powers of management, but is also specifically referred to in CPR 24.6. An application for summary judgment by the defendant that is filed before he has filed his acknowledgement of service or defence also has the effect of preventing the claimant seeking default judgment until after the summary judgment application has been heard.

- the application will usually be supported by written evidence and this written evidence must be served on the other party at least fourteen days before the hearing;
- if the application is being opposed, that written evidence must be served on the other party at least seven days before the hearing;
- any evidence in reply needs to be filed and served at least three days before the hearing;
- the application notice (usually in Form N244) must precisely identify and specify the application being made, and should state when any evidence to oppose the application should be filed and served;
- any written evidence to be relied on that is already filed at court and on the other party need not be served again, although reference to that evidence will need to be made in the application notice;
- if the defendant does not attend the hearing, any order made may be set aside on just terms;
- skeleton arguments and court bundles should be prepared in all but the most straightforward applications;
- a draft order should be prepared and filed with the application; and
- the parties must file a costs schedule in Form N260 twenty-four hours before the hearing.

14.3.4 THE EVIDENCE FOR A SUMMARY JUDGMENT APPLICATION

The essence of any evidence supporting an application for summary judgment will need to establish the two grounds set down under CPR 24.2. It must cover both elements—that is, the 'no real prospects' test, as well as the 'no other compelling reason' test.

The burden of proof is on the applicant. There is no trial of the issues in a summary judgment hearing, and the applicant needs to satisfy the court that the claim or the defence has 'no real prospect of success'. Accordingly, where assertions are made in the written evidence, the court will not be able to make an order for summary judgment if any issues arise that make it clear that a proper investigation should be made of the facts asserted—that proper investigation being at trial, where there can be a testing of the evidence by oral examination and cross-examination. The evidence must also satisfy the second part of CPR 24.2—that is, that there is 'no other compelling reason why the matter should go to trial'—and an application may fail under this criterion even where it may have succeeded under the first: for example, where the applicant has behaved in a way that is not in keeping with the ethos of litigation or within the guidelines of the overriding objective, especially when that behaviour may have prevented the other party obtaining evidence that would reveal 'real prospects of success'. Another example of this second element arising (and causing the application to fail) may be when the defendant needs more time to investigate, and there is reason to believe that time and investigation may provide 'real prospects', although they are not evident at the time of the application.

 Practical Considerations

The fine distinction between facts that should be tested at trial and those that the court can accept as supporting the application for summary judgment is one that is best learnt and understood by experience. For a practitioner new to litigation, much can be learnt from reading the judgments of important cases that have considered such applications. Cases such as *Swain v Hillman* [2001] 1 All ER 91 and *Three Rivers District Council v Bank of England (No 3)* [2001] 2 All ER 513 are good examples. However, a reasonable electronic search with the key words 'summary judgment' will produce an array of cases from which to learn and understand the distinction better. The Court of Appeal set out some useful guidelines for making successful applications for summary judgment in *S v Gloucestershire County Council* [2000] 3 All ER 346.

14.3.5 ORDERS THAT MAY BE MADE IN AN APPLICATION FOR SUMMARY JUDGMENT

14.3.5.1 Successful applications

Where the application is successful, the court will order (for the claimant) summary judgment on the claim or issue, and that will be the end of the claim or issue, or it will order (for the defendant) that the claim or issue be struck out. Once summary judgment has been obtained, enforcement can proceed in the usual way (see the Additional Chapter 'Enforcement of Judgments' in the online resources for details of enforcement options).

14.3.5.2 Partially successful applications

If the application has failed to establish the criteria for summary judgment, the application must fail. But this does not necessarily mean that the application will have had no benefit for the applicant. In a situation in which, for example, the defendant has raised a defence that has 'prospects', but which the court believes may not succeed, or if the motives of the defendant in raising the defence are in question, the court can make a conditional order instead of dismissing the application. This conditional order may include an order to pay part of the claim into court or to take a step in the action within a specified time (for example, for the defendant to 'file his defence'). The consequence of not complying with the condition may be that his right to defend will be struck out.

In this way, lesser orders may have the effect of ending the case.

 Practical Considerations

It is wise to specify, in any advance letter to your opponent, the intended application for summary judgment and to state further that an application for a conditional order will be made if the application should fail. The court will not usually make such an order if the party is unable to comply with the condition. The burden will be on the party subject to the condition imposed to show that he cannot comply.

14.3.5.3 Unsuccessful applications

If the application has failed or failed in part, as described in paragraph 14.3.5.2, the court will proceed to make an order for the progress of the action. The order may include directions for the time to file the defence, for allocation, or for substantive directions for the future management of the case. In effect, at the conclusion of the hearing, the court may treat the hearing as a case management conference (CMC—see Chapter 12).

14.4 INTERIM PAYMENTS

14.4.1 WHAT IS AN 'INTERIM PAYMENT'?

An interim payment made to a party in an action—usually the claimant—is another of the more significant interim applications that can be made. CPR 25 deals with interim remedies in general; CPR 25.6–25.9 deal with the grounds and procedure specific to an application for an interim payment. The remedy can alleviate hardship for a claimant caused by the delays of the litigation process. It may also be appropriate to make an application when the claimant's injuries have not yet stabilized and it is not, yet, appropriate to have a final hearing. An interim payment award may assist a claimant and avoid them feeling under pressure to accept a low offer because of the stress caused by the litigation or the time it is taking to be concluded. An award (of an interim payment) is always discretionary; there is no right to an order. Once the court has concluded that a ground has been established, it will first exercise its discretion whether to make an order at all and then will consider what the sum of the order should be.

 Practical Considerations

This remedy, though most commonly used in personal injury litigation, may be equally appropriate to seek in other litigation, as it may be used to secure an early payment for a commercial client who is experiencing cash flow problems whilst awaiting the process of his case claiming a large debt from the defendant against whom the interim payment application is made.

CPR 25.7 sets out several grounds on which an application may be made. The guiding principle for any award of an interim payment is to ensure that any award made does not cause an injustice. An early payment to the claimant who does not succeed in his case at the final determination of the case at trial has the potential to create a grave injustice to the defendant. Equally, an award that is higher than the sum finally secured by the claimant at trial can also cause an injustice to the defendant.

CPR 25.9 provides that any interim payment that has been made, whether it is by agreement or by order, should not be disclosed to the trial judge until after judgment of both liability and quantum has been made, unless the defendant consents.

 See the online resources for a video clip of an interim payment application, combined with a CMC.

14.4.2 THE GROUNDS ON WHICH AN INTERIM PAYMENT APPLICATION CAN BE MADE

CPR 25.7 contains five 'grounds' on which an order can be made. The burden for the claimant to persuade the court to make the award will increase in line with the potential for risk of injustice. Each of the grounds sets out clearly the remit and discretion that the district judge has when considering an application. It goes without saying that in the making of any interim application, or in opposing an application, the persuasive arguments needed to persuade the district judge to make the order or not make the order must directly address the criteria set out in the relevant CPR. Any application for an interim payment must be supported with evidence.

The five grounds set out are as follows:

- where the defendant has admitted liability (CPR 25.7.1(a));
- where the claimant has obtained judgment, but the sum to be paid is not yet assessed (CPR 25.7.1(b));

- when the court is satisfied that if the action were to go to trial, the claimant would obtain judgment for a substantial sum (CPR 25.7.1(c));

- in a claim in which there are two or more defendants and an order is sought against any one or more of the defendants, the court must be satisfied that if the action were to go to trial, the claimant would obtain judgment for a substantial sum against at least one of the defendants (but the court does not need to be sure which one), and in these circumstances, each of the defendants must be insured in respect of the claim (whether directly, or under s. 151 of the Road Traffic Act 1988, or the Motor Insurers' Bureau), or be a public body (CPR 25.7.1(e)). The court has powers to make orders between defendants as to reimbursement of the award, provided that the defendant seeking reimbursement or contribution has made a claim against the other defendant for a contribution, indemnity, or other remedy; and

- the other ground relates to an action for the possession of land, which is outside the scope of this manual (CPR 25.7.1(d)).

 Practical Considerations

CPR 25.7.1(c) is distinctly different from the grounds set down in CPR 25.7.1(a) and (b), because in this ground, there is the potential that any order granting an interim payment to the claimant *could* create an injustice to the defendant—the claimant may lose at trial. The words 'would obtain judgment' and 'substantial' are not defined by the rules. They will be given their 'natural' meaning. 'Would' means that, on the balance of probabilities, the claimant will probably win; it does not mean that he will definitely win, but the region of doubt should be narrow. Again, 'substantial' does not necessarily mean a large sum; rather, it will be a figure that, to *this* claimant, would be substantial.

14.4.3 THE PROCEDURE FOR MAKING AN APPLICATION FOR AN INTERIM PAYMENT

Before an application is made and filed at court, the defendant should be invited, by written request, to agree to make an interim payment.

The CPR provide that an application cannot be made before the end of the period for the filing, by the defendant, of the acknowledgement of service. A claimant may make more than one application for an interim payment in an action, but, clearly, each application would need to be made with the overriding objective in mind, and be proportionate, fair, and just (CPR 25.6).

There is a specific CPR designed for this interim application and the rules of procedure set out in the specific CPR must be followed. These are set out in CPR 25.6 and PD 25B.

The application must be supported by evidence which must be filed and served at the same time as the application notice.

The time limits set out in CPR 25.6.3–25.6.6 and PD 25B are as follows:

- The application notice and evidence in support must be served 'as soon as practicable' (see the 'Practical Considerations' box in Chapter 13, paragraph 13.8.1), but this must not be less than fourteen days before the hearing date.

- If the defendant wishes to rely on written evidence at the hearing, he must file the written evidence at court and serve the claimant at least seven days before the hearing.

- If the claimant wishes to respond to the written representations served by the defendant, he must file his written representations at court and serve them on the defendant at least three days before the hearing.

The written evidence supporting the application must comply with PD 25B.2.1 and include details of:

- the sum of money sought;
- the items or matters in respect of which the payment is sought;

- an estimate of the likely sum of any final judgment (and reports that support that estimate, such as medical reports, should be exhibited);
- the reasons why the application meets the requirements of CPR 25.7;
- any other relevant matters;
- in claims for personal injury, details of the special damages, and past and future loss, and in a claim under the Fatal Accidents Act 1976, details of the person(s) on whose behalf the claim is made and the nature of the claim; and
- a costs schedule in Form N260 must be filed twenty-four hours before the hearing.

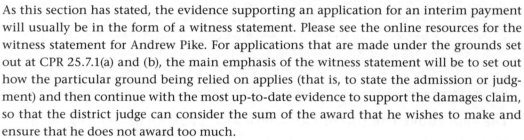

Practical Considerations

Applications for an interim payment may, when it is appropriate to do so, be combined with an application for summary judgment. For example, where a claimant has sought, and obtained, summary judgment in a claim for personal injuries and for damages to be assessed at a later hearing, it would be an advantage to the claimant to seek an interim payment pending the assessment hearing. The application for an interim payment would then proceed immediately after a successful (or partially successful) application for summary judgment. Where this is done, care should be taken when indicating the time estimate for the hearing to allow sufficient time for the application to deal with both interim applications.

As this section has stated, the evidence supporting an application for an interim payment will usually be in the form of a witness statement. Please see the online resources for the witness statement for Andrew Pike. For applications that are made under the grounds set out at CPR 25.7.1(a) and (b), the main emphasis of the witness statement will be to set out how the particular ground being relied on applies (that is, to state the admission or judgment) and then continue with the most up-to-date evidence to support the damages claim, so that the district judge can consider the sum of the award that he wishes to make and ensure that he does not award too much.

For applications made under the grounds set out at CPR 25.7.1(c) and (e), there is a risk that the claimant may fail in his case, so in these circumstances, the witness statement will need to state arguments that directly address the district judge's concern not to make an award when failure by the claimant is a real possibility, as well as contain detail and evidence of the damages claim.

Chapter 17, paragraph 17.4, sets out further guidance on the form of witness statements.

14.4.4 ORDERS THAT MAY BE MADE IN AN APPLICATION FOR AN INTERIM PAYMENT

14.4.4.1 How much can be awarded?

The court must not make an award of an interim payment that is more than a reasonable proportion of the likely amount of the final judgment (CPR 25.7.4). In assessing the sum to award, the court must take account of contributory negligence, as well as any set-off or counterclaim (CPR 25.7.5).

In *Fiona Jordan and Philippe Jordan v Dean Geason (No 2)* [2007] EWHC 2270, the Technology and Construction Court (TCC) set out some relevant guidelines to consider the amount of an interim payment award. These include:

- a consideration of a sum that was just and would not exceed a reasonable proportion of the estimated final judgment award (in this case, the TCC awarded an interim payment approximately 15 per cent below the sum sought by the claimant);
- the claimant's ability to repay the sum, as well as the financial position of the defendant to make a payment (a provision that is only likely to have any real significance in interim payments made under CPR 25.7.1(c)); and
- the court should not be overly (or at all) concerned with the claimant's 'need' for the money, nor should it be concerned with what the claimant intends to do with the money.

Practical Considerations

It would be a very brave applicant, making his application under CPR 25.7.1(c), who did not seek to add weight to his application by setting out what the money was needed for and how it might ultimately benefit the claimant. Equally, if it can be shown that an interim payment now might have the outcome of assisting the claimant's recovery and might help to reduce the sum of the final award, it would be prudent to include such evidence.

14.4.4.2 Can payments by instalment be ordered?

The court has the power to make an interim payment award payable by instalment under CPR 25.6.7, and where such an order is made, the order should contain:

- details of the total sum awarded;
- the amount of each instalment;
- the number of instalments; and
- to whom the payments should be made.

14.4.4.3 Social Security benefit payments

In the making of an interim payment award in a personal injury claim, the defendant should notify the court of any sum that is to be deducted under the Social Security (Recovery of Benefits) Act 1997. These are amounts that the claimant has received in respect of certain benefits, such as statutory sick pay. Any amount of an interim payment will be net of those (relevant) benefits that the claimant has received and with the relevant sum so deducted being repaid. The defendant will do this by obtaining a 'certificate of recoverable benefits' and filing this at court before or at the hearing of the application. (For further detail of the operation of the CRU see Chapter 7, paragraph 7.6.3.1.1.)

14.5 AN APPLICATION FOR SPECIFIC DISCLOSURE

Note: This section should be read in conjunction with Chapter 16, and Chapter 8, paragraph 8.7.

14.5.1 WHAT IS 'SPECIFIC DISCLOSURE'?

The purpose of disclosure generally is to make available documents that either support or undermine the respective parties' cases. It is designed to maintain the 'all the cards on the table' approach to litigation. As part of its management role, the court will usually make an order for standard disclosure (see Chapter 16, paragraph 16.4.1). The court can also order that certain specific documents, or classes of document, are disclosed, or it may order that further specific searches are conducted where there is evidence that a party is in breach of its disclosure obligations. The underlying purpose of specific disclosure is to ensure that justice is done between the parties and to avoid a situation in which a party may have, or obtain, an unfair advantage, or suffer an unfair disadvantage as a result of a document not being produced for inspection under standard disclosure.

Under PD 31A.5.5(1)(b), the court can make a specific disclosure order requiring a party to disclose, or to search for and disclose, documents that:

- 'it is reasonable to suppose may contain information' that will assist the applicant's case or damage the respondent's case or
- 'which may lead to a train of enquiry which has either of those consequences'.

Where a party believes that another party's disclosure is inadequate, he can apply to the court for an order for specific disclosure under CPR 31.12(1).

14.5.2 WHEN CAN AN APPLICATION FOR SPECIFIC DISCLOSURE BE MADE?

An application for specific disclosure is usually made after standard disclosure under CPR 31.5 has taken place. However, it may be made before service of the list of documents (CPR 31.12—see *Dayman v Canyon Holdings* (unreported, 11 January 2006, Ch D)). This will be subject to the specific procedural requirements in each track and any specific requirements in each of the divisions of the High Court.

14.5.3 APPLICATIONS AT A LATE STAGE OF PROCEEDINGS

There is no reason why the court will not order specific disclosure even a couple of weeks before trial, or even at trial, provided that it can be shown that the likely significance of the specific disclosure sought is substantial, the cost of complying is not disproportionate, and compliance with the order is within the capabilities of the respondent to the application even at a late stage in the proceedings (*Legal & General Assurance Society Ltd v Taulke-Johnson* [2002] EWHC 120).

14.5.4 IN WHAT CIRCUMSTANCES IS THE COURT LIKELY TO MAKE AN ORDER?

Under CPR 31.12, the court may make an order for specific disclosure if the court believes that the disclosure given has been inadequate (PD 31A.5.1). 'Inadequate' has not been precisely defined, but it may arise when:

- it is clear on the face of the opponent's list of documents that it is inadequate—for example, if there are gaps in dates in a list of chronological documents;
- important documents that are known to exist, or to have existed, have not been disclosed;
- it is apparent that the search undertaken by the opponent was inadequate—for example, if there are documents that fall into a specific category, or which were created before or after a certain date that were not searched for, but which you believe support your case or adversely affect your opponent;
- documents are referred to in a statement of case, but not provided following a request under CPR 31.14;
- documents are referred to in correspondence, but are not included;
- documents to which your client or your potential witnesses have referred as existing, but which do not appear in the list;
- the disclosure statement is limited in a way that would mean that relevant documents would not be disclosed—for example, where your opponent objects to you inspecting on the grounds of proportionality and you believe that inspection would be proportionate; or
- there appear to be documents set out in your opponent's list in the section withheld from inspection on the grounds of privilege, but which you believe may not be privileged (see Chapter 16, paragraph 16.9).

It should be remembered that standard disclosure is not now the norm in multi-track non-PI claims. These claims will apply the 'menu option' approach to disclosure. It is yet to be seen whether this will result in fewer applications for specific disclosure made in these actions.

 Practical Considerations

Was the opponent's search unreasonably limited? Look carefully at the disclosure statement. Was it unreasonable to exclude documents pre or post a certain date, or in a certain category?

Remember also that the disclosure obligation is a continuing one. Documents that may have come to light after your opponent has served his list of documents still need to be disclosed. In practice, the list of documents is amended mutually. If the documents are not forthcoming, then an application for specific disclosure may follow.

14.5.5 WHAT WILL THE COURT ORDER?

Under CPR 31.12(2), if an order for specific disclosure is granted, the court may order a party to do one or more of the following:

- disclose documents or classes of documents specified in the order;
- carry out a search to the extent specified in the order; and
- disclose any documents located as a result of that search.

However, in deciding whether to grant an order, the court will (under PD 31A.5.4):

> Take into account all the circumstances of the case and, in particular, the overriding objectives. But if the court concludes that the party from whom specific disclosure is sought has failed adequately to comply with the obligations imposed by an order for disclosure (whether by failing to make a sufficient search for documents or otherwise) the court will usually make such order as is necessary to ensure that those obligations are properly complied with.

14.5.6 THE FORM OF AN ORDER FOR SPECIFIC DISCLOSURE

Under CPR 31.12, the court may order specific disclosure by ordering a party to:

- prepare a supplemental list of documents, specifying the documents available for inspection;
- give disclosure of specific documents, or a specific class of documents; and
- carry out a new specified search and disclose documents revealed by that search.

14.5.7 'FISHING EXPEDITIONS'

When you have a belief that documents exist, but have no substantive evidence, your application for specific disclosure may be more akin to a 'fishing expedition' (that is, a search undertaken only in the hope that the documents will show up). This is known as the '*Peruvian Guano* test' (after *Compagnie Financière du Pacifique v Peruvian Guano Co* (1882) 11 QBD 55).

PD 31A.5.5(1) provides that, in appropriate cases, the court may direct a party to carry out a search for documents that may:

> (a) enable the party applying for disclosure either to advance his own case or to damage that of the party giving disclosure; or
>
> (b) lead to a train of enquiry which has either of those consequences.

Under the CPR and the definition applied to 'standard disclosure', the ability to insist on a search that could lead to relevant, but as yet unknown, documents being discovered was effectively removed. However, because of the grounds set out in PD 31A.5, the ability to seek 'train of enquiry' disclosure can be made in an application for specific disclosure. As always, such an application would need to be justified under the principles of the overriding objective, and be 'fair', 'just', and 'proportionate'.

Documents that need not be disclosed on a standard basis may well be disclosable on a specific disclosure order, which can extend the duty to 'a train of enquiry'.

 Example

> Document A may be a letter referring to bank statements of a party. Whilst Document A, in itself, may not fall within the scope of standard disclosure (CPR 31.6), the underlying bank documents referred to may contain information that could assist the other party's case. On an order for specific disclosure, it may be possible to obtain an order for the disclosure of the letter and the bank statements, because such disclosure may lead to 'a train of enquiry' if the applicant has established that they may assist his case.

14.5.8 STEPS TO TAKE BEFORE MAKING AN APPLICATION

To avoid the unnecessary cost penalties that may be incurred by making a premature application, the party seeking disclosure should make a written request to its opponent before making an application for specific disclosure.

- This request should explain what is wanted and why—that is, it should explain in detail what part of the opponent's list is inadequate and why. If documents are required that would lead to a 'train of enquiry', evidence will need to show that it is reasonable to ask for these and why.

- If the applicant believes that the search was inadequate, it would be appropriate to seek full particulars of the search that has been made. The application can ask more directly whether a search was made for a particular type of document, or it could directly ask why there are no documents in a particular category.

- The written request should give the opponent sufficient time in which to respond, but it should also impose a deadline (usually fourteen days, depending on urgency). The letter can say that an application for costs (including indemnity costs) will be made if the application has to proceed. The deadline should be noted and an application made if there has been no, or an inadequate, response.

14.5.9 THE APPLICATION

The procedure for making a specific disclosure application is set out in PD 31A.5.2–31A.5.5.

The evidence in support of the application must include a statement of belief that the disclosure of documents by the disclosing party is inadequate. The grounds for the order may be set out in either the application notice (Form N244, Part C), or in a supporting witness statement. It may include some, or all, of the following points:

- a description of the document, or classes of document, and the extent of the search sought;

- an explanation of why it is reasonable and proportionate for each class or category of documents to be disclosed, having regard to the overriding objective;

- an explanation of how the requested documents are relevant to the matters in issue;

- a statement of the source (if relevant) and the grounds for believing that such documents are, or have been, in the control of the opponent;

- if the application might raise concerns from the other party as to trade secrets or other confidential matter, an offer of a safeguard—such as agreeing to a limit on the numbers of copies of the document(s) sought, and the number of people entitled to view the documents—and provision for their return to the other party at the end of the litigation. The court will also seek to balance the interests of a party seeking disclosure and a party whose trade secrets may be put at risk. In such cases, the court will consider what safeguards should be put in place to provide adequate protection of any trade secrets; and

- The parties should file a costs schedule in Form N260 twenty-four hours before the hearing.

The only guidance given in the CPR as to the factors that the court will take into account in deciding whether to make the order are as set out in PD 31A.5.4. Further guidance can be found in the Court Guides, which will give an idea of the way in which the High Court may approach the application.

 Practical Considerations

Take care when drafting the class of documents or the extent of the search sought: if defined too broadly, the court may refuse disclosure of the whole class.

In the High Court (QBD Guide, paragraph 10.7.6), additional guidance is given as follows:

- Specific disclosure must be 'necessary'.
- The cost must be proportionate.
- A party's ability to continue the litigation must not be impaired by the order. For example, if the request for specific disclosure places very onerous costs demands on a party, with the result that he could not continue to bring the claim or defend the proceedings if the order were to be made, it is unlikely that the order will be made.
- Any specific disclosure ordered must be appropriate to the particular case, taking into account the financial position of the parties, the importance of the case, and the complexity of the issues.
- The court will also consider whether the provisions of CPR 18 (requests for further information) might eliminate the need for a specific disclosure order.

14.5.10 THE EXERCISE OF THE COURT'S DISCRETION

There is very little guidance in the CPR as to the circumstances in which the court will grant an order for specific disclosure, other than as set out in PD 31A.5.4—that is, taking into account all of the circumstances of the case and, in particular, the overriding objective. In practice, it seems likely that the court will consider the following matters:

- Is standard disclosure inadequate? For example, is the search or categories of document listed inadequate? What is the importance of the documents sought to the case as a whole?
- Are there gaps in the list?
- Whilst relevance on its own may no longer be sufficient to obtain an order, the court will still want to be satisfied that the documents are relevant to the issues in the case.
- What is the complexity and nature of the issues?
- What are the costs and burden to the disclosing party of complying with the order?
- What is the amount at stake in the litigation and what is the financial position of the parties?

The court will seek to balance the ECHR, Art. 6(1) right to a fair hearing with the opponent's Art. 8 right to respect for private life.

The court must be satisfied that:

- there is prima facie evidence that the documents are (or have been) in the control of the party; and
- although relevance is no longer a sufficient test upon which the court will grant the order, the court will still want to be certain that the documents sought are relevant.

The court may inspect documents for relevance (although it is only likely to do so where there is a disputed claim to privilege).

Where an application is based on mere probability arising from the surrounding circumstances, the court will take into account all of the circumstances of the case and, in particular, the overriding objective.

14.5.11 WHAT GROUNDS TO OBJECT TO AN ORDER FOR SPECIFIC DISCLOSURE COULD AN OPPONENT CONSIDER?

14.5.11.1 Before an application has been made

On receipt of correspondence from the other party requesting specific disclosure, an opponent should consider if the request is reasonable, bearing in mind CPR 31 and the overriding objective.

Particular points that the opponent to the application may consider are as follows:

- Are there issues of confidentiality? If so, can these be overcome by agreeing to disclosure in a limited way?

- Have the documents in question already been referred to in the defence? If so, the claimant may have a right to inspect under CPR 31.14.
- Can specific disclosure be avoided by agreeing to provision of information under CPR 18 or staged disclosure?
- Have duties regarding electronic disclosure, if appropriate, been complied with?

If specific disclosure is not appropriate, give a reasoned explanation why in correspondence. Remember that this correspondence will be shown to the court and may be relevant on the question of costs.

14.5.11.2 Once an application has been made

On receipt of an application for specific disclosure, it will almost always be sensible to file evidence in response. When preparing this evidence, consideration should be given to the following matters:

- Has a proper search been made for the documents requested?
- Have any issues of confidentiality been sufficiently dealt with?
- Should you obtain a witness statement from any third party who may be affected by an order for specific disclosure? Remember that the court will seek to balance the right to a fair trial with the right to respect for private life.
- Is your opponent seeking specific disclosure at an early stage in the proceedings? If so, has he provided adequate reasons why this is necessary and are there valid reasons for objection?

14.5.12 COSTS

The usual order is that the costs will be awarded to the successful party in the application. However, bear in mind that costs are always at the discretion of the court and that a party's conduct may be drawn to the court's attention on the question of costs, if relevant. (See Chapter 4 for further detail of the likely costs orders that may be made.)

Specifically, in applications for specific disclosure and the issues that the court will consider when deciding the appropriate costs order, the following points should be considered:

- As an applicant, have you set out the grounds for your application in correspondence before making an application and given sufficient time for a response?
- As a respondent, have you responded to any correspondence in a timely way and set out in full any reasons for refusing to give specific disclosure?
- Have you considered fully:
  - staged disclosure?
  - the provision of further information?
  - whether a costs budget has been agreed or approved (in appropriate multi-track cases) and included a contingency for such an application?

14.6 PRE-ACTION DISCLOSURE—CPR 31.16

An application for pre-action disclosure is contained in this chapter, as it is an interim application that a legal practitioner may quite commonly encounter. This section, as well as section 14.5, should be considered along with Chapter 16.

14.6.1 PROTOCOL DISCLOSURE

Early disclosure of relevant documents is an important feature of civil procedure. In any dispute, parties are expected to comply with either a specific Pre-Action Protocol, or if the dispute is not one that is governed by a specific Pre-Action Protocol, then within the PDPACP in general.

Pre-Action Protocols are designed to:

- encourage the exchange of early and full information about the prospective legal claim;
- enable parties to avoid litigation by reaching a settlement before proceedings are commenced; and
- support the efficient management of proceedings where litigation is not avoided.

Further detail of pre-action work including disclosure is contained in Chapter 8.

The general expectation is that parties to an action will be expected to disclose any *relevant* and *essential* documentation at the pre-action stage. Prospective claimants can, and usually do, set out a list of the documents that they wish to see and there is the expectation that the responding party will either comply, or say why they will not or why they believe the requested documents not to be relevant.

Failure to comply with the Pre-Action Protocols can, and generally will, be penalized in costs if the action is commenced. The courts have demonstrated a willingness to impose sanctions or penalties if a party has failed—unreasonably—to cooperate with the aims of Protocol practice. In the case of *Chapman v Tameside Hospital NHS Foundation* (unreported, 15 June 2015) (at Bolton County Court), the defendant was ordered to pay the claimant's costs where she had discontinued her case shortly before the trial (a situation where, normally, the claimant would be expected to pay the defendant's costs) because the defendant had failed to disclose a significant document (which failure had encouraged the claimant to commence litigation). The aims of protocol practice should ensure that there are fewer applications to court for pre-action disclosure under the CPR.

Note: See also Chapter 8, paragraph 8.7.

14.6.2 APPLICATION FOR PRE-ACTION DISCLOSURE

A party who is dissatisfied with the response to their request of documents pre-action can apply to the court before proceedings are issued for an order for disclosure, provided that their request meets the requirements of CPR 31.16. It should be noted that the provisions under CPR 31.16 are the exception to the general principle that a party who is dissatisfied with the pre-action behaviour of a party does not have the right to apply to the court for an order that the 'uncooperating' party cooperate. This is because the Pre-Action Protocols are not part of the CPR and, therefore, the courts do not have jurisdiction to order compliance with the Protocol *in general*.

14.6.2.1 What are the provisions of CPR 31.16?

An application for pre-action disclosure can be made under the provisions of CPR 31.16, provided that:

- the application is by, and sought against, parties who are 'likely to be parties in a subsequent action'. In this context, 'likely' does not mean 'probable', it means 'no more than "may well"' (*Herbert Black and Others v Sumitomo Corp* [2002] 1 WLR 1562, [71], *per* Rix LJ). The jurisdictional threshold is not 'intended to be a high one' (*Herbert Black and Others v Sumitomo Corp* [2002] 1 WLR 1562, [73], *per* Rix LJ). This aspect has been clarified by the Technology and Construction Court in *PHD Modular Access Services Ltd v Seele GmbH* [2011] EWHC 2210 (TCC), where it was held that proceedings should be 'anticipated' and there must be a real prospect, if not a certainty or likelihood, of proceedings between the parties. An order will not be made 'routinely'—and it must be justified;
- the application relates to documents that fall within the definition of 'standard disclosure'; and
- the advance disclosure is necessary to:
  - dispose fairly of the anticipated proceedings; and/or
  - save costs; and/or
  - assist resolution of the dispute without the need to commence proceedings.

In the *Sumitomo* case, the judge addressed himself to four questions in turn in determining whether to order pre-action disclosure:

1. Are proceedings (between the parties) likely?
2. Do the documents sought fall within the scope of standard disclosure?
3. Is pre-action disclosure desirable for any of the three reasons set out in CPR 31.16?
4. Should the court order disclosure in the exercise of its discretion?

In *Total E & P Soudan SA v Edmonds and Ors* [2007] EWCA Civ 50, the Court of Appeal also seems to be adding to this guidance by stating that an application for pre-action disclosure may be granted if the applicant can show that such early disclosure would 'enable the prospective claimant to plead their case in a more focused way'. The case of *Moduleco v Carillion* [2009] EWHC 250 (TCC) also suggests that a party who unreasonably refuses an application for pre-action disclosure may be penalized in costs.

It should not be assumed that the courts will readily grant an order for pre-action disclosure. It will not. Two recent cases have highlighted this: *Assetco plc v Grant Thornton LLP* [2013] EWHC 1215 and *BUAV v Secretary of State for the Home Dept* [2014] EWHC 43. In both cases application for pre-action disclosure was refused on the grounds that protocol practice should cover the expectation for the early disclosure sought.

 Practical Considerations

The judgment delivered by Rix LJ in the *Sumitomo* case is useful and essential reading before preparing any application for pre-action disclosure. The four questions set out would be followed (and 'answered') in any supporting evidence for an application. It guides any application beyond the words of CPR 31.16. The more focused the application and the more limited the disclosure sought, the more likely that the court will exercise its discretion in the applicant's favour.

14.6.2.2 The availability of other types of pre-action disclosure

Other types of pre-action disclosure may be available in applications for:

- a freezing injunction under the provisions of CPR 25.1 and PD 25.6;
- a search order under CPR 25.1, which may have the effect of providing information early;
- an application for the preservation of property under CPR 25.5, which can be made pre-action; and
- *Norwich Pharmacal* orders.

These substantive applications are outside the scope of this book.

14.7 AN APPLICATION FOR SECURITY FOR COSTS

14.7.1 WHAT IS 'SECURITY FOR COSTS'?

An order for security for costs offers protection to a party (usually a defendant) from the risks of their opponent not being able to pay the party's litigation costs if ordered to do so (see Chapter 10, paragraph 10.7.3). The provision is designed to protect a defendant who is facing an action where, even if he defeated the claimant's claim, the claimant would be unlikely to be able to pay any or all of the defendant's costs of defending the action. A successful application will mean that the opponent (usually the claimant but it could also be a third party) will be required to pay money into court or provide a bond against which the winning party can subsequently enforce an order for costs. Before making an order for security the court will consider, on the totality of the evidence before the court, whether it is satisfied that there is reason to believe the claimant (or third party) will be unable to pay the defendant's costs if ordered to do so. The court does not have to be satisfied that the claimant (or third party) will be unable to pay, only that there is reason to believe he will not. This is, therefore, a lower standard of proof than 'the balance of probabilities'.

14.7.2 WHEN CAN AN APPLICATION FOR 'SECURITY FOR COSTS' BE MADE?

An application for security for costs can be made:

- by a defendant/respondent against a claimant/appellant;
- by a defendant against someone other than claimant; or
- at the court's initiative or by a party pursuant to CPR 3.1(3) and CPR 3.1(5) (seeking security as a sanction or condition).

The court can impose a security for costs order as a condition, as an alternative to granting summary judgment or setting aside default judgment (PD 24.5.1–2 and CPR 13.3). There are restrictions which apply to security for costs applications.

14.7.3 WHEN MAY AN APPLICATION FOR 'SECURITY FOR COSTS' BE OBTAINED?

The overarching condition that needs to be satisfied is that the court will only make the order if all the relevant conditions under CPR 25.13.2 are met and also it is just to do so.

- Security for costs is only available for specific situations set out in statute and/or the court rules and is subject to the court's discretion.
- The court rules include that an application may not be made unless:
  - the claimant is resident outside the jurisdiction (of the court), although residents of a Brussels Contracting State (as defined by the Civil Jurisdiction and Judgments Act 1982) are excluded, or
  - where the claimant is a company or other body (whether incorporated inside or outside Great Britain), and
  - there is reason to believe that it will be unable to pay the defendant's costs if ordered to do so, or
  - where the claimant has changed his address since the claim was commenced with a view to evading the consequences of the litigation, or
  - where the claimant has failed to give his address on the claim form (or given an incorrect address), or
  - where the claimant is acting as a nominal claimant and there is reason to believe that he will be unable to pay the defendant's costs if ordered to do so, or
  - where the claimant has taken steps in relation to his assets that would make it difficult to enforce an order for costs against him.
- An order will only be made when it is 'just' to do so.
- Security for costs is only available within litigation, thus it is not available as a pre-action application. This applies even though the emphasis is on pre-action preparation and when the prospective defendant may already have incurred costs in refuting the claim in the pre-action stage.
- Security for costs is not available for small claims.
- A claimant who is a defendant to a counterclaim can apply for security for costs, but unless the counterclaim is 'of substance' it may not be granted.
- Security under CPR 3.1 cannot be sought independently. It must be sought alongside another application, such as summary judgment.
- Delay in applying for security for costs can be fatal and result in no security being granted or in the applicant being deprived of some or all of the costs they have already incurred.
- In the Commercial Court, in appropriate cases, defendants who seek security for costs orders must undertake to compensate a winning claimant against losses he may have suffered by having his funds tied up.

Practical Considerations

This list of exceptions and restrictions should make it clear that applications for security for costs are not commonplace applications. A failed application only adds to the costs burden of the defendant and an application should perhaps not be made where there may be other, more appropriate, interim applications to make—for example, an application to strike out under CPR 3, or an application for summary judgment where the court has power to make alternative orders that are tantamount to an order for security for costs (CPR 3.1 and 24.2).

14.7.4 WHAT CPR APPLY?

- CPR 25.12 and CPR 25.13.
- CPR 25.14—concerns security for costs applications against someone other than the claimant.
- CPR 3.1(3) and CPR 3.1(5)—govern security for costs as a sanction or condition.
- PD 24.5.1–24.5.2—sets out the court's power to order security for costs as an alternative to granting an application for summary judgment.
- CPR 13.3—refers to the court's power in CPR 3.1(3) to attach conditions to orders when it is deciding whether or not to set aside a default judgment.
- CPR 20.3—concerns security for costs and Part 20 claims.

14.7.5 WHEN SHOULD AN APPLICATION FOR 'SECURITY FOR COSTS' BE MADE?

Applications for security for costs should be made promptly. This will usually be after the acknowledgement of service or the defence has been filed. The application should be served at least three clear days before the hearing. There is no specific time limit for a response, but this should be served in good time for the hearing.

14.7.6 THE PROCEDURE

As with most interim applications a request for security should be made first, and only when that has been refused or the terms are unacceptable, the applicant will follow this procedure:

- Apply on notice in Form N244, including the grounds being relied on. A draft order should be lodged with the application and evidence may be included on Form N244 (though this is unlikely) or in a witness statement.
- The written evidence will seek to substantiate the ground relied on, include the factors relevant to the court's discretion, state the amount of security, and may refer to the pre-application request.
- Include the fee.
- The parties should file and serve a costs schedule in Form N260, twenty-four hours before the hearing.
- Usually, the parties will also provide skeleton arguments and the relevant (to the application) court bundle in advance of the hearing.

14.8 INJUNCTIONS: PRACTICE AND PROCEDURE

14.8.1 INTRODUCTION TO THIS SECTION

On the online resources there is a section on the law relating to injunctions, and specific detail of search orders and freezing orders and other equitable remedies. That section should be read in conjunction with this section, which is more practical in nature.

14.8.2 **WHAT IS AN INJUNCTION?**

An injunction is a court order that requires a party to an action to do or stop doing a certain act. Breach of an injunction is punishable as a contempt of court.

Injunctions are at the very top end of the 'weaponry' a party can use. They are a high-risk strategy, but they can give high rewards (the application for an injunction can in effect 'end' an action as it starts) and can prevent the opponent from further action which would not only be unlawful, but which could be potentially devastating to your client's legitimate legal and business interests.

14.8.3 **WHEN CAN AN APPLICATION FOR AN INJUNCTION BE SOUGHT?**

CPR 25 deals with injunctions. An injunction can be sought at any time during proceedings. Injunctions can only be granted 'within' an action; they cannot, therefore, be granted in isolation. There needs to be a pre-existing action in law upon which the injunction is based. For example, your clients seek your advice because they understand that there are plans for an exceptionally noisy event to take place next door to the church where they are getting married on the very same day. Your clients claim this will ruin their wedding and that the noise is unjustified (it could be held elsewhere or on another day). In any application for an injunction order to prevent the noisy event proceeding, it will be the excessive noise that will constitute a nuisance. The claim in nuisance will be the cause of action.

In some instances an injunction may be obtained before proceedings have commenced, but such applications will require the applying party (or, more likely, his legal representative) to give an undertaking to the court to issue proceedings forthwith. The usual purpose of the injunction will be to preserve the legal standing of the parties until their rights have been determined. For this reason the applicant will always have to show that there is good reason why the defendant's rights should be restricted for a period when it is not yet known whether the claimant's claim will succeed. Once obtained, an injunction will remain in force until the 'return date', if it was a without notice application, or usually until trial if the application had been with notice, at which point the court will decide whether to make the injunction final. The return date in a without notice application is usually listed within days of the first hearing, as it will be the first opportunity the defendant has to put his case to the court, and at that hearing the court will decide whether to continue the order until the trial of the action or, if the defendant is able to persuade the court that the injunction should not have been made, dismiss the injunction order. Any application by the defendant to set aside the injunction order must be made on notice. Occasionally the court will make a without-notice application 'until the trial of the action', but the defendant will have the opportunity to apply for an earlier date if he seeks to set aside the interim injunction that has been granted.

Injunctions are an equitable remedy and, therefore, are not granted as a 'right'. The court always has discretion whether to grant an order or not.

14.8.4 **IN WHICH COURTS CAN INJUNCTIONS BE GRANTED?**

All types of interim injunctions can be granted by the High Court. However, the County Court has limited jurisdiction with regards to injunctions. In particular, no search orders can be granted in the County Court and there are limited circumstances where freezing injunctions are available.

Therefore, where the County Court has no power in respect of the order being sought, the application must be made in the High Court. If the case has already been issued, and is in the County Court, an application for transfer to the High Court will have to be made for the application for an injunction to be heard.

14.8.5 IN WHAT CIRCUMSTANCES ARE INJUNCTIONS SOUGHT WITHIN LITIGATION?

There are three types of injunction, namely injunctions:

- to prevent someone from taking certain steps;
- to require the defendant to take action to do something; and
- to require the defendant to take steps to prevent harm occurring.

These can be either interim or final orders.
Circumstances when they can be sought include:

- to seek the immediate return of unpaid goods where there is a clear retention of title clause in the contract and the goods will otherwise be converted to other manufactured goods or deliberately moved from their current location;
- seeking a freezing order preventing the disposal of assets, including freezing bank accounts where there is a fraud;
- seeking a search order allowing the search of premises or the seizure of assets or documents (where there is a likelihood that they will otherwise be destroyed);
- seeking an order which requires the return of stolen confidential information and to restrain ongoing misuse;
- seeking an order to prevent an intended breach of confidence;
- seeking an order to enforce employment contract restrictive covenants so as to prevent former employees poaching clients or staff;
- seeking an order to prevent dealings with particular customers or suppliers;
- seeking an order to enforce intellectual property rights such as breach of copyright, unlawful use of trademark, and passing off;
- in shareholder disputes when there is a real risk that steps will be taken that will harm the company;
- to restrain the publication of obvious or defamatory lies;
- to restrain trespass to land by persons or structures; or to compel the removal of overhanging structures; or to order the removal of a tree whose roots are causing damage to a wall;
- to exclude a defendant from his home so as to stop a serious nuisance committed against a neighbour. Such an order may arise under the Housing Act 1996, s. 152 relating to anti-social behaviour;
- to restrain an infringement of a right to light; and to compel the removal of structures so built;
- to protect a licence to occupy premises;
- to restrain the sale of land to a third party when the vendor has already agreed to sell it to the claimant;
- to enforce a local authority's right to buy;
- seeking an order to restrain a subletting or assignment in breach of the terms of a lease;
- seeking an order to restrain harassment;
- to compel the landlord to allow peaceful re-entry; or
- seeking an order to enforce the landlord's liability to repair under the Defective Premises Act 1972.

This is not an exhaustive list. The courts are prepared to recognize the need for flexibility in determining when such relief might be justified. In the recent decision of *Vastint Leeds BV v Persons Unknown* [2018] EWHC 2456 (Ch), the High Court in England has granted a final *quia timet* (since it fears) injunction against persons unknown preventing such individuals from entering or remaining on portions of land within the former Tetley brewery site in Leeds. This is the latest decision that pushes the injunction jurisdiction into novel areas as courts have sought to use its flexibility to fit modern commercial needs. In the case of *Boyd and another v Ineos Upstream Ltd and others* [2019] EWCA Civ 515, the Court of Appeal, partially allowing an appeal regarding injunctions against fracking protestors, provided guidance and set out requirements on obtaining injunctions against persons unknown.

14.8.6 HOW QUICKLY CAN AN INJUNCTION BE OBTAINED?

For very serious matters, where your client has provided you with the required evidence and you have the right legal team in place, it can be possible to obtain an injunction in as little as forty-eight to seventy-two hours after your client is aware of the breach or serious threat to their legal rights and has consulted you. Applications can be made over the telephone and 'out of hours'.

If the injunction order is made by the court on a without notice application, the order must be personally served on the injuncted party very quickly and another hearing will be arranged a very short time later at which the defendant can apply to have the injunction set aside or varied.

When an injunction is granted without notice, the respondent has not had the opportunity to put forward its case. To afford some measure of protection to the respondent, the applicant has a duty to disclose to the court all matters relevant to the exercise of the court's discretion, including all material facts of which the court should be made aware. It must give a fair account of the case for and against the respondent, identifying any defences that would have been available to the respondent had it been present. This is known as the duty of full and frank disclosure and is an onerous one. The duty applies to matters known by the applicant and matters that ought to have been known had proper enquiries been made. The duty of disclosure continues and the applicant must return to court, as soon as it becomes apparent, to correct any misinformation or omission.

It is crucial to make the applicant aware of the extent of its obligations in relation to disclosure. Failure to provide proper disclosure can lead to the injunction being discharged and damages being payable to the respondent for any losses suffered as a result of the injunction together with any costs.

 Practical Considerations

Except where secrecy is essential, an applicant who does not have time to give proper notice of the application should give as much informal notice as possible (PD 23.4.2 and 23.2.10, and PD 25). This informal notice could include phoning the respondent and giving him details of the application. This may enable the respondent to attend and participate in the hearing. Such an application will be called an application 'opposed but without notice'. Giving informal notice may result in delays, because the respondent who attends the hearing after informal notice may well succeed in obtaining an adjournment while he prepares evidence to oppose the application. This possibility does not give the applicant good reason for not giving informal notice when it is felt that such notice would ordinarily be given but for the shortage of time.

14.8.7 ENFORCING AN INJUNCTION

An injunction order will include a penal notice, which means that once served, an interim injunction is enforceable by a charge for contempt of court if the defendant fails to comply with the terms of the order. Compliance is usually provided to be 'on service', that is, the defendant must comply with the terms of the injunction immediately upon service on him of the order. Such orders:

(a) avoid malicious and/or spiteful damage to assets covered by the interim injunction that might otherwise take place during the usual notice period;

(b) stop the defendant taking steps to tamper with evidence; and

(c) may require the defendant to 'do' something immediately, for example deliver up passwords, or stop doing something.

14.8.8 WHAT ARE THE KEY CONSIDERATIONS BEFORE MAKING AN APPLICATION FOR AN INJUNCTION?

The key points to be aware of when considering with your client whether to apply for an injunction are:

- The expense—applying for an injunction can easily require a team of lawyers working for days, often at very short notice, to prepare for, and make, the application.

- Your client will have to give the court an undertaking in damages if you succeed on the basis that if the defendant successfully applies to have the order set aside, your client will be ordered to pay damages and costs to their opponent. This undertaking may have to be supported with immediate payment into court.

- If the application is being made pre-action, the legal representative will be asked to give an undertaking to the court to issue proceedings forthwith, so instructions need to be obtained and documents quickly prepared to comply with this. The expense of this also needs to be taken into account.

- Urgency—if your client is applying to the court for an urgent order, based on the evidence of a real and immediate danger to their business, they, and you, will need to act quickly. If the application is not made speedily, the judge will take this into account. Delay can cause an application to fail.

- An application should never be used to 'bully' an opponent. A client may wish you to use the procedure to threaten their opponent, as this is a way of harrying their opponent and flexing their muscles. It is always a mistake to threaten something you are not prepared to follow through. If you do so, you will lose credibility with the opponent, and it may be seen as a sign of weakness, not strength.

- In a without notice application the client must be prepared to give 'full and frank' disclosure. This includes reference to any weaknesses in their application for an injunction application. A failure to give full and frank disclosure can again cause an application to fail on the return date and will often trigger the payment of damages to the opponent.

Injunctions will not be granted where damages would be an adequate remedy.

The principles laid down in *American Cyanamid Co v Ethicon Ltd* [1975] AC 396 need to be considered (see the online resources). The case outlines certain criteria to be considered by the courts prior to the grant of an injunction. These include consideration of whether there is a serious question to be tried, whether damages would be an adequate remedy (instead of an injunction), and whether undertakings given by the applicant to protect the defendant from loss would be 'adequate'. In addition, they also consider where the balance of convenience lies.

14.8.9 A PRACTICAL LOOK—SEEKING AN INJUNCTION TO PREVENT THE PRESENTATION OF A WINDING UP ORDER

Your client has instructed you having heard that one of its creditors has presented a winding up petition against the company and intends to proceed to advertise (as required in an action to wind up a company) the presentation of that petition. Obviously this would cause damage to your client and is a damage (to reputation) that cannot adequately be compensated by a payment of damages. Your client states that they are not insolvent, and the debt in question to the petitioning company is disputed.

What matters would need to be covered in the witness statement you would draft for your client in support of the application for an injunction order preventing the presentation of the advertisement?

The witness statement would need to cover:

- evidence to show that your client has a defence to the claim (for the winding up of the client company) and that this has a 'prospect of success'; and

- evidence that your client company is solvent.

The key requirement to establish in the evidence supporting this application is that a petition (for winding up) should not be allowed to proceed. The reasons for this will, of course, be based on the evidence your client has supplied you with, but for the purpose of this example we could include:

- the debt (to the petitioning company) is genuinely disputed—provide full and frank details of the grounds for stating this;

- the debtor has a cross-claim or right of set-off against the creditor that exceeds the amount claimed in the demand—if so, giving full (and frank) details of that cross-claim or set-off;

- the company has another reasonable excuse for not paying the debt—if so, fully (and frankly) stating what this is.

- Additionally we would expect the witness statement to provide a clear chronology of relevant matters between the two parties up to the time when the winding up petition was presented. If that chronology included correspondence where your client company had invited the petitioning company not to proceed with the petition, this should also be included. Or, if there were any matters that showed the petitioning company to have acted unreasonably, this should also be included. These would be relevant on the question of costs and an application for indemnity costs could be sought if your client's application succeeds. However, this applies to both parties, and if your client had behaved in any way that could be construed as unreasonable, then they may be at risk as to costs or such may cause the application to fail.

- A statement that the company is solvent with evidence and accounts, to establish this. While this is not strictly necessary to the issue the court is considering (whether to grant an injunction), it is something that will assist the court to consider that the petition (for winding up) should not have been presented.

- Information of the effect on the company if a petition is advertised.

14.8.10 AN ALTERNATIVE ORDER? WHEN WOULD AN EXPEDITED TRIAL BE APPROPRIATE?

An injunction is a draconian remedy, and the costs and risks of the application will sometimes preclude a party proceeding. In all cases where an injunction application is a consideration, the legal representative should consider whether an alternative process would be a better option.

The courts will sometimes grant an order for an expedited trial as an alternative to an injunction, or to limit the time when an interim injunction will remain in force. If an expedited trial cannot be ordered, the court may consider a trial of preliminary issues.

It is open to any party in civil proceedings to make an application for an expedited trial and although the CPR contain no specific provisions on expedited trials, the power will come within the court's general powers of management granted under the CPR Parts 1 and 3. However, a body of case law exists which gives guidance on the principles the court will apply when a party seeks an expedited trial. Notably see *CPC Group Qatari Diar Real Estate Investment Company* [2009] EWHC 2018 (Ch) and *Warner-Lambert v Teva UK Ltd & Ors* [2011] EWHC 3204 (Ch).

The principles the court will apply include:

- cases should be bought to the court as soon as reasonably practical (in line with the overriding objectives set out in CPR 1);

- deciding whether to grant an order (for an expedited trial) is within the discretion of the judge;

- that discretion must be exercised judicially—it is partly a question of principle and partly of practice;

- the court will take account of the fact that the order will involve a re-allocation of court time and this will impact on other cases;

- the applicant must satisfy the court that there is an objective urgency—this does not have to be immediate urgency, but a need for a decision before the 'normal process' would provide one;
- the procedural history of the case will be taken account of. Delay in seeking an order may prejudice an application;
- the respondent, if opposing the application, will need to show real prejudice if the trial is expedited; and
- the court should resolve timetabling in a way that is the least unjust to all the interests concerned.

 Practical Considerations

The alternative order, for an expedited trial, needs to be considered with care, as it can leave the parties with the problem of preparing for a speedy trial which may not always be the best option.

KEY POINTS SUMMARY

- An interim application must comply precisely with the rule providing for it.
- The evidence supporting an interim application should, wherever possible, be given added 'weight' by the inclusion of material evidence.
- All interim applications must be justified within the terms of the overriding objective.
- Nearly all interim applications should be preceded with an informal request.
- Most interim applications that are listed for less than one hour will be heard by way of a telephone conference call.
- Interim applications, such as setting aside, default judgment, and summary judgment, are significant and important applications, because they can bring an end to proceedings if successfully defended or made. Make sure that your evidence is accurate, articulate, and persuasive.
- Always discuss the purpose of making or defending an application with your client, as well as the prospect of success, and costs incurred and/or recoverable.
- Ensure that you have specific instructions to proceed to make or oppose the application.
- Interim injunction applications carry severe risks and penalties if wrongly sought. Clients need to be fully aware of these responsibilities.
- Parties will need to file a costs schedule in Form N260 twenty-four hours before any hearing.

Case Study *Andrew James Pike v Deep Builders Ltd*

Question 1

You have a witness statement of Andrew Pike dated 17 November 20?? and an application notice dated 20 November 20??. You have also received a draft order and case summary. Assume that it is now 20 November 20??, and that the partner supervising the case has instructed you to attend to service of, and preparation for, this application. Consider the following:

- the purpose of this application and witness statement;
- the formalities relating to the making of the application, such as when and how you will serve the application;

- whether the statement is either necessary or adequate in terms of its compliance with any formalities and its substantive contents;
- determine whether the application complies with the requirements of the CPR and PD; and
- what other preparations you would make for the hearing and what you would expect to be the outcome of the hearing.

Question 2

Assume that you are acting for the defendant in this matter. For the purposes of this stage, you are a legal representative with Rasputin & Co, and you have just received the application and witness statement. Your instructions from the insurer of the defendant are to resist the application with a view to ensuring that the claimant's application is refused or that any payment ordered is as small as possible. John Deep has told you that, at the time of the accident, he may have had 'a pint or two at lunchtime', and that he may possibly have been in a hurry to get to an appointment and so drove 'a little over the speed limit'. However, he is adamant that he was not over the centre lines and points out that he passed a breathalyzer test. The accident was, in his view, the fault of the claimant, who was over the centre lines.
Draft a short witness statement to resist the application.

Question 3

What would happen at the hearing—for example, who would be present, in what order would things happen, and what matters may be discussed, apart from simply whether or not an order for a payment would be made? If you were to be present, what would you need to do at the end of the hearing and following the hearing?

What document will have been lodged at court (and served on your opponent) at least twenty-four hours before the hearing? What is the purpose of this document?

Case Study *Bollingtons Ltd v Mrs Elizabeth Lynch t/a The Honest Lawyer*

Question 1

You now have instructions to pursue the matter privately for Mrs Lynch. You have informed her that the judgment was entered correctly, but have advised that it will be necessary to apply to have judgment set aside if she wishes to defend the claim. What documentation will you need to prepare? Prepare the documents that you believe are appropriate for this type of application. If you believe that a defence is necessary, then, for the purposes of this exercise, you do not need to draft a defence, but you may wish to refer to one if you think that, in making the application, you would have prepared one.

Question 2

Consider the prospects of success of the defendant's application and the likely costs orders.

 Any documents referred to in these case study questions can be found in the online resources—simply click on 'Case study documentation' to access the documents that you need for Chapter 14 and to be reminded of the questions. Suggested answers to these case study questions can be accessed in the Student Resources section of the online resources.

Relevant court forms relating to this chapter:

• N242A Court Forms

Relevant parts of the CPR and its PDs: 36, 44, and 45.

15.1 INTRODUCTION

Offers to settle pervade the practice of dispute resolution and litigation. Whilst this chapter is self-contained, the proactive legal representative should constantly be aware that it may be appropriate to make an offer to settle at any time.

ADR considerations

You should read Chapter 5 in conjunction with this chapter, on the basis that offers to settle may form part of the negotiation spectrum—usually as the first step in attempting to settle a claim.

It is extremely rare that a dispute is resolved or proceeds to trial without some type of offer being made. There does not, however, appear to be a limit on the number of offers that can be made, although credibility and common sense would indicate that offers to settle should be made purposefully, but not irrationally.

LITIGATION TRAIN: PART 36 OFFERS AND CONCLUDING A CLAIM

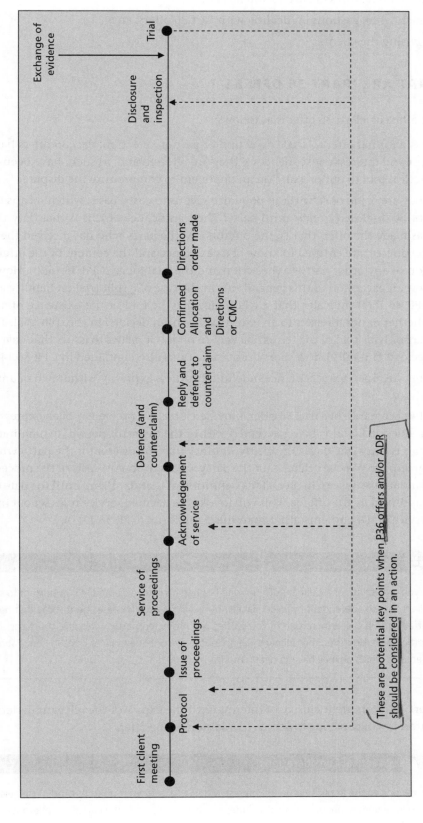

These are potential key points when P36 offers and/or ADR should be considered in an action.

Because the provisions of Part 36 are highly technical and are always something with which students and those new to practice struggle, this chapter considers:

- the main features of Part 36 and its PDs;
- practical suggestions on dealing with Part 36 offers; and
- advising the client.

15.2 WHAT ARE 'PART 36 OFFERS'? — *offer to settle!*

The ethos of a Part 36 offer is as follows:

- It is a formal offer to settle an action or part of an action. Part 36 offers have significant cost and interest consequences if they are rejected and, as such, have been designed as a tactical tool to put pressure on an opponent to compromise the dispute.

- They are made on a 'without prejudice save as to costs' basis, which means that they cannot be disclosed to any third party. The significance of this is that only the party who has made the offer, that is, the offeror, and the party who has received the offer, that is, the offeree, are entitled to know of its existence and the content of the offer to the exclusion of any other party to the action and the trial judge (CPR 36.16(2)). However, there is now an exception to this general rule in the case of a split trial on liability and quantum. CPR 36.16(4) indicates that a trial judge may be told of the existence of a Part 36 offer whether or not it relates to an issue that has been decided in the split trial. The trial judge may only be told of the terms of a Part 36 offer if it relates to issues that have already been decided or it falls into a short list of exceptions also contained in CPR 36.14(4).

- They are open for acceptance indefinitely unless expressly withdrawn or amended by the offeror.

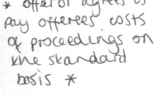
* offeror agrees to pay offerees' costs of proceedings on the standard basis *

- The acceptance of a Part 36 offer, provided it has not previously been expressly withdrawn or amended, and is being accepted within the 'relevant period' (which must be not less than twenty-one days), implicitly signifies that the offeror (or the party who is to pay) is agreeing to pay the offeree's (or the party who is to accept) costs of the proceedings on the standard basis (see Chapter 4 for a definition of 'standard'), up until the date of acceptance was served by the offeree. This will invoke the deemed service rules set out in CPR 6.26 for service of 'Documents other than the claim form' (CPR 36.13(1)).

 Costs

If you are acting for a claimant offeror who has had his offer accepted, it is important to stress to your client that the defendant offeree's liability for his costs usually ceases on the day that he accepts the offer (or in a case where one of the parties is a protected party, when the court has approved the settlement). However, the claimant will undoubtedly continue to incur costs in negotiating a cost settlement, which he may have to bear himself.

- Part 36 offers are inclusive of interest until the expiry of the relevant period, after which interest will continue to accrue in addition to the offer.

✓ Practical Considerations

In relation to the implicit nature of interest within a Part 36 offer up to the end of the relevant period, the settlement figure put forward includes interest calculated to the end of the relevant period (that is, an advance interest calculation). It is, therefore, good drafting practice to make provision for interest to run in the wording of your Part 36 offer after the expiry of the relevant period.

15.3 THE FORM AND CONTENT OF A PART 36 OFFER

For the offer to be CPR 36-compliant and to take advantage of the cost consequences detailed in paragraphs 15.7 and 15.8, there are five mandatory requirements under CPR 36.5. The Part 36 offer must:

- be made in writing—usually in letter format or Form N242A. This form appears in the online resources;
- state clearly—usually in bold in the heading—that it is made pursuant to Part 36 (CPR 36.5);
- specify a period of not less than twenty-one days (the relevant period) within which the paying party will be automatically liable for the receiving party's costs if the offer is accepted within the relevant period (unless it is less than twenty-one days before the start of a trial), in accordance with CPR 36.13;
- state whether the offer is made in respect of the whole or part of the claim, or to the whole or part of an issue; and
- state whether the offer takes into account any counterclaim.

[handwritten margin note: requirements for Part 36]

Careful drafting of Part 36 offers is crucial, and many cases that reach the courts on Part 36 are in relation to poorly drafted offers and their effect. In *Potter v Sally Montague Hair and SPA* (unreported, 7 October 2016) (at Nottingham County Court), it was held that an offer which does not comply with the strict mandatory requirements of CPR 36.5 (subject only to the express modifications in CPR 47.20) will not attract Part 36 consequences. CPR 36.5(4) provides that a Part 36 offer to pay or accept a sum of money will be treated as inclusive of interest. Stating that the offer was exclusive of interest had taken it outside the Part 36 regime.

These requirements set out in the bullet points above are the bare minimum and additional information can be included in a CPR 36 offer. For example, if the claim is for personal injuries, then there can be other specific information that needs to be included in the offer. These additional requirements are set out briefly in paragraph 15.10.

An offer may also specify interest provision once the relevant period has expired. In the recent case of *Calonne Construction Ltd v Dawnus Southern Ltd* [2019] EWCA Civ 754 the court clarified that a Part 36 offer may specify the rate of interest to be applied after expiry of the relevant period and will not render an offer invalid.

Figure 15.5 at the end of this chapter is a basic template claimant Part 36 offer letter, which can be used as a starting point for the drafting of Part 36 offers in individual cases (this can be amended for a defendant offer in accordance with the specific provisions of Part 36). If the offer is not made in accordance with CPR 36.5, the offer is not likely to have the cost consequences set out in this chapter.

There is also a Defendant Part 36 offer letter in the online resources in respect of the Andrew Pike case study.

15.4 WHEN CAN PART 36 OFFERS BE MADE?

Part 36 offers can be made in any type of dispute or proceedings including the following:

- all Part 7 and Part 8 claims;
- additional claims (CPR 20);
- proceedings involving a protected party or a child. However, if the offeree is a protected party or a child, then whilst the offeree can indicate a willingness to accept, acceptance is not, in fact, valid unless the court approves the settlement (CPR 21.10); or
- detailed assessment proceedings (CPR 47.20(4)) (see Chapter 20 on assessment of costs).

The only type of proceedings where Part 36 offers are not permitted are cases allocated to the small claims track (CPR 27.2).

Part 36 offers can be made at any time during proceedings (including trial) and also before proceedings are issued (CPR 36.7(1)) and be made on an unpleaded counterclaim (*Calonne Construction Ltd v Dawnus Southern Ltd* [2019] EWCA Civ 754). They can even be made in appeal proceedings (CPR 36.4).

By definition, the time at which a CPR 36 offer is actually made is when it is served on the offeree (CPR 36.7). CPR 6.20–6.26 deal with permitted methods of service and deemed service that apply in calculating when Part 36 offers are made.

15.4.1 TACTICALLY

The timing of Part 36 offers can be important from both a tactical and a costs point of view.

Generally, making a Part 36 offer, or any 'without prejudice save as to costs' offer, should be discussed with your client as soon as a firm view can be given on liability and quantum. As can be seen from the 'litigation train' diagram that features in this chapter, there are key times at which Part 36 offers should be considered to be made: for example, after disclosure and inspection of documents. It may also be helpful to look at the online Litigation Train in this regard. However, Part 36 offers can be made for more tactical reasons.

> ### 💡 Example
>
> Your client has not yet been minded to make a Part 36 offer in a dispute. Proceedings have not been issued and little information has been exchanged. He instructs you to make a low Part 36 offer directly before a mediation—that is, less than twenty-one days beforehand—to put pressure on the opponent and to 'test the water'.
>
> What is the impact of this offer? One school of thought is that this could speed up the process on the day of the mediation, and that the offeree can consider the cost consequences of not accepting it in light of the further work to be done on the case and make a balanced and informed decision. However, the whole purpose of mediation is to understand and explore the strengths and weakness of your own and your opponent's case with a view to considering settlement options. A derisory pre-mediation Part 36 offer may hamper this process. In practice, it would be better to make any first-time or renewed Part 36 offers during the mediation itself (rather than immediately before), because they are likely to be taken more seriously, having then been made on a full appraisal of your opponent's case.

Part 36 offers can also be made on purely commercial grounds to dispose of a time-consuming and expensive litigation.

> ### ✓ Practical Considerations
>
> Legal practitioners often consider with their defendant commercial clients in a fast-track litigation making a commercial Part 36 offer where there is a claim and a counterclaim. The defendant may have raised a counterclaim because he has a legal entitlement to do so, but with a time-consuming litigation ahead, where legal costs can easily become disproportionate, a Part 36 offer abandoning the counterclaim and offering either a 'walk away' settlement or a small contribution to the claimant's claim often has the effect of persuading the claimant to accept the offer, especially as it has the implicit provision within it to pay the claimant's reasonable costs.

15.4.2 COSTS ON PRE-ACTION PART 36 OFFERS

We can see from paragraph 15.4.1 that pre-action Part 36 offers can be made. If the offer is not accepted and proceedings are issued, it is possible to recover the costs of any pre-action work, as well as the costs of the litigation itself. However, what of the position when the Part 36 offer is accepted before proceedings are issued? This has sensibly now been clarified by the new Part 36 at CPR 36.13(1), where it states that recoverable costs may include pre-action costs.

15.5 **CLARIFICATION OF PART 36 OFFERS**

Once a Part 36 offer has been made, the offeree has seven days within which to request clarification of the offer (CPR 36.8). Requests for clarification are usually made where the offeree is seeking a breakdown of the overall settlement figure to enable him to consider how much the offeror has allocated for different issues or heads of damage. Although there are no stipulations that the request should be in writing, it is good practice to make it in letter form. Under the provisions of CPR 36.8, an offeree who has not received any, or adequate, clarification requested within seven days of the offeror receiving its request may apply to the court for an order that he do so. If the court makes an order, it must also specify the date on which the offer is deemed to have been made. This provision does not, however, apply if the trial has started (CPR 36.8(2)). Where the court has made such an order, the district judge (or master) who made the order will not have any further involvement in the action.

Responses to clarification requests should also be in writing and should be done on a 'without prejudice' basis, because you are explaining the basis of a Part 36 offer. It should also be noted that a failure to provide the offeree with the clarification information to enable him to decide whether to accept the offer or not does not invalidate the offer, although the conduct of the offeror in this regard may be taken into account when the court is considering whether to make the usual Part 36 costs order.

 Practical Considerations

It should be borne in mind that, often, claimant legal representatives will make a request for clarification and use this as an excuse for not properly assessing their own case. Defendants frequently make offers based on commercial grounds to promote settlement and apply a global figure for damages—especially when there are numerous heads of damages. Figures are often not arrived at by way of scientific calculation. Some defendants, in practice, are reluctant to reveal exact figures, because this may, in turn, reveal their strategy or tactics. These requests for clarification are therefore designed to force a defendant to provide a breakdown of its assessment of an opponent's case where it may be impracticable or unreasonable.

15.6 **HOW AND WHEN CAN PART 36 OFFERS BE ACCEPTED?**

15.6.1 **HOW?**

As with the making of a Part 36 offer, the mode of its acceptance is also in writing. There is no guidance in CPR 36 or its PD as to the form that the notice of acceptance should take, but CPR 36.11 states it is accepted by serving written notice, making specific reference to the CPR 36 offer made and sent to the offeror. It should also be noted that there is a notice of acceptance attached to the N242A which can be used if the Part 36 offer was made by using that form.

15.6.2 **WHEN?**

A Part 36 offer can be accepted at any time, even outside the relevant period, by the offeree without seeking the court's permission. There is, however, a proviso to this concerning withdrawal or amendment of the offer.

15.6.3 **WITHDRAWAL AND AMENDMENT OF PART 36 OFFERS**

The withdrawal and amendment of the terms of a Part 36 offer are now contained in CPR 36.9 and 36.10. The main considerations focus on the ability to withdraw or amend the offer before the expiry of the relevant period and after the expiry of the relevant period and we will look at both of these situations. However, before doing so there are some general points to note:

- A withdrawal of a Part 36 offer must be done expressly in writing. It is now possible in light of CPR 36.9(4)(b) to make an express provision in the offer itself that provides for its own automatic withdrawal at a certain date, rather than wait until the expiry of the relevant period and then withdraw it. The downside of including such a provision is that, if the offer is not accepted within the time stipulated, it will not have the consequences of Part 36 once it is withdrawn (CPR 36.17(7)).

- If a Part 36 offer is varied to make it *more advantageous* to the offeree, the original offer does not have to be withdrawn and the revised offer will be treated as the new offer (CPR 36.9(5)). The implications of this are twofold: firstly, if both the original offer and the revised offer turn out to be effective, the costs consequences will run from the first offer. Secondly, there will be a new relevant period when the revised offer is made.

 Example

If a defendant makes a Part 36 offer in the sum of £20,000 on 1 March with a relevant period for acceptance of 22 March and then on 1 June makes an improved offer of £25,000, the offer of £20,000 does not need to be withdrawn, and there will be a new relevant period starting from 1 June. Further, if the claimant only secures £19,000 at trial then the costs consequences will run from 23 March.

15.6.3.1 Withdrawing or amending offers within the relevant period

If the offeree has not served a notice of acceptance and the offeror serves a notice of withdrawal of a Part 36 offer or of a change in its terms to make it *less advantageous* to the offeree before the end of the relevant period, then at the end of the relevant period:

- If the offeree has not served notice of acceptance of the offer in the meantime, the offeror's notice will take effect.

- If the offeree has served notice of acceptance, that acceptance will take effect unless the offeror applies for permission to withdraw the offer or change its terms within seven days of the offeree's notice, or before the first day of the trial, if earlier. The court will only grant permission if satisfied that there has been a change of circumstances and that it is in the interests of justice.

15.6.3.2 Withdrawing or amending offers outside the relevant period

The offeror can withdraw or amend the offer in writing to make it *less advantageous* to the offeree outside the relevant period without the court's permission, provided, of course, that the offeree has not accepted it in writing (CPR 36.9(4)). However, it is important to remember the provisions of CPR 36.9(5) discussed at the beginning of this section in relation to amending an offer to make it more advantageous: there is no requirement to withdraw that offer.

Please also note that if a Part 36 offer is withdrawn either within or outside the relevant period, then it will not have the usual Part 36 cost consequences (CPR 36.17(7)).

 Practical Considerations

In practice, the decision to withdraw a Part 36 offer is mostly case specific. However, tactics can play a large part in this decision. The withdrawal of a Part 36 offer is often done to put additional pressure on the opponent, as this can have the effect of altering the 'position of power' in negotiations. The withdrawal can be read as a signal that the party withdrawing the offer is taking the bolder negotiating position. Offers can always be 're-made', but clear client instructions would need to be taken if an offer is to be withdrawn. Best practice would suggest that all Part 36 offers are kept under close review at all times.

There are, however, provisions set out in CPR 36.11(3) and (4) in which, in specific circumstances, a Part 36 offer can only be accepted with the permission of the court. Perhaps the most significant one is where the trial is in progress (CPR 36.11(3)(d)).

The application of the costs consequences of a Part 36 offer has always been complex and this complexity accounts for the vast amount of case law. There are two positions when the court will consider the application of an adverse costs consequence where an offer has been made:

- for a fully Part 36-compliant offer, Part 36 cost consequences will be enforced automatically, unless the court considers it unjust to do so;
- for any other offer, the residual discretion of CPR 44.2 can be applied.

Much of the next section is devoted to the provisions of CPR 36 generally. At this juncture we should highlight the fact that certain types of personal injury claims noted in paragraph 15.10 have their own specific rules in relation to Part 36 cost consequences, and these should be noted separately.

Cases discussing Part 36 offers usually concern whether they were accepted after expiry of the relevant period, their withdrawal, and the costs associated with their acceptance or rejection. But what happens if a party makes a Part 36 offer which they allege is a mistake, and that offer is accepted by the other side?

In the recent case *Atiba-Davies v William Hill Organisation Limited*, 16 January 2019 at Clerkenwell and Shoreditch County Court, this issue was explored, when a claimant accepted an offer considerably higher than the value of the claim which the defendant sought to say was a mistake. The case—albeit a County Court case—is a cautionary tale for those making Part 36 offers, unless the mistake is effectively an obvious one, which does not make sense in the circumstances, such offers are likely to stand.

15.7 CLAIMANT OFFERS

This section discusses what happens when a defendant receives a Part 36 offer made by a claimant. There are some helpful flowcharts at the end of this chapter to assist in the understanding of these complex rules.

15.7.1 THE PROCEDURE AND COST IMPLICATIONS OF ACCEPTING THE CLAIMANT'S OFFER

15.7.1.1 Procedure

Once the decision has been made by the defendant to accept the Part 36 offer, as stated in paragraph 15.6.1, this is simply done by letter or the notice of acceptance attached to the N242A. If proceedings have not yet been issued, then the defendant notifies the claimant in writing and the parties proceed to comply with the terms of the Part 36 offer. If proceedings have been issued, then the defendant sends a notice of acceptance, written usually in letter form, to the claimant and files a copy with the court. The claim is then automatically stayed (CPR 36.14(1)).

The Part 36 offer and subsequent acceptance may not have been in respect of the whole claim, and any subsequent stay would therefore only affect the part of proceedings to which the Part 36 offer related (CPR 36.14(3)).

15.7.1.2 Cost implications

By accepting the Part 36 offer within the relevant period, the defendant is liable to pay the claimant's costs up until the date on which the letter accepting the Part 36 offer is served on the claimant (CPR 36.13(1)). The claimant has an automatic entitlement to these costs, which are assessed on the standard basis (CPR 44.3(2) explains what this means).

So what happens if the defendant decides that he wants to accept the Part 36 offer, but outside the relevant period? CPR 36.13(4)(b) provides that the parties can try to agree liability for costs, but in the absence of agreement, the court must decide the liability for costs. CPR 36.13(5) further states that the court will decide, unless it is unjust, the following in relation to those costs: that the defendant pays the claimant's costs up until the end of the relevant period and the offeree—in this case, the defendant—will be liable for the claimant's costs incurred thereafter on the standard basis. In considering what is 'unjust' the court must take into account the factors listed in CPR 36.17(5).

15.7.2 **THE PROCEDURE AND COST IMPLICATIONS OF REJECTING THE CLAIMANT'S OFFER**

15.7.2.1 Procedure

If the defendant decides that he does not wish to accept the claimant's offer, he merely notifies the claimant in writing or simply fails to respond to the offer. The rejection of the offer by the defendant does not have the effect of withdrawing the offer. This can only be done by the claimant and must be done expressly by letter or notice. If this is not done, the offer will remain open for acceptance indefinitely.

 Practical Considerations

There is no requirement to give reasons for the rejection and it is unhelpful when the opponent simply fails to respond to the offer at all, although practically, to encourage further negotiation, there is no reason why the claimant cannot be informed of the reason for the rejection. It is in circumstances such as these that a without-prejudice chat over the telephone with the claimant's legal representative may be worthwhile. However, any proactive practitioner should be considering a Part 36 counter offer and alternative dispute resolution (ADR) when an offer is not acceptable.

15.7.2.2 Cost implications

The cost consequences for a defendant of rejecting a claimant's Part 36 offer are different from those of a claimant rejecting a defendant's Part 36 offer.

The current position is outlined at CPR 36.17(4), as follows. Where the defendant rejects the claimant's offer made more than twenty-one days before trial and the matter eventually proceeds to trial, if the claimant is successful and is awarded a sum that is the same or greater than his Part 36 offer, then the claimant is entitled to:

- interest on the entirety of the claim (not just the principal sum, awarded (*Bolt Burdon v Tariq* [2016] EWHC 1507 (QB)) at an enhanced rate of up to 10 per cent above base rate for some or all of the period from the date upon which the Part 36 offer's relevant period expired to the end of the trial;

- his costs, in respect of the period from the date on which the relevant period expired, to be assessed on the indemnity basis rather than the standard basis; and

- interest on those costs at an enhanced rate of up to 10 per cent above base rate.

If the claimant failed to equal or beat his own offer at trial, the costs will be decided in the usual way, in accordance with CPR 44.2. This would, therefore, make a claimant offer 'non-effective', save for being taken into account in a party's general conduct in an action.

15.7.2.3 Penalty damages

A payment of an additional amount of damages to a successful claimant also now forms part of the Part 36 regime in CPR 36.17(4)(d). These damages are based on percentages, which will be discussed shortly, and are payable in the following circumstances:

- the claimant has made a valid CPR 36 offer;

- the defendant has not accepted the offer; and

- the court has given judgment for the claimant which is 'at least as advantageous to the claimant as the claimant's offer'.

These new additional sanctions are calculated based on whether the claim is a damages-only claim, a mixture of monetary and non-monetary claims, or a non-monetary claim.

15.7.2.3.1 *Damages-only or mixed claims*

The amount to be paid by the defendant will be calculated as a percentage of the damages awarded to the claimant, as shown in Table 15.1.

TABLE 15.1 DAMAGES-ONLY OR MIXED CLAIMS

Amount awarded by the court	Prescribed percentage
Up to £500,000	Up to 10% of the amount awarded
Above £500,000	Up to 10% of the first £500,000 and 5% of the amount awarded above that figure

TABLE 15.2 NON-MONETARY CLAIMS

Costs ordered to be paid to the claimant	Amount to be paid by the defendant
Up to £500,000	Up to 10% of the costs ordered to be paid
Above £500,000	Up to 10% of the first £500,000 and 5% of any costs ordered to be paid above that figure

15.7.2.3.2 *Non-monetary claims*

In a non-monetary claim only the amount to be paid by the defendant will be calculated as a percentage of the costs ordered to be paid to the claimant, as shown in Table 15.2.

In these circumstances the amount to be paid is also subject to a cap of £75,000.

It is, therefore, interesting to note that in damages-only and mixed damages cases, the additional payment is likely to be received when the main damages payment is made to the claimant, whereas in non-monetary cases, the additional sanction is unlikely to be received until either costs have been agreed or formally assessed. This is usually sometime after the final hearing.

 Example

The claimant in an action for breach of contract made a Part 36 offer on 1 April in the sum of £75,000 shortly after the defence was filed. The defendant rejected the Part 36 offer and proceeded to a two-day trial on 1 December. Judgment was given to the claimant in the sum of £80,000. The claimant is therefore entitled to costs and interest as follows:

- costs on the standard basis from date of first instruction to 22 April;

- costs on the indemnity basis from 22 April to 2 December;

- interest on £80,000 from 22 April to 2 December at up to 10 per cent above base rate;

- an additional £8,000 in damages; and

- interest on costs from 22 April at up to 10 per cent above base rate.

15.8 DEFENDANT OFFERS

This section discusses what happens when a claimant receives a Part 36 offer made by a defendant. There are also some helpful flowcharts at the end of this chapter to assist in the understanding of these complex rules.

15.8.1 THE PROCEDURE AND COST IMPLICATIONS OF ACCEPTING THE DEFENDANT'S OFFER

15.8.1.1 Procedure

Generally, where a claimant decides that he wants to accept a Part 36 offer made by a defendant, the procedure is the same as that set out in paragraph 15.7.1.1.

Where the Part 36 offer made by the defendant includes an offer to pay a single sum of money, in addition to there being a stay of proceedings, on acceptance of the lump sum, the defendant is obliged to pay the sum accepted directly to the claimant within fourteen days of the date of acceptance (CPR 36.14(6)), failing which the claimant is entitled to enter judgment.

The parties can agree—usually in writing—an alternative time limit for payment of the monies, but the significant feature of this arrangement is that if the lump sum is not paid over to the claimant within the stipulated time frame, the claimant may enter judgment for the unpaid sum.

Where there are multiple defendants to an action and the claimant wishes to accept a Part 36 offer from one of them, the claimant needs to seek the court's permission to accept. CPR 36.15 sets out the criteria that the court will consider in granting permission, based on the nature of the liability of each defendant (joint and several, or just several) to the claimant.

15.8.1.2 Cost implications

The cost implications of a claimant accepting a defendant's offer are the same as those of a defendant accepting a claimant's Part 36 offer (CPR 36.13(5)), as set out at paragraph 15.7.1.2.

 Practical Considerations

There is some merit when acting for a claimant, in terms of adverse cost consequences, to accepting a Part 36 offer within the relevant period if at all possible. The information given to any claimant client when a Part 36 offer is made should include the possibility of adverse cost consequences if the offer is accepted after the relevant period.

15.8.1.3 The creation of a legally binding contract

The Part 36 offer of both a claimant and defendant and the letter of acceptance create a contractually binding arrangement between the parties. Consequently, should the receiving party not abide by the agreement, then it can be enforced within the same set of proceedings without having to go to the time and expense of issuing fresh proceedings on the breach of that agreement. The procedure is even simpler where there is a defendant offering a lump sum, as has been highlighted in paragraph 15.8.1.1.

15.8.2 **THE PROCEDURE AND COST IMPLICATIONS OF REJECTING THE DEFENDANT'S OFFER**

15.8.2.1 Procedure

As with paragraph 15.7.2.1, if the claimant wishes to reject the defendant's Part 36 offer, this is simply done in writing, and unless the defendant expressly withdraws the offer, it is open for acceptance at any time.

15.8.2.2 Cost implications

If the claimant makes the decision to reject the defendant's offer and proceed to trial, but fails to secure a judgment that is more advantageous than the defendant's Part 36 offer—that is, if the judgment is for an amount less than or equal to the Part 36 offer—then the court has a discretion to make the following orders unless it is unjust to do so (CPR 36.17(3)):

- award the defendant his costs on the standard basis from the date upon which the relevant period has expired and
- award interest on those costs.

It is important to note here that the claimant has to do better than the Part 36 offer. What this means is that if the defendant offered £20,000 and the claimant rejected this, but at trial was only awarded £20,000, then the court may invoke the costs and interest penalties. Compare this to the situation in paragraph 15.7.2.2, in which the defendant rejects the claimant's Part 36 offer: in that case, the claimant only has to achieve a sum that is the same or greater. So if it was the claimant who had offered £20,000 and the defendant who rejected the same, and at trial the judgment of £20,000 was still made, the court has the discretion to award the costs penalties set out in CPR 36.17(4).

If the claimant beats the defendant's offer, even by the smallest of margins, then his costs will be decided in the usual way, in accordance with CPR 44.2. This would, therefore, mean that the defendant's offer has been 'non-effective', save for being taken into account in a party's general conduct in an action.

15.8.2.3 How can the court decide if a Part 36 offer has been beaten?

In many cases, owing to the difference in the amount offered and the amount recovered at trial, the fact that a Part 36 offer has been beaten will be apparent. However, in cases in which it is a closer call—usually in unspecified sum claims—it may not be so easily ascertainable whether an offer has been truly beaten. This is usually either because the amount recovered in comparison to the offer is negligible (see paragraph 15.9 for a further discussion on this), or because of the interest awarded.

Remember that Part 36 offers are inclusive of interest, and this is where the difficulty can sometimes lie. However, in *Hurry Narain Purrunsing v A'Court and Co (a firm) & Another* [2016] EWHC 789 (Ch), the court held that interest awarded between the expiry of the relevant period of the Part 36 offer and judgment was not to be taken into account when determining whether or not the claimants had secured more than the sum they had offered to settle for. This does not mean the interest calculation should not be made and that the claimant will not recover the interest but that the interest will not be taken into account when determining whether the Part 36 offer has been beaten.

15.8.2.4 Part 36 and conditional fee agreements in non-personal injury cases (CFAs)

Consider the situation in which your claimant client, operating under a conditional fee agreement (CFA) with a success fee and after the event (ATE) insurance, rejects a defendant's Part 36 offer and, at trial, is awarded less than the offer. In accordance with CPR 36.17(3), unless it is unjust to do so, the claimant will probably be ordered to pay the defendant's costs from the end of the relevant period to trial. It would follow that the claimant would pay his own costs for that period too, the success fee and the ATE premium himself, not just for that period, but for the whole action.

Two issues arise here: firstly, because the claimant has ATE in respect of an adverse cost order, he will not be required to find the funds to pay the defendant, because his ATE insurers will pay—but, secondly, who will pay the claimant's own costs for that period? Unless the claimant purchased ATE to protect against him paying his own costs in this situation (which is unusual and expensive), the claimant will be responsible for payment of these to his legal representative in accordance with the terms of the CFA. This is because the CFA only stipulates 'no win, no fee' if the claimant fails to recover damages, but in this case, he has done so: he has just failed to beat a Part 36 offer.

 Practical Considerations

As a legal practitioner, you will need to discuss this with your client, because the usual terms of CFAs allow the legal representative to use his discretion as to whether to claim back these base costs.

15.9 HOW THE COURT EXERCISES ITS DISCRETION ON COSTS IN 'UNBEATEN' PART 36 OFFERS AT TRIAL

It is important to remember that all costs awards made by the court, not only those in respect of Part 36 offers, are discretionary and that whilst CPR Part 36 may stipulate cost consequences for rejection of offers, it is for the court to decide whether it wishes to implement those sanctions or not.

Specifically in relation to CPR Part 36, the court will only award the penalties set out in CPR 36.17(3) and (4), unless it is unjust to do so, based on considerations set out in CPR 36.17(5). These are:

- the terms of the Part 36 offer;
- when the offer was made;
- the information available to the parties when the offer was made;

- the conduct of the parties in relation to providing information to enable the offeree to give proper consideration to the offer; and

- whether the offer was a genuine attempt to settle the proceedings.

The courts, in accordance with CPR 36.17(2), will decide whether to award the costs consequences where a claimant fails to obtain a judgment that is more advantageous than a defendant's Part 36 offer, or where judgment against a defendant is at least as advantageous to the claimant as the defendant's Part 36 offer. Sometimes it is not obvious when a Part 36 offer has been beaten, or if it has, by how much. Consequently, there has been a plethora of case law on how the court deals with awarding the costs sanctions in CPR Part 36, and the most noteworthy cases are as follows:

- *AB v CD and Ors* [2011] EWHC 602 (Ch) held that the claimant's purported Part 36 offer was not valid because the offer merely replicated the entirety of the claimant's claim and as such there had been no concession made by the claimant. If the offer were allowed to stand as a Part 36 offer, then every claimant could obtain favourable costs consequences simply by making an offer to settle, requiring total capitulation by the defendant. This was seen as so important that it formed the basis for one of the new Part 36 rules in CPR 36.17(5)(e).

- *Ted Baker Plc and another v AXA Insurance UK Plc and others* [2014] EWHC 4178 sets out what exceptional circumstances could be in deciding whether it was unjust to displace the general rule in CPR 36.17 where the overall result was that the claimants had failed to beat the defendant's Part 36 offers. The circumstances included the defendant's approach to the central issue, which left no stone unturned and increased costs hugely. The court also commented that the fact that a defendant may make a Part 36 offer did not give him 'carte blanche' to run any defence whatsoever so as to entitle him to expect that the Part 36 consequences would automatically apply.

- The case of *Bellway Homes Ltd v Seymour (Civil Engineering Contractors) Ltd* [2013] EWHC 1890 (TCC) held that owing to all the circumstances of the case, it would be unjust to invoke the cost consequences under CPR 36.14(2) because the parties had not constructively engaged in settlement negotiations in a messy building dispute and had pursued a pointless litigation.

- The case of *RXDX v Northampton BC* [2015] EWHC 2938 (QB) has confirmed the correct application of 'unless it considers it unjust' in CPR 36.17(4), concluding that the court is entitled to consider for each of the separate sub-paragraphs, whether its application would be unjust in the circumstances of the case.

It should perhaps be mentioned here that if either the claimant or defendant to an action make an offer and they do not beat their own offer at trial, then it is of no consequence as far as cost sanctions are concerned.

15.10 PERSONAL INJURY LITIGATION AND PART 36

These provisions are pertinent to certain personal injury claims, but not all. The Rules are very specific, and, consequently, it would be prudent to review the nature and extent of any personal injury claim you handle in order to ascertain whether any of these Rules apply.

15.10.1 ADDITIONAL REQUIREMENTS TO THE CONTENT OF A PART 36 OFFER

15.10.1.1 Where the claim includes a future pecuniary loss claim (CPR 36.18)
Damages for future pecuniary loss in larger personal injury actions need to be particularized in a Part 36 offer if the offer is to be treated as a Part 36 offer with all the cost consequences that flow from such an offer. These future pecuniary losses are usually expressed to be paid

by way of a lump sum, a periodical payment, or a combination of both. In terms of articulating this, the Part 36 offer must explicitly set out the amounts which relate to the lump sum and/or periodical payments, as well as the duration of the periodical payments. In addition, if the offer is accepted, not only must a written acceptance be provided to the opponent, but the claimant must also apply to the court for an order for an award of damages in the form of periodical payments within seven days of accepting the Part 36 offer.

15.10.1.2 Where the claim includes a provisional damages claim (CPR 36.19)

If the claimant's claim also includes a claim for provisional damages, as discussed in Chapter 7 at paragraph 7.6.3.6, a Part 36 offer must specify whether or not the offeror is offering to agree to an award for provisional damages. If this is the case, then the Part 36 offer must detail the damages offered in this regard, the medical conditions which could trigger a further claim, and the period within which the further claim could be made. Again, here, if the Part 36 offer is accepted, the claimant must apply to the court for an order within seven days of acceptance.

15.10.1.3 The CRU and Part 36 (CPR 36.22)

When drafting a Part 36 offer in a personal injury claim, the issue of deductible welfare benefits must be dealt with. For a discussion on the nature of these CRU benefits, see Chapter 7, paragraph 7.6.3.

The Part 36 offer can be made either without regard to any liability for the recoverable benefits (in which case the opponent will pay the benefits in addition), or the Part 36 offer can state that it is intended to include any deductible benefits.

Therefore, the Part 36 offer must state the gross amount of the damages before the CRU benefits are offset, the name and amount of any deductible benefit by which the gross amount is reduced, and the net amount after deduction. This information is essential, as it clarifies the exact figures sought under the Part 36 offer when it comes to ascertaining whether a Part 36 offer has been beaten. The crucial figures to 'beat' are those after the deduction of the benefits, i.e. the net figure offered.

As a final point here, if a claimant accepts a Part 36 offer after the relevant period has expired and the CRU repayment figure has increased (because the claimant has continued to receive a deductible benefit), the court has a discretion to deduct the additional benefits from the net offer.

15.10.1.4 QOCS and Part 36

The advent of QOCS (as discussed in detail in Chapter 4 at paragraph 4.2.3) and other April 2013 changes (such as the non-recovery of success fees and ATE premiums from the defendant) have had a significant impact on personal injury litigation for both claimants and defendants alike. As regards Part 36 offers, the balance continues to be attempted to be redressed, because now CPR 44.14 permits costs orders to be made against a claimant in a personal injury claim, subject to them not being unjust, where that claimant has failed to beat the defendant's offer to settle, including Part 36 offers. The likely costs order to be made will be that the claimant will be required to pay the defendant's costs (an adverse costs order) from the expiry of the offer, as well as paying his own costs. However, the adverse costs order will be capped at the level of damages and interest recovered by the claimant. Legal practitioners are, therefore, questioning the true benefit of QOCS to these claimants, as most defendants in personal injury actions will at some point make an offer of settlement of some sort, and if this is made early on in the dispute process, there is little comfort to be had from the QOCS regime.

 Example

The defendant, in an action for personal injuries, made a Part 36 offer on 1 April in the sum of £80,000, shortly after its defence was filed. The claimant rejected the Part 36 offer and proceeded to a two-day trial on 1 December. The claimant was not funded and had not purchased ATE. Judgment was given to the claimant in the sum of £75,000. The costs and interest order that was made was as follows:

- The claimant was entitled to its costs on the standard basis up to 22 April.

- The claimant was ordered to pay the defendant's costs, as it was held not unjust to do so, from 22 April to 2 December on the standard basis. As the claimant had not purchased ATE the costs payment to the defendant would more than likely come from his £75,000.

- The claimant was ordered to pay his own costs from 22 April to 2 December on the standard basis. As the claimant was privately funding his claim, these would have been paid monthly to his legal representative and, therefore, would not be reimbursed.

The defendant was entitled to interest on its costs at the standard rate of 8 per cent from 22 April onwards.

15.10.1.5 The pre-action protocol claims for low-value RTA, EL, and PL claims

These claims are looked at in Chapter 4 at paragraph 4.7.2, from a general costs perspective, and in Chapter 9 at paragraph 9.2.8, from a procedural perspective.

These processes do not escape the Part 36 regime. Part 36 needs to be considered in light of those claims that remain in the Portal up to and including Stage 3, and those that exit the Portal at an earlier stage.

In relation to those cases that reach Stage 3, CPR 36.25(1) requires the offer to be made to be called a 'Protocol Offer', and it will be a valid Protocol Offer in accordance with CPR 36.25(2) if it is set out in the Court Proceedings Pack (CPP) and contains the final total amount of the offer from both parties exclusive of interest. If the matter proceeds to a final assessment of damages hearing, there are three possible outcomes for the court to consider once the assessment has been made:

- If the claimant is awarded damages that are less than or equal to the defendant's offer, the court will order the claimant to pay the defendant's Stage 3 fixed costs and interest on those costs.

- If the claimant is awarded more than the defendant's offer but less than his own, the court will order the defendant to pay the claimant's fixed costs.

- If the claimant is awarded the same or more than his own offer, the court will order the following:
  - the defendant to pay interest on all of the damages at a rate not exceeding 10 per cent above base rate for some or all of the period, beginning on the date the offer was made;
  - the defendant to pay the claimant's fixed costs and interest on those fixed costs at a rate not exceeding 10 per cent above base rate; and
  - the defendant to pay an additional 10 per cent of the amount awarded.

In relation to claims that exit the Portal, remember that Section III of CPR 45 contains costs provisions on a fixed costs basis, as mentioned in Chapter 4 at paragraph 4.7.2. Part 36, therefore, also provides separately for these Protocol claims that have left the Protocol process before Stage 3. The Rules have been drafted to deal with the cost consequences of accepting a Part 36 Offer after leaving the Portal before Stage 3, and the cost consequences of rejecting a Part 36 offer and proceeding to trial.

15.10.1.5.1 *Cost consequences of accepting a Part 36 Offer—CPR 36.21*

These are divided into four different categories as follows:

- If the claimant accepts a Part 36 offer within the relevant period, the claimant is entitled to fixed costs, as set out in Section IIIA of CPR 45, but the level of those fixed costs will depend upon the date the Part 36 offer was accepted in relation to the stage reached in the Table of Fixed Costs in Section IIIA.

- If the claimant accepts the Part 36 offer outside the relevant period, the claimant is entitled to the fixed costs applicable at the date on which the relevant period expired, but the claimant will also be required to pay the defendant's costs from the date of expiry of the relevant period to the date of acceptance.

- If a Protocol Offer was made but only accepted by the claimant after exiting the Portal, the claimant is entitled to Stages 1 and 2 Protocol fixed costs, but the claimant is also liable for the defendant's costs from the date on which the Protocol Offer was made until the date of acceptance.

- If a defendant accepts a Part 36 offer out of time and after the claim has exited the Protocol, the current position according to *Whalley v Advantage Insurance Company Ltd* (unreported, 5 October 2017) (Kingston Upon Hull County Court) is that unless there are exceptional circumstances (in accordance with CPR 45.29J), or there has been conduct 'out of the norm' to justify indemnity costs, the fixed costs regime applies to the late acceptance of an offer under CPR 36.13(4)(b). This decision is not, however, binding and Court of Appeal authority remains urgently required.

15.10.1.5.2 *Cost consequences of a Part 36 Offer after judgment—CPR 36.29*

In these circumstances, the costs order made will depend on when the offer was made as follows:

- If the claimant failed to secure a judgment that was more advantageous than the defendant's Part 36 offer after the claim exited the Portal, the claimant is entitled to the fixed costs for the Stage reached at the point in time the relevant period expired, but the claimant is also required to pay the defendant's costs from the date on which the relevant period expired to the date of judgment.

- If the claimant failed to beat a defendant's Protocol Offer, the claimant is only entitled to Stages 1 and 2 fixed costs, but the claimant is also liable to pay the defendant's costs from the date on which the Protocol Offer was made until the date of judgment.

- If the claimant beats his own Part 36 offer and by virtue of CPR 36.21(1) becomes entitled to the enhancements in CPR 36.17, in particular indemnity costs, the Court of Appeal has recently clarified the position in the case of *Broadhurst and Anor v Tan and Anor* [EWCA] Civ 2016. Previous case law had concluded that the interaction of CPR 45.29A and CPR 36.17 was inconsistent with one case concluding that fixed costs did not apply where indemnity costs had been awarded as a result of the claimant beating his own Part 36 offer, and the other case deciding that costs did apply notwithstanding that the claimant beat his own Part 36 offer at trial. The Court of Appeal has decided that claimants who beat their own Part 36 offers are entitled to indemnity costs. It, therefore, appears that the provisions of Part 36 override the provisions of Part 45 in this regard.

- It is worth noting here that where the claimant is ordered to pay the defendant's costs as described in this section, these costs cannot exceed the level of fixed costs as set out in Section IIIA of CPR 45.

15.11 ISSUES TO DISCUSS WITH YOUR CLIENT ON MAKING OR RECEIVING A PART 36 OFFER

Having now discussed the substantive requirements of CPR 36, as a legal representative, there are a number of matters that you will need to consider and discuss with your client when either making or receiving a Part 36 offer, as follows:

- Consider what type of offer should be made: a Part 36 offer, or a non-Part 36 offer—that is, a 'without prejudice save as to costs' offer, also sometimes referred to as 'global' or 'Calderbank' offers, without the penalties under Part 36? You will need to explain to your client what Part 36 offers and 'without prejudice save as to costs' offers are, because he is unlikely to understand this unless he has been involved in dispute resolution before. You will also need to bear in mind that a Part 36 offer can amount to the rejection of an earlier global/Calderbank offer as a result of the judgment on *DB UK Bank (T/A DB Mortgages) v Jacobs Solicitors* [2016] EWHC 1614 (Ch). The effect of this is that an earlier offer would no longer be open for acceptance. Therefore, as with Part 36 offers, these global/Calderbank offers will also need to be kept under review. There are, however, several tactical reasons why your client may wish to make one or the other, as follows, and you will need to discuss these with him:

– He may wish to make a global non-Part 36 offer to settle, incorporating a provision for costs in addition to damages and interest (remember that Part 36 offers are not valid Part 36 offers if they include provisions for costs) either for tactical or commercial reasons. You must therefore advise your client—preferably in writing—that any global offer if not beaten at trial is very likely to attract the court's discretion on costs under CPR 44.2 and not CPR 36.13.

– He may wish to make sequential Part 36 offers—that is, to make an optimistic Part 36 offer early on that, if rejected or once the relevant period expires, a revised lower offer is made—to encourage negotiation and settlement.

– More often in personal injury claims, it may be a prudent step in most cases to make an early Part 36 offer on liability alone, which need not be withdrawn.

In any event, you should always consider with your client the importance of making a Part 36 offer as soon as you have been able to evaluate liability, causation, and quantum, highlighting to your client the tactical advantage of an early offer.

• Check compliance with CPR 36.5—you will need to check the wording of the Part 36 offer, whether making or receiving it, especially if there are special requirements in addition to the basic points set out in paragraph 15.3.

• Seek clarification—if a Part 36 offer is unclear, then do not make assumptions about what it may or may not include. You have the benefit of CPR 36.8, which allows you to seek clarification of the offer, as discussed in paragraph 15.5.

• Advise on the procedural and cost consequences of accepting or rejecting the Part 36 offer— as soon as a Part 36 offer is made to your client, it is incumbent on you as a legal representative to act quickly if there is to be acceptance within the relevant period. You will need to advise your client, both in writing and then verbally either over the telephone or at a face-to-face meeting. The key point here is that the advice that you are seeking to give is not whether your client should accept or reject the offer (despite the fact that this is probably the first question that your client will ask you), but how well or not he may do at trial—that is, whether your client will beat the offer. Also ensure that you have discussed with him all of the relevant information to enable him to make his *own* decision on the offer. In essence, he needs to understand the risks of accepting or not accepting the offer in light of the fact that the costs of an action dramatically increase as the action proceeds to trial.

To provide such information to your client and discuss matters with him takes experience and professional judgment, neither of which a legal representative new to litigation is able to acquire at the outset. However, there are a number of important considerations, as follows, through which you can take your client to demonstrate as a starting point whether the Part 36 offer is well pitched or not, or whether it might be construed to be derisory. This exercise will then assist your client in coming to his decision.

1. You will need to undertake a risk assessment of your case and explain to your client the risk on liability (including contributory negligence, set-offs, and counterclaims), any causational difficulties (both in respect of liability and quantum), and the risk on quantum, considering the likely level of interest that may be awarded.

2. In some cases, prospects of success can turn on what evidence might be allowed or disallowed, or how well your witnesses perform in the witness box. These are matters that will also need to be taken into account.

3. Your client is entitled to know the reasons for your advice and, as such, you may need to review the file in its entirety to ensure you have all of the requisite information to hand when conducting your overall risk assessment.

4. If your client is under a CFA or DBA, review the terms in relation to Part 36 offers.

 Costs

When undertaking your risk assessment, it may be appropriate to provide your client with a costs estimate (or a costs budget if appropriate) for costs already incurred and costs to be incurred to trial. This will deal with the proportionality aspect and focus your client's mind on a realistic settlement.

5. Consider any tactics with your client on the receipt of a Part 36 offer—these should generally have the effect of moving the dispute resolution process forward and may include the following:

   (a) It may be genuinely difficult for your client to decide whether he should accept the offer within the relevant period: for example, because the case is large and complex, or because the case is at such an early stage that a true valuation of the case is problematic. In this situation, you can try to agree an extension of the relevant period with your opponent.

   (b) Do not formally reject the offer because there is no CPR requirement to do so, because Part 36 offers remain open for acceptance until withdrawn or amended.

   (c) Make a counter-offer either in the form of a CPR 36-compliant offer or a global/Calderbank offer. Either may be a useful and effective tactic depending on how much it is for and when exactly it is made.

   (d) Suggest ADR.

15.12 OFFERS IN GENERAL AND THOSE THAT ARE NOT PART 36 OFFERS

There are pros and cons of different types of settlement offers. The level of the offer may be crucial, but so too will be the type of offer. (See also Chapter 19, paragraph 19.8.2.)

Practitioners will need to have in mind the purpose of making an offer, this is not only to attempt to settle a case, but also to gain a cost advantage should an offer not be accepted. This is of course a balancing exercise as any offer made must be at an appropriate amount as it can be accepted by the opponent, ending the litigation.

As can be seen from paragraph 15.3, any Part 36 offer must comply with the form and content required under CPR 36.5. An offer which does not comply with the rule will not attract the costs benefits afforded by Part 36 (see *Mitchell v James* [2004] 1 WLR 158).

Other types of offers can still be made but which may fall outside of the regime of Part 36, see CPR 36.2(2), such as:

• Calderbank offers. These derive their name from the family case of *Calderbank v Calderbank* [1975] 3 ALL ER 333. These offers can be used to form submissions at the end of case, when the issue of costs arises. Such offers will be brought to the attention of the court when it excerises its discretion as to costs under CPR 44.2 (4). That is why such offers are labelled 'without prejudice save as to costs' so that they attract privilege during the case but can be used at the conclusion where the question of costs arises. They do not attract the same benefits as Part 36, but may offer some costs protection.

- Open offers. Open offers can also be used during a case. These are also capable of being accepted and thereby ending the litigation. They do not attract privilege and therefore can be disclosed during proceedings. The benefits of such offers are that they focus the mind of the opponent. Any judge dealing with the proceedings can see the position of the offering party. This sends a very clear signal to the judge and the opponent that the offering party is comfortable with their position and is content for the judge to see it and draw conclusons as to the reasonableness of that party.

The advantages of Part 36 offers are:

- The regime of Part 36 offers a degree of certainty to the parties on the cost consequences which may arise. These offers are still subject to some discretion, albeit not as potentially wide as the discretion of CPR 44.2.

- A second or subsequent offer does not withdraw the first or previous offer. Those offers remain open and can only be withdrawn in the circumstances set as out in paragraph 15.6.3, CPR 39.9, and 36.10 (*Gibbon v Manchester CC* [2010] EWCA Civ 726).

- The advantage of the costs protection for the claimant at CPR 36.17(4).

- The advantage of the costs protection for the defendant at CPR 36.13(5) and 36.17(3).

When other, non Part 36 offers could be considered:

- If a part 36 offer is accepted, CPR 36.6 states that a single sum of money has to be paid and CPR 36.14 states it must be paid within 14 days of acceptance of the offer. Therefore, if the defendant wanted to pay by instalments or later than the 14 days specified, the offer made should not be a Part 36 offer.

- The period of acceptance for a Part 36 offer is at least 21 days, CPR 36.5. In certain situations, a party may not want the offer to remain open that long. An example would be where a party wanted to attempt to settle a matter before a hearing which was due to be heard before the expiry of the 21 days. It maybe that the offering party would not want the offer to remain open after the hearing, should the hearing change the position of the party making the offer.

Strategically, offers will need to be considered at many different points during litigation. The practitioner will need to decide not only when an offer should be made, but also the amount and type of offer depending on the circumstances of the case. This process of review will need to continue throughout the litigation. Consideration will also need to be given to the different types of offer that could be made.

KEY POINTS SUMMARY

- Part 36 offers represent one of the most important tactical steps that a party to a dispute can take.

- If you are acting for a party who is offering to pay a sum of money in settlement and this is formulated in a Part 36 offer, you must explain to the client that the payment of damages is not the end of his liability to his opponent, because there is an implicit duty to pay the opponent's costs up to the date of acceptance, if within the relevant period, on the standard basis.

- It is the client's decision to decide whether to accept or reject a Part 36 offer. The role of the legal representative is to ensure that the client has all of the requisite information before him to enable him to make that decision on an informed basis.

- Control your client's expectations on costs awards. Remind your client that costs are at the discretion of the court, and that the cost sanctions that are a feature of CPR 36 may not be awarded even if offers are equalled or beaten at trial.

- Because Part 36 offers can be accepted at any time as long as they have not been withdrawn or amended, it is important that you keep your own client's offers under review and withdraw them if appropriate. Therefore, it is important to consider at all key stages whether these offers should be made, accepted, withdrawn, or revised, and if withdrawn, to ensure your client understands that the offer then loses the cost implications of a Part 36 offer.

See Figures 15.1 to 15.4 at the end of this chapter, for illustrations of various Part 36 offer scenarios.

Case Study *Andrew James Pike v Deep Builders Ltd*

Andrew Pike has now been medically examined by Mr Higgins, but the report was not wholly conclusive as further investigations need undertaking. Proceedings have now been issued and a defence and counterclaim filed by Deep Builders Limited. The case has been allocated to the multi-track and directions set for the action. At the time of completing the directions questionnaire, the claimant's solicitor made an application for an interim payment.

The directions set at the CMC have not yet been complied with by either party as the timetable set by the court has not yet started. Shortly after the interim payment application, the defendant made a valid CPR36 offer of £20,000. A copy of the letter appears in your online resources. You have telephoned your client to inform him of the offer and that you will be writing to him about the offer.

Question 1

At this particular stage in the action, consider what advice you would give to Andrew Pike on the timing of the offer? Consult the 'litigation train' both in the book and online to help you to contextualize where we are in the litigation.

Question 2

Please consider the contents of the defendant's Part 36 offer letter and draft a letter to Andrew Pike on the timing of the offer made by the defendant.

Helpful hints to consider for the letter:

- Note the type of letter that this will be in terms of style, length, formality, and content. Gauge the intellect of your client.
- Where we are in the litigation? What has happened? What will happen?
- Consider the impact of the timing of the offer on your advice?
- Is there any additional information needed to help you advise Andrew Pike?
- What about Andrew Pike's funding arrangements?
- How can you move the action along proactively.

Case Study *Bollingtons Ltd v Mrs Elizabeth Lynch t/a The Honest Lawyer*

A Defence and Counterclaim has been filed and served by Mrs Lynch. Acting for Bollingtons Limited, you are completing the directions questionnaire (DQ) and have prepared a cost estimate, which shows that costs to date are £2,000 but anticipated costs to trial in light of the disputed nature of the debt are likely to be an additional £10,500. Mrs Lynch has now made a Part 36 offer of £8,000.

Question 1

Consider the proportionality issues in this case and the discussions that you will need to have with Mr Green of Bollingtons Limited.

Question 2

How will this impact on your advice to him?

Any documents referred to in these case study questions can be found in the online resources—simply click on 'Case study documentation' to access the documents that you need for Chapter 15 and to be reminded of the questions. Suggested answers to these self-test questions can be accessed in the Student Resources section of the online resources.

FIGURE 15.1 FLOWCHART SHOWING WITHDRAWAL AND ACCEPTANCE OF A PART 36 OFFER

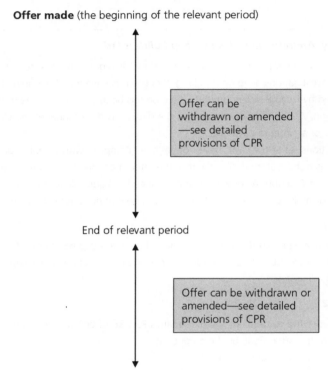

Offer made (the beginning of the relevant period)

Offer can be withdrawn or amended —see detailed provisions of CPR

End of relevant period

Offer can be withdrawn or amended—see detailed provisions of CPR

Offer is capable of being accepted **at any point from the date it is made until the start of the trial**, provided it has not been withdrawn or amended

FIGURE 15.2 FLOWCHART FOR THE CLAIMANT'S ACCEPTANCE OF A DEFENDANT'S PART 36 MONETARY OFFER FOR THE WHOLE CLAIM

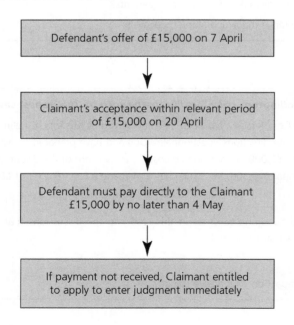

Defendant's offer of £15,000 on 7 April

Claimant's acceptance within relevant period of £15,000 on 20 April

Defendant must pay directly to the Claimant £15,000 by no later than 4 May

If payment not received, Claimant entitled to apply to enter judgment immediately

FIGURE 15.3 FLOWCHART FOR THE COST AND INTEREST CONSEQUENCES OF A CLAIMANT NOT 'BEATING' A DEFENDANT'S MONETARY OFFER

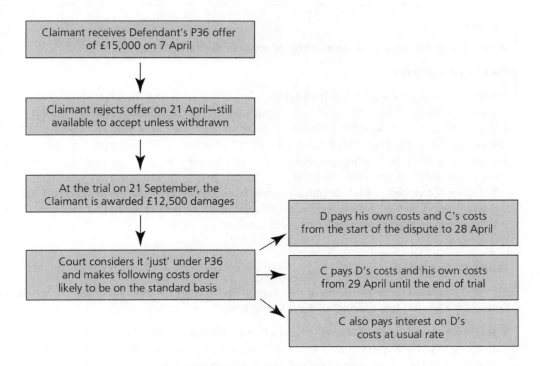

FIGURE 15.4 FLOWCHART FOR THE COST AND INTEREST CONSEQUENCES OF A DEFENDANT NOT 'BEATING' A CLAIMANT'S MONETARY OFFER

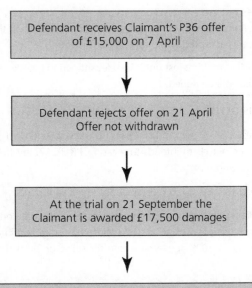

FIGURE 15.5 A TEMPLATE CLAIMANT PART 36 MONETARY OFFER LETTER

Dear Sirs,

Without prejudice save as to costs—Offer to settle under Part 36

(Heading of matter)

We refer to the above matter in which we act for . . . . Our client is confident that it has a strong case against your client, ..., and is entitled to substantial damages, [as set out in its particulars of claim OR as set out in correspondence OR for the reasons set out below]. Nevertheless, our client is [keen to resolve this matter amicably OR mindful that under the Civil Procedure Rules litigants are expected to try to resolve their disputes whenever possible]. We are, therefore, authorised by our client to make the following offer to settle under Part 36.

This Offer is intended to have the consequences set out in Part 36 of the Civil Procedure Rules. In particular, your client will be liable for our client's costs up to the date of notice of acceptance which must be in writing in accordance with CPR 36.10, if the offer is accepted within . . . . (the relevant period).

TERMS OF THE OFFER

Our client is willing to settle [the whole of the claim referred to above OR specify which part of the claim or issue the client is willing to settle] on the following terms:

• Your client to pay our client, within [14 or such other number as client is willing to accept] days of accepting this Offer, the sum of £ . . . . by [means of payment—e.g. electronic transfer] into [give account details] or [set out precise terms of offer in a non-money claim].

• This Offer [takes OR does not take] account of your client's counterclaim [or/and any other claims your client may have against ours] in this matter.

• The settlement sum does not include costs and, as mentioned above, your client will be liable to pay our client's costs on the standard basis, to be assessed if not agreed, up to the date of service of notice of acceptance if this Offer is accepted within the relevant period.

• The settlement sum is inclusive of interest until the relevant period has expired. Thereafter, interest at a rate of . . . .% p.a. will be added.

FAILURE TO ACCEPT THIS OFFER

If your client does not accept this Offer, and our client obtains a judgment which is equal to or more advantageous than this Offer, our client intends to rely on CPR 36.17. In other words, our client will be seeking an order in the following terms:

• Your client to pay our client's costs up to the expiry of the relevant period.

• Your client to pay our client's costs on the indemnity basis from the date on which the relevant period expired, with interest on those costs of up to 10% above base rate and interest on the whole or part of any sum awarded at up to 10% above base rate for some or all of the period starting from the same date.

• Your client to pay an additional amount of £xxx by way of an additional sanction.

If you think that this offer is in any way defective or non-compliant with Part 36, please let us know.

We look forward to hearing from you.

Yours faithfully,

16 | DISCLOSURE AND INSPECTION

LITIGATION TRAIN: DISCLOSURE AND INSPECTION

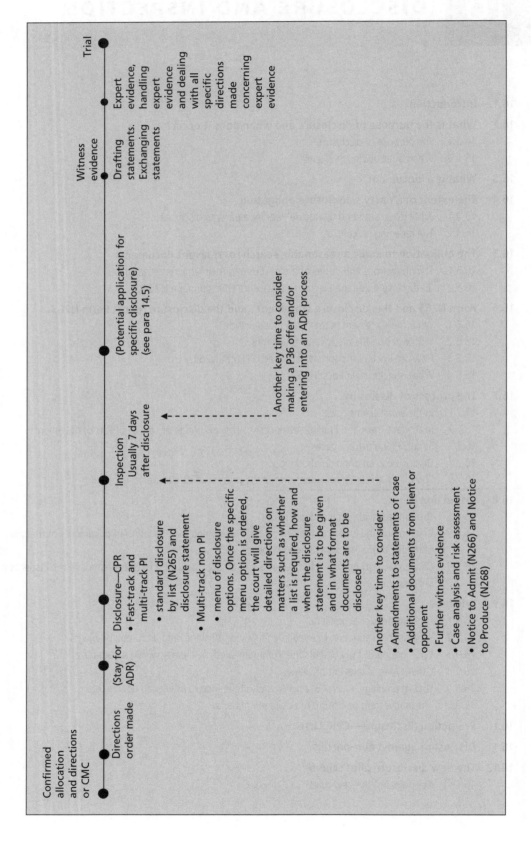

Relevant court forms relating to this chapter:

- N265 List of Documents (for all fast-track and PI multi-track cases)
- The Disclosure Report N263—for all multi-track (other than PI) cases
- N264—The Electronic Disclosure Questionnaire
- N244 Interim Application (for pre-action disclosure applications dealt with in this chapter)

Relevant parts of the CPR and its PDs: 23 and 31.

Note: This section should be read in conjunction with Chapter 8, paragraph 8.7, and Chapter 14, paragraph 14.5.

16.1 INTRODUCTION

In this chapter, we will consider the definition of 'disclosure', its *purpose*, its *extent*, and the *process* whereby it is implemented.

During litigation, the parties have a duty to disclose and permit inspection of certain documents. The process of formal disclosure is usually the first directions order that the parties to an action must comply with in the litigation process. Disclosure can be a very 'expensive' part of the litigation process—comprising the need to search for, list, and disclose the documents to be disclosed in the action. For this reason the courts are increasingly determined to ensure that the number of documents made available to the parties and the court for the hearing of the matter are only those documents that are 'proportionately' as to value and costs, 'fairly', 'efficiently', and 'justly' needed. The duty to disclose relevant (to the issues of the case) documents is based on the premise that litigation is conducted on a 'cards on the table' approach, i.e. that all of the information that will be available to the court at trial will already have been made available to the parties.

However, we will see in this chapter that not all of the 'cards' need be 'face-up' at the time at which disclosure must be made. Some documents may be **disclosed**, but be 'face-down' and unavailable for **inspection** by your opponent. Whether these documents remain unavailable for inspection may depend on the directions order in the case which may have directed that the documents be 'exchanged'—and, therefore, available to be seen by the opponent—at a later date. We will consider these situations later in this chapter.

The essential point to note in relation to disclosure and inspection is that any document that is to be used and referred to at trial will, at some time before the trial, have been made available to all of the parties.

This chapter will also look at other types of disclosure and the times at which such disclosure may take place—some of which may be *before* litigation has been commenced (see paragraph 8.7).

The formal provisions for disclosure are contained in CPR 31 and its accompanying PD. The formal disclosure rules apply to cases in the fast track and the multi-track. They do not automatically apply to the small claims track (CPR 27.2(1)(b)). The process of disclosure is slightly different in the fast-track and personal injury (PI) multi-track cases to the disclosure process for non-PI multi-track cases.

The future: It is important to read paragraph 16.12, as this sets out details of a pilot scheme for a fundamental change in the way 'disclosure' is handled by the courts.

16.2 WHAT IS THE PURPOSE OF DISCLOSURE AND WHEN DOES IT OCCUR?

16.2.1 THE PURPOSE OF DISCLOSURE

The purpose of disclosure is to provide details of all of the documents (and the word 'documents' is not restricted to paper documents—see paragraph 16.3) that either support *or* undermine the respective parties' cases. This purpose is a general one that applies to both parties. In this way, the obligation to disclose documents that either party has that are relevant to the issues of the case applies whether they support or do not support that party's case. The aim of the obligation to disclose those documents that might undermine a party's case or support its opponent's case, as well as those documents that a party has that support its own case, is to do *justice* between the parties. Additionally, the court will look to define (or restrict) the extent of the search for, and disclosure of, documents for the action according to what is 'proportionate' for the case.

Disclosure is one of the most important stages of an action, and is a time when the relative strengths and weaknesses of each party's case may be more clearly revealed. It is after disclosure and inspection that both parties will probably fully review their case, consider making, repeating, increasing, decreasing, or withdrawing Part 36 offers (see Chapter 15), and consider again the options for alternative dispute resolution (ADR).

It is important to remember the distinction between 'disclosure' and 'inspection'. Disclosure means identifying the existence of all of the documents that should be disclosed. Inspection identifies which of the documents—that have been disclosed—may be inspected (seen) by the opponent. The process of disclosure does *not* make all of the documents available to be seen ('inspected') when disclosure is made.

16.2.2 WHEN DOES DISCLOSURE OCCUR?

Disclosure is a stage in the process and progress of an action to trial. The order for parties to give 'disclosure' will often be defined as one of the first directions orders that the court makes that detail how the case will be managed and progress. This can be seen in the 'Litigation train' diagram at the beginning of this chapter. The timing and extent of the disclosure obligations of each party are within the court's discretion. In most cases, an order for disclosure will be defined and made as part of the 'directions order' which will be made after the parties have filed their directions questionnaire (DQ; for all fast-track and PI multi-track cases), or have filed their disclosure report in Form N263 (for all multi-track, non-PI cases) or Electronic Disclosure Questionnaire in Form N264 at the first case management conference if one has been listed (CMC—see Chapter 12, generally). If a CMC is held after the DQs have been filed then the directions order (including the provisions for Disclosure) will usually be defined and made at the CMC. If no CMC is called then the court will make the directions order as a paper exercise and after considering the parties responses in their DQs. Defining the extent of the disclosure obligations of the parties in the case and making the 'disclosure order' is usually the first opportunity that the court will take to manage the case actively and the obligation for the parties (or just one of the parties if appropriate) to make disclosure will often be the first 'direction' in the directions order that the parties must act upon. It will thus usually begin the timetable for the progress of the case to trial.

In the fast track, 'disclosure' will often be ordered to take place within four weeks of the case being confirmed as allocated to that track. PI multi-track cases will be similarly managed, but the timescale for the parties to comply with their disclosure obligations may, where it is justified, be longer than four weeks. The time the parties are given to comply will be dependent on the value of the claim and the extent of disclosure to be made. In non-PI multi-track cases, where directions for the progress of a case towards trial may be more specific to the factors of the case, the extent of the directions orders the parties must comply with will still often be one of the first stages with which the parties will comply, although the time within which it should be undertaken may be (but again, not necessarily) longer. When the court has set down the time when the disclosure exercise must be completed, it is important that the parties ensure that they meet that obligation within the time set. Any application to extend the time should be fully justified and be made before the deadline date that has been set.

The parties may agree, or the court may order, that disclosure takes place in stages (CPR 31.13). This might happen if a decision has been made for a 'split trial' (see Chapter 12, paragraph 12.7.3.4.2). For example, in a case that proceeds on issues of liability, first, an order for disclosure on the issues relating to liability will be made, and only after the liability issue has been determined, and if necessary, will an order for disclosure on issues of quantum be made. In hotly contested actions that may have complex and costly evidence to produce for issues of quantum, it can have significant costs savings for the parties to have disclosure (and, in part, evidence gathering) in stages.

Sometimes, an action can have a clear division of the issues, and the court may seek to restrict the issues to be tried within its case management powers (to ensure that the action proceeds within the aims of the overriding objective), or the parties may agree to restrict the number of issues. Where such a restriction occurs, there will be an equal restriction on the scope of the parties' disclosure obligations.

It is important to note that the obligation to disclose documents may, and commonly does, arise at other times. The provisions of CPR 31.16 provide the circumstances under which an application for pre-action disclosure may be sought (see Chapter 8, paragraph 8.7, and paragraph 16.10 in this chapter). In compliance with a Pre-Action Protocol or the Practice Direction on Pre-Action Conduct and Protocols (PDPACP), the parties are expected to exchange documents that will help to clarify issues. Where parties have conducted their pre-action behaviour in accordance with Protocol, it is likely that some disclosure will have already taken place between the parties (see Chapter 8). It is also important to note, however, that if a party has failed to abide by Protocol and has not given any disclosure before commencement of proceedings, the sanction for this noncompliance is likely to be in an adverse costs order within the action. Remember (see Chapter 8), the courts do not have the power to order compliance with Protocol. However, the provisions enabling an order for pre-action disclosure, where one can be made under those provisions, is CPR 31.16. The effect of such an application can *appear* to have the effect of ordering a party to comply with this aspect of Protocol.

It is also important to note that the obligation to give disclosure continues until the conclusion of the proceedings. Accordingly, if a relevant document comes to light after the parties have complied with the direction to give disclosure, it must be disclosed to the other side immediately.

16.3 WHAT IS A 'DOCUMENT'?

A definition of 'document' is contained in CPR 31.4. It is not restricted to paper or only to originals. It extends to anything upon which information of any description is recorded and will include electronically held information, such as databases, emails (including deleted emails), electronic personal organizers, file servers, backup tapes, and hard drives, as well as hard-copy correspondence, faxes, memoranda, reports, photographs, plans, maps, diaries, and board minutes, as well as objects. This definition includes, therefore, several possibly different versions of a document when one has been amended or annotated, and the dates of those amendments or annotations may be an important part of the document.

The rules dealing with the disclosure of real evidence, such as plans, maps, models, and photographs, are contained in CPR 33.6.

16.4 THE EXTENT OF A PARTY'S DISCLOSURE OBLIGATION

The obligation to make disclosure will arise from either a court order or the parties' agreement. CPR 31.5 gives the court the power to make an order:

- that dispenses with disclosure;
- that requires disclosure on an issue-by-issue basis;
- that requires disclosure on the 'standard basis'; or
- that requires disclosure on such basis as the court directs.

The court will order, and will expect the parties, to seek to agree the disclosure obligations as being those that best suit the case and those that meet the overriding objectives. In the fast-track and multi-track PI cases, the parties will usually be ordered to give 'standard disclosure', but, depending on the replies and requests the parties have made in their DQ, the court may order, or the parties may have agreed, to limit their disclosure obligations to less than even 'standard disclosure' (see the definition of 'standard disclosure' in paragraph 16.4.1). In non-PI multi-track claims, parties will have to file the 'disclosure report' in Form N263. In this document the parties must state what relevant documents exist or may exist (as form N265 requires), but this report also requires the party to provide details of the likely cost of giving relevant disclosure. The parties are also required to discuss their report and, if possible, agree the scope of their disclosure obligations. If they cannot agree, the court will impose the extent of their disclosure obligations.

16.4.1 WHAT DOES 'STANDARD DISCLOSURE' REQUIRE A PARTY TO DISCLOSE?

'Standard disclosure' requires a party; to disclose:

- documents on which it relies and
- documents that:
  - affect its own case adversely;
  - affect the other party's case adversely; and
  - support the other party's case; and
- documents that, in particular types of claim, are specified by the court.

This relates to all documents within a party's 'control'.

The question of whether a document should be disclosed is determined by reference to the issues raised in the parties' statements of case. Only those documents that have reference to the issues between the parties are to be disclosed. It is important, therefore, that where parties (or the court) limit the number of issues between them, the disclosure obligation will be reduced to meet only those issues remaining. In order to meet with the overriding objective—that is, the requirements of proportionality, fairness, and justice—parties are encouraged to be both realistic and reasonable in determining with which issues to proceed. It is often at the stage of disclosure—or later, at the stage at which witness statements of fact and expert reports are exchanged—that a party is able to determine more clearly the strengths and weaknesses of parts of (or the whole of) its case. Where a part of the case seems unlikely to succeed, it may be sensible for that party to seek to agree those parts, and in this way further restrict the amount of disclosure and documents to be referred to at trial. Obviously, if the reappraisal process determines that that party's whole case has been seriously undermined, then settlement of the whole should be sought.

Further examination of the definition of 'standard disclosure' reveals that:

- the obligation is a wide-ranging one and clients will usually need specific guidance on the extent of their obligation;
- it does not include documents, or classes of document, that are, in effect, documents that may simply lead a party on a 'train of enquiry'.

A legal representative is under a professional duty to advise clients of their disclosure obligations. This advice should be given at the earliest opportunity to avoid clients removing documents from their possession that they consider to be harmful to their position. Where a client does deliberately remove or destroy harmful documents in their possession, the legal representative has further duties to the court. These would expect him to advise the court and the other party in the disclosure process of the existence of the document so removed or destroyed, together with the circumstances of its removal or destruction. The court would be entitled to draw adverse inferences from the client's behaviour. If a client will not give

↳ if destroy documents on purpose

instructions to give that information, the legal representative would be expected not to continue acting for the client. The professional duties relating to disclosure are onerous.

16.4.2 THE MEANING OF 'CONTROL'

The obligation to disclose documents includes those that are within a party's control. 'Control' extends to documents of which a party:

- has physical possession;
- has a right to possession, or to inspection, or to take copies; or
- had, but no longer has.

This definition will mean, therefore, that a party has an obligation to give disclosure not only of documents that it has, but also of documents that it does not have, but which it has the right to reclaim or of which it has the right to obtain copies. This could include, for example, documents that are held by a party's accountants, or documents held by a subsidiary company in an action in which the parent company is a party.

It also includes the obligation of a party to disclose documents that it did have, but does not have anymore. At one end of the spectrum, this will include letters that have been sent, and at the other end of the spectrum, it can include documents that have been deliberately destroyed (see paragraphs 16.4.1 and 16.5.1). In the case of 'letters sent', it is likely that a duplicate of that original letter is still retained by the party and that, also, is a document that must be disclosed. With the degree of electronically created documents and the extent to which these can be 'retrieved', the preparation of a party's list of documents in order to comply with its disclosure obligation can be very onerous indeed. However, some restriction on the potential scope of this obligation is provided by CPR 31.9(1)—that is, that 'A party need not disclose more than one copy of a document'. This rule would not apply, however, if any amendments or annotations were to have been made to the document in its exchanges to and fro, and the amendments on it met the definition of 'standard disclosure'.

16.5 THE OBLIGATION TO MAKE A REASONABLE SEARCH FOR RELEVANT DOCUMENTS

16.5.1 THE OBLIGATIONS AND DUTIES OF THE PARTIES AND THEIR LEGAL REPRESENTATIVES

Each party that has an obligation to give disclosure is required to make a reasonable and proportionate search for documents. The duty of a party in an action to disclose is qualified by the principles of 'reasonableness' and 'proportionality'.

Determining what is a 'reasonable and proportionate' search includes a review of the nature, the importance, and the value of the case. It also includes a consideration of the costs and the ease of retrieval of the documents.

Clients will need guidance on the extent of the search that the client should make so that he can make an honest and true 'disclosure statement or disclosure report'. A legal representative has an obligation to the court to ensure that his client makes proper disclosure.

When the client declares, when he makes disclosure, that he has conducted a 'reasonable search' for documents, he is saying that he *understands* the duty to disclose and that, to the best of his knowledge and belief, *he has discharged* that duty. The disclosure report that the parties will complete in non-PI multi-track cases includes a statement of truth. The declaration that he has carried out his disclosure obligation has a profound influence on the way parties should approach their obligations of disclosure. The client will, therefore, need to have a clear understanding of the issues of the case in order to carry out the search effectively. It will be for the legal representative to ensure that the client has this level of understanding. The case of *CMCS Common Market Commercial Services AVV v Taylor* [2011] EWHC 324 (Ch) confirms the risks for a legal representative who fails to undertake his disclosure obligations. In this case the court made a wasted costs order against the legal representative for their failure to supervise the client in undertaking their disclosure obligations.

As an 'officer of the court', a legal representative owes a duty to the court to have gone through his client's disclosure list carefully in order to make sure, as far as is possible, that no relevant documents have been omitted.

It is, therefore, good practice to give clients timely advice, both orally and in writing, about the types of document that are to be disclosed and the appropriate person in the client's organization to make the search, as well as advice concerning the retention, storage, and filing of documentation. The burden on the legal representative to ensure that he meets all of the professional obligations relating to disclosure is a heavy one.

16.5.2 'E'-DISCLOSURE AND THE ELECTRONIC DISCLOSURE QUESTIONNAIRE N264

PD 31B contains guidance for all e-disclosure.
'Documents' under the CPR include:

- emails and other electronic communications;
- word-processed documents;
- databases;
- documents readily accessible from computer systems, and other electronic devices and media, such as memory sticks, CDs, and mobile phones;
- documents stored on servers and back-up systems;
- electronic documents that have been deleted; and
- metadata.

The growth in recent years of the number of electronic documents created during the course of a matter has increased greatly and this has increased the e-disclosure obligations during litigation. Parties can seek to limit the extent of this disclosure and the methods of searching for such documents in order to limit the costs of the exercise.

PD 31B(10–13) provides guidance for the completion of the Electronic Documents Questionnaire (EDQ) in Form N264, which will be completed along with the List of Documents where electronic disclosure is undertaken. The purpose of the EDQ is to enable the parties to investigate, categorize, and agree the nature of electronically held documents that the parties must potentially disclose. Parties are expected to discuss and agree the extent of a reasonable electronic search before they undertake the search, and if they cannot agree, make representations to the court at the first CMC where the issue of the disclosure order is being dealt with. The potential extent of e-disclosure can be very great, so parties must take care to agree the extent of it such that it is proportionate. As technology develops this process will hopefully become more simplified by the development of predictive coding, which uses sophisticated technology to identify relevant documents and code them by issue. In the case of *Pyrrho Investments Ltd & Another v MWB Property Ltd & Others* [2016] EWHC 256 (Ch), the use of predictive coding to search for e-documents was approved as a suitable way to reduce the costs of the process.

The Technology and Construction Court has adopted the e-disclosure Protocol. Though the specific procedures in this specialist court are outside the scope of this manual it would be helpful for a legal representative to review this Protocol, which may act as guidance for the e-disclosure in their case. If these protocol guidelines are successful, the Protocol may be adopted by the courts in general.

 Practical Considerations

Any legal representative engaged in the process of disclosure must think carefully about the range and extent of e-disclosure required of the client. There is a misconception that deleted files can very easily be retrieved; they can be retrieved—but not always that easily. Files often become fragmented when placed in the 'deleted files bin'. Does an isolated fragment found in an unallocated fragment or cluster on a disk constitute, for the purposes of disclosure, the document that is relevant to disclose? Advising a client of their disclosure obligations and blithely stating that this includes 'deleted electronic materials' is likely to cause great consternation in the client's IT department, or, for a smaller company client, great concern because of the man hours, and expense, of complying with the advice given. Any early advice to a client about its obligations of disclosure in any action in progress or that might affect it in a possible future action should include advice that might result in its reviewing the way in which the company processes, stores, retains, or deletes data. This can be done in a standard 'disclosure letter' to the client. An example of such a letter appears in the online resources.

There are additional questions that must be asked of the client that will assist them in complying with an order for e-disclosure. There are also further questions that will be asked in a review of a list of documents provided by an opponent. These might include the following:

- Has all equipment holding electronic data been searched?
- Are individuals (within the client's or opponent's workplace) able to store documents on their local hard drives, and have they been doing so?
- Is material on local hard drives routinely backed up onto the client's central server?
- What type of, and how many, servers are used? If they are web-based, does the client have 'control' of documents backed up this way?
- Do individuals have documents on their personal computers at home?
- Does the company operate a 'hot-desk' system, whereby employees may use more than one computer?
- How are documents backed up? (A full, detailed explanation is needed.)
- How is data stored? (A detailed explanation of the methods used is required.)
- Are mobile phones used to store documents and data?
- Do individuals use memory sticks, flash cards, external hard drives, CD-Rs, or DVD-Rs?
- What is the client's (or opponent's) email policy (particularly in relation to storage and deletion)?

Parties should meet early on in the litigation to discuss potential issues regarding electronic disclosure and that, where used, keyword searches should be agreed as far as possible. Where the extent of the search for e-documents is challenged by a party, the proper interim application to make is not one for specific disclosure, but instead should be an interim application for specific inspection.

The court may take the following matters into account when considering the correct level of e-disclosure to order the parties to undertake:

- the potential value of appropriate electronic searches to identify important documents that might otherwise be missed;
- but the rules do not require that 'no stone should be left unturned'; and
- it will be the court which ultimately decides what the scope of the e-search and e-disclosure should be.

16.6 FORM N265 AND THE 'DISCLOSURE STATEMENT', AND THE DISCLOSURE REPORT FORM N263

When a party complies with his obligation to give disclosure within the directions order made by the court in fast-track and PI multi-track cases, he will usually do so on Form N265. In non-PI multi-track cases the parties will complete a 'disclosure report' in Form N263 at least fourteen days before the first CMC. Inevitably, detailed consideration of the disclosure to be made in the case will need to be undertaken earlier. The disclosure report (N263) only contains a simple statement of truth, not the full statement or declaration that is contained in Form N265 by the party making disclosure that the search for documents has been carried out properly and with an understanding of his obligations. Form N263 seems to indicate that it may be signed by the legal representative. Careful consideration will have to be given to who is the most appropriate signatory. The simpler statement of truth in the disclosure report may be because it is filed before full disclosure and the filing of the N265 is made (authors' comment), and it will be on the Form N265 that the full disclosure declaration is made.

16.6.1 WHAT THE STATEMENT IN THE N265 MUST INCLUDE

The disclosure statement must:

(a) detail the extent of the search that has been made to locate documents that are required to be disclosed;

(b) certify that the person signing the statement understands the duty to give disclosure;

(c) certify that, to the best of his knowledge, that person has carried out that duty;

(d) declare that he believes that the extent of the search made is a reasonable one, in all of the circumstances; and

(e) if a particular search has not been carried out, specify the search that has not been carried out and give reasons for not carrying it out, or declare, if any searches made were limited in any way, what those limitations were and why the limitation was imposed.

16.6.1.1 In relation to (d)

In 'all of the circumstances' means what it is reasonable to have done having regard to the value and/or importance of the case. 'Importance' here means important in terms of either a legal principle or issue. All cases are important to the parties, but a low-value case, albeit one of great importance to the party, will not have a higher degree of the duty to 'search for documents' than it is proportionate, in terms of the value of the case, to carry out. This may not be the position if the case is one of relatively low value, but which may have a significant contribution to make in terms of legal principle or legal clarification.

16.6.1.2 In relation to (e)

The usual reason that will be given for any restriction in terms of time or extent of the search will be that it is 'not proportionate' to make that search. In a relatively simple road traffic accident (RTA), this could be a restriction of the search for documents 'from the date of the accident and not before it'. It is open to a party to challenge any restriction declared. For example, if the claim being made is one against the local authority and concerning its duties to maintain the highway, it may be appropriate to challenge the extent of the search and to seek to widen it to include statistics on accidents that may have occurred at the spot before the accident that is the subject of the claim, in order to establish that the place at which the accident occurred was an 'accident black spot'.

Very frequently, limitations or restrictions will be placed on the extent of any electronic search for documents. An example might be that the search has been restricted to 'existing emails'. Again, it will be open to the opposing party to seek to challenge whether it would be reasonable to make a search that included 'deleted emails' and the extent of that further search. A further example could be a restriction on the search for electronic documents to have been by defined 'keywords'. Again, any such restriction may be open to challenge by the opposing party.

16.6.2 WHO WILL SIGN THE DISCLOSURE STATEMENT?

Under CPR 31.10(6), a disclosure statement is defined as 'a statement made by the party disclosing the documents'.

In the great majority of cases, it will be the client, or a representative of the client, who signs the statement. It will not usually be the legal representative, because it is the client who will declare his understanding of his disclosure obligations and who will have carried out a reasonable search for the documents. Under CPR 31.10(6) it *may* be most appropriate for another person to make the disclosure statement. The legal representative's duty is to ensure that the client understands the obligations and carries out the obligations accordingly (PD 31.4.4). See paragraph 16.6, which discusses the differing statements in the disclosure report (Form N263) and the full disclosure declaration signed on the list of documents (Form N265).

✓ Practical Considerations

When considering who will sign the disclosure statement, ensure that the appropriate person is available to sign the list before exchange. This is of particular relevance when the client is a company and the person signing the statement is away on business or on holiday. It is good practice to check the availability of the person to sign to avoid being in breach of the direction for disclosure by the date set by the court.

In certain circumstances, a person other than the client or a representative of the client may sign the disclosure statement and this is provided for in CPR 31.10(9)—that is, 'A disclosure statement may be made by a person who is not a party where this is permitted by a relevant practice direction'. PD 31.4.7 sets out circumstances in which an insurer or the Motor Insurers' Bureau (MIB) may sign the disclosure statement on behalf of a party.

Where the party making disclosure is a company, firm, association, or other organization, CPR 31.10(7) provides that the party signing the disclosure statement must also:

- identify the person making the statement; and
- explain why or certify that he is the appropriate person to make the statement; and
- give his name, address, and position in the organization.

16.6.3 HOW ARE DOCUMENTS SORTED AND LISTED ON FORM N265?

CPR 31.10, PD 31A, and PD 31A–31B set out the detailed instructions for compiling the list in Form N265. There are three sections in Form N265, and documents to be disclosed need to be placed in one of the three sections. A blank N265 can be found in the online resources, and a completed one can be found in Appendix 7 at the back of the manual.

In the 'top' section on the list, the party making disclosure lists and numbers all of those documents that it does not object to the opponent inspecting. As stated in paragraph 16.8, this inspection process includes physically inspecting the documents listed and/or seeking copies of them.

In the 'middle' section on the list, the party making disclosure lists and numbers all of those documents that it does object to the other party being able to inspect. In this section, the disclosing party also needs to give the reason for withholding the documents from inspection. There is usually standard wording for this section.

In the 'bottom' section on the list, the party making disclosure lists and numbers all of those documents that it no longer has in its control, and goes on to state when they were last in its control and where the documents are now. There is also usually standard wording for this section.

16.6.4 WHAT IS INCLUDED IN FORM N263?

In non-PI multi-track cases the parties will need to complete a disclosure report on Form N263 not less than fourteen days before the first CMC CPR 31.5(3) (or, if no CMC has been listed, along with the DQ—authors' comment). This report will include:

- a statement of truth;
- what documents exist, or may exist, that are, or may be, relevant to the issues of the case;

- where, and with whom, the documents described are;

- how any electronic documents are stored (authors' comment: it is thought that where electronic documents are disclosed, the Electronic Documents Questionnaire should also be completed);

- the estimated costs of giving 'standard disclosure' in the case (which should include the cost of searching for and disclosing any electronically held documents); and

- which directions orders from the menu options (CPR 31.5(7) and (8)) are sought (with justification where appropriate).

16.7 THE PROCESS OF DISCLOSURE

16.7.1 IN THE SMALL CLAIMS TRACK

When the defence has been filed and the court has made a provisional allocation of the case to the small claims track (in Form N149A), the court is likely to impose limited (proportionate) directions orders. Where a party is a litigant in person, the court will send a hard copy of the DQ (in Form N180) to the party, which they must complete and file within at least fourteen days (and serve on the other parties). Parties are expected to cooperate with each other about the directions requests that they make in the DQ. Before giving the directions order, the court will ask the parties to state whether they are prepared for the case to be referred for mediation (or other form of ADR), and only if this is refused will the court set down management decisions (being a 'directions order'), which will include such limited disclosure as the court feels is proportionate to the case. The court will either deal with the case as a paper hearing after that disclosure has taken place, or, if they think it appropriate, set the matter down for a hearing.

16.7.2 IN THE FAST-TRACK AND PI MULTI-TRACK CASES—THE EXCHANGE OR SERVICE OF LISTS OF DOCUMENTS

Directions Questionaire

In the fast-track or in PI multi-track cases an order for disclosure will usually be made after the parties have completed and filed (at court and with each other) the DQ (in Form N181), or at the first CMC if one has been listed. Once the defence has been filed, the court will make a provisional decision as to which track is appropriate based on the value of the claim, and will send out notices to all parties requiring them to download and complete the DQ (unless they are an unrepresented party, in which case they will be sent a copy). Along with the completed DQ the parties will be expected to cooperate with each other and file the suggested directions that they would like the court to make, or, if they have not agreed the directions they require, each party will state which directions orders they require. The DQs must be filed within twenty-eight days from the deemed date of service of the Notice from the court of Proposed Allocation to track (in Forms N149A, B, or C). There is guidance on the Ministry of Justice website, which sets out and makes accessible a very full list of different directions orders that can be sought.

The court will make a directions order either as the parties have agreed (if the court feels that such an order is appropriate for the case and meets the overriding objectives), or as it deems appropriate. The directions order made will include not only details of the scope of the directions order (which is likely to be for 'standard disclosure' or less than standard disclosure), but also a date by which the parties' lists of documents are to be made available to each other. The order will usually provide for either exchange of lists (where both parties are to give disclosure), or service of lists where only one party may have disclosure obligations, or that the service of the lists is to be sequential. Generally, the order will provide that the lists should be contained within Form N265. CPR 31.10 assumes 'service' of lists. This, it could be argued, does not assume 'exchange' of lists. In most cases, it would be sensible to agree—or, in the absence of agreement, to ask for—a direction for 'exchange'.

The directions order made will also specify a time period when 'inspection' (of the documents that are, at that time, available for inspection) may take place.

 Practical Considerations

Legal representatives should consider the form of the order for disclosure they intend to ask for before completing the DQ (Form N181), or before attending the first CMC. Consideration should be given not only to the dates by which parties should serve their lists of documents, and whether these should be simultaneous or sequential, but also what the scope of the disclosure obligation should be and the dates, or period, in which the search for documents should be made. Requests for disclosure that is outside the scope of 'standard disclosure' can be made, but should be justified (within the provisions of the overriding objective).

When listing is complete, the parties will:

- confirm to each other that they are ready to exchange or serve their lists;
- exchange or serve their lists;
- in the case of the party in receipt of an opponent's list of documents, consider the list served and give notice to exercise its rights of inspection; and
- carry out inspection.

There may also be either requests or applications for specific disclosure, or a challenge to the list supplied by a party. These matters are now considered further.

16.7.3 IN NON-PI MULTI-TRACK CASES

In these cases, as with other cases that have been issued, the court will make a provisional decision as to which track is appropriate based on the value of the claim, and will send out notices to all parties requiring them to download and complete the DQ (in Form N181) and prepare a disclosure report in form N263.

The disclosure report in Form N263 (see paragraph 16.6.4) must be filed at least fourteen days before the first CMC (authors' comment: or if no CMC has been listed, along with their DQs). The disclosure report must be accompanied by a statement of truth. In the preparation of their disclosure reports, the parties must discuss and seek to agree a proposal for disclosure (that meets the overriding objectives). When there is to be electronic disclosure, the parties will also file the EDQ, form N264 (see paragraph 16.5.2), which will be filed with the disclosure report.

At the CMC the parties should have also filed a summary of the matters (relating to disclosure) that they agree and those that they do not agree.

With this degree of consideration, cooperation, and information from the parties, the courts will be in a good position to make appropriate directions orders for the case. The court will be looking to restrict the extent of disclosure wherever possible. The court has the power to dispense with disclosure altogether, to restrict it to specific issues, or to extend the scope of disclosure beyond 'standard disclosure', but only if it is considered proportionate, fair, just, and efficient to do so.

 Practical Considerations

The impact of the disclosure obligations and the requirement to give detailed information and proposals so early in the litigation means that parties and their legal representatives will need to consider 'documents' (for the case) very early on and require both to get organised. Legal representatives, and their clients, will also have to have regard for the estimated costs of the extent of the disclosure obligations they wish the court to impose, as they will need to give an estimate of these costs as part of the justification for their preferred option and in their costs budgets.

16.7.4 **DISCLOSURE IS AN ONGOING OBLIGATION**

The duty of disclosure continues until proceedings are concluded and this probably means after judgment, but before the judgment has been handed down (*Vernon v Bosley (No 2)* [1997] 3 WLR 683).

Often, the list of documents prepared and served or exchanged may be incomplete. This may be because investigations are ongoing. Where this occurs, the fact that further documents will be disclosed should be stated in the disclosure statement. It may be because documents come to light later. If the reason for a failure to disclose is because the client felt the document to be damaging, then this reason and the client's reluctance will need to be explained. A legal representative who is not given instructions to explain the failure or delay to disclose a document will have to cease acting.

 Practical Considerations

It is important to remind clients of the ongoing duties of disclosure, as well as of the disclosure obligations referred to in previous 'Practical Considerations' boxes. Clients should be reminded not only of the ongoing duty, but also of the possible consequences of a breach. Any costs implications of late disclosure should also be raised.

If additional material does come to light after the list of documents has been served, CPR 31.11(2) provides that the other party must be notified immediately. A supplemental list should be prepared and served. If there are only a small number of additional documents, these can be simply added to the original list. There is no prescribed form of the supplemental list, although Form N265 could be adapted for this purpose.

 Practical Considerations

If new material arises, it may be necessary to review your client's case again in the light of the new documents and then to update any advice to the client in the light of the new information. A further review of the documents listed should also be made to ensure that no further documents have slipped through the net of the 'reasonable search'.

16.7.5 **THE ROLE OF THE LEGAL REPRESENTATIVE IN THE PROCESS OF DISCLOSURE**

Part of the legal representative's role in the process of disclosure will be to ensure that the client understands their disclosure obligations and ensure that disclosure has been properly made and then to ensure that the organization of the documents is appropriate, so that the documents being disclosed are placed in the right part of Form N265.

16.7.5.1 Considerations of the legal representative when compiling a list of documents
In relation to each document being considered, the following will need to be considered:

- Is the document, in principle, one that is to be disclosed?

- Does the client have the right (or a duty) to withhold inspection?

Thus, in the first part of the process, the documents that have been revealed by the 'reasonable search' may be sorted into five categories, as follows:

- **Documents that are to be disclosed, but disclosure of which is being withheld.** There will not usually be many documents, if any, in this category. If a document is to be disclosed, then few grounds will justify it *not* being contained within the list of documents being disclosed. One such reason might be a claim for 'public interest immunity'. This may happen, for example, in proceedings involving sensitive political or state information.

- **Documents that are to be disclosed, but inspection of which is being withheld.** These will most often be privileged documents. A full discussion of 'privilege' arises in paragraph 16.9. These documents will be listed in the middle section of Form N265. Some of the documents listed here may be withheld from inspection at the time that parties are ordered to 'disclose by an exchange of lists of documents' because they are, for example, privileged. However, the client may waive the privilege at a later stage and make the document available to the opponent. Thus, draft (or final) witness statements may be withheld from inspection, but will ultimately be made available to the opponents at the time at which the parties have been ordered to 'exchange witness statements' in the court's directions order made after allocation. This direction will usually be after the order for 'disclosure by list' (see Chapter 12).

- **Documents that are to be disclosed, and which will be disclosed and inspection of which will be permitted.** These are the documents that the opponent will be entitled to see once they exercise their rights of inspection. These documents may make up the bulk of the list and will be listed in the first section of the list. How the parties exercise the rights of inspection is detailed in paragraph 16.8.

- **Documents that are partly to be disclosed.** Part of such documents will be redacted. Privileged or irrelevant commercially sensitive material can be 'blanked out' of (that is, redacted from) a document that otherwise needs to be disclosed. The description of the document in the list should make it clear that it has been redacted (see also the case of *CMCS Common Market Commercial Services AVV v Taylor* [2011] EWHC 324 referred to at paragraph 16.5.1, a case concerning the redaction of documents).

- **Documents that are not to be disclosed.** The search for documents in an action may reveal documents that are either not relevant to the issues of the case and/or do not fall within the ambit of order to disclose. Most likely, it will be that they do not fall within the definition of 'standard disclosure', because that is the most likely definition of a party's duty to give disclosure (see paragraph 16.4).

 Practical Considerations

When documents are being sorted for disclosure, a file note should be made in respect of each document (or class of documents) of the reason for the category in which it has been placed. The transparency of the disclosure process in this way both shows that a proper consideration has been given to the process and will record the time spent on the process (and thus justify the charges applied to the process). A proper recording will also ensure that the whole team involved on the case is able to see the work done on the process, as well as the reasons for the categories into which the documents have been placed. The recording in this way will also be a starting point for dealing with any challenges that may be made to that party's disclosure or in responding to any application for specific disclosure. (For specific disclosure applications see Chapter 14, paragraph 14.5.)

When the documents have been categorized, sorted, and listed in Form N265, the client will be asked to sign off the prepared list and make the disclosure statement on the front page of the form. At this stage, the legal representative will indicate to his opponent that he is ready to effect exchange. Where both parties have been ordered to give disclosure—and this may not always be the case—when a party is ready to effect exchange, he may write a letter, email, or fax to the opponent as follows:

In accordance with the Order of [example: 'Mr District Judge'] made on the [date of the order] at paragraph [relevant paragraph of the order], we confirm that we are ready to effect exchange of our client's list of documents. Please confirm that you are ready to exchange your client's list.

16.7.5.2 Considerations of the legal representative when receiving a list of documents

When a party receives the opponent's list, he will undertake the following:

- The legal representative should review the list. This review will initially compare each party's list to ascertain what documents both parties have and do not have. The revision will also need to consider whether there are any obvious omissions from the documents being inspected: perhaps a reference to another document is made in a document that has been disclosed for inspection, but which is not itself in the list. A review could reveal whether there are any surprises in the documents: for example, where a copy has been made available, but not the original. It could equally show up any queries of the scope of the search that has been made for documents or the extent of the documents that are held back from inspection (whether the claim for privilege can be justified, and whether it should be challenged). The review should include a review of the disclosure statement and whether any restrictions in the search for documents are reasonable. Has an appropriate person signed the disclosure statement?

- As a result of the review undertaken, that party's legal representative will prepare correspondence setting out any concerns and, at the same time, decide how they wish to exercise 'inspection', giving notice of same.

- The legal representative will serve a notice to inspect the documents available for inspection. The procedure for inspection is set out in CPR 31.15—that is, that a request to inspect should be given in writing and that the party disclosing the documents must permit inspection within seven days after receiving notice to inspect. The request to inspect may specify that the party requires copies and it is provided in the rules that they are also agreeing to pay the reasonable photocopying charges. It is good practice to seek to agree these charges.

- It is open to the inspecting party to inspect the originals either before or after receiving photocopies. There is no prescribed form of the 'notice to inspect'. Typically, the notice to inspect takes the form of a letter specifying the documents, or categories of document, inspection of which is sought—specifying whether this is by the provision of photocopies (or on disk) or by physical inspection.

 Practical Considerations

The process of inspection is often a paper exercise, with each party requesting certain documents from its opponent's list and agreeing to pay reasonable photocopying charges. It is, therefore, unusual for legal representatives and/or clients to attend inspection of the documents personally. But it should be remembered that it is the client's right to 'inspect' and that his legal representative is carrying out that right on the client's behalf. There may be situations in which it would be appropriate for the client to attend the inspection. Personal inspection will happen, however, when the numbers of documents to inspect are great and/or in a complex action, or where the list has been compiled in such a way as to make identification of specific documents difficult and unreliable.

If the list of documents for inspection is lengthy, it is important to ensure that the documents are made available to you to inspect in the order in which they appear in the list. If they are not, it can make inspection more time-consuming and, therefore, more costly for your client. Given the work that can take place in a review of a party's list of documents, the time limits are tight and should be diarized as a 'key date'.

16.8 INSPECTION

The time period for inspection of documents is invariably set out in the directions order and, as indicated earlier, is usually seven days after disclosure. If the time for inspection has not been fixed in the directions order, reference should be made to CPR 31.15, which contains default provisions on the timing of the provision of copies and inspection.

The place at which inspection should take place will often be at the offices of the disclosing party's legal representatives, but the court may order, or the parties may seek an order, that inspection should take place at another (more convenient) location.

When a party formally discloses a document in civil proceedings by stating that it exists, his opponent will have the right to inspect the document unless the disclosing party claims a right or duty to withhold inspection. Inspection means physically looking at the document, calling for a copy of it, or calling for a copy and then physically inspecting it. Specific provision should be made regarding inspection of electronic materials.

If the disclosing party is claiming a duty or a right to withhold inspection, the basis of that claim must be set out on the Form N265. If the disclosing party is claiming that it would be 'disproportionate' to make the document available for inspection, this reason should also be given. Any claim to withhold inspection may be challenged by the opponent.

Unless the list of the documents available for inspection states that they are 'copies', the assumption will be that the document available is the original. A document that has been amended in any way from the original is treated as a separate document.

 Practical Considerations

If there is any doubt about the authenticity of a document, it will be important to inspect originals. Important information can be observed by inspecting original documents, because they can reveal differing ink colours, the use of highlighters, pencil annotations, or other information that shows a transition in the form of the document. These additions to a document can provide valuable evidence when reviewing the documents.

CPR 32.19 provides that 'A party shall be deemed to admit the authenticity of a document disclosed to him under CPR Part 31 unless he serves notice that he wishes the document to be proved at trial'. Any notice under this provision must be served by the latest date for serving witness statements, or *within seven days of disclosure of the document*, whichever is later.

16.8.1 GROUNDS FOR WITHHOLDING INSPECTION

Under CPR 31.3, a party to whom a document has been disclosed has a right to inspect that document unless:

- the document is no longer in the control of the party disclosing it—in which case, the disclosing party is simply stating a fact that inspection of the document with them is not possible. In this situation, the opponent will need to consider the meaning of the word 'control' and determine whether examination of the document should be sought in the hands of another person, who may not be a party in the action (see paragraph 16.4). It may also involve consideration of an application for non-party disclosure under the provisions of CPR 31.17 (see paragraph 16.11);

- the party disclosing it has a right or a duty to withhold inspection of it—where a party claims a right to withhold inspection, it is usually on the basis (or ground) that the disclosed documents are 'privileged'. There are a number of different types of privilege, including:

- legal advice privilege;

- litigation privilege;

- common interest privilege; and

- without-prejudice privilege.

A detailed examination of 'privilege' is contained in paragraph 16.9:

- the party disclosing it considers that it would be disproportionate to the issues in the case to permit inspection of it. This is in keeping with the overriding objective. Whether or not this claim will withstand a challenge from the opponent will depend on the facts of the case. A claim might be made to withhold inspection, for example, when there are large numbers of documents held abroad, and it would be 'disproportionate' and would little assist the court's ability to deal with the issues of the case 'fairly', 'justly', or 'expeditiously' to enforce inspection of these documents.

16.8.2 CHALLENGING THE EXTENT OF THE SEARCH AND CHALLENGING THE ALLOCATION OF DOCUMENTS TO THAT PART OF THE LIST THAT IS NOT 'AVAILABLE TO INSPECT'

Any party in receipt of another party's list of documents needs to undertake a careful review of the documents listed. The existence of the disclosure statement of the listing party does not mean that the receiving party has to take at face value the accuracy or the completeness of the list provided. Where you have identified concerns about the list provided, there are several steps that can be taken to ensure that an accurate or complete list is provided.

CPR 31.23 provides that proceedings for contempt of court can be brought against a party who makes, or 'causes to be made', a false disclosure statement without an honest belief in its truth. Such proceedings are quite rare and other options will usually be taken before contempt proceedings are considered. These 'other options' include the following:

- You might choose to set out your specific concerns by letter to your opponent's legal representative. This should include a full explanation of the reasons for your concerns, as well as, if possible, details of the documents that you feel are not included in the lists. The letter could have included in it advance warning that if an application has to be made to the court, then indemnity costs for the application will be sought.

- You might consider making a specific disclosure application (see Chapter 14, paragraph 14.5). Under CPR 31.12(2), the court may order a party to:

  - disclose documents, or classes of document, specified;

  - carry out a search as specified; and/or

  - disclose any further documents revealed by the search or as ordered.

- Any application for specific disclosure will need to consider the overriding objective: is the further disclosure *necessary* to do *justice* between the parties? Is it *proportionate* to the issues of the case? Is it *economic* to make the order for further disclosure?

- You might consider whether it is appropriate to serve a 'notice to admit facts' (see Chapter 17, paragraph 17.6.1). Under CPR 32.18(1), a party may serve another party with a notice requiring him to admit the facts or the part of the case that the party serving the notice states in the notice. The aim of the notice is to seek admissions on evidence or stated issues of the case, thereby avoiding the serving party having to prove the stated facts or issues set out in the notice. The provisions have the benefit of both narrowing issues and saving costs, both of which are important aspects of the CPR. The notice to admit facts can be used effectively to put pressure (usually costs pressure) on an opponent.

- In either of these applications, you should consider asking the court to include an 'unless order' that is intended to ensure that a party complies (see Chapter 13, paragraph 13.10). An 'unless order' is one that provides for a further step to be taken—usually to debar a party from proceedings with a step, or more critically, their action, if they do not comply with the initial part of the order. It would always be appropriate to seek an 'unless order' where the opponent has repeatedly failed to comply, or has unreasonably failed to respond to an early request, or when his good faith in not responding to the order is in doubt in some other way.

16.8.3 CHALLENGES MAY BE RAISED FROM A REVIEW OF AN OPPONENT'S LIST OF DOCUMENTS AND THE INSPECTION PROCESS

The following is a non-exhaustive list of the grounds on which challenges may be made to an opponent's list of documents:

- a failure to disclose a document referred to in documents that are disclosed and that have been inspected;

- that there are documents that, as a matter of common sense, should be in the list;

- in relation to documents that may be in the 'middle' section of the list and unavailable for inspection, but the claim for privilege of which can be challenged;

- that the disclosure statement has not been signed by an 'appropriate person';

- that the parameters of the search for documents are too narrow or otherwise too restricted either as to the search made or the period in which the search is made;

- in relation to e-disclosure (see paragraph 16.5.2), that the keyword search is too narrow, or the search has not been wide enough; or

- that the listing is too vague and is inadequate, and/or it is not possible to have a clear enough idea of the documents being listed.

In any request or challenge to a party's list of documents, consideration must be given to 'relevance', as well as to the aims of the overriding objective. The request and, especially, any application to the court should be supported with details of the likely cost (to the party) of complying with the application, so that the court can apply the concept of proportionality to the application, as well as the need for the further disclosure or verification in terms of fairness, justice, or expedition. Consideration can also be given to any alternative means of achieving the aim: for example, by CPR Part 18 requests if they would achieve a more efficient and cheaper, as well as fairer, outcome.

The CPR do not specify the format of most applications that may be made to challenge a party's list of documents. Most applications would include a written request first, then an application, either by letter or on Form N244, with supporting evidence.

 Costs

The process of scrutinizing your opponent's list of documents and inspecting the copies of documents that you request can be time-consuming and, therefore, costly to your client. The time spent on this is regularly challenged at costs assessments (both summary assessment and detailed assessment). Make a careful note of the time spent and, with that note, your notes justifying the time spent. Inform your client before the cost is incurred in the larger 'document dense' cases, so that he is aware of the impact on proportionality and his overall costs, which he may not fully recover, even if he is ultimately successful and secures a costs order in his favour.

16.9 PRIVILEGE

'Privilege' entitles a party to withhold evidence from production to a third party, an opponent in proceedings, or the court. Once privilege has been established, an absolute right to withhold the document in question arises. In litigation, 'privilege' entitles a party to withhold the 'inspection' of the privileged document; it does not provide a right not to 'disclose' the document. So privileged documents must still be contained within the list of documents, but they will be contained in the middle section of that part of Form N265 that lists the documents being disclosed but which are not available for inspection. However, some documents listed in this part may become available for the other party to see later in the action. An example of this is draft witness statements; these will not be disclosed to the other party until the date when the court has ordered exchange of witness statements. These statements may have been amended since the disclosure stage, but the final version will lose its privilege if the party relying on it wants to subsequently disclose it. Other documents may never be made available for the opponent to see.

Where privilege is claimed, neither the court nor the opponent can ask the court to draw adverse inferences by the exclusion of the document from the proceedings.

In paragraph 16.8.1, the types of privilege were identified as:

- legal advice privilege;
- litigation privilege;
- common interest privilege; and
- without-prejudice privilege.

The exclusion of privileged documents from the litigation process is extremely important—not least because the documents that are being withheld may be highly relevant to the issues of the case. In only four areas will documents be excluded from the court irrespective of the court's attitude to them:

(a) documents that are irrelevant;

(b) documents containing opinion evidence (save where expressed by an expert appointed for that purpose);

(c) where the document is privileged; and

(d) where public immunity interest applies.

Irrelevant documents—that is, area (a)—and opinion evidence that is not authorized by it being given by an appointed expert—that is, area (b)—are often included in a party's case, sometimes through mistake or, more commonly, because of a lack of good preparation by the legal representative. The courts do not exclude this type of evidence; they instead usually adopt the response of 'attaching very little or no weight' to such evidence.

However, in the case of evidence that is covered by privilege (that is, area (c)) or public interest immunity (that is, area (d)) the rights attaching to them for individuals amount, in practice, to an important personal constitutional right. These rights are underwritten by Arts 6 and 8 of the European Convention on Human Rights (ECHR). Accordingly, a person who has a (possibly highly relevant) document to which privilege or public interest immunity attaches may:

- refuse to give oral evidence or to produce the document to the court at any trial or hearing;
- refuse to disclose the information under any Pre-Action Protocol;
- refuse to answer a witness summons to answer questions or to produce documents relating to the privileged information;
- refuse to permit inspection of the document either pre-action or during the action or at trial;
- refuse to give any access to the documents to any person with a search warrant or search order; and
- refuse to answer any questions relating to the privileged materials from a police officer or other investigator.

The importance of these rights cannot be overemphasized—especially because it is also to be noted that these rights may apply regardless of how relevant or otherwise admissible the materials might be, and, further, no adverse inferences can be drawn by the court from the exclusion of the material.

16.9.1 LEGAL PROFESSIONAL PRIVILEGE

Legal professional privilege includes 'legal advice privilege' and 'litigation privilege'. Privilege cannot be claimed unless the evidence in question is confidential, so where the information or the document has ceased to be confidential, the document containing it can no longer be subject to a claim for privilege. For the same reason, no privilege can attach to communications between opposing parties (unless they are subject to 'without prejudice' privilege). Equally, and for the same reason, when it is no longer 'confidential to one party', there can be no privilege in:

- transcripts of proceedings in chambers, in open court, or before arbitrators;
- attendance notes of meetings at which both parties were present; and

- telephone attendance notes of conversations between legal representatives of both sides. (The exception to this is if the notes contain additional notes by one party's legal representative that detail strategy, advice, or the merits of a party's case.)

The underlying purpose of legal professional privilege is to allow a party access to legal advice, to the lawyer's professional skill and judgment, without compromising his position with the opponent. In this context, 'lawyer' includes all members of the legal profession: solicitors; barristers; in-house lawyers, in part of their work; and foreign lawyers. It also covers supervised legal executives and trainees. The narrow definition of 'legal adviser' would probably exclude legal advice given by lay advisers at advice centres.

The position of in-house lawyers is more complex. Some of what they do is covered by legal professional privilege, but that part of their work that deals with business advice or administration will not be privileged. In-house lawyers should distinguish in their work between the giving of legal advice and work that, for example, ensures compliance with regulations for the business for which they work or which relates to their executive functions.

The case of *R (on the application of Prudential plc & another) v Special Commissioner of Income Tax & another* [2013] UKSC 1 has stated that such legal advice privilege relates to legal advice by lawyers, it cannot extend to *tax advice* given by accountants. However, in respect of such advice given by accountants and where litigation arises, the position will be different, and, provided the 'dominant purpose' test is satisfied (see paragraph 16.9.2.2), an accountant's advice to his client will be privileged.

Legal professional privilege belongs to the client, and it is, therefore, only the client, or an agent of the client with ostensible authority, who can waive the privilege applying.

16.9.2 WHAT IS THE DISTINCTION BETWEEN 'LEGAL ADVICE PRIVILEGE' AND 'LITIGATION PRIVILEGE'?

Legal advice privilege and litigation privilege are distinct types of legal professional privilege. See also Figure 16.1 at the end of this chapter.

16.9.2.1 Legal advice privilege

Legal advice privilege can apply whether or not litigation is pending or contemplated, whereas litigation privilege can apply only when litigation is pending or contemplated. 'Pending' or 'contemplated' means a real likelihood, rather than a mere possibility. A distinct possibility that sooner or later someone might make a claim, or a general apprehension of future litigation, is not enough.

Legal advice privilege protects against compulsory disclosure of all types of communication made between a client and his lawyer in which advice is sought or given within a relevant legal context. The subject matter of the advice sought or given is irrelevant, so long as it is in a legal context. Therefore, legal advice privilege protects advice sought by, or given to, a client in relation to both contentious and non-contentious matters. The key test of what constitutes 'legal advice' was considered in *NRG v Bacon and Woodrow* [1995] 1 All ER 976, in which Colman J stated that the advice must be 'directly related to the performance by the solicitor of his professional duties as legal advisor'. This position, although threatened in the Court of Appeal decision in *Three Rivers District Council v Governor and Company of the Bank of England (No 5)* [2002] EWHC 2730, was restored by the House of Lords in *Three Rivers District Council v Bank of England (No 6)* [2004] 3 WLR 1274, where it was confirmed that:

- legal advice privilege covers advice relating to public rights, liabilities, and obligations; and hence,
- includes presentational advice given by lawyers to a party whose conduct might be the subject of public criticism; and
- would extend to advice and assistance given with reference to a range of enquiries, including coroners' inquests, and statutory and ad hoc enquiries; but

- if the lawyer became the client's 'man of business' advising across a wide range of non-legal topics, such as investments and other business matters, the advice might lack the relevant legal context to uphold the privilege; and

- there does not appear to be a 'dominant purpose' test as there is in litigation privilege.

The privilege does not apply in other types of 'confidential' discussion that a person may have with another person who is not their lawyer: for example, their doctor or priest. This applies even if the discussions with that person relate to legal matters. However, the court will consider the position carefully before compelling such persons to divulge the confidential information. This ability to include otherwise confidential information in proceedings has been held to apply in many situations in which the client may find it hard to understand, in the light of the absolute privilege that arises with legal advice privilege: for example, information held by personnel consultants (*New Victoria Hospital v Ryan* [1993] ICR 201) and industrial relations consultants (*M and W Grazebrook Ltd v Wallens* [1973] 2 All ER 868).

More recently in the *RBS Rights Issue Litigation* [2016] EWHC 3161 (Ch), the court has put a narrow interpretation on who can be considered to be a lawyer's client for the purposes of legal advice privilege. In this case it was held that notes taken of employee interviews during internal investigations by the bank did not attract legal advice privilege. This will have implications for lawyers in providing legal advice when conducting investigations unless litigation is imminent. Care is, therefore, required in any investigation if privilege might be important.

16.9.2.2 Litigation privilege

Legal advice privilege does not, however, protect third-party communications—that is, a communication between either a client or his lawyer and a third party, such as a factual or expert witness. The latter privilege can only be protected within litigation privilege, and for that to arise, litigation must be pending or contemplated. A further distinction is that, where litigation privilege is being claimed but the document had more than one purpose, the courts will look at the dominant purpose of the document to determine whether litigation privilege applies. The 'dominant' purpose of the document must be to prepare for the litigation in progress or in contemplation.

Provided that the communication is made with one of the following as its sole or dominant purpose in relation to the actual litigation in process or in contemplation, the document will be privileged:

- giving advice or

- obtaining evidence or

- collecting evidence.

Once established as this, litigation privilege will attach to the communications themselves (for example, the letter of instruction to the expert, although this will be lost if that party intends to use that expert to give evidence at the trial of the action), the documents or materials used to provide the advice (unless those documents are already out in the open and no longer confidential), and the documents generated from the communications—that is, the reports that are prepared.

The 'dominant purpose' test is one of dominance and not exclusivity. Documents are frequently brought into existence for more than one purpose, and close scrutiny of the purpose of the existence of the document will be made by the court to determine its 'dominant purpose'. The actual wording in the document may not be conclusive so, for example, if the document states on it that it was for the particular purpose of enabling litigation advice to be given, or was for another unrelated main purpose, the courts will look beyond the stated purpose of the document to determine its 'dominant' purpose.

The leading decision in seeking to define the 'dominant purpose' test is still *Waugh v British Railways Board* [1980] AC 521. The case involved the preparation of statements after a fatal rail accident. The courts decided that in order for litigation privilege to attach to a document, it must satisfy the 'sole dominant purpose' test. If the purposes for which the document were of equal weight, then the privilege would not attach. This decision has had significant repercussions for all compliance investigations, because as a result of the conclusions of this case, much of the collected material from enquiries and investigations will not attract litigation privilege. And it may not attract legal advice privilege as a result of the decision in *Three Rivers (No 5)*. In *Axa Seguros SA De CV v Allianz Insurance plc & Ors* [2011] EWHC 268 (Comm), the court again considered the extent and impact of the 'dominant purpose' test—and here concluded that the engineering reports in question had two purposes, one of which was to determine whether the highways in question had been constructed to internationally accepted standards. They concluded that the 'dominant purpose' test was not satisfied sufficiently to secure a finding of privilege. The test to claim litigation privilege is a high one and was restated recently in the case of *Tchenguiz & Anor v Rawlinson & Hunter Trustees SA & Others* [2013] EWHC 2297 (QB). In this case, the judge emphasized that the mere fact that a document is produced for the purpose of obtaining information or advice in connection with pending or contemplated litigation, or of conducting or aiding in the conduct of such litigation, is *not* sufficient for a claim to litigation privilege—it is only if that was the 'dominant' purpose of the document's creation.

The burden of proof in a claim for litigation privilege rests with the party seeking to assert privilege.

 Practical Considerations

Advising clients in this area is fraught with uncertainties and difficulties. It is important to give advice concerning the existence or not of 'privilege' to a document only after careful thought and research. Problems tend to arise in relation to documents not privileged in themselves and collected from the client or third parties, or copied during the course of preparing for litigation. The 'start point' for your considerations will be that all documents that are within the definition of standard disclosure or within the definition of any specific disclosure order that has been made, and that have, at any time, been within the client's control are to be disclosed and available for inspection *unless* privilege is available (or there is some other reason why it would be wrong to make it available—for example, that it is disproportionate to do so). The mere fact that the client seeks legal advice or that the document has been assembled for litigation does not cloak all otherwise unprivileged documents with privilege.

'Litigation' in this context means proceedings before the courts, but also before arbitrators and tribunals when exercising judicial functions. Thus, it will probably not apply in forums that are designed to be 'fact-finding', or those that are not 'adversarial'. Litigation privilege can normally be claimed in proceedings in which a judicial function is being exercised, but if the proceedings are merely fact-finding (for example, an inquiry under the Banking Acts—see the *Three Rivers* case again) or the tribunal has an administrative function, it is unlikely that litigation privilege can arise. The distinction is a fine one, because often an inquiry or inquest will result in litigation once the inquiry or tribunal has reached its conclusions.

The main difference between the two types of legal professional privilege is that litigation privilege enables the client or the lawyer to communicate under the protection of privilege with a third party, but is confined to situations in which litigation is in process (or contemplated). Legal advice privilege does not. On the other hand, legal advice privilege applies to communications between client and lawyer that may relate to both contentious and non-contentious matters.

Because legal professional privilege is a substantive right, it can be asserted in any situation and regardless of how old the document is (see *Calcraft v Guest* [1898] 1 QB 759, in which documents that were a hundred years old were still privileged).

Practical Considerations

When advising clients of their disclosure obligations and the existence of legal professional privilege, it is important that both you and the client have an understanding of the consequences of actions taken. Being over-efficient can sometimes have unexpected and unwanted consequences, so, for example, take care in gathering evidence too early. If evidence is gathered before there is any reasonable prospect of litigation, then only 'legal advice' will be protected by privilege. Conversely, sending off a 'letter before action' or an early notice letter too early can equally have the effect of covering all of your opponent's 'fact-finding' steps as 'evidence gathering' covered by litigation privilege.

16.9.3 WHAT HAPPENS IF DOCUMENTS ARE 'COMMUNICATED' BY A PARTY WITHIN ITS ORGANIZATION?

So what happens if documents are communicated by a party within its own organization? Will this result in the document no longer being 'confidential' and no longer capable of attracting privilege?

where client = corporate entity

The *Three Rivers* litigation has placed important practical limitations on the scope and availability of legal advice privilege where the client instructing the legal representative is a corporate entity (or similar). In *Three Rivers (No 5)*, the Court of Appeal decided that, in such circumstances, the client is not the corporate entity itself, but a narrow group of individuals employed by the entity charged with seeking and receiving legal advice on its behalf. Others outside this group of individuals who make communications related to the legal advice run the risk of exposing those communications, because they will not attract legal advice privilege (and they may not fit the criteria of litigation privilege either). This position applies even in relation to documents generated by employees (who are outside the group of employees defined as 'the client') that are necessary to provide information to the lawyers to advise (although here litigation privilege may apply).

Practical Considerations

Because of the practical effects of *Three Rivers*, there is a view that dissemination of advice given by the legal representative to others within the corporate entity should be made subject to appropriate confidentiality obligations. Consider whether your clients should be asked to exercise caution and accompany such notes disseminating legal advice with words such as 'privileged' or 'this communication does not amount to a waiver of privilege', and ask for an acknowledgement that the information will be held in confidence.

Designating the whole workforce of the organization as 'the client' is very unlikely to work; nor does it seem to be an answer to channel all communications through the in-house lawyer. Equally, it is impractical to construct an 'inner client' for every single legal issue that confronts any large entity. These very real problems, only very briefly highlighted here and the in-depth study of which is outside the scope of this book, are set out to alert any practising legal representative of the extent of the knowledge that they must have to advise clients about the complex issues of disclosure and privilege.

16.9.4 OTHER TYPES OF RELEVANT PRIVILEGE

16.9.4.1 Common interest privilege

Common interest privilege is a relatively new variant of legal advice privilege. It operates to preserve privilege in documents that are disclosed to third parties. It may occur in group actions, or in cases in which there is more than one claimant or defendant—that is, situations in which the group (who may not be parties to the action) or co-litigants have the same self-interest. All of these parties may collect information for the purposes of the litigation, and all may take copies of documents and relevant information.

The privilege is applied as follows: if party A has a sufficiently common interest in communications that are held by party B, then party A can obtain disclosure of those communications from party B even though, as against third parties, the communications would be privileged from production. In *Buttes Gas and Oil Co v Hammer (No 3)* [1981] QB 223, Lord Denning MR concluded that, for the purposes of disclosure, the court should treat all of the persons interested as if they were partners in a single firm. Each can avail himself of the privilege. Where common interest privilege applies, the document remains privileged in the hands of the recipient. The recipient can assert the disclosing party's privilege as against the world. For common interest privilege to be asserted, the common interest between the communicators must have existed at the time of disclosure between them. The principle of common interest privilege can apply in both arms of legal professional privilege: legal advice privilege and litigation privilege. Guidance as to when common interest privilege arises was given more recently in *Winterthur Swiss Insurance Company and Anor v AG (Manchester) Ltd and Ors* [2006] EWHC 839 (Comm).

Common interest privilege could be used as a 'sword' (to obtain disclosure), as well as a 'shield' (to prevent disclosure). It has been held to apply between companies in a group, insurer and insured, and agent and principal. However, the case law remains uncertain, and each situation needs to be considered on its own merits.

 Practical Considerations

Because the case law is relatively uncertain in this quite modern form of privilege, it is best to be cautious when considering or advising clients about the disclosure of documents to third parties who could be considered to have a 'common interest'. If in doubt, consider disclosure only on the basis of express contractual undertakings that privilege in the document is not being waived.

16.9.4.2 Joint interest

Where a third party can establish a joint interest with another, then even though there is no confidentiality between them, each can assert joint privilege if they should subsequently fall out. That joint privilege enables each to assert the privilege against the 'rest of them', and, importantly, the privilege arising can only be jointly, not severally, waived. In situations in which joint privilege arises, documents can be shared between the parties without the risk that they have waived privilege by making the documents no longer 'confidential' by their exchanges. It also means that neither party can assert privilege against the other in respect of the communications between them (before they fell out). It also means that neither will be able to deny the other the right to access to the documents held by the other. As stated earlier, both can assert the privilege to prevent disclosure to others.

Examples of joint privilege have been held to arise in a subsequent conflict of interest arising between beneficiaries and trustees, a company and its shareholders, partners, and a parent company and its subsidiaries.

16.9.4.3 The privilege against self-incrimination

A person is entitled to refuse to give evidence or disclose information if the revelation of the information would have the effect of increasing the likelihood of his being prosecuted for a criminal offence or being subjected to a penalty. This privilege, or right, can be asserted at any stage, including within the process of disclosure. It is an important facet of Art. 6 of the ECHR and the 'right to silence'.

It does not arise commonly, but may arise, for example, in a claim based on fraud or corruption. It could be assumed that it could commonly arise in many RTA claims when criminal proceedings (against a driver) often ensue, or in employer liability cases, but in these cases, the civil claim will usually get going after the conclusion of any criminal proceedings. It should be noted that any *relevant* criminal prosecutions that have been made may be stated in a party's case under the provision of s. 11 of the Civil Evidence Act 1968.

The right to withhold information that may have a tendency to incriminate is based on s. 14(1) of the 1968 Act. There are several exceptions to this right: under s. 31 of the Theft Act 1968, under s. 72 of the Senior Courts Act 1981, under s. 291 of the Insolvency Act 1986, and under s. 434 of the Companies Act 1985.

16.9.4.4 'Without prejudice' negotiations

It is within the spirit of the Woolf reforms for civil litigation and the ensuing CPR that every encouragement should be given to parties to settle their disputes. Any genuine attempt to settle proceedings will be regarded as 'without prejudice' and parties may not make any reference to those offers or concessions made in the action. Any such document or negotiation that meets the definition—a genuine attempt to settle the dispute or an issue within the dispute—will be 'without prejudice' even if it has not been marked 'without prejudice'. It is, however, always better to mark such letters, documents, and negotiations as 'without prejudice'. The principles established play an important role in the concept of protective offers on costs made within the provisions of CPR Part 36 (see Chapter 15).

The protection conferred by the 'without prejudice' principle means that neither party to the 'without prejudice' negotiations may put in evidence the content or detail, or the fact that an offer or concession has been made at all. This is provided that it was made:

- as part of attempts made in good faith to negotiate a settlement of the case or some of the issues, and
- expressly or impliedly 'without prejudice'.

This is also unless:

- all parties consent to revealing the existence of or detail of the negotiations;
- a concluded settlement is reached (that is, a new agreement is formed);
- it has been made 'save as to costs' (this applies whether or not it complies with CPR Part 36); and
- disclosure is sought by an individual who is not a party to the proceedings in which the negotiations took place.

However, in *EMW Law LLP v Scott Halborg* [2016] EWHC 2526 (Ch), it was held that where the documents—on which without prejudice privilege was being claimed—were relevant to an issue in dispute, they could be admitted into evidence where appropriate arrangements could be made to ensure that there was no prejudice to the parties who owned the privilege. This case shows that disclosure can be made for a limited purpose to a limited group of people. Therefore, not all documents marked 'without prejudice' will be protected from possible discosure in the future.

16.9.4.5 Public interest immunity

Under CPR 31.19, a party is entitled to 'withhold disclosure of a document on the ground that disclosure would damage the public interest'. This right is a form of privilege, and it is a right to withhold a document from disclosure itself, not just from withholding 'inspection' of a disclosed document. Its aim is to prevent disclosure of material that would harm the nation or the administration of justice.

Claims to withhold disclosure on this ground are relatively rare, and to apply it, a without-notice application must be made. Courts may adopt a more active role in monitoring the assertion of this right than they used to do and the court is required to carry out a balancing exercise to determine whether the 'public interest' identified by the party resisting disclosure outweighs the potential value that it may have for the party who would otherwise have access to it.

Public interest immunity differs from 'privilege' in that, once the public interest is established, the court has no choice and the document must not be disclosed.

16.9.5 LOSS OF PRIVILEGE, WAIVER OF PRIVILEGE, AND REFERENCE TO PRIVILEGED DOCUMENTS

There are no definitive rules setting out the circumstances in which privilege may be lost. Usually, for privilege in a document to be lost, some act must have occurred that results in an implied or actual loss of the right. Thus, enabling inspection of a previously privileged and 'withheld from inspection' document will usually result in the right of privilege being lost. This can happen because of a deliberate intention to waive privilege, or it may happen because of an accident: for example, if the document is inadvertently referred to in a statement of case, or inadvertently made available for inspection. Privilege may also be lost if the document becomes no longer 'confidential'. Privilege may be lost if it is necessary to refer to the privileged document in order to establish a claim or defence.

Whenever a document is referred to in a statement of case, witness statement, or affidavit, any privilege attached to it may be lost. CPR 31.14 deals with applications for inspection of documents (or categories of documents) referred to in a witness statement. The case of *W M Morrison Supermarkets plc & Others v Mastercard & Others* [2013] EWHC 2500 (Comm) provides a useful example of the court's approach to such applications, and highlights that the decision whether to order inspection will be a matter for judicial discretion and subject to whether it is in the interests of justice and the overriding objectives. It must also be borne in mind that the court may permit redacting from a document being disclosed that contains privileged material in part of it. If a document is inadvertently included or referred to, it will usually be possible to retain the privilege, provided that the party ceases to rely on the document.

Service of an expert report waives privilege in the report and in documents referred to in it. Experts' reports are not disclosed subject to any confidentiality. Therefore, privilege cannot be claimed in any subsequent action against a third party.

 Practical Considerations

The whole arena of 'experts' and the 'instructions given to an expert' within the context of disclosure and privilege is complex. Often, litigation requires both expert guidance (for the party preparing his case) and expert opinion for the court. In exceptional cases at trial, two experts could be retained: one to provide advice, and one to provide the expert evidence for the court. However, where this is not economic or practicable, consideration needs to be given to the issues surrounding disclosure and privilege. For the expert's report, as a CPR Part 35 expert, the content of the instructions to that expert will form part of the documentation that is to be disclosed; so too will the information on which the expert has relied to prepare his report, which may include information, instructions, and discussions that he had *before* he was retained as the CPR Part 35 expert and when he was only giving 'advice' to the party in the preparation of his case. Guidance has been given by the Court of Appeal in *Lucas v Barking, Havering & Redbridge Hospitals NHS Trust* [2003] EWCA Civ 1102.

16.9.6 THE INADVERTENT DISCLOSURE OF PRIVILEGED MATERIAL

CPR 31.20 provides the court with discretion to consider the position of privileged documentation being inadvertently revealed to an opposing party. In general, it provides that the court will consider the nature of the material inadvertently disclosed and decide whether to grant permission for it to be used by the party who has seen it. A full discussion of the factors that the court will take into account in deciding whether to grant permission or not is set out in the Court of Appeal's judgment in *Al Fayed v Commissioner of Police of the Metropolis* [2002] EWCA Civ 780.

ADR considerations

In large commercial cases, the whole process of disclosure and inspection can be challenging, time-consuming, and expensive. After inspection of documents, it is often a good time to take stock of where you are in the litigation and consider what you are trying to achieve for your client. It is all too easy to become embroiled in expensive arguments over privilege and lose sight of your client's goals (which may change as the case progresses), but you must remain in 'tune' with the overriding objectives. Consideration should, therefore, be given to whether it is an appropriate time to enter into an ADR process (see the 'litigation train' diagram at the beginning of this chapter).

16.10 PRE-ACTION DISCLOSURE—CPR 31.16

Pre-action disclosure applications are contained in Chapter 14 at paragraph 14.6.

16.11 DISCLOSURE AGAINST NON-PARTIES

It must be noted that an application for pre-action disclosure under the provisions of CPR 31.16 is only available against a person who is likely to become a party to proceedings. An order to disclose may be available against persons who are not parties to the proceedings under the provisions of CPR 31.17 in:

- *Norwich Pharmacal* orders;
- freezing injunctions;
- search orders;
- applications for the preservation of property;
- *Bankers Trust* orders; and
- requests for further information under the provisions of CPR 18.

Again, this substantive application is outside the scope of this book.

16.12 THE NEW DISCLOSURE PILOT SCHEME

The pilot disclosure scheme commenced in the Business and Property Courts on 1 January 2019, this does not include proceedings in the County Court. The pilot will run for two years from that date and will apply to new proceedings in certain Business and Property Courts of England and Wales. The extent of the pilot should be checked by any High Court user as some Courts and claims do not fall within the scheme. Further details can be found at PD51U.

16.12.1 KEY POINTS OF THE NEW RULES

The rationale for the pilot scheme is to reduce the burden and therefore, the cost of disclosure. It is intended that documentation to be disclosed is to be kept only to that which is strictly relevant.

The stages are as follows:

- Duties in relation to disclosure;
- Preservation of documents;
- Initial disclosure;
- The extended disclosure models.

16.12.1.1 Duties in relation to disclosure

A party should be warned that if they are a party in proceedings or are to be a party involved in proceedings that they should take reasonable steps to preserve documentation. Once proceedings have commenced any party with adverse documentation must disclose this regardless of any order for disclosure. Orders for disclosure should be complied with and parties are under a duty to carry out any reasonable search in a responsible and consciencious manner. There is also a duty to act honestly both when giving disclosure and reviewing disclosure by another party. There is a positive duty to avoid providing documents that have no relevance, thereby reducing excessive documentation.

A legal representative has a positive duty to the Court to take reasonable steps to preserve documents within their control that may be relevant to any issue in proceedings. They must also take reasonable steps to advise and assist the party to comply with their duty of disclosure. They must liaise and cooperate with the other parties, act honestly in relation to giving disclosure, reviewing disclosure and to undertake a review to satisfy themselves that any claim by the party to privilege is properly claimed and explained. Importantly, where there is a known adverse document that has not been located, the duty is met by that fact being disclosed.

16.12.1.2 Preservation of documents

There is a positive duty to preserve documents that may otherwise be deleted in the normal course of business. This duty ensures that there is an obligation to suspend any documents that may be part of a documentation deletion or destruction processes. There is also an obligation to send written notification to relevant employees, former employees, agents, and third parties for any documents they may hold and that should not be destroyed or deleted.

Legal representatives must within a reasonable period of being instructed, notify their clients of the need to preserve documentation, even if litigation is not yet commenced but is contemplated. Written confirmation will need to be obtained that they have taken steps to suspend document deletion or destruction, inform relevant employees and former employees, agents, and third parties. This must be confirmed in writing when serving particulars of claim or defence that steps have been taken to preserve relevant documentation.

16.12.1.3 Initial disclosure

Parties must provide in their statement of case an intial disclosure list of key documents. These are the doucments that they will rely upon to support their case. This is known as the initial disclosure stage. However, it may not be required in some circumstances where the parties have disposed of it, or the court has dispensed with it, or it would mean more than 1000 pages or 200 documents (whichever greater). There is at this stage no obligation to carry out a search.

16.12.1.4 The extended disclosure models

Within 28 days of the filing of the final statement of case, parties must indicate in writing whether they seek any additional disclosure, known as extended disclosure. If the parties do not require extended disclosure, the disclosure for the case will amount to the initial disclosure and any adverse documentation.

Where a party seeks additional disclosure after intitial dislosure, or where intitial disclosure did not take place, extended disclosure must be requested. This will be in line with one of the models listed below.

The following is an overview of the extended disclosure models, a revised Disclosure Menu comprising of five models:

Model A 'Disclosure confined to known adverse documents'—the previous model 'No order for disclosure' is re-named to emphasize that the obligation to disclose known adverse documents will always apply.

Model B 'Limited Disclosure', consisting of known adverse documents, plus Initial Disclosure to the extent this has not already taken place

Model C 'Request-led search-based disclosure', consisting of known adverse documents plus documents specifically requested by another party

Model D 'Narrow search-based disclosure', broadly equivalent to the current 'standard disclosure' model in which a party discloses all documents that either support or are adverse to its own case or another party's case

Model E 'Wide search-based disclosure', consisting of all standard disclosure documents, plus 'train of enquiry' documents that may lead to the identification of further documents for disclosure; reserved for exceptional circumstances and anticipated to be used most commonly in fraud cases.

Parties must then agree a list of issues for disclosure and decide which extended disclosure models are required. A disclosure review document is completed by the parties and reviewed by the court. If they require request-led searches, that is to say any of the extended disclosure models C–E, parties should complete a questionnaire which can be found within the second part of the disclosure review document. Parties can request a disclosure guidance hearing if they are unable to resolve disputes between themselves or it may take place within the case management conference.

KEY POINTS SUMMARY

- Consideration of the documents necessary to a case should be undertaken at the earliest opportunity.

- The legal representative's duties in relation to disclosure are onerous. 'Retained' clients should be given general advice about their disclosure obligations in litigation, and all new clients should be advised of their obligations for any ensuing litigation.

- Ensure that the client is told, and understands, what disclosure means and that the client understands the key message not to destroy documents that might be relevant to the matters in issue, not to create new documents without consideration of the disclosure obligations, and not to ask third parties to send you documents or to send documents out to others without consideration of the disclosure obligations.

- Not disclosing a document means not listing it. A failure to do this can be serious, because the 'cards on the table' approach to litigation is entrenched within the CPR.

- Not permitting inspection means listing a document and putting your opponent on notice that it exists, but, for the reason claimed, withholding it.

- Ensure that the 'appropriate person' in the client's organization signs the disclosure statement.

- Carry out 'inspection', and make a thorough and careful review of the opponent's list.

- Challenge grounds to withhold from inspection or challenge the substance of an opponent's list when it is proportionate, fair, and just to do so.

- Treat the use of privilege with respect. It is a complex area of litigation, and if in any doubt on any aspect of privilege, then seek advice from a more experienced colleague.

Case Study *Andrew James Pike v Deep Builders Ltd*

Acting for the defendant, assume that it is 16 December 20?? and that you are a trainee with the defendant's solicitors. You have just received the letter dated 14 December 20?? from LPC & Co, enclosing the claimant's list of documents.

Question 1

What directions orders could be made in this case? When do they come into effect? When is there a duty to give disclosure? Which documents do you have to disclose, but not allow inspection of?

Question 2

Draft a letter replying to the letter dated 14 December 20?? You will, of course, need to consider whether there are any documents that you would wish to see and would want to ask the other side for.

 Any documents referred to in these case study questions can be found in the online resources—simply click on 'Case study documentation' to access the documents that you need for Chapter 16 and to be reminded of the questions. The suggested answer to these self-test question can be accessed in the Student Resources section of the online resources.

FIGURE 16.1 LITIGATION PRIVILEGE AND ADVICE PRIVILEGE FLOW CHART

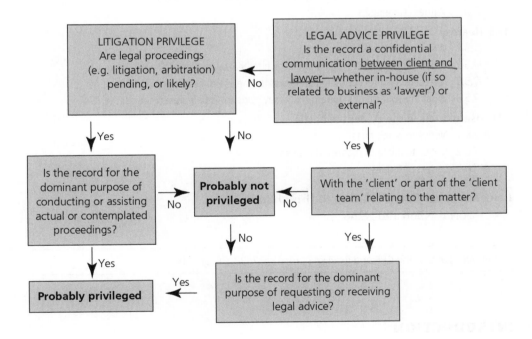

17 WITNESS STATEMENTS AND DOCUMENTARY EVIDENCE

Relevant court forms relating to this chapter:
- Forms N266 and N268

Relevant parts of the CPR and its PDs: 3, 13, 22, 32, 33, 35, and 44.

17.1 INTRODUCTION

A case can readily be won or lost on the strength of witness evidence at trial. Similarly, important applications may fail if a witness statement does not adequately deal with all of the issues. A legal representative must, therefore, understand both the underlying theory behind the use of witness evidence and documentation during the course of litigation, including the rules on hearsay, as well as the practical requirements and challenges encountered in the preparation of witness statements.

LITIGATION TRAIN: WITNESS STATEMENTS AND DOCUMENTARY EVIDENCE

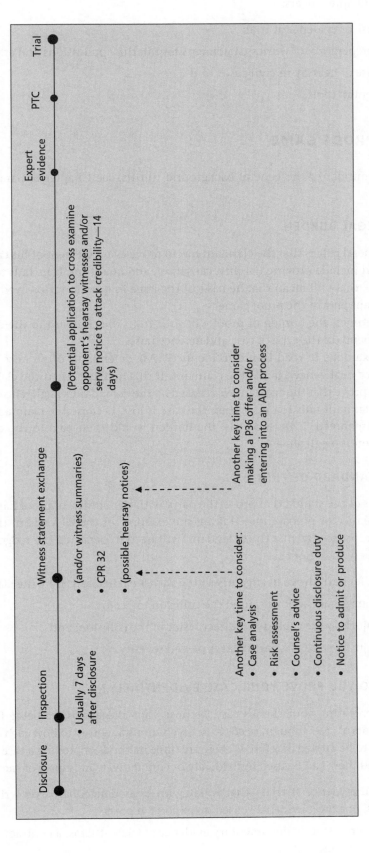

The relevant parts of the CPR are Parts 32 and 33. The governing statute is the Civil Evidence Act 1995.

This chapter covers:

- the use of evidence at trial;
- the preparation of witness statements for interim applications and at trial;
- the use of hearsay in civil cases; and
- evidential tools.

17.2 THE PROOF GAME

As a reminder of the general background to this, see Chapter 6, paragraphs 6.4.2.3 and 6.4.3.6.

17.2.1 THE LEGAL BURDEN

The general rule is that the claimant has to prove every element of his case. In most claims, this will include proving liability, causation, and quantum. If he fails to prove any part of his case, that will mean that he has lost the issue in question. However, what part does the defendant play in the proof game?

Sometimes, the burden of proof will shift from the claimant to the defendant, and this will depend on the type of case and defence raised.

For example, in road traffic accidents (RTAs), defendants often raise allegations of contributory negligence against the claimant. If this happens, then the claimant will initially have to prove that the accident was caused by the defendant's negligence (primary liability). If the claimant fails to do so, then the case is lost, because the claimant's burden has not been discharged. If he succeeds, the burden would then pass to the defendant to prove contributory negligence.

17.2.2 THE STANDARD OF PROOF

In terms of the standard of proof, the party with the burden of proof has to prove his claim on a balance of probabilities. Taking the example of the RTA again, the claimant, when proving his case against the defendant, will need to persuade the judge at trial that it was more likely than not that:

- the defendant drove negligently in the way(s) particularized by the claimant;
- those negligent actions caused the collision to occur;
- the injuries were caused as a direct result of the collision; and
- the injuries were of a particular type and severity.

17.2.3 HOW DO YOU PROVE YOUR CASE EVIDENTIALLY?

When preparing your client's case, because your allegations are being formulated in your statements of case, thought needs to be given simultaneously to how each of those allegations is going to be proved or refuted. There are three methods of proving a case evidentially, as follows, and these can be used individually or cumulatively in respect of each allegation made:

- by oral evidence at trial—that is, lay witness evidence, based on written witness statements, or expert evidence, based on experts' reports;
- by the provision of documentary evidence at trial—that is, a contract, expert's report, or hospital notes; and/or
- by real evidence being available at trial—for example, a faulty machine or defective car.

However, as can be seen from paragraph 17.3, the court can control whether or not you are allowed to use a type of evidence at trial. This chapter concentrates on lay witness evidence and documentary evidence. (For a discussion of the use of expert evidence, see Chapter 18.)

17.2.4 THE CONCEPT OF PROPORTIONALITY AND WITNESS EVIDENCE

The concept of proportionality may influence the decisions that you make concerning the collection of witness evidence. The lower the 'value' of the action, the more likely it will be that you will have to undertake some considered 'pruning' of the numbers of witnesses that you wish to use. This will be more prevalent with the proportionality test in CPR 44.3(5). Please see Chapter 4, paragraph 4.3.2.4.

17.3 CAN ALL TYPES OF EVIDENCE BE USED AT TRIAL?

A party to litigation is at liberty to obtain any type of evidence to prove or disprove the case against him. However, whether that party will be permitted to use and rely on that evidence at trial will depend on mandatory requirements and the court's discretion.

17.3.1 EVIDENCE THAT MUST BE EXCLUDED

In your early practice as a legal representative, it is unlikely that any of these exclusionary rules will be problematic. However, you are required to know that the following categories of evidence cannot be used or relied upon at trial:

- irrelevant evidence, such as some similar fact evidence and previous judgments or convictions;
- opinion evidence, except from that of an expert in his field;
- privileged evidence;
- without prejudice communication (this includes any Part 36 offers); and
- evidence protected by public interest immunity.

(See Chapter 16 for a fuller discussion on privileged evidence, without prejudice communications, and public interest immunity.)

17.3.2 EVIDENCE THAT MAY BE EXCLUDED

The court has a discretion to exclude evidence that is ordinarily admissible and its powers to do so are derived from the CPR. The most common areas are as follows:

- The court's discretionary powers under CPR 32.10, CPR 32.12, and CPR 35.13, regarding lay and expert witness evidence, respectively, permit the court to exclude the use of oral witness evidence at trial, and to rely on experts' reports and oral testimony at trial. Therefore, where the party wanting to use the evidence has failed to disclose it in accordance with directions set by the court, the court can exclude it altogether.
- The court's powers under CPR 32.1 are general and far-reaching, to the extent that the court can exclude evidence that would otherwise be admissible—for example, a second witness statement attesting to the same facts as appear in another witness statement obtained by you.
- The court's case management powers specifically under CPR 3.1(2)(m) mean that the court can take any other step or make any other order for the purpose of managing the case and furthering the overriding objective.

> ✓ **Practical Considerations**
>
> In practice, you are far more likely to have material evidence excluded as a result of the court exercising its discretion under any one of these parts of the CPR. It is, therefore, advisable to raise the admissibility issue with your client before you incur the fee or cost of obtaining the evidence, so that he is aware that there is a possibility that the court may disallow it.

17.4 WITNESS STATEMENTS

This section deals with some early considerations of which a legal representative should be aware in order to ensure that witness statements are well prepared and presented in the correct format, whether the statements are for use at an interim hearing, at which the witness is not generally required to attend, or for use at trial, at which the witness is obliged to attend.

17.4.1 WITNESS STATEMENT OR AFFIDAVIT?

In most aspects of High Court and County Court litigation, evidence at interim hearings and at trial is given by way of witness statements. However, Practice Direction (PD) 32.1.4 sets out the occasions on which an affidavit must be used—most notably, in applications for search and freezing orders, parts of insolvency proceedings, and in applications for contempt of court. These applications fall outside the scope of this book (but see the Additional Chapter 'Injunctions and Other Equitable Remedies' in the online resources).

17.4.2 WITNESS STATEMENTS FOR TRIAL

17.4.2.1 First steps

The preparatory work that is needed to prepare an effective witness statement of fact for trial starts well in advance of the issue of proceedings. For example, if you act for the claimant, you will want to obtain a proof of evidence (a 'warts and all' record of what was first said by your client or witness, including a full commentary on any documents) to help you to draft your letter of claim and statement of case. Conversely, if you act for the defendant, you will require your client's proof of evidence to assist in the response to the letter of claim and the preparation of the defence. The importance of drafting the witness statements for a trial that do include the evidence the case has been set down to prove is vital. The recent case of *Clutterbuck & Paton v Cleghorn* [2018] EWHC 2125 (Ch) is a helpful reminder that litigants must closely examine their case and what evidence they require to substantiate it.

Such steps should be taken prior to issuing the claim. If litigants do not have their house in order at the start of the trial, then the Court is highly unlikely to permit that party to take late steps to address that, as it could result in de-railing the trial. This would mean that the gaping evidential holes cannot be plugged and the case is highly likely to fail.

17.4.2.2 Preparing the witness statement

With this in mind, once you are in a position to commence the preparation of the witness statements for trial, which may be many months after you have taken the proof, there are a number of important points to note, as follows:

- You only need to refer to facts that are in issue. Therefore, review the statements of case, and assess which facts are agreed and which are not agreed.

- Decide which party has the burden of proving those facts.

- Assess which witness(es) can prove which facts, and if there is more than one, assess which witness is in the best position to prove the fact in issue.

- If you have not already made contact with a witness, do so, explaining who you are, who you represent, and why you would like to speak to them.

- Arrange a meeting and send any key documents in advance.

- At the meeting, let the witness tell his story and take him through the relevant documents, ensuring that you ask questions to clarify his evidence.

- After the meeting, prepare the witness statement as soon as possible. This must be in the witness's own words, not yours. The statement may take some careful drafting to achieve this. Remember that the witness can be cross-examined on any part of his witness statement and so be sure how the witness would respond on cross-examination.

- Send the statement in draft to the witness, with a covering letter inviting him to make any amendments, approve, and sign the statement of truth. This may need to be explained to the witness.

Practical Considerations

The witness statement may need to be passed between the witness and yourself many times before it is finalized. Once a final draft has been signed, create a witness statement section in your paper or electronic file. Any witness who is not your client may have no interest in the outcome of the trial, and so treat them with respect and keep them fully informed of their impending attendance at trial. There is no 'property' in a witness; therefore, you may approach any witness who has already been approached by your opponent, asking them to talk to you and to provide a witness statement. Whilst interviewing the witness, it would, therefore, not be sensible to give the witness a view of the merits of the case or details of your tactics. However, you must never try to persuade the witness to change his evidence. There may be a risk, if you do decide to interview your opponent's witness, that such allegations will be made. Therefore, to avoid this, either record the interview or ask the other side to attend.

Practical Considerations

Discuss with your client, at the outset of the claim or defence of the claim, which facts need to be proved and how. If your client is to give evidence in the form of a witness statement, then he should be aware of the fact that his statement will contain a statement of truth. Remember that a list of witnesses and the facts/issues to which they will be attesting is to be inserted in the Directions Questionnaire, although, in practice, it is often too soon to have the identities of all of your witnesses at this early stage. The more up-to-date list of witnesses will go in section B of the pre-trial checklist.

17.4.2.3 Formatting the witness statement

Every witness statement must contain certain information to make it compliant with CPR 32 and its Practice Direction. If it is not in the required form, then, in accordance with PD 32.25.1, the court may disallow the use of the evidence and the costs arising from it. It is, therefore, important that you are aware of these basic formalities that appear in PD 32.17–20, starting from the beginning of the statement as follows:

1. The top right-hand corner of the witness statement must include five points and these are usually numbered for ease:

    (a) the party on whose behalf the statement is made;

    (b) the initials and surname of the actual witness;

    (c) the number of the statement for that particular witness in the litigation—that is, is it the first statement, second statement, etc.;

    (d) the initials of the witness and the number of exhibits attached to the statement;

    (e) the date on which the statement was made; and

    (f) the date of any translation.

2. The statement must be headed with the title of the action. This can be obtained from an indorsed claim form or the particulars of claim. The heading stays the same even if, for example, it is the defendant who makes the interim application.

3. The statement should set out in heading form, usually in bold, the full name of the witness. This is helpful to the parties to the action and the court when sifting through large numbers of statements, because it makes it easily identifiable.

4. The maker of the statement must then set out his name (again), address, occupation, and whether he is a party to the proceedings or employed by a party to the proceedings.

5. Numbered paragraphs must also be used throughout.

6. The statement will be in the first person.

7. A standard introductory paragraph must be used for all witness statements for trial and includes the following:

   (a) who the maker of the statement is in relation to the claimant or defendant, if not a party to the action;

   (b) that the witness, if not a party to the action, has authority to make the statement on behalf of that party—remembering that, if a party is a limited company, it will always need a representative to speak for it and so 'the authority point' will need to be dealt with;

   (c) the witness must declare that the information he will give in the statement is either from his own knowledge and are matters of information or belief, or from the source stated (and then, when appropriate, to say in the statement the source of a particular fact—that is, 'I am informed by xxx that …').

8. As from April 2020, all witness statements are required to state the process by which it has been prepared, for example, face-to-face, over the telephone and/or through an interpreter (PD32.18.1(5)). This rule was introduced during the coronavirus pandemic when social isolation was in force and statements could not be taken face-to-face.

9. Also from April 2020, is a new requirement that a witness statement must be drafted in the witness' own language. If a witness statement is to be translated, the translator must sign the original statement and certify that the translation is accurate.

10. A statement of truth must conclude the witness statement as required by CPR PD 22.2: 'I believe that the facts stated in this witness statement are true. I understand that proceedings for contempt of court may be brought against anyone who makes, or causes to be made, a false statement in a document verified by a statement of truth without an honest belief in its truth'. Alternatively, a better and more complete statement of truth can be:

'I have care and conduct of this matter and am duly authorized to make this statement on behalf of the Claimant/Defendant. Save where otherwise stated, the facts and matters I address in this witness statement are within my own personal knowledge, or obtained from information supplied to me by the Claimant/Defendant including by the documents referenced in this statement. Where the facts and matters referred to in this witness statement are within my own knowledge they are true. Where they are not within my own knowledge they are true to the best of my knowledge, information and belief. I understand that proceedings for contempt of court may be brought against anyone who makes, or causes to be made, a false statement in a document verified by a statement of truth without an honest belief in its truth.'

The statement of truth must be dated and be in the witness' own language.

New rules introduced in April 2020 require the solicitor to explain the importance of the statement of truth, through an interpreter if necessary.

The importance of a legal representative's compliance with these rules is paramount. The High Court has criticized witness statements for failing to state that the witness was speaking from his own knowledge, the source of the information, and the relevant facts. In the case of *Brownlie v Four Seasons Holdings Inc* [2014] EWHC 273 (QB), the court indicated that it was unacceptable for legal representatives to breach the rules and directed that in such circumstances, an application for permission to file a defective witness statement under PD 32.25.2 should have been made along with a detailed explanation as to the need for such an application. Otherwise, the statement should not have been filed at all, as non-compliant statements waste time and costs, and could attract sanctions.

17.4.3 WITNESS STATEMENTS FOR INTERIM APPLICATIONS

In order to be successful at an interim hearing, you will need to prepare evidence to prove your case. This very often takes the form of a witness statement. The party making the application is called the 'applicant' and the party opposing the application is known as the 'respondent' (but they may also be referred to as if 'claimant' or 'defendant' is their title in the action). Many of the points in paragraph 17.4.2.3 also apply to witness statements prepared for interim applications. However, there are also a number of additional considerations. It may also be helpful to refer to Chapters 13 and 14 when considering the drafting of witness statements for interim applications.

17.4.3.1 Preparing the witness statement

17.4.3.1.1 *Facts or submissions*

Whatever type of interim application you are preparing for or opposing, it is very likely that you will be outlining facts to the court at the hearing, having regard to the order that you are asking the court to make or oppose. You will also be making written submissions in relation to your legal arguments to be put to the court to persuade the district judge or master to grant or dismiss the order.

For example, if you act for a defendant who has had default judgment entered correctly against him in an alleged debt action, an application to have that judgment set aside under CPR 13.3 can be made on his behalf. A factual background will need to be set out in the witness statement to highlight the fact that the defendant does not believe it to be an undisputed debt case, but a contested dispute. Those facts can then be drawn upon when the written submissions are made in relation to the requirements of CPR 13.3.1 being 'a real prospect of successfully defending the claim', or 'another good reason why the defendant should be allowed to defend the claim'. In essence, there must be a marrying up of the facts to the legal submissions (see Chapter 14 for further discussion).

17.4.3.1.2 *Who should make the statement?*

In light of the fact that an interim application is likely to contain both facts and submissions, you will need to give some thought as to in whose name the witness statement should be: you as the legal representative, the client, or another witness. This will depend on who is best placed to give first-hand evidence on the information that you intend to place before the court.

Where detailed legal submissions are to be made, it is more usual for the legal representative to make the witness statement, but this still leaves the problem of the factual submissions in relation to which the client or another witness may have first-hand knowledge. If this is the case, there are two options: either prepare two witness statements for the application, one being a factual statement for the client or witness, or a carefully worded statement from the legal representative covering both facts and submissions. The latter is the most common way of dealing with this problem and how to achieve this is highlighted here.

17.4.3.1.3 *Where the legal representative makes the statement*

The following important features will also need to be included where a legal representative makes the witness statement:

- In relation to the point made in paragraph 17.4.2.3, rather than state whether you are a party to the proceedings, it is more usual to state that you are the legal representative for the claimant or defendant, and include your firm's address.

- In addition to the points raised in paragraph 17.4.2.3, as a new legal practitioner, you are required to state that you 'have the care and conduct of the matter on behalf of the claimant (or defendant), subject to the supervision of [your] supervising partner'. Obviously, on qualification, the supervision point can be relinquished.

- It is important to remember that where you, as the legal practitioner, are making reference to the factual background to the case, you must use the words 'I am informed by ...', or 'the claimant/defendant has informed me that ...', to ensure that you are relaying the source of your knowledge to the court.

17.4.3.2 Formatting the witness statement

Much of paragraph 17.4.2.3 applies to witness statements for interim applications, but the following additional features should be noted:

- The second paragraph of the statement should inform the court of the purpose of your witness statement. As with the earlier example of the application to set aside default judgment, an appropriate sentence to achieve this would be: 'I make this statement in support of the defendant's application to have default judgment set aside.'

- In terms of formatting the structure to the statement, subheadings may be useful—especially to identify any relevant factual background and any legal submissions. Alternatively, when opposing an application, your witness statement in response may flow better if you respond to the witness statement in support, and, where appropriate, make additional relevant factual and legal arguments.

- It is helpful, when you come to making the written submissions in the statement, to state the part of the CPR (if there is a relevant part to your application) under which you are seeking the order, such as CPR 13.3.

- After the introductory statements and declaration of what the witness statement seeks to achieve (to make or oppose an application), it is usual for the applicant to set out a brief chronology of the relevant facts or the progress of the case. This should, in effect, make it clear that the application has been made at the correct time. Unless this is contested by the respondent to the application, the respondent will be able to agree this brief chronology.

- Once you have completed your submissions, conclude by repeating what it is that you are requesting: 'I therefore respectfully ask this honourable court to set aside default judgment in accordance with the terms of the draft order annexed to this application.'

- Finally, the statement of truth is as in paragraph 17.4.2.3, but because you are not a party to the action, this statement must be qualified with an authority sentence as follows: 'I am duly authorized to make this statement on behalf of the claimant/defendant ...'

 Practical Considerations

When setting out the persuasive elements of your client's case, you can be as articulate as you like, making reference to parts of the CPR. Here, you are seeking to persuade the district judge that he should make the order sought. The degree of persuasion needed may vary with the particular interim application or ground under the CPR on which the case relies. Another way to look at how these 'persuasive' elements of the witness statement should be drafted is to consider the discretion that the district judge or master has in relation to the application and, in effect, draft arguments that enable the district judge or master to make the order that you seek within the remit of his discretion.

Figure 17.1 at the end of this chapter is a template for a witness statement for an interim hearing.

17.4.4 EXHIBITS TO WITNESS STATEMENTS

A witness statement for trial or for an interim application can refer to documents. If this is the case, the documents must be exhibited to the witness statement. Reference to the number of exhibits is made at point (4) in the information given in the top right of the front page of the statement itself.

When referring to an exhibit in the body of the witness statement, the witness should state, 'I refer to [description of the document including a date] marked "TS 1/2/3 etc."'. Detailed provisions relating to exhibits can be found in PD 32.11–32.15. Each exhibit, or bundle of exhibits, should have a covering sheet featuring (or should have expressly written upon it) the court heading, the name of the witness, and that 'this is the exhibit marked "TS 1/2/3 etc." referred to in the statement of … '.

17.4.5 DISCLOSURE AND SERVICE OF WITNESS STATEMENTS

17.4.5.1 Witness evidence for trial

Witness statements for use at trial must be disclosed to your opponent (CPR 32.4), in default of which a party will be unable to rely on such evidence and call the witness to trial. The court has, unsurprisingly, a discretion to allow a party to rely on new evidence at trial even where that evidence has not been disclosed in accordance with the case management directions on exchange of witness statements. The criteria which must be satisfied for an application to rely on and adduce such evidence at trial is set out in *The Nottinghamshire and City of Nottingham Fire Authority v Gladman Commercial Properties* [2011] EWHC 1918 (C). The terminology for this is 'exchange of witness evidence'. This must be done in accordance with the directions laid down by the court as a result of the DQ or at a case management conference (CMC). As can be seen from Chapter 12, the usual order is for exchange of lay witness evidence, which should be mutual and simultaneous among all parties to an action, to be effected by 4 p.m. on a specified date. Sanctions are likely to apply if the deadline is missed.

Practical Considerations

Once you are ready to exchange witness statements, it is good practice to telephone or write to your opponent to confirm that you are in a position to exchange in accordance with the order of the court. If your opponent is also ready, then exchange can proceed, and both parties usually confirm during the telephone call or in the reciprocal letters when and how they will serve their witness statements: for example, by putting the statements in first-class post on a particular date.

Professional Conduct

If your opponent is not ready to exchange witness statements in accordance with the order given, with your client's instructions, you may wish to grant an extension of time, but you can only do so if the original order does not prohibit you from doing so. If you do agree to an extension, ensure that the revised date does not conflict with any other direction laid down by the court; do not serve your witness statements on your opponent, but either give them to the court to keep, or send in a sealed envelope to the opponent only to be opened when they have served theirs on you. If you were to serve your statements unilaterally, then your opponent would be given an unfair advantage in the final preparation of its own evidence. This may not be in your client's best interests (Principle 4). If you do not agree to an extension, then your opponent will be forced to make an application to the court for an extension of time.

17.4.5.2 Witness evidence for interim applications

Witness evidence in respect of interim applications is usually required to be unilaterally served either in accordance with the specific provisions of a part of the CPR, such as CPR 24, or if the CPR are silent on this, then the evidence should be served as soon as possible, but in any event at least three days before the hearing (CPR 23.7(1), (4), and (5)).

17.4.6 **WHAT DO YOU DO ON RECEIPT OF YOUR OPPONENT'S WITNESS EVIDENCE?**

17.4.6.1 Witness evidence for trial

This is probably one of the key points in litigation at which to reassess your client's claim by undertaking a file review and conducting a risk assessment. You should specifically look at:

- checking the statement is CPR 32 compliant;
- a review of the prospects of success;
- costs to witness exchange and on to trial;
- any additional evidence (lay, expert, or documentary), or investigations to deal with any issues raised on exchange of witness statements;
- dealing with any hearsay issues (see paragraph 17.5);
- making a Part 36 offer or revised Part 36 offer;
- requesting a stay for alternative dispute resolution (ADR);
- seeking counsel's opinion in writing or in conference; and
- strategy and tactics in moving forward to trial.

Because this is an important stage, a detailed letter to your client will be necessary, enclosing your opponent's statements, highlighting the salient points, and underlining any issues that have arisen. A meeting may also be necessary.

The 'litigation train' diagram at the beginning of this chapter illustrates how this fits in, in practice.

> **ADR considerations**
>
> As can be seen from the 'litigation train' diagram with which this chapter opens, at a time after exchange of witness statements, ADR should be reconsidered by you and discussed with your client to decide whether it is, indeed, appropriate to try to resolve the dispute by other means.

17.4.6.2 Witness evidence for interim applications

On receipt of your opponent's witness statement either in support of or in opposition to the application, it may be appropriate to:

- check their grounds for the application;
- prepare a witness statement in response, if permitted by the CPR or if appropriate;
- in larger, more complex applications, send a copy to your client and request further information or clarification if required;
- reassess the prospects of success of the application in light of the evidence; and
- consider whether it is in your client's best interests to brief counsel to attend or whether you are, in fact, capable of undertaking the advocacy at the hearing.

17.4.7 **WITNESS SUMMARIES**

If a witness is unwilling or unable to provide a statement for trial voluntarily, then you will be unable to rely on what the witness has to say at trial: for example, where you have spoken to a witness and have sent them the statement to sign, but they do not want to sign it, or are out of the country. The absence of their evidence may be potentially damaging to the success of your client's case.

If you find yourself in this situation, consider the use of a witness summary in accordance with CPR 32.9. A witness summary identifies the witness and summarizes the factual issues that his evidence will cover. In order for you to take advantage of a witness summary, you will need the permission of the court. The application is generally without notice (see the Additional Chapter in the online resources 'A Practical Guide to Court Hearings'). The witness summary must contain the witness's name and address, and must be served by the date set for exchange of witness statements. You will, therefore, need to decide some time in advance of the date set for exchange whether you wish to rely on a witness summary.

 Practical Considerations

The purpose of the witness summary is to enable you to call the witness to trial to give evidence. Witness summaries can also be used where you have not interviewed the witness and do not know what they are going to say. Caution should be exercised if you wish to call such a witness to trial and when the content of their evidence is unknown, because this could be particularly damaging to your client's case.

 Costs

As with the disclosure and inspection process, preparing and scrutinizing witness statements for trial can be an expensive and time-consuming process. Remember that costs are usually awarded on the standard basis, and that, therefore, even if your client is successful and secures an order for costs in his favour at trial, those costs must be reasonable in amount, reasonably incurred, and proportionate. Be mindful of the time taken by you in the preparation and exchange of witness statements, and remind your client that, even if successful, he is unlikely to recover all of his legal costs.

17.5 HEARSAY

Hearsay evidence is now classed as admissible evidence in civil proceedings by virtue of the Civil Evidence Act 1995 and is defined by s. 1(2) of that Act as a statement made otherwise than by a person while giving oral evidence in the proceedings, which is tendered as evidence of the matters stated. The use of hearsay evidence is regulated by the Act in terms of how and when it can be used at trial, and the weight attached to it by the trial judge.

17.5.1 WHAT IS 'HEARSAY'?

You will come across hearsay most commonly in the following situations.

17.5.1.1 When calling another witness to testify as to what the eyewitness saw

When you are interviewing your witness for the purposes of, firstly, preparing a proof, and eventually, preparing a witness statement for trial, the 1995 Act permits you to include his hearsay comments—that is, his comments in relation to what someone else told him about an issue in the claim. The witness's evidence of what he said or saw is first-hand evidence, but the evidence of what someone else told him is second-hand evidence and thus 'hearsay'. If there is more than one person removed from the original statement, then this is known as 'multiple hearsay'.

 Example

An RTA occurred on a country lane between a van and a red car, and was observed by a hill walker in the adjoining field. He proceeded to the next village and went into the local shop, where he informed the shopkeeper that he had seen an accident. He told her that he had seen the driver of the van speaking on his mobile phone immediately before the accident. Later that week, the driver of the red car came into the shop, asking if anyone in the village had seen the accident. The shopkeeper informed him of what the hill walker had told her.

The witness statement of the red car driver could potentially contain multiple hearsay, as follows: 'The shopkeeper told me that she had been told by a hill walker that the driver of the van had been speaking on his mobile phone immediately before the accident.'

17.5.1.2 Adducing the eyewitness's written statement to prove what was seen

Hearsay evidence will also arise when your witness has signed a witness statement, but is unable to attend trial. Even though you have no difficulty in proving the statement as a document, tendering his written statement in place of the witness giving oral evidence in the witness box at trial constitutes reliance on hearsay evidence.

 Example

In this example, if the shopkeeper were to have provided a written witness statement, but then disappeared, the witness statement would still be admissible evidence and can still be relied upon at trial, subject to the requirements detailed in paragraph 17.5.3.

17.5.2 WHAT WEIGHT DOES THE TRIAL JUDGE ATTACH TO HEARSAY EVIDENCE?

The most persuasive evidence that can be put before the court is first-hand evidence, as highlighted in paragraph 17.2.3—namely, oral evidence at trial by the eyewitness, or an original document or object.

In terms of witness evidence, if the maker of the statement does not attend the trial to give oral evidence, or a witness's recollection whilst in the witness box of what happened refers to what somebody else told him about a fact in issue, the court is unlikely to place as much weight on either forms of the evidence as it would if the original witness were there in court.

The question is exactly how much weight will the court give to the evidence in these circumstances? Section 4(2) of the 1995 Act confers a duty on the court to have regard to six factors, as follows:

(a) whether it would have been reasonable and practicable for the party by whom the evidence was adduced to have produced the maker of the original statement as a witness;

(b) whether the original statement was made contemporaneously with the occurrence or existence of the matters stated;

(c) whether the evidence involves multiple hearsay;

(d) whether any person involved had any motive to conceal or misrepresent matters;

(e) whether the original statement was an edited account, or was made in collaboration with another or for a particular purpose; and

(f) whether the circumstances in which the evidence is adduced as hearsay are such as to suggest an attempt to prevent proper evaluation of its weight.

The trial judge will usually explain in his judgment the weight that he has attached to hearsay evidence.

17.5.3 ARE THERE ANY PROCEDURAL REQUIREMENTS FOR THE USE OF HEARSAY EVIDENCE?

Section 2(1) of the 1995 Act requires any party wishing to adduce hearsay evidence to serve notice on his opponent. CPR 33.2 sets out the court's requirements where the hearsay evidence is to be given either by a witness giving oral evidence at trial, or where the hearsay evidence is contained in a witness statement of a witness who is not being called to give oral evidence.

17.5.3.1 Where hearsay evidence is to be given by a witness who is attending court to give oral evidence

Let us look at the driver of the red car in the example given in paragraph 17.5.1.1. The notice formalities are complied with by the service of the witness statement itself. Therefore, because the red car driver's witness statement for trial contains hearsay evidence from the shopkeeper and the hill walker, the service of the witness statement, in accordance with the directions set by the court for witness statement, exchange will suffice as formal notice.

17.5.3.2 Where the evidence is contained in a witness statement of a person who is not giving oral evidence

Remember from paragraph 17.5.1.2 that a written statement from someone who will not be attending trial is also classed as hearsay evidence. If this is the case, then a separate formal notice should be served with the witness statement, identifying the hearsay evidence, confirming that hearsay evidence will be relied upon at trial, and giving reasons why the witness will not be called.

There is no guidance given in the CPR as to the exact format of the notice. We would suggest that the template found in Figure 17.2 at the end of this chapter be used as a starting point for a hearsay notice. Please also see the hearsay notice in the Andrew Pike case study in the online resources.

Practical Considerations

In practice, very few legal representatives serve a notice, and even fewer will ever raise the point. Failure to serve the notice does not affect the admissibility of the hearsay evidence, but the court may exercise its discretion on the question of costs.

17.5.4 WHAT ARE YOUR CLIENT'S OPTIONS IF HEARSAY EVIDENCE IS BEING USED AGAINST HIM?

If, in the course of litigation, you receive a hearsay notice, you will need to consider the effect that the weight of the hearsay evidence will have on your case and whether there is anything constructive that you can do about it.

In terms of the effect of the weight of the hearsay evidence, this will very much depend on the strength of your own evidence, the type of hearsay evidence against you, the strength and type of any other evidence against you, and the six factors listed in paragraph 17.5.2.

Constructively, the best that you can hope to do, where you believe the hearsay evidence to be effective for your opponent, is to try to reduce any weight that the trial judge may attach to it. This can be done in one of two ways: either by calling the maker of the hearsay statement to court to be cross-examined, or by attacking the credibility of the maker of the hearsay statement in his absence.

17.5.4.1 Cross-examination

Section 3 of the 1995 Act allows a party who has been served with a hearsay notice to apply to the court for an order to call the maker of the hearsay statement to court to be cross-examined. The application is effected in the usual way, with a Form N244 plus witness evidence in support of the application. CPR 33.4 requires that the application be made no later than fourteen days after service of the hearsay notice.

Practical Considerations

Applications of this nature would only be used in cases in which the whereabouts of the witness is known, because the court is unlikely to make the order if the witness has disappeared. In practice, consideration should be given to cross-examination orders where your opponent has obtained and served a witness statement, but decides not to call the witness to give oral evidence at trial, relying on the statement of the absent witness as hearsay. You are permitted to apply to cross-examine. If you do succeed and cross-examine your opponent's witness, there is a risk that the witness may be uncooperative and this may damage your client's case.

17.5.4.2 Attacking credibility

Section 5(2) of the 1995 Act permits a party who has been served with a hearsay notice to attack the credibility of the maker of that hearsay evidence. This is done by serving a 'notice to attack credibility' on your opponent within fourteen days after service of the hearsay notice under CPR 33.5. There is no guidance on the form of the notice in the CPR, but it usually follows the format of the hearsay notice and will include an outline of the reasons why you seek to attack the witness's credibility.

Practical Considerations

When trying to identify the reasons for attacking a hearsay witness's credibility, try imagining that the witness is, in fact, in the witness box at trial and consider what questions you would put to him to discredit him. Go on, then, to consider what trait it is about the hearsay witness's character that you are trying to highlight to the judge: is he biased, untrustworthy, or unreliable? It is these character defects that need to be included in the notice to attack credibility, not the questions that you would have put to the witness had they attended court.

In practice, trial judges place limited weight on hearsay evidence.

Practical Considerations

You may wish to consider taking both of the steps in paragraph 17.5.4.1 or 17.5.4.2, because they both operate under the same time limits—particularly if you are trying concurrently to trace the hearsay witness. If you are unable to locate them by the time that your application comes to a hearing, you have the option of withdrawing the application—but be mindful of any costs consequences. Alternatively, you may not wish to take either step. This would probably only be the case if you were to feel you have a sufficiently strong case, but care should be taken, because if you do choose to do nothing on receipt of the hearsay notice, then, at the trial, you will not be permitted to make any representations to the judge on the character or credibility of the hearsay witness.

17.6 USEFUL TOOLS IN THE EVIDENTIAL BATTLE

Usually, at a point after disclosure and exchange of witness statements, when reviewing your client's case generally and conducting your risk assessment, as illustrated in the 'litigation train' diagram at the start of this chapter and that at the start of Chapter 16, there may be facts or parts of the case that could usefully be admitted by your opponent with a view to putting some pressure on your opponent and saving costs. There are three methods available to you, as follows.

17.6.1 NOTICE TO ADMIT FACTS

In order to ensure that the court's time at trial is not wasted in having to determine facts and issues that could be reasonably admitted, consideration should be given to serving a 'notice to admit facts' in Form N266, in accordance with CPR 32.18. This can be served at any time, but no later than twenty-one days before trial. See the online resources for a copy of the form.

If an admission in relation to the fact or issue sought is not forthcoming from your opponent, then you have the burden of proving or disproving the fact at issue at trial. If you are successful on that issue, then your opponent may be asked to pay your costs of proving or disproving those particular facts or issues, irrespective of the overall outcome of the case.

The use of the notice to admit facts is, perhaps, best explained by way of an example.

 Example

A defendant serves a defence denying liability in a personal injury claim. However, the real issue is quantum. The defendant makes a Part 36 offer to put pressure on the claimant. The claimant could serve a notice to admit facts on the defendant to put him at risk on the costs of defending the liability issue, where the costs would be significant.

17.6.2 NOTICE TO ADMIT OR PRODUCE DOCUMENTS

CPR 32.19 is concerned with the position in which a document is deemed to be authentic, unless you serve a 'notice to prove a document at trial' in Form N268 (a copy of which can be found in the online resources). This must specify the document being challenged and must be served by the latest date for exchange of witness statements, or within seven days of disclosure of the document, whichever is the later.

These notices are not as commonly used as notices to admit, but feature in cases in which the signature or date on a contract is being challenged. If such a notice is served and your opponent successfully proves the authenticity of the document, the court has a discretion to make an adverse costs order against you.

17.6.3 LETTERS OF REQUEST

Letters of request are essentially a request by a court in one jurisdiction to a court in another jurisdiction to take evidence on its behalf where there is an unwilling witness in another jurisdiction. The letters can request oral evidence or documents. There are three different scenarios:

- Letters of request from courts within the European Union (other than Denmark) are governed by EC Regulation 1206/2001 on cooperation between the courts of the member states in the taking of evidence in civil and commercial matters.

- Where a domestic court receives a letter of request from a non-EU court, the governing legislation is the Evidence (Proceedings in Other Jurisdictions) Act 1975, which applies to the domestic court's handling of the request.

- If a party is seeking a letter of request to be issued to a non-EU court in proceedings in this country, an application must be made to the High Court (even if a County Court matter) under CPR 34.

Within each of these, there are different rules to be followed, and, as such, you will need to consult the appropriate authority.

Letters of request usually feature in international commercial cases.

KEY POINTS SUMMARY

- Key witnesses need to be identified pre-action or immediately after statements of case.
- Note the wording of the order for witness statement exchange.
- Non-essential witness statements should not be exchanged.

- Be aware of the court's discretionary power to control evidence for trial.

- Take greater care than ever to ensure that witnesses' own words are used in witness statements—in particular, that the language of any contemporaneous notes is carried through into the final statement.

- Ensure the correct format of witness statements.

- Note the differences between witness statements for trial and those for interim hearings.

- Hearsay may be written or oral, and may be first-hand, second-hand, etc.

- Hearsay notices should be served at the same time as witness statements if hearsay evidence is to be relied upon at trial.

- Try to reduce the weight that the trial judge will attach to the hearsay evidence by making an application to cross-examine or by serving a notice to attack credibility.

Case Study *Andrew James Pike v Deep Builders Ltd*

Disclosure and inspection have now taken place. The only documents of which you have received disclosure and inspection from the defendant are the costs of repairs to the truck and the cost of the damaged materials. You have disclosed all of Andrew Pike's receipts in relation to his special damages claim, along with his hospital and doctor's notes. The defendant is still denying liability, causation, and quantum.

Question 1

Consider what points you will have to prove at trial.

Question 2

If the defendant's legal representatives refuse to accept any of your points, how will you prove those points and what steps will you have to take prior to trial?

Exchange of witness statements has taken place. You act for Andrew Pike and exchange only one witness statement—that of Andrew Pike based on his original proof of evidence. The defendant exchanged a witness statement of John Deep, denying that he was responsible for the accident. They also disclosed a witness statement of Raquel Hake, along with a hearsay notice. (See Raquel Hake's statement and the hearsay notice that appear in the online resources.)

Question 3

Consider how you would respond to this notice and consider the weight of Raquel Hake's evidence at trial. What are the possible lines of attack on her evidence?

Question 4

What options do you have? Prepare any documentation that you think may be necessary to carry out the step(s) that you have set out.

Case Study *Bollingtons Ltd v Mrs Elizabeth Lynch t/a The Honest Lawyer*

Question

In Mrs Lynch's witness statement prepared for trial, she mentions the fact that many of the guests at the party had tasted the beer and had commented to her on how disgusting it was. Is this hearsay evidence? Would it be necessary to obtain statements from the guests, and if you were to do so, would the court allow you to rely on them at trial?

 Any documents referred to in these case study questions can be found in the online resources—simply click on 'Case study documentation' to access the documents that you need for Chapter 17 and to be reminded of the questions. Suggested answers to these self-test questions can be accessed in the Student Resource section of the online resources.

FIGURE 17.1 TEMPLATE FOR A WITNESS STATEMENT FOR AN INTERIM HEARING

1. **Claimant/Defendant**

2. **T. Solicitor**

3. **1st/2nd etc.**

4. **TS 1/2/3 etc.**

5. **Date**

IN THE COUNTY COURT AT   **CASE NO**

BETWEEN

MR   **CLAIMANT**

AND

MR   **DEFENDANT**

WITNESS STATEMENT OF TRAINEE SOLICITOR

Witness name: insert name of trainee solicitor

Witness address: insert firm's address

Witness occupation: insert the fact that you are a trainee solicitor and that you act on behalf of either the Claimant or the Defendant

1. I am a trainee solicitor and have the care and conduct of this matter subject to the supervision of my supervising partner. I am duly authorized to make this statement on behalf of the Claimant/Defendant. I make this statement from my own knowledge, belief and from the information given to me by the Claimant/Defendant/someone else.

2. I make this statement in support of (or in opposition to) the Claimant/Defendant's application for . . . .

Chronology/facts/procedural events

Insert any relevant background here in numbered paragraphs 3–?

Submissions

Insert your legal arguments here repeating the wording of a relevant part of a CPR part if appropriate in consecutive number paragraphs.

Conclude your submissions with 'I therefore respectfully ask this honourable court to make the order as asked in accordance with the terms of the draft order annexed to this application'.

Statement of truth and authority

I have care and conduct of this matter and am duly authorised to make this statement on behalf of the Claimant/Defendant. Save where otherwise stated, the facts and matters I address in this witness statement are within my own personal knowledge, or obtained from information supplied to me by the Claimant/Defendant including by the documents referenced in this statement. Where the facts and matters referred to in this witness statement are within my own knowledge they are true. Where they are not within my own knowledge they are true to the best of my knowledge, information and belief. I understand that proceedings for contempt of court may be brought against anyone who makes, or causes to be made a false statement in a document verified by a statement of truth without an honest belief in its truth.

FIGURE 17.2 TEMPLATE FOR A HEARSAY NOTICE

IN THE COUNTY COURT AT   **CASE NO**

BETWEEN

                                                                                        Claimant

                                                    and

                                                                                        Defendant

NOTICE OF INTENTION TO ADDUCE HEARSAY EVIDENCE

Take Notice that at the trial of this action the Claimant/Defendant intends to give in evidence the statement made in the following document, namely the statement of . . . . dated . . . . a copy of which is annexed hereto.

And further take notice that the particulars relating to the said statement are as follows:

1. It was made by . . . .

2. It was made to . . . . of the Claimant/Defendant's solicitor.

3. The said statement was made on . . . . at . . . .

4. It was made in the following circumstances, namely that the Claimant/Defendant's Solicitor obtained the witness name from . . . . and attended . . . . for the purpose of obtaining a statement from him/her

And Further Take Notice that the said . . . . .cannot be called as a witness at the trial because . . . .

To: The Claimant/Defendant

Dated . . . .

18 EXPERTS AND EXPERT EVIDENCE

LITIGATION TRAIN: ACTING FOR A DEFENDANT, RESPONDING TO THE CLAIM, THE CONSEQUENCES OF FAILING TO RESPOND

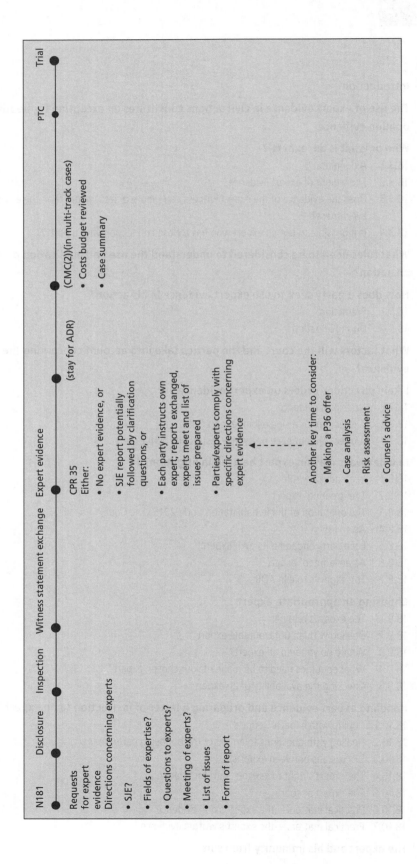

18.12 Experts and privilege

18.12.1 When will experts' reports be disclosed?

Relevant parts of the CPR and its PDs: 27, 28, 29, 32, and 35.

18.1 INTRODUCTION

In this chapter, we will consider the role of experts and the part that they may play in an action that ensures that their input to a case accords with the overriding objective set out in the Civil Procedure Rules (CPR) Part 1—most notably, for the court to ensure that 'justice' is done between parties in an action, 'fairly' and 'proportionately'.

Legal representatives need to be fully conversant with the times at which expert evidence is *needed* in an action and, in engaging an expert, to be fully clear of the *role* that expert will take. The Civil Justice Council's Guidance for the Instruction of Experts in Civil Claims 2014 (the Guidance Note) sets out very useful information for the legal practitioner in the use of, and instruction of, expert witnesses.

CPR 35 also provides very firm guiding principles to make the role of experts in litigation effective and fair. In this chapter we will see that the use of expert evidence in actions will be strictly controlled by the court, not the parties. However, as with all directions orders the court makes to manage a case, the type of order it makes concerning the use of expert evidence (if any is permitted) in an action can be influenced by the representations made by the parties' legal representatives (see Chapter 12, paragraph 12.7). We will also see that the experts are required to make declarations that they understand their duties (to the court). It will be for the legal representative to ensure that the expert understands his role, irrespective of who is paying the expert's fees. The expert's job is to give a full appraisal of the views (opinion) that he puts forward and he should also seek to evaluate these views in the light of other scientific (or technical) opinion, outcomes, or views. The judge should, at all times, be *assisted* in his deliberations by the involvement of expert evidence.

This chapter will consider:

- when expert support is *needed*—whether that is as part of the *evidence submitted* in the action, or as part of the *advice sought* to prepare the client's case, or perhaps for both situations;

- the *role* that the expert will take in both of the situations identified;

- when *permission* of the court is needed to engage and submit expert evidence in the action;

- understanding the need to provide a cost estimate of using an expert and the *costs consequences* for the client in engaging expert evidence for advice or as part of the evidence submitted to the court;

- the management and suitable direction of steps taken in advising your client and proceeding with an action, so as to meet the *court's overall discretion* to control the evidence in relation to the inclusion of expert evidence (or not to include it); and

- the important matters to consider in the *engagement* of an expert and in managing several experts in a case.

Whether a party is permitted to use its 'own' expert or 'share' one (as a single joint expert), CPR 35 clearly imposes significant duties and obligations upon that expert. The expert's overriding duty is to the court (CPR 35.3). We will see from this chapter that no expert who will be giving evidence (whether oral or written) to the court, even if appointed by a party to give evidence for that party, is actually *that party's* expert. Under the CPR, the expert has to take responsibility for ensuring that his own objectivity is both demonstrated and preserved. This very objectivity of the expert is often the area in which an attack on that expert's evidence may be made by the other party in cross-examination at the trial. These duties of objectivity, integrity, and independence of the expert from the parties make a legal representative's job of working alongside an expert perhaps more difficult. This manifests itself in relation to difficulties over issues such as retaining privilege in instructions and materials given to an expert, and, so far as is possible, ensuring that the expert is, ultimately, on the client's side, but without being tainted with the client's or his legal representative's views. Apart from the technical rules concerning expert evidence, these other matters must be fully understood by any practitioner and are also considered in this chapter.

18.2 THE USE OF EXPERT EVIDENCE IN CIVIL ACTIONS CONSTITUTES AN EXCEPTION TO THE RULE AGAINST OPINION EVIDENCE

Experts are permitted to give opinion evidence. As a general rule, opinion evidence is inadmissible because it is the role of the court to form its opinion of the evidence presented to it. However, in providing this exclusion to this rule and permitting an expert to give opinion evidence, the court is acknowledging that, in some areas, it requires guidance and assistance on matters that are outside the expertise of the judge to determine. The evidence from the expert may do any one or more of the following whenever the judge needs the expert's assistance to decide the key issues and make a judgment on the issues before him:

- deal with the valuation of an asset;
- explain a physical or mechanical process;
- clarify technical jargon;
- make an assessment of 'risk' or likelihood (of an event happening);
- give evidence on standard or benchmark behaviour or practices; or
- give an assessment of 'blame'.

Section 3 of the Civil Evidence Act 1972 sets out the test for calling an expert witness in civil proceedings:

(a) The expert may give his opinion on any relevant matter; and

(b) The expert must be qualified to give the opinion.

We shall see that both 'relevance' and 'qualified to give' are important matters to consider whenever seeking leave of the court to adduce expert evidence.

18.3 WHO OR WHAT IS AN 'EXPERT'?

18.3.1 A DEFINITION

The CPR defines an 'expert' as a person who has been 'instructed to give or prepare expert evidence for the purpose of proceedings' (CPR 35.2). Further, the rules define a 'single joint expert' (SJE) as an expert instructed to prepare a report for the court on behalf of two or more of the parties to the proceedings. The reality of these definitions is that an 'expert' can be anyone with knowledge or experience of a particular field or discipline beyond that to be expected of a layperson. The expert witness is allowed to give an opinion to the court on matters that they may not have seen directly, but in which matters they are an 'expert'. Anyone who can convince a judge of their knowledge, skills, or training in an area of knowledge that the court needs to understand to try the case fairly can act as an expert. A professional qualification is not necessarily required but is preferred. The expertise of the 'expert' is gauged from their professional training, but also their employment or experience in other ways.

18.3.2 **THE WEIGHT OF EXPERT EVIDENCE**

There are a number of factors that will determine the weight that the judge will attribute to the expert witness's evidence. These include the extent to which he backs up his opinions with current scientific thinking and the degree to which he accepts and analyses alternative views and conclusions. The expert's opinion evidence will also be 'weighed' against the evidence of fact of lay witnesses who have seen, or had direct involvement in, the issues of the case.

In civil litigation, an ordinary witness is called to tell the judge, and is only allowed to tell, what he himself actually perceived. An expert witness may, however, draw an inference from his conclusions of the facts. It is always for the judge to decide if the alleged facts are true; he will do this by balancing the evidence that he hears or reads from both types of witness. The expert witness differs fundamentally from the ordinary witness: he did not see or hear the incident in dispute; he gives evidence of scientific fact; and he gives his opinion based on professional knowledge and experience. Although the expert witness may subsequently see the injured person, the damaged equipment, the accounts, or the scene, his evidence of the 'facts' of the event are his 'opinion' of it.

For example, a lay witness may not say that a vehicle was being driven recklessly, only that it ended up in the ditch. It is the function of the court to decide the cause of the accident, based on the evidence placed before it. It is the task of the expert witness (say, in this example, an accident investigator) to assist the court in reaching its decision, with technical analysis and opinion inferred from the factual evidence: for example, by an expert determination of skid marks on the road.

An expert witness can give evidence based on opinion, or his conclusions, if four basic conditions are met, as follows:

1. The opinion, inferences, or conclusions must depend on special knowledge, skill, or training that is not within the ordinary experience of the judge.

2. The expert must be shown to be qualified as a true expert in the particular field of expertise.

3. The expert must give evidence to a reasonable degree of certainty regarding his opinion, inferences, or conclusions.

4. The expert must be able to demonstrate, or persuade from scientific fact, the basis of his opinion, inference, or conclusions.

The 'weight' to be attached to the expert's evidence is a matter for the judge to determine. Critical matters will be his status, qualifications, interests, experience, reputation, bearing, and response.

It is essential that the expert's report and evidence is a frank statement by the expert of the limits of the accuracy of his opinion, inferences, or conclusions. He must be prepared to indicate, whether asked to do so or not (but the legal representative instructing the expert also has a duty to ensure that the expert fully understands the extent of his duties and obligations), what his evidence suggests as likely. Just as litigants are obliged under the rules of disclosure (see Chapter 16, paragraph 16.4.1) to disclose documents that are against his case or support the other party's case, the expert is under an obligation to make sure that the court does not, unwittingly, use his evidence without realizing its scientific limitations.

The three 'i's of an expert are: independence, integrity, and impartiality. All of these are vital if an expert's opinion is to carry weight. Any expert who is more concerned in the outcome of the case will find himself the subject of sustained attack in cross-examination—he will be asked to comment, in the witness box, on contradicting authoritative materials or publications or to comment on the effect of his hypotheses on a differing statement of facts. Any expert witness who has not fully appraised the conclusions that he makes without proper regard to alternative conclusions will find his evidence discredited. The same can be said of written experts' reports so the opposing party may raise questions on the content of the report setting out contradicting conclusions and evidence. In paragraph 18.8.1, there is a discussion of circumstances in which an expert may be used to assist a party in the preparation of *his* case—that is, the 'behind the scenes' expert. These experts, who will not be 'trial' experts, will assist a party to prepare a trial strategy plan. This may include questions to ask the opposing party's expert witness in cross-examination and prepare written questions to that expert on the contents of his report.

It is the aim of a good trial expert to ensure that the judge not only understands the words, terms, and expressions that the expert uses, but also to ensure that the judge is able to do so without too much effort. The expert must build this bridge between science and knowledge to every conclusion that he states.

18.3.3 DOES THE EVIDENCE OF THE EXPERT WITNESS CARRY MORE OR LESS WEIGHT THAN THE EVIDENCE OF THE EYEWITNESS?

The court is not required to accept the evidence of the expert over the evidence of witnesses of fact (who are giving evidence of what they have actually perceived).

In the case *Van Oord UK Ltd & Another v Allseas UK Ltd* [2015] EWHC 3074 (TCC), Coulson J rejected the claimant's quantum's expert evidence in its entirety. He set out 12 reasons why he was rejecting it! The judge concluded that the expert had unwittingly allowed himself to be a 'mouthpiece' for the claimant. The case is a timely reminder of the potential pitfalls of using an inexperienced expert or the legal representative failing to monitor or supervise his input to the case.

There are other cases that quite clearly highlight that the court does not have to favour the expert's evidence over that of a party. Two cases illustrate this clearly: *Armstrong & O'Connor v First York* [2005] EWCA Civ 277 and more recently *Robshaw v United Lincolnshire Hospital NHS Trust* [2015] EWHC 247 (QB). For those handling expert evidence in cases these cases are worth reading.

It is clear that the court will, when necessary, uphold decisions that prefer the evidence of an eyewitness to that of an expert. This makes logical sense, because the expert is giving his *opinion* and, in doing just that, is not giving a guarantee or assurance that every view that he expresses is necessarily 100 per cent correct.

18.3.4 IS IT POSSIBLE TO USE AN EXPERT WHO HAS A CLOSE CONNECTION WITH A PARTY?

It has previously been thought that it would be inappropriate to use an expert who has a close connection with a party. The requirement to be 'independent' is crucial for an expert to assist in the litigation process. The Civil Justice Council has stated that experts should provide opinions which are independent, regardless of the pressures of litigation. In this context a useful test of 'independence' is that the expert would express the same opinion if given the same instructions by an opposing party. Experts should not take it upon themselves to promote the point of view of the party instructing them or engage in the role of advocate. Provided this very 'independence' can be shown, the courts have concluded that, in certain circumstances (for example when the number of available experts in the field required are very limited), using an expert who has a close connection to a party may not always be a bar to instructing the expert. This clear 'independence' could be shown in a number of ways. In *Gallagher International Ltd v Tlais Enterprises Ltd* [2007] EWHC 464 (Comm), the judge permitted the use of an expert who was employed by the claimant and adopted the reasoning set down in an earlier case (*Armchair Passenger Transport Ltd v Helical Barr plc* [2003] EWHC 367 (QB)) of the circumstances in which it may be appropriate to permit a person to give expert evidence despite a close connection with a party as follows:

- The fact (of the expert's employment with the claimant) was openly declared.

- The terms of engagement of the expert have been clearly defined within the provisions of the CPR, and the claimant had done as much as it could to 'isolate and separate' the expert from the affairs of the company in the litigation and his duties as an expert in the proceedings.

- The expert had relevant experience and was wholly aware of his duties to the court.
- Experts in the field were scarce—and further, the timescale before trial indicated that it would be unfair for the claimant to have to try to seek another expert in the field at the late stage of the proceedings.
- The expert would be open to cross-examination.
- The claimant bore the risks that the weight of the expert's evidence may be reduced by the judge at trial because of the connection to the party calling him.

Clearly, these reasons would not apply in many situations and the principle remains that an independent expert should be sought whenever possible.

18.4 WHAT RULES NEED TO BE CONSIDERED TO UNDERSTAND THE USE AND APPLICATION OF AN EXPERT IN AN ACTION?

CPR Part 35, its supporting Practice Direction (PD), and the Guidance Note are the rules that govern the use of experts in litigation.

However, CPR 32 also needs to be considered, because this provides the power for the court to control the evidence before it and this will include the control of expert evidence.

18.5 HOW DOES A PARTY SEEK TO USE EXPERT EVIDENCE IN HIS ACTION?

18.5.1 PRE-ACTION

A party can decide himself when and how to use an expert in the pre-action stage. This may be to help him to formulate his case, or to add strength and weight to his arguments.

Whether it is one specifically designed for the action or within the Practice Direction on Pre-Action Conduct and Protocols (PDPACP), the Protocol sets down guidelines for the use of expert evidence. Detailed guidance can be found at paragraph 7.2–7.11 of the Pre-Action Protocol for Personal Injury Claims. Some specialist proceedings may be covered by other specific rules (CPR 49) but these are outside the scope of this manual. The aim in Protocol is that parties should seek to agree how to use an expert and who to use. However, the ultimate decision will lie with the claimant. The legal representative's role will be to ensure that the client has given instructions to engage the expert and that he understands the costs implications of engaging the expert. There is no certainty that the courts will allow any costs recovery of the fees of retaining the services of an expert in the pre-action stage.

18.5.2 DURING LITIGATION

If the action does not settle in the Protocol stage and proceedings are issued, any future use of evidence will be strictly controlled by the court under CPR 35 and parties may only use expert evidence at trial if given permission to do so. The court will also define the way in which expert evidence will be used (see paragraph 18.6).

Where a party has defined a need to use expert evidence in his action, he should make a request for that evidence as soon as is practicable. The request must include an estimate of the costs involved. The arguments for permission to adduce expert evidence will usually be set down in the Directions Questionnaire (DQ) and at a later stage, regarding oral evidence of the expert, in the pre-trial checklist (see Chapter 12). Any further requests for the permission of the court to define the use of expert evidence by the parties further, or for permission for additional expert evidence, must be made by an interim application or at a subsequent case management conference (CMC).

18.6 WHAT FACTORS WILL THE COURT AND THE PARTIES TAKE INTO ACCOUNT CONCERNING THE USE OF EXPERT EVIDENCE?

The court will consider at the first opportunity—usually on receipt of the completed DQs—whether expert evidence will be required. Both parties' legal representatives should have considered their requirement for expert evidence in the action and should have justified their request in their completed Form N180 or N181 (the DQs), or come prepared to address the court on their reasons for expert evidence and the extent of it at a subsequent CMC. No expert evidence may be adduced without the permission of the court (CPR 35.4(1)), so any perceived need for it must be fully set out as 'necessary' within the aims of the overriding objective. CPR 35.1 provides that expert evidence should be restricted to that which is reasonably required to resolve the proceedings.

Expert evidence may be sought for actions in any of the tracks, but clearly issues of proportionality will apply and therefore, for cases in the small claims track, careful consideration will have to be made about the use of expert evidence. CPR 27 restricts the cost of any expert permitted in a small claims track case to a maximum of £750 for each expert (PD 27.7.3). However, in any of the tracks the court will consider a 'cost capping' provision stating the sum that may be spent on any expert evidence permitted. Any request for permission to have experts to provide evidence in a case should be accompanied by an estimate of the cost of it.

Expert evidence may be central to issues of liability and causation, and/or quantum. Although parties are expected to cooperate in the preparation of their cases, the need for expert evidence is often one area in which the parties are unable to agree. The disagreement may concern:

- whether expert evidence is needed at all;
- whether expert evidence is needed in a particular field;
- whether an SJE should be used; and
- the cost of it.

The case of *(1) Kenneth Alex Wattret (2) Laurie Grace Wattret v Thomas Sands Consulting Ltd* [2015] EWCH 3455 (TCC) highlights the degree of consideration by the court as to whether an expert is *needed* in an action. The case highlights the need in any application by a party, or the parties, for an order that expert evidence may be permitted in the action, the parties should not only seek to *justify* why expert evidence is needed but also should identify exactly what *issues* the expert should cover.

18.7 LIKELY DIRECTIONS ORDERS ON EXPERT EVIDENCE

If the court concludes that expert evidence may be adduced at trial, the following are examples of directions orders that may be made.

18.7.1 NO EXPERT EVIDENCE

No expert evidence being necessary, no party has permission to rely on expert evidence.

18.7.2 A DIRECTION FOR A SINGLE JOINT EXPERT (SJE)

In the small claims track or fast track, any permission for expert evidence to be adduced will *normally* only be given to call expert evidence on a particular issue from one expert (CPR 35.4(3A)). This is intended to provide consistency and directly refers the courts to PD 35.7, which sets out the criteria to apply when the court considers whether to direct the use of expert evidence in a matter. However, in the multi-track also the question of *proportionality* will be at the forefront in the consideration of expert evidence and the use of a SJE will always be a consideration.

Any direction order for an SJE must use the term 'single joint expert'. A direction for an SJE could include some or all of the following directions:

- 'Permission is given to the parties to rely on the written evidence of an SJE in the field of [specify field], instructed jointly by the parties on the issue of [specify issue], and the parties have agreed to use [name expert].'

- 'If the parties cannot agree who the SJE should be, any party may apply to the court to obtain further directions.'

- 'In the event that the parties cannot agree the identity of the SJE by [date], the parties shall, on or before [date], apply to [specify who—for example, the President of the Royal Institute of Chartered Surveyors] to nominate a suitable SJE.'

- 'The claimant shall inform the court, in writing, when the SJE has been appointed.'

- 'Instructions are to be provided to the SJE by [date], and the report is to be simultaneously served by [date] on both parties.'

- 'The parties are to serve any written questions on the SJE and the other party by [specify timescale—for example, within 28 days of receipt of the expert's report], and the SJE shall file and serve the answers to any such questions on both parties by [time—for example, 28 days thereafter].'

- 'Unless the parties agree in writing or the court orders otherwise, the SJE's fees and expenses shall be paid by the parties [equally or in the proportions agreed or ordered], and the total amount of the SJE's fees and expenses shall be limited to £x [amount].'

- 'The evidence of the SJE shall be given at trial by [written report *or* oral evidence of the SJE].'

- Where more than one expert is giving evidence the court may direct that some or all the experts give their evidence concurrently (PD 35.11.1). The court may make further directions concerning the use of multiple experts at a trial in accordance with PD 35.11.2.

18.7.3 A DIRECTION THAT EACH PARTY MAY INSTRUCT ITS OWN EXPERT

A direction that each party may instruct its own expert might include the following options:

- 'Where, at the first CMC, the parties have decided in principle that they will want experts, but have not yet decided on the area of expertise [for example, whether it should be expert evidence of a quantity surveyor or a chartered surveyor], a further CMC can be held to deal with expert evidence [and any other outstanding matters], to be fixed for the first available date after [date], and to be reserved to [specify master or district judge], if possible.'

- Where the parties have decided that they each want to rely on their own expert:
  - 'permission is given to each party to rely upon the written evidence of [specify number of] in the field of [specify field] expert(s) addressing the following issues [list issues]. [Specify which party] intends to use [name expert] and [specify other party] intends to use [name expert]';
  - 'the parties shall exchange their lists [of issues] and the experts of both parties shall consider both parties' issues in their reports';
  - 'the experts' reports shall be exchanged simultaneously by [date]', *or* 'there shall be sequential exchange of experts' reports, the claimant's [specify field] expert's report to be served by [date] and the defendant's [specify field] expert's report to be served by [date]';
  - 'written questions may be put to the experts on their reports within [number of days—usually 28 days] of the report being served. The experts are to respond to the questions in writing within [number of days] of being served the questions';

- – 'the reports are to be agreed if possible';
- – 'if not agreed, the experts shall hold a without prejudice meeting for the purpose of identifying the issues, if any, between them and, where possible, reaching agreement on those issues. The experts shall by [specify date] prepare and file [at court] and serve a statement showing:
  - – those issues on which agreement has been reached; and
  - – those issues on which they have not agreed, with a summary of the reasons why they disagreed.'

- • 'All supplemental experts' reports shall be limited to [specify number of] pages, excluding supporting documentation and appendices, and shall be served by [date].'
- • 'No party shall recover from any other party more than £[amount] for the fees and expenses of an expert.'
- • 'The parties have permission to rely upon the oral evidence of [specify the experts] at trial'; *or*
- • 'Each party has permission to use in evidence their [name expert] reports and the court will consider when the claim is listed for trial whether expert oral evidence will be allowed'; *or*
- • 'If the experts' reports cannot be agreed, the parties are at liberty to rely on and call expert witnesses to give oral evidence at trial, limited to those experts whose reports have been served pursuant to paragraph [number] above.'
- • Further directions may be made under the provisions of PD 35.11.1 and 35.11.2 concerning the giving of the evidence of several experts concurrently.

ADR considerations

As can be seen from the 'litigation train' diagram at the beginning of this chapter, in addition to disclosure and inspection, and exchange of witness statements, expert evidence is another key stage in the litigation at which the case needs to be reassessed, another risk assessment needs to be carried out, and consideration given to whether an alternative dispute resolution (ADR) process would be appropriate. Once expert evidence has been dealt with, this often signifies the end of the 'information gathering' in an action and the matter now moves towards trial preparation, which is another costly part of the litigation. The courts expect parties to embrace resolving their dispute by an ADR process and will question them on their attempts at this in any forthcoming pre-trial hearing or review, and questions are asked concerning this in the pre-trial checklist (Form N170).

18.8 IN WHAT WAYS MAY AN EXPERT BE USED IN LITIGATION?

18.8.1 IN AN ADVISORY ROLE

An expert witness is different from an 'expert adviser', sometimes also known as an 'independent expert'. The expert adviser is a person who advises a party on a specialist or technical matter within his expertise at any stage of a problem, dispute, or claim. He may also assist with the formulation of the case, and thus be employed in the pre-action phase, or he may assist in the drafting of a witness statement (this could be pre action). There may be considerable advantages, or certainly some justification in a high-value case (in which the additional costs of instructing an expert adviser can be justified), of instructing an expert early on in an action, because his expertise may assist the client (and his legal representatives) to assess the strengths and weaknesses of their case so as to decide whether to pursue or defend it. Using an expert adviser later on, during the course of the action, may also assist the client (and his legal representatives) to assess the strengths and weaknesses of any evidence that has been disclosed and revealed either by inspection, or at the exchange of witness statements and expert's report stage. The disadvantages of their use is that the costs of the expert advisers are not likely to be recoverable and, if used pre-action, that expert may not be acceptable as an expert witness in the action, because he may no longer be considered sufficiently independent. The differences between the different 'experts' who have had involvement in the action or with the party are important when considering the duties of the expert, the communications that the legal adviser or client may have with him, the expert's immunity from suit, and in several other respects.

 Practical Considerations

It is always essential, when considering using an expert to advise on a case to assist you to understand the technically difficult matters or facts arising, or to assist you to formulate your case, to think first whether you might wish to seek the court's permission to use your instructed expert adviser to act as your expert witness in the action (as an SJE or as your client's expert). If you have previously used the expert as an adviser, he may no longer be considered sufficiently independent to be used as an expert witness. Even if the court does permit his use, the court is likely to order that all of your communications with that expert, even during the time that he acted as your expert adviser, be disclosed. Care must always be taken in any communications with an expert at any stage and for whatever purpose.

 Costs

It is important, whenever considering the use of an expert in litigation, at whatever stage of the action, that the legal representative informs the client of the cost consequences of instructing the expert and gives appropriate advice concerning the likely recoverability (or not) of those costs. At all times, the client's specific instructions should be obtained to retain an expert in the action. It may also be necessary to obtain from the client the expert's fees in advance. Further in any application for permission to use an expert the costs of that expert should form part of the request.

18.8.2 **THE 'TREATING' EXPERT**

Understanding the fundamental differences of 'role' between the litigation expert and the treating expert is vital.

A litigation expert (no matter who instructed him) owes primary duty to the court over and above any duty to any party (CPR 35.3). CPR 35 controls his participation in the proceedings. His very existence as an expert is subject to the court's permission (CPR 35.4). His evidence is to be 'objective, unbiased opinion'.

The treating expert owes primary duties to the party or client. That relationship is governed not by the court, but by the ethical requirements of the treating expert's profession for providing such treatment. That relationship will usually have arisen pre-action. The records of such a treating expert are, prima facie, documents that are to be disclosed within the proceedings. Additionally, if he becomes a witness in the proceedings, he is a witness of fact, not an expert.

 Practical Considerations

All too often in low-value cases and in an attempt by the parties to consider the sum of costs being expended, a claimant's legal representative will seek to put forward the claimant's 'treating expert' as the litigation expert in the action. In terms of proportionality, this may be sensible, but in doing so the legal representatives must be sure not to lose sight of the roles and duties of the expert in the role that he has had compared with the one that he will have if he becomes the litigation expert. The treating expert may have a conflict of interests—a conflict between his professional obligations to the claimant as a patient and the duties that he owes to the court as a litigation expert. If the legal representatives have lost sight of the different 'roles' of the chosen expert (who has been a treating expert), this conflict will not become apparent until long into the action (the judge is unlikely to know from the allocation questionnaire that the proposed 'selected joint expert' was the claimant's treating expert). By that stage, time and expense will have been lost and incurred, as well as significant embarrassment caused to the legal representatives of both parties. Also, because of the mistake, the court could readily impose 'wasted costs' orders against the lawyers' firms involved. Using the 'treating' expert as the expert in litigation should be avoided wherever possible, but if it is not avoided the expert must make it clear that he understands his position. The guidance in PD 35 makes it clear that the expert will 'need to give careful consideration as to whether they can accept a role as expert witness'.

18.8.3 THE OPERATION OF THE REHABILITATION CODE 2015 (THE CODE) AS UPDATED IN 2019

The Code is incorporated into the Pre-Action Protocol on Personal Injury at paragraph 4. The Code also applies to clinical negligence cases.

The Code is predicated on the idea that it is in everyone's interests to get the claimant into as recovered a state as possible. The purpose of the Code is to encourage claimants' lawyers and insurance companies to cooperate as soon as possible after the claimant's injury to procure appropriate treatments, without either side feeling that this will disadvantage them in the future conduct of the litigation. The Code has, to a limited extent, achieved this, although many claimants' representatives remain wary of giving too much away at an early stage.

The Code primarily provides for an 'independent assessment', either by a treating physician or surgeon or (more usually in practice) an agency that is suitably qualified and/or experienced in such matters, which is financially and managerially independent of the claimant's solicitor's firm and the insurers. The assessment is carried out on a joint instruction basis and the report should cover:

- the claimant's injuries and present condition;
- the claimant's domestic circumstances;
- for what injuries intervention or rehabilitation is suggested; and
- what is the intervention, its cost, and its likely benefit.

The report does not deal with diagnosis, causation, or long-term care requirements. It is an 'immediate needs' report only.

In some ways, the rehabilitation assessor is treated like an SJE, because the report is disclosed simultaneously and each party can raise questions, but must disclose those questions and any answers to the other party. However, the report is explicitly and specifically produced outside the litigation process, and is described as 'covered by legal privilege', although it is hard to see exactly what is meant by this in the Code, because the document is disclosed to both parties, but the report, all notes, and all correspondence is not referred to in any legal proceedings. But it is important to remember that this only applies to the report and ancillary documents. Any treatment or therapy that the claimant receives as a result of the report is subject to the same general principles as relate to any other 'treating expert', because the relationship is that between a patient and doctor (or therapist), and the treating expert, if he gives evidence, is giving evidence of fact, not opinion.

However, once the distinction between a treating expert and a litigation expert is clear, the next matters about which you must be clear are the distinctions between, and appropriate times to use, a 'single' joint expert, when each party may instruct and use the evidence of their own expert, and when an 'agreed' expert is used.

Supplemental to the Code is the Serious Injury Guide (the Guide) which came into effect on 12 October 2015 and updated on 25 January 2019. This guide is designed to assist with the conduct of complex personal injury claims with a potential value of £250,000 and above. Its key objectives include early notification, prompt disclosure, and a commitment to resolve liability issues within six months. This Guide does not, however, extend to clinical negligence or asbestos-related disease claims.

18.8.4 **AS AN SJE**

CPR 35.7(1) states that where two or more parties wish to submit expert evidence on a particular issue, the court may direct that the evidence on that issue is to be given by one expert only. The court will consider the overriding objective when deciding whether to allow the parties to have their own experts or insist on an SJE. CPR 35.7(2) provides that where the parties cannot agree who should be the SJE, the court may select an expert from a list prepared by the parties, or it may direct that the expert be selected in such manner as the court directs.

Under the provisions of the overriding objective and the drafting of the CPR, the court is clearly under a duty to consider, where expert evidence is identified and justified as necessary to the case, directing SJEs when giving case management directions (see Chapter 12). Equally, the parties have a duty to conduct their cases within the spirit of the overriding objective and, therefore, should have already considered whether the appointment of an SJE is the appropriate way forward. In the fast track, the court must 'give directions for an SJE unless there is good reason not to' (PD 28.3.9(4)). Similar provisions apply in the multi-track, where the court is urged to 'give directions for the appointment of an SJE on any appropriate issue unless there is good reason not to do so' (PD 29.4.10(4)). The emphasis therefore is on the use of SJEs. However, limiting the use of expert evidence in this way (to an SJE) will often not be possible in cases in which the expert evidence is central to liability. This is especially so in high-value cases and clinical negligence cases.

In view of the wording of PD 28.3.9(4), SJEs are most commonly appointed in cases allocated to the fast track, where it will often be difficult to justify the cost of two experts in the claim. Also, in the multi-track, because the value band for actions in this track can start at a figure 'exceeding £25,000', it would be equally difficult to justify the cost of two experts for actions at the lower end of the spectrum of cases, in value terms.

The use of an SJE necessarily means that only one view is being expressed. Paragraph 18.9.4 sets out the safeguards that are in place within the CPR to ensure that the SJE's views are not partisan. However, the court must have proper regard to the evidence of the SJE when looking at the evidence as a whole and does not have to accept everything that the expert says (see paragraph 18.3.2).

18.8.4.1 The advantages and disadvantages of using an SJE

18.8.4.1.1 *Advantages that can be identified*

- It is usually cheaper—but not always: for example, when the parties have already each appointed experts in the pre-action phase.

- It is usually quicker, because there is no need to meet to address the opposing issues of another expert.

- It is less likely that the expert will attend trial to give oral evidence, and this also will usually produce a cost and time saving.

- The use of an SJE often helps to encourage settlement negotiations.

18.8.4.1.2 *Disadvantages that may arise*

- It is not possible to have discussions or a conference with counsel on the more difficult parts of the report, or where a party wishes to challenge some parts of the report, without also involving the other party.

- It may be difficult to dispute the evidence of the SJE if it does not support the client's case.

- A party will not have had unfettered choice as to which expert should be appointed, and if agreement cannot be reached as to the identity of the expert, the court may choose the expert or direct a default mechanism for the appointment of the expert, which would leave the parties with no control of the identity of the expert to be appointed.

- It may still be necessary for a party to have its own expert to comment and advise (the advisory expert) on the report of the SJE, and the costs of this advisory expert are usually not recoverable.

- The courts are often reluctant to order the SJE to attend trial for questioning.

18.8.4.2 Instructing an SJE

Once an SJE has been selected, CPR 35.8 and paragraph 20 of the Guidance Note give guidance on the instructions to the expert. It is clear that both parties are at liberty to send separate instructions to the expert, although they must send a copy of their instructions (and of any other communications that they may have with the expert) to the other party in the action. Ideally, the letter of instruction to the expert should be agreed, because this is more likely to create a clearer list of the issues on which the expert is being asked to report. If any instructions are given by telephone or in person, then the content of the instructions should be confirmed in writing. All communications from the SJE should be addressed to all parties.

The instructing parties are jointly and severally liable for the SJE's fees unless the court directs otherwise. The court will often also direct that the sum of the SJE's fees shall not exceed a certain figure (that the court will set) and further direct the proportion of those fees that each party should pay. This is often an equal division. The court also has the power to order either or both parties to pay that sum into court (see also *Smolen v Solon Co-operative Housing Services Ltd* [2003] EWCA Civ 1240).

 Costs

The direction by the court as to how the SJE's fees should be divided between the parties does not decide the issue of which party will ultimately bear the costs of the expert—this will depend on the ultimate order for costs that the court makes. The earlier direction indicating the share each party should pay of the SJE's fees merely ensures that the expert gets paid. Any party seeking expert evidence must, in their request, provide the court with an estimate of the costs of doing so.

When sending instructions for a report, it is necessary to ensure that the expert is aware of all of the issues in the case, where the burden of proof lies, and what the relevant standards of proof are. This will ensure that the expert produces the right kind of report.

18.8.5 EACH PARTY ENGAGING ITS OWN EXPERT

For each party to be able to adduce its own expert evidence at the trial of an action, a direction for each party to have its own expert must be made.

Given that there is so much emphasis on the use of SJEs in actions, when would it be appropriate to oppose the appointment of an SJE and seek instead an order that each party may instruct 'its own' expert?

The use of more than one expert may be justified if:

- there are several tenable schools of thought on the relevant issue;

- the issues on which the expert will be advising are very complex;

- the issues on which the expert will be advising are so important to the likely outcome of the case that the parties should be allowed to instruct their own expert;

- the value of the claim is sufficiently high that the appointment of separate experts would not be disproportionate;

- the parties have already appointed their own experts before proceedings began and it will be more cost-effective to continue using them, and to try to resolve the expert evidence issues through written questions and experts' discussions, rather than to appoint a new SJE; or

- the expert is being asked to report on difficult issues of liability and causation. It is more difficult to persuade the court of the need for separate experts where the issue to be addressed is quantum only, unless those issues are particularly complex and substantial.

Where the court has made an order that each party should have its own expert, it will normally wish to state the purpose or field of expertise required.

18.8.6 AS AN 'AGREED' EXPERT

The distinction of what is an 'agreed' expert is not an easy one to define and the word is perhaps used by legal representatives without clearly defining what they mean by it, and where they are, in reality, referring to an SJE.

For clarity, an 'agreed' expert (otherwise referred to as a 'jointly selected expert' or a 'mutually accepted expert') is one proposed by the Personal Injury Protocol and is an expert retained in the **pre-action phase**. Under the Protocol, an expert (or a list of experts) is proposed by one party (usually, but not always, the claimant) to his opponent. If an expert is 'agreed' from that list, the expert remains that party's own, solely instructed expert, but the other party has the right to raise questions. If the expert is not 'agreed', the parties may instruct experts of their own choice.

18.8.7 THE EXPERT'S ROLE IN ADR

An expert may have a relevant and positive role to play in any ADR process—particularly in any mediation into which the parties enter. The parties may agree, or the mediator may require, that some areas of expertise be one of the areas that require examination in a mediation. If both parties have retained experts, they can be asked to explain their differences in a joint session in the mediation, so that all participants can get a better understanding of the different points of view. The expert's role in a mediation may be helpful in assisting the decision-making processes. Any legal representative in the process should also be aware of the difficulties that can arise in the use of experts in mediation: they could create further divisions; they may make admissions or concessions that may damage the strength of a party's negotiating position; costs will be increased; and issues of privilege may arise if the mediation does not result in a settlement and litigation proceeds. It is also worth noting, however, that using experts in ADR may have consequences in any subsequent proceedings on the issue of privilege. In *Aird v Prime Meridian Ltd* [2006] EWCA Civ 1866, the Court of Appeal held that a joint statement by experts used in a mediation could be disclosed and could be ordered to be produced within the proceedings, and concluded that it was not privileged just because it was used in the mediation.

18.9 CHOOSING AN APPROPRIATE EXPERT

It is important to choose an expert wisely, but equally it is important to select an expert who is available in the timescale that the court directions have allowed. A failure to find the right expert and instructing one who proves to be unable to deliver his report in time can be disastrous (see paragraph 18.3.3), and the court will not readily permit extensions of time for the preparation of a report, or to attend to questions, or to attend a meeting between experts without regard to the overriding objective.

18.9.1 THE EXPERT'S RETAINER

PD 35 and paragraphs 16–20 of the Guidance Note contain useful advice on appointing an expert. The terms of the retainer with an expert are suggested to include:

- the capacity in which the expert is to be appointed (that is, as an SJE, an expert adviser, or an expert for one party);

- the services required (that is, to prepare a report, answer questions, have a meeting with any other expert appointed, participate in the preparation of an expert's schedule of issues, attend court, etc.);

- the time for the delivery of the report; and

- the basis of the expert's fees, and how disbursements will be dealt with and whether any cancellation charges have been agreed. How and when the expert will be paid and whether his fees will be subject to assessment by a costs officer.

✓ Practical Considerations

It may be helpful to set out the terms of the retainer with the expert separately from the letter of instruction to that expert. If this is done, the expert should be asked to acknowledge the retainer letter and confirm that he accepts the terms of appointment. A sample letter of retainer is available in the online resources as part of the Andrew Pike case study.

18.9.2 DEALING WITH AN UNFAVOURABLE EXPERT

Because of the need for impartiality of the expert evidence, it can be difficult to deal with the expert who proves to be unfavourable, whether this is an SJE or an expert for one party only. Where this happens, any application to the court for permission to obtain an alternative expert report or for leave to appoint a new expert is likely to be met either with an order refusing permission (because it would not be within the provisions of the over-riding objective to give permission), or, where permission is being granted, an order that the earlier report also be disclosed with the alternative expert's report. On the basis that any subsequent expert is likely to have had sight of the earlier report and have been asked to comment on it, any privilege attaching to the earlier report will be lost. The decision of *Odera v Ball* [2012] EWHC 1790 (TCC) highlights the court's view that when a further expert is being sought by a party, any permission for a further expert to be used should be conditional on the first expert's report being disclosed, but that view is not 'fixed in stone' and the courts will look at the facts of the case when deciding whether to order disclosure of the first report. *Guntrip v Cheney Coaches Ltd* [2012] EWCA 392 has also confirmed that an expert whose report is unfavourable is not 'good reason' to seek permission for an alternative expert to be appointed.

18.9.3 WHERE DO YOU FIND AN EXPERT?

One of the most effective ways of selecting an expert will be by recommendation, and in this, your client (possibly with the exception of personal injury claims) may be an obvious starting point. They will have a feel for who is rated in their industry. However, whenever taking the client's views, it is important to ensure that there is no possibility of a conflict arising for the expert or a finding that the expert is not sufficiently impartial (but note the special circumstances referred to in paragraph 18.9.2).

However, a search for an appropriate expert may also be made by:

- reviewing any lists of experts previously used that your client may hold—usually with an assessment of that expert and whether it is worth using them or not;

- consulting Judicial College publications;

- consulting the Expert Witness Institute; or

- consulting the Academy of Experts—which advances the role of expert evidence in the following ways:

- it keeps and provides a directory of members, categorized according to discipline and experience;

- it develops and maintains the standards of excellence—vetting all applicants for practising membership; and

- it is cooperating with, and making representations to, judicial and legal authorities, government departments, official enquiries, and tribunals to ensure that the best use is made of experts' advice;

• following the recommendation of other lawyers working in that field, colleagues, opponents, the Association of Personal Injury Lawyers (APIL), counsel, and other experts.

Clearly, the 'type' of expert needed will be indicated by the nature of the case and the issues on which the expert will be expected to comment: for example, in a case needing technical expertise in manufacturing, an engineer may be what is required; on accounting matters, an accountant. It is necessary to be clear of exactly what the expert is needed for and this may not necessarily be directly related to the subject matter of the cause of action.

It is also important that the retained expert is well respected in his field. Notoriety, or a person who has a reputation for novel and untested theories, is not what is needed.

Additionally, the expert will ideally be a person who has some experience of being an expert witness—that is, a person who will not be undermined or intimidated by the judicial process or by cross-examination (see paragraph 18.3.3). Although it is perfectly proper to advise your expert of the *form* of their report and thereby assist them with the judicial process, it is not in any way acceptable to make any attempt to guide or influence the expert as to his *findings and conclusions*.

18.9.4 WHAT ENQUIRIES NEED TO BE MADE OF YOUR CHOSEN EXPERT?

Your chosen expert will need to provide you with a curriculum vitae (CV) and references before they are engaged. The Academy of Experts' Judicial Committee has published a model form of CV for expert witnesses. This is not a standard form, but it offers useful guidance to legal practitioners and to experts in the provision of the expert's CV.

You will also need to assess whether they have the required experience for your case. One way in which you can do this is to give brief details of the case in which they will be expected to act as expert and to ask directly whether they think they have the requisite experience. Alternatively, you can make enquiries of them regarding details of:

• in which courts they have previously appeared;

• the nature of the cases in which they have previously been engaged; and

• their previous court experiences—for example, whether they have been cross-examined.

You will also need to ensure that there is no conflict of interest with engaging your chosen expert. To ensure this, you will need to advise the expert of the names of the other parties in the action, any other experts that have been engaged, and the names of the other party's legal representative, asking the expert to confirm that he has no conflict of interest. It has also been suggested that an expert should be required to make an additional statement at the end of his report in relation to conflicts of interest, although there is no formal requirement for this.

Despite the fact that it is, in certain circumstances, acceptable to utilize an expert who is connected to a party (see paragraph 18.3.4), it is generally best to avoid any connection with the instructing party and care should, wherever possible, be taken to ensure that:

• the recommendation does not come from colleagues or friends of the expert;

• the expert does not have any out-of-court contact with judges, or the parties, or their legal representatives, on their cases.

18.9.5 **CHECKING THE AVAILABILITY OF AN EXPERT**

With the timetable of an action being strictly controlled by the court and because, particularly in the fast track, the timetable of the time to trial is short (within thirty weeks from allocation), the availability of the expert to be able make his enquiries, deliver his report, deal with any questions, and take any further steps directed by the court, as well as be available at trial if he is required to give oral evidence, is vital. The courts will not readily adjourn the proceedings to fit in with the availability of expert evidence. It is the responsibility of the legal representative to ensure that the chosen expert will be available within the timescale set down by the court.

18.10 **HANDLING EXPERT EVIDENCE AND PREPARING A LETTER OF INSTRUCTION TO AN EXPERT**

A copy of any order concerning expert evidence must be served on the expert by the party instructing him. If the expert is an SJE, then the claimant must serve the expert (PD 35.8). The duties of an expert are clearly set down in CPR 35.3:

(1) *It is the duty of an expert to help the court on matters within his expertise.*

(2) *This duty overrides any obligation to the person from whom he has received instructions or by whom he is paid.*

It will be for the legal representative to ensure that the expert understands his duties. A good letter of instruction will be well structured and, it is suggested, should include (at least) the following:

- basic information, such as names, addresses, and contact details of those instructing the expert;
- notice that the report should be addressed to the court, be in the first person, and should set out the expert's qualifications;
- other contact details—for example, those of the client;
- guidance on whom to contact in the first instance if queries or instructions need amending or clarifying;
- advice that there should be no formal or informal unrecorded discussions;
- a summary of the case and the purpose of the report, or of the issues that it should cover, including specific questions to address;
- a chronology, which should include a programme of the key dates of which the expert should be aware;
- reference to, and a list attached of, all documents and/or relevant evidence (that is, relevant to the expert);
- general points that the expert should address and advice on the 'form' of the report (but not, of course, its content). This may include the guidance set down in CPR PD35 paragraph 2.4, which states the form of the expert's statement of truth and declaration of awareness;
- suggested training in report-writing skills or courtroom skills—these may be tax-deductible and will provide continuing professional development (CPD) points for the expert;
- an emphasis of the overriding duty to the court;
- a request that the report be signed and contain the expert's statement of truth; and
- many practitioners will also send a copy of CPR Part 35 or the Expert Protocol, with particular reference to guidelines for the expert.

The obligations of an expert witness were summarized and clarified (by Cresswell J in the Court of Appeal) in the *Ikarian Reefer* case (*National Justice Compania Naviera SA v Prudential Assurance Co Ltd (No 1)* [1993] 1 Lloyd's Rep 455, [2000] 1 WLR 603, [2001] WL 753347:

(a) Expert evidence presented to the court should be seen to be the independent product of the expert uninfluenced as to form or content by the exigencies of litigation.

(b) An expert witness should provide independent assistance to the court by way of objective unbiased opinion in relation to matters within his expertise. An expert witness in the court should never assume the role of advocate.

(c) An expert witness should state the facts or assumptions on which his opinion is based. He should not omit to consider material facts which detract from his concluded opinions.

(d) An expert should make it clear when a particular question or issue falls outside his expertise.

(e) If an expert's opinion is not properly researched because he considers that insufficient data is available, then this must be stated with an indication that the opinion is no more than a provisional one.

(f) If, after exchange of reports (if there is more than one expert), or at any other time, an expert witness changes his view on a matter, such change of view should be communicated to the parties (or party) instructing him without delay and, when appropriate, to the court.

Further guidance of what should be included in an expert's report is contained in the case of *Bowman v Fels* [2005] EWCA Civ 226 and PD 35.3:

(a) Details of the expert's academic and professional qualifications, experience, and accreditation relevant to the opinions expressed in the report, and the range and extent of the expertise and any limitations upon his expertise.

(b) A statement setting out the substance of all the instructions received (written and oral), questions asked, the materials provided and considered, and the documents, statements, evidence, information, or assumptions which are material to the opinions expressed or upon which the opinions are based.

(c) Information relating to who has carried out measurements, examinations, tests, etc. and the methodology used, and whether or not such measurements etc. were carried out under the expert's supervision.

(d) Where there is a range of opinion in the matters dealt with in the report, a summary of the range of opinion and the reasons for the opinion given. In this connection any material facts or matters which detract from the expert's opinions and any points which should fairly be made against any opinions expressed should be set out.

(e) Relevant extracts of literature or other material which might assist the court should be referred to and may be attached.

(f) A statement to the effect that the expert has complied with his duty to the court to provide independent assistance by way of objective unbiased opinion in relation to matters within his expertise. An acknowledgement that the expert will inform all parties, and where appropriate, the court, in the event that his opinion changes on any material issues.

(g) Where, on exchange of experts' reports (where there is more than one expert) matters arise which require a further, or supplemental, report, the above guidelines should be complied with.

A synopsis of this is contained in CPR 35.10, PD 35.2, and the Guidance Note at paragraphs 48–62.

A sample letter of instruction is available to students in the online resources.

18.10.1 **COPING WITH EXPERTS' REPORTS**

To be effective, the expert's report needs to be comprehensible to the parties, the legal representative, and any other professional employed to assist in the case, as well as the court.

When an expert's report has been received, not only will the report need to be carefully read, but the implications of it will also need to be understood. Additionally, there will be more peripheral matters to consider. These include a need to check whether:

- there has been full disclosure regarding all documents upon which the expert relies;

- the chronology schedule to the particulars of claim accords with the expert's chronology;

- there are any discrepancies or inconsistencies in the lay evidence that is being adduced. If there are, have all discrepancies or inconsistencies been identified and explained? Alternatively, check that the expert evidence dovetails with the witness statements and pleadings in the case; and

- the evidence covers all of the issues.

 Practical Considerations

The following represents a template 'checklist' that might be used when receiving any expert report.

Content A legal representative cannot influence the content and conclusions of the expert, but the following is a list of the matters that should be considered when an expert's report is received.

- Can you understand it?

- Is it in a layperson's language? Are technical terms explained?

- Is it independent?

- Does it have the 'declaration' (understanding expert's role and duty)?

- Is it authoritative?

- Is it persuasive?

- Does the expert avoid going outside his area of expertise?

- Have opinions been qualified where they are outside the area of expertise?

- Are 'facts', 'assumptions', and 'opinions' clearly defined?

- Is it signed?

Form Under the provisions of CPR 35, the report should be in proper form. Has the expert:

- given his name?

- given his address?

- identified his specialist area?

- included his qualifications and experience?

- confirmed his instructions?

- added a summary?

- inserted paragraph numbers and/or headings?

- inserted page numbers? (Is an index necessary?)

- included a glossary?

- dealt with the issues to be addressed?

- dealt with the facts (research, experiments, investigation)?

- given his opinion?

- stated the range of opinions in the field and commented on the reasons for this?

- concluded his report?

- included any necessary appendices for his investigations, references, or exhibits, etc.?

 Practical Considerations

When instructing an expert in a personal injury claim, whether as your own expert or an SJE, it is important that the expert is asked to cover all the 'lifestyle' aspects of your client's case so that the expert can comment on the way the claimant's injuries have affected his pre-accident lifestyle. In this way, where the expert agrees, the claimant's own witness statement will be supported by the medical report. This will give considerable evidential weight to the claimant's claim under the heads of damage. The expert should be asked to allow sufficient time in his appointment with the claimant to discuss these aspects of his lifestyle changes.

Please see Appendix 9 for a sample expert's report in a personal injury claim.

18.10.2 DEALING WITH QUESTIONS TO AN SJE OR THE OPPOSING PARTY'S EXPERT

CPR 35.6 contains the provisions that permit either party to put questions to an SJE or to the opposing party's own expert. It includes provisions that:

- questions may be put to that expert once;
- questions be put to the expert within twenty-eight days of receipt of the report; and
- questions must be for the purpose of clarifying the report.

The court may, however, modify these provisions either on its own initiative or upon the application of a party.

The written questions to experts should be 'proportionate'. This is intended to avoid instances when the questions put to an expert go beyond the issues identified in the case. Where parties are to have permission to put questions to an expert, a direction to this effect should be sought within the directions orders giving permission to use expert evidence (see paragraphs 18.4 and 18.7).

The expert will be required to answer the questions put to him as directed and in the time ordered by the court. His answers will be treated as part of his report. If the expert fails to answer questions put to him, the court may direct that the expert's evidence cannot be relied on and/or provide that the costs of that expert shall not be recoverable by the party who has engaged him. A party raising questions should serve a copy of the questions on the other parties in the action. The party asking the questions must initially bear the costs of the expert in answering the questions, but this does not affect any decision that the court may make concerning the costs orders that it may make at the conclusion of the case.

The CPR state that the questions to an expert should only be 'for the purpose of clarifying the report'. This is not defined by the rules. In *Mutch v Allen* [2001] EWCA Civ 76, the Court of Appeal considered the meaning of 'clarification' and concluded that it did enable a party to put a question to the expert that would have the effect of extending his report—that is, a question may be put on a matter not covered in the report. However, if the questions put to the expert are oppressive, in number or content, the court will not hesitate to disallow or restrict the questions asked.

18.10.3 DISCUSSIONS BETWEEN EXPERTS

Experts' discussions may take place at any time by arrangement between the parties, but they are usually ordered by the court in a directions order (see paragraph 18.7) (CPR 35.12). The court may also direct that the experts produce a statement after their discussions, setting out those areas on which they agree and those on which they do not. In the areas in which they disagree, they should give reasons (CPR 35.12(3)).

 Practical Considerations

The CPR do not specify exactly how meetings of experts should be set up. The Guidance Note, at paragraphs 70–83, and the Practice Direction on Experts and Assessors, at paragraph 9, sets out guidelines on how the parties and their legal representatives should cooperate in preparing an agenda, and making all of the necessary arrangements. It specifically states that instructing solicitors must not seek to restrict these discussions in such a way to 'avoid reaching areas of agreement on areas within their competence', but they can be reminded not to disclose certain confidential information of their client's. Equally, the legal representative must not instruct the expert to submit any schedule of agreed issues for 'approval' before it is finalized.

The Practice Direction on Experts and Assessors states, at paragraph 19.4, that legal representatives should not be present at the meeting of experts unless all parties and their experts have agreed, or the court orders the presence of legal representatives. In practice, many meetings of experts take place over the telephone for convenience and costs reasons.

18.10.4 THE EXPERT'S RIGHT TO ASK THE COURT FOR DIRECTIONS

Experts are entitled to ask the court for directions to assist them in carrying out their responsibilities and duties to the court, and where they feel that they need assistance (CPR 35.14). If the expert does ask the court for directions in this way, he is required to let his instructing party have a copy of his request to the court at least seven days before filing it at court, and all other parties, at least four days before his request is filed (these times can be varied by the court in the directions order that it makes concerning expert evidence).

 Practical Considerations

It may be a good idea to include in your terms of engagement with the expert a provision concerning the notification of any request to the court for directions. This will give the legal representative the chance to explore with the expert whether it is possible to resolve the difficulties that the expert has identified, and if it is not possible to resolve the issue that the expert has identified, to assist him in formulating the request to the court.

18.10.5 THE EXPERT AT COURT

Oral evidence at trial can only be given with the court's permission, and this includes expert oral evidence. In the fast track, the court is more likely to order that expert evidence be adduced in writing and that there is no oral expert evidence. Where oral expert evidence is provided for, the order will probably not be given until after the pre-trial checklist, which will be after the conclusion of experts' meetings and the preparation of the schedule of issues between the experts. If a party seeks an order for expert oral evidence, he will be expected to establish all, or one, or some, of the following:

- that the expert oral evidence is likely to have an impact on the outcome of the case;
- that the expert oral evidence will assist the judge;
- that there is a risk of injustice if the expert evidence is not tested at trial; or
- that the costs of expert oral evidence are not disproportionate.

Under the provisions of PD 35.11 the court will consider whether multiple experts in an action should give their evidence concurrently and, if so, will make orders as to how this will be achieved.

 Practical Considerations

If your expert is giving oral evidence at trial, it is important that you make the necessary arrangements concerning the expert's availability (that is, serve a witness summons—see Chapter 19, paragraph 19.4.1), and that he is aware what to expect and of the likelihood of cross-examination. If the trial is listed for several days, consideration should have been given in the trial timetable to provide on which day(s) the expert should be available. It is important, though, that the expert is in court not only for the time of his own oral evidence, but also for the time during which other evidence is being given that is within his area of expertise, so that he is able to comment on it and explain its significance. A single expert may assist his instructing party in the cross-examination of a witness or expert of the opponent. If the expert is not giving oral evidence or is not in court when judgment is given, as a matter of courtesy, make sure that you inform the expert of the outcome of the case.

18.10.6 PRACTICAL MATTERS—THE EXPERT'S ORAL EVIDENCE

Prior to attending court to give evidence, you need to ensure that the expert being called as a witness is aware that he will be expected:

- to speak clearly, briefly, and in simple, non-technical terms, where possible;
- to look at the judge, rather than the legal representative;
- not to be evasive, obstructive, hostile, or obstinate when his opinion is shown to be wrong—particularly if the point is not detrimental to the client;
- to be detached and concerned for the truth at all times, and not to be perceived as always allied with only one side;
- to be positive and assured about having his experience tested under cross-examination and not be resentful or antagonistic;
- not to become emotionally involved with the client;
- to stay within the boundaries of his own expertise and experience;
- to come up to proof;
- to be well prepared and as knowledgeable about the case as possible, including his opinion on prognosis; and
- not to be misled by omissions—you need to ensure that he has, and has considered, all of the material facts.

18.10.6.1 Concurrent expert evidence: 'hot-tubbing' PD 35.11

The court can direct that some or all of the expert's evidence from like discipline can give evidence concurrently (PD 35.11). This is also known as 'hot-tubbing'.

PD 35.11 sets out the procedure and allows for flexibility in the way that experts can give oral evidence at trial, bearing in mind that concurrent expert evidence is not appropriate in every case.

Experts can give their evidence in any appropriate manner as directed by the court. This could mean that experts of like discipline give evidence, and are cross-examined, on an issue by issue basis (PD 35.11.2). Where expert evidence is to be given concurrently the court may follow the steps set out at PD 35.11.4.

18.10.7 PRACTICAL MATTERS—THE EXPERT'S WRITTEN EVIDENCE

If experts look for and report on factors that tend to support a particular proposition, the report should still:

- provide a straightforward, not misleading, written opinion that the court will readily understand;
- be objective and not omit factors that do not support the expert's opinion—remembering that you may find that the expert has to give an opinion that is adverse to your client, and if this occurs, you need to consider how to inform the client;
- be properly researched—if the expert considers that insufficient data is available, then he should say so and indicate that his opinion is no more than a provisional one.

Where an expert's report contains opinion evidence (that the expert is not qualified to give), the view has been that those parts of the report should be redacted. This view has been questioned by the High Court in *Hoyle v Rogers* [2014] EWCA Civ 537, with the suggestion that applications to redact are unnecessarily expensive—the whole document should be admitted without redaction and the judge can ignore that which is inadmissible.

18.11 THE EXPERT AND HIS IMMUNITY FROM SUIT

The common law concept of witness immunity is that all witnesses, including expert witnesses, are immune from civil suit. However, in the judgment of *Jones v Kaney* [2011] UKSC 13, the Supreme Court by a majority decision concluded that the immunity from suit that experts have had in the work they undertake in legal proceedings should be abolished. This judgment may well mean that experts can be expected (and directed) to be more careful when preparing their opinion and report.

18.12 EXPERTS AND PRIVILEGE

An expert's report, which is prepared for the purpose of contemplated or pending civil actions for obtaining or giving legal advice, is privileged. There is no obligation to disclose a report on which the party does not intend to rely at trial. Provided that a report is not used as a source of evidence, it may be used in cross-examination of the other side's expert—to test the strength of his opinion. However, once a report has been disclosed by a party, notwithstanding any later decision not to adduce it as evidence at trial, the opponent is permitted to rely on it if he so wishes. This is because once a report has been disclosed, it loses its privilege.

Any advice given by an expert acting in an advisory role for a party will be privileged (*Carlson v Townsend* [2001] EWCA 511), provided the dominant purpose test is satisfied (see Chapter 16, paragraph 16.9.2.2).

18.12.1 WHEN WILL EXPERTS' REPORTS BE DISCLOSED?

In personal injury claims, the claimant must disclose a report when issuing proceedings. Any further use of expert evidence in personal injury actions will be controlled by the court in the normal way (see paragraph 18.3).

In all other cases, the courts will usually make orders detailing the exchange of experts' reports as part of its case management directions. Usually, reports will be ordered to be exchanged after an appropriate period of time, but usually after disclosure and exchange of witness statements. Generally, disclosure of expert evidence should be simultaneous. PD 29.4.11 provides that if it appears that expert evidence will be required both on issues of liability and on the amount of damages, the court may direct that the exchange of those reports that relate to liability will be exchanged simultaneously, but that those relating to the amount of damages will be exchanged sequentially.

KEY POINTS SUMMARY

- The key provisions of CPR Part 35 are:
  - CPR 35.1—there may be no experts at all;
  - CPR 35.2—expert evidence defined;
  - CPR 35.3—expert's duty to court prevails;
  - CPR 35.4—court control;
  - CPR 35.6—questions to experts;

- CPR 35.9—sharing unilateral expertise;

- PD 35.11—'hot-tubbing' provisions;

- CPR 35.12—experts' discussions;

- CPR 35.14—experts applying to the court.

- Experts have a variety of roles (and uses) in litigation—be sure to understand the distinctions.

- Expert evidence can only be adduced in litigation with the permission of the court. Essentially, it will only be permitted if it can be shown to be probative, useful, and cogent, and the cost of obtaining it must be proportionate. Any request for expert evidence must be accompanied with a statement of the costs of having it.

- Be clear about the difference between a single joint expert (SJE) and a jointly selected expert.

- The duties and obligations of the expert to the court take precedence over any obligations that he may feel to the party who engages or is paying him. Remember the three 'i's of an expert: integrity, independence, and impartiality.

- A legal representative may influence and guide the expert of the form of his report, but not its content or the conclusions reached by the expert. There must be complete transparency of communication between expert and legal representative.

- The trial judge is ultimately the person who decides on which of two conflicting opinions he will rely and he can reject expert opinion in favour of the evidence of witnesses of fact.

- Handling experts and expert evidence takes considerable care and skill.

Case Study *Andrew James Pike v Deep Builders Ltd*

Question 1

In this case and acting for Andrew Pike, you have now downloaded and completed the DQ (Form N180 or N181). Do you feel that you should ask for a direction that each party may instruct, and rely on, their own expert? If so, what are your reasons for this and what directions do you think you should ask the court to make? If you think the appropriate order should be for an SJE, give your reasons for this and suggest the directions order that you will seek.

Question 2

Prepare a letter instructing an SJE in this matter.

 Any documents referred to in these case study questions can be found in the online resources—simply click on 'Case study documentation' to access the documents that you need for Chapter 18 and to be reminded of the questions. Suggested answers to these self-test questions can be accessed in the Student Resources section of the online resources.

Relevant court forms relating to this chapter:

- N20 Witness Summons

- N260 Statement of Costs for Fast-Track Trials

- N292 Draft Consent Order (Children's Claims)

- N320 Court Funds Form (Children's Claims)

Relevant parts of the CPR and its PDs: 5, 8, 18, 21, 33, 34, 36, 38, 39, 40, 44, 46, and 52.

In the online resources there is a short podcast that will help you to understand the nature and purpose of Tomlin orders.

LITIGATION TRAIN:

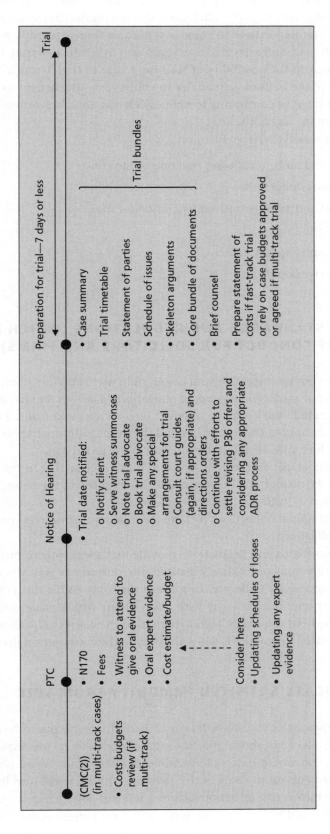

PTC
(CMC(2))
(in multi-track cases)

- Costs budgets review (if multi-track)

- N170
- Fees

- Witness to attend to give oral evidence
- Oral expert evidence
- Cost estimate/budget

Consider here
- Updating schedules of losses

- Updating any expert evidence

Notice of Hearing

- Trial date notified:
  o Notify client
  o Serve witness summonses
  o Note trial advocate
  o Book trial advocate
  o Make any special arrangements for trial
  o Consult court guides (again, if appropriate) and directions orders
  o Continue with efforts to settle revising P36 offers and considering any appropriate ADR process

Preparation for trial—7 days or less

- Case summary
- Trial timetable
- Statement of parties
- Schedule of issues
- Skeleton arguments
- Core bundle of documents
- Brief counsel
- Prepare statement of costs if fast-track trial or rely on case budgets approved or agreed if multi-track trial

Trial bundles

Trial

19.1 **INTRODUCTION**

Despite the fact that the whole philosophy of litigation today is to avoid trial by engaging in and complying with Protocol, alternative dispute resolution (ADR), and case management, all legal representatives need to know how to run a case up to trial and through the trial day itself. A high percentage of civil cases settle well in advance of trial, but it is still important for you to look to the possibility of running a case to trial, because this is, in essence, the benchmark of the basis of your advice to your client—the benefit to your client of settling at an earlier stage, or continuing to fight or defend a case, is measured against what is likely to happen on the day of the trial.

This chapter will therefore focus on:

- fast-track and multi-track cases that proceed to trial;
- professional conduct issues;
- procedural and administrative preparation for trial;
- the day of the trial;
- judgment and appeals; and
- settlement without trial.

19.2 **THE SRA STANDARDS AND REGULATIONS (WHICH INCLUDE THE CODES OF CONDUCT FOR SOLICITORS AND FIRMS)**

Throughout your retainer with your client, right up to and including the trial, you must be mindful of your professional conduct obligations. The SRA Standards and Regulations (see Chapter 1) include the Codes of Conduct for solicitors and firms. They make it clear that solicitors must uphold the rule of law and the proper administration of justice, and ensure that his conduct upholds public confidence in the profession.

The SRA Standards and Regulations also make it clear that in the event of any conflict between the Principles, then the Principle that best serves the public interest in the proper administration of justice will take precedence.

These professional obligations include the legal representatives conduct in litigation and advocacy obligations.

The SRA Standards and Regulations provide that a legal practitioner must not attempt to deceive or knowingly or recklessly mislead the court in any way, whether this be him or by assisting someone else to deceive or mislead the court. What this effectively means is that a legal practitioner must comply with court orders which place obligations on him, and, of course, the need to comply with his duties to the court at all times. The main challenge that may be faced in practice is when the duty to the court outweighs the duty to the client.

19.3 **AN ADVOCATE'S LIMITED IMMUNITY FROM SUIT**

A solicitor-advocate or counsel will only be liable in negligence in respect of his work as an advocate when it can be shown that 'the error was one that no reasonably competent member of the profession would have made' (*Arthur JS Hall & Co v Simons* [2000] UKHL 38). Mere 'error of judgment' on the part of the advocate will not make him liable in negligence. In practice, this means that an action against a solicitor-advocate or counsel who acts honestly and carefully is unlikely to succeed. It has also been suggested that the level of competence could also be related to the advocate's level of expertise (or seniority) (*McFaddens (a firm) v Platford* [2009] EWHC 126). However, it cannot be finally concluded from this cases that the 'seniority' test can be relied on in all situations in which a solicitor-advocate or barrister is in court.

19.4 IMMEDIATE ACTION ON RECEIPT OF THE TRIAL DATE

In most fast track claims, the court may fix the trial date on receipt of the directions questionnaire. In other more substantial fast track claims and multi-track claims, only once the court has dealt with the pre-trial checklist (PTC) and any necessary pre-trial review or hearing, will the court then list the matter for trial. In either case, once this has been done, it will then dispatch to all parties a Notice of Trial Date, informing the parties of the trial date. There are a number of important matters that a legal representative needs to deal with, and these are outlined here.

19.4.1 ISSUE WITNESS SUMMONSES

As soon as you receive the Notice of Trial Date from the court, you will need to consider which witnesses and experts will be required to attend the trial, either to give oral evidence or to produce specified documents. You should already have, by this stage, permission from the court to rely on and adduce such evidence at trial. It is, therefore, extremely important that you prepare, issue, and arrange for the service of a witness summons in respect of each witness and expert in Form N20 (see the online resources for a copy of the form). The purpose of the summons is to compel attendance at trial. A court fee and conduct money (to compensate the witness for expenses of attending trial) are required and should have been requested from the client in anticipation of the hearing date.

If a witness or expert subsequently fails to attend trial having been validly served with a witness summons, then they will either be fined if in the County Court (County Courts Act 1984, s. 55(1) and (2)), or be found to be in contempt if in the High Court. If, however, you omit to deal with the issue and service of witness summonses, and one of your witnesses fails to attend court, you are likely to be in breach of your professional conduct obligations and possibly be the subject of a wasted costs order if the trial is adjourned, or be faced with a professional negligence action if the evidence of the absent witness was crucial to the success of the case.

In order for the witness summons to be valid, Form N20 must be correctly completed and sent to the court. You can decide whether you wish to serve the witness summons yourself, in which case, you will need to send three copies to the court. If you decide that you want the court to serve the summons, then the court requires only two copies. In either case, the summons will only be valid if you enclose a court fee and a sum of money in respect of the witnesses' reasonable expenses and compensation for loss of time (known as 'conduct money'—see CPR 34.7). Service must be effected at least seven days before the date of the trial (CPR 34.5).

 Practical Considerations

Some legal representatives prefer not to serve experts with witness summons because they feel this is disrespectful, and that it is implied in the expert's duty to the court and acceptance of instructions that he will attend the trial of the matter. However, others believe that all witnesses giving oral evidence or producing documents to the court at trial should be summonsed to 'cover their backs' against the risk of a potential professional negligence claim should the expert fail to attend. We would recommend that a politely worded covering letter to the expert explaining the purpose and nature of the summons would alleviate any professional discomfort on the part of the legal representative, whilst affording him the protection that he and his client deserve. In any event, witnesses, such as the police, will not attend trial unless served with a witness summons. Further, witness summonsing your expert allows him to clear his diary and to prevent non-attendance by a supervening incident—particularly if a medical expert.

19.4.2 CONTACT COUNSEL

Unqualified practitioners are not permitted to act as trial advocates in fast track or multi-track cases, although you may have the opportunity to undertake trial advocacy in small claims cases. You will need to ensure that you have the appropriate solicitor-advocate or barrister to undertake the advocacy. In this section, we refer to the trial advocate as 'counsel'.

There is an additional chapter, 'Guide to Preparing Instructions to Counsel', available in the online resources.

When considering whether to advise the client that counsel should be instructed to undertake the advocacy at trial, you are under a duty to act in the best interests of your client. For example, you may have chosen a competent, relatively inexpensive, but fairly inexperienced counsel to advise on the prospects of success at the outset of the case, but you have managed the case without further input from this counsel. As the trial approaches, you will need to consider with your client whether counsel with more trial experience would be more appropriate, even if that would entail instructing a more expensive counsel. You will also need to consider the timing of the change of counsel. Any change in counsel for this reason before trial should be detailed in a written note on the file and a letter to the client.

Once you have the trial date from court, practitioners will have the task of booking counsel for the trial and considering with the client and counsel whether a pre-trial conference is required. The simplest and quickest way of booking counsel is to contact the counsel's clerk directly over the telephone or by email. Remember that you will have already sought counsel's general availability for the trial window when completing the PTC. The court may have taken several weeks to list the matter and dispatch the notice of hearing to you, so you will need to act expeditiously, because counsel may, in the interim, have other commitments.

Counsel's clerk will place the details of the trial in the diary and this secures counsel for the trial. At this stage, there is no need to send any papers to counsel or to agree a fee. The terminology for this, when you come to undertake them, is important: when sending papers to counsel to advise, draft, or attend a conference (if you are seeking a conference with a Queen's Counsel (QC, otherwise known as a Silk), then it is called a 'consultation'), you are said to be 'instructing counsel', and the papers are known as 'instructions to counsel'. When you send papers to counsel to attend any interim or final hearing, you are said to be 'briefing counsel', and the papers are known as 'a brief'. The key point with a brief is that, as soon as this is 'delivered' to counsel, the brief fee is incurred—and there will be a liability to pay for counsel whether or not the trial or hearing goes ahead. This is the reason why briefing counsel is only done a matter of days before the hearing, because settlement efforts are at a premium at that stage.

✓ Practical Considerations

It is always worth ensuring you have a good relationship with counsel's clerk, because if they are on your side, they will be more likely to waive a brief fee for an aborted or adjourned hearing, or to squeeze in an urgent conference. It is the clerk who is responsible for agreeing all fees and arranging conferences with counsel. These are never discussed with counsel.

The brief fee that you agree covers counsel's preparation for the trial; his skeleton argument, excluding the time spent at any pre-trial conference; plus his attendance at court for the first day of the trial, no matter how long he is there. If the trial is listed for more than one day, then the clerk will discuss a refresher fee with you, which represents a percentage of the brief fee. For example, if the brief fee is £6,000 and the trial is listed for three days, the refresher fee for each of the two remaining days could be £1,500 per day, making total counsel's fee for the trial £9,000.

19.4.3 LIAISE WITH YOUR CLIENT

Another immediate task that you must undertake is to contact your client to inform him of the trial date. Again, you will have already obtained his available dates and inserted them in the PTC. It would also be sensible to ask your client to keep his diary relatively free for the few days in the run-up to the trial for settlement negotiations and generally, to enable you to seek instructions from him without delay. There is no requirement to witness summons your client.

19.4.4 CHECK YOUR DIARY

The trial date needs to be inserted into your diary, with the weeks before left relatively clear to focus on the final preparations for the trial bundles (see paragraph 19.5.2) and settlement opportunities. The run-up to trial is an extremely busy time for legal representatives, whose workload for the week before the trial becomes almost exclusively taken up with the matter in hand.

 Practical Considerations

It is good practice to have a central diary scheme on which details of the trial date and venue can be posted, so that others in the department are aware that a trial is coming up or is taking place. This will indicate that you will be busy and out of the office for extended periods of time. Delegation of tasks on other files may have to be considered if another file demands attention whilst you are unavailable.

19.5 PREPARATION FOR TRIAL

19.5.1 ADMINISTRATIVE TASKS

19.5.1.1 Paying the trial fee

The Civil Proceedings Fee (Amendment) Order 2016 removed the ability to seek a refund of the trial fee if the matter settles or is discontinued after the fee has been paid. This order also provides that a claim (or counterclaim) will be struck out if the trial fee is not paid. CPR 3.7A1(7) also states that the strike out for non-payment of the trial fee will be automatic. The defaulting party retains a right to apply to reinstate the claim; however this must be made within seven days of service of the order and will be conditional on payment of the fee.

In terms of time limits within which to pay the fee, this will depend on when the court gives the Notice of Trial (or the trial period). Where there are more than thirty-six days until the trial from the date of issue of the Notice, the fee must be paid within twenty-eight days (or by the Monday of the first week of the trial period). Where there are less than thirty-six days until the trial (or the Monday of the first week of the trial period) from the date of issue of the Notice, the fee must be paid within seven days of the Notice being given.

In light of these changes, the court will now issue a Notice to Pay Fee (N173) to avoid any confusion as to when the fee is due to be paid.

19.5.1.2 How is the evidence at trial to be given

It is extremely important that the trial flows without a hitch in terms of presentation of the evidence to the judge. You do not want to irritate your judge for any reason, so it is worth spending some time considering, both at the PTC stage and directly before trial, how the judge will hear the evidence. Special requirements in relation to the presentation of the evidence at trial should have been set out in the PTC. (See Chapter 12, paragraph 12.7.3.3, for a discussion on the PTC.)

A witness or expert may be giving evidence by video link, for which permission of the court is required. You may have video or audio recordings to play to the judge, some documents may need to be displayed electronically, or you may need access to the Internet. Similarly, an interpreter may be required. You will need to arrange all of these for the day of the trial by ensuring that there is a working video link facility at court, a video or DVD player available, a laptop and projector, an Internet connection, and a variety of visual displays, such as flip charts. The choice and costs of the interpreter are also important.

19.5.1.3 Transcripts

In some lengthy trials, it may be appropriate to arrange for a daily transcript to be produced. There are two types of transcription service available: a daily transcript, which is available a few hours after the day's hearing has finished, and a realtime transcription, such as LiveNote. This is more expensive than the daily transcript, but allows you to follow the trial by reading the text on a laptop in court, which, in complex matters and lengthy cross-examination, allows you and your advocate to highlight salient points.

19.5.1.4 General arrangements

There are also a number of good general 'housekeeping' tasks for a legal representative to consider, such as ensuring that the court has sizeable and numerous conference rooms for meetings with counsel and the client before the trial starts and in which to debrief at the end of the day. Is there a canteen or restaurant at the court, and if not, what alternative arrangements can be made for lunch and general refreshments? Is the court near a railway station or car park? (Sometimes voluminous documentation is required to be taken to the court on the day of the hearing.)

19.5.1.5 Preparing your witness of fact for trial

Whilst witness summons have usually already been served in the run-up to trial, witnesses should be contacted shortly before the trial to firm up on final arrangements for meeting up at court, how to prepare for the trial, and what to expect when giving evidence. You should:

- ensure that the witness knows the location of the court and has made adequate travel arrangements;

- explain the layout of the court and where he will be giving evidence;

- advise him of the appropriate attire for his court appearance;

- outline what he should do to prepare to give evidence—he should be asked to review his and other relevant witness statements, and any relevant documentation;

- advise him on giving his evidence. You should explain to him when and how long he is likely to be in the witness box, that he will be asked to take an oath or affirmation, how to address the judge, and remind him to address his answers to the judge, not counsel. It would also be useful to explain to him the process of cross-examination and re-examination, and to give him some tips on keeping calm in the witness box; and

- in more complex cases where the witness is likely to be in the witness box for some time, consider witness training with an independent organization.

19.5.2 PREPARING THE TRIAL BUNDLES

19.5.2.1 What documentation goes into a trial bundle?

Trial bundles must be prepared for all trials, and this is a task that usually falls to those new to practice. There are several points of reference to help you to decide when and what documentation is used to compile the trial bundles, as follows:

- the court order following the PTC and/or review or hearing;

- the Court Guides; and

- CPR 39 and its Practice Direction (PD).

The trial bundles are prepared by the claimant's legal representative (CPR 39.5(1)), and getting the bundles right requires structured planning and attention to detail. They are very time-consuming to prepare and this should not be underestimated. The process begins with a review of all non-privileged documentation and the preparation of a trial bundle index. This should be sent to your counsel and opponent for approval before the actual documents are copied.

 Practical Considerations

When drafting the index, use your common sense as to what documents to include and in what order they should appear, remembering to exclude all privileged and without-prejudice documents, and to include only those that are necessary for the trial. For example, there is little point enclosing copy correspondence with the court, because this is unlikely to go to any issue in the case or the emailed duplicate version of a letter unless sending the letter by email will help prove a point. Try to make the bundles as user-friendly as possible for the judge and counsel: a bundle that contains irrelevant, poorly copied, and obliterated material is unlikely to impress the judge.

The claimant must file the bundles between three and seven days before the start of the trial, unless the court has made a different order (CPR 39.5, and PD 39A 3.1 and 3.4). In more lengthy and complicated matters, the trial bundle can consist of a substantive bundle, an authorities' bundle, and a procedural bundle. Alternatively, depending on the amount of documentation, there may only be one substantive bundle, containing the following documents:

- the trial timetable* and statement of parties;*
- a schedule of issues;*
- a skeleton argument* and list of authorities* (plus a reading list, where appropriate);
- a case summary* and/or chronology,* where appropriate;
- the claim form and all statements of case;
- CPR 18 requests and replies;
- witness statements and summaries;
- notices of intention to rely on hearsay evidence and corresponding notices to attack credibility;
- notices of intention to rely on evidence, such as plans and photographs, under CPR 33.6;
- notices to admit;
- experts' reports;
- relevant orders for directions; and
- any relevant necessary documents.

19.5.2.2 Documentation specifically prepared for trial

The documents marked with an asterisk are documents that are specifically prepared for the trial as a result of a court order or as per the requirements of the Court Guides. All of these documents, save for the skeleton arguments and list of authorities, are usually prepared by the claimant's solicitor and are usually agreed by the opponent.

- The trial timetable sets out what will happen in what order and for how long on the day(s) of the trial. The judge does not always follow it. The statement of parties identifies who will be representing each party in terms of the legal team, including counsel, and details the party to the action and who will be attending on their behalf, if appropriate.
- The schedule of issues will list the main issues still outstanding between the parties on liability, causation, and quantum.
- The skeleton argument and list of authorities will be prepared by each party's trial advocate, and will set out in writing the legal basis for the party's case and the main submissions to be made on the day of the hearing. It may attach cases or statutes for the judge to read. Therefore, in line with the 'cards on the table' approach to litigation, both you and your opponent will have an outline of the major submissions to be made at trial.
- The case summary and chronology provide an outline of the case facts, and what is being claimed or refuted. Chronologies are not always necessary, but can be useful when dates and conduct are crucial to a case, such as in a breach of contract action.

19.5.2.3 The trial bundle index and the bundles

Once you have prepared, and your trial advocate has approved, the trial bundle index, this should be sent, usually by email, to your opponent's legal representative for agreement.

* See paragraph 19.5.2.2.

Invariably, their counsel will want to approve the index too, so planning your preparation of the trial bundle index in advance is essential. It is not unusual for your opponent to request that additional documents be added to the index. The trial bundle is an agreed bundle, and it may take a little 'toing and froing' before agreement is reached.

Once it is agreed, the first bundles created can be paginated and the page numbering inserted in the index. Then, the copying begins. There should be a minimum of six duplicate bundles prepared: one each for the judge, yourself, and your counsel; one each for your opponent and his counsel; and one for the witness in court. It is probably a good idea to prepare a further trial bundle for your client and an extra copy to be left at the office. The copies for the judge and witness box must be filed within the deadlines stipulated, but it is probably a good idea to liaise with the court clerk regarding the practical arrangements for delivery if the bundles are numerous or cumbersome.

 Practical Considerations

Questions often arise as to how best to deal with large documents, such as plans, poor-quality copies, hole-punching, and pagination. CPR 39 and its Practice Direction are helpful, as are the Court Guides, although most of the principles are based on common sense—for example:

- consider using separate files for very large documents, rather than including them in chronological order in the bundles;
- insist on the best copy quality and avoid copying from faxed versions;
- hole-punch only where text will not be obliterated; and
- paginate where the number can be clearly seen and not omitted by the photocopier.

A final thought on the preparation of trial bundles is to focus on making the bundles as user-friendly as possible for the judge and counsel. Trial bundles that are too heavy, and overflowing with irrelevant materials and poor copies, are likely to frustrate your trial judge.

19.5.3 PART 36 OFFERS AND ADR

Now that most of the substantive matters in the action have been dealt with, you have attended to the filing of the PTC, and your trial preparation is in hand, this is another ideal time at which to continue your attempts to settle the case to avoid trial.

The 'litigation train' diagram at the beginning of this chapter highlights that this is a good time to seek counsel's advice in conference for the purpose of defining views on liability, causation, and quantum, as well as for advice on making a well-pitched Part 36 offer or revised offer. In line with the overriding objective, it may now also be appropriate to reconsider ADR again (especially if you have not yet tried one of the processes). Counsel can also be asked for his views on which is the most suitable process.

19.5.4 REVIEW FUNDING COVER

Very often, there will be a need if your client is funded by insurance—whether after the event (ATE), before the event (BTE), or even a litigation funder (for example, a trade union), or if your client is publicly funded—to report the pre-trial position to the funder and seek authority to proceed to trial.

19.5.5 UPDATE DOCUMENTATION

In some actions, from the initial preparation of documentation (particularly medical evidence and a variety of schedules) to trial, a significant amount of time has elapsed and the information contained in such documentation may need updating to ensure that the court has the most up-to-date and accurate information before it on the day of the trial. In the case of the medical report, for example, if the expert examined the claimant over a year before trial, you will need to check with the expert that the prognosis is still accurate, and he may need to re-examine the claimant and provide an up-to-date report. Similarly, if the schedule of losses in the particulars of claim has changed since issue (and this is very likely due to items being agreed or changed), this will also need revising, as will the defendant's counter-schedule.

 Costs

> In the run-up to trial, costs are being incurred at a tremendous rate. In fast-track cases, costs estimates will have been periodically prepared and updated for the court and for your client throughout the action. In multi-track cases, costs budgets will have been prepared and either agreed with the opponent be subject to a CMC or simply approved by the court and copied to your client. This is a final opportunity to consider—and discuss with your client—the overall costs of the action (with projected figures for the trial itself). In fast-track cases, Form N260 is required to be filed at least two clear days before the trial. In relevant multi-track cases, there is no requirement to file a separate costs schedule, although the costs budget will have contingencies built into the overall figure and regard must of course be had to any CMOs.

19.6 THE DAY OF THE TRIAL

19.6.1 MEETING UP

Arrive at court early to ensure that you have a conference room for discussions with counsel and your client before the trial commences. As an alternative, if the court centre is local to either counsel or your firm's offices, this conference can take place at either of these locations, but ensure you allow ample time to make your way across to court in time for the 10 a.m. or 10.30 a.m. start. Once at court, you will need to keep an eye out for your witnesses as they arrive, and remind them that they are not allowed to discuss the case with either party and its respective legal team. It is part of your role on the day of the trial to ensure that the witnesses are prepared and ready to give evidence.

19.6.2 TRIAL ETIQUETTE

There are a number of important points to note and whilst some of these may seem elementary, the intensity of the run-up to trial and the trial day(s) can mean that these are sometimes overlooked.

- When the judge enters or leaves the room, the court usher will say 'Court rise'. Everybody must stand until the judge is seated or has left the room. The judge has his own private entrance to the courtroom and, on entering and leaving, he will bow to the court. Everybody must reciprocate. If you enter or leave the courtroom whilst the judge is sitting, then you should stand to face the judge and bow before sitting or leaving. It is important not to turn your back to the judge.

- Formal dress should be worn by all those attending court. Usually, dark-coloured suits are appropriate.

- All mobile phones, laptops, and tablets should be switched to silent.

- If you must talk, this must be done as quietly as possible, only to communicate a message to your counsel or the court clerk, and only if urgent, otherwise you should wait until a break in the proceedings. Traditionally, legal representatives sitting behind counsel write a message and tug on counsel's gown to attract his attention to enable him to reach for the note. Take a pack of sticky notes in with you on which you can pass short notes to counsel.

Practical Considerations

As the trial day progresses, there may be times during the day at which your counsel is making good progress in his cross-examination. It is very important for you, as well as your client, not to react in any way to evidence or submissions, because the judge sees all reactions. For example, if your counsel trips up your opponent's witness in your favour, under no circumstances should you laugh, or even smile. Similarly, if you disagree with what your opponent's counsel or witness is saying, then you are not to sigh or show signs of frustration.

19.6.3 A TYPICAL DAY IN COURT

The judge usually sits between 10 a.m. and 4 p.m., but, on occasions, he may sit later, depending on the progress of the trial and the availability of the court staff.

The usual format of the trial is as follows:

1. Opening submissions for the claimant.

2. Opening submissions for the defendant.

3. Any preliminary issues (these sometimes involve dealing with unforeseen events that arise on the morning of the trial).

4. Claimant's witnesses of fact.

5. Claimant's expert evidence.

6. Defendant's witnesses of fact.

7. Defendant's expert evidence.

8. Closing submissions for the claimant.

9. Closing submissions for the defendant.

Depending on the nature of the case and the judge, opening submissions may be dispensed with if the skeleton arguments are sufficient. This is happening more frequently, as it saves time on the day of the trial. Therefore, give thought to abandoning these opening submissions and discuss this with your trial advocate. In terms of all of the witnesses, they are subject to an examination-in-chief by their own counsel (although this is limited to confirming their name, address, and that the witness statement in the trial bundle is their own, unless the court gives permission for the witness to add anything, for example new information), cross-examination by the opponent's counsel, and re-examination by their own counsel.

 Practical Considerations

The main function of the legal representative during the trial is to take detailed notes, irrespective of transcription services, and to be aware of any issue that needs to be brought to counsel's attention during trial. This is hard work, so ensure that you are alert and focused on what is being said in court at all times by all persons present. Ensure that you have enough paper; counsel notepads are often used by the legal team to make notes and an array of coloured pens is also useful to highlight the salient points that you may want counsel to consider at a break in the proceedings, or for the purposes of cross-examination. The notes can be reviewed at the end of the trial day. Laptops and tablets are also permitted in court to assist both counsel and legal representatives during the trial to make notes and cross-examination points.

19.6.4 UNFORESEEN EVENTS

On the eve of the trial, or even on the morning of the hearing, certain matters often arise, the most common of which are new evidence and attempts to amend statements of case on the part of your opponent. If something does arise, it is important to discuss it with counsel and your client, taking the time to assess the potential impact on your client's case, and whether and to what extent the late change should be opposed.

Occasionally, the trial will need to be adjourned, but this is really a last resort. When this happens, costs orders will need to be considered. If the trial is to go ahead, then you may wish to make the appropriate costs representations to the judge if the unforeseen event has an impact on your own client's costs, such as a new witness, which extends the length of the trial, or an amended particulars of claim, which requires an amended defence to be prepared.

19.7 AFTER THE TRIAL

There are a number of considerations that you will need to bear in mind when both parties have made their closing submissions and the trial has effectively finished. These are in relation to the judgment, costs, and appeals.

19.7.1 JUDGMENT

Fast-track trials or trials that have been relatively straightforward are more likely to have judgments available immediately after the completion of the closing submissions. In these cases, the judge may retire to his rooms to consider his judgment before coming back into the court to 'hand it down' to the parties' advocates. Once judgment has been given in these circumstances, then representations are made to the judge on the question of costs (see Table 4.2 in Chapter 4 for the different types of costs order) and for permission to appeal. These are discussed in paragraph 19.7.2.

In most other cases, judgment is not usually handed down on the last day of the trial, because the judge requires time to evaluate all of the evidence heard and review any legal authorities. After closing submissions, the judge will inform the court that he will reserve judgment, and will fix a date, there and then, with the court clerk and the parties for the formal handing down of the judgment, which is frequently several weeks—or even months—from the completion of the trial.

 Practical Considerations

In some cases, clients have been waiting a long time for their case to come to trial. It is sensible to manage their expectations not only of the trial procedure itself, but also as to when they are likely to know whether they have substantially won or lost. The trial day(s) are the most expensive part of litigation and whether your client is under a conditional fee agreement (CFA), is paying privately, or is funded by insurance, there may be additional legal fees and disbursements relating to the trial that need to be paid out before the judgment is handed down. A well-informed client is more likely to be patient and content during the period between trial and judgment.

Once the judge has prepared his judgment and the date that has been fixed for the formal handing down approaches, the judge may release his draft judgment to the parties. Draft judgments are technically confidential and should not be released to your client, although the judge may not, in every draft judgment, attach an embargo in this regard. PD 40E contains provisions dealing with how draft judgments should be treated.

Judgments are sometimes released in draft a day before the judgment is to be delivered, to allow the parties time to consider whether they wish to seek any consequential orders or permissions to appeal, and to identify any typographical errors or other minor errors before the formal handing down, which is when the judgment becomes effective.

At the handing-down hearing, the judge will sit and recite his judgment, after which the parties can make various representations to the court on the question of costs.

Practical Considerations

In order to be prepared for the handing down of judgment hearing, which is only a short hearing, revisit the Court Guides on draft judgments and handing down, and be clear about what potential orders you may be required to apply for.

19.7.2 COSTS

Your client should have been given the requisite information on costs at the outset of your retainer with him and at appropriate intervals throughout his case. This information would include funding the litigation, the extent of costs recovery against the opponent, and the various costs orders that can be made by the court, including the basis upon which those costs are assessed. (See Chapter 3, paragraph 3.2, and Chapter 4, paragraph 4.3, for full details of your duty to your client in this regard.)

Therefore, by the time that the judgment is handed down, the costs consequences of winning or losing should come as no surprise to your client, even if the terms of the judgment do. The important feature here is to ensure that, at the hearing, you are in a position to do your best for your client when counsel is making representations to the judge on costs, either asking for an order for costs, or opposing an order for costs.

Practical Considerations

You may wish to prepare in advance of the hearing a bundle for your counsel containing all of the Part 36 offers or Calderbank or 'Global' offers that have passed between the parties in the event that, should your client be successful, you have to hand information to help the judge decide what costs order to make (whether this is for standard or indemnity costs) and whether any costs and interest enhancements should be made; conversely, should your client have effectively lost, the bundle may assist the judge in deciding whether any penalties should be imposed as a result of your opponent not beating an offer.

Remember that, if it is a fast-track trial, you should have prepared a statement of costs in a form similar to Form N260, as a summary assessment will be made. Fixed costs usually apply to fast-track trials (see Chapter 4, paragraph 4.7.3, and CPR 45, Section VI, 45.37–45.45.40).

19.7.3 THE SHORTER TRIALS SCHEME (STS) AND THE FLEXIBLE TRIALS SCHEME (FTS)

The shorter trials scheme (STS) and the flexible trials scheme (FTS) (previously a pilot under PD 51N) both became permanent with effect from 1 October 2018 in the Business and Property courts nationwide. The practice and procedure is contained under CPR Practice Direction 57AB.

The STS scheme creates a streamlined procedure with a docketed judge leading to judgment within twelve months of proceedings being issued. Trials are limited to a maximum of four days with judgment published within six weeks. Claimants initiate the process and approach defendants about resolving the case, with a judge able to intervene if the parties cannot agree.

19.7.4 APPEALS

19.7.4.1 Introduction

Where a party is unhappy with a court judgment or order at either a final or interim hearing, including a costs order, that party may be entitled to appeal that judgment or order. The practice and procedure is the same for appeals in the County Court, the High Court, and the Court of Appeal which are all governed by CPR 52 and its revised PDs. The PDs have now been subdivided into five separate PDs as follows:

- PD 52A Appeals general provisions;
- PD 52B Appeals in the County Court and the High Court;

- PD 52C Appeals to the Court of Appeal;

- PD 52D Statutory Appeals and appeals subject to special provision; and

- PD 52E Appeals by way of case stated.

CPR 52 has been revised on a number of occasions in recent years, notably in October 2016. The Court Guides are also very useful to help you to prepare for these types of appeals and should be consulted in addition to CPR 52 and the relevant PD. Legal representatives should, however, remember that the main procedure governing appeals is contained in CPR 52 and that the purpose of the PD is only to supplement CPR 52.

It is, however, very different in the Supreme Court, which has its own rules: Supreme Court Rules 2009, SI 2009/1603, which are supplemented by 14 Practice Directions.

We will cover here the basic provisions relating only to appeals in the County Court and the High Court, as these are likely to be the most common appeals to those new to legal practice.

19.7.4.2 To which court do you appeal?

The identity of an appeal court is contained in the destination of appeals tables found in Table 1 PD 52A.3.5 as follows for civil (other than family or insolvency) matters only:

TABLE 19.1 DESTINATION OF APPEALS

Court	Deciding judge	Decision Under Appeal	Destination
County	DJ	Any, other than a decision in non-insolvency proceedings brought pursuant to the Companies Acts	CJ (CC)
		A decision in non-insolvency proceedings brought pursuant to the Companies Acts	HCJ or Registrar
	CJ	Any	HCJ
High	Master, Registrar or	Any	HCJ
	DJ	Any	CA
Intellectual property Enterprise Court	DJ	Any	Enterprise Judge
	Enterprise Judge	Any	CA

It is also possible to 'leapfrog' to a different court or judge and the rules relating to 'leapfrogging' are set out in CPR 52.23.

To assist in the understanding of terminology, the 'lower court' is the court whose decision is to be appealed and the 'appeal court' is the court which will hear the appeal.

19.7.4.3 Permission to appeal

In virtually all cases of appeal from a County Court and the High Court, you must obtain permission to appeal. This can be undertaken in a number of ways. Firstly, by way of oral submission when the judgment you wish to appeal has been handed down in the lower court (CPR 52.3(2) and PD 52A 4.1); secondly, should that submission be unsuccessful (or simply not made), then permission must be sought from the appeal court by way of paper application known as an Appellant's Notice plus the application for permission to the relevant appeal court within twenty-one days after the date of the decision of the lower court, unless of course the lower court orders further time (CPR 52.12(2)(b)) or specific time limits apply (to specialist cases) in CPR 52.8–11 and PD 52D. The Appellant's Notice and the application for permission are usually heard without an oral hearing. Where permission is refused, then thirdly, there is a further right to have the decision refusing permission reconsidered at an oral hearing (CPR 52.4 and PD 52B 7.2), the time limit for which is seven days after service of the notice that permission had been refused.

Permission will ultimately only be granted if the appeal has a real prospect of success or there is some other compelling reason why the appeal should be heard (CPR 52.6).

Practical Considerations

Should your client lose the trial, it may be worth considering making an application for permission to appeal in any event after judgment, even if you are unsure whether the appeal will eventually be lodged—it is more difficult and costly to apply for permission to appeal out of time.

19.7.4.4 Time limits

The case of *McDonald v Rose* [2019] EWCA Civ 4 is a timely reminder that the time limits for applying for permission runs from the date of the decision to be appealed, which in the case of a reserved judgment, is the date it was formally handed down. Time does not run from the date the lower court's order is sealed or (where the party has first applied to the lower court for permission, as is usual) the date the lower court refuses permission to appeal.

If a party wants more time to file its application with the Court of Appeal, it must seek an extension of time from the trial judge, either when the judgment is handed down or when requesting an adjournment of the hand-down hearing (so as to give it more time to apply to the lower court for permission). An adjournment in itself will not extend time.

It is possible to apply to the Court of Appeal to extend time retrospectively, but this is treated as an application for relief from sanctions and therefore the three-stage test from *Denton v TH White Ltd* [2014] EWCA Civ 906 (considered here) will apply, namely:

1. the seriousness and the significance of the failure to comply with the rules;

2. why the default occurred;

3. an evaluation of all the circumstances of the case, so as to enable the court to deal justly with the application.

In this case, the court noted that the failure was serious and relatively significant, and there was no good reason for it. On a consideration of all the circumstances, it would have been a borderline case for relief. However, because of how the case was listed, the court was in a position to consider the merits of the application for permission to appeal more fully than would normally be appropriate. It concluded that the appeal would have no real prospect of success in any event, and therefore it did not need to reach a definitive view on the question of an extension.

CPR 52.3(2) provides that an application for permission to appeal may be made: to the lower court at the hearing at which the decision to be appealed was made; or to the appeal court in an appeal notice.

Under CPR 52.12(2), the appeal notice must be filed within twenty-one days after the date of the decision of the lower court which the appellant wishes to appeal—or such longer or shorter period as may be directed by the lower court.

This case usefully summarized the effect of the relevant authorities and the procedure that should be followed, including the following points:

1. Time begins to run under CPR 52.12 on the date of the hearing at which the decision is given, which may be extempore or by the formal hand down of a reserved judgment.

2. A party who wishes to apply to the lower court for permission to appeal should normally do so at the decision hearing itself. Where the judgment is to be handed down and counsel have been excused from attending, that can be done by applying in writing before the hearing.

3. If (exceptionally) a party is not ready to make an application at the decision hearing, it must ask for the hearing to be adjourned to give it more time to do so. The judge will then set a timetable for written submissions and will normally decide the question on the papers without the need for a further hearing.

4. If no permission application is made at the original decision hearing, and there has been no adjournment, the lower court is no longer seized of the matter and cannot consider any retrospective application for permission to appeal.

5. Whenever a party seeks an adjournment of the decision hearing they should also seek an extension of time to file the appeal notice. Otherwise, they risk running out of time before the permission decision is made. An adjournment of the decision hearing does not automatically extend time.

The court also noted (although the point was not addressed in the authorities considered by the court) that, if the judge announces his or her decision with reasons to follow, that too will start time running. In those circumstances, it should be standard practice for the court to adjourn the decision hearing and extend time for filing the appeal notice until a specified period after the reasons are given.

19.7.4.5 Grounds for appeal

There are only two grounds for appealing the decision of a lower court: the decision was wrong, either in fact, law, or in the exercise of the court's discretion; or it was unjust because of a serious procedural or other irregularity in the proceedings.

 Practical Considerations

In drafting your grounds for appeal, it is helpful to set out the reasons why one or both of the grounds apply and specify whether the ground raises an appeal on a point of law or against a finding of fact.

19.7.4.6 Documents for appeals

The appellant must prepare the Appellant's Notice (Form 161) plus a court fee. Skeleton arguments are not, however, automatically required in every County Court and High Court appeal. There is also now no express requirement for the appellant to file a bundle at the same time as the N161 although some documents will still inevitably need to be filed and bundled at a later stage. All that is required at this stage is:

- three copies of the N161 and one additional copy for each respondent;

- a copy of the sealed order under appeal;

- if permission was not granted or applied for, the application for permission to appeal and the grounds of appeal.

The twenty-one-day time limit already mentioned commences from the date of the judgment or order and not from the date it was drawn up.

The Respondent's Notice (Form 162) is only required to be filed if the respondent wishes to seek permission for a cross appeal from the appeal court (the same rules as to permission will apply) or he wishes to ask the appeal court to uphold the decision of the lower court for different reasons to those given by the lower court (and as such no permission is required). If the Respondent merely wishes to maintain the decision of the lower court for the reasons given, then there is no requirement to file an N162. If an N162 is to be filed, it must be filed within fourteen days of receiving the N161 unless the court orders otherwise.

It should also be noted here that if the case had been allocated to the small claims track, the correct form for the Appellant is the N164.

In *Kovarska v Otkritie* [2017] EWCA Civ 1485, the Court of Appeal upheld an application by *Otkritie* to set aside an earlier *ex parte* order of that court which had granted *Ms Kovarska* permission to appeal and had been decided on the papers. Citing serious misrepresentations and material non-disclosures, the Court of Appeal found that it had been misled and that there were compelling reasons to set aside its previous order.

Following changes to the Court of Appeal's procedure in October 2016 whereby applications to appeal are to be determined on the papers unless the court considers that an application should be heard at an oral hearing, the judgment provides useful guidance on avoiding certain pitfalls which could result in permission to appeal being set aside.

Specific points arising from the judgment:

1. where an application for permission to appeal is made under CPR 52.3 and is decided on the papers under the usual 'essentially "without notice" procedure' to the respondent, the applicant has a duty to make full and frank disclosure of all the material facts;

2. under the old rule CPR 52.9 (now CPR 52.18), the court may set aside permission to appeal, in whole or in part, where there is a compelling reason to do so. In its judgment, the court held that material non-disclosure and serious misrepresentations were compelling reasons for setting aside permission to appeal; and

3. in any event, the court also has the power under CPR 3.1(7) to vary or revoke any aspects of orders made in circumstances where it is misled as to the correct factual position, for example because of material non-disclosure or serious misrepresentations.

19.7.4.7 The appeal hearing

Every appeal is limited to a review of the decision of the lower court. The exceptions to this are:

- where the court believes it would be in the interests of justice to hold a rehearing or

- a Practice Direction makes provision (CPR 52.21 (1)).

Generally the appeal court will not allow a party to rely on a matter that was not included in its N161/N162 without permission, although the court will always apply the overriding objective.

19.7.4.8 Costs

In so far as costs are concerned for the appeal, the costs rules are generally the same as for other applications and hearings. However, it should be noted that the appeal court has a discretion over the costs of the appeal hearing, but also over the costs in the lower court. Your client will need to be informed of the cost implications before the appeal is launched.

19.7.4.9 Part 36

Part 36 offers can also be made in relation to the costs of an appeal. However, what needs to be noted here is that a Part 36 offer made during a first instance hearing does not protect the maker against the costs of a subsequent appeal. Therefore, a fresh Part 36 offer should be made on appeal (CPR 36.1(1)). As always, you must remove all references to any Part 36 offers already made in any documentation that you are filing in support of an application for permission or for the appeal itself. This rule, however, does not apply if the Part 36 offer is relevant to the substance of the appeal.

19.8 CONCLUDING A CASE WITHOUT TRIAL

Parties can choose to settle their dispute either before proceedings are issued or during the litigation itself. Here, we look at how this can be done.

19.8.1 SETTLEMENTS REACHED BEFORE PROCEEDINGS

Settlements achieved without the need to issue proceedings are often as a result of an ADR process, such as negotiation or mediation.

However, once the terms of settlement have been reached, it is important to consider the cost provisions of the settlement, because there is no strict entitlement in the absence of an express agreement. As regards costs, the position is the same unless there is a contractual or statutory provision applicable. If the settlement concluded that one party would pay the other party's costs, but the terms of settlement have not confirmed the sum of those costs or a method by which they will be settled, then the receiving party can issue a Part 8 claim in respect of those costs under the provisions of CPR 44.5.

19.8.1.1 Settlements generally

Once the terms of the settlement have been agreed, the agreement needs to be recorded in writing. Sometimes, it is sufficient for an exchange of correspondence between the parties to represent the agreement reached adequately. However, most legal representatives would prepare a separate document, commonly known as a 'compromise agreement', which would include all of the agreed terms. This compromise agreement, in effect, creates a legally binding contract between the parties that, if breached, enables a claim to be pursued for breach of the compromise agreement. (See also Chapter 15, paragraph 15.12.)

 Practical Considerations

If a compromise agreement were to be breached, it is likely that the action that would follow would be commenced as a Part 7 claim in which a prompt application for summary judgment would be made. (See Chapter 14, paragraph 14.3, for details of a summary judgment application.)

19.8.1.2 Compromising a claim for a child or protected party

When a compromise of the action is reached before proceedings are issued on behalf of a child or protected party, then the party paying over the sum of the agreed settlement will not obtain a valid discharge unless the court has approved the settlement. Approval is sought by issuing a CPR Part 8 claim form (CPR 21.10(2)).

PD 21 sets out those documents that should be provided to the court. These are:

- a draft consent order in Form N292;
- a court funds Form 320; and
- the litigation friend's approval of the proposed settlement terms.

In personal injury actions, the following additional documents or details must be provided to the court:

- the circumstances of the accident;
- the (up-to-date) medical reports;
- the (up-to-date) schedule of loss and damage; and
- counsel's opinion (relating to the terms of the settlement).

If there is a claim for future pecuniary loss, the court must be satisfied that the parties have considered whether the damages should take the form wholly or partly as periodical payments.

Cost recovery by the litigation friend: It should be noted that an amendment to CPR 21 (Children and protected parties), clarifies that the restriction in CPR 21.12, which allows a litigation friend to recover their costs and expenses from damages awarded to the claimant for whom they acted, only applies where the claimant is a child, and not a protected party.

 Practical Considerations

The courts do not take 'infant approval settlements' lightly (also known as 'protected party settlements'). Common problems arise with a failure on the part of the legal representative to address minor important details and include: a failure to provide the birth certificate; failure to obtain a supplemental report where the child's injuries have persisted beyond the prognosis period outlined in the original medical report; or a failure of the medical report to address certain issues that may impact on the amount of the damages that the child or protected party might be awarded. Usually, the child and his litigation friend will attend this hearing, and the judge will ask the child questions if he is old enough to understand and answer the questions put to him.

19.8.2 **SETTLEMENTS REACHED AFTER PROCEEDINGS**

19.8.2.1 Consent orders

If settlement has been reached during litigation, again by an ADR process, a consent order will need to be prepared (where both parties are legally represented) to record the terms of settlement of the dispute and the provision relating to costs. Care must be taken when drafting consent orders to ensure that all parties understand to what they are agreeing. In practice, it is rare for the court to interfere in the terms of settlement agreed between parties.

The term 'consent order' is a generic description for all orders that record settlements. As with pre-action settlements, the consent order is a legally binding contract and, if breached, the innocent party is entitled *to issue fresh proceedings* for breach of contract—that is, of the consent order.

A template consent order appears as Figure 19.1 at the end of this chapter.

19.8.2.2 Tomlin orders

In commercial claims, another piece of litigation on the back of the original claim may be frustrating, because a further action, even if short-lived, will be time-consuming, will necessitate the following of Protocols, and will incur costs and disbursements, during which time the breaching party may have absconded or become insolvent.

You are likely to be in breach of your professional conduct duties if you failed to draft a Tomlin order, but instead prepared a generic consent order, and your opponent subsequently disposed of its assets or became insolvent, rendering a recovery unlikely because of the time constraints of issuing fresh proceedings.

In an attempt to remedy this inconvenient position, a consent order can be drafted in a particular manner to *avoid the need to issue fresh proceedings*, and, consequently, shorten the overall timescale and costs implications for your client. This particular type of consent order is known as a 'Tomlin order'.

It is essentially split into two parts: the first part is the order itself, and the second part is the schedule (or sometimes a settlement agreement) annexed to the order. The schedule often contains a confidentiality clause, so that the terms of settlement remain confidential. However, even where confidential schedules are annexed to the order, there are occasions on which the court may order their disclosure (see *L'Oreal SA v eBay International AG* [2008] EWHC 313 (Ch)). There may, however, be instances where parties would be well advised to draft the order stating that the agreed terms in the schedule are confidential and are not to be filed at court. The court has, on occasions, kept a copy of the confidential schedule on the court file in a sealed envelope. This would prevent a non-party being able to obtain a copy under CPR 5.4C(1) (see *ABC v Y* [2010] EWHC 3176 (Ch)).

The order does not set out the details of the agreement between the parties, but merely states that:

- the parties have agreed terms of settlement;

- all further proceedings are stayed;

- the stay is based on the terms set out in the schedule being complied with;

- if the terms in the schedule are not complied with, then the innocent party can make an application to the same court in which the proceedings were issued and ask the court to allow it to enforce the terms agreed in the schedule (by way of one of the enforcement options set out in the Additional Chapter 'Enforcement of Judgments' available in the online resources)—a procedure formerly known as 'liberty to apply', but which is now referred to as 'permission to apply'; and

- there is a provision for the payment and assessment of costs.

The order essentially sets out all of the items that the court is able to order. The order must also be dated.

The schedule usually appears at the end of the Tomlin order and includes (where the agreement involves the payment of money):

- who is paying the money, how much, and when;
- that the agreement is in full and final satisfaction; and
- a default provision on interest should the monies not be paid.

The court has the power to vary the terms incorporated into the order but not to vary the terms of the schedule (except on the usual basis for interfering with a contract). The court only has the power to enforce the terms of the schedule if not adhered to by either party.

 Practical Considerations

Tomlin orders are frequently used in litigation to record settlement of terms. They are mainly used when a payment is to be made sometime in the future. Their main advantage is that, should the terms of the schedule be breached, then like a Part 36 settlement, there is no need to issue fresh proceedings for breach of the agreement; rather, you are permitted to go back into the original set of proceedings (by virtue of the 'permission to apply' clause in the order) and ask the court, by way of an application— probably without notice and hearing—for permission to proceed straight to enforcement.

A template Tomlin order appears as Figure 19.2, at the end of this chapter.

19.8.2.3 Compromising an action for a child or protected party

If an action on behalf of a child or protected party is compromised by settlement, the court must approve the settlement before it can be a valid settlement.

Here, the requirement to obtain the court's approval of the settlement is mandatory (whereas the reason to obtain approval in paragraph 19.8.2.1 is in order that the payer obtains a valid discharge). The approval is sought by issuing an ordinary application notice. The information set out in paragraph 19.8.2.1 should be provided to the court.

Whenever the court has made a judgment for the child or protected party in an action or is approving a settlement, the court will also give directions how the money shall be dealt with. In the case of large orders or settlements for a protected party, the court will usually direct that an application should be made to the Court of Protection to appoint a receiver and for the funds to be transferred to the Court of Protection. For orders or settlements for a child, or for smaller settlements or orders for a protected party, the court will administer and invest the funds.

The provisions for accepting a CPR Part 36 offer are the same as in paragraph 19.8.2.1, save in circumstances in which there has been a payment in the High Court. Children or protected parties are also entitled to the interest accrued on the payment from the date of valid acceptance and it is from the date of a valid acceptance that the court approved the settlement. The court also made it clear that it was the claimant's (or his litigation friend's) responsibility to make the application for court approval promptly.

19.8.3 DISCONTINUANCE OF PROCEEDINGS

CPR 38 governs the discontinuance of proceedings by a claimant.

At any point during proceedings, even at trial, a claimant can decide that he no longer wishes to pursue the whole, or any part, of his claim, even though no settlement has been reached, and the action is, therefore, ended. The usual reasons for discontinuance are that the defendant is no longer worth suing, or that the claimant no longer believes that his own claim will substantially succeed at trial.

Generally, the claimant can discontinue of its own volition, but provisions relating to when the claimant will need permission are contained in CPR 38.2 for example multi- party claims, interim payments, undertakings have been given or interim injunctions.

In order to discontinue, the claimant must file and serve a notice of discontinuance on all other parties to the action, and whilst the defendant can apply to have the notice set aside (where no permission was required by the claimant) within twenty-eight days, this is rare.

The main feature of a claimant's entitlement to discontinue is that he is liable to pay the defendant's costs on the standard basis for the whole action or the part of the action that has been discontinued. It is, therefore, very important that this is explained to your client. However, in exceptional cases, the court will exercise its inherent discretion and reduce the claimant's costs' liability, but only where the claimant can show cogent reasons and can demonstrate a change of circumstances. The courts adopt a robust approach here, as in the cases of *Brookes v HSBC Bank PLC* [2011] EWCA Civ 354 and *Jemitus v Bank of Scotland PLC* [2011] EWCA Civ 854. However, if the claimant can prove that proceedings were only issued because the defendant failed to respond to any pre-action correspondence, then the court may also disapply the default costs rule here. The recent case of *Nelson's Yard Management Company and others v Eziefula* [2013] EWCA Civ 235 has held that the defendant should only pay a proportion of the claimant's costs on discontinuance because there had been an abject failure to reply to any pre-action correspondence. One wonders if the same decision would have been reached by the Court of Appeal if there had been late or inadequate responses.

In the case of *Ward v Hutt* [2018] EWHC 77 (Ch), the court considered whether the claimant can bring a new claim after discontinuance. CPR, r. 38.7 provides that 'A claimant who discontinues a claim needs the permission of the court to make another claim against the same defendant if (a) he discontinued the claim after the defendant filed a defence . . .'. Matthew HHJ held that the defendant will be the same even if he or she is sued in a different capacity in the proposed second claim.

KEY POINTS SUMMARY

- Issue and serve witness summons, and liaise with witnesses directly before trial.

- Book and brief counsel, and consider whether a pre-trial conference is appropriate with the client and any experts or witnesses.

- Allow plenty of time to prepare accurate and user-friendly trial bundles. Keep a spare one at court and at the office.

- Ensure that you are familiar with every aspect of the case before the trial commences.

- Put administrative arrangements in place for the smooth running of the trial.

- Keep in close contact with counsel and the client in the days running up to the trial.

- Be clear as to the arrangements for the handing down of judgment, and if a draft judgment is released, adhere to any embargo placed on it by the judge.

- Know the new Appeals procedures and the strict time limits for appeals, and instruct counsel to be prepared to seek permission or to oppose an application for permission to appeal when the judgment is handed down.

- Understand the mechanics of settling before and after the issue of litigation.

- If settlement is concluded by a non-Part 36 offer, ensure that the correct consent order is agreed and drafted.

Case Study *Andrew James Pike v Deep Builders Ltd*

All of the directions have now been complied with, and the PTC has been filed and served. You have now received a notice of hearing, listing the trial for three days. Acting for Andrew Pike, consider the following questions.

Question 1

On who should you serve a witness summons and why?

Question 2

Is it necessary to have a conference with counsel at this stage? Give reasons for your answer.

Question 3

If Andrew Pike does not beat Deep Builders' Part 36 offer of £20,000, what are the likely cost consequences for each party and how will the court deal with this?

Question 4

You have been instructed by your supervising partner to help prepare a trial bundle index for the trial of this matter. He informs you that all special damages have been agreed subject to liability, although medical evidence has not been agreed, because the defendants obtained an order seeking their own evidence. There is no order for expert oral evidence at trial.

The trainee who was helping your principal has departed on annual leave, but has left you his notes on what he would include in the bundles. These may or may not be of assistance to you. These appear in the online resources.

Based on your knowledge of the case for Andrew Pike and the information that your colleagues have provided, draft the trial bundle index.

Case Study *Bollingtons Ltd v Mrs Elizabeth Lynch t/a The Honest Lawyer*

Question 1

The fast-track trial has been listed. As the day of the trial approaches, Mrs Lynch is getting nervous and asks you to attend the trial with her. What costs advice would you give her?

Question 2

Mrs Lynch lost the fast-track trial both on the claim against her and her counterclaim, the judge indicating in his judgment that he preferred the evidence of Mr Green. Permission to appeal was obtained. Consider what advice you would give to her on the prospects of successfully appealing and the costs implications in relation to costs hearings or the costs of an appeal.

 Any documents referred to in these case study questions can be found in the online resources—simply click on 'Case study documentation' to access the documents that you need for Chapter 19 and to be reminded of the questions. Suggested answers to these self- test questions can be accessed in the Student Resources section of the online resources.

FIGURE 19.1 TEMPLATE CONSENT ORDER

IN THE HIGH COURT OF JUSTICE   20??-P-3003

QUEEN'S BENCH DIVISION

DISTRICT REGISTRY

Between

                                                                        Claimant

and

                                                                        Defendant

CONSENT ORDER

Upon the Claimant and Defendant having agreed to settle this matter

By Consent it is ordered that:

1. The Defendant do pay the Claimant the sum of £ . . . . by Friday 25th January 20?? in full and final settlement of his claim.

2. The CMC listed on 14th December 20?? be vacated.

3. The Defendant do pay the Claimant's costs of the action to be the subject of a detailed assessment if not agreed.

We consent to the terms of this order

. . . .

For the Claimant

. . . .

For the Defendant

Dated . . . .

FIGURE 19.2 TEMPLATE TOMLIN ORDER

IN THE HIGH COURT OF JUSTICE   20??-P-3003

QUEEN'S BENCH DIVISION

        DISTRICT REGISTRY

Between

                                                            Claimant

                               and

                                                       Defendant

TOMLIN ORDER

Upon the Claimant and Defendant having agreed to the terms set out in the Schedule attached, By Consent it is ordered that:

1. All further proceedings in this action be stayed on the terms set out in the attached schedule to this order, except for the purpose of carrying the said terms into effect and for that purpose there is permission to apply.

2. Each party shall have permission to apply to the court to enforce those terms without the need to bring a new claim.

3 There be no order as to costs **OR** each party shall bear its own costs **OR** the claimant **OR** the defendant shall pay the defendant's **OR** the claimant's costs on the standard **OR** the indemnity basis to be subject to a detailed assessment in default of agreement.

Schedule

1. The Defendant do pay the Claimant the sum of £xxx within xx days of the date of this order.

2. The order is made in full and final settlement of claims subsisting or capable of subsisting between the parties.

3. In the event of late payment, the Defendant will pay interest on the sum of £xxx . . . . . . or any part thereof at a daily rate of xx . . . .%.

Relevant parts of the CPR: 44, 45, and 47.

20.1 INTRODUCTION

This chapter is primarily concerned with the practical considerations and procedures involved in assessing costs once the litigation is concluded. It should, however, be read with reference to the underlying costs principles, formulas, and likely costs orders that were discussed in Chapter 4 on 'The Nature, Extent, and Recovery of Legal Costs'.

The client must understand that, despite receiving a costs order in his favour, agreeing a liability to pay, or being ordered to pay costs, if the amount of costs cannot be agreed between the parties, then further proceedings and costs are incurred before a resolution is secured.

 Practical Considerations

A 100 per cent costs recovery is very rare, even if a party was wholly and fundamentally successful in his case and obtained a 'cost of proceedings' order from the court. While there is nothing set in stone, practitioners adopt an unwritten guide when advising clients on the amount of cost recovery. A successful party usually recovers between 65 per cent and 80 per cent of what they have been charged and, in privately paying cases, have also paid their legal representatives. It is important to highlight this with the client, as they need to understand that what they are responsible for paying to you as their legal representative is not likely to be covered by any amount that they recover from their opponent. Eliminating enhanced expectations of costs recovery at an early stage will avoid additional time and further costs in negotiating with your opponent the figure your client is prepared to accept.

This chapter will cover:

- the procedures for the assessment of costs;
- costs only disputes.

20.2 SUMMARY ASSESSMENT OF COSTS

This is governed by CPR 44.6 and CPR 47, along with PD 44, as well as the specific Court Guides for High Court matters.

20.2.1 WHAT IS IT AND WHEN DOES IT TAKE PLACE?

This is the procedure whereby the court will assess the costs immediately in the following situations:

- at the end of an interim application;
- at the end of a one-day fast-track trial.

There are of course circumstances where a summary assessment may not be appropriate and PD 44 subsection 9 at paragraph 9.2 suggests that there would need to be good reason not to do so. Further, Part 1 of the Legal Aid, Sentencing and Punishment of Offenders Act 2012 lists the other cases where there will be no summary assessment of costs, notably legally aided clients.

The process is intended to be brief and does not involve the lengthy consideration of each item claimed as occurs in a detailed assessment (see paragraph 20.3 and Figure 20.1). In assessing the costs, the court will assess either on the standard or indemnity basis (depending on the costs order made). These terms were discussed in Chapter 4 at paragraph 4.3.2. It will include a consideration of the amount of work done in terms of hours, the grade of the fee earner who has undertaken the work and his hourly rate, VAT, and any disbursements including counsel's fees. Once the court has assessed the costs summarily, those costs are required to be paid within fourteen days, CPR 44.7 to the successful party, and this order will not change irrespective of the final outcome of the matter.

Practical Considerations

If at an interim application a costs order is made in favour of a party funded by way of a CFA with a success fee, the court should still summarily assess the base costs (unless there is a good reason not to do so). In practical terms, this means that the statement of costs for summary assessment should only contain details of the base costs and not of any additional liability.

20.2.2 HOW DOES A SUMMARY ASSESSMENT PROCEED?

The parties must assist the court in the summary assessment, and a statement of costs in a form similar to Form N260 must be completed. This must be filed, and served no later than twenty-four hours in advance of the actual time of the hearing for an interim hearing and no later than two days before a fast-track trial PD 44 9.5(4). If this is late or overlooked without a reasonable explanation, the court will take this into account when making its costs order, although it may not be a complete bar to entitlement and recovery. Form N260 is used by most legal representatives.

Please refer to the online resources for a copy of the N260. It should contain details of the work done as highlighted earlier, and must be signed by a fee earner confirming that the indemnity principle is not being breached.

As a summary assessment of costs can be made at the conclusion of a fast-track trial, it is especially important to complete the N260 as fully as possible because, with fast-track trials, the legal representative may not have undertaken the advocacy at the trial himself and may have instructed counsel to appear. In this situation, it will rarely be proportionate to arrange to 'sit behind' counsel at trial (see Chapter 4 at paragraph 4.7.3). The trial advocate will, therefore, not have the intimate knowledge of the file to enable him, at the conclusion of the trial, to meet any challenges raised on the content of the N260 (where your client has succeeded in securing a costs order in his favour) or raise a challenge to the opponent's N260 (if your client has been ordered to pay the opponent's costs).

There is no fee for a summary assessment and no requirement to provide any additional documentation to the court in support of a statement of costs, although supporting papers should be taken to the hearing.

 Practical Considerations

Once you have received your opponent's statement of costs, you should consider it as against your own. If you believe it is reasonable, then, with your client's instructions, the costs can be agreed subject to the outcome of the hearing. If they cannot be agreed in advance, then submissions will need to be made at the hearing.

20.2.3 INTEREST

The entitlement to interest on the legal costs of the main action is derived from the Judgments Act 1838, s. 17, although interest only accrues on County Court costs orders if the sum of costs is £5,000 or more in accordance with s. 74 of the County Courts Act 1984.

Interest accrues from the date of the order at the rate currently set at 8 per cent per annum (Judgment Debts (Rate of Interest) Order 1993).

20.3 DETAILED ASSESSMENT OF COSTS

This is governed by CPR 47 and PD 47, as well as the relevant Court Guides for High Court matters.

20.3.1 WHAT IS IT?

This is the procedure whereby the court will scrutinize the costs in a separate set of proceedings which takes place up to several months after the conclusion of the main action, unless of course the costs can be agreed between the parties. Detailed assessments of costs usually take place in multi-track cases, but sometimes, at the discretion of the court, in some lengthy interim applications and in some appeal cases. In assessing the costs, the court will assess either on the standard or indemnity basis (depending on the costs order made) and will consider the amount of work done, the grade of fee earner, any disbursements including counsel's fees, and any costs budgets and costs management orders (CMOs) made in the course of the proceedings. The court will also consider proportionality at a detailed assessment on the standard basis.

 Practical Considerations

At the end of the trial, CPR 44.2(8) permits the court to order the paying party to make a payment on account of costs where a costs order has been made against that party. The purpose of doing this is to expedite funds to the receiving party and to reduce the interest that will accrue, as the detailed assessment hearing is likely to be many months in the future. The court will know approximately how much it would be safe to award as a payment on account of costs, as costs estimates/budgets will have been filed in the run-up to the trial setting out the party's estimated costs of proceedings and trial.

20.3.2 WHERE DOES IT OCCUR AND WHO CONDUCTS THE HEARING?

The venue of detailed assessment proceedings is determined by the location of the main action. For those cases that proceeded in London or in surrounding areas (as listed in CPR 47.4) in the County Court, the assessments are commenced in the Costs Office and are heard by authorized court officers.

For all High Court and County Court actions outside London, costs judges and district judges will conduct the detailed assessment hearings.

20.3.3 WHEN DOES IT TAKE PLACE?

A detailed assessment usually occurs after the main action has concluded and is for all intents and purposes a separate set of proceedings. As with any form of litigation, it can be avoided by negotiation and compromise either before the proceedings are formally up and running or during the detailed assessment procedure itself. The time limit for the commencement of detailed assessment proceedings is generally three months after the date of the judgment or order, giving the entitlement to costs.

20.3.4 NEGOTIATING A COMPROMISE ON COSTS

Once the final order or judgment is made, it is good practice to try to agree the amount of costs with your opponent, as this is quicker and cheaper than proceeding to a judicial determination by way of detailed assessment.

In the first instance, you will need to send to your opponent a draft bill of costs, or at the very least, some formal calculations for them to consider. A bill of costs is basically a chronological list of all the steps taken in the action and a summary of all the work done by a variety of fee earners and disbursements incurred. The nature of the work done is very much the same as covered in the N260, summary assessment of costs as discussed in paragraph 20.2, except that it is set out in much more detail.

In complex and lengthy litigation, a law firm will often engage a costs draftsman to do this. The entire file is sent to him and a detailed bill in accordance with one of the costs precedent bills A–D as appears in the annexe to PD 47 will be prepared. If settlement is not achieved, then the bill can be used for the detailed assessment procedure itself.

 Practical Considerations

Many firms will have a policy on whether costs draftsmen are instructed at a fee or whether a fee earner, usually the fee earner involved in the file, prepares the bill in accordance with one of the costs schedules mentioned earlier. The time taken or the fee paid for the preparation of the bill is ultimately included in the total amount sought from the opponent at the detailed assessment hearing. The Court of Appeal in *Nicholas Crane v Canons Leisure Centre* [2007] EWCA Civ 1352 held that the costs draftsman's fees were base costs. Costs draftsman's fees are, therefore, not disbursements.

Once the bill or calculations are prepared, these are sent to the opponent for their consideration. Copies of any fee notes and disbursement invoices could also be sent at this stage, although there is no obligation to do so. Where counsel has been used and experts instructed, it often assists negotiations to let your opponent see the fee notes at this early stage.

When trying to secure an early compromise and sending the bill to the opponent, it is good practice to also make an offer of settlement and this is usually done in accordance with CPR 36. However, it is not clear who will necessarily have the more advantageous result as it will depend on the wording of an effective offer. There is now case law which suggests that CPR 36.17(4) 10 per cent enhancement applies to the amount of costs awarded *Horne (as executrix of the estate of Edward Horne deceased) v Prescot (No 1) Ltd* [2019] EWHC 1322.

20.3.5 THE DETAILED ASSESSMENT PROCEDURE

There are now two possible ways of proceeding to the detailed assessment of costs: a detailed assessment hearing, or a provisional assessment on paper (if the amount of costs sought is £75,000 or less CPR 47.15, PD47 14.1), which can take place partway through the detailed assessment procedure.

Practical Considerations

The detailed assessment process can be quite complicated and drawn out in larger cases. Your client will need to have sufficient information to be able to understand what is likely to happen. You should, therefore, consider discussing with your client who should draft the bill, the layout of the bill of costs in one of the precedent forms, what steps are likely to take place in moving to the final hearing, CPR 36 offers, and what principles and factors the costs judge will take into account at the hearing. These discussions should be followed with a detailed file note, which should either be sent to the client or used as a base for a letter to the client repeating matters discussed.

20.3.5.1 Notice of Commencement of detailed assessment proceedings

In paragraph 20.3.4 we discussed trying to negotiate the costs to avoid the need for detailed assessment proceedings. This should be done within the three-month time limit as there is a limited time to which detailed assessment proceeedings can be commenced CPR 47.7. If a settlement cannot be reached, then proceedings are formally commenced by the receiving party (i.e. the party in whose favour the costs order was made), serving on the opponent:

- a Notice of Commencement in Form N252 signed by a party or his legal representative (not a costs draftsman);
- a copy of the Bill of Costs;
- copies of disbursement receipts (only those that exceed £500); and
- copies of counsels' and experts' fee notes.

These documents are only served on the opponent; they are not filed at court at this point, and, therefore, there is no fee payable at this stage. Legally aided parties have their own rules and forms contained in PD 47.18.

If the three-month time limit is missed, there are two different sanctions. CPR 47.8(2) states that if the receiving party commences outside the three-month time limit and the paying party has made no application to the court compelling them to commence, then the only sanction available to the court is to disallow some or all of the interest on those costs. However, *Haji-Ioannou and Others v Frangos and Others* [2006] EWHC 1663 confirmed that the court does have a discretion to disallow some of the paying party's costs in certain circumstances where the delay was inordinately long and the conduct of the receiving party was tantamount to wilful misconduct.

If, however, the paying party does issue an application compelling the receiving party to commence, then the court, in accordance with CPR 47.8(1), does have the discretion to disallow some or all of those costs.

If a party is facing difficulties in commencing detailed assessment proceedings within the three-month time limit, it is best to agree an extension of time in writing. Reasons for the delay should be given. If agreement cannot be reached, then the receiving party should apply to the court for an extension, thus safeguarding its position on costs and interest.

20.3.5.2 Points of dispute

After the notice of commencement has been served with supporting documents, your opponent is entitled by CPR 47.9 to dispute any item in the bill by serving points of dispute on the receiving party within twenty-one days of service of the N252. This time period can be extended by agreement between the parties.

The points of dispute should be concise and follow Precedent G in the schedule of costs precedents in PD 47. It is helpful when completing the points of dispute to identify each item in turn, explain why you object to it, and suggest a reasonable alternative. For example, you may object to the grade of fee earner dealing with part of a case at a particular hourly rate. You would therefore give a reason, such as the claim was relatively straightforward, and put forward your own suggestions.

The points of dispute must be signed by the paying party or his legal representative.

20.3.5.3 Default costs certificate

If the paying party fails to serve points of dispute, CPR 47.9(4) permits the receiving party to file at court, along with a court fee, Form N254, requesting a default costs certificate. On receipt of this, the court will deem that the paying party has no objection to the bill of costs and issue Form N255, which is the default costs certificate. The amount specified to be paid will be the total amount stated on the bill plus interest and must be paid within fourteen days.

The default costs certificate can be set aside if there is good reason as set out in CPR 47.12.

The whole default costs certificate procedure can be likened to a default judgment (although there is a fee required for the default costs certificate request) and potentially having that judgment set aside in the main action (CPR 12 and 13).

20.3.5.4 Replies to points of dispute

CPR 47.13 permits the receiving party to reply to the points of dispute within twenty-one days after service. This is entirely optional. Some legal representatives believe there is little point in conceding items in the replies, as it is better to do this in separate negotiations where concessions can be made. Others believe that if an item cannot be substantiated, it is better to get it out of the way early on.

20.3.5.5 Requesting a detailed assessment hearing

Settlement negotiations can take place at any time. It is usual to try to negotiate costs as soon as the draft bill has been prepared right up until the hearing itself. If negotiations have failed and the steps detailed in paragraphs 20.3.5.1–20.3.5.4 have been completed, then it is time to proceed to a final hearing.

This is done by filing at court (this is the court's first involvement in the detailed assessment procedure) a Request for Hearing (Form N258), the bill of costs plus receipts and court fee, the points of dispute, any replies, any costs budgets, and a hefty cheque. This must be done within three months of the expiry of the first three-month time limit discussed in paragraph 20.3.5.1. Form N258 requires the receiving party to give a time estimate for the hearing and careful consideration must be given to this.

Again, there are sanctions for missing the second three-month time limit as follows:

- If the receiving party misses the second three-month time limit and the paying party issues an application to compel a Request for Hearing to be sought, unless it is sought by the receiving party within a revised time limit stipulated by the court, all or part of the receiving party's costs and/or interest may be disallowed.

- If the receiving party misses the second three-month time limit and the paying party does nothing, there is no automatic sanction imposed. Although, if matters are left too long the court may disallow all or some of the receiving party's costs and interest.

Once the N258 plus supporting documentation and cheque have been filed with the court, the court will fix a hearing date and serve the opponent. It is, therefore, important to ensure that you have filed enough copies of the requisite documentation with the court.

When serving the Notice of Hearing Date, the court will usually request that the receiving party lodge its full file of papers with the court seven days before the actual hearing.

20.3.5.6 Provisional Assessment of Costs

This paper-based part of the process applies to any detailed assessment proceedings where the costs claimed are less than or equal to the amount set out in CPR 47.15 PD 47 14.1 being £75,000.

The provisional assessment will commence after all the documents have been filed at court in accordance with PD 47.14.3, save for the fact that a sealed envelope marked 'Part 36 or similar offers' containing any such offers made by any party must also be filed at court. The court will try to conduct the provisional assessment on paper within six weeks, and once assessed, it will return the points of dispute with the court's decisions noted thereon to the parties. The parties must then agree the total sum due to the receiving party based on the court's decisions. CPR 47.15 permits the court to list the case for a detailed assessment hearing where it believes the matter is not suitable for a provisional assessment. It also allows either party to request an oral hearing to challenge the provisional assessment with in twenty-one days of the return of the points of dispute. If no such challenge is made, the provisional assessment is binding on both parties.

20.3.5.7 Interim costs certificate and final costs certificate

20.3.5.7.1 *Interim costs certificate*

The detailed assessment hearing will usually be listed at least fourteen days in advance of the hearing itself. If it is evident that the matter is contested and the hearing is in fact some time in the future, CPR 47.16 permits the court to issue an interim costs certificate and PD 47.16 permits a party to also apply by way of a Part 23 application for an interim costs certificate.

20.3.5.7.2 *Final costs certificate*

This can be issued at two separate points:

(1) If settlement is achieved between the request for the hearing and the detailed assessment hearing itself, the parties draft a consent order. This is to be signed by both parties and filed at court along with a court fee for approval, with a view to obtaining a final costs certificate.

The procedure on the final costs certificate is akin to the manner in which a main action can be concluded by consent.

(2) If the parties proceed to the final hearing, at the conclusion of the hearing, the receiving party has fourteen days to complete the bill with the figures ordered by the costs or regional costs judge and return it to the court. The court will serve the final costs certificate once this is received.

20.3.5.8 What happens at the detailed assessment hearing?

Persons with a thorough knowledge of the file should attend the hearing. In practice, costs draftsmen frequently attend. A costs draftsman may have prepared the bill, but his ability to argue on your behalf for the work undertaken can only be as good as the instructions and information that you give to him, so it is important to engage with issues raised on the bill. The court will go through each and every item claimed in the bill that is in dispute from start to finish and allow both parties to make submissions on these issues. This process is laborious and time-consuming, and detailed assessment hearings can take half a day or more, even in smaller cases.

The court's powers at the detailed assessment hearing, in terms of what it will take into account, have already been set out in Chapter 4 at paragraph 4.3.2. In addition to this, in considering the level of costs to award, the court will also take account of costs budgets filed at the directions stage of the main action, as a result of which such budgets have been approved in accordance with PD 44 3.

However, this practice direction only sets out the impact of costs budgets on detailed assessment proceedings where a costs management order (CMO) has not been made under CPR 3.15. Remember, in many cases, CMOs are not routinely made. It states that if, on assessment, there is a difference of 20 per cent or more between sums claimed and the costs budget filed by the receiving party, the receiving party must provide with his bill of costs, a statement of reasons for the difference. If the paying party reasonably relied on the exceeded budget, then the court may restrict those costs to a lesser amount than appears in the bill or to the amount of the original costs budget, especially where the court does not believe the receiving party has supplied a satisfactory explanation for the difference. It is, therefore, crucial that costs budgets are prepared carefully so that they do not adversely affect any later costs recovery.

In cases where there has been a CMO, *Harrison v University Hospitals Coventry and Warwickshire NHS Trust* [2017] EWCA Civ 792, has confirmed that the future (estimated costs) element of the Precedent H costs budget is binding on a subsequent detailed assessment.

The figure for those costs should not be departed from (upwards or downwards) unless a 'good reason' can be shown. However, the incurred costs element of the budget is not binding on a later assessment. Those costs fell to be assessed in the usual way. What this essentially means is that there is virtually no scope to argue against the level of estimated costs in the Precedent H leaving only the incurred costs up to the CMO to be challenged in most multi-track cases.

20.3.5.9 Costs of the detailed assessment hearing

The costs are usually awarded to the receiving party unless the costs or district judge feels that the detailed assessment proceedings had been conducted unjustifiably or where a CPR 36 offer had been validly made and beaten.

The amount of the costs of the detailed assessment proceedings are summarily assessed, and the receiving party should provide details to the court and opponent, although there is no requirement to serve a statement of costs in N260.

The costs are usually ordered to be paid within fourteen days of the final costs certificate. Should payment not be made, then orders for costs can be enforced in the usual way as money judgments. Please see the Additional Chapter on 'Enforcement of Judgments' in the online resources.

20.3.5.10 Interest

As already stated in paragraph 20.2.3, interest on costs of the main action accrues from the date of the final judgment or order if over £5,000. Similarly, interest on the costs of the detailed assessment hearing begins to run on the same basis from the date of the order.

20.4 COSTS ONLY PROCEEDINGS

These are governed by CPR 46.14 and PD 46 and were developed to deal with the situation where, before proceedings are issued, the parties had settled the dispute and determined who should pay the costs, but could not agree on the level of costs to be paid. The procedure allows the parties to quickly and relatively cheaply obtain an order for costs which can then provide the basis for those costs to be assessed.

This simple procedure is a CPR 8 claim seeking an order for costs (see Chapter 9 on 'Starting your Claim' at paragraph 9.3.6 for the procedure on CPR 8 claims) followed by a detailed assessment of those costs.

The court will consider the basis of the costs to be assessed and will usually order that the costs of the application are to be in the assessment, i.e. the party in which the court holds favour makes an order for costs at the end of the detailed assessment proceedings and will be entitled to the costs of this application.

Once an order for costs has been made, there are no short cuts to a detailed assessment final hearing and CPR 47 will apply.

KEY POINTS SUMMARY

- Advise your client at the outset of the nature of costs recovery proceedings and the likely percentage recovery to be made.

- Ensure your client file is well documented to enable you to prove each item of work done that is being claimed for.

- Understand the procedures for summary and detailed assessment of costs.

- Prepare accurate costs budgets.

- Do not forget to claim interest on costs of the main action and of the detailed assessment proceedings.

SELF-TEST QUESTIONS

1. What form is generally used for a summary assessment of costs?

2. When must a Detailed Assessment commence?

Suggested answers to these general questions can be accessed in the online resources.

FIGURE 20.1 DETAILED ASSESSMENT FLOWCHART

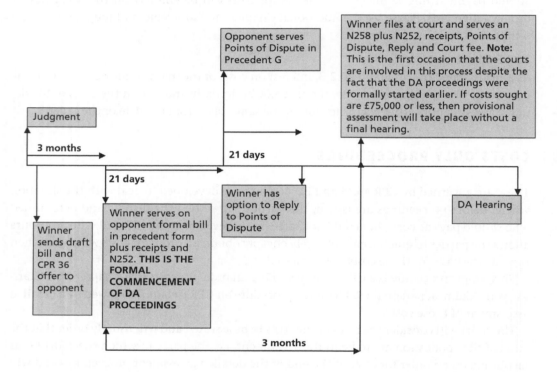

APPENDIX 1

ADDITIONAL CHAPTERS

Additional chapters to accompany this text can be found at the following location: www.oup.com/he/civillit20-21/.

INJUNCTIONS AND OTHER EQUITABLE REMEDIES

This online chapter supplements Chapter 14, paragraph 14.7 of the manual and provides further detail on the law, practice, and procedure for seeking an 'injunctive remedy'.

The chapter is divided into two sections:

In Section A, injunctions will be considered, including the purpose, effect, and the consequences of the different types of pre-emptive relief that can be obtained by way of an injunction.

In Section B, there is a brief overview of the remedies of 'rectification', 'specific performance', and 'a declaration'. Section B will not set out the detail of practice or procedure in respect of these equitable remedies, as this is beyond the scope of this book, but it is felt that any new legal practitioner should be aware of the existence of these remedies.

A PRACTICAL GUIDE TO COURT HEARINGS

This chapter provides practical guidance and advice to the student or young legal representative on how to prepare for and attend formal applications to the court and eventual trials. It also gives helpful suggestions on how to behave both in person and at telephone hearings, as well as how to interact with counsel at court.

This chapter is wholly vocational in nature and is intended to enhance the confidence of those new to litigation practice.

GUIDELINES FOR PREPARING INSTRUCTIONS TO COUNSEL

This chapter provides practical guidance and advice to the student or young legal representative on the practical steps in preparing a brief or set of instructions to counsel. It also gives guidance on the ways counsel may be used in litigation.

This chapter is purely vocational in nature and is intended to enhance the confidence of those new to litigation practice.

ENFORCEMENT OF JUDGMENTS

This chapter provides essential information on debt recovery in both the High and County Court. It focuses on the most common enforcement methods.

There is also a short section dealing with cross-border enforcement, which helps highlight the basic rules, and directs those new to foreign enforcement regulations to the appropriate legislation for further advice. However, this section may be subject to further review as negotiations for the UK's exit from the EU progress and we become aware which of the cross-border agreements on the enforcement of UK-wide judgments are to be maintained or amended.

APPENDIX 2

COURT FORMS

Online Resources

Links to the following Court Forms are provided in the book's online resources at www. oup.com/he/civillit20-21/:

N1 Claim form (CPR Part 7)
N9 Response Pack
N9A Form of admission (specified amount)
N9B Defence and Counterclaim (specified amount)
N9C Admission (unspecified amount and non-monetary claims)
N9D Defence and Counterclaim (unspecified amount)
N11 Defence form
N251 Notice of funding of case or claim
N211 W3 Claim Form (CPR Part 20—additional claims)
N265 Standard disclosure list
N181 Directions Questionnaire (fast and multi-track)
N263 Disclosure Report
N 264 Electronic Documents Questionnaire
N170 Listing questionnaire (pre-trial checklist)
N215 Certificate of service
N225 Request for judgment and reply to admission (specified amount)
N255A Notice of part admission (specified amount)
N227 Request for judgment by default (amount to be decided by the court)
N244 Application notice
N244 Notes Application notice (Form N244)—Notes for Guidance
N20 Witness Summons
N260 Statement of Costs (summary assessment and fast-track trial)
N266 W3 Notice to admit facts
N268 W3 Notice to prove documents at trial
Precedent H
Form R

APPENDIX 3

CLAIM FORM

<table>
<tr><td colspan="2"></td><td colspan="2">In the
County Court Money Claims Centre</td></tr>
</table>

Claim Form

In the	County Court Money Claims Centre
Fee Account no.	
Help with Fees - Ref no. (if applicable)	**H W F** – ☐☐☐ – ☐☐☐

	For court use only
Claim no.	
Issue date	

You may be able to issue your claim online which may save time and money. Go to www.moneyclaim.gov.uk to find out more.

Claimant(s) name(s) and address(es) including postcode

SALESMARSH INVESTMENTS LIMITED
Eagle Lodge
Lower Hexgreave, Farnsgate
Newmoor
NE26 5ST

SEAL

Defendant(s) name and address(es) including postcode

Mr Simon Hill (1) Mrs Patricia Hill (2)
25 Borough Road, Church Alton
Mansfield, Nottinghamshire, NG4 5RT

Brief details of claim

Claim for payment of monies due and owing under three Loan Agreements totalling £80,270.82 plus interest in the sum of £11,159.07 to 30 November 20?? and continuing

Value

The Claimant expects to recover the sum of £80,270.82 plus interest of £11,159.07

You must indicate your preferred County Court Hearing Centre for hearings here *(see notes for guidance)*

County Court at Newmoor

Defendant's name and address for service including postcode	Mr Simon Hill Mrs Patricia Hill 25 Borough Road Church Alton Mansfield Nottinghamshire NG4 5RT		£
		Amount claimed	91,429.89
		Court fee	4,571.49
		Legal representative's costs	100.00
		Total amount	**£96,101.38**

For further details of the courts www.gov.uk/find-court-tribunal.
When corresponding with the Court, please address forms or letters to the Manager and always quote the claim number.

© Crown Copyright 2016

	Claim No.	

Does, or will, your claim include any issues under the Human Rights Act 1998? ☐ Yes ☑ No

Particulars of Claim (attached)

Statement of Truth
*(I believe)(The Claimant believes) that the facts stated in these particulars of claim are true.
* I am duly authorised by the claimant to sign this statement

Full name _____

Name of claimant's legal representative's firm _____

signed _____ position or office held _____
      *(Claimant)(Litigation friend)   (if signing on behalf of firm or company)
       (Claimant's legal representative)
                                                              *delete as appropriate

LPC and Co
27 Leek Road
Stoke on Trent
Staffordshire
ST1 8ED

Claimant's or claimant's legal representative's address to which documents or payments should be sent if different from overleaf including (if appropriate) details of DX, fax or e-mail.

APPENDIX 4

PARTICULARS OF CLAIM

IN THE COUNTY MONEY CLAIMS CENTRE   **CLAIM NO. BY2LY87650**

BETWEEN:

SALESMARSH INVESTMENTS LIMITED

<u>Claimant</u>

and

(1) MR SIMON HILL
(2) MRS PATRICIA HILL

<u>Defendants</u>

PARTICULARS OF CLAIM

---

1.   The Claimant company advanced to the First and Second Defendants sums of monies pursuant to three Private Loan Agreements made in writing as follows:

    1.1.   Private Loan Agreement for £65,000.00 dated the 20 November 20?? ('the first Loan Agreement');

    1.2.   Private Loan Agreement for £15,000.00 dated the 20 April 20?? ('the second Loan Agreement');

    1.3.   Private Loan Agreement for £2,000.00 dated the 29 May 20?? ('the third Loan Agreement');

    Copies of these three Agreements are attached to the Particulars of Claim.

2.   The following were express terms of the first Loan Agreement:

    2.1.   The loan of £65,000.00 was in respect of an interest only Agreement subject to capital repayments being made by the First and Second Defendants following refinancing by themselves at a date after the 20 February 20?? being the review date;

    2.2.   Interest was to accrue on the £65,000.00 at a rate of 7% gross per annum payable monthly in arrears directly to the Claimant company's bank account.

3.   The following were express terms of the second Loan Agreement:

3.1.   The loan for £15,000.00 was an interest and capital repayment loan over a period of forty-eight months commencing on the 20 April 20??;

3.2.   The interest was to accrue on the balance at 7.5% gross per annum payable monthly in arrears directly to the Claimant company's bank account.

4.   The following were express terms of the third Loan Agreement:

4.1.   The loan for £2,000.00 was an interest and capital repayment loan over a period of 48 months commencing on the 29 May 20??;

4.2.   The interest was to accrue on the balance at a rate of 7.5% gross per annum payable monthly in arrears directly to the Claimant company's bank account.

5.   The First and Second Defendants have made the following payments:

5.1.   In respect of the first Loan Agreement, the First and Second Defendants have made no payments in respect of the capital amount of the loan in the sum of £65,000.00. However, interest payments in the sum of £379.16 per month were made until October 20??, after which no further payments were received by the Claimant company save for a 'one off' payment of £500 on 17 December 20?? which was allocated to outstanding interest by the Claimant company;

5.2.   In respect of the second Loan Agreement, the First and Second Defendants made five capital and interest repayments between May 20?? and September 20?? each in the sum of £362.68. No further payments have been received by the Claimant company;

5.3.   In respect of the third Loan Agreement the First and Second Defendants made four payments between June 20?? and September 20??, each in the sum of £48.36. No further payments have been made.

6.   In respect of the first Loan Agreement, the Claimant company has made a number of requests since the 29 February 20??, requesting repayment of the capital loan of £65,000.00, but no payments have been made. However, as stated in paragraph 5.1, above, some interest payments have been made in respect thereto. As regards the second and third Loan Agreements, the loan period of forty-eight months has now expired, and, as detailed in paragraph 5.2 and 5.3, above, no further payments have been made in respect of capital or interest since those dates. Consequently, the First and Second Defendants are indebted to the Claimant company in respect of the following sums:

PARTICULARS

6.1. First Loan Agreement

Capital sum outstanding	£65,000.00
Interest at a monthly rate of £379.16 from October 20?? to date (less a payment of £500.00 made towards interest in December 20??)	£ 9,737.32

6.2. Second Private Loan Agreement

Capital sum outstanding as a result of payments set out in paragraph 5.2	£13,437.50
Interest at a rate of £50.18 per month from October 20?? to date	£ 1,254.50

6.3. Third Loan Agreement

Capital sum outstanding as a result of payments set out in paragraph 5.3	£ 1,833.32
Interest at a monthly rate of £6.69 from October 20?? to date	£ 167.25

Total of capital and interest due to date of issue   £91,429.89

7. Further, the Claimant company is entitled to continuing interest on the said capital sums of £80,270.82 at the contractual rates as set out in the three private Loan Agreements at a daily rate of £14.53 until judgment or sooner payment. Alternatively, the Claimant company will seek interest pursuant to Section 69 of the County Courts Act 1984 at a rate of 8% per annum from the date of issue until judgment or sooner payment.

AND the Claimant claims:

(1) £91,429.89;

(2) Interest from date of issue to judgment or sooner payment at a contractual rate of 7% in respect of the first Loan Agreement and a contractual interest rate of 7.5% per annum in respect of the second and third Loan Agreements or pursuant to Section 69 of the County Courts Act to be assessed.

STATEMENT OF TRUTH

I believe that the facts stated in these Particulars of Claim are true. I understand that proceedings for contempt of court may be brought against anyone who makes, or causes to be made, a false statement in a document verified by a statement of truth without an honest belief in its truth.

I am duly authorized by the Claimant company to sign this Statement of Truth.

Signed ....

Director of Claimant company

Dated ....

Address for receiving documents:

LPC and Co
27 Leek Road
Stoke on Trent
Staffordshire
ST1 8ED

Ref: KE.SJW.Sa13/1

APPENDIX 5

DEFENCE AND COUNTERCLAIM

IN THE COUNTY COURT MONEY CLAIMS CENTRE   **Claim No. BY2YK78231**

BETWEEN

           (1) Mr Martin Oakes
           (2) Mrs Moira Sarah Oakes   <u>Claimants</u>

           and

           Nuneaton Leisure Ltd   <u>Defendant</u>

DEFENCE AND COUNTERCLAIM

DEFENCE

1. Paragraph 1 is admitted.

2. Paragraph 2 is admitted.

3. No admissions are made in relation to paragraph 3 as to the date the Claimants decided to sell the caravan or who would undertake the negotiations. Further, it is denied, save for the fact that as at January 20?? both Owen Davies and Patrick Statham were employees of the Defendant, that the commission rate was agreed at 10%. The commission rate in accordance with the site agreement had always been 15% plus VAT and neither Owen Davies and Patrick Statham had authority on behalf of the Defendant to agree a reduction thereto if that is indeed what they did purport to agree, which is denied.

4. No admissions are made regarding paragraph 4.

5. No admission is made regarding paragraph 5.

6. No admissions are made in relation to paragraph 6. The Defendant additionally contends that the figure of £17,500 for a caravan of that age/condition is grossly inflated. Glasses Caravan Guide currently values the said caravan at £5,125.00 just eighteen months after the alleged agreement for sale.

7. The Defendant denies that their employee, Bernard Williams, was negligent as alleged in paragraph 7 of the Particulars of Claim or at all. The statement made by the Defendant's employee regarding the time the caravan can remain on the site was in fact correct if he did in fact make that statement which is not admitted. No caravan is permitted to remain on the site if more than fifteen years old. The Claimants' caravan was seven years old at the time of the purported sale. It is further denied that the sale would have otherwise proceeded to completion and the Claimants are put to strict proof on this point.

8. Paragraph 8 is noted but no admissions are made in relation thereto. The Defendant would further aver that it is the Claimants' prerogative as to whether to sell the caravan for the price offered or not.

9. Paragraph 9 is denied for the reasons articulated in paragraphs 3–8, and the Claimants are put to strict proof as to the entitlement to the items claimed.

10. The Defendant denies that the Claimants are entitled to interest as claimed in paragraph 10 of the Particulars of Claim or at all.

11. Paragraph 11 is noted.

COUNTERCLAIM

12. The Defendant repeats paragraphs 1–8 of the Defence.

13. On or about 1 April 20?? the Claimants sold the caravan via an online auction site. This contravenes the terms of the site agreement.

14. The Claimant subsequently failed to pay the defendant commission following the sale of the caravan. The site agreement states that 15% plus VAT commission is payable on all caravan sales.

15. By reason of the matters aforesaid, the Defendant has suffered loss and damage.

PARTICULARS OF LOSS

• Commission of 15% plus VAT of the £7,300.00 sale price: £1314.

16. The Defendant claims interest under Section 69 of the County Courts Act 1984 on the sum of £1314.00 at a rate of 8% per annum from the 1 April 20?? amounting to £35.42 and thereafter continuing until judgment or sooner payment at a rate of £0.29 per day.

AND THE DEFENDANT COUNTERCLAIMS

1. £1314.00;
2. Interest under Section 69 of the County Courts Act 1984.

STATEMENT OF TRUTH

I believe that the facts stated in this Defence and Counterclaim are true. I understand that proceedings for contempt of court may be brought against anyone who makes, or causes to be made, a false statement in a document verified by a statement of truth without an honest belief in its truth.

I am duly authorized to sign this Defence and Counterclaim on behalf of the Defendant.

....

Dated ....20??

DIRECTIONS ORDER

IN THE COUNTY COURT AT CHESTER   **Claim No 7YT98560**

BETWEEN

MILTON DEVELOPMENTS LTD

Claimant

AND

KNIFTON AND CO (A FIRM)

Defendant

On 5 October 20??, Deputy District Judge Smith sitting at the County Court of Chester, considered the papers in the case and **Ordered** that:-

1. The Claim is allocated to the Fast Track.

2. There be a stay for a period of three months until 17 December 20??, in which period the Parties are to endeavour to settle this matter.

3. Should settlement not be achieved then either party may apply to the Court for a further stay by no later than 24 December 20?? should this be appropriate and/or necessary, OR THE FOLLOWING DIRECTIONS shall be ordered.

4. Each Party shall give standard disclosure by list by no later than 4 p.m. on Monday 14 January 20??.

5. Inspection shall take place by no later than 4 p.m. on Monday 21 January 20??.

6. Each Party shall serve Witness Statements of any witness upon whom it intends to rely by way of simultaneous and mutual exchange no later than 4 p.m. on Monday 18 February 20??.

7. No permission is given for expert evidence.

8. Each Party must file a completed Pre-Trial Checklist no later than 4 p.m. on Monday 18 March 20??.

9. A Trial of this claim will take place on a date to be fixed between Monday 22 April 20?? and Monday 13 May 20??, with an estimated length of hearing of one day.

10. By no later than 4 p.m. on Monday 18 March 20??, the parties must file with court their availability for trial, preferably agreed with a nominated single point of contact. They will be notified of the time and place of trial.

11. Not more then seven and not less than three clear days before trial, the claimant must file at court and serve an indexed and paginated bundle of documents which complies with the requirements of CPR 39.5 and PD 39A. The parties must endeavour to agree the contents of the bundle before it is filed. The bundle will include a case summary, chronology with list of issues, and a trial timetable.

12. The parties must file at court and exchange skeleton arguments at least three clear days before trial by email.

13. Costs in the case.

The parties are reminded of the provisions of the Practice Directions to CPR 28 or 29 concerning variation of directions and failure to comply with directions, and that in particular such applications must be made without delay. They should not be left until the filing of pre-trial checklists.

Each party must inform the court immediately if the case is settled whether or not it is then possible to file a draft consent order to give effect to their agreement.

APPENDIX 7

DISCLOSURE STATEMENT

List of documents:
standard disclosure

Notes
- The rules relating to standard disclosure are contained in Part 31 of the Civil Procedure Rules.
- Documents to be included under standard disclosure are contained in Rule 31.6.
- A document has or will have been in your control if you have or have had possession, **or** a right of possession, of it **or** a right to inspect or take copies of it.

In the The County Court at Brighton	
Claim No.	7TG23510
Claimant (including ref)	**Mr David Anderson**
Defendant (including ref)	**South Meadow Holidays Limited**
Date	**2 November 20??**

Disclosure Statement

I, the above named

☐ Claimant　　　☐ Defendant

☒ Party (if party making disclosure is a company, firm or other organization identify here who the person making the disclosure statement is and why he is the appropriate person to make it)

> Stewart Coaster, Managing Director of the Defendant Company. Individual with the relevant knowledge and authority in this litigation.

state that I have carried out a reasonable and proportionate search to locate all the documents which I am

required to disclose under the order made by the court on (date of order)　　 5 JULY 20??

☒ I did not search for documents:-

　☒ pre-dating　　October 20??

　☒ located elsewhere than
> South Meadows Holidays Ltd's Head Office

　☒ in categories other than
> The circumstances surrounding the contract for the adventure holiday

☐ for electronic documents

　I carried out a search for electronic documents contained on or created by the following:
　(list what was searched and extent of search)

> The desk top computers at South Meadows Holidays Ltd's head office in Cambridge. All emails and documents created in respect of the holiday contract and information.

[x] I did not search for the following:-

[x] documents created before | October 20??

documents contained on or created by the [ ] Claimant [x] Defendant

[ ] PCs   [x] portable data storage media
[ ] databases   [x] servers
[x] back-up tapes   [x] off-site storage
[x] mobile phones   [x] laptops
[x] notebooks   [x] handheld devices
[x] PDA devices

documents contained on or created by the [ ] Claimant [x] Defendant

[ ] mail files   [ ] document files
[x] calendar files   [x] web-based applications
[ ] spreadsheet files   [x] graphic and presentation files

Documents other than by reference to the following keyword(s)/concepts
(delete if your search was not confined to specific keywords or concepts)

I certify that I understand the duty of disclosure and to the best of my knowledge I have carried out that duty. I further certify that the list of documents set out in or attached to this form, is a complete list of all documents which are or have been in my control and which I am obliged under the order to disclose.

I understand that I must inform the court and the other parties immediately if any further document required to be disclosed by Rule 31.6 comes into my control at any time before the conclusion of the case.

[ ] I have not permitted inspection of documents within the category or class of documents (as set out below) required to be disclosed under Rule 31(6)(b) or (c) on the grounds that to do so would be disproportionate to the issues in the case.

Signed | Stewart Coaster | **Date** | 2 November 20??

Defendant's Representative

List and number here, in a convenient order, the documents (or bundles of documents if of the same nature, e.g. invoices) in your control, which you do not object to being inspected. Give a short description of each document or bundle so that it can be identified, and say if it is kept elsewhere i.e. with a bank or solicitor

I have control of the documents numbered and listed here. I do not object to you inspecting them/producing copies.

1. Emails from Claimants to Defendant dated 05.01.?? – 09.04.??
2. Customer enquiry form undated
3. Sales invoice dated 14.04.??
4. Agreement Terms Summary dated 31.03.1??
5. Sales invoice dated 11.10.??
6. Statements of Case in this action
7. Correspondence and copy correspondence between the Claimants' and Defendant's solicitors
8. Correspondence and copy correspondence between the Claimants' solicitor and Defendant

---

List and number here, as above, the documents in your control which you object to being inspected. (Rule 31.19)

I have control of the documents numbered and listed here, but I object to you inspecting them:

1. Confidential correspondence and copy correspondence and communications and attendance notes written by the Defendant's solicitor for the Defendant for the purpose of giving legal advice relating to this action.
2. Statements and proofs of evidence, drafts, and copies thereof.
3. Documents brought into existence solely for the purpose of this action.

Say what your objections are

I object to you inspecting these documents because:
They are privileged by legal professional privilege and/or litigation privilege

---

List and number here, the documents you once had in your control, but which you no longer have. For each document listed, say when it was last in your control and where it is now

I have had the documents numbered and listed below, but they are no longer in my control.

The originals of any correspondence referred to above. The originals were last in the Defendant's possession on the dates when they were posted to the recipients at the address noted.

APPENDIX 8

WITNESS STATEMENT

1. Claimant
2. S Bowen
3. First
4.
5. Date

IN THE HIGH COURT OF JUSTICE   **Claim NO: 3-HT-78**
QUEENS BENCH DIVISION
STOKE ON TRENT DISTRICT REGISTRY

Between   **MRS RACHEL DAY**   **Claimant**

                             and

              IDEAL CARAVANS LTD   **Defendant**

WITNESS STATEMENT of SUSAN BOWEN

WITNESS NAME: Susan Bowen

WITNESS ADDRESS: 24 Newcastle Road, Newton Bridge, Near Birmingham, B745GJ

WITNESS OCCUPATION: Head Mistress

1.   I am duly authorized to make this witness statement on behalf of the Claimant and I make this statement from my own knowledge and belief in support of the Claimant's claim for the value of the lost sale of a lodge to myself. This statement was provided in a face to face meeting with the Claimant's solicitor.

2.   I am a Head Mistress of a private girls' school in Birmingham and live with my partner Peter Phelps. I wanted to buy a lodge and my daughter, Gillian, helped me to do this. My recollection as to dates is not exact but I remember visiting the Undermere Holiday Park with my daughter Gillian 14th April 20??. I did not see the Claimant when we first visited but I dealt with a man called John who was acting on her behalf. I know that my daughter had emailed Ideal Caravans Ltd as we wanted to come over and view a selection of lodges and one of those lodges was owned by the Claimant.

3. I wanted to buy a lodge that would be suitable for me to live there for most of the school holidays but not all of the time. The Claimant's lodge was noted as A17 and it was a deluxe model with double glazing, central heating and outdoor hot tub. As far as I can recall, it was priced at £85,000.00.

4. I wanted to think about this with my daughter Gillian but the next day I rang the site manager, Felicity Madeley to offer the asking price as I had fallen in love with the lodge. I asked when we could move in and she said that she would speak to the Claimant and agree on a date after she had moved out her belongings.

5. A few weeks later however I received a call from Felicity Madeley, who told me, that the lodge owned by the Claimant in her view was over priced compared to others of a similar type and that she had another lodge, slightly newer, with an in built sauna for the same price. I took on board what she told me and in reliance on her statement I decided to withdraw my offer and purchase the newer lodge.

The facts stated in this witness statement are true to my best knowledge and belief. I understand that proceedings for contempt of court may be brought against anyone who makes, or causes to be made, a false statement in a document verified by a statement of truth without an honest belief in its truth.

Signed ....
          Susan Bowen

Dated ....

APPENDIX 9

MEDICAL REPORT

<u>MEDICAL REPORT</u>

- on -

<u>Mr Malcolm Smith</u>

7 Meir Road, Stoke-on-Trent, Staffordshire, ST7 2PY

- by -

<u>PROFESSOR M. HARRIS MB. FRCS(Ed)</u>

Consultant Orthopaedic Surgeon at the University Hospital of South Manchester

<u>ADDRESSED TO:</u>	**THE COURT**
<u>INSTRUCTED BY:</u>	**LPC & Co Solicitors** **17 Leek Road, Stoke-on-Trent, Staffordshire,** **ST1 3AD**
<u>OUR REFERENCE:</u>	**Ref: KE/PEW/MAL7/2**
<u>DATED:</u>	**5 October 20??**

Medical Report dated 5 October 20??
Professor M. Harris

QUALIFICATION

I am a Consultant Orthopaedic Surgeon with over 35 years experience in this field. I became a Consultant in 1976. My full CV is attached to this report.

INSTRUCTIONS

This Medical Report was produced on the instruction of LPC & Co. Malcolm Smith is a sixty-year-old General Practitioner who has worked in Manchester since 1980. He lives with his wife.

In March 20?? he was hit by a car. I interviewed and examined him on 5 October 20?? to prepare this report which describes his injuries, treatment, and prognosis. I have been provided with photocopies of his medical records and his hospital records to enable me to prepare this report.

THE ACCIDENT

On 18 March 20??, Mr Smith was standing behind his car. He was just about to open the boot when a car immediately behind him lurched backwards striking the back of leg. He felt two impacts before he started to fall to the ground. Some friends who were standing close by caught him and lowered him onto the road. Later an ambulance took him to the University Hospital of South Manchester.

SUBSEQUENT HISTORY

Mr Smith was in hospital for ten to twelve days. He underwent an operation on 21 March 20?? in which the fracture of his left tibial plateau was fixed with a plate and screws. He went home in a plaster cast which remained in place for several weeks. When the cast was removed he had physiotherapy. He is still working as a General Practitioner. He had to stop work on the day of the accident and returned to work on 26 September 20??.

PREVIOUS MEDICAL HISTORY

Mr Smith has diabetes for which he takes tablets, has high blood pressure also for which he takes tablets. In 20?? he underwent an angioplasty but has not had any further problems with his heart. He takes aspirin and a statin. He is a non-smoker.

PRESENT SITUATION

Mr Smith tells me his left leg is still painful. The pain seems to be worse when he is resting than when he is walking but he finds it difficult to walk more than a short distance. He gets pain at night which often wakes him. He started driving five months after the accident and has an automatic car. When he walks he feels that he tends to draw his left foot.

Medical Report dated 5 October 20??
Professor M. Harris

The plate is still in place and he has been told that it could be removed. He has decided to leave it in place however. I asked him about hobbies and sports but he tells me that although he played cricket many years ago he no longer does any sport or hobbies and did not do so at the time of the accident.

MEDICAL RECORDS

I have seen photocopies of the 336 pages from the hospital records and the General Practitioner notes-including-x-rays.

All sections within quotation marks are verbatim. Comments in square brackets are mine. I will only refer to the entries that I consider relevant to this report.

I cannot find any reference to any significant pre-existing condition affecting his left knee.

21-3-??	A letter from Mr Dawson, Consultant Orthopaedic Surgeon states 'Mr Smith was admitted yesterday. He was between two cars and caught between the bumpers of the car in front and the car behind. When the car behind was started it was in gear and lurched forward crushing his tibia. He has a small abrasion in the distal third of his tibia. He has sustained a fracture of his proximal tibia which is minimally displaced. There is some extension of the proximal posterior tibial component. There is a significant coronial split.'

The options of management have been discussed with Mr Smith and he wishes to consider surgical intervention by way of a left proximal lateral tibial plate.

8-4-??	A letter from Mr Dawson, Consultant Orthopaedic Surgeon states, 'Surgical wound has healed. He has a good range of motion of the knee . . . radiographs . . . show that the fracture is in a good position. Whilst he was here he mentioned pain over the left thigh. There is clinically nothing abnormal to find. He may have sustained a strain of his quadricep muscles.'
18-5-??	A letter from Mr Jones, Consultant Neurologist states '. . . as you can see you have a relatively mild acute partial left femoral nerve lesion which will either be related to the accident itself or possibly be related to your diabetes. From our last conversation I understand that the pain was beginning to resolve and I would expect things to gradually improve. . . .'
13-6-??	A letter from Phillippa Griffiths, Physiotherapist states. 'He has full active movement in his left knee but has had tightness in his ilio-tibial band. These issues have settled with massage. He can straight leg raise but has weak quads which will need further work. . . .'

Medical Report dated 5 October 20??
Professor M. Harris

2-9-??   A letter from Mr Dawson, Consultant Orthopaedic Surgeon states, 'Radiographs show that the proximal tibial fracture appears to be well on its way to healing with good callus formation at the fracture site. He is mobilizing independently without a stick now with a good range of motion. The alignment clinically is satisfactory and the plate is prominent proximally. He wishes to have this removed, this can be arranged in twelve months.

Review in one year, with x-rays on arrival for a final check. . . .'

EXAMINATION

I interviewed and examined Mr Smith on 5 October 20?? at The Nuffield Hospital, Benjamin Lane, South Manchester. He was not wearing any form of support or bandage on the left leg and walked without a stick or crutch but had a noticeable limp.

Left Leg

There was a curved antero-lateral surgical scar over the proximal left tibia, measuring 10 cms in length. There were three 1 cm scars more distally from insertion of the percutaneous screws of the LISS plate. The proximal end of the plate is easily palpable just under the skin. It is not tender. The knee is cool and there is no effusion. There is no deformity and he has a normal valgus angle I could not detect any significant ligament laxity. The knee flexes and extends fully but there is some crepitus palpable through parts of the range of movement. Some of the crepitus appears to be patello-femoral but some may becoming from medial or lateral compartments.

RADIOLOGIAL EXAMINATION

I have examined the x-rays, and all the relevant x-rays are of the left knee and tibia.

18-3-20??   X-rays taken on admission show a long oblique fracture of the proximal left tibia extending proximally into the tibial plateau. The fracture line runs up between the tibia plateau and into the lateral plateau. CT scans confirm an unusual fracture pattern as there is a very long oblique component to the fracture. The proximal fragment is continuous with the postural part of both tibial plateaux but there is a separate anterior fragment which is displaced. There is some comminution or shattering laterally.

20-3-20??   Post operative x-rays show that the fracture has been nicely fixed with two inter-fragmentary screws and a bridging anterior–lateral locking plate. There are six screws approximately, and three screws distally in the plate.

The most recent x-rays taken on 2 September 20?? confirm the fractures have all healed and are in good alignment.

Medical Report dated 5 October 20??
Professor M. Harris

PROGNOSIS AND OPINION

Mr Smith describes how he was standing behind his own car when the car behind him suddenly reversed striking the back of his legs. He felt two impacts before he started to collapse. He was caught by some friends who lowered him to the ground. He was immediately aware that he had injured his leg.

He was taken by ambulance to the University Hospital of South Manchester, where he was admitted and told that he had sustained a left tibial plateau fracture.

He underwent an operation three days later in which the fracture was internally fixed with an LISS plate. He was discharged from hospital after twelve days with a plaster cast on his leg and used crutches for several months.

He found it very difficult to get around and was unable to return to his work as a General Practitioner. He underwent nerve conduction studies owing to the fact that there does not appear to have been any direct crushing of the part of the thigh where the femoral nerve lies. It is more likely that the abnormalities and the femoral nerve identified by the conduction studies are due to diabetes than to the trauma.

Mr Smith has undergone physiotherapy and the movement in his left knee has slowly improved. The pain initially has improved but it has not settled completely. After 5 months he was able to return to driving. After six months he started work again as a General Practitioner.

I would suggest that the time absent from work was perfectly reasonable in view of the nature of the injury and the treatment which it necessitated.

Mr Smith still suffers from aching in the left knee which tends to be worse when he is resting. The pain often wakes him in the night. When I examined him on 5 October 20??. I found that he had regained full movement in the knee although there was some crepitus as he flexed and extended his knee. This crepitus is likely to be coming from the arthritic patello femoral joint. As explained earlier, the degenerative change in the patello femoral joint is likely to have pre-dated the accident and was not made worse by the affects of the accident.

It is likely that the residual aching in his knee will improve over the next two and a half years. By three years from the date of the accident, the aching will have become mild and intermittent.

The articular surfaces of the tibial plateau have been nicely restored by the internal fixation. The injury has not, therefore, increased any risk of arthritis in the knee. It has not increased the rate at which any pre-existing degenerative changes will progress.

The plate can be felt quite prominently into the skin but he is not keen to have it removed at the moment. There is no absolute reason for the plate to be removed but if the protruding proximal

Medical Report dated 5 October 20??
Professor M. Harris

end starts to irritate him, then he could have the plate taken out at a later stage. Removal of the plate would require a further operation under general anaesthetic.

When Mr Smith was seen by Mr Dawson in Clinic on 2 September 20??, it was decided that matters would be reviewed in twelve months, hence when a final decision would be made about whether to remove the plate.

DECLARATION

I understand that my overriding duty is to the Court both in preparing this report and in giving or evidence. I have set out in my report what I understand from those instructing me to be the questions in respect of which my opinion as expert is required. I have done my best in preparing this report to be accurate and complete. I have mentioned all matters which I regard as relevant to the opinions I have expressed. All of the matters on which I have expressed an opinion lie within my field of expertise.

I have drawn to the attention of the Court all matters which I am aware which might adversely affect my opinion. Wherever I have no personal knowledge I have indicated the source of factual information. I have not included anything in this report which has been suggested to me by anyone including the lawyers instructing me without forming my own independent view of the matter.

Where in my view there is a range of reasonable opinion, I have indicated the extent of the range in the report. At the time of signing the report, I consider it to be complete and accurate. I will notify those instructing me if, for any reason, I subsequently consider that the report requires any correction or qualification.

I understand this report will be the evidence I will give under oath, subject to any correctional qualification I may make before swearing to its veracity.

I confirm that I have made clear which facts and matters referred to in this report are within my own knowledge and which are not. Those that are within my own knowledge I confirm to be true. The opinions I have expressed represent my true and complete professional opinions on the matters to which they refer.

....

PROFESSOR M. HARRIS MB. FRCS(Ed)
Consultant Orthopaedic Surgeon
University Hospital of South Manchester

APPENDIX 10

LISTING QUESTIONNAIRE (PRE-TRIAL CHECKLIST)

Listing questionnaire
(Pre-trial checklist)

Name of court	The County Court Hearing Centre Burnley

To be completed by, or on behalf of,

Brunswicks Limited

Claim No.	CHG98765
Last date for filing with court office	XX/XX/20??
Date(s) fixed for trial or trial period	25/XX/20??- 15/XX/20??

who is XXXXXXXX[   ][Claimant][Defendant]
[XXXXXXXXXXXXXXXXXXXXXXXX in this claim

This form must be **completed** and **returned** to the court no later than the date given above. If not, your statement of case may be struck out or some other sanction imposed.

If the claim has settled, or settles before the trial date, you must let the court know immediately.

Legal representatives only: If no costs management order has been made.You must **attach** estimates of costs incurred to date, and of your likely overall costs. In substantial cases, these should be provided in compliance with CPR.

For multi-track claims only, you must also **attach** a proposed timetable for the trial itself.

A Confirmation of compliance with directions

1. I confirm that I have complied with those directions already given which require action by me. ☑ Yes ☐ No

   If you are unable to give confirmation, state which directions you have still to comply with and the date by which this will be done.

Directions	Date

2. I believe that additional directions are necessary before the trial takes place. ☐ Yes ☑ No

   If Yes, you should attach an application and a draft order.

   *Include in your application all directions needed to enable the claim **to be tried on the date, or within the trial period, already fixed**. These should include any issues relating to experts and their evidence, and any orders needed in respect of directions still requiring action by any other party.*

3. Have you agreed the additional directions you are seeking with the other party(ies)? ☑ Yes ☐ No

B Witnesses

1. How many witnesses (including yourself) will be giving evidence on your behalf at the trial? *(Do not include experts - see Section C)* `4`

Continued over ⇗

Witnesses continued

2. If the trial date is not yet fixed, are there any days within the trial period you or your witnesses would wish to avoid if possible? *(Do not include experts - see Section C)*

Please give details

Name of witness	Dates to be avoided, if possible	Reason
Karen Dale	25-30 XXX 20??	Holiday
Jane Reid	9 and 11 XXX 20??	Work prior commitments

Please specify any special facilities or arrangements needed at court for the party or any witness (e.g. witness with a disability).

Karen Dale is an elderly lady who is rather deaf. She wears a hearing aid. A hearing loop at the trial centre would be necessary so she can hear clearly.

3. Will you be providing an interpreter for any of your witnesses? ☐ Yes ☑ No

C Experts

You are reminded that you may not use an expert's report or have your expert give oral evidence unless the court has given permission. If you do not have permission, you must make an application (see section A2 above)

1. Please give the information requested for your expert(s)

Name	Field of expertise	Joint expert?	Is report agreed?	Has permission been given for oral evidence?
Mr O Coulsen	Electrical Engineer	☐ Yes ☑ No	☐ Yes ☑ No	☐ Yes ☑ No
		☐ Yes ☐ No	☐ Yes ☐ No	☐ Yes ☐ No
		☐ Yes ☐ No	☐ Yes ☐ No	☐ Yes ☐ No

2. Has there been discussion between experts? ☑ Yes ☐ No

3. Have the experts signed a joint statement? ☑ Yes ☐ No

4. If your expert is giving oral evidence and the trial date is not yet fixed, is there any day within the trial period which the expert would wish to avoid, if possible? ☐ Yes ☐ No

If Yes, please give details

Name	Dates to be avoided, if possible	Reason

D Legal representation

1. Who will be presenting your case at the trial?   ☐ You   ☑ Solicitor   ☐ Counsel

2. If the trial date is not yet fixed, is there any day within the trial period that the person presenting your case would wish to avoid, if possible?   ☐ Yes   ☑ No

   If Yes, please give details

Name	Dates to be avoided, if possible	Reason

E The trial

1. Has the estimate of the time needed for trial changed?   ☐ Yes   ☑ No

   If Yes, say how long you estimate the whole trial will take, including both parties' cross-examination and closing arguments   ☐ days   ☐ hours   ☐ minutes

2. If different from original estimate have you agreed with the other party(ies) that this is now the **total** time needed?   ☐ Yes   ☐ No

3. Is the timetable for trial you have attached agreed with the other party(ies)?   ☑ Yes   ☐ No

Fast track cases only

The court will normally give you 3 weeks notice of the date fixed for a fast track trial unless, in exceptional circumstances, the court directs that shorter notice will be given.

Would you be prepared to accept shorter notice of the date fixed for trial?   ☐ Yes   ☑ No

F Document and fee checklist

Tick as appropriate

I attach to this questionnaire -

☐ An application and fee for additional directions   ☑ A proposed timetable for trial

☑ A draft order   ☑ An estimate of costs

☑ Listing fee **or** quote your Fee Account no. 12345GH

Signature	Your name and full postal address		If applicable
Melanie Price	LPC and Co, 24 Leek Road Stoke on Trent, Staffs,		
[Legal Representative for the] [1ˢᵗ][2ⁿᵈ][3ʳᵈ][ ] [Claimant][Defendant][Part 20 claimant]	Legal representatives for the Claimant	Telephone no. 01782 1111111
		Fax no. 01782 111111
		DX no. 20954 Sekot
	Postcode S T 5 1 T T	Your ref. KE/BL/SIL12/1
Date 2 1 / X X / 2 0 ? ?	E-mail m.price@LPC.co.uk	

3 of 3

CLAIM NOTIFICATION FORM (PL1)

This is a formal claim against you, which must be acknowledged by email immediately and passed to your insurer.

Claim notification form (PL1)
Low value personal injury claims in public liability accidents (£1,000 - £25,000)

Before filling in this form you are encouraged to seek independent legal advice.

Date sent	2	0	/	0	8	/	2	0	?	?

Items marked with (✱) are optional and the claimant must make a reasonable attempt to complete those boxes. All other boxes on the form are mandatory and must be completed before being sent.

What is the value of your claim? ☑ up to £10,000   ☐ up to £25,000

Please tick here if you are not legally represented? ☐ *If you are not legally represented please put your details in the claimant's representative section.*

Claimant's representative - contact details	**Defendant's details**
Name	**Defendant's name**
Samira Jones	Cotters Playground
Address	**Defendant's address***
HPS Personal Injury Solicitors 12th Floor HPS House High Street Chester	Cotters Playground Oakes Town Near Chester Cheshire
Postcode C H 1 2 D F	Postcode C H 2 5 7 J K
Contact name	**Policy number reference (if not known insert not known)**
Samira Jones	Not Known
Telephone number	**Insurer/Compensator name (if known)**
xxxxx 23456	Not Known
E-mail address	
sj@HPSsolicitors.co.uk	
Reference number	
SJ/CP.12/2106	

Section A — Claimant's details

☐ Mr.   ☐ Mrs.   ☑ Ms.
☐ Miss ☐ Other

Claimant's name

Claire Peakston

Address

57 Oakes Town Centre Street
Oakes Town
Near Chester

Postcode C H 2 5 · 7 G K

Date of birth
1 3 / 0 4 / 1 9 8 0

Is this a child claim? ☐ Yes ☑ No

National Insurance number
N B 2 2 1 3 7 8 Y

If the claimant does not have a National Insurance number, please explain why

Occupation

Teacher (Part time)

Date of accident
2 4 / 0 7 / 2 0 ? ?

If exact accident date is not known please select the most appropriate date and provide further details in Section B 1.1

Section B — Injury and medical details

1.1 Please provide a brief description of the injury sustained as a result of the accident

Bruising to her left hip, thigh, arm, elbow and cheek. Small laceration to her left forehead. Left black eye

this section continues over the page ⇨

1.2 Has the claimant had to take any time off work as a result of the accident?　　☑ Yes　☐ No

1.3 Is the claimant still off work?　　☐ Yes　☑ No

If No, how many days in total was the claimant off work?

`3`

1.4 Has the claimant sought any medical attention?　　☑ Yes　☐ No

If Yes, on what date did they first do so?

`2 4 / 0 7 / 2 0 ? ?`

1.5 Did the claimant attend hospital as a result of the accident?　　☐ Yes　☑ No

If Yes, please provide details of the hospital(s) attended

1.6 If hospital was attended, was the claimant detained overnight?　　☐ Yes　☑ No

If Yes, how many days were they detained?

Section C — Rehabilitation

2.1 Has a medical professional recommended the claimant should undertake any rehabilitation such as physiotherapy?　　☑ Yes　☐ No　☐ Medical professional not seen

If Yes, please provide brief details of the rehabilitation treatment recommended and any treatment provided including name of provider

Physiotherapy. Ultra Sound.
Shore Side Physiotherapy Clinic.

2.2 Are you aware of any rehabilitation needs that the claimant has arising out of the accident?　　☑ Yes　☐ No

If Yes, please provide full details

See section 2.1 above.

Section D — Accident time, location and description

3.1　Estimated time of accident (24 hour clock)

11.15

3.2　Where did the accident happen?
Please provide sufficient detail to identify
the precise accident location (e.g. road name,
house number, permanent location feature,
grid reference etc.)

Cotters Playground, Oakes Town, CH25 7JK

3.3　Please give a description of the accident and
provide a sketch or photograph, if appropriate

The Claimant's daughter had been using one of two swings. The other swing was also
occupied by a child. When the claimant's daughter had finished using the swing, she and the
claimant walked away from the swings (but not directly behind the other swing). As they
walked away the other swing suddenly detached itself from the swing frame and flew through
the air hitting the claimant and knocking her to the ground. The claimant's child was not hit.

3.4　Was the accident reported?　　　☑ Yes　　☐ No　　☐ Not known

If Yes, please confirm the date the accident was
reported and to whom it was reported (if known)

By telephone to Mrs Cotter on the 24th July 20?? shortly after the accident.

Section E — Liability

4.1 Why does the claimant believe that the defendant was to blame for the accident?

Cotters Playground (the premises) is in breach of its statutory duty under section 2 of the Occupiers Liability Act 1957 (the Act) and/or is negligent in that the firm:
1. Failed to take any or any reasonable care to ensure that the claimant would be reasonably safe on the premises
2. Caused or permitted unsafe swings to be used
3. Failed to institute or enforce any or any adequate system for the inspection and/or maintenance of the equipment at the premises, notably the swings
4. Failed to take any or any adequate care for the safety of the claimant
5. Exposed the claimant to a danger and foreseeable risk of injury
6. In the circumstances, failed to discharge the common duty of care to the claimant in breach of the Act

PL1 6

Section F — Funding

5.1 Has the claimant undertaken a funding arrangement within the meaning of CPR rule 43.2(1)(k) of which they are required to give notice to the defendant?

☑ Yes ☐ No

If Yes, please tick the following boxes that apply:

☐ The claimant has entered into a conditional fee agreement in relation to this claim, which provides for a success fee within the meaning of section 58(2) of the Courts and Legal Services Act 1990

Date conditional fee arrangement was entered into

☐☐/☐☐/☐☐☐☐

☐ The claimant has taken out an insurance policy to which section 29 of the Access to Justice Act 1999 applies.

Name of insurance company

Address of insurance company

Policy number

Policy date ☐☐/☐☐/☐☐☐☐

Level of cover

Are the insurance premiums staged? ☐ Yes ☐ No

If Yes, at which point is an increased premium payable?

☐ The claimant has an agreement with a membership organisation to meet their legal costs.

Name of organisation

Date of agreement ☐☐/☐☐/☐☐☐☐

☐ Other, please give details

Section G — Other relevant information

Section H — Statement of truth

Your personal information will only be disclosed to third parties, where we are obliged or permitted by law to do so. This includes use for the purpose of claims administration as well as disclosure to third-party managed databases used to help prevent fraud, and to regulatory bodies for the purposes of monitoring and/or enforcing our compliance with any regulatory rules/codes.

Where the claimant is a child the signature below will be by the child's parent or guardian or by the legal representative authorised by them.

☑ I am the claimant's legal representative. The claimant believes that the facts stated in this claim form are true. I am duly authorised by the claimant to sign this statement.

☐ I am the claimant. I believe that the facts stated in this claim form are true.

Signed

Date

2 0 / 0 8 / 2 0 ? ?

Position or office held
(if signed on behalf of firm or company)

Solicitor

☑ I have retained a signed copy of this form including the statement of truth.

Claim notification form (PL1)

Low value personal injury claims in
public liability accidents (£1,000 - £25,000)

Compensator response

Section A — Liability

Please select the relevant statement

Defendant admits: Accident occured

Caused by the defendant's breach of duty

Caused some loss to the claimant, the nature and extent of which is not admitted

The defendant has no accrued defence to the claim under the Limitation Act 1980

☐   The above are admitted

☐   The defendant makes the above admission but the claim will exit the process due to contributory negligence

If the defendant does not admit liability please provide reasons below

```
```

Section B — Services provided by the compensator - Rehabilitation

Is the compensator prepared to provide rehabilitation?   ☐ Yes   ☐ No

Has the compensator provided rehabilitation?   ☐ Yes   ☐ No

If Yes, please provide full details below

```
```

Section C — Response information

Date of notification ☐☐/☐☐/☐☐☐☐

Date of response to notification ☐☐/☐☐/☐☐☐☐

Defendant's compensators details

Address

Contact name

Telephone number

E-mail address

Reference number

HPS Personal Injury Solicitors
12th Floor HPS House
High Street
Chester CH1 2DF

Tel: xxxxx 23456
www.HPSsolicitors.co.uk

e-mail:sj@HPSsolicitors.co.uk

20 August 20??

Cotters Playground

Oakes Town

Near Chester

CH25 7JK   ref: SJ/CP.12/2106

Dear Mr and Mrs Cotter,

Ms Claire Peakston   Accident 24 July 20??

We refer to the above accident and enclose a copy of the Claim Notification Form.

Under the Civil Procedure Rules, 'Pre-action Protocol for Low Value Personal Injury (Employer Liability and Public Liabilty) Claims Portal' you must confirm receipt of the Claim Notification Form by email within one day of receipt of this letter. You must also provide us with your insurers full details including your policy number.

We look forward to receiving the above details along with your confirmation that your insurers have been sent a copy of the enclosed Claims Notification Form. A duplicate of the form is enclosed for this purpose.

Yours faithfully

HPS Personal Injury Solicitors

Enc: Two copies of PL1.

HPS Personal Injury Solicitors
12th Floor HPS House
High Street
Chester CH1 2DF

Tel: xxxxx 23456
www.HPSsolicitors.co.uk

e-mail:sj@HPSsolicitors.co.uk

25 August 20??

Cotters Playground

Oakes Town

Near Chester

CH25 7JK   ref: SJ/CP.12/2106

Dear Mr and Mrs Cotter,

Ms Claire Peakston   Accident 24 July 20??

We refer to our letter dated 20 August 20??.

We note that you have failed to provide your insurer's details to allow us to submit this claim to them via the Portal. You are now in breach of rule 6.10 of the Civil Procedure Rules 'Pre-action Protocol for Low Value Personal Injury (Employer Liability and Public Liabilty) Claims Portal' and we are consequently entirely justified in commencing court proceedings against you.

However, in an attempt to avoid costly litigation, we will provide you with a further seven days to provide us with your insurers details, with policy number.

Your reply is awaited in that time.

Yours faithfully

HPS Personal Injury Solicitors

**HPS Personal Injury Solicitors
12th Floor HPS House
High Street
Chester CH1 2DF**

Tel: xxxxx 23456
www.HPSsolicitors.co.uk

e-mail:sj@HPSsolicitors.co.uk

31 August 20??

Cotters Playground

Oakes Town

Near Chester

CH25 7JK   ref: SJ/CP.12/2106

Dear Mr and Mrs Cotter,

Ms Claire Peakston   Accident 24 July 20??

We refer to your letter dated 27 August 20??, with enclosed response.

We note that you are seeking to deny our client's claim. As a result of this the claim will enter the Pre-Action Protocol for Personal Injury claims and the Claims Notification Form sent to you under cover of our letter dated the 20 August 20?? will act as the Letter of Claim within that Protocol.

Under the provisions of the Pre-Action Protocol for Personal Injury claims you now have 3 months from the date of your acknowledgment (27 August 20??) to provide us with a decision on liability. We calculate that date to be 27 November 20??.

As you have chosen for the claim not to be dealt with under the Portal, the relevant costs shall apply.

We look forward to hearing your detailed response on liability by 27 November 20??.

Yours faithfully

HPS Personal Injury Solicitors

HPS Personal Injury Solicitors
12th Floor HPS House
High Street
Chester CH1 2DF

Tel: xxxxx 23456
www.HPSsolicitors.co.uk

e-mail:sj@HPSsolicitors.co.uk

20 November 20??

Cotters Playground

Oakes Town

Near Chester

CH25 7JK

ref: SJ/CP.12/2106

Dear Mr and Mrs Cotter,

Ms Claire Peakston   Accident 24 July 20??

We refer to our letter dated 31 August 20?? and write to remind you that your decision on the issue of liability, in accordance with the Pre-Action Protocol for Personal Injury claims (the protocol) falls due on the 27 November 20??.

We expect compliance with the Protocol and we give you notice that, in the event that your decision is not provided by the due date (27 November 20??), or if liability continues to be denied and you do not simultaneously provide disclosure, we shall make an application, without further notice, for pre-action disclosure pursuant to Civil Procedure Rules 31.16.

For the avoidance of any doubt, we shall be seeking disclosure of the following documents:

1. Accident report form
2. Accident report
3. Risk assessments
4. Inspections records for the relevant area (the swings) of your playground for one month prior to our client's accident
5. Copies of any warning signs and markings present in the relevant area
6. Records of similar (or any) accidents in the playground for the twelve months prior to our client's accident
7. Records of any complaints made of any facilities within the playground for the twelve months prior to our client's accident
8. Details of the frequency and type of inspections taken place of the equipment in the playground in the twelve months prior to our client's accident

In the event that an application does become necessary, we shall draw to the attention of the court your breach of the Protocol and, in addition to an order for disclosure of the above documents, we shall be seeking payment of costs on the indemnity basis.

We look forward to hearing from you.

Yours faithfully

HPS Personal Injury Solicitors

INDEX

Tables and figures are indicated by an italic *t* and *f* following the paragraph number.

A